Diatessarica
PART X, SECTION IV

THE FOURFOLD GOSPEL
THE LAW
OF THE NEW KINGDOM

THE FOURFOLD GOSPEL

SECTION IV

THE LAW OF THE NEW KINGDOM

BY

Edwin A. Abbott

Honorary Fellow of St John's College, Cambridge
Fellow of the British Academy

"Bear ye one another's burdens, and so fulfil the law of Christ"
The Epistle to the Galatians, vi. 2.

WIPF & STOCK · Eugene, Oregon

Wipf and Stock Publishers
199 W 8th Ave, Suite 3
Eugene, OR 97401

The Fourfold Gospel; Section IV
The Law of the New Kingdom
By Abbott, Edwin A.
Softcover ISBN-13: 978-1-6667-0087-9
Hardcover ISBN-13: 978-1-6667-0088-6
eBook ISBN-13: 978-1-6667-0089-3
Publication date 2/9/2021
Previously published by Cambridge University Press, 1916

This edition is a scanned facsimile of the original edition published in 1916.

PREFACE

THE subject with which this volume begins is Christ's teaching in parables and His object in thus teaching. The subject with which it concludes (or draws towards its conclusion) is Christ's precept to His typical follower: "Let him deny himself and take up his cross." There are few Synoptic traditions that are more obscure as to their meaning and origin than these two. An attempt will be made in the following pages to shew that the Fourth Evangelist, who nowhere mentions the word "parable," and who nowhere represents Jesus as mentioning the word "cross," constantly refers to Christian thoughts about both these terms, and helps us not only to understand why he, the writer, left the terms unmentioned, but also to draw nearer to what we may believe to have been thought about them by our Lord Himself.

Mark's Gospel is taken as the starting point for investigation, for three reasons, first, because it has been proved to contain Synoptic tradition in its earliest form, secondly, because Matthew and Luke have largely borrowed from it, and thirdly, for a reason that cannot be quite so briefly expressed.

It is, that Mark appears to have been, to a surprising extent, let alone by early editors and scribes. Victor of Antioch, writing not earlier than the fifth century, complains that Mark's is the only Gospel on which he has not been able to find a single continuous commentary. The result is that Mark often retains, in a brief, rough, and obscure shape, some tradition, altered or omitted in Matthew, and

PREFACE

still more frequently in Luke, which takes us back, closer than we are taken by their later and smoother traditions, to the original thought.

In these cases, where the thought is of importance, John often intervenes in such a way that he explains Mark's tradition. The instances of intervention are so frequent that it has been found expedient to regard such Johannine intervention as a rule, and to undertake the task of discussing all important exceptions.

This has added greatly to the bulk of the work, and must add not a little to the labour of the reader. But it seemed the only fair course To select some twenty or thirty instances where John obviously intervenes in behalf of Mark would have been easy, brief, and momentarily effective. But it would have left the thoughtful reader unsatisfied and inquiring—after he had had time to reflect—"But what about those instances of peculiar Marcan tradition where John has not intervened?"

By the inclusive method adopted in these pages that question is anticipated and answered. The answer is "The instances of peculiar Marcan tradition are all given. Sometimes it is admitted—as, for example, in traditions relating to the Baptist—that John has not intervened Sometimes you may think that non-intervention ought to have been admitted more freely as to other matters. Sometimes the evidence for intervention may appear to you thin, tedious, and unsatisfactory. But in any case you cannot complain that anything is kept back The phenomena unfavourable to the theory of Johannine Intervention are to be found in the continuous text of Mark which you can compare with the texts of Matthew and Luke in parallel columns. You can judge for yourself. The facts are placed fully before you."

PREFACE

Take, as an instance, the following tradition about parables, where Matthew omits part, and Luke the whole, of a tradition in Mark:—

Mk iv. 33—4	Mt. xiii 34	Lk. om
And with many such parables spake he *the word unto them, as they were able to hear it*. And without a parable spake he not unto them *but privately to his own disciples he expounded all things*.	All these things spake Jesus in parables unto the multitudes, and without a parable spake he nothing unto them	

John substitutes the word "proverb" for "parable" when he says about the allegorical parable of the Good Shepherd "This *proverb* [i.e. *parable*] spake he unto them." He also represents Jesus as saying, on the night before the Crucifixion, "These things have I spoken unto you in *proverbs* [i.e. *parables*]; the hour cometh when I shall no longer speak unto you in *proverbs* [i.e. *parables*] but shall tell you plainly of the Father." But the substitution of a different *word* does not affect the inference that John is here intervening as to Synoptic *thought*. We shall endeavour to shew that his object was to modify, explain, and place in its right order, the Marcan tradition omitted partially by Matthew and wholly by Luke.

It will be maintained that in the Fourth Gospel *all Christ's teaching is regarded as having been of the nature of parables, proverbs, or dark sayings, to His disciples*, until the Holy Spirit was given to them after His death and resurrection. According to this view, Mark's tradition needed to be placed later. It was a mistake to suppose that Jesus used parables at any time to make His teaching obscure. The obscurity was a necessity. In that case, we may suppose John's interpretation of the motives of Jesus, and of the historical fact at the bottom of Mark's tradition, to have been something of the following kind: "All the words of the Lord Jesus before His death, not only those to the multitudes but also those to His disciples, were of the nature of parables or proverbs, which He spoke unto them '*as they were able to hear*,' in order to lead those who were willing to be led, step by step, to the truth. But after His resurrection, after He had been manifested to those of His household, the disciples, and after He had bestowed on them the Holy Spirit, from that time forward He spoke no longer in parables but told them plainly of the Father. Mark's tradition is based on fact. But he has placed it before its time. The fact became fact after the Lord had risen from the dead."

Whether this Johannine intervention is correct is a point to be discussed later on. The point for us at present is that John does appear to intervene, and that we ought not to allow his intervention as to Synoptic thought about "parables" to be concealed from us by the fact that he avoids (as he almost always does) the technical Synoptic word. It may also be added that, whether John is right or wrong, we gain something by studying the difficult Synoptic statements about Christ's parables in the light of his intervention.

Let us now consider what, if anything, John has to teach us about the second of the two subjects mentioned at the beginning of this Preface, the command that bids every Christian "take up his cross." At first sight it seems that there is nothing Johannine that even remotely

PREFACE

corresponds to this. But it has been urged in a previous part of Diatessarica that when Jesus said "Take my yoke upon you," that is to say, "Take my service upon you," He implied a precept that might be expressed in some circumstances (where the "service" was hard and dangerous) by the phrase "take my cross upon you." The original may not have enjoined, and probably did not enjoin, mere readiness to face death. It enjoined service to the Son of Man, including service to all the sons of man whom He came to serve and to save.

Turning to the Fourth Gospel for some command or precept of this kind—some precept enjoining service such as the Son of Man enjoined—many of my readers may be surprised to find how few commands or precepts that Gospel contains—not more than three or four—as compared with the numerous commands recorded by the Synoptists. Among these three or four by far the most prominent is that one which Jesus Himself literally fulfilled for His disciples and then bade them fulfil for one another: "If I then, the Lord and the Master, have washed your feet, ye also ought"—literally, "ye owe it as a debt"—"to wash one another's feet."

Even this precept is not expressed by an imperative. The Fourth Evangelist dislikes imperatives. Yet how much more than an ordinary imperative is implied by this "owe-it-as-a-debt" may be seen from the Johannine Epistle, which tells every Christian that "he *owes-it-as-a-debt* to walk even as he [*i.e.* Jesus] walked," and that "we *owe-it-as-a-debt* to love one another," and "Hereby know we love because he [*i.e.* Jesus] laid down his life for us, and we also *owe-it-as-a-debt* to lay down our lives for the brethren." To the same effect the Epistle to the Romans says "*Owe not a debt* to anyone except to love one another,"

PREFACE

and "We that are strong *owe-it-as-a-debt* to bear the weaknesses of those that are not strong."

It may be fairly and reasonably argued that, when John describes Jesus as thus ministering to His own disciples, who recline at the table while He waits on them like a servant, he has in view the tradition of Mark and Matthew, omitted by Luke, "Verily the Son of man came not to be ministered to, but to minister, and to give his life a ransom for many." But, apart from this, we ought to learn much from these Johannine traditions about "*owing-as-a-debt.*" They connect the "debt" of a Christian with Christ's "washing the feet" of the disciples; and with "walking" even as He walked (that is to say "following" Him); and with "loving one another"; and with "laying down life for the brethren." Is not this last phrase equivalent to "taking up the cross for the brethren"? And are we not thus brought round by these stages of tradition from the Johannine precept "wash one another's feet" to the Synoptic precept "take up the cross" —with this new light on the latter, that we perceive its meaning to be, not, "Face martyrdom, and practise asceticism that you may save your own souls," but "Follow the Son of Man whose love of men constrained Him to make Himself the Servant of those whom He loved"?

It may seem somewhat venturesome to say that Jesus was "constrained" to do anything. But in reality it is more reverent, as well as more true, than to say that He "was not constrained to do anything," or that He "could do as He pleased." The expressed doctrine of the Fourth Gospel is that Jesus "was not able to do" anything except that which He saw the Father doing. And its implied doctrine is, that the Son, being the incarnate Love of God, was constrained by His own love to take up the yoke, or

PREFACE

the cross, and to lay down His life for His brethren, to whom, when He departed from them, He bequeathed Himself, that is to say, the Spirit of His own "constraining" love.

The great need of Christendom, at the present time, is the sense, or rather the indwelling fervour, of this constraining love. The Fourth Evangelist and the Apostle of the Gentiles both speak of it as a "debt." And "debt" may seem a cold word to connect with love. So also may "constraint." But there is no coldness in the Pauline words "The love of Christ *constraineth* us because we thus judge, that one died for all, therefore all died; and he died for all, that those who live should no longer live unto themselves, but unto him who for their sakes died and rose again." John takes this fervid doctrine a little further by saying, in effect, that men "should no longer live unto themselves but unto the brethren for whose sake Christ died."

Thinking of this debt, as expressed by these two great exponents of Christian thought, we perceive at once that it is not of a commercial character. It may be instructively (though not completely) regarded in a military aspect, as the debt owed by the soldiers of the army of righteousness, in the first place to their Leader the Prince of righteousness—who both died for them as their comrade, and led them to victory as their Lord—and in the second place to their fellow-soldiers, whom their Leader identified with Himself. Even men of the world would admit that Christians, if they believed in the existence of such a debt, ought to regard it as "a debt of honour." Yet how very far are those who are striving to become "sons of the light" below those who frankly admit that they are "sons of this world," in feeling a whole-hearted and passionate

PREFACE

determination that, whatever else may remain unpaid, their "debt of honour" shall be discharged!

To inspire Christians with a passionate determination of this kind, passionate yet not military—merging duty in love, and "I must" in "I will"—is (doubtless) the object of all the Evangelists But the Fourth, more than the Three, seems to reveal Jesus as the natural source of such an inspiration. The Three teach us about the Law of the Seed and about the Law of the Cross, but separately, and without much suggestion of their naturalness, or of any connection between the two. The Fourth combines the doctrines, shewing (in one and the same lesson) that the seed must fall in order to rise, and that the death implied by the Cross means self-sacrifice for others, not asceticism for oneself. The seed is drawn up by the sun from the darkness of its decaying integument into light, life, and fruitfulness; so is the crucified and buried Saviour drawn up to the Father, with power to draw up into Himself and into His eternal life the souls of those who have shared His death.

Hence it is that from the Fourth Gospel imperatives are almost banished, and commands in it are almost superseded by silent drawing. The "almost" is required by a notable exception—the last of the few Johannine imperatives, "Follow thou me" As this command was addressed to Philip at the opening of the Gospel, so it is to the penitent Peter at its close.

The exception is indeed noteworthy. But we should also note, in the same passage, an instance of silent "drawing." For there we find, besides Peter, another disciple following Jesus; and he follows uncommanded. What made him follow? We are not told. But we are led, with Johannine indirectness, to surmise the cause. "Peter,

PREFACE

turning about, seeth *the disciple whom Jesus loved* following." We must be dull indeed if we cannot infer that the cause of that "following" was Christ's "constraining love."

With the following of this unnamed disciple the following of Peter appears to be both compared and contrasted. Peter is to have the privilege of "glorifying God" by the "manner" of his "death." This probably means that he is to follow literally on the path of the Cross, and to be a crucified martyr. In any case it means that he is to be a *martyr*—that is to say, a *martus*, or "witness."

The other disciple is to have no such privilege of special following. Perhaps he is not to follow at all in any such sense but merely to wait ("If I will that he tarry?"). Tertullian said, "The blood of Christians is seed." If that were the only seed, the unnamed disciple would be no sower. But may not the life and work of Christians also be "seed"? May not this also "witness" for Christ? The Gospel implies that it may. The unnamed disciple, it says, "witnesses" in a way of his own:—"This is the disciple that *witnesseth* concerning these things, and we know that his *witness* is true."

And surely, whatever may be its historical defects, "his *witness* is true"—spiritually, most true. No other disciple of Christ, not even Paul, has so powerfully helped us to discern, in the words and deeds and posthumous influence of Jesus, the Law of the Seed and the Law of the Cross, and to recognise, beneath both, the Law of eternal Life and Growth revealed as triumphant through the transitory appearances of death.

PREFACE

I gratefully acknowledge the help of my friends Mr W. S. Aldis, Mr H. Candler, and Rev. J. Hunter Smith in revising the proofs of this volume, as also those of preceding volumes of Diatessarica. Their criticism has enabled me to see and to correct many obscurities, and some errors, that would otherwise have escaped my notice.

EDWIN A. ABBOTT.

Wellside, Well Walk
Hampstead, N W.

20 *Dec* 1915.

CONTENTS

		PAGE
REFERENCES AND ABBREVIATIONS	. . . . .	xxi

CHAPTER I

THE PARABLES OF SOWING
[Mark iv. 1—34]

§ 1	Christ's "parables" or "things hidden" . .	1
§ 2	"Hear ye," in Mark	8
§ 3	When did the disciples "ask Jesus the parables"?	10
§ 4	"The mystery of the kingdom," in Mark .	15
§ 5	"The word," in Mark	19
§ 6	"The word," in John, how first mentioned by Jesus .	21
§ 7	"There is nothing hid save that it should be manifested," in Mark . . .	27
§ 8	"He knoweth not how," and "the earth beareth fruit of herself," in Mark	36
§ 9	"Less than all the seeds," and "greater than all the herbs," in Mark and Matthew . .	41
§ 10	Private "expounding," in Mark . . .	45
§ 11	"The word," in the Fourth Gospel as a whole . .	49

CHAPTER II

THE STILLING OF THE STORM
[Mark iv. 35—41]

§ 1	Why does John omit this?	52
§ 2	(R V) "They take him with them, even as he was, in the boat," in Mark .	55
§ 3	"And other boats were with him," in Mark	60
§ 4	"On the cushion," in Mark .	62

CONTENTS

CHAPTER III
THE DEMONIAC AND THE SWINE
[Mark v. 1—20]

		PAGE
§ 1	Reasons for discussing this narrative . .	66
§ 2	"Gerasenes," "Gadarenes," or "Gergesenes" .	71
§ 3	"Two" demoniacs in Matthew, and "two thousand" swine in Mark	74
§ 4	Why does Matthew omit "legion"? . . .	75
§ 5	"Beseeching," "exhorting," or "comforting" .	78
§ 6	Versions of the narrative in an Apocryphal Gospel .	82
§ 7	"Outside the country" in Mark, and "into the abyss" in Luke	86
§ 8	"Outside," applied to the "casting out" of "the ruler of this world," in John	89

CHAPTER IV
JESUS RESTORING TO LIFE
[Mark v. 21—43]

§ 1	Differences in the Synoptic narratives . . .	94
§ 2	"Knowing that she was dead" in Luke, "Lazarus is dead" in John	100

CHAPTER V
JESUS IN HIS OWN COUNTRY
[Mark vi 1—6 a]

§ 1	The agreements and disagreements of the Four Gospels	107
§ 2	"His country" and "his own country," in all the Gospels	109
§ 3	"And his disciples follow him," in Mark . .	111
§ 4	"Were astonished" in Mark and Matthew, how expressed in Luke	113
§ 5	"Cast down a precipice" and "hang," confused in a version of Luke	115
§ 6	Attempts on Christ's life, in John . . .	118
§ 7	"Wisdom" and "mighty works," in Mark and Matthew	119
§ 8	"The carpenter," in Mark and Matthew . . .	120
§ 9	"Offended," in the Synoptists	124
§ 10	"Offended," in John	128

CONTENTS

		PAGE
§ 11	"Not without-honour," in Mark and Matthew	133
§ 12	"And he was not able to do there any mighty work," in Mark	137
§ 13	"And he marvelled because of their unbelief," in Mark	143

CHAPTER VI
THE SENDING OF THE APOSTLES
[Mark vi 6 b—13]

§ 1	Johannine "sending of the apostles"	148
§ 2	Jesus "going round the villages in a circle," in Mark	152
§ 3	"He began to send them out by two and two," in Mark	155
§ 4	"Save a staff only," in Mark	158
§ 5	A parallel from the Essenes	161
§ 6	What corresponds to "the staff" in John?	165
§ 7	"Shod (R V) with sandals," in Mark	167
§ 8	What corresponds to "sandals" in John?	168
§ 9	"Scrip," "girdle," "purse"	170
§ 10	"Anointing with oil," in Mark and James	175
§ 11	"The sin unto death"	178
§ 12	"Anointing" among the Jews	180
§ 13	"Anointing [with oil]" metaphorical	183
§ 14	"Many that were infirm," in Mark	184
§ 15	Johannine tradition	187

CHAPTER VII
JOHN THE BAPTIST'S DEATH
[Mark vi 14—29]

§ 1	What was said after the Baptist's death	190
§ 2	The cause of the Baptist's death	195

CHAPTER VIII
CHRIST'S MIRACLES OF FEEDING
[Mark vi 29—44, and see vii 24—ix 1]

§ 1	The complexity of the evidence	203
§ 2	Traces of metaphor underlying the narratives about the "baskets"	209
§ 3	The immediate sequel of John the Baptist's death	216
§ 4	"And he saith unto them, Come ye. .and rest a little," in Mark	219

CONTENTS

		PAGE
§ 5	"Come ye, [by] yourselves, apart, into a desert place," in Mark	223
§ 6	The concourse of "many," in Mark	226
§ 7	"They had no leisure so much as to eat," in Mark	233
§ 8	"To a desert place apart," in Mark and Matthew	237
§ 9	"In the boat," in Mark	241
§ 10	Signs of conflation in Mark	243
§ 11	"On foot," in Mark and Matthew	245
§ 12	"He had compassion," in Mark and Matthew	247
§ 13	"They were as sheep not having a shepherd," in Mark and Matthew	252
§ 14	"Shepherd" (*sing*) nowhere mentioned by Luke	254
§ 15	"And he began to teach them many things," in Mark	256
§ 16	"When the day was now far spent," in Mark	261
§ 17	"They continue with me now three days," in Mark and Matthew	263
§ 18	"Buying" or "Whence?"	269
§ 19	"Two hundred pennyworth," in Mark and John	274
§ 20	"How many loaves have ye? Go [and] see," in Mark	283
§ 21	"There is a lad here," in John	286
§ 22	"Here," in all the Gospels	294
§ 23	"By companies," "by ranks," in Mark	296
§ 24	"On the green grass," in Mark	302
§ 25	"By hundreds and by fifties," in Mark	309
§ 26	"Taking," "blessing," and "looking up to heaven"	315
§ 27	"Breaking in pieces" or "breaking"	321
§ 28	"And the two fishes he divided among [them] all," in Mark	328
§ 29	"Twelve basketfuls" (R V), in Mark	336
§ 30	"They that ate the loaves," in Mark	344
§ 31	"Five thousand men" or "about five thousand [men]"	348
§ 32	Irenaeus and Origen on the "five thousand" in the Acts, and Clement of Alexandria on the "five loaves"	352
§ 33	"Give ye them to eat," why omitted by John	355
§ 34	"Eating" in the presence of the Lord	357
§ 35	"That he should give something to the poor," in John	360
§ 36	"We all partake of the one loaf"	363
§ 37	"Jesus...taketh the loaf and giveth to them," in John	365
§ 38	Christ's "leaven"	370
§ 39	The passionateness of the Eucharist	375
§ 40	The "kiss of love"	378
§ 41	"Testament" or "Covenant"	384
§ 42	"Testament" in the Gospels	392

CONTENTS

CHAPTER IX
JESUS WALKING ON THE SEA
[Mark vi 45—52]

		PAGE
§ 1	The sequel of the Feeding of the Five Thousand	403
§ 2	Christ's journeying in North Palestine	407
§ 3	"Having (?) bidden them farewell," in Mark	413
§ 4	"Distressed" and "the fourth watch of the night," in Mark and Matthew	418
§ 5	"Distressed," differently applied in Mark and Matthew	421
§ 6	How Peter "was grieved" by Jesus	426
§ 7	"For they all saw him," in Mark	429
§ 8	"An apparition," in Mark and Matthew	430
§ 9	"But their heart was hardened," in Mark	438

CHAPTER X
THE NEW LAW OF PURIFICATION
[Mark vi 53—vii 23]

§ 1	Jesus is followed at first by the multitudes	442
§ 2	Jesus is attacked by the Pharisees concerning the washing of hands	445
§ 3	The reply of Jesus to the Pharisees, in Mark and Matthew	451
§ 4	The doctrine of Jesus on "purifying," in Matthew and Luke	455
§ 5	Johannine Intervention	458

CHAPTER XI
THE NEW LAW OF SACRIFICE
[Mark vii 24—ix 1[1]]

§ 1	The Syrophoenician woman	464
§ 2	The first "sighing" of Jesus, in Mark	467
§ 3	The second "sighing" of Jesus, in Mark	474
§ 4	The disciples are said for the second time to have their "heart hardened," in Mark	478
§ 5	Jesus lays His hands twice on a blind man and heals him, in Mark	483

---

[1] See p 464, n. *.

CONTENTS

			PAGE
§ 6	The Johannine healing of blindness	. .	489
§ 7	"Prophet," "Son of Man," "Christ"	. .	493
§ 8	"Get thee behind me, Satan," in Mark and Matthew .		498
§ 9	Variations in the expression of the New Law	. .	501
§ 10	"Denying oneself"		506
§ 11	"Taking up the cross" and "following"	. .	507
§ 12	"For my sake and the gospel's," in Mark	. .	511
§ 13	"For what could a man give in exchange for his soul?" in Mark and Matthew	.	512
§ 14	"In this adulterous generation," in Mark	. .	515
§ 15	"With the angels that are holy," in Mark	. .	518
§ 16	"When he cometh in the glory of his Father"	. .	522

INDICES

I	Scriptural Passages	. . . .	529
II	English .	. .	543
III	Greek .		570

REFERENCES AND ABBREVIATIONS

REFERENCES

(i) *a*. References to the first nine Parts of Diatessarica (as to which see pp. 574—5) are by paragraphs in black Arabic numbers —

    1— 272 = *Clue*.
    273— 552 = *Corrections of Mark*
    553—1149 = *From Letter to Spirit*.
    1150—1435 = *Paradosis*.
    1436—1885 = *Johannine Vocabulary*
    1886—2799 = *Johannine Grammar*.
    2800—2999 = *Notes on New Testament Criticism*.
    3000—3635 = *The Son of Man*
    3636—3999 = *Light on the Gospel from an ancient Poet*.

(i) *b* References to the Sections of the Tenth Part of Diatessarica, entitled *The Fourfold Gospel*, are by pages The four Sections now completed are —

    (Section 1) *Introduction*.
    (Section 2) *The Beginning*
    (Section 3) *The Proclamation of the New Kingdom*
    (Section 4) *The Law of the New Kingdom*

(ii) The Books of Scripture are referred to by the ordinary abbreviations, except where specified below. But when it is said that Samuel, Isaiah, Matthew, or any other writer, wrote this or that, it is to be understood as meaning *the writer, whoever he may be, of the words in question*, and not as meaning that the actual writer was Samuel, Isaiah, or Matthew.

(iii) The principal Greek MSS are denoted by ℵ, A, B, etc , the Latin versions by *a*, *b*, etc , as usual The Syriac version discovered by Mrs Lewis on Mount Sinai is referred to as SS, *i e*. "Sinaitic Syrian " It is always quoted from Prof Burkitt's translation. I regret that in the first three vols of Diatessarica Mrs Lewis's name was omitted in connection with this version.

(iv) The text of the Greek Old Testament adopted is that of B, edited by Prof. Swete; of the New, that of Westcott and Hort.

(v) Modern works are referred to by the name of the work, or author, vol., and page, *e.g.* Levy iii. 343 *a*, *i e* vol. iii. p. 343, col. 1.

REFERENCES AND ABBREVIATIONS

ABBREVIATIONS

Aq = Aquila's version of O T
Brederek = Brederek's *Konkordanz zum Targum Onkelos*, Giessen, 1906.
Burk. = Prof F C. Burkitt's *Evangelion Da-mepharreshe*, Cambridge University Press, 1904
Chr = *Chronicles*
Clem Alex 42 = Clement of Alexandria in Potter's page 42.
Dalman, *Words* = *Words of Jesus*, Eng. Transl. 1902; *Aram. G.* = *Grammatik des Judisch-Palästinischen Aramäisch*, 1894
En = Enoch ed Charles, Clarendon Press, 1893
Ency = *Encyclopaedia Biblica*, A. & C. Black, 1899.
Ephrem = Ephraemus Syrus, ed Moesinger.
Etheridge = Etheridge's translations of the Targums on the Pentateuch
Euseb = the Ecclesiastical History of Eusebius
Field = Origenis Hexaplorum quae supersunt, Oxford, 1875, also Otium Norvicense, 1881.
Gesen = the Oxford edition of Gesenius
Goldschm = *Der Babylonische Talmud*, 1897—1912, ed Goldschmidt
Goodspeed = Goodspeed's *Indices*, (i) *Patristicus*, Leipzig, 1907, (ii) *Apologeticus*, Leipzig, 1912
Hastings = Dictionary of the Bible, ed Hastings (5 vols)
Hor Heb = *Horae Hebraicae*, by John Lightfoot, 1658—74, ed Gandell, Oxf 1859
Iren. = the treatise of Irenaeus against Heresies
Jer. Targ or Targ Jer (abbrev for Jerusalem Targum), or Jon. Targ (i e Targum of Jonathan, abbrev for the Targum of Pseudo-Jonathan) = the Targum of Pseudo-Jonathan on the Pentateuch, of which there are two recensions—both quoted (*Notes on N T Criticism*, Pref. p viii) by ancient authorities under the name "Jerusalem Targum." The two recensions are severally denoted by Jer. I and Jer II. On other books, the Targum is referred to as simply "Targ "
Jon Targ , see Jer Targ
Justin = Justin Martyr (*Apol.* = his First Apology, *Tryph.* = the Dialogue with Trypho)
K = *Kings*
Krauss = Krauss's *Griechische und Lateinische Lehnworter* etc., Part ii, Berlin, 1899.

REFERENCES AND ABBREVIATIONS

Levy = Levy's *Neuhebräisches und Chaldäisches 'Worterbuch*, 4 vols, Leipzig, 1889; Levy Ch = *Chaldäisches Worterbuch*, 2 vols., 1881.

L S. = Liddell and Scott's Greek Lexicon

Mechilta, see Wu(nsche).

Onk. = the Targum of Onkelos on the Pentateuch.

Origen is referred to variously, e g *Hom. Exod.* 11 25 = lib. 11. ch. 25 of Hom. Exod , but Orig on Exod. 11 25 = the commentary *ad loc.*, Lomm 111 24 = vol. 111. p 24 of Lommatzsch's edition.

Oxf Conc = *The Oxford Concordance to the Septuagint*

Pec. = peculiar to the writer mentioned in the context.

Pesikta, see Wu(nsche).

Philo is referred to by Mangey's volume and page, *e g.* Philo 11. 234, or, as to Latin treatises, by the Scripture text or Aucher's pages (P A.).

Pistis = *Pistis Sophia*, ed. Petermann (marginal pages).

Ps Sol = *Psalms of Solomon*, ed Ryle and James, Cambr 1891.

R, after Gen, Exod, Lev. etc means *Rabboth*, and refers to Wunsche's edition of the Midrash on the Pentateuch, e g. *Gen. r.* (on Gen. xii 2, Wu p 177)

Rashi, sometimes quoted from Breithaupt's translation, 1714

S = *Samuel*; s = "see"

Schottg = Schottgen's *Horae Hebraicae*, Dresden and Leipzig, 1733.

Sir = the work of Ben Sira, *i e* the son of Sira It is commonly called Ecclesiasticus (see *Clue* 20 *a*) The original Hebrew used in this work is that which has been edited, in part, by Cowley and Neubauer, Oxf 1897, in part, by Schechter and Taylor, Cambr. 1899; in part, by G Margoliouth, *Jewish Quart. Rev*, Oct. 1899 (also printed in *About Hebrew Manuscripts* (Frowde, 1905) by Mr E. N Adler, who discovered the missing chapters).

SS, see (iii) above

Steph. Thes = Stephani *Thesaurus Graecae Linguae* (Didot).

Sym = Symmachus's version of O T

Targ. (by itself) is used where only one Targum is extant on the passage quoted

Targ. Jer., Targ Jon, and Targ. Onk, see Jer. Targ, Jon. Targ., and Onk., above.

Tehillim = Midrash on Psalms, ed. Wunsche (2 vols.).

Test xii Patr = Testaments of the Twelve Patriarchs ed. Charles, 1908 (Gk, Clarendon Press, Eng., A. & C Black).

Theod. = Theodotion's version of O T.

Thes. Syr = Payne Smith's *Thesaurus Syriacus*, Oxf. 1901

Tromm. = Trommius' *Concordance to the Septuagint*.

REFERENCES AND ABBREVIATIONS

Tryph. = the Dialogue between Justin Martyr and Trypho the Jew.

Walton = *Biblia Sacra Polyglotta*, 1657.

Wetst = Wetstein's *Comm. on the New Testament*, Amsterdam, 1751.

W.H. = Westcott and Hort's New Testament.

Wu. = Wunsche's translation of *Rabboth* etc., 1880—1909 (including *Mechilta, Pesikta Rab Kahana, Tehillim* etc.).

(a) A bracketed Arabic number, following Mk, Mt , etc indicates the number of instances in which a word occurs in Mark, Matthew, etc , e g ἀγάπη Mk (0), Mt. (1), Lk. (1), Jn (7).

(b) Where verses in Hebrew, Greek, and Revised Version, are numbered differently, the number of R.V. is given alone

(c) In transliterating a Hebrew, Aramaic, or Syriac word, preference has often, but not invariably, been given to that form which best reveals the connection between the word in question and forms of it familiar to English readers   Where a word is not transliterated, it is often indicated (for the sake of experts) by a reference to Gesen , *Thes. Syr* , Levy, or Levy *Ch.*

CHAPTER I

THE PARABLES OF SOWING
[Mark iv. 1—34]

§ 1. *Christ's "parables" or "things hidden*[1]*"*

MATTHEW concludes his exposition of what he calls Christ's "parables" with the words "That it might be fulfilled which

---

[1] In this chapter it has not been found possible to treat of small differences of expression in the Synoptic texts printed below. One of them—the passage where Luke (viii 13) substitutes "in time of temptation they *fall away*," for the tradition of Mark (closely followed by Matthew) "When tribulation or persecution ariseth because of the word, straightway they *stumble*"—will be referred to later on in discussing Mk vi 3 "and they were offended in him." The present chapter does not enter into verbal detail except where some Marcan phrase omitted or altered by Luke demands consideration.

In the parallel passages printed below, and for the most part in others printed in footnotes, R V text is followed (with a very few occasional deviations indicated by brackets) as being convenient for rapid reference enabling the reader to take a broad view of the subject under consideration. But in the detailed study of the Greek text, R V text is frequently departed from.

Here and elsewhere the parallel Synoptic texts are printed below in full, not for continuous reading along with the remarks made above, but for the convenience of rapid reference when the reader desires to know the context of any passage under discussion.

Mk iv 1—20 (R V)	Mt. xiii. 1—23 (R V.)	Lk viii. 4—15 (R V)
(1) And again he began to teach by the sea side. And there is gathered unto him a very great multitude, so that he entered into a boat, and	(1) On that day went Jesus out of the house, and sat by the sea side (2) And there were gathered unto him great multitudes,	(4) And when a great multitude came together, and they of every city resorted unto him, he spake by a parable

A. L   I (Mark iv 1—20)   I

THE PARABLES OF SOWING

was spoken by the prophet, saying, 'I will open my mouth in

Mk iv 1—20 (R V) contd	Mt xiii 1—23 (R.V) contd.	Lk. viii 4—15 (R V) contd
sat in the sea, and all the multitude were by the sea on the land	so that he entered into a boat, and sat, and all the multitude stood on the beach	
(2) And he taught them many things in parables, and said unto them in his teaching,	(3) And he spake to them many things in parables, saying, Behold, the sower went forth to sow,	(5) The sower went forth to sow his seed and as he sowed, some fell by the way side, and it was trodden under foot, and the birds of the heaven devoured it
(3) Hearken Behold, the sower went forth to sow	(4) And as he sowed, some [seeds] fell by the way side, and the birds came and devoured them	
(4) And it came to pass, as he sowed, some [seed] fell by the way side, and the birds came and devoured it		
(5) And other fell on the rocky [ground], where it had not much earth, and straightway it sprang up, because it had no deepness of earth	(5) And others fell upon the rocky places, where they had not much earth and straightway they sprang up, because they had no deepness of earth	(6) And other fell on the rock, and as soon as it grew, it withered away because it had no moisture
(6) And when the sun was risen, it was scorched, and because it had no root, it withered away	(6) And when the sun was risen, they were scorched, and because they had no root, they withered away	
(7) And other fell among the thorns, and the thorns grew up, and choked it, and it yielded no fruit	(7) And others fell upon the thorns, and the thorns grew up, and choked them	(7) And other fell amidst the thorns, and the thorns grew with it, and choked it
(8) And others fell into the good ground, and yielded fruit, growing up and increasing, and brought forth, thirtyfold, and sixtyfold, and a hundredfold	(8) And others fell upon the good ground, and yielded fruit, some a hundredfold, some sixty, some thirty	(8) And other fell into the good ground, and grew, and brought forth fruit a hundredfold As he said these things, he cried, He that hath ears to hear, let him hear.
(9) And he said, Who hath ears to hear, let him hear	(9) He that hath ears (*some anc auth add* to hear), let him hear	
(10) And when he was alone, they that	(10) And the disciples came, and said	(9) And his disciples asked him

THE PARABLES OF SOWING

parables, I will utter [*things*] *hidden* from the foundation [of the

Mk iv 1—20 (R V.) *contd*	Mt. xiii 1—23 (R V.) *contd*	Lk viii 4—15 (R V.) *contd.*
were about him with the twelve asked of him the parables	unto him, Why speakest thou unto them in parables?	what this parable might be
(11) And he said unto them, Unto you is given the mystery of the kingdom of God but unto them that are without, all things are done in parables	(11) And he answered and said unto them, Unto you it is given to know the mysteries of the kingdom of heaven, but to them it is not given	(10) And he said, Unto you it is given to know the mysteries of the kingdom of God but to the rest in parables, that seeing they may not see, and hearing they may not understand.
(12) That seeing they may see, and not perceive, and hearing they may hear, and not understand, lest haply they should turn again, and it should be forgiven them	(12) For whosoever hath, to him... (13) Therefore speak I to them in parables, because seeing they see not, and hearing they hear not, neither do they understand	
(13) And he saith unto them, Know ye not this parable? and how shall ye know all the parables?	.... (15) Lest haply they should and should turn again, and I should heal them	(11) Now the parable is this The seed is the word of God.
(14) The sower soweth the word	....	(12) And those by the way side are they that have heard, then cometh the devil, and taketh away the word from their heart, that they may not believe and be saved.
(15) And these are they by the way side, where the word is sown, and when they have heard, straightway cometh Satan, and taketh away the word which hath been sown in them	(18) Hear then ye the parable of the sower	
	(19) When any one heareth the word of the kingdom, and understandeth it not, [then] cometh the evil [one], and snatcheth away that which hath been sown in his heart This is he that was sown by the way side	
(16) And these in like manner are they that are sown upon the rocky [places], who, when they have heard the word, straightway receive (λαμβάνουσιν) it with joy, (17) And they have no root in themselves, but endure	(20) And he that was sown upon the rocky places, this is he that heareth the word, and straightway with joy receiveth (λαμβάνων) it, (21) Yet hath he	(13) And those on the rock [are] they which, when they have heard, receive (δέχονται) the word with joy, and these have no root, which for a while believe,

THE PARABLES OF SOWING

world]¹'" This is a free quotation from a Psalm of Asaph, "I will open my mouth in a parable², I will utter *enigmas*, or, *riddles* of old³." The "riddles" appear to be the mysterious dispensations by which God is described in this long Psalm as

Mk iv 1—20 (R V.) contd.	Mt xiii 1—23 (R V) contd	Lk viii 4—15 (R V) contd
for a while, then, when tribulation or persecution ariseth because of the word, straightway they stumble	not root in himself, but endureth for a while, and when tribulation or persecution ariseth because of the word, straightway he stumbleth	and in time of temptation fall away.
(18) And others are they that are sown among the thorns, these are they that have heard the word, (19) And the cares of the world (*or*, age), and the deceitfulness of riches, and the lusts of other things entering in, choke the word, and it becometh unfruitful (20) And those are they that were sown upon the good ground, such as hear the word, and accept it, and bear fruit, thirtyfold, and sixtyfold, and a hundredfold	(22) And he that was sown among the thorns, this is he that heareth the word, and the care of the world (*or*, age), and the deceitfulness of riches, choke the word, and he becometh unfruitful (23) And he that was sown upon the good ground, this is he that heareth the word, and understandeth it, who verily beareth fruit, and bringeth forth, some a hundredfold, some sixty, some thirty	(14) And that which fell among the thorns, these are they that have heard, and as they go on their way they are choked with cares and riches and pleasures of [this] life, and bring no fruit to perfection (15) And that in the good ground, these are such as in an honest and good heart, having heard the word, hold it fast, and bring forth fruit with patience

¹ Mt xiii 35 ἀνοίξω ἐν παραβολαῖς τὸ στόμα μου, ἐρεύξομαι κεκρυμμένα ἀπὸ καταβολῆς.

² Ps lxxviii 2 (LXX) ἀνοίξω ἐν παραβολαῖς (Aq ἐν παραβολῇ, Sym διὰ παροιμίας) τὸ στόμα μου

³ Ps lxxviii 2 (LXX) φθέγξομαι προβλήματα ἀπ' ἀρχῆς, Aq. ὀμβρήσω αἰνίγματα ἐξ ἀρχῆθεν, Sym ἀναβλύσω προβλήματα ἀρχαῖα The Heb חידה=αἴνιγμα (4), διήγημα or διήγησις (2), πρόβλημα (10) Πρόβλημα (Judg xiv 12—19) means (8 times) "riddle" In Ps xlix 4 "I will open my *enigma* on the harp," the "enigma" appears to be the temporary prosperity of those who fear not God and who are (*ib* 20) 'like the beasts that perish" Matthew paraphrases "riddle" as

THE PARABLES OF SOWING

permitting Israel to rebel against Him and to need His chastening in the course of their national growth. The growth went on, but, along with it, there went apparent waste. Isaiah puts such a "riddle" venturesomely before us when he represents Israel as crying "O Lord, why *dost thou make us to err* from thy ways, and *hardenest our heart* from thy fear[1]?" Isaiah also writes "Thou art *a God that hidest thyself*, O God of Israel the Saviour[2]"; and he represents even the Chosen Servant, in apparent discouragement, as saying—or at all events as having once said to the Lord—"I have laboured in vain, I have spent my strength for nought and vanity[3]."

Jesus is brought before us by all the Synoptists, in the Parable of the Sower, as recognising the danger of converting the God of Israel into "a God that hides Himself." According to Mark and Luke, He places this danger before His disciples in language borrowed from Isaiah about a judicial sentence of blindness ("in order that, seeing, they may see and yet not

---

κεκρυμμένα But Paul retains the thought in 1 Cor xiii 12 βλέπομεν γὰρ ἄρτι δι' ἐσόπτρου ἐν αἰνίγματι—the only N T instance of αἴνιγμα

In Mk iv 11 ἐκείνοις δὲ τοῖς ἔξω ἐν παραβολαῖς τὰ πάντα γίνεται, "for those outside *all things take place* in parables," τὰ πάντα γίνεται has a force that seems to have escaped Matthew and Luke. The parables were not wholly "parables" (that is, obscure sayings, as in Ezek xx 49 "Doth he not speak *parables* (משל)?") to those who had some power of spiritual hearing and seeing. Jesus endeavoured to teach with clearness, as the actors in a play try to speak with clearness. But "all things took place in parables" for those who were deaf to the voice of the Spirit that inspired the Teacher. Similarly, for the deaf, in a theatre, "*all things take place* in dumb show."

[1] Is lxiii 17 (where R V margin refers us to Is vi. 10, and Jn xii 40) Ibn Ezra accepts the words on the ground that "God is the highest, first cause of everything," but adds other explanations

[2] Is xlv 15, where Ibn Ezra protests against the paraphrase "an invisible God." Comp *ib* lvii 17 "For the iniquity of his covetousness. I hid [myself]"

[3] Is xlix 3—4 "He said unto me, Thou art my servant, Israel, in whom I will be glorified. But I said, I have laboured .."

5 (Mark iv 1—20)

behold ")[1] The language seems to represent the teaching by parables as itself causing, and intended to cause, the blindness. Matthew softens this. John, on the other hand, commenting on the reasons why the Jews did not accept the teaching of Jesus, says, "For this cause *they were not able to believe*, because Isaiah said again, *He hath blinded their eyes and he hardened their heart, lest they should see with their eyes and perceive with their heart*, and should turn, and I should heal them[2]."

This "riddle," or "dark saying," about the "hardening" of Israel's heart by God, is one side of what Paul calls a "mystery" when he says to the Romans "I would not, brethren, have you ignorant of this *mystery*...that a *hardening* in part hath befallen Israel[3]." But there is another side, expressed in the following words—"*until the fulness of the Gentiles be come in*"—so that the "mystery," as a whole, means the issue of good out of evil, and of redemption out of stumbling. The recognition of this particular "mystery" is a comfort to Paul as a teacher of the Gospel[4]. A similar recognition of the general "mystery" of the Gospel's success through apparent failure seems to be implied in the Parable of the Sower, or rather in the explanation of it subsequently given by Jesus when He says to the disciples—in Mark—"Unto you is given the mystery of the kingdom of God." Justin Martyr says, in his only reference to this Parable, "As my Lord said, 'The sower went forth to sow the seed, and some fell...and some on good ground'." I must speak, then, in the hope that there may be

---

[1] So Mk iv 12 with "*in order that*," ἵνα μὴ ἴδωσιν and sim. Lk viii 10 ἵνα μὴ βλέπωσιν, but Mt xiii 13 with "*because*," ὅτι βλέποντες οὐ βλέπουσιν.

[2] Jn xii 39—40. Comp *ib* ix 39 "For judgment came I into this world, that they that see not may see, and that they that see may become blind," with the following question of the Pharisees "Are we also blind?" and Christ's reply.

[3] Rom xi 25.

[4] Rom xi. 25—33 concluding "O the depth of the riches both of the wisdom and of the knowledge of God!"

THE PARABLES OF SOWING

good ground somewhere[1]" And Origen, quoting words peculiar to Mark, "He that soweth soweth the word," says "Who are they that sow? It is those who bring forth the word of God in the Church Let the teachers therefore hearken...," and the context warns us that the word of God must not be "contaminated by those who sow it[2]"

These two ancient references warn us against assuming that the Parable of the Sower was intended merely to teach every disciple of Christ to be on his guard against the evil influences that might destroy the seed of the Gospel in his own soul It teaches that, but it teaches also more than that. It is adapted for him as a preacher of the Gospel—which every disciple of Christ is supposed to be—as well as for him as a hearer of it. In the Psalm already referred to, Asaph begins by saying "Give ear, O my people, to my law," and terminates his "riddles," or "dark sayings," by shewing how Israel, through innumerable failures, was led at last successfully into the fold of its Shepherd[3]. Jesus, preparing His disciples to proclaim the New Law, teaches them that there are as many phases of failure as of success[4]; and His allusion to Isaiah indicates that He perceived Israel itself, the Chosen People—with its bewildering mixture of arrogance and ignorance, spiritual possibilities and carnal realisations—to be in some sense a failure and a "riddle[5]."

---

[1] *Tryph* § 125

[2] Origen, *Levit Hom* xii 7 (Lomm ix 396) Origen is referring to the "contamination" mentioned in Lev xxi. 14—15 But his words suggest that the "birds" and "thorns" and other influences that destroy the seed of the Gospel, might be mentioned in warnings to teachers as well as to hearers

[3] Ps lxxviii 1, 70—72

[4] The three classes of success, recognised in Mk iv 8 (Mt xiii 8), Mk iv 20 (Mt xiii 23) are not recognised in the parall. Lk viii 8, 15.

[5] Compare Pope's sceptical couplet on Man as the angels regard him —
"Sole judge of truth, in endless error hurled,
The glory, jest, and riddle of the world"
Essay on Man, ii 17—18.

THE PARABLES OF SOWING

But every Hebrew prophet knew that there was to be a solution to the "riddle" of Jehovah and a success through His temporary appearances of failure, so that when Isaiah heard the astounding message, "Make the heart of this people fat, and make their ears heavy, and shut their eyes, lest they see with their eyes, and hear with their ears," he answered at once, "Lord, how long[1]?" knowing that this was but a means to an end. Jesus could not have fallen below this standard of prophetic hopefulness. The three Synoptists have variously reported His quotation of Isaiah's words, and the Fourth Evangelist has quoted them in his own person in a separate form[2]. These variations must be carefully studied But we must study them always on the lines of Hebrew and Jewish thought, and always in adherence to the rule that, where the Gospels vary, a difficult and rough Hebraistic tradition is probably truer than a smooth Hellenistic form of it

§ 2. "*Hear ye*," *in Mark*[3]

Matthew and Luke omit this, and so does the Diatessaron. It might allude to the "*hear thou*" in Deuteronomy ("*Hear thou*, O Israel, the Lord our God is one Lord[4]"). But there would seem to be more appropriateness in an allusion to the Psalm of Asaph above quoted "*Hearken thou*, O my people, to my law...I will open my mouth in *a parable*[5]" Matthew and

---

[1] Is vi 10—11

[2] Jn xii 40

[3] Mk iv 2—3 "...and said unto them in his teaching, *Hearken* (ἀκούετε) " om in Mt xiii 3, Lk viii 4—5 Comp the answers to the question as to which was the "first" or great commandment — Mk xii 29 (to "one of the scribes") "The first is, *Hear* (ἄκουε), O Israel, the Lord our God, the Lord is one, and thou shalt love ," Mt. xxii 37 (to "a lawyer") "Thou shalt love " Luke, in a different context, represents "a lawyer" as replying to Jesus (x 27) "Thou shalt love...," without the prefatory "*hear* "

[4] Deut vi. 4.

[5] Ps lxxviii 1—2 LXX "attend ye (προσέχετε)," Aq ἐνωτίζου The Heb = forms of ἀκούω (3), ἐνωτίζομαι (26), προσέχω (7)

THE PARABLES OF SOWING

Luke may have omitted "Hear ye" as being too strong a phrase to introduce a single parable in a course of parabolic teaching in which Jesus (as Mark and Matthew say) "taught" the people "many things in parables." But if the parable introduces a new spiritual "law" in which two kinds of "hearing" are distinguished, and the right kind of "hearing" is regarded as resulting in a regeneration of the hearer, then Mark is justified in the prominence that he gives to the Saviour's initial command to "hearken."

John—though he never represents Jesus as saying "Hearken ye," or as quoting the formula "Hear, O Israel"—distinguishes in a very careful and subtle way between passive hearing and receptive hearing[1]. When Jesus for the first time mentions "hearing," it is in a dialogue with Nicodemus to whom He is attempting to explain the doctrine of regeneration through the Spirit[2]. After first stating it in general terms ("except *any one* be born from above") He insists that it applies to Nicodemus himself and to his associates, the Pharisees, who are deaf to the inner meaning of the Spirit "Marvel not that I said unto thee that *thou and thy associates*[3] must be born from above The Spirit breatheth, or bloweth, where it willeth[4], and *thou hearest* [the mere sound of] its voice, but knowest not whence it cometh, and whither it goeth," that is to say its source or motive, and

---

[1] See *Joh Voc* **1614** *b—c* on the Johannine ἀκούω with accus and with genit In Jn v 25 Westcott rightly paraphrases οἱ ἀκούσαντες as "those who receive it." The meaning is "those who take it in through hearing."

[2] Jn iii 3—8.

[3] "Thou and thy associates" = ὑμᾶς, in δεῖ ὑμᾶς γεννηθῆναι ἄνωθεν Ὑμᾶς is made emphatic by its superfluousness The natural phrase would have been δεῖ γεννηθῆναι, "one must needs be born." But Jesus means "*You and your friends the Pharisees*, who think yourselves superior to such a need."

[4] On the play on the word πνεῦμα, see *Joh Voc* **1655**, and add that πνεῦμα is taken as the Spirit by Origen *Num Hom* xxvii 13 (Lomm x 363), *De Princip* i 4 (Lomm xxi 76), and by Jerome (*Letters* lviii 3)

THE PARABLES OF SOWING

its object or purpose. This is an appeal as it were to all the Scribes or Teachers of Israel, in the person of Nicodemus, to whom Jesus says "Art thou the teacher of Israel and dost thou not recognise these things¹?"

Later on, an instance of this sound, or voice, of the Spirit, and of its being misunderstood—but on this occasion not by Pharisees, but by the multitude and by others—is presented dramatically: "There came *a voice* from heaven, 'I have both glorified it and will glorify it again' The multitude therefore that was standing *and heard* [*it*] said that it had thundered; others said 'An angel hath spoken to him².'" Here the misunderstood voice follows immediately on a proclamation of the doctrine about the grain of wheat, "If it die, it beareth much fruit³" This is, in effect, a brief repetition of the doctrine of regeneration through the Spirit and at the same time a suggestion of a new aspect of a detail in the Parables of Sowing And both the Johannine passages call attention to the importance of the right kind of "hearing"—as Mark does in the tradition under discussion.

§ 3. *When did the disciples "ask Jesus the parables"?*

The Synoptists differ here. Mark writes, "And when he was alone, they that were about him with the Twelve began to ask (*or*, used to ask) [of] him *the parables*⁴" Mark has

---

¹ Jn iii. 10.   ² Jn xii 28—9
³ Jn xii 24

Mk iv 10 καὶ ὅτε ἐγένετο κατὰ μόνας ἠρώτων αὐτὸν οἱ περὶ αὐτὸν σὺν τοῖς δώδεκα τὰς παραβολάς, Mt xiii 10 καὶ προσελθόντες οἱ μαθηταὶ εἶπαν αὐτῷ, Διὰ τί ἐν παραβολαῖς λαλεῖς αὐτοῖς, Lk viii 9 ἐπηρώτων δὲ αὐτὸν οἱ μαθηταὶ αὐτοῦ τίς αὕτη εἴη ἡ παραβολή In Mk, Codex D has (instead of τὰς παραβολάς) τίς ἡ παραβολὴ αὕτη, and so have *a, b, c* etc (see Swete) Origen (*Comm Matth*, Lomm iv 193), after quoting Mt. and Lk correctly, says "Marcus vero sic, 'Et cum *facti fuissent secreti*, interrogabant eum discipuli quae esset parabola haec'" Diatess also has "And when *they were alone*" See p. 45 foll., "*Private 'expounding' in Mark*"

THE PARABLES OF SOWING

previously written, "Jesus began (*or*, used) to teach them *many things* in parables, and said to them in [the course of] his teaching[1]," after which he places the Parable of the Sower. The two statements imply that the disciples did not ask the meaning of the Parable of the Sower separately, and immediately But the parallel Luke expressly says that they did ("they began to question him *what this parable was*"). Matthew gives the question quite a different turn, "Why speakest thou to them in parables?" But he does not say that the disciples waited to ask this till Jesus was "alone." He merely says that they "came to" Jesus to ask it. This does not imply an interval of any long duration. Mark's tradition appears to have been corrected by Matthew and Luke partly because of its verbal, and partly because of its historical, difficulty. Verbally, though "ask" could be used with two accusatives in such phrases as "ask him *the name*," "ask him *the meaning*," it could hardly be used in "asked him *the parables*," unless it meant "asked him what secret meaning he implied[2]."

That Mark does actually use "parable" here to mean "secret meaning of the parable," appears probable from another passage where Jesus maintains that a man is defiled not by what goes into him but by what comes out of him. Concerning this astounding paradox—as it would appear to most Jews—Mark says that Christ's disciples "*questioned him* [*about*] *the parable*," where Matthew avoids the word "question" and

---

[1] Mk iv 2 καὶ ἐδίδασκεν αὐτοὺς ἐν παραβολαῖς πολλά, καὶ ἔλεγεν αὐτοῖς ἐν τῇ διδαχῇ αὐτοῦ

[2] Steph. *Thes* in a very long note on ἐρωτάω = "ask concerning," quotes only (1) "Aristoph [?] ἐρωτᾶν πόλιν," an error (see Aristoph *Pax* 688), and (2) Plato *Pol.* 508 A τὸν ἥλιον ἐρωτᾷς The latter follows the question "Whom can you mention as the Causer of light?" and means "You are asking me [the name of] the Sun "

THE PARABLES OF SOWING

represents Peter as saying to Jesus, "*Tell us the parable*[1]." In both narratives, "*parable*" seems to mean "*the secret at the bottom of the parable*"

If that is Mark's meaning, his language may be illustrated (as often) from Hermas—almost the only very early Patristic writer that uses the word "parable[2]." Hermas gives us a whole book of Parables, written down at the direction of the Shepherd The sense he sometimes attaches to the word may be inferred from his replying—when the Shepherd tells him that grief destroys man and crushes out the Holy Spirit—"My Lord, I am of no understanding and do not understand *these parables*, for I do not perceive how grief is able to crush and [yet] again to save[3]." This usage is not that of literary Greek—a fact that may be illustrated by Justin Martyr's non-use of the

---

[1]   Mk vii 17   Mt xv 15
Καὶ ὅτε εἰσῆλθεν εἰς οἶκον ἀπὸ   Ἀποκριθεὶς δὲ ὁ Πέτρος εἶπεν
τοῦ ὄχλου, ἐπηρώτων αὐτὸν οἱ μαθηταὶ   αὐτῷ Φράσον ἡμῖν τὴν παραβολήν.
αὐτοῦ τὴν παραβολήν

Here Mark describes Jesus as going into a "house" where Matthew does not, and it becomes necessary to remember that "the *house* of Hillel" would be a familiar phrase for "*the disciples* of Hillel" (*Son* **3460** c)

Ἐπερωτᾶν is quoted by Steph *Thes* from Herod ix 93 ἐπειρώτεον τοὺς προφήτας τὸ αἴτιον, and from Dion Cass lvii 15 δίκας ἐπερώτων, "disceptans," but not in such a phrase as Mark's

[2] Besides Hermas, Goodspeed gives only Barn vi 10 "What then is the meaning of (λέγει) 'unto the good land...(Exod xxxiii. 1, 3)?.' The prophet means (*or*, says) (λέγει) *a parable of the Lord* [i e Jesus]," and *ib* xvii 2 "If I write to you about things impending or future ye will not understand, because they are involved in parables (διὰ τὸ ἐν παραβολαῖς κεῖσθαι)"

[3] Herm *Mand* x 1 3 The context calls such sayings (*ib* 4) τὰς παραβολὰς τῆς θεότητος. They may be sometimes called "spiritual paradoxes" Comp. *Mand* xi 18 foll "listen, then, to the *paradox* (παραβολήν) I am going to tell you" It is (among others) this—that a drop of water, which going up from below does nothing, when coming [down] from above does much, whence we are to infer that "the divine Spirit coming [down] from above is powerful," and to "believe" in that Spirit, but to "abstain" from the other, i e from the spirit of this world

THE PARABLES OF SOWING

word "parable" in his Apologies. In the Dialogue with the Jew he uses it a dozen times, but in the Apologies not once[1]. In literary Greek "parable" means comparison or illustration, without any suggestion of obscurity, paradox, or riddle[2]

Accepting, then, the Marcan meaning of "parables" to be something like "dark sayings," "riddles," or "paradoxes," we have to ask—since Matthew and Luke omit the Marcan statement about Christ's being "alone"—"How and where, if at all, does John intervene? As regards the *word* 'parable,' we know that John never mentions it. But he does introduce the *thought*, under the word *paroimia*, or 'proverb.' What then has John to say about Christ's use of 'proverbs' to His disciples either 'when he was alone' (as Mark says) or otherwise?"

John appears to have a definite and consistent theory about Christ's "proverbs," and to believe that Jesus *did not and could not explain them to the disciples while He was on earth*[3] The reason may be because the application of the proverbs was personal, and the Person, the Son, was not to be comprehended by the disciples till the Holy Spirit, the Paraclete, should come into their hearts. In any case John gives us the impression that, before the departure of the Son to the Father, everything that Jesus had said was a "proverb" to them, that is to say, an obscure saying[4]. It is true that, when Jesus Himself warns the disciples of this, the disciples contradict Him: "Now

---

[1] He uses it always about O.T. and always in the dative ("in a parable," or "parables") often along with words implying (*Tryph.* § 52) "hidden meaning," (*ib* § 68) "mysteries or symbols," (*ib.* § 77) "similitudes," (*ib* § 78) "mystery," (*ib* § 90) "types," etc, and often with a mention of the Holy Spirit (*ib* §§ 36, 52, etc.).

[2] See Steph. *Thes.* and L.S. which explain the Aristotelian use of παραβολή.

[3] See *Proclamation* pp 438—43

[4] Jn xvi 25 "These things I have spoken unto you *in proverbs*, the hour cometh when I shall no more speak unto you in proverbs..." On this, Westcott says "It seems to be unnatural to limit the reference to the answer to the question in xvi 17. The description applies in fact to all the earthly teaching of the Lord."

THE PARABLES OF SOWING

speakest thou plainly and speakest *no proverb*." They suppose that they are safe in an intellectual conviction of Christ's omniscience and consequent divinity ("Now know we that thou knowest all things...by this we believe that thou camest forth from God"). But they are woefully mistaken. In a few minutes they will abandon Him[1].

This leads us to a fairly probable conclusion about the historical fact latent in Mark (the time when Jesus was "alone"), and to a highly probable conclusion about John's view of Mark Mark seems—or at all events seemed to John—to have placed out of order, and before Christ's resurrection, a course of post-resurrectional revelation concerning Christ's parables that was not given till Jesus was "alone," that is, in the circle of the disciples and the Twelve[2]. Matthew and Luke, being misled by Mark's order, retained his order but altered his tradition[3]. John has altered Mark's order but retains a recognition that Christ's parables, or proverbs, were obscure, and needed to be explained by the Holy Spirit[4].

---

[1] See Jn xvi 29—32

[2] Such a circle of disciples, which might be described by Jews (*Son* **3460** c) as "the household," or "house," of Jesus, is described in Acts i 15   Those who were outside that circle might be described as Mk iv 11 ἐκείνοις τοῖς ἔξω   Mt xiii 11 ἐκείνοις and Lk viii 10 τοῖς λοιποῖς omit ἔξω, which perhaps some interpreted literally as meaning "outside the house"

[3] Luke's view—that the questioning related merely to the single (viii. 9) "parable" of the Sower—had some justification   No other parable presented so many difficulties   Why did the Sower sow seed "by the way side"?   Why had he not removed the stones and the thorns?   How different from the planter of the vine in Isaiah, who (v 2) "made a trench," and "gathered out the stones," and was able to say (v 4) "What could have been done more?" The difference could perhaps be explained   But it appeared to need explanation

[4] If this Marcan tradition refers to a period after the Resurrection what have we to say as to the mention of (Mk iv 10) "*those around Jesus*," along with the Twelve?   Does John represent them at the end of his Gospel, as well as at the beginning, in the person of

THE PARABLES OF SOWING

§ 4. *"The mystery of the kingdom," in Mark*[1]

Delitzsch renders "mystery" here by the Hebrew "secret," meaning "confidential intercourse." This has quite a different meaning from that of the Greek word *mustērion*, which meant "initiation." The Hebrew word is never used in the plural[2] Both in English and in Greek the word "mystery" is quite unfit to represent the phrase "the secret of God" as it is used in the Bible[3].

A Greek "mystery" implied that some Greek God or Goddess (for example Demeter in her temple at Eleusis) was "manifested" to his or her initiated worshippers by some visible form or sign. Hence, to Greeks, Philip's appeal to Jesus "Shew us the Father" would seem to imply "Reveal to us *a mystery*", and the reply of Jesus to another disciple, a little afterwards, that He with His Father would "come" and "abide with" anyone that "loved" and obeyed Him, would

---

Nathanael? It is possible, but in any case it is not an instance of Johannine intervention For Luke also (xxiv 18, 27, 43) represents Cleopas (and a companion) as receiving from Jesus an exposition of the Scriptures concerning Himself, and afterwards as receiving proofs of His resurrection

[1] Mk iv 11 Ὑμῖν τὸ μυστήριον δέδοται τῆς βασιλείας τοῦ θεοῦ, Mt. xiii 11 Ὑμῖν δέδοται γνῶναι τὰ μυστήρια τῆς βασιλείας τῶν οὐρανῶν (Lk viii. 10 τοῦ θεοῦ)

[2] See Gesen 691 b

[3] Ps xxv 14, Prov iii 32 In Job xxix 4 "*the secret of God* was upon my tent" the reading is disputed, but it seems to make good sense, meaning "the stamp of God's favour." During the days of Job's prosperity there was, as it were, written on his tent, "Here is one of the intimates of God" (Gesen Ps xxv 14, "intimacy with Jehovah") Comp *Odes of Solomon* viii 11—14 "Guard my secret, ye that are guarded by it Guard my faith. know my knowledge .Love me with fervent-love, ye that are loving"
On "the secret of the Lord" see *Light* **3797—817**, and on "mysteries" see **3798** foll and **3802 b—j**.

15 (Mark iv 1—20)

fill the mind of the ordinary Greek with astonishment[1]. Yet that is the meaning of the Hebrew phrase "the secret of God." It meant "confidential intercourse," or "intimacy," with Jehovah

Independently of this difference between Hebrew and popular Greek thought, there is also a great difference between those to whom "*the mystery of the kingdom of God has been given*" and those to whom "*it has been given*" merely "*to know*" its "*mysteries.*" Mark has the former phrase, Matthew and Luke the latter[2]. By "*the mysteries*" might be meant—at all

---

[1] Jn xiv 9, 23 We must however distinguish "the ordinary Greek" from such a philosopher as Epictetus Epictetus believes man to be, by right, "a god"—a god in all the most homely acts of life—and reproaches him for ignoring his own divinity (ii 8 12) "When thou art eating.. knowest thou not that thou art sustaining a god ? Thou carriest about (περιφέρεις) (comp 2 Cor iv 10) God, poor-wretch, and knowest it not!" comp ii 16 33 "But if thou followest-faithfully (παρακολουθείς) Him who swayeth the universe, and *carriest Him about* (περιφέρεις) *in thyself*" Also, in the only passage (iii 21 13—16) where Epictetus mentions "mysteries," he pours scorn on those who think they can reproduce the mysteries of Eleusis by reproducing the material circumstances —the "building," the "hierophant," the "herald," the "torch-bearer," "the very same voices" There is need, he says, that a man should "have previously purified himself and be predisposed by the reflection that he is on the point of drawing near things holy [in themselves] and holy by reason of their antiquity" This passage is preceded by the saying "Men do not sow till they have invoked Demeter" The only other mention of Demeter is contained in the ironical reproach against certain philosophers who denied what most people would call the evidence of the senses (ii 20 32) "Grateful creatures and reverent! They eat their daily bread and yet are not deterred from saying 'We know not whether there is a Demeter or a Proserpine or a Pluto'"—that is, the gods whose action typified the seed and the harvest, death and resurrection

[2] It should be noted that מסטירין is used in New Hebrew (Levy iii 166, "gr. τὸ μυστήριον, od τὰ μυστήρια") and in Aramaic (Levy Ch ii 51 "gr. μυστήρια") and is variously regarded as sing or pl (Krauss 346 "das Geheimniss, oft irrthumlich als Pl behandelt") Walton and Etheridge render it "secrets" in Gen xxviii 12 (Jer I) "because they had revealed the *secrets* of the

THE PARABLES OF SOWING

events for Christians at the end of the first century reading the Synoptic Gospels—the mysteries of the incarnation, death, and resurrection of Jesus, and of Baptism and the Eucharist for His disciples. But by "*the mystery*" must be meant some supreme and all-including "mystery," such as Paul suggests when he speaks about the "recognition of *the mystery of God*, [*namely*] *Christ*[1]." About "*the mysteries*" we may say "we know them," more appropriately than about "*the mystery*," which is better regarded as being received into our souls through faith and feeling (and not merely through evidence and proof).

If we ask what the Marcan mystery is, we find the answer somewhat complicated by various possibilities as to the time and circumstances in which Jesus uttered the word, and by doubts whether He referred to one particular parable, or to many, and to the principle underlying them all. But many reasons may be given for concluding that He referred to the underlying principle, the principle of the divine redemption of the soul. This is confirmed by the earlier Clement's comment on "The sower went forth[2]," and by Isaiah's likening of God's forgiveness of sins to "the rain that cometh down from heaven" and "giveth seed to the sower[3]." It appears to be the mystery of life through death or dissolution. Clement points out how "the Sower casteth into the earth each one of the seeds,"

Lord of the world," but "secret" in Numb xvi 26 "they betrayed my *secret* when I slew the Egyptian" Levy *ib* quotes (*inter alia*) Pesikt r s 5 Anf 7 b, where the Gentiles say to God "Worin bestehen denn deine *Mysterien*?" and God replies "Das ist die Mischna" There the Heb seems better represented by "*mysteries*" than by "*mystery*"

[1] Coloss ii. 2 εἰς ἐπίγνωσιν τοῦ μυστηρίου τοῦ θεοῦ, Χριστοῦ. This recognition would not imply exactly "knowing" the mystery. It would be a feeling of approximation like that implied in (Eph iii. 19) "knowing the love of Christ which passeth knowledge" There is much to be said also for the reading of W H txt and R.V txt in 1 Cor ii 1 τὸ μυστήριον τοῦ θεοῦ

[2] Clem Rom *Cor.* § 24
[3] Is lv 9—11

THE PARABLES OF SOWING

which, "dry and bare, falling into the earth, dissolve Then, from the dissolution, the mightiness of the Master's providence raiseth them up" so that "from the one [seed]" they increase manifold and bring forth fruit[1]. Origen applies Isaiah's words, "my ways are not as your ways," to prove that "with God, nothing is useless"; even the censers of Corah and his sinful companions are used for God's glory[2].

Clement's expression about "the seeds dry and bare, falling into the earth" and afterwards "raised up" by the Master, so that each seed brings forth manifold fruit, resembles in thought, though not exactly in word, the Johannine saying about the "grain of wheat," which "except it fall into the earth and die, abideth by itself alone, but if it die it beareth much fruit[3]" The antithesis to "by itself alone" would naturally be "in company with others" And this gives to the Johannine parable a suggestion of altruism not conveyed by Clement Clement teaches that each human soul may pass by a resurrection, through death, to a developed and more fruitful existence. But the context in the Fourth Gospel brings out the truth that the death and the increased fruitfulness are to be for the sake of others as well as for the sake of the particular soul that passes through death The scene in which Jesus enunciates the law of "the grain of wheat" that is to "die" and, by dying, to bear much fruit, contains also, in effect, a prediction of the redemption of the Gentiles (typified by the "Greeks" who come to Jesus); it contains also a recognition,

---

[1] Clem Rom. *Cor* § 24 ἡ μεγαλειότης τῆς προνοίας τοῦ δεσπότου ἀνίστησιν αὐτά [ι e τὰ σπέρματα] καὶ ἐκ τοῦ ἑνὸς πλείονα [? σπέρματα or καρπόν] αὔξει καὶ ἐκφέρει καρπόν, Lightf has "and from being one they increase manifold and bear fruit," but adds that αὔξει is treated as a transitive in the Syriac ("The mightiness. .increases them")

[2] Origen *Num Hom* ix (Lomm x 74)

[3] Jn xii 24, where πολὺν καρπὸν φέρει may be compared with Mk iv 8 ἐδίδου καρπὸν ἀναβαίνοντα καὶ αὐξανόμενα καὶ ἔφερεν. , Mt xiii 8 ἐδίδου καρπόν, Lk viii 8 φυὲν ἐποίησεν καρπόν, Clem Rom *Cor* § 24 πλείονα αὔξει καὶ ἐκφέρει καρπόν

THE PARABLES OF SOWING

through a Voice from heaven, that the hour of supreme glory is at hand, in which the Father will be glorified by the death of His Son, not for His own sake but for the sake of others[1]. The Marcan word, "mystery," is not mentioned; but the whole of the narrative leads us to "the recognition of the mystery of God, [namely] Christ."

§ 5. *"The word," in Mark*

Mark mentions "the word" absolutely whereas Matthew and Luke call it, severally, "the word of the kingdom" and "the word of God." But further, Mark introduces his mention of "the word" with a preface uttered by Jesus but omitted by Matthew and Luke "And he saith unto them, Know ye not this parable? And how [then] will ye come-to-know all the parables? The sower soweth *the word*[2]"

Comparing Mark with the parallels, we are led to infer that Matthew and Luke did not understand why "this parable" should be singled out as if it contained the key to the explanation of "all the parables" They also thought that "the word" should be defined, and they accordingly define it in phrases apparently intended to signify the proclamation of the Gospel—that is to say, the spoken or written Gospel—but capable also of a wider significance[3] Just as a Jewish tradition, quoted above,

---

[1] Jn xii 20 foll, concluding with the words (*ib* 32—3) "And I, if I be lifted up from the earth, will draw all men unto myself But this he said signifying by what manner of death he was to die"

[2] Mk iv 13—14 καὶ λέγει αὐτοῖς Οὐκ οἴδατε τὴν παραβολὴν ταύτην, καὶ πῶς πάσας τὰς παραβολὰς γνώσεσθε, Ὁ σπείρων τὸν λόγον σπείρει, comp Mt xiii 18—19 a Ὑμεῖς οὖν ἀκούσατε τὴν παραβολὴν τοῦ σπείραντος Παντὸς ἀκούοντος τον λόγον τῆς βασιλείας.., Lk viii. 11 ἔστιν δὲ αὕτη ἡ παραβολή· Ὁ σπόρος ἐστὶν ὁ λόγος τοῦ θεοῦ.

As regards Matthew's version, "the word of the kingdom," it is worth noting that Matthew uses "kingdom" 56 times, as against 69 in the other three Gospels taken together

[3] Comp Acts vi 7 (and xii 24 "*the word of God* increased (RV grew) (ηὔξανεν) and multiplied") "And *the word of God* increased (ηὔξανεν) and the number of the disciples multiplied...," which

THE PARABLES OF SOWING

said that the Mishna was "the mystery" or "mysteries" of God, so Christian tradition toward the end of the first century might begin to narrow down "the word of God" to the word written in the Gospels[1]

Luke's change of "word" into "word of God" may be illustrated by the LXX "*word of the Lord*" substituted for Jeremiah's absolute use of the term: "The prophets shall become wind and *the word* is not in them[2]" Also, where one Psalm has "The Lord giveth *the word*," the Targum has "The Lord gave *the words of the Law*[3]," and where another has "He sendeth *his word* and healeth them," the Targum has "He will send *the words of His healing* and will heal them[4]" In all these cases the expansion indicates the natural desire of a later writer to explain an obscurity in an earlier one[5].

---

perhaps means that it "increased," like a fire, in intensity as well as in extent

[1] It was difficult for a Jew to regard "the Law," or "the Word," as a seed that must die and be assimilated in the heart of man In *Ezr-Apoc* ix 31 foll, when God says "Behold, I sow my Law in you, and it shall bring forth fruit in you," Ezra replies that the Law abides, but Israel has to say "we perish " Ezra has previously (*ib* viii 6 Lat) requested (if the text is correct) "the seed of a [new] heart and cultivation to our perception, whence fruit may spring"

Origen, on the other hand (*Exod Hom* 1 4, Lomm ix 7)—emphasizing the necessity that the "seed," or "word," should die—connects, in a most fanciful but instructive way, (Jn xii 24) the "death" of the "seed," (Acts vi 7) the "increase" of the "word," with the "death" of "our Joseph," betrayed "by one of his brothers Juda(s)," followed by (Exod 1 6—7) the "increase" of the children of Israel! Comp Tertull *Adv Jud* § 10 "Joseph was sold into Egypt just as Christ was sold by Israel.. when He is betrayed by Judas (*or*, Judah) (*Iuda*)"

[2] Jerem v 13   [3] Ps lxviii 11.
[4] Ps cvii 20

[5] But "the word" might also be omitted by a later writer as being superfluous For example, where Mark has (iv 33) "*was speaking .the word*," Matthew (xiii 34) has simply "*spake*" (Lk om)

THE PARABLES OF SOWING

Mark's use of "the word" is not improbably Petrine. At all events a Petrine speech in the Acts appears to allude to the Psalmist's phrase "He sendeth *his word* and *healeth* them," when Peter says that God "sent *the word* unto the children of Israel, preaching the gospel of peace through Jesus Christ," and adds that Jesus was "anointed with the Holy Spirit and with power," and "went through [the land] doing good and *healing* all that were oppressed by the devil[1]". In the Psalm, both Origen and Jerome take *"his word"* as meaning the divine Logos, or Son[2]. In the Acts, it seems to mean, not the Logos, but the effective utterance of the Logos. But the passage is instructive as shewing that "the word" may sometimes be an ambiguous term. It may mean the Principle, or Mystery, of Redemption, the Healing Power, or it may mean the Person exercising that power[3].

§ 6. *"The word," in John, how first mentioned by Jesus*[4]

In John, when Jesus uses the term *logos*, it is mostly in such phrases as "my word," or "his [i.e. God's] word," or

---

[1] Acts x. 34—8, Ps cvii. 20. The text is involved and possibly corrupt, being a Lucan conglomeration of old traditions, but the allusion to the Psalm is manifest.

[2] Jerome *ad loc*, and Origen *Cels* ii. 31.

[3] Mk ii. 2 "he was speaking unto them *the word*" (Mt om.) is parall to Lk v. 17 "and *the power of the Lord was toward his healing*," and Luke may have understood "the word" to mean the effective and healing word. Comp. 1 Cor. iv. 20 "The kingdom of God is *not in word* but *in power*," 1 Thess. 1. 5 "not *in word only* but *in power*," Acts iv. 29—30 "grant unto thy servants to speak *thy word* ...while thou stretchest forth thy hand *to heal*."

[4] Jn iv. 37 ἐν γὰρ τούτῳ ὁ λόγος ἐστὶν ἀληθινὸς ὅτι ἄλλος ἐστὶν ὁ σπείρων καὶ ἄλλος ὁ θερίζων. See *Joh. Gr.* **2799** (iii) "On λόγος (sing. and defined) in Christ's words." Λόγος refers to a passage in the Psalms in Jn xv. 25 "that there might be fulfilled *the word* that is in their own law [there] written that (Ps xxxv. 19) 'They hated me without a cause'" Jn x. 35 "If he called them 'gods' unto whom *the word of God* came" refers to Ps lxxxii. 6. A.V. has "saying," instead of R.V. "word," in Jn viii. 51, 52, 55, xv. 20.

"the word of God," and nowhere means a mere "saying" of ordinary people Here, however, both our Versions render it by "saying," "Herein is *the* (A V *that*) *saying* true, One soweth and another reapeth." Perhaps the translators regarded this as a mere popular "saying," beneath the level of a "word" (as used in such phrases as "word of God").

But, if they are right, there are two exceptional points in this sentence. Not only does Jesus use *logos* here to mean a mere "saying," but also the Greek *alēthinos*, which means "real," or "ideal," is here confused with *alēthēs*, which means "true." John uses both words frequently But *alēthinos* is almost peculiar to him among the evangelists[1], and it implies something quite different from what we call "true" in a true and accurate statement. It means something that is free from all admixture of transient, earthly and corruptible nature. Hence Origen, commenting on Christ as "the *real* (*alēthinon*) light," says "But Christ, being the light of the world, is the *real* (*alēthinon*) light *in contrast with the* [light] *received-by-the-senses, since nothing that is received-by-the-senses is real* (*alēthinon*)[2]."

"keep *my word*   keep *my word*.   keep *his* [i e *God's*] *word*," "if they (have) kept *my word* "

Apart from Christ's utterances, A V has "saying" and R V "word," the Gk being λόγος, in Jn iv 39 "because of *the word* of the woman," vii 36 "What is this *word* that he said...?" xii 38 "that *the word* of Isaiah .might be fulfilled," xviii 9 "that there might be fulfilled *the word* that he spake, namely (ὅτι) 'Of those whom thou hast given me I have lost none,'" xviii 32 "that *the word* of Jesus might be fulfilled which he spake, signifying by what death he should die " R V follows A V in Jn vi 60 "this is a hard *saying*" etc

[1] The only Synoptic instance of ἀληθινός is Lk. xvi. 11 where τὸ ἀληθινόν means "the real and heavenly [treasure]" as opposed to "the mammon of unrighteousness."

[2] Origen, on Jn i 9, *Comm Joann.* i 24 (Lomm i. 54) Ἔστι δὲ ὁ Χριστὸς φῶς ἀληθινὸν, πρὸς ἀντιδιαστολὴν αἰσθητοῦ, οὐδενὸς αἰσθητοῦ ὄντος ἀληθινοῦ He adds "But it does not follow that, because that which

THE PARABLES OF SOWING

This use of *alēthinos* accords with its use in the best Greek authors. For example, when Plato says "not an artificial myth but *a real logos*," he means, not "*a true narrative*"—as though vouching for its complete accuracy—but "*a real history*" as distinguished from a myth[1]. Also a second century grammarian has given the title "About *alēthinos logos*" to a treatise on the *logos* regarded as a conception inherent in the soul and not verbally expressed[2]. Hence Westcott, in the Johannine text under consideration, instead of "*is true*," substitutes "*finds its complete, ideal, fulfilment.*" With this alteration, the whole passage may be paraphrased thus "Lift up your eyes from the cornfields on earth to the cornfields in heaven, and see there the spiritual harvest, the harvest of souls, white and ready for reaping. Others have sown, Moses and the Prophets and all the Messengers of God, these have sown, and you have entered into their labours. In this harvest the common proverb—often repeated as a complaint of injustice, namely, that the sower is indeed[3] one and the reaper quite another—finds

---

is received by the senses is not *real* (ἀληθινὸν), it is consequently false."

Comp Jn iv 23 "the real [*and spiritual*] worshippers," vi 32 "the bread from heaven, the *real* [*and spiritual*] bread," vii 28 "he that sent me is *real*," viii 16 "my judgment is *real* [*and spiritual*]," xv 1 "I am the *real* [*and spiritual*] vine," xvii 3 "thee, the only *real* God." The last instance is xix 35 καὶ ἀληθινὴ αὐτοῦ ἐστιν ἡ μαρτυρία where the word ought to be rendered consistently with the saying of Origen "*real* in contrast with that which is received by the senses"

John also uses ἀληθής about fourteen times—including the context of the last-quoted sentence—(as against two Synoptic instances) so that we cannot suppose him to be using ἀληθινός where other writers would use ἀληθής

[1] Plato *Tim* 26 E

[2] Steph *Thes* i 1453 quoting from Hermog "*De id.* ii. 7 Περὶ ἀληθινοῦ λόγου Init cap. ὁ ἐνδιάθετος καὶ ἀληθὴς καὶ οἷον ἔμψυχος λόγος"

[3] "Indeed" is implied by ἐστίν It might have been omitted (ἄλλος ὁ σπείρων καὶ ἄλλος ὁ θερίζων). But it is inserted for emphasis

THE PARABLES OF SOWING

its divine fulfilment. For indeed, God, the heavenly Sower, sows, and those men who are most like God, they also sow, that others may reap."

This corrects the erroneous substitution of "true" for "real," but it leaves a possible error in the rendering of *logos* as a mere "saying" or "common-proverb." For the statement that "the common-proverb is a genuine and spiritual common-proverb" is not like the statement "my judgment is a genuine and spiritual judgment[1]." A "judgment" can be genuine and heavenly and remain a "judgment," but a "common-proverb" can hardly be heavenly and yet remain what it is. Hence we are led back to doubt whether this exceptional rendering of *logos* in an utterance of Jesus can be correct[2] And the doubt is confirmed by the fact that some very good authorities take *logos* as meaning "*word*," and insert the article before *alēthinos*, so that the meaning becomes "Herein is the Word of Truth" or "Herein is the Word that is real [and spiritual][3]."

The Word of Truth, in such a context, would seem to be regarded as the Word from above, about which God says, in Isaiah, "As the rain...giveth seed to the sower and bread to the eater, so shall *my word be*[4]" Irenaeus interprets this as being

---

[1] Jn viii 16 ἡ κρίσις ἡ ἐμὴ ἀληθινή ἐστιν
[2] Hence I now doubt the complete accuracy of the explanation given in *Joh Gr* **2795** "This worldly proverb is 'really and genuinely true' in another interpretation, and that a spiritual one"
[3] Jn iv 37 SS "For in this is the word of truth," *d* "in hoc est enim verbum veritatis," D ἐν γὰρ τούτῳ ἐστὶν ὁ λόγος ὁ ἀληθινός, ℵ ὁ λόγος ἐστὶν ὁ ἀληθινός B, followed by W H , has ὁ λόγος ἐστὶν ἀληθινός. But the dropping of O in a confused text would be an easy error, which has been shewn (*Joh Gr* **2652**) to be frequent in B. Chrys quotes ὁ λόγος ἐστὶν ὁ ἀληθής and adds "These things the people (οἱ πολλοὶ) used to say and [Jesus] says that this saying here especially finds its truth (ὅτι οὗτος ὁ λόγος ἐνταῦθα μάλιστα τὴν ἀλήθειαν ἔχει)" Origen *ad loc* (Lomm 11 94—5) (1) quotes as B, (2) has πῶς ἀληθινὸς ὁ [v. r. om ὁ] λόγος ἐστί, (3) represents Heracleon as apparently quoting ἐν τούτῳ ἐστὶν ὁ λόγος ἀληθινός.
[4] Comp. Iren iv 25 3 (Jn iv. 37) "*In hoc enim*, inquit, *sermo est verus, quoniam alter quidem est qui seminat* populus [i e Israel],

THE PARABLES OF SOWING

the Word of the one true God, which came first to Israel the sower, and afterwards to the Christian Church the reaper. But that does not appear to go to the bottom of the meaning of the Johannine saying, which (interpreted as above) teaches us not so much about man's history as about God's nature. It indirectly leads us to recognise, as the Word of Truth, this Law of the heavenly Harvest.—"It is more blessed to give than to receive[1]," pointing to the One God, who sows that others may reap, and who is glad that it should be so[2].

---

alter qui metet [i e the Church], *unus autem Deus praestans utrisque quae sunt apta*, (Is lv 10) *semen quidem seminanti, panem vero ad edendum metenti.*

[1] Acts xx 35

[2] Space does not allow an examination of Heracleon's comments (possibly corrupt) on Jn iv 37, about which Origen says "He is not at all clear in his exposition of the nature of the two Sons of Man of whom one sows and the other reaps." The impression left by it is that Heracleon interpreted *logos* as "[divine] word," and not as "[popular] saying."

Origen's introductory remarks about the spiritual harvest in heaven (Jn iv 35) contain frequent references to the Creation in Genesis, and to the action of the divine Logos and to the several *logoi* of created things (*Comm Joann* xiii 42) πάρεστιν ὁ τοῦ θεοῦ λόγος σαφηνίζων καὶ φωτίζων πάσας τὰς χώρας τῆς γραφῆς,... παρισταμένου τοῦ περὶ ἑκάστου λόγου . ἐνεῖδεν ὁ θεὸς τοῖς λόγοις ἑκάστου καὶ εἶδε πῶς καθ᾽ οὓς γέγονεν ἕκαστον τῶν κτισμάτων λόγους ἐστὶ καλόν.. ὁ λόγος [? ὁ λόγος ὁ] περὶ ἑκάστου τούτων ἐστὶν ὁραθεὶς θεῷ τὸ καλόν.. Πῶς γὰρ καλὸν τὰ θηρία...εἰ μὴ ἄρα ὁ λόγος ὁ περὶ αὐτῶν ἐστι τὸ καλόν,... προτρέποντος τοῦ παρόντος τοῖς μαθηταῖς λόγου τοὺς ἀκροατὰς ἐπαίρειν τοὺς ὀφθαλμούς...

In the first instance Origen introduces the incarnate Logos of God as enlightening and illuminating all the cornfields of scripture, and in the last as exhorting His hearers to lift up their eyes to the harvest of heaven

Later on, coming to Jn iv 37, he says that (*Comm Joann* xiii 47) "whether we take the words in this passage (τὰ κατὰ τὸν τόπον) κατὰ τὸ ἀπὸ τῶν τεχνῶν καὶ τῶν ἐπιστημῶν ληφθὲν παράδειγμα, in that case it is clear how (σαφὲς πῶς) ἀληθινὸς ὁ λόγος (v r. λόγος) ἐστὶ .,," or, whether it be taken to refer to Moses and the Prophets, "so too it is clear how one soweth and another reapeth." This favours the view that Origen took λόγος to mean "a popular saying," but possibly

THE PARABLES OF SOWING

If John does indeed connect "the *logos* of truth" with "sowing" in the first passage where Jesus mentions the *logos*, the connection affords some grounds for thinking that John had in view the Synoptic Parables of Sowing and especially the tradition peculiar to Mark, "The sower soweth the *logos*." But such an allusion, though not unimportant, is subordinate to the deeper purpose of the Johannine doctrine, namely, to take the term out of a dangerous position where it might be confused with the oral "word" of catechists or the written "word" of evangelists, and to personify it as the Mind or Purpose of the divine Giver of all good. The Evangelist writes as if he knew that the Synoptic Gospels had omitted that saying of Jesus which is almost the only one preserved by Paul, and as if he were determined to inculcate its meaning on his readers "Jesus said, It is more blessed to give than to receive."

The first Johannine tradition about "giving" follows close after the mention of the Logos as being "with God," and as including "light" and "the life of men." It says "As many as received him, to them he gave authority to become God's children[1]" This is the first mention of "*giving*." The next refers to the inferior gift of the Law as compared with the higher gift of grace and truth· "The Law was *given* through Moses, the [gift of] grace and the [gift of] truth came into being through Jesus Christ[2]." Before this, and after it, the text speaks of an "Only begotten," who is "in the bosom of the Father," and who has "declared" God, and the next mention of God's "*giving*" says "God so loved the world that he *gave his only begotten Son* that whosoever believeth on him should

---

with a play on the meaning It is difficult to understand how he can call this "clear ($\sigma\alpha\phi\acute{e}s$)" without any attempt to explain $\dot{\alpha}\lambda\eta\theta\iota\nu\acute{o}s$—unless he supposes that he has made it clear by his long previous account of the relation between the *Logos* and the *logoi*.

[1] Jn 1 12
[2] Jn 1 17. See also *Joh Gr* 2411 *e*, *Son* 3566

26 (Mark iv 1—20)

THE PARABLES OF SOWING

not perish but have eternal life[1]" Thus the Son dies in the flesh that men should not perish in the spirit. In the language of Isaiah, He "seeth of the travail of His soul and is satisfied[2]" Or, according to the metaphor of the harvest, the Love of the eternal Sower in heaven sows His Word upon earth, and reaps His harvest from the redeemed souls of men It is probably not too much to say that when John wrote down "*The Word* was with God" in the first sentence of his Gospel, he had also in mind the thought that "the Sower soweth *the word*," and that he was preparing the way for what he was to write later on: "Except a grain of wheat fall into the earth and die, it abideth by itself alone, but if it die it beareth much fruit...he that hateth his life in this world shall keep it unto life eternal[3]."

§ 7   "*There is nothing hid save that it should be manifested,*" *in Mark*[4]

The Parable of the Sower, as explained in Mark and Matthew, concludes with the mention of three classes of fruit-bearers as the result of the seed in the good ground Luke mentions but one class If the sowing typifies a spiritual generating of believers, then we may perhaps point to the three stages of belief apparently denoted in the Johannine Epistle, as corresponding to what Luke omits[5]

---

[1] Jn i 14, 18, iii 16 "Giving" is more frequently mentioned in the Fourth Gospel than in any of the Three, and mostly refers to divine "giving" Mk iv 25 implies divine giving but does not mention the Giver ("to him shall be given"), Mt vii 11, Lk xi 13 describe the Father as "giving" severally "good things," or "the Holy Spirit," to those who ask After Mk ii 12, Mt ix 8, Lk v 26 "they glorified God," Mt alone adds "who had given such power unto men" But no Synoptist approaches John in the emphasis that he lays on giving.

[2] Is liii 11

[3] Jn xii. 24—5

[4] Mk iv. 22 οὐ γάρ ἐστιν κρυπτὸν ἐὰν μὴ ἵνα φανερωθῇ.

[5] 1 Jn ii. 12 foll.

THE PARABLES OF SOWING

After this—which describes the result of the seed that is hidden rightly in the ground—comes a brief parable about a lamp that ought not to be hidden under a bushel; and then Mark adds that "hiding"—that is to say the right kind of hiding—takes place *"with a view to manifestation."* The disciples are not to hide their light, but to impart it to others. If they do not, they will lose it[1]

---

[1] The parallel columns given below are printed for the purpose of reference, so that the reader may turn back to them and see the context of the particular expressions discussed in the pages that follow

Mk iv 21—5 (R V)	Mt v 14—16, x 26, xi 15, vii 2, vi 33, xiii 12 (R V)	Lk viii 16—17, xiv 35, viii 18 a, vi 38, xii 31, viii 18 b (R V)
(21) And he said unto them, Is the lamp brought to be put under the bushel, or under the bed, [and] not to be put on the stand? (22) For there is nothing hid, save that it should be manifested, neither was [anything] made secret, but that it should come to light	(v 14) Ye are the light of the world A city set on a hill cannot be hid (15) Neither do [men] light a lamp, and put it under the bushel, but on the stand, and it shineth unto all that are in the house (16) Even so let your light shine before men, that they may see your good works, and glorify your Father which is in heaven (x 26) Fear them not therefore for there is nothing covered, that shall not be revealed, and hid, that shall not be known	(viii 16) And no man, when he hath lighted a lamp, covereth it with a vessel, or putteth it under a bed, but putteth it on a stand, that they which enter in may see the light (17) For nothing is hid, that shall not be made manifest, nor [anything] secret, that shall not be known and come to light
(23) If any man hath ears to hear, let him hear (24) And he said unto them, Take heed what ye hear with what measure ye mete it shall be measured unto you and	(xi 15) He that hath ears to hear (*some anc auth omit* to hear), let him hear (vii 2) For with what judgment ye judge, ye shall be judged and with what measure ye	(xiv 35) . He that hath ears to hear, let him hear (viii 18 a) Take heed therefore how ye hear.. (vi 38) Give, and it shall be given unto you, good measure,

THE PARABLES OF SOWING

It will be seen that Matthew and Luke give quite a different turn to Mark's words as if they meant "There is nothing hidden by man that shall not be revealed in the day of judgment." But that does not appear to be the meaning. Ben Sira (and probably *Aboth*) condemns the teacher that hides his knowledge[1] Philo fiercely attacks the disreputable "initiations" and "mysteries" practised among the Greeks by "three or four" of the initiated "in the dark[2]." But he praises the "mysteries" implied in the recognition of God, the Father of the Universe, as the Sower of all good[3]. The same contrast was probably at the bottom of Mark's tradition. But Matthew, transposing the parable of the lamp, appears to have missed the meaning

Mk iv 21—5 (R V) *contd*	Mt v 14—16, x 26, xi 15, vii 2, vi 33, xiii 12 (R V) *contd*	Lk viii 16—17, xiv 35, viii 18 a, vi. 38, xii 31, viii 18 b (R V) *contd*
more shall be given unto you (25) For he that hath, to him shall be given and he that hath not, from him shall be taken away even that which he hath	mete, it shall be measured unto you (vi 33) But seek ye first his kingdom, and his righteousness, and all these things shall be added unto you (xiii 12) For whosoever hath, to him shall be given, and he shall have abundance but whosoever hath not, from him shall be taken away even that which he hath	pressed down, shaken together, running over, shall they give into your bosom For with what measure ye mete it shall be measured to you again (xii 31) Howbeit seek ye his kingdom (*many anc auth* the kingdom of God), and these things shall be added unto you (viii 18 b) . .for whosoever hath, to him shall be given, and whosoever hath not, from him shall be taken away even that which he thinketh he hath (*or*, seemeth to have)

[1] Sir xli 14—15, rep xx. 31, comp. iv 23, *Aboth* 1 14 (see Taylor's note)

[2] Philo ii 260

[3] Philo i 147—8 He appeals to Jeremiah (Jer iii 4) as being a μύστης See *Light* 3799 b—c which quotes Philo fully on ὁ σπείρων and τὰ ἱερὰ ὄντως μυστήρια

29 (Mark iv 21—5)

THE PARABLES OF SOWING

And Luke, although he keeps Mark's order, agrees (erroneously) with Matthew in altering Mark's meaning.

So far as "hiding" refers to seed hidden in the ground we may say that John expresses the doctrine, though without the exact word, when he implies that the grain of corn "falls to the ground" and "dies" in order that it may "bear much fruit." There is a doctrine of "hiding," or non-recognition, of a future deliverer of Israel that may be traced in Jewish Apocrypha (based on several Biblical precedents)[1]; and this implies a hiding with a view to manifestation. Also in Jewish Haggadic literature that speaks of the rose or lily of Israel among thorns[2], we find Israel described as "hidden" in, or under, various adversities and oppressions that precede its blossoming. The last of these is Sheol —"The congregation of Israel crieth before the Eternal, 'Lord of the world, I am *hidden* in the depths of Sheol; but as soon as the Holy One will lead me forth from the abyss of surge and from the depths of Sheol, I will blossom in good works like the lily[3].'"

In the Gospels, the doctrine of productive "hiding" is perhaps best illustrated by the "hiding" of the "leaven" in "three measures of meal" mentioned by Matthew and Luke, where the leaven may be said to "die," as leaven, and to live again in the nature of bread[4]. But Epictetus definitely connects

---

[1] See *Notes* **2998** (lv) *d—m* on "The Doctrine of Hiding." Comp Is xlix 1—2

[2] Cant ii 1—2 "a rose (חבצלת) .a lily among thorns." See Gesen 287, חבצלת. There is a play on this word and words signifying "love" and "shadow." "Shadow" implies "hiding."

[3] *Tehill* on Ps 1 4 (Wu pp 18—19). Previously Israel is described as "hidden" (1) in the shadow of Egypt, (2) at Sinai (Exod. xix 17), (3) in the shadow of the conquering Empires

In the context, the Earth says to the Lord "All the dead of the world are *hidden in my shadow* (Is xxvi 19 *my dead bodies shall arise*) and if the Holy One demands them from me, I give them back to Him and blossom like a lily."

[4] Mt xiii 33, Lk xiii 21, on which see *Notes* **2998** (lv) *k*. Mt xiii 44 says that a man found a treasure "hidden" in some one

THE PARABLES OF SOWING

"hiding" with "sowing" thus "First make a practice of being ignored as to what you really are. Be philosopher to yourself [*i e* give your philosophic lectures to yourself] for a short time That is the way to produce fruit The seed, for a time, must be *buried*, must be *hidden*, must grow by little and little, that it may come to perfection[1]." That seems to supply the link of thoughts necessary to connect the Synoptic Parables of "sowing" with those of "hiding," and both of them with the Johannine brief Parable—if it may be so called—of the grain of corn falling into the ground and dying

---

The preceding observations have not noticed the Synoptic parallels to Mark's tradition about the proper place for "the lamp"—namely, on "the stand," and not under "the bushel" or "the bed[2]" Referring to those parallels, the reader will perceive that Luke here passes continuously to "the lamp" from the "good ground" in the explanation of the Parable of the Sower, as though there were some connection between them[3] Matthew, on the other hand, here proceeds from the Parable of the Sower to "another parable[4]" But in the Sermon on the Mount he adds to the Marcan tradition an interpretation and a moral The lamp is the disciples ("ye

---

else's field and "hid" the treasure and bought the field—an action not very satisfactorily explained by Origen and Jerome Mt xiii 33 ἐνέκρυψεν suggests an allusion to Gen xviii 6 (LXX) ἐγκρυφίας, on which see Philo i 173, Clem Alex 694, and Origen *ad loc*.

[1] Epict iv 8 35—6 (quoted in *Notes* **2998** (lv) *j*) where κατορυγῆναι δεῖ means "must be [as it were] *buried alive*" as freq in Steph *Thes* , and probably in Epict ii 22 10, the only other Epictetian instance

[2] Mk iv 21

[3] Lk viii 15—16 "And that in the good ground these. . bring forth fruit with patience But no one (οὐδεὶς δέ) having lighted a lamp covereth it with a vessel "

[4] Mt xiii 23—4 " some thirty Another parable set he forth " (The Wheat and the Tares)

THE PARABLES OF SOWING

are the light of the world[1]") The moral is "Let your light shine[2]" Luke elsewhere places another version of the Marcan saying immediately after a denunciation of "this evil generation" as being worse than Nineveh, and before the saying "The lamp of thy body is thine eye[3]" This saying Matthew places in the Sermon on the Mount after the warning to seek treasure in heaven[4]

These facts indicate very early differences of tradition as to the meaning and context of "the lamp" The reasons for these there is not space to discuss[5] But whatever may be the reasons the fact remains that Mark's single mention of "the lamp" is obscure, and that he nowhere supplements it by any doctrine concerning "light[6]" The only instance of the

---

[1] Mt v 14

[2] Mt v 16—17 "Even so let your light shine before men, that they may see your good works, and glorify your Father who is in heaven Think not that I came to destroy the law . "

[3] Lk xi 32—4 " . a greater than Jonah is here No one having lighted a lamp putteth it into a cellar or under the bushel but on the stand, that those who enter may see the light The lamp of thy body is thine eye ."

[4] Mt vi 19—22 "Treasure ye not .for where thy treasure is there will thy heart be also The lamp of the body is the eye "

[5] The regular Heb for λύχνος (first mentioned in Exod xxv 37) is נר but sometimes it is ניר or ניר Now ניר (Gesen 644 b) means "tillable ground" But in Aram it = "yoke" (Levy Ch ii 109 a) Comp 1 K xi 36 "lamp" ניר, LXX θέσις, al ex θέλησις, Aq. Sym λύχνος, Targ "regnum", Prov xxi 4 "the lamp (marg the tillage)," Jerem iv 3 "break up your fallow ground," Syr "kindle your lamp" On Numb xxi 30 (R V) "we have shot at them (נירם)" Onk has "their kingdom," apparently taking ניר as "yoke" (which Onk has for Heb על "yoke" in Gen xxvii 40 etc) If Matthew had before him some tradition taking ניר as עיר, "city," it might explain his placing here "a city that is set on a hill cannot be hid"

The Heb for "lighting" the lamps in Exod xxv 37 etc is עלה, R V. txt "light," marg "set up" This word is rendered in LXX by (a) ἔρχομαι in various forms, (b) καίω, (c) ἅπτω in various forms These three words are used severally in Mk iv 21, Mt v 15, Lk viii 16

[6] Mk xiv 54 "warming himself in the light [of the fire]" is the only instance of φῶς in Mark

32 (Mark iv 21—5)

THE PARABLES OF SOWING

word "light," in Mark, is where Peter warms himself "by the light" of a fire so that he is seen and accused of being a Galilaean, with the result that he denies his Master.

In the Sermon on the Mount, each disciple is regarded as a "lamp," and is exhorted not to let his light be hid. Elsewhere Matthew implies that the "eye," not the disciple, is a "lamp," and in the context the eye is apparently called "the light", but the metaphors are not clear, and the parallel Luke, though more fully expressed, gives the reader no definite notion of what the "eye" is to see[1]. The context in both Gospels, mentioning the "evil," or "wicked," eye in opposition to the "single" one, suggests to us that we are commanded to "see" in a spirit of straightforward kindness and goodness without the obliquity of jealousy and malice. But it does not tell us whether that which we are thus to "see" is in ourselves —as suggested by the Delphian oracle to Socrates "know thyself"—or in all mankind, or in some few, or in the inanimate as well as animate creation[2].

What course does John take in order to lead us to the understanding of the doctrine latent under Mark's homely

---

[1] Mt vi 22—3 (R V.)
(22) The lamp of the body is the eye if therefore thine eye be single, thy whole body shall be full of light
(23) But if thine eye be evil, thy whole body shall be full of darkness If therefore the light that is in thee be darkness, how great is the darkness!

Lk xi 34—6 (R V)
(34) The lamp of thy body is thine eye when thine eye is single, thy whole body also is full of light, but when it is evil, thy body also is full of darkness
(35) Look therefore whether the light that is in thee be not darkness
(36) If therefore thy whole body be full of light, having no part dark, it shall be wholly full of light, as when the lamp with its bright shining doth give thee light

[2] See Origen *Cels* vi 3 replying to a quotation of Celsus from a letter of Plato who writes that the Supreme Good, ἐκ πολλῆς συνουσίας γινομένης περὶ τὸ πρᾶγμα αὐτὸ καὶ τοῦ συζῆν ἐξαίφνης, οἷον ἀπὸ πυρὸς πηδήσαντος ἐξαφθὲν φῶς, ἐν τῇ ψυχῇ γενόμενον αὐτὸ ἑαυτὸ ἤδη τρέφει. Origen's quotation differs slightly

tradition of the lamp under the bushel¹? In the Prologue to his Gospel, he strikes a note accordant with the words of the Psalmist "Thy lovingkindness, O Lord, is in the heavens... the children of men take refuge under the shadow of thy wings...for with thee is the fountain of life, in thy light shall we see light²." Not that John mentions "lovingkindness." That is the outcome, not the outset, of his Gospel, John leads us up to it by introducing the Word, who is "with God," and in whom there is a "life" that is "the light of men," and through whom men receive "authority to become children of God." Whereas Mark speaks of "the lamp" as "coming," John speaks of "the light" as "coming" ("*the light* that lighteth every man—*coming* [*continually*] into the world.") But the Prologue goes on to say also that this Word "became flesh" and "tabernacled among us," and it concludes by telling us what men consequently saw and what they did not and could not see "We beheld his glory, glory as of the only begotten from the Father....No man hath seen God at any time. the only begotten Son, who is in the bosom of the Father, he hath declared [him]³."

What John here thus adds does not deny, but supplements, the Synoptic doctrine, and at the same time protects his readers from an error of such "philosophy" as goes hand in hand with "vain deceit⁴." He tells us, in effect, that we are not to think of "the light" as being something of our own to be obtained by self-absorption, by meditating on our own faculties, or by meditating on a God that can be described as Alone. God is revealed to us in the Fourth Gospel as the Father in the beginning, never disconnected from the Son Later on, the

---

¹ It may be assumed that this was in the original tradition Mk iv 21 μόδιον may have been altered by Luke (viii 16) into σκεῦος, because of some differences as to the *modius*, the *medimnus*, the *ephah*, and the *seah* But *modius*, a Hebraized word, is retained in Lk xi 33.
² Ps xxxvi 5—9.   ³ Jn i 14—18
⁴ Coloss ii 8

THE PARABLES OF SOWING

thought of "the fountain of life" comes before us when we see Jesus sitting by a "fountain" or "spring"—visibly by "the fountain of Jacob," but invisibly by the fountain of life in heaven—and teaching the Samaritan woman the doctrine of "the living water[1]." There is no mention of light here, but there is a suggestion that the same Eye of God that "saw" Hagar also "saw" the daughter of Samaria ("He told me all things that ever I did") and that both women received a revelation that was illuminative as well as nutritive[2].

Thus gradually John leads us up to the proclamation implied but not expressed in the Prologue. "I am *the light of the world*, he that followeth me shall not walk in the darkness, but shall have the light of life[3]" Even though we may find it impossible to believe that Jesus uttered these identical words, we may be certain that He meant them The Synoptists themselves represent Jesus as saying that whosoever "received" the Son of Man "received" God As an inference from this, the reception of the Son of Man as the Light of the World, is regarded in the Fourth Gospel as bringing a higher light and life, making humanity more truly humane, in contrast with that bestial or infra-bestial existence into which it had too often

---

[1] See *Proclam* pp 344—5 "What she calls (Jn iv 11, 12) '*well* (φρέαρ)' the Evangelist calls (Jn iv 5, 6) '*fountain* (πηγή)'" Also Jesus (Jn iv 14) speaks of πηγή ὕδατος Comp Gen xvi 7, 14, where what is called at first *Ain*, πηγή, "*fountain*," is afterwards called by Hagar *Beer*, φρέαρ, "*well*" Neither of these Hebrew words is the same as that in Ps xxxvi 9 (מקור) In LXX, πηγή never = Heb *Beer*

[2] The only Johannine mention of a "lamp" is in a reference to John the Baptist (Jn v 32—6) "There is another that beareth witness of me, and I know that the witness that he witnesseth of me is true Ye have sent unto John, and he hath borne witness unto the truth . .He was *the lamp* that burneth and shineth . But the witness that I have is greater than [that of] John" The "greater" witness is that of the Father, from whom the Son is inseparable "The lamp" is mentioned by contrast as an inferior thing

[3] Jn viii 12

THE PARABLES OF SOWING

lapsed   Yet "reception" was only a partial expression of that spiritual metamorphosis.   It was not so true to say that men saw or possessed the Light, as to say that the Light entered into and possessed men, regenerating their souls so that from being the children of earth they became children of heaven[1]

§ 8   *"He knoweth not how," and "the earth beareth fruit of herself," in Mark*[2]

The parallel columns given below describe a "man" that sows   But in Matthew this is the "householder," that is,

---

[1] Comp Plato *Pol* vi 509 B τὸν ἥλιον τοῖς ὁρωμένοις οὐ μόνον, οἶμαι, τὴν τοῦ ὁρᾶσθαι δύναμιν παρέχειν φήσεις, ἀλλὰ καὶ τὴν γένεσιν καὶ αὔξην καὶ τροφήν   The context implies that the sun is regarded as the image or pattern (comp Plato *Tim* xviii 49 A μίμημα δὲ παραδείγματος δεύτερον) of the Supreme Good which is the source of the ideal birth, growth, and sustenance

This thought of the "sun" as representing the source of birth may throw light on Philo's abrupt transition from Sarah's giving birth to Isaac to "the lamp" in the tabernacle   In the only passage in which Philo's Index refers to Exod xxv 31, he writes thus (1 520) "For she is wont to bring forth children to God alone ..For he [Moses] also says that the (lit) lampstand (λυχνίαν), the archetypal pattern of the imitation (τὸ ἀρχέτυπον τοῦ μιμήματος παράδειγμα) shines on one side, that is the side toward God   For being seventh (ἑβδόμη) and in the midst of the six branches . it sends its rays upward to the ONE (πρὸς τὸ ἕν) thinking its light too brilliant to be met by mortal sight   Wherefore he does not say that Sarah did not bring forth . "

Elsewhere again (ii 151 ὁ γὰρ ἥλιος, ὥσπερ ἡ λυχνία, μέσος τῶν ἐξ τεταγμένος) Philo applies the term λυχνία to the central light   These passages from Plato and Philo shew how, by contrast, Mark's homely metaphor about "the lamp under the bushel," along with Matthew-Luke traditions about "the light of the body," and also with Matthew's *logion* "Ye are the light of the world," when presented to educated readers, might leave them dissatisfied   These Synoptic traditions were true, but they were not the fundamental truth   The truth at the bottom of the Three Gospels was that Jesus Himself brought into the world a regenerating Light, and this latent truth the Fourth Gospel draws to the surface

[2] Mk iv 26—9 (R V)   Mt xiii 24—7, 30 (R V)

(26) And he said, So is the kingdom of God, **as** if a man should cast seed upon the earth ,

(24) Another parable set he before them, saying, The kingdom of heaven is likened unto a

THE PARABLES OF SOWING

God In Mark it is not God, but simply a common human being That is shewn by Mark's phrase "*he knoweth not how*" This could not be applied to God or to the Son of Man except by a very forced interpretation[1] Matthew's combination of the Marcan words "*blade*" and "*bud* (R V *spring up*)"—uniquely used here in the Gospels—shews that he had before him either Mark or some version of Mark's tradition modified to suit the interpretation of "man" as householder[2] Luke may have

Mk iv. 26—9 (R V) *contd*	Mt xiii 24—7, 30 (R V) *contd*
(27) And should sleep and rise night and day, and the seed should spring up (βλαστᾷ) and grow, he knoweth not how. (28) The earth beareth (*or*, yieldeth) fruit of herself, first the blade (χόρτον), then the ear, then the full corn in the ear (29) But when the fruit is ripe (*or*, alloweth), straightway he putteth forth (*or*, sendeth forth) the sickle, because the harvest is come	man that sowed good seed in his field (25) But while men slept, his enemy came and sowed tares also among the wheat, and went away (26) But when the blade sprang up (ἐβλάστησεν ὁ χόρτος), and brought forth fruit, then appeared the tares also (27) And the servants of the householder came .. (30) Let both grow together until the harvest and in the time of the harvest I will say to the reapers, Gather up first the tares, and bind them in bundles to burn them but gather the wheat into my barn

[1] Ephrem Syrus tries indeed to explain it about God thus (p 126) "Et quod dicit '*Ipse nescit*, quod terra e se ipsa fert fructum,' non ac si ignoraret quod plantavit, sed quia *in hoc suo opere non defatigatur*" He seems to mean that the seed is drawn up by God with such ease and unconsciousness of effort that He may be said "*not to know*" that He is doing it Pseudo-Jerome says that the man casting the seed is the Son of Man, and that the sleeping of the man is the death of the Saviour "Exsurgit semen nocte et die Post somnum Christi numerus credentium germinabat in fide et crevit in opere dum nescit ille Tropica est ista locutio." He adds "*nescire nos fecit* quis fructum in finem afferat," which seems to be another attempt to explain "*he knoweth not*"

[2] Βλαστάνω occurs (in N T) only in Mk iv 27, Mt xiii 26, Heb. ix 4 (of Aaron's rod that budded) and Jas v 18 ἡ γῆ ἐβλάστησεν τὸν καρπὸν αὐτῆς Χόρτος in the sense of "blade" occurs only here, see below, p. 305

THE PARABLES OF SOWING

omitted the whole owing to the doubtfulness of interpretation.

There are several indications that Mark's peculiar Parable is based upon Jewish traditions concerning the first Biblical narrative of sowing: "And Isaac sowed in that land, and found in the same year an hundredfold; and the Lord blessed him, and the man waxed great, and grew more and more until he became very great[1]" "The ground was bad," says the Midrash, "and the year was bad"; and indeed the preceding context says that "there was a famine in the land." Yet Isaac "*found*"—not "reaped," says Philo, but "*found*"—a hundredfold. It is implied that the "blessing" did everything; Isaac, who was himself a son (as it were) of the blessing bestowed on Abraham, was blessed by the spontaneousness of the earth in a supernatural way. To Adam it was said "Cursed is the ground for thy sake, in toil shalt thou eat of it...thorns also and thistles shall it bring forth to thee[2]," but to Isaac we may apply the words of the Psalm "Blessed is every one that feareth the Lord and walketh in his ways, for thou shalt eat the labour of thine hands[3]."

Passing to the Marcan phrase "beareth *of herself*," literally "*automatically*," we note that "*automatic*" occurs in N T only here and in the story describing how the gate of Peter's prison "automatically opened[4]." The word "*automatic*" is applied in Greek literature to the earth in the Golden Age bringing forth her fruits of her own accord, and in LXX to the spontaneous fruit that springs up, of its own accord, in the seventh or sabbatical year "*That-which-groweth-automatically* of thy harvest thou shalt not reap[5]." To this apparently allusion is

---

[1] Gen xxvi 12—13, on which see Philo, the Midrash, Rashi, and Origen
[2] Gen iii 17—18 [3] Ps cxxviii 1—2.
[4] Acts xii 10 αὐτομάτη [sc ἡ πύλη] ἠνοίγη αὐτοῖς
[5] Lev xxv. 5, 11 Heb ספיח, LXX αὐτόματα ἀναβαίνοντα.

38 (Mark iv. 26—9)

THE PARABLES OF SOWING

made in the words of Isaiah, "This shall be the sign unto thee, ye shall eat this year *that-which-groweth-automatically*[1]."

Philo connects this Levitical precept (about "that which groweth automatically") with Isaac, as being the type of "the self-taught and self-instructed wise man"—what we should call, "the genius"; and he says "As to those things which we light upon, coming to us *automatically* from Nature, of these we do not find either the beginnings or the ends in ourselves as though we were their causers   The sowing is the beginning, the reaping is the end   But it is better to accept that [saying] 'Every beginning and every end is *automatic*,' [as] equivalent to 'It is Nature's work, not ours[2].'" Later on, he says that Isaac "'*sowed*' indeed, setting forth the virtue that is hostile to envy and malice, but is said to have '*found*,' not '*reaped*[3],'" apparently meaning that the good seed of kindness not only exterminates the weeds and thorns of envy and malice, but also elicits from the earth a spontaneous and unexpected fruitfulness

Regarded in this way, the Marcan Parable is an encouragement to the Christian sower to believe that, if he sows the right seed, all things, as Paul says, will "work together for good" for it   He may sleep, he may wake, but whether he sleeps or wakes his work will go on, though "he knoweth not how"   Possibly he may die   But, as Origen says, "You will find, even under the Law, martyrs whose fruit was a hundredfold," and Tertullian says "The blood of Christians is seed[4]"   The

---

[1] 2 K xix 29 Heb ספיח, LXX αὐτόματα, rep in Is xxxvii 30, where, however, LXX has ἃ ἔσπαρκας but οἱ λοιποί have αὐτόματα (or αὐτομάτως)   Αὐτόματος does not represent Heb correctly in Josh vi 5, Job xxiv 24

[2] Philo i 571—2.   In οἷς γὰρ ἀπαυτοματίζουσιν ἐκ φύσεως ἐπιτυγχάνομεν παρ' ἑαυτοῖς ὡς ἀναιτίους (ed Richter)—I have assumed that ἀναιτίους is a misprint for ἂν αἰτίοις

[3] Philo i 619, quoting Gen xxvi 12

[4] Origen on Gen xxvi 12 (Lomm viii 238), Tertull *Apologet* § 50   Comp Pseudo-Jerome on Mk iv 29 "justi gaudebunt qui 'in lacrymis seminaverunt' (Ps cxxvi 5)"

THE PARABLES OF SOWING

martyr after death rests from his labour and "sends in the sickle" that others may reap what he sowed[1], so that, like Isaac, the martyr may be regarded as a type, not only of the Resurrection but also of the sowing of the seed of the Holy Spirit[2].

John appears to express the automatic nature of spiritual growth in the Dialogue where Jesus says to Nicodemus "That which is born of the Spirit is spirit," and then, "The Spirit *breatheth where it listeth*[3]" If there is an allusion to "wind" as well as to "Spirit," that makes it all the more certain that the expression implies a spontaneous influence uncontrolled by man, the influence of Nature acting "of herself," that is, automatically We cannot add, in the same definite way, that the Johannine passage also implies man's ignorance of the nature of the spiritual growth For the words "*Thou knowest not* whence it cometh and whither it goeth[4]" may possibly be intended to apply to the special ignorance of the Pharisee, Nicodemus But still the impression left on us by the Fourth Evangelist is that he felt a valuable truth to be contained in the Marcan "he knoweth not how," namely, that every human teacher, every sower of the seed of truth,

---

[1] Comp Jn iv 38 "others have laboured and ye have entered into their labours"

[2] Comp Eccles xi 5—6 "As thou knowest not what is the way of the wind (*or*, spirit), [nor] how the bones [do grow] in the womb of her that is with child, even so thou knowest not the work of God who doeth all In the morning sow thy seed, and in the evening withhold not thine hand for thou knowest not which shall prosper, whether this or that"

On this, *Gen r* (on Gen xxv 1, Wu p 290) says "R Akiba said 'Hast thou made disciples in thy youth, make them also in thine old age, since thou knowest not in which of them thy teaching will endure'." It is added that twelve thousand of his earliest disciples died at one time, but at the last there were seven, some of the most famous of all the Rabbis (rep *ad loc* on Eccles xi 5—6, somewhat differently)

[3] Jn iii 6, 8   [4] Jn iii 8

(Mark iv 26—9)

THE PARABLES OF SOWING

has to sow and then wait—waiting in ignorance of the exact nature of the spiritual agencies that bring the seed to perfection. Those teachers especially need this warning who are proud of their teaching. Jesus addresses it to a teacher of the Pharisees to whom He says, "Art thou *the teacher of Israel* and knowest thou not these things[1]?" But the same warning was needed by Christian Pharisees later on[2], and is needed still.

§ 9 *"Less than all the seeds," and "greater than all the herbs," in Mark and Matthew*[3]

Luke omits these two phrases. The omission of the former is explicable because the mustard-seed is not "less than all the seeds"; the omission of the latter may be similarly explicable in a writer like Luke, who would not care to commit himself

---

[1] Jn iii 10.
[2] Acts xv 5 "But there rose up certain of the sect of the Pharisees…" They wished to exclude uncircumcised converts. Peter reminds them of God's action (*ib* 8) "giving them the Holy Spirit even as he did unto us."

[3]
Mk iv 30—32 (R V)	Mt xiii 31—2 (R V)	Lk xiii 18—19 (R V)
(30) And he said, How shall we liken the kingdom of God? or in what parable shall we set it forth? (31) It is like (*lit* As unto) a grain of mustard seed, which, when it is sown upon the earth, though it be less than all the seeds that are upon the earth, (32) Yet when it is sown, groweth up, and becometh greater than all the herbs, and putteth out great branches, so that the birds of the heaven can lodge under the shadow thereof.	(31) Another parable set he before them, saying, The kingdom of heaven is like unto a grain of mustard seed, which a man took, and sowed in his field: (32) Which indeed is less than all seeds, but when it is grown, it is greater than the herbs, and becometh a tree, so that the birds of the heaven come and lodge in the branches thereof.	(18) He said therefore, Unto what is the kingdom of God like? and whereunto shall I liken it? (19) It is like unto a grain of mustard seed, which a man took, and cast into his own garden; and it grew, and became a tree, and the birds of the heaven lodged in the branches thereof.

THE PARABLES OF SOWING

to the assertion that no "herb" grew to a greater height than that of the mustard. Elsewhere, in Matthew, Jesus speaks of the effectiveness of *"faith as a grain of mustard-seed"* This is explained by Origen (obscurely followed by Jerome) as meaning, not "little faith," but "all faith"—called "little" by men of the world, though spiritually great[1]. But Clement of Alexandria and Macarius explain it (entirely or partially) as referring to the biting and purifying nature of mustard[2] The Naassenes and Simon Magus are said to have applied "grain of mustard-seed" to a doctrine of generation "from an indivisible point," from which they drew fanciful and sometimes vicious inferences[3] These facts lead us to ask whether John anywhere intervenes by suggesting to us some truth equivalent to the doctrine of "the less" as generating "the greater," here implied by Mark and omitted by Luke.

If there is intervention, it is, as usual, indirect John never uses the word "little-one," or the adjective "little" in any context (except in the phrase "a little time"), throughout his Gospel[4] Of course he is obliged to speak of those whom Jesus called His "little ones" But he does it in a way of his own, a way that precludes any materialistic comparison between "little" and "great" The Evangelist first calls them, in the Prologue of his Gospel, "children," saying that the Logos, or Light, "gave authority to become God's *children*" to as many as received Him[5] Then, at the close of Christ's life on

---

[1] Mt xvii 17—20, on which see Origen (Lomm iii 219) and Jerome

[2] Clem Alex 155, 643—4, 966 (where it is classified with "spark," "pupil of the eye," and "leaven"), Macar iv 17 (p 192)

[3] See *Son* **3364** *e—f*, quoting Hippol v 4, vi 9 and 12, and illustrating from Levy ii 107a and 176a the Jewish use of "mustard-seed," *e g* "a mustard-seed (*i e* drop) of blood"

[4] He uses μικρόν adv frequently—nine times, against four (μικρόν (2), μετὰ μικρόν (2)) in the Synoptists—but not μικρός (except (Jn vii 33, xii 35) with χρόνος)

[5] Jn i. 12.

THE PARABLES OF SOWING

earth, he represents Jesus as using to the disciples something like what Origen calls "the language of the nursery," saying "*[Dear] little-children*, yet a little while am I with you[1]." Jesus here speaks to them in the language of a mother, as Paul does, to his converts, in the Epistle to the Galatians. Later on, changing the metaphor, Jesus says to them "And ye now therefore have sorrow", and He likens their present sorrow to that of "a woman when she is in travail," and their future joy to that of the same woman rejoicing "for the joy that a man is born into the world"—meaning, apparently, that the "man" Christ, the risen Saviour, shall then be, as Paul says, "[fully] shaped in them[2]."

This passage detaches us from unprofitable speculations about the precise size and material nature of the mustard-seed, and concentrates our attention on the lesson to be learned from birth and growth But it adds something of importance. In Mark, the lesson is simply the growth of the great from the little But when applied to human beings does not this growth often imply pain? A child's body is sometimes said to have "growing pains" And may not a child's mind—and a man's mind as long as he is spiritually an undeveloped child—have its corresponding spiritual "pains"? The ascent through pains of growth to a higher life suggests a thought of Resurrection Isaiah encourages such a suggestion when he writes "Like as a woman with child, that draweth near the time of

---

[1] Jn xiii 33 Τεκνία, to which Origen applies the term (Lomm ii 474) ὑποκοριστικόν, occurs almost certainly in Gal iv 19 τεκνία (v r τέκνα) μου οὓς πάλιν ὠδίνω μέχρις οὗ μορφωθῇ Χριστὸς ἐν ὑμῖν, where the language is that of a mother, and freq in 1 Jn ii. 1 etc. (always pl) Steph *Thes* gives no instance of it earlier than those in N T Aristoph has (*Lysistr* 889) τεκνίδιον, but not τεκνίον. It would sound to a Greek probably more homely than "darling," and more like "dearie "

In Jn, Christ's only mention of τέκνα is (viii 39) "if ye are *children (τέκνα) of Abraham.*"

[2] Jn xvi 21—2, Gal iv 19.

THE PARABLES OF SOWING

her delivery, is in pain and crieth out in her pangs, so have we been in thy presence, O Lord," and then, "Thy dead shall live, my dead bodies shall arise Awake and sing, ye that dwell in the dust, for thy dew is [as] the dew of herbs, and the earth shall cast forth the dead[1]"

In Isaiah, instead of "herbs," many authorities here substitute "illuminations," and LXX goes quite astray. We cannot therefore suppose that the Marcan Parable of the uprising of the mustard-seed to be the greatest of "herbs" originally alluded to this passage of Isaiah, and was typical of the Resurrection as well as of the spread of the Gospel But we may feel fairly confident that the Fourth Evangelist had in his mind this passage of Isaiah as a type of various kinds of resurrection If that was so, the poetry of the Hebrew "dew of herbs" might naturally be contrasted in his mind with prosaic Christian discussions about the mustard-seed as "greater than the herbs" This would confirm him in his purpose to subordinate the *size* of the growth (from "little" to "great") and to emphasize its regenerating *nature*, according to the words of the Psalmist "In the beauties of holiness, from the womb of the morning, thou hast the dew of thy youth ... Thou art a priest for ever, after the order of Melchizedek[2]." At all events the fact remains that the Fourth Gospel never mentions Christ's "little-ones," but does mention "children of God," and those whom Jesus Himself calls His "[dear] little children[3]"

---

[1] Is xxvi 17—19, R V marg "dew of light," and so Targum Ibn Ezra places this interpretation before "herbs" Rashi mentions only "herbs"

[2] Ps cx 3—4

[3] Specimens were given above (p 30, notes 2, 3) of Jewish doctrine about mystical "hiding," called "hiding *in the shadow*" It is worth noting that Mark describes the mustard-seed, which itself has been first hidden in the ground, as putting forth such branches that the birds of the air "find lodging *under its shadow*" (Mt and Lk "in its branches")

Also Lk 's substitution of (xiii 19) "his own garden" for (Mt)

44 (Mark iv 30—32)

THE PARABLES OF SOWING

§ 10. *Private "expounding," in Mark*[1]

Matthew omits two Marcan statements, 1st, that Jesus adapted His parables to the ability of His hearers, 2nd, that He used afterwards to explain[2] all things privately to His own disciples. Luke omits the whole. The versions of Mark vary, and an ancient comment on Mark says that Jesus explained only *all those parables about which He was questioned*[3]. "Expounded *all things*" might well seem incompatible with subsequent statements about the blindness of the disciples to some of the truths taught them by Jesus. Matthew's parallel

---

"his field" (Mk has "the earth") may have been partly due to a desire to shew that the seed here mentioned was not of corn but of something select and separate. Comp. Is lxi 11 "As the earth bringeth forth her bud, and as the *garden* causeth to bud her *sowing*, so the Lord will cause to bud righteousness..." on which Gesen. 283 *a* refers only to Lev xi 37, explained by Rashi from Dan i 12 (comp. 1 16) "*sowings* to eat," R V "*pulse*," marg. "*herbs*," Theod. "*seeds*," LXX ὀσπρίων (of which Steph *Thes* gives Galen's interpretation as "any seeds from which bread is not made").

[1]   Mk iv 33—4 (R V)
(33) And with many such parables spake (ἐλάλει) he the word unto them, as they were able to hear it
(34) And without a parable spake (ἐλάλει) he not unto them but privately to his own disciples he expounded (ἐπέλυε) all things

Mt xiii 34—5 (R V)
(34) All these things spake (ἐλάλησεν) Jesus in parables unto the multitudes, and without a parable spake (ἐλάλει) he nothing unto them
(35) That it might be fulfilled which was spoken by (*or*, through) the prophet, saying, I will open my mouth in parables, I will utter things hidden from the foundation of the world (*many anc. auth. omit* of the world)

[2] By the imperfect ἐπέλυε, "used to explain" or "proceeded to explain," and by "privately," an interval is implied between the utterance, and the explanation, of the parable

[3] Cramer, on Mk iv 34, "Let us understand '*expounded all things*' [to mean] that [He expounded] *all things as many as they sought to understand from Him*, as [for example] the parable of the seed and that of the tares. For the rest He left uninterpreted, having said to them, (Mt xiii 51) Have ye understood all these things? They said, Yea, Lord"

THE PARABLES OF SOWING

statement that Jesus was fulfilling the words of the Psalmist, "I will *utter things hidden from the foundation of the world*[1]," gives us the impression that he may mean, by "things hidden," something corresponding to "the word" in Mark. But there is nothing in Matthew parallel to the Marcan "expounding."

We must return to the question, touched on above, "*When did Jesus 'expound' these parables?*" Here, ancient commentators give little or no light. Origen, it is true, twice or thrice quotes the Marcan tradition[2]. But he couples his first quotation with a statement that Jesus appeared with a different appearance to the multitudes from that which He assumed to His disciples, at all events to "the eyes of their soul," and, in his opinion, "also to the eyes of their body[3]." This gives no indication as to the interval between the parables and the "expounding." It would be compatible with the view that the "expounding," at all events in some cases, did not take place till after Christ's resurrection.

---

[1] Mt xiii 35, comp Ps lxxviii 2

[2] The quotation is undoubted where he uses the Marcan ἐπιλύω, not used elsewhere in the Gospels, Cels ii 64, iii 46. It is also probable in Cels vi 6 ὅτι μὲν ἐλάλει τὸν τοῦ θεοῦ λόγον τοῖς μαθηταῖς κατ' ἰδίαν, καὶ μάλιστα ἐν ταῖς ἀναχωρήσεσιν, εἴρηται. τίνα δ' ἦν ἃ ἔλεγεν, οὐκ ἀναγέγραπται

[3] Cels ii 64 "Ἀλλὰ καὶ εἴπερ "κατ' ἰδίαν τοῖς ἰδίοις μαθηταῖς ἐπέλυε" τὰς παραβολὰς...ὥσπερ ταῖς ἀκοαῖς ἦσαν κρείττους οὕτω καὶ ταῖς ὄψεσι πάντως μὲν τῆς ψυχῆς, ἐγὼ δ' ἡγοῦμαι, ὅτι καὶ τοῦ σώματος. In T and T Clark's translation, this is not printed as a quotation from Mark. In Lommatzsch it is printed as from Mt xiii 10, 11, seqq. In Cels. iii 46 "κατ' ἰδίαν γὰρ τοῖς ἰδίοις μαθηταῖς ἐπέλυεν ἅπαντα" ὁ Ἰησοῦς —as also in Philocal § 18 (Lomm xxv 120)—Lomm prints the words as from Mark, but T and T Clark's transl. does not. Mk iv 34 is apparently referred to in Clement Hom xix 20 (ed Clark, "He explained to His disciples privately the mysteries of the kingdom of heaven") in connection with an alleged saying of Jesus "Keep the mysteries for me and the sons of my house," but I have found no other early reference except perhaps Tertull De Praescript § 20. In the Index to Jerome's *Letters* (transl. Fremantle) p 468 "Mark iv. 34" is an error for ix 34

THE PARABLES OF SOWING

Startling as this may be, it is certainly the conclusion to which John leads us—and that, in more ways than one First, negatively, though he often represents Jesus as speaking in private to His disciples, he never represents Him as explaining to them in private what He had said to others in public. Secondly, he represents Jesus as saying "I have spoken openly to the world; I ever taught in synagogue, and in the temple, where all the Jews come together; and in secret spake I nothing[1]." Thirdly, he represents Jesus as having taught what would be called the essential "mystery" of the Christian religion—the doctrine of His flesh and blood as the food of the world—publicly in the synagogue of Capernaum[2]. Fourthly, he calls the Parable of the Good Shepherd a "proverb"—that is (apparently) a dark saying, "not understood" by those to whom it was addressed[3]. Subsequently Jesus is represented as telling His disciples in effect (though they almost refuse to believe it) that all His past teaching has been "dark sayings" to them, and must be so till He sends the Holy Spirit or Paraclete to explain their meaning[4].

Let us suppose that John is here intervening to explain the meaning of the Marcan tradition transmuted by Matthew and rejected by Luke In that case his view would seem to be to this effect "Mark is referring here to Christ's method of teaching as a whole. It was not intended to hide mysteries from the multitudes outside the circle, or 'house' (as the Jews call it) of His disciples, and to reveal them immediately afterwards in that 'house[5].' It was the desire of Jesus to prepare all for the knowledge of '*the word*' as far as possible, that is, '*even as*

---

[1] Jn xviii. 20, see *Joh Voc* **1694** *b*   [2] Jn vi 59
[3] Jn x 6   By "understood" John means "morally understood." Every man "understands" what "a shepherd" means, but no self-absorbed man "understands" what "the good shepherd" means To the Pharisees (Westcott *ad loc*) "the spiritual conceptions of the fold, the door, the sheep, the shepherd, were all strange "
[4] Jn xvi. 25 foll.   [5] On "house," see *Son* **3460** *c*

they were able to hear [and understand].' But they were able to go but a little way, even the most zealous of the hearers, in understanding. As long as He was in the flesh with them, *He did not, [and could not] speak to them without a parable* But afterwards *in private,* in the days that followed His resurrection, to *His own [true] disciples He expounded all things*[1]."

If all this seems to us indefinite, circuitous, and historically unsatisfying, perhaps the reason is that we attach more importance than the Fourth Evangelist did to believing definite historical statements about the words and deeds of the incarnate and the risen Saviour, apart from the spirit in which we believe them. It seems clear from the whole tenor of the Johannine Gospel and Epistle that the author cannot conceive of a soul as being really Christian unless it permanently possesses, and is possessed by, the quickening and instructing Spirit of the ever-living Christ. A book that strives to impart to its readers the conception of the influence of such a Life and such a Spirit may well be regarded by many as less definite, direct, and satisfying than a history (like Luke's) that devotes itself to "tracing the course of all things accurately from the first[2]"

---

[1] If that is the historical fact, we must suppose that Mk iv 10 "*quite-alone* (κατὰ μόνας)" has a special significance In N T it does not occur elsewhere except Lk ix 18 ἐν τῷ εἶναι αὐτὸν προσευχόμενον κατὰ μόνας συνῆσαν (marg συνήντησαν) αὐτῷ οἱ μαθηταί where Mk-Mt mentions (Mk viii 27, Mt xvi 13) "Caesarea Philippi" Καταμόνας does not occur in Goodspeed's Concordances except Hermas *Mand* xi 8 οὐδὲ καταμόνας λαλεῖ Lat *secrete* (but ? by himself, apart from God's help) The *Pistis Sophia*, after much discourse (1—4) about the "mystery" that is "the head of all things" and "surrounds (*or*, explores) the universe," says (4) "the disciples were sitting by themselves on the mount of Olives" and Jesus "sat at a little distance from them (sedit remotus ab iis paululum" (rep 5) Presently He comes to them and says (9) "From this day I will speak with you openly (ἐν παῤῥησίᾳ) from the beginning of the truth even to the end thereof, and I will speak with you face to face without parable" Comp Acts 1 6—12 which describes the disciples as questioning Jesus on the Mount of Olives

[2] Lk. 1. 3

THE PARABLES OF SOWING

But if we are wise we shall accept the Fourth Gospel as wholesomely supplementing the Third. And we may do well to ask ourselves whether this "unsatisfying" writer might not say to us "The Church is in danger of being too easily satisfied by books. I would have my readers rise from their reading unsatisfied, and desiring something that can be given them by no book, but only by the Saviour Himself[1]."

§ 11. *"The word," in the Fourth Gospel as a whole*

Reviewing the preceding sections we find much to justify the conclusion that John's interventions in favour of Mark—as in the phrases "he knoweth not how," and "hidden that it may be revealed," and "to you is given the mystery"—are part of a general attempt to shew that the divine Logos, or Word, is to be distinguished not only from the mere intellectual Logos that would be connected by Greeks with "logic," but also from Scripture on the one side and Voice on the other[2], and that it is to be regarded as "sown," or incarnate in humanity, in order to produce Love, the Love of the Son of Man. In Christ's first mention of the Logos we have seen reason for supposing that this mystery is suggested: "Herein is the Word of Truth (*or*, the Word ideally true) that one soweth and another reapeth," that is to say, God "sows" His Word and man reaps salvation[3].

---

[1] Comp. Jn xxi. 25.

[2] Comp. Papias, in Euseb. iii. 39. 4, on the importance he attached to "what comes from living voice," τὰ παρὰ ζώσης φωνῆς as compared with τὰ ἐκ τῶν βιβλίων. He does not mention Scripture. On the other hand, Irenaeus iii. 2. 1 describes heretics as objecting to N.T. taken by itself, on the ground that "it was not delivered by [written] letters but *through living voice* (per vivam vocem)." John (xxi. 25) speaks of "books" as an inadequate representation of Christ's actions. He also represents the Baptist as saying (i. 23) "I am [but] the voice of one crying...," that is, in effect, "I am *only a voice*, not the Word."

[3] See § 6 above.

THE PARABLES OF SOWING

In the expression of this doctrine, and more particularly in the marked distinction between "real" and "true" (*alēthinos* and *alēthēs*), John may have been influenced by Greek philosophy. Epictetus ascribes to the *logos* a cleansing power. The Gods, he says, are "clean by nature," and men, so far as they draw nigh to the Gods in accordance with the *logos*, grasp that which is clean and that which is cleansing (*or*, cleanly). "But since it is impossible that their substance should be entirely clean, being blended of such matter (*hylē*) [as is inherent in it], the *logos, received from [the Gods by men] attempts to make this [substance] cleanly as far as possible*[1]" No doubt Epictetus implied that there is to be in this "cleansing" some infusion of love, good will, and respect for one's fellow creatures. But he does not say so here; and it is significant that in the whole of the Dissertations the word "good-will" occurs only incidentally[2].

The Fourth Evangelist also represents the *logos* as "cleansing." But in how different a form! And with an appeal to motives how different! He represents Jesus, on the last night of His intercourse with His disciples, as washing their feet like a servant, and as saying to them, some time afterwards, "Already are ye *clean because of the logos that I have spoken*

---

[1] Epict iv 11 3—4 ἐπεὶ γὰρ ἐκεῖνοι φύσει καθαροὶ καὶ ἀκήρατοι, ἐφ' ὅσον ἠγγίκασιν αὐτοῖς οἱ ἄνθρωποι κατὰ τὸν λόγον, ἐπὶ τοσοῦτον καὶ τοῦ καθαροῦ καὶ τοῦ καθαρίου εἰσὶν ἀνθεκτικοί ἐπεὶ δ' ἀμήχανον τὴν οὐσίαν αὐτῶν παντάπασιν εἶναι καθαρὰν ἐκ τοιαύτης ὕλης κεκραμένην, ὁ λόγος παραληφθεὶς εἰς τὸ ἐνδεχόμενον ταύτην καθάριον ἀποτελεῖν πειρᾶται

[2] The only mention of εὔνοια is in iv 1 22 "he asks for a sword, and is angry with the man who, out of good will, refuses it" But it occurs also in the Fragments ed Schenkel, pp 472, 480 Φιλία occurs more frequently, and there is a passionate detestation (ii 4 3) of the selfish licentiousness that destroys neighbourhood, friendship and citizenship, but the treatise on φιλία shews that the philosopher's main thought is of that which is (ii 22 20) "profitable (συνοίσει)" to himself, that is to his true Self, the Man within him (as opposed to the Beast)

50 (Mark iv 33—4)

THE PARABLES OF SOWING

to you, abide in me, and I too in you[1]." Herein Jesus is referring to what He had said immediately after the washing, "Ye are *clean*, but not all[2]"—"not all," because Judas had not "received the *logos*" into himself As soon as Judas goes out of the chamber, Jesus promulgates the New Commandment "*A new commandment* I give unto you, that ye love one another[3]."

Few, very few, are he commandments or precepts that Jesus gives to His disciples in the Fourth Gospel In Matthew and Luke they abound In Mark they are perhaps not more than a dozen But in John the precepts of Jesus to the Disciples, up to the night of the Last Discourse, are not more than three: (1) "Lift up your eyes," (2) "Make the people sit down," (3) "Gather up the fragments[4]." It is perhaps not an accident that the Fourth Gospel represents Jesus as giving to the Twelve, up to the time of the Washing of the Feet, no precepts at all except such as concerned them, either (1) as reapers of the spiritual harvest, or (2) as preparers of the people for the reception of the spiritual bread, or (3) as recipients (in full measure) of bread for themselves in return for the bread given to others.

---

[1] Jn xv 3—4 [2] Jn xiii 10
[3] Jn xiii 34
[4] Jn iv 35, vi 10, 12 Some might add, as being at all events an imperative, Jn xii 7 ἄφες But this is in the singular, and the context, mentioning Judas by name, suggests that Judas is addressed The above remarks refer to precepts addressed to *more disciples than one*

CHAPTER II

THE STILLING OF THE STORM
[Mark iv 35—41]

§ 1. *Why does John omit this?*

WE now come to a point where criticism, if it is to be practised at all, will have to include minute verbal analysis, a close study of words and minute phrases, as well as an attempt to re-imagine (as it were) the mingled reminiscences and imaginations of the Galilaean fishermen who formed an important part in the circle of Christ's disciples, and who, after His resurrection, sang songs of praise and adoration to their Lord in heaven while waiting day by day till He should return to them on earth.

An instance of such minute verbal analysis was given in a previous volume where it was shewn[1] that a single Greek word used by Luke pointed to early divergent interpretations of one of what we might call the Gennesaret-traditions. Luke represented Peter in a fishing-boat as "*making signs*" to his partners in another fishing-boat to come and help him, in consequence of a miraculous draught of fishes so vast that the boats were "*beginning to sink*[2]." It was shewn that the Greek word *kateneusa* used by Luke did not elsewhere mean "*made signs*" (though it might mean "*made a sign of assent*") but that

---

[1] *Proclamation* pp. 91—7

[2] Lk v 7 ὥστε βυθίζεσθαι αὐτά. Βυθίζομαι does not occur in canon LXX. Goodspeed gives it only in Clem. Rom. *Cor* § 51 of the Egyptians in the Red Sea. Βύθος in canon LXX refers almost always to the Red Sea, or metaph. to the "sinking" or "drowning" of the soul. Βυθίζω, in N.T. elsewhere, occurs only in 1 Tim. vi 9 of spiritual "drowning."

THE STILLING OF THE STORM

it did sometimes mean "*swam to [shore]*" Now John does, in effect, describe Peter as *swimming to shore*, toward Jesus, from a fishing-boat on Gennesaret, after Christ's resurrection. Hence it was inferred that John regarded Luke as having misinterpreted and placed before the Resurrection an event that he should have placed after it

These facts, though discussed under the Calling of the Fishermen, will demand some attention later on when we are confronted with the question why, and with what differences, John describes the Walking on the Sea, which Mark and Matthew insert but which Luke omits For we must there note that in that description Matthew inserts an account of Peter's coming to Jesus across the sea and "*beginning to be drowned*[1]." This John omits, presumably regarding it, like Luke's version, as erroneous and antedated.

The object of these remarks is to bespeak more than usual patience for the study of some details in the Stilling of the Storm, on the ground that, in such a narrative, even a single word or phrase may have a meaning not visible on the surface and not fully intelligible till we perceive that it refers to a post-resurrectional period

It will be convenient to dwell separately on the traditions peculiar to Mark in the parallel texts as given below Putting aside unimportant verbal differences, and also the exorcistic address to the sea ("Be silent, be thou muzzled") which is alien from the Fourth Gospel[2], we find the following three

---

[1] Mt xiv 30 ἀρξάμενος καταποντίζεσθαι (not elsewhere in N T except Mt xviii 6 implying condemnation) In LXX, once of the Red Sea, elsewhere always metaphorical

[2] Mk iv 39 Σιώπα, πεφίμωσο Comp Mk i 25, Lk iv 35, where "Be thou muzzled" is used exorcistically John, later on, speaks of "*a great wind* that blew," vi 18 ἥ τε θάλασσα ἀνέμου μεγάλου πνέοντος διηγείρετο (as א etc) "*Great wind*" (of which three instances are mentioned in *Lev r* on Lev xiii 2) suggests God as the Sender in the case of Jonah (i 4) The other instances are Job i 19 ("there came a great wind") where Satan is apparently

THE STILLING OF THE STORM

(1) "they take him [i e Jesus], as he was, in the boat," (2) "and other boats were with him," (3) "he was in the stern on the cushion[1]"

---

[1] permitted to send it, and 1 K xix. 11 where the Lord apparently sends it, but "the Lord was not in the wind"

Mk iv 35—41 (R V)	Mt viii 18, 23—7 (R V)	Lk viii 22—5 (R V)
(35) And on that day, when even was come, he saith unto them, Let us go over unto the other side (36) And leaving the multitude, they take him with them, even as he was, in the boat And other boats were with him (37) And there ariseth a great storm of wind, and the waves beat into the boat, insomuch that the boat was now filling (38) And he himself was in the stern, asleep on the cushion and they awake him, and say unto him, Master (or, Teacher) (διδάσκαλε), carest thou not that we perish? (39) And he awoke, and rebuked the wind, and said unto the sea, Peace, be still And the wind ceased, and there was a great calm (40) And he said unto them, Why are ye fearful? have ye not yet faith? (41) And they ·feared exceedingly, and said one to another, Who then is this, that even the wind and the sea obey him?	(18) Now when Jesus saw great multitudes about him, he gave commandment to depart unto the other side .... (23) And when he was entered into a boat, his disciples followed him (24) And behold, there arose a great tempest in the sea, insomuch that the boat was covered with the waves but he was asleep (25) And they came to him, and awoke him, saying, Save, Lord, we perish, (26) And he saith unto them, Why are ye fearful, O ye of little faith? Then he arose, and rebuked the winds and the sea, and there was a great calm (27) And the men marvelled, saying, What manner of man is this, that even the winds and the sea obey him?	(22) Now it came to pass on one of those days, that he entered into a boat, himself and his disciples, and he said unto them, Let us go over unto the other side of the lake and they launched forth (23) But as they sailed he fell asleep and there came down a storm of wind on the lake, and they were filling [with water], and were in jeopardy (24) And they came to him, and awoke him, saying, Master, master, (ἐπιστάτα), we perish And he awoke, and rebuked the wind, and the raging of the water and they ceased, and there was a calm (25) And he said unto them, Where is your faith? And being afraid they marvelled, saying one to another, Who then is this, that he commandeth even the winds and the water, and they obey him?

THE STILLING OF THE STORM

§ 2. (R.V.) *"They take him with them, even as he was, in the boat,"* in Mark[1]

No explanation of "even as he was" is alleged from any early commentator. Euthymius paraphrases it, "as He was sitting in the boat." This is said to mean that Jesus was "already on board—a point which Matthew and Luke overlook —and He now put to sea without going ashore to make preparations[2]." But (1) there is no other instance in which the disciples are said to "take" Jesus "with them" in this literal sense, (2) the divergences of Matthew and Luke indicate that they dissented from the Marcan tradition, (3) the Diatessaron omits the Marcan clause, though inserting the Marcan words that precede and that follow; (4) an ancient commentator on Mark reads "*He* took them with *him*," and explains why He did it, namely, that He might *"make them witnesses"* of the miracle that was to follow[3].

The precise meaning of the Marcan word is "*take, or receive, from.*" Applied to things, it is often used of "*receiving [tradition] from*" a teacher. Applied to persons, it may mean "*receiving [children] from [parents]*" with a view to instruction, but it also means, generally, "*taking charge of*," "*taking into one's own circle*," "*taking as a companion*[4]." In LXX it is used of Abraham, Laban, Joseph etc. "*taking, from [one place to another]*," servants, or friends, to accompany them on some journey or business[5]. In the Synoptic Gospels, it is frequently

---

[1] Mk iv 36 παραλαμβάνουσιν αὐτὸν ὡς ἦν ἐν τῷ πλοίῳ

[2] So Prof. Swete quoting Euthymius, and adding "In the Gospels the word is commonly used of the Lord 'taking' the Twelve, e.g. ix 2, x 32, xiv 33, cf. Jo xiv 3, but here the disciples, as owners and navigators of the boat, 'take' Him with them."

[3] Cramer *ad loc*. He uses first ἔλαβε and then παρέλαβε, thus τοὺς μὲν οὖν μαθητὰς μεθ' ἑαυτοῦ ἔλαβεν. παρέλαβε δὲ οὐ μάτην οὐδὲ εἰκῆ, ἀλλ' ὥστε ποιῆσαι θεατὰς τοῦ μέλλοντος ἔσεσθαι θαύματος.

[4] See Steph *Thes* παραλαμβάνω

[5] See LXX *Oxf Concordance*, παραλαμβάνω

THE STILLING OF THE STORM

used of Jesus taking all, or some, of the Twelve apart, as companions. But it is never thus used by John. His three instances of it are (1) (narrative) "He [*i.e.* the Logos] came unto his own and his own *received* him not," (2) (Jesus to the disciples) "If I go and prepare a place for you, I come again and will *receive* you unto myself," (3) (narrative) "Then therefore he [*i.e.* Pilate] delivered him unto them [*i.e.* the Jews] to be crucified. They therefore *received* Jesus[1]."

As to this last, it is worth noting that the only Synoptic instances of "*receiving Jesus*" are in Matthew's accounts of the Temptation and the Passion. In the former, there is some obscurity since the devil is twice described as "receiving" Jesus[2]. Origen, in a comment on Satan and the "delivering up," or *paradosis*, of Jesus, after saying that the Father "delivered up the Son, as in the case of Job, to the opposing powers," says that "it was to the destruction of their own kingdom and dominion, contrary to their expectation, that they *received* the Son from the Father[3]." In the account of the Passion Matthew says "Then the soldiers of the governor *received Jesus* [from Pilate and took him] into the praetorium[4]." It is perhaps not without a touch of Johannine irony that John begins his Gospel by saying that when the incarnate Logos came to "his own"—*i.e.* to the Jews—*from God*, "his own *received him not*," but when He was delivered to them *by Pilate*, then "they *received him*."

---

[1] Jn 1 11, xiv 3, xix 16—17
[2] Mt iv 5 R V "*Taketh* (παραλαμβάνει) him into the holy city," A V "*taketh him up*," rep *ib* 8. Luke avoids the difficult word, having ἀνάγειν and ἄγειν. Origen (Lomm xxi 511, rep xxv 21) uses ἀναβιβάζοντος, perhaps blending (see context) Luke and Matthew.
[3] Origen *Comm Matth* xiii 8, 9 εἰς κατάλυσιν τῆς ἰδίας βασιλείας καὶ ἀρχῆς παρὰ προσδοκίαν παραλαβόντες ἀπὸ τοῦ πατρὸς τὸν υἱόν
[4] Mt xxvii 27 τότε οἱ στρατιῶται τοῦ ἡγεμόνος, παραλαβόντες τὸν Ἰησοῦν εἰς τὸ πραιτώριον. The other Synoptists do not use the word in describing the Passion. See *Joh Gr* **2570** *d* quoting *Evang Petr* §1 καὶ τότε κελεύει Ἡρώδης ὁ βασιλεὺς παρ[αλημ]φθῆναι τὸν Κύριον

THE STILLING OF THE STORM

The Pauline Epistles say (1) "As therefore *ye received Christ Jesus the Lord*, [so] walk in him," (2) "*Having received* from us the word of hearing [*i e* the word of the Gospel] [which is the word] of God, ye welcomed [it] not [as the] word of men, but—even as it truly is—[the] word of God, which also inwardly-worketh in you that believe," (3) (in a passage where "*learn* Christ" means in effect "*receive* Christ") "Ye did not so *learn Christ*, if so be that ye have heard him, and were taught in him, even as truth is in Jesus[1]" All these imply that we are, in some spiritual sense, to "*receive Jesus as He is*," not merely to *receive words about Jesus* The phrase "*as He is*" may be illustrated from the Johannine Epistle, which uses it of the ultimate revelation for which men may hope "We know that, if he shall be manifested, we shall be like him, for we shall see him *even as he is*[2]."

In the Walking on the Sea, it is said by John alone, "They therefore desired to *take* (or, *receive*) him into the boat[3]." John here uses the uncompounded form "*take*" (not "*take-from*") No doubt there is a difference between the two, as may be seen from his Prologue, where he uses the compounded along with the uncompounded form, thus "He [*i e* the Logos, or the Son] came unto his own, and his own did not *receive him from [the Father]*; but, as many as *received* him, to them gave he authority to become children of God[4]" In the Prologue, the meaning perhaps is that, "when the Son of God came to His own family, none *received Him [fitly as coming] from [the Father]*, but some *received Him [though imperfectly]*[5]." So here, on the hypothesis that the Johannine clause ("they desired to receive him into the boat") is to be taken

---

[1] Coloss ii 6, 1 Thess ii 13, Eph iv 20, 21.
[2] 1 Jn iii 2 καθώς ἐστιν
[3] Jn vi 21 ἤθελον οὖν λαβεῖν αὐτὸν εἰς τὸ πλοῖον.
[4] Jn i 11—12 παρέλαβον ἔλαβον
[5] Quoted from *Joh Gr* **2570**, where see the difference between λαμβάνω and παραλαμβάνω, illustrated from Epictetus.

57 (Mark iv 35—41)

THE STILLING OF THE STORM

metaphorically, we may suppose that some clause of this kind in the original tradition referred to the spiritual "reception" of Jesus after the Resurrection, when He returned to them across the waters of Sheol, and when they recognised that He was no "phantasm" or "bodiless spirit" or "demon," but their true Lord, so that they "received Him *as He was*,"—though (even now) imperfectly, because the Holy Spirit had not yet descended[1].

Of course to modern readers all this seems extremely fanciful But we should put ourselves in the position of the Galilaean fishermen during that night of despair when their Master—as they afterwards believed and as the Christian Creeds teach us still to believe—actually passed across the Sea of Death in order to "preach to the spirits in prison" Then we ought to attempt to realise something of the nature of those songs which Paul and Silas sang in the dungeon of Philippi and which Christians must have sung from the beginning of the Gospel that they preached in His name. Thus, and only thus, shall we be prepared to do justice to the supposition that these narratives of what happened on the Sea of Galilee are described in language originally used in Songs of Resurrection

---

[1] "*Phantasm*," in N T, occurs only in Mk vi 49, Mt xiv 26 (the Walking on the Sea) where SS has "*devil*," and in Lk xxiv 37 (D) (the Resurrection) "they thought they saw *a spirit* (πνεῦμα) (D φάντασμα)" Ignatius has (*Smyrn* § 3) "For I know that also after the resurrection when He came to Peter and his friends [*lit* to those around Peter], He said to them, *Take* (or, *receive*) (λάβετε), handle me, and see (ἴδετε) that I am not a bodiless *demon* (δαιμόνιον ἀσώματον)" Lk xxiv 37—8 adds that the disciples were "terrified and *full-of-fear* (ἔμφοβοι)" and that Jesus said to them "Why are ye *troubled* (τεταραγμένοι)?" Comp μὴ φοβεῖσθε in Mk vi 50, Mt xiv 27, Jn vi 20 and ἐταράχθησαν in Mk vi 50, Mt xiv 26 (Jn vi 19 ἐφοβήθησαν) The Johannine account of the Resurrection makes no mention of "*fear*" except in Jn xx 19 "the doors being shut where the disciples were *for fear of the Jews*, there came Jesus and stood in the midst . "

THE STILLING OF THE STORM

It is not proof, but only supposition—supposition, however, derived from many lines of evidence pointing to one conclusion. It must be reserved for later occasions—when we come to discuss the Walking on the Sea and the Resurrection—to collect in detail the evidence for the hypothesis that the Resurrection is the historical fact, on which are based the two earlier narratives of Mark-Matthew (one omitted by John and one by Luke) which are of the nature of poetry. The phrase "of the nature of poetry" (not "poetry") is intended to leave us free to believe that there may have been some actual scenes of storm on Lake Gennesaret, which, after Christ's resurrection, were recorded in Galilaean poetry as being typical of that which came to pass later on when Christ "fell asleep[1]." If the hypothesis had not been stated here, the reader might have complained that, in dealing with the phrase "they took him with them even as he was," we had passed over an instance of the failure of the rule of Johannine Intervention. We maintain on the contrary that it will be found to be an instance not of failure, but of fulfilment, if the reader will keep his mind open for the evidence as a whole.

---

[1] Compare Origen *Cant Hom* ii 9 (Lomm xiv 272—3) "To this day in the faithless, and in those of doubtful heart, the divine Word sleeps. sleeps in those who are tossed by storm-waves . Straightway comes a calm when He awakes (eo vigilante) Straightway all the mighty masses of waters become still, all the opposing spirits (*or*, winds) (spiritibus) are rebuked, the rage of the waves is silent While He sleeps, there is storm, death, and despair" Origen also expressly accepts the narrative in its literal sense as well as spiritually (Lomm v 269—70) "Although at all times, when He is awakened (excitatur) by disciples, He restrains the whirlwinds or storm-blasts of the Church, yet it is certain that also at the time the events recorded in the history actually took place (tamen certum est etiam tunc gesta esse ea quae per historiam referuntur)"

Origen's words are capable of a partial illustration from a poetical conception of the Saviour's Descent into Sheol When Jesus fell asleep on earth, the opposing spirits raged in exultation When He passed into Sheol and led captivity captive, they were rebuked and became silent

THE STILLING OF THE STORM

§ 3 *"And other boats were with him," in Mark*[1]

The text in Mark varies. Several MSS or versions insert "many" and omit "other"[2]; or insert "but" as well as "and"[3], or omit "boats," or substitute "little boats"[4]; or have "with them" for "with him"[5]. Codex D, instead of *ploia*, "*boats*," has, apparently under an erasure, a feminine form *ploiai*, non-existent in Greek[6]. It is possible to explain the variations as to "*other*" and "*but*" from a passage about "boats" in John where Nonnus and Chrysostom take the Greek to mean "*other boats*," but R V and W H take it as "*but boats*"[7]. The Greek, in ancient MSS which are unaccented, may mean either "*other*" or "*but*," so that the Greek MSS are of no interpretatory value on this point

This Johannine passage has an obvious bearing on our

---

[1] Mk iv 36 καὶ ἄλλα πλοῖα ἦν μετ' αὐτοῦ, om in parall Mt -Lk

[2] Confusion has arisen owing to the ambiguity of αλλα meaning (1) "*but*" (adversative), (2) "*other*". Those who took it to mean "other" might add δέ meaning "but" (supplementary) See below Codex *b* inserts "simul" as well as "multae" "et *multae naves simul* erant cum illo," codex *e* ("many *persons*") has "et *simul multi* erant cum eo"

[3] See Swete *ad loc*

[4] See Swete as to "little boats (πλοιάρια)," but add that codex *e* has "many [*persons*]," and that codex *b* has, first, "navicula" ("in the *little-boat*"), and then "naves" ("many *boats*")

[5] So Syr in Walton "naviculae autem aliae cum eis erant"

[6] Mk iv 36 και αλλαι δε πλοιαι πολλαι ησαν, consistently making the adj ἄλλος feminine pl and the verb ἦσαν pl instead of singular

[7] Jn vi 23 (W H) ἀλλὰ ἦλθεν πλοῖα Probably the harshness of "other boats came"—without "but" or "and" to introduce the clause—has induced W H to accent αλλα as "but" This harshness (doubtless) explains why many authorities insert δέ Alford reads ἄλλα [δέ] ἦλθεν πλοιάρια Blass rewrites the text as ἐνέβησαν εἰς πλοιάρια ἐπελθόντα ἐκ Τιβεριάδος But if that had been the original, why should scribes have altered a sentence so simple and easy? The chaotic condition of the text in Jn vi 23 (for which see Blass *ad loc*) is best explained as an attempt of John to clarify an old Marcan tradition about αλλα πλοια

THE STILLING OF THE STORM

Marcan tradition about *"other boats"* And if *alla,* *"but,"* were placed before the Greek *ploia,* it might be read as *all'aploia* Now *aploia* means "weather not fit for sailing." That might seem appropriate in Mark· "Jesus was already in the boat, desirous to depart, *but the weather was not fit for sailing."* Moreover the word *aploia* had a kind of literary history which would make it specially appropriate at the outset of a narrative that was to suggest to Christians a thought of their Lord as being in the circumstances of Jonah, yet rising superior to them For *aploia* in Herodotus, Æschylus, and Euripides, means *unfavourable winds sent by the Gods and propitiated by human sacrifice*[1]. It was known to all the world that the Greek fleet sailing for Troy had been detained at Aulis till Iphigenia had been offered up as a sacrifice to Artemis. It was also known to all Jews that Jonah had been, in a manner different but somewhat similar, cast into the deep at his own request, for the sake of the safety of his companions.

The word is not alleged to occur in later Greek[2]. We should therefore note the use of it in the Dissertations of Epictetus, where he says that, instead of concentrating ourselves on one thing alone—namely, our mind—we foolishly attach ourselves to external things: "For this cause, if there be *foulweather* (*aploia*) we sit, distracted, and peering constantly 'What wind is it?' we say, 'Boreas? What do we want with Boreas? When will Zephyrus blow?'" The philosopher replies to the distracted man "When Zephyrus pleases, my good

---

[1] See ἄπλοια in Herod II 119 (pl.) and Aesch *Ag* 150 (Dindorf) (pl.), also sing in Aesch *Ag* 188, Eurip *Iph Aul* 88, *Iph Taur* 15 Plutarch *Mor* 857 B is quoting Herodotus, though loosely In all these cases, human sacrifice is the result, resorted to in order to terminate ἄπλοια

[2] It is not in the Concordances to Aristophanes, Aristotle, Demosthenes, nor in the Index to Lucian, nor in the Indices to Berlin Urkunde and Egypt Expl Papyri (Sept 1915) In Plutarch it occurs merely as part of a free quotation from Herodotus.

THE STILLING OF THE STORM

friend, or when Æolus pleases. For the Gods did not make you steward of the winds, but Æolus[1]"

Whatever may be the explanation of the variations in the MSS they indicate that the phrase caused difficulty in early times; and the Johannine clause and its variations, when compared with the Marcan clause and its variations, appear to constitute an instance of Johannine Intervention This increases the probability that as to the Marcan clause in the context, discussed in the last section ("they took, *or*, received, him"), John has again intervened; for an intervention that is only slightly probable as to a particular text becomes more probable if we can shew that the writer intervened as to the context[2].

§ 4 "*On the cushion,*" *in Mark*[3]

No satisfactory evidence has been hitherto produced that "*the cushion,*" in a literal sense, was "a regular part of the boat's

---

[1] Epict. 1. 1. 16. "Ἀπλοια occurs nowhere else in Epictetus. The text varies Might Epictetus here be jibing against the Christian representation of Jesus as Æolus and reproducing some version of the tradition about αλλαπλοια? Or might the scribe of D be influenced by traditions about the ἄπλοια that befell Jonah?

[2] Whatever uncertainty may attend the explanation of this Johannine parenthesis about ΑΛΛΑΠΛΟΙΑ, one conclusion is fairly certain, that it does not proceed from the Evangelist's invention And this is important because of the great number of Johannine parentheses (see *Joh Gr* Index "*Parenthesis*"). Some of these suggest, at first sight, that the Gospel has been "worked over" by an editor, with doctrinal bias, who has not always taken the trouble to fill the gaps between the evangelic text and the editorial interpolations But the clause under consideration, when studied along with Mark, does not favour the hypothesis of an editor adding anything of his own invention It rather favours the hypothesis of an evangelist or sub-evangelist, inserting an ancient explanation, for which he did not consider himself responsible

[3] Mk iv 38 ἐν τῇ πρύμνῃ ἐπὶ τὸ προσκεφάλαιον καθεύδων D omits τό Instead of "*puppe* (stern)," codex *e* has "*priora*," apparently for "*prora*," followed by "super pulvinum dormiens" An ancient commentary says "Mark has also told us how He slept, namely, that

THE STILLING OF THE STORM

equipment[1]." Codex Bezae alters *"the cushion"* into *"a cushion."* But how came *"the"* into the Greek text? And why do the parallel Matthew and Luke avoid the word altogether instead of adopting this simple alteration? These questions call for an answer, and at the same time, although John omits the whole of this narrative, we are bound to ask, in accordance with our rule, whether he has anything that bears on the Marcan word.

In the first place we must note that the Greek for "cushion" is literally "head-rest," or "pillow," and that it is only occasionally and irregularly used for a rower's cushion. In the next place, the Syriac Thesaurus has a form of the word "pillow" not only in Mark but also in John, "She saw two angels in white sitting, one *at the pillow*, and one at the feet, where the body of Jesus had been put[2]" Then, looking into the Scriptural Hebrew that corresponds to the Syriac "pillow,"

---

it was ἐν προσκεφαλαίῳ, plainly shewing His simplicity (ἄτυφον) " I do not understand the force of ἐν, if it is deliberately substituted for ἐπί

[1] Concerning the προσκεφάλαιον, Theophylact (writing about A D. 1071) says ξύλινον δὲ πάντως ἦν τοῦτο But it is not shewn by competent evidence that in boats on the Sea of Galilee or elsewhere there existed a structure of this kind that was called *"the head-rest,"* τὸ προσκεφάλαιον On the other hand Steph *Thes* illustrates the use of προσκεφάλαιον for ὑπηρέσιον ("rower's cushion") and quotes Lysias p 121, 36 προσκεφάλαια εἰς τὴν ταφήν as shewing that the word was applied to a part of funeral clothing The evidence of Macgregor (*Rob Roy on the Jordan*, 4th ed p 321) begs the question ("evidently a regular part of the boat's equipment, from the use of the definite article") and is of no value

[2] Jn xx 12 So Walton. *Thes Syr* 293 has "cervical" here and in Gen. xxxviii (error for xxviii) 11, 18, 1 S xix 13, xxvi 12, etc., and adds that in the place of the sing (which is non-existent) there is used in Mk iv 38 a shortened form with a prefix Castell 173 renders the Chaldaic in O T and the Syr in Jn xx 12 by "cervical " SS for Mk is wanting, for Jn it is rendered (Burk) "one *at the head of the place*"—Walton, "unum *a cervicali*"—"that Jesus had been lying in and one at the feet "

THE STILLING OF THE STORM

we see that it is a plural noun meaning *"place at the head"* or *"head-place,"* but it is rendered by A V *"pillows"* in Genesis, and *"bolster"* in Samuel, and by A V. marg and R V. *"head-tires"* in Jeremiah[1]. This indicates that a word rendered in Mark's version of the Stilling of the Storm *"pillow"* or *"cushion,"* may have been rendered in a Johannine narrative of the Resurrection *"the place at the head,"* but it would not shew, or even suggest, that John was alluding to Mark, unless other evidence of allusion were produced

The only instance of the Marcan word "pillow" in the canonical LXX corresponds to a form of a Hebrew word meaning "cover," so that it might naturally mean "covering" or "veil," and Origen (followed by Jerome) takes it as a woman's veil thrown over the face of a man—a thing that ought not to be[2]. Now John, in the same narrative in which he mentions Mary as seeing an angel *"at the head* (Syr. *head-place,* or *pillow),"* mentions also Peter, a little before, as seeing *"the napkin that had been on his head...*[3]" This is not the place to discuss what Origen calls the "tropology[4]"—that is to say mystical metaphor—of all these Johannine details, which suggest the thought of Jesus bound and veiled in the grave by well-meaning Jewish friends, but released and glorified in the Resurrection All that we can say here is, first, that we ought not to conclude at present that John has *not* intervened as to

---

[1] Gesen 912 quoting Gen xxviii 11, 18 etc and Jerem xiii 18 (where Gesen proposes to read "from your heads")

[2] Ezek xiii 18—20 (*bis*) See Origen on Ezek xiii 18 (Lomm xiv 43—5) "Si quis vero confusionis velamen gerit et peccati, iste quasi muliebria velamina habet super caput suum "

[3] Jn xx 7 "the napkin that had been on his head apart, wrapped up (lit) *into one place"*—a rare phrase (Gesen 880 *a*) suggesting that the napkin was rolled away like the waters (Gen i 9, comp Ps civ 8—9) that once veiled the face of the earth

[4] Origen *Cels* v 56 δηλωτικόν τινος εἶναι τροπολογίας τῆς περὶ τῶν προφαινομένων τοῖς τὴν ἀνάστασιν τοῦ Λόγου θεωρεῖν παρεσκευασμένοις

THE STILLING OF THE STORM

this particular Marcan phrase until we have weighed the cumulative evidence for such intervention as a whole; secondly, that these "Gennesaret-traditions" lend themselves to variety of interpretation and chronological arrangement; thirdly, that if John has intervened, the intervention may be illustrated by his description of Peter as swimming from his boat to the Lord, whereas Luke describes him as in a boat that is "beginning to sink," and Matthew as himself "beginning to be drowned."

CHAPTER III

THE DEMONIAC AND THE SWINE
[Mark v. 1—20]

§ 1 *Reasons for discussing this narrative*

It was necessary to print the narratives given below, for the sake of completeness, in order that the reader might feel that no facts are kept back from him that are unfavourable to the theory of Johannine Intervention[1] But at first sight no

---

[1]

Mk v 1—20 (R V)	Mt viii 28—34 (R V)	Lk viii 26—39 (R V)
(1) And they came to the other side of the sea, into the country of the Gerasenes	(28) And when he was come to the other side into the country of the Gadarenes, there met him two possessed with devils, coming forth out of the tombs, exceeding fierce, so that no man could pass by that way	(26) And they arrived at the country of the Gerasenes (*v r* Gergesenes, *or*, Gadarenes) which is over against Galilee
(2) And when he was come out of the boat, straightway there met him out of the tombs a man with an unclean spirit,		(27) And when he was come forth upon the land, there met him a certain man out of the city, who had devils, and for a long time he had worn no clothes, and abode not in [any] house, but in the tombs
(3) Who had his dwelling in the tombs and no man could any more bind him, no, not with a chain,		
(4) Because that he had been often bound with fetters and chains, and the chains had been rent asunder by him, and the fetters broken in pieces and no man had strength to tame him.		

THE DEMONIAC AND THE SWINE

comment appeared to be needed except that John records no exorcisms, and that the Synoptic narratives contain nothing

Mk v 1—20 (R V) *contd*	Mt viii 28—34 (R V) *contd*	Lk viii 26—39 (R V) *contd*
(5) And always, night and day, in the tombs and in the mountains, he was crying out, and cutting himself with stones		
(6) And when he saw Jesus from afar, he ran and worshipped him, (7) And crying out with a loud voice, he saith, What have I to do with thee, Jesus, thou Son of the Most High God? I adjure thee by God, torment me not. (8) For he said unto him, Come forth, thou unclean spirit, out of the man	(29) And behold, they cried out, saying, What have we to do with thee, thou Son of God? art thou come hither to torment us before the time?	(28) And when he saw Jesus, he cried out, and fell down before him, and with a loud voice said, What have I to do with thee, Jesus, thou Son of the Most High God? I beseech thee, torment me not. (29) For he commanded the unclean spirit to come out from the man. For oftentimes (*or*, of a long time) (πολλοῖς χρόνοις) it had seized him and he was kept under guard, and bound with chains and fetters, and breaking the bands asunder, he was driven of the devil into the deserts
(9) And he asked him, What is thy name? And he saith unto him, My name is Legion; for we are many. (10) And he besought him much that he would not send them away out of the country (11) Now there was there on the mountain side a great herd of swine feeding.	(30) Now there was afar off from them a herd of many swine feeding (31) And the devils	(30) And Jesus asked him, What is thy name? And he said, Legion, for many devils were entered into him (31) And they intreated him that he would not command them to depart into the abyss. (32) Now there was there a herd of many swine feeding on the mountain and they intreated

THE DEMONIAC AND THE SWINE

that, either in word or thought, could claim to belong to the Fourfold Gospel On closer examination, however, there

Mk v 1—20 (R V) *contd*	Mt viii 28—34 (R V) *contd*	Lk viii 26—39 (R V) *contd*.
(12) And they besought him, saying, Send us into the swine, that we may enter into them (13) And he gave them leave And the unclean spirits came out, and entered into the swine and the herd rushed down the steep into the sea, [in number] about two thousand, and they were choked in the sea (14) And they that fed them fled, and told it in the city, and in the country And they came to see what it was that had come to pass (15) And they come to Jesus, and behold him that was possessed with devils sitting, clothed and in his right mind, [even] him that had the legion and they were afraid (16) And they that saw it declared unto them how it befell him that was possessed with devils, and concerning the swine (17) And they began to beseech him to depart from their borders (18) And as he was entering into the boat, he that had been possessed with devils besought him	(*lit* demons) (δαίμονες) besought him, saying, If thou cast us out, send us away into the herd of swine (32) And he said unto them, Go And they came out, and went into the swine and behold, the whole herd rushed down the steep into the sea, and perished in the waters (33) And they that fed them fled, and went away into the city, and told everything, and what was befallen to them that were possessed with devils (34) And behold, all the city came out to meet Jesus and when they saw him, they besought [him] that he would depart from their borders	him that he would give them leave to enter into them And he gave them leave (33) And the devils came out from the man, and entered into the swine and the herd rushed down the steep into the lake, and were choked (34) And when they that fed them saw what had come to pass, they fled, and told it in the city and in the country (35) And they went out to see what had come to pass; and they came to Jesus, and found the man, from whom the devils were gone out, sitting, clothed and in his right mind, at the feet of Jesus and they were afraid (36) And they that saw it told them how he that was possessed with devils was made whole (*or*, saved) (ἐσώθη) (37) And all the people of the country of the Gerasenes (*v r* Gergesenes, *or*, Gadarenes) round about asked him to depart from them, for they were holden with great fear and he entered into a boat, and returned (38) But the man from whom the devils

68 (Mark v 1—20)

THE DEMONIAC AND THE SWINE

appeared to be one point that might repay investigation, a point common to all the Synoptists, the mention of *"the tombs."*

"In the tombs," in John, is connected with the future resurrection of the dead· "The hour cometh in which *all that are in the tombs* shall hear his [i e the Son of man's] voice, and shall come forth, they that have done good, unto the resurrection of life, and they that have done ill, unto the resurrection of judgment[1]" *"Tombs,"* in the plural, is of rare occurrence in the New Testament, and *"out of the tombs"*—apart from Mark-Matthew here—occurs nowhere else except where Matthew mentions a resurrection of the saints following immediately on Christ's death: "And *the tombs* were opened; and many bodies

Mk v. 1—20 (R V.) *contd*	Mt viii 28—34 (R.V.)	Lk viii. 26—39 (R V.) *contd*
that he might be with him (19) And he suffered him not, but saith unto him, Go to thy house unto thy friends, and tell them how great things the Lord hath done for thee, and [how] he had mercy on thee (20) And he went his way, and began to publish in Decapolis how great things Jesus had done for him and all men did marvel		were gone out prayed him that he might be with him but he sent him away, saying, (39) Return to thy house, and declare how great things God hath done for thee And he went his way, publishing throughout the whole city how great things Jesus had done for him

[1] Jn v 28—9 οἱ ἐν τοῖς μνημείοις   Mk v 3, 5, Lk viii 27 have ἐν τοῖς μνήμασιν   Mk v 2, Mt viii 28 have ἐκ τῶν μνημείων   Sometimes such a variation might point to a difference of documentary origin   Matthew and John, who severally use μνημεῖον about seven and sixteen times, never use μνῆμα   Mark and Luke use both   Comp Xen *Hellen* iii 2 15 ἐκ τοῦ ἀντιπέρας. ἐπὶ τῶν μνημάτων... εἰς τὰ παρ' ἑαυτοῖς μνημεῖα καὶ τύρσεις τινας, where "*the tombs* [in the distance] over against them" are mentioned first, and then "*the memorials* and various kinds of tower-shaped structures on their own side."

THE DEMONIAC AND THE SWINE

of the saints that had fallen asleep were raised, and coming forth *out of the tombs* after his resurrection, they entered into the holy city and appeared unto many[1]." Origen, commenting on this passage, which he illustrates from John, takes Matthew in a spiritual as well as a literal sense. Both passages might be regarded as predicting, or describing, the Preaching of Christ to the spirits in prison, which was believed to have taken place during the "three days" that followed His death[2].

The question arises whether "in the tombs" may have had originally a similar significance. Several facts brought forward in our last Chapter pointed to the conclusion that the Stilling of the Storm, whatever may have been its basis in literal fact, was primarily a spiritual poem describing the condition of the disciples tossed in tempests of doubt during the "three days" that followed Christ's death. Now we have to consider whether the sequel in Mark may contain another version of what happened during those "three days." If it does, then according to this second version, Jesus was not, as in the first version, "sleeping on the pillow." He had passed across the waters of Sheol to the land of "tombs," the prison-house of the dead. In that case, who is it that comes out from the tombs to meet Jesus? Is it "two" demoniacs as Matthew says? Or is it "one," as Mark and Luke say, but one possessed by "many" devils? And is there any explanation of the fact that the Mark-Luke term "legion" is omitted by Matthew? And is there any connection between "*two*," used by Matthew alone to describe the two demoniacs, and "*two thousand*," used

---

[1] Mt xxvii 52—3
[2] See Lightfoot's numerous quotations on Ign *Magn* §9. Add Origen *Comm Matth* on Mt xxvii 52—3 (Lomm v 70) and *Evang Petr* §10. The latter describes Christ as being carried up to heaven from the tomb in the sight of the soldiers, while the Cross follows "They heard a voice from heaven saying, 'Hast thou preached to them that are sleeping?' And an answer was heard from the Cross, 'Yea.'"

THE DEMONIAC AND THE SWINE

by Mark alone to denote the number of a herd of swine apparently corresponding to the number of a legion?

§ 2 "Gerasenes," "Gadarenes," or "Gergesenes[1]"

Reviewing the questions that conclude the preceding section, the reader may perhaps ask why the first place was not given to a question about the scene of the miracle. According to R V, it is called by Mark and Luke's text "the country of the *Gerasenes*"; by Matthew, "that of the *Gadarenes*"; but Luke's margin has "*Gergesenes*" or "*Gadarenes*." Why do we not ask first of all "What was the name of the place?"

The answer is "Because it is impossible to ascertain the fact." Even in Origen's time there was uncertainty owing to variations of readings in MSS as well as differences between the Gospels. And Origen gives us a clue to the explanation of these variations when he says that the names of the places where Jesus wrought mighty works are "*eponymous*," that is to say, named in accordance with the works[2]. He himself favours the name "Gergesenes," which he explains as if it were two words, "the sojourning of those-who-cast-out." One might have supposed that if the word was derived from "cast-out," the "casting out" would be the act of Jesus "casting out" the devils. But Origen refers it to the inhabitants, as if they were, in effect, "casting out" Jesus when they "besought" or "asked" Him to depart from their borders[3]. Jerome in his

---

[1] Mk v 1, Mt viii 28, Lk viii 26

[2] Origen *Comm Joann* x 10 (Lomm 1 295) ἴσμεν γὰρ καὶ τόπων ὀνόματα ἐπώνυμα τυγχάνοντα τοῖς κατὰ τὸν Ἰησοῦν πράγμασιν. His meaning—strange though it may seem—must be that these ancient names were prophetically appropriate to the future Messianic actions. Clark renders it "We know that the names of places agree in their meaning with the things connected with Jesus."

[3] Mk v 17 ἤρξαντο παρακαλεῖν αὐτὸν ἀπελθεῖν ἀπὸ τῶν ὁρίων αὐτῶν, Mt viii 34 παρεκάλεσαν ὅπως μεταβῇ ἀπὸ τῶν ὁρίων αὐτῶν, Lk viii 37 καὶ ἠρώτησεν αὐτὸν ἅπαν τὸ πλῆθος τῆς περιχώρου τῶν Γερασηνῶν ἀπελθεῖν ἀπ' αὐτῶν. R V renders παρακαλεῖν here "beseech," but in Lk iii 18 (of John the Baptist) "exhortations," and similarly in Acts ii 40

THE DEMONIAC AND THE SWINE

commentary on Matthew takes no notice of the differences of name in Gospels or MSS and gives no interpretation to the form ("Gerasenes") which he adopts

The name "Gadarenes" might be regarded by some as "eponymous," because it was connected with "fold," "flock," "herd," so that it might refer to the swine[1]. "Gerasenes" might refer to the "casting out" of the demons[2]. "Gergesenes" might be derived from "the ancient Canaanite stock of the *Gergashites*, or from the word *Gargushta*, which signifies *clay* or *dirt*[3]."

This last explanation is not so improbable as it at first sight seems. Daniel, speaking of the resurrection, says, according to the literal Hebrew, "Many of them that sleep in the *ground of the dust* shall awake", but Theodotion has "in the *heaped-up-dust* (or, *mound*) *of the earth* (or, *land*)," using a word (*chôma*) that is often used to mean a "hillock-tomb" or "cairn," but also means a "mound" of any kind[4]. Now this word *chôma* occurs in the whole of the early Fathers and Apologists *only once, in the following charge against the Jews brought by Justin Martyr*. "And from the words of the aforesaid Jeremiah they have likewise cut out this, 'But the Lord God remembered His dead [that were from] Israel that had fallen asleep in[to] *the earth* (or, *land*) *of the heaped-up-dust*, and came down to proclaim unto them His salvation[5].'" This saying is

---

(of Peter preaching) etc. Comp. Rom. xii. 8 ὁ παρακαλῶν ἐν τῇ παρακλήσει, "he that exhorteth in his exhortation." It would be appropriate to Christ "exhorting" the spirits imprisoned in Hades

[1] Ἀγέλη is used here by all the Synoptists to represent "herd." Comp. 1 S. xxiv. 3 (4) "*enclosures* (ἀγέλας) *of the flocks*," Heb. g[e]dērah

[2] See Gesen. 176 b on *gârash* "*cast out*"

[3] *Hor. Heb.* on Mt. viii. 28

[4] Dan. xii. 2 (Theod.) ἐν γῆς χώματι

[5] Justin Mart. *Tryph.* § 72, Ἐμνήσθη δὲ κύριος ὁ θεὸς ἀπὸ Ἰσραὴλ τῶν νεκρῶν αὐτοῦ τῶν κεκοιμημένων εἰς γῆν χώματος, καὶ κατέβη πρὸς αὐτοὺς ἀναγγελίσασθαι αὐτοῖς τὸ σωτήριον αὐτοῦ. Perhaps we ought to read τῶν

THE DEMONIAC AND THE SWINE

repeatedly quoted by Irenaeus as from Jeremiah or Isaiah. The Greek is wanting, but the Latin renderings of *"the earth of the heaped-up-dust"* are *"terra"* with *"sepultionis," "defossionis," "sepelitionis,"* but once with *"limi," "*mud[1]"

This brings us round to the suggestion of Horae Hebraicae, agreeing with that of Origen as to the name, though not as to the interpretation. The word *Gargushta,* "clay," "dirt," or "clod," which is frequently used in the Targums, occurs pertinently in the Targumistic rendering of Job's aspirations for a resurrection, "My body is clothed with worms and with *clods (gargushta)* of dust[2]" This lends itself to a symbolism like that of Origen, not unknown also in Greek as well as Hebrew literature, "The bodies of sinful souls, that is, souls dead unto God, are called '*tombs*[3]'"

These Gergesenes may have been regarded in some Christian poetry as "clods[4]" But this would not exclude a different class of metaphors, in which they may be regarded as bound in the prison-house in chains of their own sinful desires, or else enslaved by Satan and Death

---

ἀπὸ 'Ισραήλ Otto, in his long and valuable note, omits to mention that Justin reproduces Dan Theod ἐν γῆς χώματι in εἰς γῆν χώματος. I dare say subsequent editors have supplied this omission

[1] Iren III 20 4, IV 22 1 [IV 33 1, incomplete], IV 33 12 ("limi"), V 31 1 It is probable that this quotation came to Irenaeus from several authors of early date

[2] Job VII 5 quoted in Levy *Ch* 1 152—3, with other instances.

[3] Origen on Mt xxvii 51—3 (Lomm v 70) See Steph *Thes* on σορός and τύμβος Mk v 5 "in the tombs *and in the mountains*" may be compared with Is xiv 19 "from thy *sepulchre*," ἐν τοῖς ὄρεσιν See *Clue* **146** *a* quoting Taylor's conj σοροῖς for ὄρεσιν. Another explanation would be that χῶμα was sometimes interpreted as "hill"

[4] George Fox, in his Diary, describes himself as sitting among a dead congregation, round a dead preacher, and seeing them revealed to him as "clods"

THE DEMONIAC AND THE SWINE

§ 3 *"Two" demoniacs in Matthew, and "two thousand" swine in Mark*[1]

There are other instances where Matthew, differing from the other Synoptists, mentions "two[2]". But those (which will be discussed in their order) will be found to differ from the present. Here, the parallel Mark mentions "two," but in a different context ("about *two thousand*," referring to the swine "choked" in the sea); and the conduct of the "two" in Matthew is quite different from that of the "one" in Mark-Luke. The "two," instead of being bound in chains (as Mark and Luke say), practically bar the way themselves against all passers-by. They are "exceeding fierce (*or*, terrible) so that no man was strong enough to pass along through that way[3]". In ancient poetical descriptions of Jesus descending to Hell to rescue the imprisoned spirits, a mention of "two fierce demons" would be suitable in the scene where Satan goes forth outside to meet Jesus, while Hades says to his demons "Shut the gates (*or*, the cruel gates) of brass, . and resist bravely, that we, holding captivity, may not be taken captive[4]" Macarius says that the "two" mentioned by Matthew were "exarchs," that is chiefs, of demons[5] One word for *"chief"* or *"captain"* in Hebrew is closely similar to the Hebrew for *"thousand*[6]*"* Hence *"chief"* might be taken as *"thousand,"* or as *"chief of a*

---

[1] Mt. viii 28, Mk v. 13

[2] Mt ix 27, xxvi 60

[3] Mt viii 28 Χαλεπός, "fierce," applied to persons, occurs in the whole of the Greek Bible (including Apocrypha) nowhere else except Is xviii 2 (Heb) "terrible" It is applied by Homer to a δαίμων in *Od* xix 201, and to hard, cruel, persons as well as things, in Greek literature

[4] Comp *Descens ad Inf* § 5 (21) (Tisch p 376) reading "captivemur" for "captivemus" For traditions about the "Descent" see above, p 70, n 2.

[5] Macar ed Blondel, p 76

[6] See Gesen pp 48—9, אֶלֶף "thousand," אַלּוּף "chief," "chiliarch"

THE DEMONIAC AND THE SWINE

*thousand*¹" Thus an original "*two leaders*" referring to Satan and Hades might be taken by Mark to mean "*two leaders of thousands*," so that the total number of their host was "two thousand"

That Mark is wrong appears probable from the fact that he himself represents the demoniac as saying "My name is Legion, because we are many" Now a legion, in imperial times, would number six thousand or even more, and probably never so few as two thousand

§ 4 Why does Matthew omit "legion"?

If Matthew's original regarded the two demoniacs as demon "princes" or "chiefs," they could not say, "We are many," but only "We have many under our command" In Jewish tradition, the Latin word "Legion," transliterated as a Jewish word, meant *either "legion" or "commander of a legion"* Matthew appears to have taken it in the latter sense We have seen that he applies the rare epithet "*hard*" (meaning "cruel") to his two demoniacs The same epithet, in Hebrew, is repeatedly applied to "the commander of a legion²"

In the light of these facts, it is possible to explain Mark's additions, as attempts to combine two quite different pictures. One is that of Christ, confronted by Satan and Hades, two "chiefs" of Hell, who bar its doors and draw fast its chains to prevent His ingress and the release of their captives From this, Mark borrows the "chains," but he applies them to the demoniac, who (according to Mark) has been chained for his

---

¹ See Zech ix 7, xii 5, 6 where "*leader*" is rendered χιλίαρχος, "*leader of a thousand*"

² Levy ii 474 b "zwei *strenge Feldherren* (oder *Leibgarden*) .. jenen *strengen Feldherren*," Levy Ch 1 403 a "dieser *Befehlshaber* ist *streng*" In all these cases the noun is "*legion*" (meaning "legionary commander") and the adj is the Heb word for (Gesen. 904) "*hard*," "*severe*," "*fierce*"—exactly corresponding to the Greek χαλεπός

THE DEMONIAC AND THE SWINE

own benefit and has broken the chains to his own injury Mark also borrows "*two chiefs.*" But he takes it as meaning *two thousand*, and as implying that the demoniac, though but one, was possessed by two thousand devils, who pass into swine of a corresponding number ("two thousand swine")

Another picture is that of Israel in Egypt, the captive nation "bound" in the "misery and iron" of Egyptian bondage. In Exodus, the Lord conspicuously calls the Captive out of the Tyrant's dungeon But the Lord may also be regarded as calling the Tyrant out of the prison where he has held Israel captive. The Tyrant is Pharaoh In Exodus, Pharaoh, greedy for Israel as his prey, is led on by God to drown himself in the Red Sea In Mark, the Tyrant, in accordance with his own desire, is "permitted" to pass into swine, who hurry him and his hosts into the Sea of Galilee, where his legion, according to Mark and Luke, is "choked[1]"

This "choking," or "suffocation," must not be passed over without notice. The LXX describes Saul as being "choked" by an evil spirit[2]. And the word here used in the Syriac of Mark-Luke[3] is connected with "legions" in a Targum on Esther, which uses the phrase "*the legions that choke you on your beds*[4]" It would be in accordance with the Jewish Law

---

[1] Mk v 13 ἐπνίγοντο, Lk viii 33 ἀπεπνίγη (but Mt viii 32 ἀπέθανον).

[2] 1 S xvi 14 ἔπνιγεν, Heb "troubled"

[3] See *Thes Syr* 1323—4 where it is also quoted from Ephrem as referring to the Egyptians

[4] Levy *Ch* 1 270 *b*, Esth ii 1, 2 I am informed by my friend Mr E N Adler that it occurs in a letter (Targum Scheni, Esth 1 3 (not 1 2)) supposed to be written to the queen of Sheba by Solomon who threatens her with his "kings, *legions*, and horsemen " The "kings" are "the beasts of the field " The "horsemen" are "the birds of the heavens " Then it is added "My hosts (חילי) are the legions that choke you on your beds "

Gen r on Gen 1 7 explains why the Scripture, after describing God's work on the second day of the Creation—when He divided the waters above from the waters below—does not say, as on the other six days, "and God saw that it was good " The reason was,

THE DEMONIAC AND THE SWINE

of Retribution that *the evil spirits that "choke" men should be "choked" themselves* Both the thought, therefore, and the word, point to a Jewish origin for this tradition

Horae Hebraicae, commenting on the Marcan "legion," quotes the saying of Jesus in Matthew about "twelve *legions* of angels," and also one of Caesar's about the "ten *legions*" of Rome which could "pull down heaven itself[1]" In the East as well as the West, "legion" was an expressive word The demoniac's language sprang from a national dread of the Roman power symbolized by "legion" The "legion" is Rome in its darker aspect—not Rome exercising authority from above to judge justly, but Rome enforcing injustice. John regards the whole of "this world" as being possessed and dominated by a spirit of fear, which is the instrument employed by "the ruler of this world" to keep his slaves in subjection This is symbolized by Rome or by Caesar[2] The rulers of the Jews are thus dominated when they say, as an excuse for murder, "*The Romans* [that is, *the legions*] will come and take away our place and our nation[3]" The Roman judge in Jerusalem is himself dominated by the servile spirit, though in a different way, when he allows himself to be forced into partnership with murderers by their cry, "If thou let this man go thou art not *Caesar's friend*[4]." The rulers of the Jews themselves confess their slavery to this Demon or Master of many legions when they exclaim "We have no king but *Caesar*[5]"

---

that the water was to be used as an instrument of wrath in the Deluge God is compared to a King who has a "*cruel* (lit *hard*) *legion*," and who says "Since this *legion* is so cruel, my name shall not be placed thereon"

[1] Mt xxvi 53, Caes *Bell Civ* vi 42

[2] Epictetus says (i 29 60 foll) that when Caesar comes thundering and lightening with threats of death or bribes of pleasure to which we yield, then we are mere slaves "But take away these adjuncts and see how calm I shall be [in his presence]"

[3] Jn xi 48, see *Joh Gr* **2645**   [4] Jn xix 12

[5] Jn xix 15 Comp *Joh Gr* **2645** "the trees of the field chose the bramble to be their king"

77 (Mark v 1—20)

THE DEMONIAC AND THE SWINE

§ 5. *"Beseeching," "exhorting," or "comforting"*

The verb here repeatedly rendered by R V. "beseech" is *paracalein*, from which comes the noun *Paraclete*, 1 e. "called-in-to-help"—commonly known as the "Advocate" or "Comforter[1]." In literary Greek, the verb means "I call to my side [a friend to aid me]," and also "I exhort," "stimulate"; but in LXX it often means "I call aside [from trouble or sorrow]," that is "I console[2]" Some such meaning, in connection with good tidings, is frequent in Isaiah (LXX)[3]. Besides the variation in meaning, the verb also varies in construction according as it is found in different kinds of Greek. In LXX, outside Maccabees, it is not used in the sense of "exhorting" with a dependent clause ("exhorting some one *to do something*"), but in Maccabees a dependent clause about "doing" is sometimes added, mostly in the infinitive ("to do")—which is a frequent construction in literary Greek[4]

---

[1] 1 Jn 11 1 R.V marg "Or, *Comforter*, or, *Helper*" Παρακαλέω (*Joh Voc* **1674**) occurs in the Gospels, Mk 9, Mt 9, Lk 7, Jn 0 In Mk v 10—23 it occurs five times Outside the Triple Tradition, it sometimes means "comfort," "exhort," *e g* in Mt 11 18, v 4, Lk iii 18, xvi 25

[2] Steph *Thes*, after giving a column of other meanings, says, finally, "Consolor, unde παράκλησις, consolatio" And that is all But it is frequent in LXX In Is xl 1, li 12, 18 (Sym) and liv. 11 (Theod) the LXX παρακαλέω is replaced by παρηγορέω, "I talk over," "soothe"

[3] Is xxxv. 4 "*say* to them that are of a fearful heart," LXX παρακαλέσατε, οἱ ὀλιγόψυχοι τῇ διανοίᾳ, where "comfort" (like our vernacular "cheer up") is perhaps intransitive Clem Rom § 59 παρακάλεσον τοὺς ὀλιγοψυχοῦντας seems to allude to this passage, Barn. (apart from one instance in a quotation) uses παρακαλέω absolutely thus, (§ 19) πορευόμενος εἰς τὸ παρακαλέσαι, *i e* "going [to people's homes] to give them the comfort of the gospel" In Is xl 2 "*call* to her" the context speaks of "comfort" In Is. xli 27 παρακαλέσω represents "*one-that-bringeth-good-tidings*," usually translated εὐαγγελίζομαι

[4] See *Oxf Conc* quoting 2 Macc ii 3, iv 34, vii 5 etc No instance of the use with ἵνα is given in *Oxf Conc* (but the context

THE DEMONIAC AND THE SWINE

In the Marcan narrative under consideration the construction is strangely varied. The verb is used twice with the conjunction "that[1]," besides being used once with the infinitive[2], and once absolutely, with "saying[3]." There is a passage in Mark where the verb, with "that," introduces a petition to be allowed to do something—"They besought him *that* they might touch ...[4]" In this sentence if we substitute "he" for "they," we perceive there may be ambiguity. Greek makes no distinction between "*that he might*" and "*that he would*" in such a sentence as "He besought him that *he might* (or, *would*) touch." Go a step further, and substitute "go out" for "touch," and then who is to decide between the two meanings (1) "that he, *the beseecher, might be allowed to go out*," and (2) "that he, *the person besought, would consent to go out*"?

Let us consider how these facts may bear on the interpretation of the following passage, which describes how "they,"

---

of 4 Macc iv 11, x 1 has ὅπως). There is no instance with ἵνα in the Indices to Plato, Aristotle, Aristophanes, and Marcus Antoninus, and there are only two in Epictetus (who uses παρακαλέω fairly often with prepositions)

[1] Mk v 10 παρεκάλει αὐτὸν πολλὰ ἵνα μὴ αὐτὰ ἀποστείλῃ, *ib* 18 παρεκάλει αὐτὸν ὁ δαιμονισθεὶς ἵνα μετ' αὐτοῦ ᾖ (where ἵνα does not introduce something to be *done*, but something to be *permitted*, as also in vi 56). But Mk viii 22 παρακαλοῦσιν αὐτὸν ἵνα αὐτοῦ ἅψηται introduces something to be *done*

[2] Mk v 17 παρακαλεῖν αὐτὸν ἀπελθεῖν

[3] Mk v 12 παρεκάλεσαν αὐτὸν λέγοντες, Πέμψον ἡμᾶς (comp. Mt viii 31 οἱ δὲ δαίμονες παρεκάλουν αὐτὸν λέγοντες, Εἰ ἐκβάλλεις ἡμᾶς, ἀπόστειλον ἡμᾶς... Lk viii 32 παρεκάλεσαν αὐτὸν ἵνα ἐπιτρέψῃ αὐτοῖς ..) In Mk v 12 several authorities insert "the devils" or "all the devils" before the pl "they besought," but the correct text of Mk has the pl. here in spite of the sing in v 10 καὶ παρεκάλει αὐτὸν πολλά. R V expresses it correctly "And *he besought* him much .. And *they* (A V *all the devils*) besought him." Mark oscillates between the thought of the *one* demoniac, and the *many* demons in him

There is a strange mixture in Mk v 23 παρακαλεῖ. λέγων ὅτι Τὸ θυγάτριόν μου . ἵνα . ἐπιθῇς (comp vii 32 παρακαλοῦσιν αὐτὸν ἵνα ἐπιθῇ)

[4] Mk vi 56, Mt. xiv. 36

THE DEMONIAC AND THE SWINE

meaning everyone "in the city," as Matthew implies, or everyone "in the city and in the country" (as Mark and Luke imply)[1]—practically rejected Jesus —

Mk v 17	Mt viii 34	Lk viii. 37
And they began to *beseech* him to depart from their borders	And seeing him, they *besought* [*him*] that he would pass-away (*lit* change [his] place)[2] from their borders	And all the multi-tude of the country of the Gerasenes round about asked him to depart[3] from them

It should be noted that the subject of the verb "besought" is variously and vaguely stated by Mark-Matthew, and that Luke amplifies and defines it This was not unnecessary. For in Mark, if we supply the subject of the verb in the verse above quoted, from the verse preceding it ("they that saw it"), the meaning is "*The seeing* [*ones*]"—that is the eye-witnesses—"related to them [*i e* to the citizens] how it had befallen the demoniac...*and* [*they*] *began* to beseech him to depart " This might be taken to mean that "the seeing [ones]" besought. Matthew uses "*seeing*"—superfluously, it would seem, and out

---

[1] Mk v 14 "in *the city and the country*, and they came ," sim. Lk viii 34 Mt viii 33—4 "into *the city* all *the city*"

[2] "Change-his-place (μεταβῇ)" It implies a complete change of place and does not occur in the Synoptists elsewhere except Mt xi. 1, xii 9, xv 29 μεταβὰς ἐκεῖθεν (of Jesus) and xvii 20 (about the "removing" of a mountain) μετάβα καὶ μεταβήσεται, and Lk x 7 μὴ μεταβαίνετε ἐξ οἰκίας εἰς οἰκίαν John represents Christ's brethren as saying to Him (vii 3) μετάβηθι ἐντεῦθεν, i e "go hence from the quiet of Galilee into the publicity of Jerusalem " Elsewhere in Jn (v 24, xiii 1, 1 Jn iii 14) it means passing out of death into life or out of this world to the Father Elsewhere in N T it occurs only once (Acts xviii 7 "departed thence"), after Paul has said to the "blaspheming" Jews "Your blood be upon your own heads from henceforth I will go unto the Gentiles "

[3] "Asked (ἠρώτησεν) him to depart (ἀπελθεῖν) " Luke retains the Marcan "depart," but not the Marcan "beseech " In Lk viii 37 "multitude"=πλῆθος, i e the population, not quite the same as ὄχλος in viii 40

THE DEMONIAC AND THE SWINE

of place ("*seeing* him [*i e* Jesus] they besought")—in such a way as to suggest that, in his Original, "*seeing*" may have meant "*those seeing* him [*i.e* the man]," and that "the seers" were the beseechers Luke sets this right by repeating "*see*" thrice —"Having *seen that which had come to pass* the herdsmen fled and reported to the city... and [they, *i e* the citizens] came out *to see that which had come to pass*... and *the seers* reported to them... and *the whole population of the surrounding country of the Gerasenes asked* him to depart[1]" This makes it quite clear, negatively, that "the beseechers," or (as Luke prefers to say) "the askers," were not "the seers," and, positively, that they were the whole of the Gerasenes.

From these bewildering obscurities, and from the freedom with which Luke attempts to make them clear, there emerge at least three conclusions —The plural and the singular are liable to be interchanged in this narrative owing to the plurality of the spirits of the demoniac The rejection of parts of the Marcan narrative by Matthew points to the conclusion that Matthew believed them to be "conflations," or repetitions, such as abound in Mark[2] Foremost among the words that appear to be suspiciously repeated is the word "beseech"

---

[1] In Lk viii 34 "they *reported* (ἀπήγγειλαν)" is parall to Mk v 14 (Mt viii 33) ἀπήγγειλαν But in Lk viii 36 ἀπήγγειλαν is parall to Mk v 16 διηγήσαντο, "they *related*" Later on, Lk viii 39 "*relate* (διηγοῦ)" is parall to Mk v 19 "*report* (ἀπάγγειλον)" The Lucan repetitions, ἰδόντες. τὸ γεγονός, ἰδεῖν τὸ γεγονός, and οἱ ἰδόντες are remarkable Perhaps Luke means, in effect, "The traditions about οἱ ἰδόντες vary We must distinguish the *eye-witnesses*, i e the herdsmen, from those who came out *to see*, i e the Gerasenes Matthew, it is true, speaks of all the citizens as '*having seen him*' But Matthew means '*having seen Jesus*' The truth is, that, 'when they came to Jesus they found the demoniac clothed and in his right mind, sitting at the feet of Jesus' This was really what they '*saw*'"

[2] On Marcan "conflations" generally, see *Clue passim*, and the Indices to Diatessarica ("conflations," "Mark") In Mk v 1—20, note, besides the repeated παρακαλέω, the repetition of μνημεῖα or μνήματα in *ib* 2, 3, 5 whereas "tombs" occurs but once in the parallel Matthew-Luke

THE DEMONIAC AND THE SWINE

Hence we have something more than mere conjecture, though a great deal less than demonstration, in the hypothesis that the above-quoted verse from Mark "began to *beseech* him to depart" was originally "began to *exhort* him to depart," and that it referred originally to a tradition about Jesus "*exhorting*" those oppressed by the devil to pass out of the devil's prison into the freedom of God, somewhat as Peter "*exhorted* them [*i.e.* the Jews] saying, Save yourselves from this crooked generation[1]."

In that case, the call would be somewhat similar to the summons in a saying of Jesus which Matthew places a little before this narrative, "Follow me, and leave the dead to bury their own dead[2]" Those words seem to imply that the man addressed was living in some "city of the dead" Using another metaphor, we might say that he was one of the "*fellow-citizens of the swine*"—as Origen characteristically calls the Gergesenes[3].

§ 6 *Versions of the narrative in an Apocryphal Gospel*[4]

The Arabic Gospel of the Infancy, whatever may be its date, illustrates the distinction, drawn above, between (1) the story of the Demoniacs or Devils that barred the way or attacked those who came by the way, and (2) the story of the

---

[1] Acts ii 40.

[2] Mt viii 22 To this is added in the parall Lk ix 60 "do thou go and carry-tidings of (διάγγελλε) the kingdom of God"

[3] See Origen *Comm Joann* vi 24 (Lomm 1 239) where οἱ τῶν χοίρων πολῖται is admitted to be in the text, as also in *ib* x 10 (Lomm 1 295) (though some editors have ventured to substitute χωρίων)

It should be added that, in addition to the possible confusion of thought, above mentioned, between the singular and plural, the plural of "*began* [to exhort, or beseech]," HPΞATO, might easily be confused by scribes with the singular HPΞATO, in the written text of Mk v. 17

[4] See *Evangelia Apocrypha*, 1853, Tischendorf p 175 foll

THE DEMONIAC AND THE SWINE

Demoniac that had been bound with chains, who cut himself with stones.

The first of the apocryphal stories refers to a young man, the son of a priest of an idol-temple in Egypt. The youth had been "three years[1] beset by several demons...and when the demons seized him, he rent his garments and remained naked[2], and attacked men with stones[3]." On the arrival of the babe Jesus, the idol collapsed and "all—[both the] inhabitants of Egypt and others—rushed together at the fall thereof." The demoniac enters the place where the babe's swaddling bands were lying and places one of them on his head. The demons flee forth from his mouth in the form of crows and serpents. There is no mention of swine.

The second story describes the departure of Joseph and Mary from Egypt. "Departing hence they came to a place where there were robbers, who had despoiled many [travellers] of their baggage and garments and had bound them. Then the robbers heard a mighty sound, like the sound of a great king with army and horsemen and drums coming forth from his city[4]

---

[1] *Evang. Infant. Arab.* § 10 "Erat huic sacerdoti filius *triennis* ab aliquot daemonibus obsessus." The context shews that "*triennis*" must here indicate the duration of the possession. The writer adds "multa loquebatur et proferebat," perhaps an attempt to render Mk v. 10 παρεκάλει αὐτὸν πολλά.

[2] Lk viii. 27 "he would not put on a cloak (ἱμάτιον)" is the only Synoptic phrase that suggests nakedness, or tearing off one's garments, at this point; but, later on, Mk v. 15 "cloaked (ἱματισμένον)" indicates that nakedness should have been mentioned by Mark here. Perhaps Mk v. 3—4 (mentioning "chains") originally meant that the demoniac would not bind even a girdle round him. Later on, the writer says, of a woman, § 14 "neque vestimenta pati poterat."

[3] "Homines lapidibus petebat" is probably a form of Mk v. 5 κατακόπτων ἑαυτὸν λίθοις, see below, pp 85—6.

[4] "Tum latrones regis ex urbe sua egressi" would suit the story of the *Descensus* better if we could connect "egressi" with "latrones" instead of "regis" ("the robbers came forth from their city"). But the "latrones" have only a "locus," not an "urbs."

THE DEMONIAC AND THE SWINE

Thereat, in terror, the robbers left all their spoil. But the captives arose, loosing one another's bonds, and they took back their baggage and departed. There, seeing Joseph and Mary approaching, they said to them, 'Where is that king the mighty sound of whose approach the robbers heard, and departed, leaving us safe?' Joseph replied, 'He will come behind us[1]'"

This has features resembling those of the *Descensus ad Inferos*. The writer roughly follows Matthew. He borrows nothing but the "binding" from Mark. And to that he gives a different application. It was the "robbers," he says, who "bound" the captives (not keepers of a madman, who bound the madman for his good). Also the chains were not broken beforehand (as in Mark). They were not broken till the sound of the King's arrival reached the robbers and their prisoners[2].

Next comes a narrative blending Mark and Luke, but with Luke predominant. The sufferer is a woman. "Thereafter they came into another city where there was a demoniac woman, whom Satan—accursed and rebellious—had beset[3] when once she had gone out to fetch water at night. She could neither bear clothes[4] nor live in a house, and as often as they tied her up with chains and thongs[5], she broke them and fled naked into waste places[6]; and, standing in cross-roads[7] and cemeteries, she kept pelting people with stones, but *for*

---

[1] *Evang. Infant. Arab.* § 13

[2] Comp. *Descens. ad Inf.* § 5 (21) (Tisch. pp. 306—7) "The angels of the Lord say The Lord strong and mighty. And straightway. the brazen gates were shattered, and the iron bars broken, *and all the dead that had been bound were loosed from their bonds,* and we with them."

[3] Comp. Lk. xiii. 16 "a daughter of Abraham, whom Satan hath bound, lo, [these] eighteen years."

[4] Comp. Lk. viii. 27 οὐκ ἐνεδύσατο ἱμάτιον

[5] Comp. Mk. v. 4 πέδαις καὶ ἁλύσεσι

[6] Comp. Lk. viii. 29 τὰς ἐρήμους

[7] No Synoptic narrative mentions "cross-roads (compita)." Mk. v. 5 has ὄρεσιν.

THE DEMONIAC AND THE SWINE

her own [*family*] (*suis*) she was preparing very heavy evils[1]. And when the Lady Mary saw her she pitied her; and upon this, Satan straightway left her, and, fleeing in the form of a young man, departed, saying, Woe is me because of thee, Mary, and because of thy son. So that woman was cured of her torment, and, being restored to her senses, she blushed on account of her nakedness, and, shunning people's sight, she departed to *her own* [*family*] (*suos*) After she had put on her garments, she related the matter to [her] father *and her own* [*family*] (*suisque*)[2]; and they, since they were the chief people of the country, received the Lady Mary and Joseph with the greatest honour and hospitality "

Why do these narratives all omit the "swine"? The first of the three stories mentions evil spirits in the form of "crows and serpents," but not in that of swine Perhaps those who framed the stories found that "swine" did not accord with their framework. But more causes than one might explain the exclusion of this detail The New Hebrew and Aramaic words for "*going round*," "*circle*" or "*neighbourhood*," and for "*swine*," are very similar[3] Also, in two passages of Ben Sira the Syriac Version substitutes "swine" for a form of this word meaning "go round[4]."

The phrases "pelting people with stones" and also "preparing evils for her own family," may be explained from Mark's

---

[1] *Evang Infant Arab* § 14 "Et in compitis sepulcretisque stans *homines lapidibus impetebat, suis* vero gravissima mala parabat" See below, p 86

[2] Comp Mk v 19 "Go to thy house unto (πρὸς) thine own family (τοὺς σούς)," Lk viii 39 "Go back to thy house"

[3] Levy ii 33—4 חזירה may mean (1) "going round" or "returning," (2) "a sow," and see Levy *Ch* i 248 on the meaning "round and round" It occurs in the Targ of Ps lix 6 "make a noise like a dog and *go round about* the city"

[4] See *Thes Syr* 1239 quoting Sir xxii 13 and xxxiii (Gr xxxvi) 5 and suggesting that the Syr was from a Heb or Chald version In xxxiii 5 "a rolling axle-tree" (*i e.* "that which goes round") corresponds to Syr and Arab "hog"

THE DEMONIAC AND THE SWINE

"cutting himself with stones." For the same Hebrew verb that may mean "cut" may also mean "prepare evil[1]." And "himself," when expressed by the Hebrew phrase "his own flesh," may be taken as "his family (*or*, relations)[2]"

It is interesting to note that these apocryphal narratives omit all mention of the place to which the unclean spirits were driven. Even that one of them which describes the spirits as going forth in the forms of crows and serpents does not say whither they vanished. One reason for not saying anything may be that the writer did not know what to say. The early opponent of Christianity against whom Macarius wrote lays great emphasis on the peculiar Marcan tradition that the devils besought Jesus "not to cast them out outside *the country*, or *place*, or *province*." Reiterating the word, he scoffs at the Saviour, who saved one man to ruin others, permitting these devastating devils to carry their devastations from "*country*" to "*country*," into many "*countries*," instead of suppressing them altogether[3]

§ 7 "*Outside the country*" *in Mark, and* "*into the abyss*" *in Luke*[4]

Luke apparently interprets Mark as meaning "outside the earth," *i.e.* outside the region of human life and inside the region of disembodied spirits, that is, "the abyss." But if

---

[1] Heb רעע = κακοποιέω (14) The same letters frequently (Gesen 949 b) mean "break in pieces."

[2] Prov xi 17 "troubleth *his own flesh* (LXX σῶμα αὐτοῦ)" is taken by Gesenius (985) as "troubleth *himself*," but Rashi says "*his relations (propinquos suos)*," and that is the usual meaning, as in Levit xviii 6, 12, 13 etc LXX οἰκεῖος

[3] Macar iii 4 (pp 55—7) After quoting Mark's χώρα, and saying that the devils ought to have been sent into the χωρίον, *i.e.* "the strong place, or prison," of "the abyss" (Lk viii 31) which they deprecated, he mentions χώρα, sing and pl, four times in bitter reiterations

[4] Mk v 10 ἔξω τῆς χώρας, Lk viii 31 εἰς τὴν ἄβυσσον.

THE DEMONIAC AND THE SWINE

Mark had meant "earth," he could have written it. The fact that he wrote "country" instead indicates that he meant "country" Matthew might well omit it, for it is extremely obscure

Mark's word, *chōra*, for "country (sing)" occurs in LXX for the first time in three consecutive passages of Genesis describing how Haran, the brother of Abraham, died "in the *country* of the Chaldaeans," and how God led Abraham out of that "*country*[1]." Philo and Origen agree that this "country" means hallucination, or false worship[2] The Hebrew has "Ur[3] of the Chaldaeans" The LXX, in its rendering, perhaps desired to give a suggestion of inferiority It was not a "land"—like the "land" of milk and honey—but rather a "province" or "separate region" with an implied notion of subordinate jurisdiction, and sometimes of tribute[4].

According to this view, when Luke represents Satan as shewing to Jesus "all the kingdoms of the inhabited [earth]," and as saying "To thee will I give *all this authority*...for it is given over to me[5]," this in fact describes "the ruler of this

---

[1] Gen xi 28, 31, xv. 7 χώρα in each case (but pl χῶραι in Gen x 20, 31 = pl of ארץ) Note that אור ("Ur") might be transliterated as χωρ according to the precedents of Χαάζ 1 Chr viii 35, 36, ix 42 (A), Χαιθάμ Jerem l 44 (א?), Χεμήρ Nehem vii 40 (see *Oxf Conc*)

[2] Philo 1 486 and *Quaest Gen* ad loc (P A 167), Origen *Hom Jerem* xx 4 (Lomm xv 401) "Potens est Deus qui et nobis tribuat de terra Chaldaeorum exire"

[3] "Ur," see *Son* 3369 *b*, 3501 *f* foll

[4] Comp Lam 1 1 "How doth the city sit solitary. princess among the provinces, she is become tributary" That is, as the Targum says, The provinces once paid tribute to Jerusalem, but now Jerusalem pays tribute Hence she might be called, in some sense, a *medinah* or "province" But Jews would distinguish (Nehem. 1 3) between "Jerusalem" and the "province" of Judaea (see Levy iii 30 *a*) Χώρα = *medinah*, "province" freq in Ezra, Nehem, Esth and Dan In Syriac (*Thes Syr* 844) *medinah* sometimes means "city"

[5] Lk iv. 5—6

THE DEMONIAC AND THE SWINE

world" as saying "All this is my *medinah*, my *province, place, or jurisdiction*." Hermas, who often helps us to understand Mark, uses the word *chōra* in only one passage, and there it is put into the mouth of the lord of the visible city of this present world as opposed to the Lord of the invisible City "The lord of this *country* justly says to thee, Either obey my laws or give place [and depart] from my *country*[1]." Somewhat similarly in Mark we may suppose that the Master of the Legion, who holds rule in the "place" or "city" of Mansoul, may claim it as a right that he should not be compelled to give up his jurisdiction· "It is given over to me   It is *my province*. I ought not to be driven out of it."

There remains the difficulty of believing that Jesus could have been supposed by any Evangelist to have driven out evil spirits (by act or by permission) into unoffending beasts At this point there comes to our aid the hypothesis of verbal misunderstanding   The demoniac may have felt a horror lest he and his legion should be hurled to the bottomless abyss (mentioned by Luke) and may have prayed that at all events this might not be his fate   "If it must be, permit us to go to *some place round about*." There is comparatively little difficulty in believing that Jesus permitted that   "*Round about*," as has been shewn above, may have been erroneously taken to mean "*the swine*[2]." Such an error would be all the more natural if the fact was that the madman actually saw the forms, not of

---

[1] Hermas *Sim* 1 4 ἐκχώρει ἐκ τῆς χώρας μου 'Εκχώρει "give place [and depart]" constitutes a sort of third mention of χώρα The explanation of χώρα given in *Clue* 150 is based on an insufficient collection of facts

[2] See above, p 85   It should be added that the names "Gerasa," "Gadara," and "Gergesha (clods, mud, or mire)" suggest notions of herds, and the driving of herds, and the mud in which herds of swine wallow, and are all adapted to favour the view that the inhabitants of these places were themselves of a swinish nature

THE DEMONIAC AND THE SWINE

crows or serpents[1], but of swine, the hateful swine of Rome, driven forth from himself to perish in the Lake[2]

§ 8 *"Outside," applied to the "casting out" of "the ruler of this world," in John*

Although John never mentions Christ's visible acts of exorcism, he represents Jesus Himself as saying "Now is the judgment of this world, now *shall the prince of this world be cast out* And I, if I be lifted up from the earth, will draw all [men] to myself. But this he spake signifying by what manner of death he was about to die[3]" This is the first of three passages where the Fourth Gospel mentions "*the prince of this* (or, *the*) *world*," always in utterances of Jesus[4]. The term was frequently used by the Jews to mean "the angel of death," or "the angel of the nations as distinct from Israel." It does not always imply what we should imply by Satanic hostility to man[5] John appears to use it in the sense of Satan, or Enemy, but in such a way as to imply that the enmity is exercised through this present and visible world, which often overshadows, in the mind of man, the invisible and spiritual world Thus "the world" is, in effect, the "city," "province,"

---

[1] See above, pp 83, 85
[2] Comp *Mids N Dream* v 1 9
  "One sees more devils than vast hell can hold,
  That is the madman"
[3] Jn xii 31—3 See *Son* 3391—407, 3449—51, on the "lifting up" of the Son of Man, alluding to the Crucifixion It may of course allude also at the same time to the Ascension
[4] The two others are (xiv 30) "There cometh *the prince of the world*, and he hath nothing in me" (*i e* no sin in me, nothing that falls under his dominion), (xvi 11) "Because *the prince of this world* hath been judged" Ἄρχων is rendered by R V "prince" in this phrase, and not "ruler" The rendering has the advantage of distinguishing the title from the Supreme Ruler
[5] See *Hor Heb* (on Jn xii 31) quoting Sanhedr 94 *a* "When God was about to make Hezekiah the Messiah, *saith the prince of the world* to him, 'O eternal Lord, perform the desire of this just one'"

THE DEMONIAC AND THE SWINE

or "place," mentioned in Hermas as above quoted, the prince of which says to us on earth "Obey me, or else go out of my city."

About the Johannine word "outside," if we ask "Outside of what?" we are left in doubt as to the answer. The meaning may be "Outside the *cosmos*, or *beautiful and orderly world*, where the prince has wrongfully enthroned himself." But on the other hand *cosmos* may mean the world in a bad sense, the "world" that "passeth away[1]." We may be intended to see the Prince of the *cosmos, the defiled and corrupted world*, descending, *cosmos* and all, into an abyss of darkness. And the context still further unsettles any definite local notions we may have formed about "outside" by representing the Messiah Himself as being removed "from the earth." The removal, it is true, is one of exaltation. But it is the exaltation of crucifixion. It means "If I be lifted up on the cross." This—like most of Christ's deepest teaching in the Fourth Gospel—is a paradox[2]. And then the following words "I will draw all men unto myself" contain a further paradox, suggesting the question "Whither? Are all men to be drawn up to the Cross and to stay there?" Doubtless the meaning is, that we are to be drawn first up to the Cross, and then along with the ascending Cross, up to the right hand of God[3], but it is all very mysterious and, as it were, dislocating.

Perhaps it is, in some sense, deliberately dislocating, or at all events unsettling. The Evangelist, though not directly, is indirectly polemical. He appears to be attempting, and successfully attempting, to unsettle and detach his readers from their fixed and hardened notions about local exorcism.

---

[1] 1 Jn ii 17, comp 1 Cor vii 31
[2] Concerning the Hebrew and Greek play on the double meaning of "lift up"—(1) crucify, (2) exalt—see *Joh Gr* **2211**c, **2642**b, and add *Numb r* (on Numb i 47 Wu p 9) commenting on the twofold "lifting up the head" in Gen xl 13, 19, 20
[3] See *Evang Petr* § 10 for the description of the ascending Cross.

THE DEMONIAC AND THE SWINE

They are not to think of evil spirits driven out of a local human body into a local prison-house of demons. Christians are to turn their minds to the thought of Christ's good Spirit breathed into their soul or inmost being so as to make their union with Him independent of place. We are not even to prize our own "soul," as long as it is "in this world." If we serve Christ we shall be where He is· "He that loveth his soul destroyeth it, and he that hateth his soul in this world shall keep it to eternal life. If any one be ministering to me let him follow me, and where I am there shall also be the minister that is truly mine[1]."

No mention has been made above of the textual variations in the Johannine saying "The prince of this world shall be cast out *outside*" which have induced Blass to print it "The prince of this world shall be cast *down*[2]" Several authorities substitute "*down*" for "*outside*[3]" But Epiphanius, who is one of these, indicates a motive that may have induced scribes (wrongly) to substitute "*down*," when he quotes at the same time the Lucan saying "fallen from heaven." "Down" may have seemed to express, better and more definitely than "outside," the defeat and fall of Satan[4].

Macarius has some important remarks on the meaning and variations of the text and (incidentally) on the *chōra*, or "province," placed under "the ruler of this world." After saying "Some copies have '*cast down*'," he adds "The name 'world'

---

[1] Jn xii 25—6

[2] On Jn xii 31, W H and R V give no marginal alternative, and Westcott ("*cast out* from the region of his present sway") assumes the reading "outside."

[3] SS "is thrown *down*," b, e, Corb mittetur *deorsum*, Epiphan. *Adv Haer* ii 2 66, 680 D, 681 C βληθήσεται κάτω (quoted along with Lk x 18 "fallen from heaven") and sim Chrys *ad loc*. Comp. Rev xii 9

[4] The same motive might induce Luke, instead of the Marcan "outside," to substitute "into the abyss."

THE DEMONIAC AND THE SWINE

(*cosmos*) is here tropically given to human-nature...." Then he says that, whereas the so-called ruler could not rule over non-human nature, since that is under absolute control, "he did obtain control over human nature, since that is under its own control[1]" This "ruler" is "not the Demiurgus or Lawgiver [of the universe]" but "a kind of archdemon" who "has come to rule over the licentious because of their licentiousness and has artfully enslaved those who are under their own control": and he did not attain sovereignty through violence or mere force, "but by taking counsel as it were with [men], and by versatile devices, he brought under his control the herd [that is called] rational, which herd is here called metaphorically *cosmos* (i.e. world). For man is appropriately called *cosmos* (*i.e.* order and beauty) since he is the *cosmos* of the *cosmos* and [of] an admirable frame, a creation honourable and made for honour."

In what follows, the writer speaks of the Cosmos as he might speak of the demoniac freed from the Legion, and at the close he says· "To be cast down, then, in the case of the ruler of the world, is nothing but to be hurled from his authority as ruler. The fall thus darkly suggested here is not from a literal place[2]. It consists in his being stripped of the honourable estimation that he possessed when he was actively worshipped by men in their vileness" Similarly, "to-day a king may *cast down* a ruler of a *chōra*, province,... and everyone will say that he is '*cast down*'...even though he goes on living in the same house in the *chōra*[3]" So it is, says Macarius, with "the ruler of the world"

---

[1] Macar 11 20 (p 37) τῶν ἀνθρώπων (ἦρξε) διὰ τὸ αὐτεξούσιον, τῶν δ' ἀψύχων ἀμήχανον διὰ τὸ ὑπεξούσιον

[2] Macar 11 20 (p 41) Οὐ τοπικὴν ὧδε τὴν πτῶσιν αἰνιττόμενος

[3] This sentence, combined with the above-quoted use of *chōra* in Hermas, confirms the view taken above that the original of *chōra* meant "*province,*" in Mark, and that Macarius is alluding to that meaning Perhaps, too, there is an allusion to the "*herd*" of swine in the sarcastic phrase τῆς λογικῆς ἀγέλης, "the rational *herd*," applied to humanity enslaved by the ἄρχων τοῦ κόσμου

THE DEMONIAC AND THE SWINE

The remarks of Macarius help us to realise the importance that would be attached by a writer like the Fourth Evangelist to the removal of the obstacle to belief presented to educated Greeks by Synoptic accounts of exorcism. In this particular story, the going forth of "swine" into the "abyss" is probably no invention of a Christian evangelist or poet, but based on some sayings uttered by a demoniac in all good faith about what he had himself seen and himself experienced. Yet, as related by the Synoptists, the story is liable to encourage many honest and pious readers to believe that Jesus did what, in an ordinary prophet, they would have blamed as being unjustifiable. It did not lie within the province of the Fourth Gospel to correct their possible misunderstanding. Perhaps indeed John himself accepted the narrative as mainly, if not entirely, true. But putting all exorcistic narrative aside, John has devoted himself to the object of inspiring his readers with a spiritual faith that should override difficulties arising from historical details of doubtful authenticity. He has also indicated to us that the rulers of the Jews in Jerusalem were themselves, in effect, possessed by the unclean spirit of the Roman Legion with a possession far more deadly than that of the demoniac by the Sea of Galilee.

CHAPTER IV

JESUS RESTORING TO LIFE
[Mark v. 21—43]

§ 1. *Differences in the Synoptic narratives*[1]

IN the three Synoptic narratives printed below, Matthew omits many of Mark's details. But Luke does not omit them

---

[1] Mk v 21—43
(R V)

(21) And when Jesus had crossed over again in the boat unto the other side, a great multitude was gathered unto him and he was by the sea
(22) And there cometh one of the rulers of the synagogue, Jairus by name, and seeing him, he falleth at his feet,
(23) And beseecheth him much, saying, My little daughter is at the point of death [I pray thee], that thou come and lay thy hands on her, that she may be made whole (*or*, saved) and live
(24) And he went with him, and a great multitude followed him, and they thronged him

Mt ix 18—26
(R V)

(18) While he spake these things unto them, behold, there came a ruler (W H ἄρχων ⌜[εἰς]⌝ προσελθών¹, marg ἄρχων εἰσελθών), and worshipped him, saying, My daughter is even now dead but come and lay thy hand upon her, and she shall live.

(19) And Jesus arose, and followed him, and [so did] his disciples

Lk viii 40—56
(R V)

(40) And as Jesus returned, the multitude welcomed him, for they were all waiting for him
(41) And behold, there came a man named Jairus, and he was a ruler of the synagogue and he fell down at Jesus' feet, and besought him to come into his house,
(42) For he had an only daughter, about twelve years of age, and she lay a-dying But as he went the multitudes thronged him

94 (Mark v. 21—43)

JESUS RESTORING TO LIFE

Consequently no discussion of them is necessitated by considerations of the rule of Johannine Intervention. A few however

Mk v. 21—43 (R V) *contd*	Mt. ix. 18—26 (R.V) *contd*	Lk viii 40—56 (R V.) *contd*
(25) And a woman, which had an issue of blood twelve years, (26) And had suffered many things of many physicians, and had spent all that she had, and was nothing bettered, but rather grew worse, (27) Having heard the things concerning Jesus, came in the crowd behind, and touched his garment (28) For she said, If I touch but his garments, I shall be made whole (*or*, saved) (29) And straightway the fountain of her blood was dried up, and she felt in her body that she was healed of her plague (*lit* scourge) (30) And straightway Jesus, perceiving in himself that the power [proceeding] from him had gone forth, turned him about in the crowd, and said, Who touched my garments? (31) And his disciples said unto him, Thou seest the multitude thronging thee, and sayest thou, Who touched me? (32) And he looked round about	(20) And behold, a woman, who had an issue of blood twelve years, came behind him, and touched the border of his garment (21) For she said within herself, If I do but touch his garment, I shall be made whole (*or*, saved).	(43) And a woman having an issue of blood twelve years, which had spent all her living upon physicians, and could not be healed of any, (*some anc auth*, *followed by* W H , *omit* had spent ...and) (44) Came behind him, and touched the border of his garment and immediately the issue of her blood stanched (45) And Jesus said, Who is it that touched me? And when all denied, Peter said, and they that were with him (*some anc auth omit* and they that were with him), Master (ἐπιστάτα), the multitudes press thee and crush [thee]. (46) But Jesus said, Some one did touch me for I perceived that power had gone forth from me (47) And when the

95 (Mark v 21—43)

JESUS RESTORING TO LIFE

may be profitably noticed as illustrating the nature of the difficulties placed in the way of the Fourth Evangelist by the differences of the Three

Mk v. 21—43 (R.V.) *contd*	Mt. ix. 18—26 (R.V.) *contd.*	Lk. viii. 40—56 (R.V.) *contd*
to see her that had done this thing (33) But the woman fearing and trembling, knowing what had been done to her, came and fell down before him, and told him all the truth (34) And he said unto her, Daughter, thy faith hath made thee whole (*or*, saved thee), go in peace, and be whole of thy plague (*lit* scourge) (35) While he yet spake, they come from the ruler of the synagogue's [house], saying, Thy daughter is dead why troublest thou the Master (*or*, Teacher) (διδάσκαλον) any further? (36) But Jesus, not heeding (*or*, overhearing) the word spoken, saith unto the ruler of the synagogue, Fear not, only believe. (37) And he suffered no man to follow with him, save Peter, and James, and John the brother of James (38) And they come to the house of the ruler of the synagogue, and he beholdeth a tumult, and [many] weeping and wailing greatly (39) And when	(22) But Jesus turning and seeing her said, Daughter, be of good cheer, thy faith hath made thee whole (*or*, saved thee) And the woman was made whole (*or*, saved) from that hour (23) And when Jesus came into the ruler's house, and saw the flute-players, and the crowd making a tumult, (24) He said, Give place	woman saw that she was not hid, she came trembling, and falling down before him declared in the presence of all the people for what cause she touched him, and how she was healed immediately (48) And he said unto her, Daughter, thy faith hath made thee whole (*or*, saved thee), go in peace (49) While he yet spake, there cometh one from the ruler of the synagogue's [house], saying, Thy daughter is dead, trouble not the Master (*or*, Teacher) (διδάσκαλον) (50) But Jesus hearing it, answered him, Fear not only believe, and she shall be made whole (*or*, saved) (51) And when he came to the house, he suffered not any man to enter in with him, save Peter, and John, and James, and the father of the maiden and her mother (52) And all were weeping, and bewailing her but he said,

JESUS RESTORING TO LIFE

Mark and Luke give the name of Jairus to a chief or ruler of the synagogue. Matthew omits the name, and possibly he is justified[1]. Matthew also omits the statement that Jairus'

Mk v 21—43 (R V) *contd*.	Mt ix 18—26 (R V) *contd*	Lk viii 40—56 (R V) *contd*
he was entered in, he saith unto them, Why make ye a tumult, and weep? the child is not dead, but sleepeth.	for the damsel is not dead, but sleepeth	Weep not, for she is not dead, but sleepeth
(40) And they laughed him to scorn But he, having put them all forth, taketh the father of the child and her mother and them that were with him, and goeth in where the child was	And they laughed him to scorn (25) But when the crowd was put forth, he entered in,	(53) And they laughed him to scorn, knowing that she was dead
(41) And taking the child by the hand, he saith unto her, Talitha cumi which is, being interpreted, Damsel, I say unto thee, Arise	and took her by the hand, and the damsel arose	(54) But he, taking her by the hand, called, saying, Maiden, arise
(42) And straightway the damsel rose up and walked, for she was twelve years old And they were amazed straightway with a great amazement		(55) And her spirit returned, and she rose up immediately and he commanded that [something] be given her to eat
(43) And he charged them much that no man should know this and he commanded that [something] should be given her to eat	(26) And the fame hereof went forth into all that land	(56) And her parents were amazed: but he charged them to tell no man what had been done

[1] Mk v 22 SS gives Jairus as "Ioarash" יואָרשׁ Delitzsch gives Mk's contextual words as "one of the *heads of* (ראשׁי) the synagogue" This similarity between "*Jairus*" and "*head*" (or "ruler") indicates possibilities of confusion In Gen xlvi 21, ראשׁ, *Rôsh*, is a name of one of the sons of Benjamin It is retained by Jer Targ with the addition that he was "a *chief* in his father's house," and *Gen r ad loc* explains why he was called "chief" In Ezek xxxviii 2,

JESUS RESTORING TO LIFE

daughter was twelve years old   But this may be because it was an isolated tradition, placed by Mark almost at the end, but by Luke at the beginning of his narrative[1]. Matthew may have regarded it as referring to the duration (mentioned in the context) of the disease of the woman with the issue[2]. Quite at the end of Mark's narrative come words that may be literally rendered "said [for something] to be given to her to eat[3]." This might be taken to mean that the girl (thereby proving that she was restored to life) asked for something to eat[4] Similarly a son of R Gamaliel, at the exact moment when he was cured of fever by the prayers of R Chanina, "asked for something to eat[5]" Matthew, omitting this request (after omitting the words *Talitha cumi*), has, in its place, "And there went forth this report into the whole of that land[6]" It is by no means improbable that this, too, is based on some Hebrew or Aramaic corruption[7].

3, xxxix 1 "*Rosh*" is regarded by Gesenius (912 b) as a name, but rendered by the Targ as "*head*"

[1] Mk v 42, Lk viii 42

[2] Mk v 25, Mt ix 20, Lk viii 43   In Lk , the two mentions of "twelve years" come in consecutive verses

[3] Mk v 43 εἶπεν δοθῆναι αὐτῇ φαγεῖν, Lk viii 55 διέταξεν αὐτῇ δοθῆναι φαγεῖν

[4] For Heb "say," meaning "command," see Gesen 56 b   This is unambiguously expressed by Lk διέταξεν, but not quite by Mk εἶπεν.

[5] So Schlatter (on Jn iv 53) quoting *J Berach* 9 d   A similar story in *B Berach* 34 b has "asked them for something to drink"

[6] In Mk v 41 Ταλειθά, e has *tabea acultha*, and Dr Chase suggests (*Syro-Latin Text* p 110) that this is a relic of the word מאכולתא "food"   If so, it may have some connection with the Mk-Lk tradition about "giving food"   The word תבע in Schlatter's quotation from *J Berach* "demanded food," might be rendered by *tabea*

[7] The above-mentioned word *acultha*, if the initial *a* were dropped after the final *a* in *tabea*, would become *cultha*, and confusable with words meaning (*Thes Syr* 1737) "*universim*" etc , so as to give rise to Matthew's view that "the fame went out [*everywhere*, or] *into all that land*"

Another explanation, however, of Matthew's words is that they

JESUS RESTORING TO LIFE

The Synoptists also differ as to the interval between the girl's death and restoration to life In Mark and Luke, her father describes her to Jesus as "breathing her last" or "in the act of dying"; but in Matthew he says "She has just died[1]." This needs little comment since "she is dying"—in Greek, "she *dies*"—when rendered into reported speech, might easily be taken to refer to an accomplished fact "he said *that she [had] died*"

As for Marcan peculiarities omitted by Luke, the principal one refers to the fact that physicians, attempting to cure the woman with the issue, caused her the loss of her fortune and made her worse rather than better[2]. This may possibly be explained from a Hebrew original differently translated by Mark and Luke[3]. In any case, it can hardly be regarded as a failure of the rule of Johannine Intervention

---

are a paraphrase of Mk v. 42 "*they were amazed* with a great amazement" Lk viii 56 restricts the amazement to "*the parents*," Diatess to "*her father*" Matthew extends it to "all that land" "Hearing" and "amazement" (שמע and שמם) are confusable in Heb (see *Indices to Diatessarica*, p 33)

[1] Mk v 23 ἐσχάτως ἔχει, Mt. ix. 18 ἄρτι ἐτελεύτησεν, Lk viii 42 ἀπέθνησκεν

[2] Mk v 26, parall to Lk. viii 43 οὐκ ἴσχυσεν ἀπ' οὐδενὸς θεραπευθῆναι In Lev. v. 7, xxvii. 8 οὐκ ἰσχύει with χείρ means "cannot afford," "is not rich enough," so that Luke's original may have meant "*Was not rich enough* to [pay physicians so as to] be healed by anyone"

[3] Lk viii 43 ἀπ' οὐδενὸς (not ὑπ' οὐδενὸς) is given by W H without alternative But θεραπεύω ἀπὸ in Luke elsewhere (3 or 4 times, not in Bible elsewhere, except 2 K ix 16 (LXX), nor in Steph *Thes*) means "*heal of*" some disease. Ἀπὸ, if correct, suggests that the original meant "healed from any part of her disease," and that it corresponds to Mk v 26 "not benefited, but rather made worse"

There is no space to deal with other Marcan details But see *Clue* **84** foll and **241** foll. for proof that Heb "And be thou made whole" might be confused with "And she was made whole" In Mk v 34 (*Joh Voc.* **1728** *e*) "(1) go back (ὕπαγε) in peace and (2) be whole (*or*, sound) (ὑγιὴς) from thy *plague* (μάστιγος)," there seems

There is, however, one important point as to which John does appear to intervene in order to shew the reality of Christ's power of revivification But the intervention, if there is one, is not for Mark against Luke Some might say it was for Luke against Mark and Matthew More exactly, it might be described as an intervention against an unspiritual interpretation of words assigned to Jesus by all the Synoptists "she is not dead but sleepeth" Luke attempts to meet such a misinterpretation But John meets it in a different way, as will be seen in the next section.

§ 2 *"Knowing that she was dead" in Luke, "Lazarus is dead" in John*[1]

Luke has two ways of meeting the objection that, if the girl was, as Jesus declared, *"not" really "dead,"* then no miracle followed First, he puts into the mouths of the crowd in the ruler's house an implied statement—which he does not make in his own person—that she *"was" really "dead."* Then he adds, in his own person, after Jesus has pronounced the command to *"arise,"* that *"her spirit returned"*[2] This, he might suppose, would lead his readers to conclude that it had previously passed out of her, and consequently that she *had really been "dead"* But the usage of Scripture would not justify the conclusion[3] Hence, this is not quite satisfactory Nor do

---

to be a conflation The parall Lk viii 48 has simply "go (πορεύου) in peace" Mt ix 22 has "and the woman was made sound (ἐσώθη) *from that [very] hour,"* i e at once Heb רגע "*moment*" might be confused with נגע "*plague*" or "*stroke*" (μάστιξ (3), πληγή (2)) so that "from the *plague*" might be confused with "in that same *moment*" See Exod xxxiii 5 "*moment* (רגע)," LXX πληγήν (Tromm *leg* נגע)

[1] Lk viii 53 εἰδότες ὅτι ἀπέθανεν, Jn xi 14 Λάζαρος ἀπέθανεν

[2] Lk viii 55 καὶ ἐπέστρεψεν τὸ πνεῦμα αὐτῆς

[3] See Judg xv 19 "And *his [Samson's] spirit returned*, and he lived," καὶ ἐπέστρεψεν τὸ πνεῦμα αὐτοῦ καὶ ἔζησεν, and comp 1 S xxx 12 (Heb) Neither of these cases implies anything more than recovery of strength after extreme faintness

JESUS RESTORING TO LIFE

we get much help from Jerome (who explains Matthew's "*not dead*" by saying "because all things live to God") or from other early comments[1]. Perhaps the most satisfactory explanation is the one given by Pseudo-Jerome on Mark, that Jesus meant "She is dead to you [the crowd]; she sleeps to me."

John represents Jesus (in the Raising of Lazarus) as Himself using the terms "*sleeping*" and "*dead*" in such a way as to give the disciples at first a false impression which He Himself subsequently removes[2]. Thus John meets the objection that what Christ called a mere "sleep," and "not death," Christ's disciples called "death" in order to magnify their Master's fame. He answers, in effect, "It was the custom of Jesus to describe 'death' as 'sleep.' I can give you an instance where He did thus. But on the same occasion He not only described it as 'death' but brought the dead man out of his tomb, after he had been four days dead. No one can doubt that this was real 'death.' It is said 'For three days the spirit [of the departed] wanders about the sepulchre, expecting if it may return into the body. But when it sees that the form or aspect of the face is changed, then it hovers no more but leaves the body to itself[3].' Hence some might argue against Luke's tradition 'The spirit returned to her,' in the story of the raising up of the ruler's daughter. 'This proves nothing'—they might say—'for three days had not elapsed.' But in a case that I shall mention, a sister of the dead man said to Jesus 'Lord, by this time he stinketh, for he hath been [dead] four days[4].'"

---

[1] Cramer (on Mt ix 24) prints two explanations, (1) "Those who have hope of the resurrection in Christ are not dead but sleep," (2) Jesus "makes light of the work He is about to perform," and "conceals it," afterwards saying "Tell no one." These are attributed to Origen.

[2] Jn xi 11, 14

[3] This is a tradition of Ben Kaphra in *Gen r* 114 3 (on Gen l 10, Wu p 504) quoted by *Hor Heb.* (on Jn xi 39) with other passages to the same effect

[4] Jn xi 39

As against such objections to the reality of the Synoptic revivification, the effectiveness of the Johannine narrative seems plain, but there is a great deal more that is not plain First take, in their order, the sentences that follow the message "He whom thou lovest is sick" sent to Jesus by the sisters of Lazarus: (1) "This sickness is not unto death, but for the glory of God, that the Son of God may be glorified thereby," (2) "Now Jesus loved Martha and her sister and Lazarus," and then (3)—what appears to be a *non sequitur*—"When therefore he heard that he was sick, he abode at that time two days in the place where he was"

Still more perplexing are the sentences "Our friend Lazarus is fallen asleep" and "Lazarus is dead," and then the saying to Martha "Thy brother shall rise again," followed by her answer "I know that he shall rise again in the resurrection at the last day," to which Jesus does not reply with a correction of her misunderstanding, but with words that might still further perplex her, "I am the resurrection and the life .. Whosoever liveth and believeth on me shall never die " It is difficult, even for those who are confident that all this is right, to explain *how* it is right

"Surely," we say, "Jesus could not mean, and Martha could not suppose Him to mean, that every disciple of His was immortal 'Die' must mean spiritual death 'Rise again' must mean spiritual resurrection Yet Jesus seems to have been purposing, both then and some days earlier, to raise Lazarus from a literal grave Then why does John give us the impression that Jesus is, as it were, mystifying the friends and relations of the dead? Why does he not represent Jesus as saying at once, straight out, that He intends to raise Lazarus from the tomb?"

Perhaps we may find some suggestion of an answer to this question in Origen's declaration that the raising of Jairus' daughter, like the raising of Lazarus, was in answer to a request of Jesus, though in neither case is a definite request recorded¹. John seems anxious to warn us against supposing that the Son ever performed a miracle of healing as if it were from Himself, and without some kind of special intercommunication—whether by vision, or by answer to request, to prayer, or to unuttered aspiration—between the Son and the Father And he leads us to infer that, when Jesus spoke to His disciples about such miracles, signs, or works—resulting in "life," or "soundness," or "awakening," or "rising again"—He often used such language (natural to Him but not natural to them) that they failed to understand it That is to say, they failed while He was living, but they understood it afterwards when He had died and risen again and sent His Spirit into their hearts. Before that time, Jesus, being in the position of one seeing works performed for Him (as it were) celestially before He performed them terrestrially, was wont to speak about them in the language of heaven to disciples accustomed to the language of earth

If this is the Johannine view we may find some kind of answer—a partial answer at all events—to the objection "The narrative of the Raising of Lazarus would be much more beautiful if the narrator did not represent Jesus as knowing beforehand all that He purposed to do and yet concealing it from His disciples and from the sisters of the deceased " Logically we must admit that there would be great force in

---

[1] Jn xi 41 "I thank thee that thou heardest me" implies that Jesus had sent forth some request to the Father But it is not recorded Origen says (ad loc Lomm ii 319) "We must not suppose that the soul of Lazarus was [still] present with the body after the departure [from it], and that, as being [still] present, it quickly heard Jesus when He cried and said, '*Lazarus! Hither! [Come] outside!*' But I think nearly the same thing came to pass also when He raised up the daughter of the ruler of the synagogue, praying about this (? περὶ τούτου εὐξάμενος), for He asked that the soul should come-back-again and be caused to dwell again in the body " The words "praying about this" appear to mean "praying about this [same thing in both cases]," namely, the return of the departed soul

JESUS RESTORING TO LIFE

this arraignment if Jesus were to be regarded here and elsewhere in the Gospel as having complete foreknowledge. But is that the case? Does the Fourth Gospel consistently maintain that Jesus (as in the Feeding of the Five Thousand) "knew what he was to do" in every minute detail?

It would be truer to say that Jesus is to be regarded as led by emotion blended with knowledge, and that the emotion that leads Him may be best summed up as filial Love[1]. The Son, representing the Love of the Father, is regarded as dependent at every moment on the Father, and as not knowing, not wishing to know, and even perhaps as refusing to know, all the details of that which will come to pass, until the time comes for their performance. He knows that, in some sense, the sickness of Lazarus is "not unto death but for the glory of God." But He awaits further revelation. This seems to come to Him step by step, or by oscillations. All sorts of words describing earthly "love" and "friendship" (the personal affection of Jesus for Lazarus and his sisters), "weeping," "trouble," "groaning" and passionate emotion[2], are introduced or reiterated in this narrative in such a way as to indicate that we are witnessing a gradual accumulation of human as well as divine emotions, destined to achieve—as it were by natural means, if we take enlarged views of nature—some supreme sign of the vivifying Love of the Father for all mankind.

We have seen above that one ancient comment on the Synoptic words "she is not dead but sleepeth" explains them as proceeding from Christ's desire to disparage His own wonderful work. In the Fourth Gospel, there is no desire to

---

[1] Not "love" merely, for a dog loves his master, and a babe loves its mother. But the "love" of Christ means love combined with that insight which the Son has into the Father's will, owing to unity of nature.

[2] E g $\phi\iota\lambda\epsilon\omega$ in Jn xi 3, 36, $\phi\iota\lambda os$ in xi 11 (and $\dot{a}\gamma a\pi \dot{a}\omega$ in xi 5), $\dot{\epsilon}\mu\beta\rho\iota\mu\dot{a}o\mu a\iota$ in xi 33, 38. Κλαίω is used twice, about Mary and the Jews (xi 33), δακρύω once, about Jesus (xi 35).

JESUS RESTORING TO LIFE

disparage, but to express Christ's different moods, at one moment speaking to the disciples in His own language "Our friend Lazarus is fallen asleep," at another in their language "Lazarus is dead" At the same time beneath both of these moods there is the recognition that man's life consists, not in the continued act of material breathing, but in the continued act of spiritual breathing, and this kind of breathing is a loving faith by which man passes through the Son into the Father ("whosoever liveth and believeth on me shall never die") This Jesus feels to be a solid reality Hence it is unnatural for Him to say at first to the disciples about anyone whom He dearly loves "He is dead" He says this afterwards But it is the language of the nursery The spiritual truth is "Our friend is fallen asleep," and, at the same time, He receives a special intimation that, even in the popular sense, the "sleep" is only a temporary sleep, so that He adds "But I go, that I may awake him out of sleep"

How far the Raising of Lazarus may be regarded as historical is a most difficult question, not discussed here If it is historical, then Luke—who mentions the sisters Martha and Mary but makes no mention of their brother, nor of any Lazarus except the beggar raised from the dead to Abraham's bosom—appears to forfeit all claim to be a well-informed biographer of Christ with any sense of proportion A similar forfeiture, though in a less degree, would seem to be incurred by Mark and Matthew[1]

---

[1] It has been suggested that the earlier Evangelists suppressed every written account of the raising of Lazarus because of the danger that (Jn xii 10) the Jews might kill him No doubt, such a danger might exist in the early days of the Church of Jerusalem But when Peter and John healed a lame man, though the rulers of the Jews said (Acts iv 16) "What shall we do to these men? For that indeed a notable miracle hath been wrought through them is manifest to all that dwell in Jerusalem," we do not find them attempting to kill the lame man And it is hardly probable that at the time when Mark wrote his Gospel—perhaps a generation after the alleged raising of Lazarus—in Alexandria or Rome, he would seriously say

JESUS RESTORING TO LIFE

If it is not historical, it would be best explained, not as fiction, but as narrative deduced from other traditions about Christ's acts of revivification, combined and amplified symbolically in order to shew, in one specimen, the spiritual aspect of such mighty works. But even in that case we may say that the Fourth Evangelist throws light on the Synoptic tradition "she is not dead but sleepeth." It was the custom of Jesus to regard what the world called "death" as being what He called "sleep," but in a special case, where He received an intimation that there was to be an immediate rising up from this sleep, He might mix as it were the two dialects "Not [*what you call*] death, but [*what I call*] sleep [and a sleep from which there is to be an immediate awakening]."

---

to himself "We Christians have known for thirty years that Jesus raised a man named Lazarus of Bethany from the dead, but I will not describe it and put down his name on paper—as I ventured to put down the name of Bartimaeus—for it might endanger his life."

If the Synoptists had anticipated any danger for Lazarus, they might have omitted his name, as Matthew and Luke omit the name of Bartimaeus, and as Luke omits the name of the young man whom Jesus raised from the dead at Nain. When John says (xii 10) "The chief priests *took counsel that they might put Lazarus also to death*," he implies that they did not carry out their "counsel." And he leads us to the inference that after they had killed Jesus it was not worth their while to kill Lazarus. The same thing would be true in after years. Moreover, at the time when Luke wrote, after the fall of Jerusalem, "the chief priests" had no longer the power to kill Lazarus, even if Lazarus was still alive.

CHAPTER V

JESUS IN HIS OWN COUNTRY
[Mark vi 1—6 a]

§ 1. *The agreements and disagreements of the Four Gospels*

THIS is one of the very rare occasions where the Fourth Gospel, as will be seen below[1], agrees roughly with the Three

---

[1] Mk vi 1—6 a (R V)	Mt xiii 53—58 (R V)	Lk iv 16—17, 21—24, 28 (R V)	Jn iv. 43—45 (R V)
(1) And he went ut from thence, nd he cometh into is own country, nd his disciples ollow him (2) And when he sabbath was ome, he began to each in the synaogue and (*some nc auth insert* the) any hearing him ere astonished, aying, Whence ath this man these ings? and, What the wisdom that given unto this an, and [what ean] such mighty orks wrought by is hands? (3) Is not this he carpenter, the on of Mary, and rother of James, nd Joses, and udas, and Simon? nd are not his sters here with s? And they were	(53) And it came to pass, when Jesus had finished these parables, he departed thence (54) And coming into his own country he taught them in their synagogue, insomuch that they were astonished, and said, Whence hath this man this wisdom, and these mighty works? (55) Is not this the carpenter's son? is not his mother called Mary? and his brethren, James, and Joseph, and Simon, and Judas? (56) And his sisters, are they not all with us? Whence then hath this man all these things? (57) And they were offended (*lit* caused to stumble) in him But Jesus	(16) And he came to Nazareth, where he had been brought up and he entered, as his custom was, into the synagogue on the sabbath day, and stood up to read (17) And there was delivered unto him the book of the prophet Isaiah (21) And he began to say unto them, To-day hath this scripture been fulfilled in your ears (22) And all bare him witness, and wondered at the words of grace which proceeded out of his mouth and they said, Is not this Joseph's son? (23) And he said unto them, Doubtless ye will say unto me this	(43) And after the two days he went forth from thence into Galilee (44) For Jesus himself testified, that a prophet hath no honour in his own country (45) So when he came into Galilee, the Galilaeans received him, having seen all the things that he did in Jerusalem at the feast: for they also went unto the feast

JESUS IN HIS OWN COUNTRY

in a few words attributed to Jesus, and there is a general agreement in the thought, namely, that it is difficult for a prophet to obtain full recognition "in his own country." But the verbal variations in the context are of such a kind as to lead early commentators to divergent conclusions as to what the "country of Jesus" was. Luke makes Jesus say that a prophet is not "acceptable" (lit *"received [with welcome]"*) in his own country. John says that the Galilaeans *"received"* Him because they had seen in Jerusalem the miracles that He had done in Jerusalem. Luke represents the hearers of Jesus as saying "The things that we have heard as having been done [by thee] at Capernaum"—not in Jerusalem—"do also here in thine own country." Lastly, Luke deviates from all the

Mk vi 1—6 a (R V) *contd*	Mt xiii 53—58 (R V) *contd*	Lk iv 16—17, 21—24, 28 (R V) *contd*
offended (*lit* caused to stumble) in him (4) And Jesus said unto them, A prophet is not without honour, save in his own country, and among his own kin, and in his own house (5) And he could there do no mighty work, save that he laid his hands upon a few sick folk, and healed them (6 a) And he marvelled because of their unbelief	said unto them, A prophet is not without honour, save in his own country, and in his own house (58) And he did not many mighty works there because of their unbelief	parable, Physician, heal thyself whatsoever we have heard done at Capernaum, do also here in thine own country (24) And he said, Verily I say unto you, No prophet is acceptable in his own country* . . (28) And they were all filled with wrath in the synagogue, as they heard these things

* Luke proceeds as follows (iv 25—30) —

(25) But of a truth I say unto you, There were many widows in Israel in the days of Elijah, when the heaven was shut up three years and six months, when there came a great famine over all the land, (26) and unto none of them was Elijah sent, but only to Zarephath, in the land of Sidon, unto a woman that was a widow (27) And there were many lepers in Israel in the time of Elisha the prophet, and none of them was cleansed, but only Naaman the Syrian (28) And they were all filled with wrath in the synagogue, as they heard these things, (29) and they rose up, and cast him forth out of the city, and led him unto the brow of the hill whereon their city was built, that they might throw him down headlong (30) But he passing through the midst of them went his way

JESUS IN HIS OWN COUNTRY

Gospels by representing the visit as terminated by an attempt on the part of the audience to cast Jesus down a precipice.

This last fact suggests, as a working hypothesis, that in this narrative Luke, as compared with John, has pursued the same course as in the Calling of the Fishermen[1]. That is to say, Luke has combined with the visit to what people would call "his father's house" in Nazareth an account of an attempt on Christ's life made, according to John, later on, and not at Nazareth but in what Jesus would call His Father's House (*i e* the Temple) at Jerusalem[2] Such an explanation is at all events less improbable than any that would require us to believe that Mark and Matthew, as well as John, either did not know of this attempt on Christ's life at Nazareth, or knew it but concealed their knowledge

§ 2. *"His country" and "his own country," in all the Gospels*

Writing in their own persons, the Evangelists say severally, that Jesus came—(Mark and Matthew) "*into his country*"; (Luke) "to *Nazareth where he had been brought up*, (John) "*into Galilee*[3]." Afterwards, recording the words of Jesus, all of them use the word "*country*[4]" The Greek word, *patris*, here used for country, occurs rarely in canonical LXX There

---

[1] See *Proclamation*, Preface pp vi—vii, on the Lucan story of the Draught of Fishes

[2] Comp Lk ii 49 (R V txt) "Wist ye not that I must be *in my Father's house* (ἐν τοῖς τοῦ πατρός μου)?"

[3] Mk vi 1, Mt xiii 54 εἰς τὴν πατρίδα αὐτοῦ, Lk iv 16 εἰς Ναζαρά, οὗ ἦν τεθραμμένος, Jn iv. 45 εἰς τὴν Γαλιλαίαν Mt xiii 54 "in their *synagogues* (pl)" is read by the best Latin and Syriac versions This implies that the translators regarded πατρίς as a district, not a city

[4] Mk vi 4 ἐν τῇ πατρίδι αὐτοῦ καὶ ἐν τοῖς συγγενεῦσιν αὐτοῦ καὶ ἐν τῇ οἰκίᾳ αὐτοῦ, Mt xiii 57 ἐν τῇ [W H marg ins ἰδίᾳ] πατρίδι καὶ ἐν τῇ οἰκίᾳ αὐτοῦ, Lk iv 24 ἐν τῇ πατρίδι αὐτοῦ, comp Jn iv. 44 ἐν τῇ ἰδίᾳ πατρίδι

JESUS IN HIS OWN COUNTRY

it corresponds mostly to a Hebrew word meaning "kindred," but once to "land of one's kindred[1]" It is not limited to a "city." The Syro-Sinaitic Version uses a word that in Syriac may mean either "city" or "region"; but in Aramaic it mostly has the latter meaning, as it always has in Hebrew[2]. Comparing the eight passages of the four Gospels together we see that, beneath all their variations, the *thought* in all of them was of "country" in the sense of "place of rearing," which is usually also "place of kinsfolk." This may be almost said to imply in one word all that Genesis expresses in three, "thy land and thy kindred and thy father's house[3]."

One might have supposed that all commentators from the first would have agreed that, since *patris* must here have this suggestion of "kinsfolk," the word must mean the region round Nazareth Jerome takes it so But he adds "It may however be otherwise understood, namely, that Jesus is despised *in His house and His country, that is, among the people of the Jews*, and that on this account He 'worked few miracles' there, lest they should become absolutely inexcusable But He works greater signs daily among the Gentiles through the Apostles, not so much in the healing of bodies as in the saving of souls[4]."

This latter view is that of Origen, who says that perhaps the Evangelists (that is, Mark and Matthew) did not say precisely what the *patris* was "because of something mystically signified in the passage concerning the *patris*, namely *the whole of the*

---

[1] Gesen 409 *b*, Jerem xlvi 16 (Heb) "land of our kindred"

[2] Gesen 193 *b* מדינה, Levy *Ch*. ii 10—11, *Thes Syr* 844 Delitzsch, in Mk vi 1, Mt xiii 54, has simply "*his land*," comp Gen. xii 1 "Get thee forth from (Heb) *thy land* (τῆς γῆς σου) and thy kindred and thy father's house"

[3] Gen xii 1. This is the first instance of Heb (sing) "land" with a possessive suffix The Greek πατρίς does not usually suggest allusion to "kinsfolk" Hence, perhaps, Mk vi 4 adds συγγενεῦσιν and οἰκίᾳ

[4] Jerome on Mt xiii 58.

JESUS IN HIS OWN COUNTRY

Jewish [*land*][1]" He also interprets "*His sisters, are they not all with us?*" as meaning "something of this kind, '*They have our thoughts, not the thoughts of Jesus, and they have no strange element of preeminent understanding as Jesus has*[2]'" Others might agree that *patris*, "native country," meant something larger than "city," but might urge that it ought not to be regarded as including the whole of Palestine but only the northern portion, where Christ's home lay. This would be appropriately represented by "Galilee" which John substitutes.

§ 3. "*And his disciples follow him*," in Mark

Mark alone inserts that the disciples followed Jesus[3] He also alone inserts "*the many*" (i e the majority) in the next verse "And when the sabbath came he began to teach in the synagogue, and *the majority*, hearing [him] were astonished[4]." Matthew mentions no disciples and no majority but only "them," *i e.* the natives of the *patris* just mentioned: "Having come into his *country* (*patris*) he began to teach *them* in their synagogue (*v.r.* synagogues) so that they were astonished[5]." This "astonishment" is followed both in Mark and Matthew by remarks of the hearers about their familiarity with the

---

[1] Origen on Mt xiii 53—4 appears to use ὅλης τῆς Ἰουδαίας to mean here, not "the whole of [the province of] Judaea," but "the whole of the land and people of the Jews" The context shews that he assumes the Mark-Matthew visit to be distinct from the Lucan visit, which expressly mentions Nazareth

[2] Origen on Mt xiii 56 δοκεῖ μοι τοιοῦτόν τι σημαίνειν τὰ ἡμέτερα φρονοῦσιν, οὐ τὰ τοῦ Ἰησοῦ καὶ οὐδὲν ξένον ἔχουσιν ἐξαιρέτου συνέσεως ὡς ὁ Ἰησοῦς Taken in a literal sense, the words "Are they not all with us?" Mark ("*here* with us"), could hardly mean anything but that the sisters were (perhaps married and certainly resident) in Nazareth.

[3] Mk vi 1 καὶ ἀκολουθοῦσιν αὐτῷ οἱ μαθηταὶ αὐτοῦ

[4] Mk vi 2 καὶ οἱ πολλοὶ ἀκούοντες ἐξεπλήσσοντο Οἱ is inserted by B and L

[5] Mt xiii 54 καὶ ἐλθὼν εἰς τὴν πατρίδα αὐτοῦ ἐδίδασκεν αὐτοὺς ἐν τῇ συναγωγῇ (Syr and latt mostly pl) αὐτῶν ὥστε ἐκπλήσσεσθαι αὐτούς....

JESUS IN HIS OWN COUNTRY

kinsfolk of Jesus, and then by the statement "And they stumbled because of him."

Obviously Mark does not intend us to suppose that the disciples joined in this disparaging astonishment. He represents the hearers as being, practically, divided into two sections—the disciples, who were not likely to be astonished, and the natives, of whom most[1] were astonished. Matthew recognises no such division.

Luke takes a course difficult to understand until we read his text in the Diatessaron. There we find the Lucan visit to Nazareth divided into two parts separated by a long interval so as to make two distinct visits. In neither visit is there described any division of mind. In the first Lucan visit "*all* began to bear witness to him and to marvel at the words of grace that were proceeding out of his mouth[2]." In the next Lucan visit "*all*" were "filled with wrath" and tried to kill Jesus[3].

John does not—in the present passage describing this particular visit to Galilee—mention any division of opinion. He merely implies that the Galilaeans derived most of their recognition of Jesus from what they had seen of His works in Jerusalem at the feast of the Passover, and that they "received" Him on that account[4]. But if we ask whether elsewhere John recognises divergences of opinion, and changes of mind, and divisions between a majority and a minority—such as Mark obscurely suggests—we shall find that such recognition is frequent. John thrice uses the word "schism" to express this division; and it is not in the "multitude" alone, but also among

---

[1] "Most" but not all. For Jesus is said to have healed (Mk vi 5) "a few sick folk." These would hardly disparage Him.

[2] Lk iv 16—22*a* placed in *Diatess* § 5.

[3] This is in Lk iv 23—30 (omitting 22*b* "and they said, Is not this Joseph's son?") It is placed in *Diatess* § 17 following immediately after Mt xiii 55—7 (see p. 107 above).

[4] Jn vi 45.

JESUS IN HIS OWN COUNTRY

"the Pharisees," and among "the Jews[1]." The last mention of this "schism" is followed by an attempt to stone Jesus in the Temple

§ 4. *"Were astonished" in Mark and Matthew, how expressed in Luke*

The Diatessaron, combining Mark and Matthew, says "He taught them in their synagogues so that they *were perplexed*. And when the sabbath came, Jesus began to teach in the synagogue, and many of those that heard *marvelled*, and said, Whence came these things to this [man]? And many *envied* him, and *gave no heed* to him, but said, What is this wisdom that is given to this [man] that there should happen at his hands such as these mighty works? Is not this a carpenter, son of a carpenter...?' This is a very remarkable accumulation of verbs apparently intended as renderings of Mark's *"were astonished"*

This leads us to consider the uses of the word "astonished" elsewhere in Mark and Luke. One Marcan instance is reproduced by the parallel Luke, but the other Lucan instances are not parallel to a Marcan instance[2] To two other Marcan instances Luke has either no parallel, or one that perhaps

---

[1] Jn vii 43 "So there arose a *division* (σχίσμα) *in the multitude* because of him" (see also the contrast in the context between "the officers" and the Pharisees), ix. 16 "Some therefore *of the Pharisees* said, This man is not from God .But *others* said...And there was a *division* among them," x 19—21 "There arose a *division again among the Jews*.. And *many* of them said, He hath a devil .*Others* said ..Can a devil open the eyes of the blind?" This is followed by a second attempt to stone Jesus (*ib* 31) "The Jews took up stones again to stone him '

[2] Lk iv 32 is exactly parall to Mk i 22 ἐξεπλήσσοντο ἐπὶ τῇ διδαχῇ αὐτοῦ The other instances of ἐκπλήσσομαι in Luke are Lk ix. 43 ἐξεπλήσσοντο (pec), Lk ii 48 ἐξεπλάγησαν (about the parents of Jesus seeing Him in the Temple)

JESUS IN HIS OWN COUNTRY

implies Hebrew confusion[1] A third Marcan instance requires special attention:

Mk xi. 18	Lk xix 47—8
And the chief priests and the scribes heard it, and sought how they might destroy him. for they feared him, for all the multitude *was astonished* at his teaching	.. But the chief priests and the scribes and the principal men of the people sought to destroy him and they could not find what they might do, for the people all *hung upon* (lit *from*) *him*, listening

Here Matthew begins, as Mark and Luke do, with "the chief priests and the scribes," but goes off into a separate tradition about "the children crying in the temple[2]." It seems as though Matthew, like Luke, was not satisfied with Mark's commonplace reiteration of "astonished at his teaching," and desired to substitute, or to go back to, some tradition descriptive of the passionate excitement of the multitude Luke's expression (lit.) *"hung from him"*—rendered by Delitzsch *"clave after him"*—is rather Greek than Hebrew, for the Hebrew "hang" is very rarely used metaphorically[3]; but the Syriac versions have it here ("hanging on him to hear him[4]").

---

[1] To Mk vii 37 ὑπερπερισσῶς ἐξεπλήσσοντο, Luke has no parallel On Mk x 26 περισσῶς ἐξεπλήσσοντο, Mt xix 25 ἀκούσαντες ἐξεπλήσσοντο σφόδρα, Lk xviii 26 οἱ ἀκούσαντες, see *Corrections* **392** *a*, **441**, **443**, where some Heb confusion is indicated

[2] Mt xxi 15—16 "But when the chief priests and the scribes saw the wonderful works...and the children crying in the temple, .. they were moved with indignation ..And Jesus saith unto them, Did ye never read 'thou hast perfected praise'?"

[3] See Gesen 1067 *b* on the rare form in Deut xxviii. 66 "thy life *hung up* [i e in suspense] before thee" and Hos xi 7 "(lit) *hung up to"* R V *"bent to"* (Gesen "certainly corrupt") The more usual form (Gesen 1067 *b* foll) is always literal In New Heb, "hang from" occasionally means "depend on," "trust" (Levy iv 645 *a*, Levy *Ch* ii 539 *a*)

[4] The word also occurs in Solomon's Odes iii 2, on which see *Light* **3673—6**

JESUS IN HIS OWN COUNTRY

The origin of Luke's *"hung from him"* must be discussed in its order, but the parallelism between it and the Marcan *"astonished"* is noted here because we must now call attention to the fact that in the Lucan parallel to the Marcan Visit to Nazareth, where Luke's text mentions *"casting down a precipice,"* some Syriac quotations of it mention *"hanging"*

§ 5. *"Cast down a precipice"* and *"hang,"* confused in a version of Luke

In the Lucan account of the Visit to Nazareth, the Syro-Sinaitic Version concludes thus "They were filled with fury, and they put him forth out of the city and brought him even unto the Pharos (?), the hill that their city was built on, so that they might hang him¹" The Greek has *ophrus*, "brow" (*"brow* of the hill"). *Ophrus* occurs nowhere else in the Greek Bible except where the Hebrew phrase *"the ridge of the eye"* is rendered in LXX by the single word *ophrus*, "brow²" The Hebrew for *"ridge,"* there and elsewhere, is *gab*, and Walton's Syriac has it here, "the *gab* of the hill" But further the Hebrew and Aramaic for "hang" often represents our "crucify" as in Paul's quotation "cursed is he that hangeth on a tree³." And what appears to be a form of the Hebrew *gab* is used by John in a passage describing Jesus as brought out to receive sentence before crucifixion, "at a place called the pavement, but in Hebrew *Gab-batha*⁴."

On this Westcott says "There can be little doubt that this represents *Gab Baitha*, the ridge (back) of the House,' *i.e.* of the Temple; but as the author of Horae Hebraicae

---

¹ Lk iv 29 (SS, Burkitt) The word printed "Pharos" represents Gk ὀφρύς, of which it may be a transliteration. SS "hang" corresponds to Gk κατακρημνίσαι, on which see p 117, n. 1

² Lev xiv 9

³ Gal iii 13, quoting Deut xxi 23.

⁴ Jn xix 13

expresses doubt, and Prof. Dalman has recently changed his views on the subject[1], we shall be safer in saying that in the first century *Gab-batha* might be taken by some to mean "*the brow of the House of the Lord.*" If so, it might be taken by Christians, ignorant of Jewish usage, in more senses than one Jews and some Christians would take it as a ridge near the House of the Lord, the Temple, in Jerusalem, but some Christians might take it as *a ridge near the house of the Lord Jesus in Nazareth* If however the name was found in connection with the "*hanging*" of Jesus, or an attempt at "hanging," such a tradition could only be applied to Jerusalem No one could seriously and permanently maintain that an attempt was made to "*hang*" (that is, to "*crucify*") Jesus in Nazareth

What therefore would be Luke's natural course if he came to the conclusion that the visit of the Lord Jesus to His home in Nazareth had been misunderstood by Mark-Matthew, and that it really terminated in an attempt to take away His life in a place of which the name meant something like "the ridge of the hill of the Lord's house"? We may infer his probable course from what he seems to have done in the analogous case of the Draught of Fishes which he places early, in contrast with John who places it late[2]. There Luke appears to have retained a difficult word *kateneusa*, but to have interpreted it as meaning, not "*swam to shore*" but "*made signs*," and to have adapted his context accordingly[3]. Somewhat similarly here, we could explain the difficult Syro-Sinaitic "*hang*" and the difficult

---

[1] See *Hor Heb* on Jn xix 13 quoting *Jer Sanhedr* fol 18 3 as possibly to be rendered "the elders that sit in the upper 'Gab' in the *Mount of the Temple*" (lit *House*) Westcott refers to *Jer Sanhedr* 18 *d* as mentioning "Gab of the House" This *Hor Heb* does not exactly mention See Hastings *Dict* "Gabbatha," and Dalman *Words* p 7

[2] See *Proclamation* pp 1 foll, 35 foll, 91 foll

[3] *Proclamation* pp 92—3, 97

(Mark vi 1—6)

JESUS IN HIS OWN COUNTRY

Greek *"precipitate"* by an early confusion between similar or identical Greek words that have both these meanings[1]

That Luke had some textual basis for his account of the attempt on Christ's life in Nazareth seems all the more probable because of the intrinsic improbability of the account, indicating that he could not have invented it. The traditional supposition of a Rock of Precipitation, two miles from Nazareth, is generally abandoned[2], and no other has been substituted with any probability that could resist the argument "If this *was* the real place, how came it to be supplanted by the false and traditional one?" If Jesus had been stoned just outside the synagogue, and in company with a few disciples to stand round Him, we could understand His escape, but, as Luke relates the story, the escape is manifestly miraculous Accordingly Ephrem says about it "When they threw Him from the hill, *He flew in the air*," and Aphraates, "He shewed the power of His majesty when *He was thrown from the height into the depth and was not hurt*[3]"

---

[1] Steph *Thes* iv 1107 gives κατακρήμνημι as meaning, in the middle, *"dependeo," "praeceps dependeo,"* but in the active the same thing as κατακρημνίζω *"praecipitem dejicio" Ib* 1944 emends κρεμνᾶν (*"hang* the maiden") into "κρῆμναν vel κρεμᾶν" *Ib* 1950 gives κρημνάω and κρήμνημι as 1 q κρημνίζω, according to Eustathius, but really meaning "*hang*," and quotes other instances of corruption Confusion was very natural since κρημνός "precipice" etymologically means "*an overhanging* place," like the English local term "*hanger*"

The only other Biblical instance of κατακρημνίζω is in 2 Chr xxv 12 κατεκρήμνιζον αὐτοὺς ἀπὸ τοῦ ἄκρου τοῦ κρημνοῦ, where Syr has (but see context "broken in pieces") "venerunt autem omnes vincti catenis (שׁשׁלתא)"—not mentioned in *Thes Syr* 4343

[2] *Enc Bib* 3359

[3] Burkitt vol ii pp 130, 183 It is worth noting that Luke's first use of ἐκπλήσσομαι occurs in the narrative of the first visit of Jesus to the Temple (Lk ii 48) "they were astonished (ἐξεπλάγησαν)" Mary says to Jesus "Thy *father*," meaning Joseph Jesus replies "The [house] of my *Father*," meaning God Probably Luke intends to suggest that the parents of Jesus were bewildered and almost out of their minds with astonishment

117 (Mark vi 1—6)

JESUS IN HIS OWN COUNTRY

§ 6. *Attempts on Christ's life, in John*

Mark (as also Matthew) describes no open attempt to take Christ's life There would therefore be no breach of the rule of Johannine Intervention if the Fourth Gospel were equally silent But John mentions two such attempts. Both of them were made in the Temple, and in both cases the attempt is to stone Him[1] The first of these says that Jesus "*was hidden* and went out of the temple" Our R V text renders this as "hid himself" But there are reasons for retaining the passive rendering "Luke had described Christ as 'passing through' the Nazarenes, but had not explained how this was effected John suggests that it was literal and miraculous, but also that it was typical of a spiritual blinding whereby Christ '*was hidden*' from those who rejected Him[2]"

There is less difficulty in John's narrative than in Luke's. On the only other Biblical occasion where "stoning" in the Temple is mentioned, a repairing of the Temple is described as going on at the time, so that stones might be lying about[3]. Such repairs in the Herodian Temple would be frequent, and a reference to the possibility occurs in the Talmud[4] A sudden rush of the crowd to snatch up such stones on the spot, and the escape of Jesus, hidden in part at all events by the faithful disciples round Him, are very different things from the Lucan picture which describes how a Nazarene crowd seized and conveyed Jesus—apparently by Himself and without a single disciple near Him—to a rock at a distance (traditionally estimated at two miles) from the town, and then how Jesus, "passing through the midst of them, went his way[5]."

---

[1] Jn viii 59 (on which see *Joh Gr* **2538—43**) and x 31, 39
[2] *Joh Gr.* **2543**   [3] Comp 2 Chr xxiv 21 with *ib* 13
[4] See *Hor Heb* on Jn viii 59 quoting *Sabb* 115 a "R Jose saith, They whelmed him (a heretic) under a heap of clay 'Is there any clay in the mountain of the House ?' Gloss· '*There was mortar, which they used in building.*'"
[5] Lk iv 30.

JESUS IN HIS OWN COUNTRY

§ 7 *"Wisdom" and "mighty works," in Mark and Matthew*

Mark speaks of "mighty works" as emphatically present, "through his hands [*continually*] *coming to pass*", Matthew, omitting this phrase, leaves the time an open question[1] Luke has "Whatsoever we *have heard* [as] *having come to pass* at Capernaum, do also here in thy country[2]," as though the speakers spoke of the past, and of things that they knew only by hearsay and hardly believed to be true. John says "The Galilaeans received him having seen all things *whatsoever he had done in Jerusalem* at the feast, for they themselves also had come to the feast[3]"

This appears to be an instance of Johannine Intervention, so far as concerns the nature of the evidence that led people in Christ's "country" to believe in His "mighty works", but as regards the mention of "wisdom" by Mark and Matthew we cannot say that John intervenes—at all events verbally and directly. "Wisdom," *sophia*, is a word that he never uses either in his Gospel or in his Epistle Perhaps he would have shrunk from attributing it to Jesus (except in very special contexts) because it was often associated by many, as by Paul, with "wisdom of word" and with the "wisdom" "sought after" by "the Greeks[4]," largely consisting of the disputations of those who were called "philosophers," i e. "*lovers of wisdom*"

The parallel Luke says "All. .were marvelling at the *words of grace* that were proceeding out of his mouth," and John, in

---

[1] Mk vi 2 Πόθεν τούτῳ ταῦτα, καὶ τίς ἡ σοφία ἡ δοθεῖσα τούτῳ καὶ αἱ δυνάμεις τοιαῦται διὰ τῶν χειρῶν αὐτοῦ γινόμεναι, Mt xiii. 54 Πόθεν τούτῳ ἡ σοφία αὕτη καὶ αἱ δυνάμεις,

[2] Lk iv 23 Ὅσα ἠκούσαμεν γενόμενα εἰς τὴν Καφαρναοὺμ ποίησον καὶ ὧδε ἐν τῇ πατρίδι σου

[3] Jn iv 45 ἐδέξαντο αὐτὸν οἱ Γαλιλαῖοι, πάντα ἑωρακότες ὅσα ἐποίησεν ἐν Ἱεροσολύμοις ἐν τῇ ἑορτῇ, καὶ αὐτοὶ γὰρ ἦλθον εἰς τὴν ἑορτήν.

[4] 1 Cor 1. 17—22 "*wisdom of word...the Greeks* seek after *wisdom.*"

his prologue, repeatedly mentions the "*grace*" or "*grace and truth*" that abounded in "the only begotten[1]" Mark and Matthew never mention "grace." May we then say that John here intervenes for Luke? Not in this passage There is no thought of real "grace" in the reception of Jesus by the Galilaeans as described by John For the most part Luke uses "grace" to mean "favour" or "gratitude" And here the "grace" mentioned by Luke in the reception of Jesus by the Nazarenes, "marvelling at *the words of grace* that were proceeding out of his mouth," is no real "grace" at all. It is nothing but an empty sound of "words of grace"—"words" that seemed quite out of proportion to the merit of a prophet who had not done anything in their presence to justify them, so that they elicited from the audience nothing but marvel at the speaker's presumption The marvel is followed by disparagement ("Is not this the son of Joseph?") and then by an overt act of hostility In all this there is nothing that resembles the Johannine "grace" that overflowed into the hearts of the disciples from "the only begotten"

§ 8. "*The carpenter," in Mark and Matthew*[2]

There is reason to think that "the carpenter" may not have conveyed, in Mark's original, the contemptuous impression that it conveyed to Celsus and would probably convey to the Roman

---

[1] Χάρις, "grace," is peculiar to the third and fourth Gospels (*Joh Voc* **1775** *c*) But in Luke it mostly means "favour" or "gratitude" In John it means "divine graciousness" (contrasted with Law) abounding in the incarnate Logos from whom it flows forth to those who receive Him (Jn 1 14—17) "full of grace and truth .from his fulness we all received, and grace succeeding (ἀντί) grace ..the [gift of] grace and the [gift of] truth (see *Joh Gr.* **2284—7, 2301, 2411** *e*, *Son* **3566**) came into being through Jesus Christ"

[2] Mk vi 3 ὁ τέκτων ὁ υἱός...., Mt xiii 55 ὁ τοῦ τέκτονος υἱός In Mk, some Greek cursives have ὁ τοῦ τέκτονος υἱός ., and similarly some Latin codices have "fabri filius"

JESUS IN HIS OWN COUNTRY

world[1]. The Hebrew for "carpenter," a word that means "artificer," whether in wood, or stone, or metal[2], is sometimes used in the Talmud for a distinguished Teacher[3] The word used in the Syriac of Mark and Matthew for "carpenter" is frequently used in the same way in Talmudic treatises. For example, about some difficult critical question, a Rabbi says, "There is *no carpenter and no son of a carpenter*" that could answer it, and another Rabbi, while declaring that he can answer it, adds nevertheless, in modest deprecation, that he is "*no carpenter and no son of a carpenter*[4]."

This appears to have been a frequent phrase, and there is perhaps an allusion to it when it is said "Better is the saying of the *Smith* than that of the *son of the Smith*," where "the Smith" is the name given to a Rabbi Isaac and "the son of the Smith" is the name given to the celebrated Rabbi Jochanan[5]. Jochanan's early date attests the antiquity of such titles; for he is connected with legal questions that arose before the destruction of Jerusalem, and legend tells that he predicted to Vespasian his future elevation to the imperial dignity[6].

---

[1] Origen (*Cels* vi 36) quotes Celsus as saying, about Jesus, τέκτων ἦν τὴν τέχνην and denies that any Gospel makes this statement Origen is mostly so accurate that we may pardonably conjecture that he read ΤΕΚΤΟΝΟ (i e τέκτων ὁ) as ΤΕΚΤΟΝΟϹΟ (*Joh Gr* **2652**)

[2] Gesen 360 b   [3] Levy ii 118—9

[4] *Aboda Sara* 50 b   See Levy iii 338 (נגר) who gives other instances of "carpenter and son of a carpenter"

[5] *Sanhedr* 96 a   Levy iii 419 b quotes and renders *Sanhedr* thus, but refers to *B Metz* 85 b "son of the Smith" as *a name of R Isaac*, whereas Goldschm says, in a note, that it is "*a name of R Jochanan*" Levy himself says that *Chull* 77 a "R Isaac *son of the Smith*" is an error, and refers to *Sabb* 25 b as one of many instances where R Isaac is called "*the Smith*" Comp 2 Tim iv 14 "Alexander *the Coppersmith* (χαλκεύς)" There Schottgen says "I do not believe that he was a *smith* (*fabrum*) by trade (*professione*) but that he was *a Rabbi*," and quotes *Joma* 54 b about "*Isaac the Smith*" But Alexander may have been *both*

[6] See Schurer ii 1 pp 366—7 referring to *Lam. r* on Lam. 1. 5 (Wu. p 66 foll)

121   (Mark vi. 1—6)

JESUS IN HIS OWN COUNTRY

After the fall of Jerusalem he became the most important of the scribes. It is said of him that he lived one hundred and twenty years, of which the first forty were given to "business"; and although that must not be accepted as literally true, it shews—what we know from other sources—that a training in "business" was regarded as a credit rather than a discredit to the career of an eminent rabbi[1]. It may therefore be taken for granted that the title eulogistically applied to him, "son of a Smith," and the (apparently) earlier and more general title "son of a carpenter," together with the rabbinical titles "smith" and "carpenter," were in use before Jochanan's time, and consequently in the days when Jesus came bringing the Gospel to Galilee.

In view of these facts we must clear our minds from the modern notion, which was also the ancient Greek and Roman notion, that there was something disparaging in the name "carpenter" applied to Jesus[2]. We must even prepare our minds to accept the conclusion—astonishing to us perhaps—that it was complimentary, and that it must be taken with what precedes, thus: "Whence hath this man these [gifts]? And what is the wisdom that is given to him?...*Is not this indeed a carpenter* [i.e. *a Chief among the Rabbis*]?" Along with this tradition might go one that Matthew has preferred, "Is not this *a son of a carpenter*?" Both would naturally be soon

---

[1] On Jochanan's "business" (פרנגמטיא, πραγματεία) see Levy ii 227 *a* quoting *R hasch* 31 *b*, and Levy iv 99 *b*. For other instances (very numerous) see Wagenseil's *Sota* pp. 596—600.

[2] In his comment on Mk vi 1 foll., Pseudo-Jerome reads "filius fabri," and says, "et hoc mystice, sed fabri qui fabricatus est Auroram et Solem." Origen, as we have seen, denies that Jesus was called a carpenter. The only mentions of τέκτων in Goodspeed are in Justin Mart. *Tryph* § 88 describing Jesus as "deemed (νομιζομένου) the son of Joseph the carpenter," and as "deemed a carpenter" because he wrought the "works of a carpenter," making "ploughs" and "yokes." This might mean instruments for the sowing of the seed of the Gospel, but Justin says "by which He taught the symbols of righteousness and an active life (ἐνεργῆ βίον)."

JESUS IN HIS OWN COUNTRY

taken by Greeks to mean "the carpenter, or, the son of the carpenter [whom we all knew in Nazareth]." Of course, all this does not exclude the possibility that Jesus, or Joseph, or both, were actually "carpenters" But it makes highly improbable the usual assumption that the term was employed in the first instance with a sense of disparagement.

On our hypothesis (of non-disparagement), the sentence in Mark—which originally perhaps combined "carpenter" and "son of a carpenter," meaning, in effect, "Is not this a prince of Rabbis?"—corresponds in meaning, though not in words, to a long paraphrase in the parallel Luke "And all bare witness unto him, and wondered at the words of grace that came forth out of his mouth" But Luke has erroneously added to this a more literal but incorrect version of Mark's original, in which he has substituted *"son of Joseph"* for *"son of a carpenter."*

As regards what follows in Mark and Matthew, we may suppose that, in spite of this outburst of superficial admiration for Jesus as a mere popular preacher, the Nazarenes speedily relapsed into the reflection that after all He could not be so very different from His brothers and sisters who were quite ordinary people

There is something a little grotesque and abrupt in this argument against the claims of Jesus.—"His sisters are here with us, so that he cannot be a very great prophet" Perhaps Luke the historian omitted it—though very true to human nature—because it was grotesque Mark's context favours the view that he himself interpreted "carpenter" in a disparaging sense. But about that we cannot be sure. We can be sure, however, that, in the first half of the first century[1], a disparagement of "carpenter" that would seem natural to Greeks would seem quite unnatural to Jews.

---

[1] That is, before the Christian "carpenter" had become recognised by Jews in general as their enemy, and referred to by that name, "the Carpenter," in polemical discussions

(Mark vi. 1—6)

If "the carpenter" has this metaphorical meaning, we may perhaps say that as Luke has paraphrased it here, so John has paraphrased it elsewhere in passages where the eloquence of Jesus is described as producing an effect on the crowd But we cannot maintain that there is anything in John corresponding to the Mark-Matthew mention of Christ's "sisters" About Christ's "brethren,' of whom Luke makes no mention here, John makes mention elsewhere in terms that describe them as being out of touch with Christ's disciples and not disposed to believe in Him[1]. The omission of the names James, Joses, Judas and Simon may perhaps be explained by John's general habit of omitting Synoptic names that are not essential to his narrative[2] But as to the "sisters" we must admit that John's silence constitutes an instance of exception to the rule of Johannine Intervention.

§ 9. "*Offended*," *in the Synoptists*

This narrative ("and they were offended in him") contains Mark's second use of the word "offend[3]." The first was in the Parable of the Sower, "when...persecution ariseth...they are *offended*[4]." But the discussion of it was deferred to the present occasion, that its meaning in the narrative of the Evangelist might be compared with its meaning in the lips of Christ The third Marcan instance is transitive, "whosoever shall *offend* one of these little ones[5]." In all these passages A V. has "offend," but the text of R.V. has "stumble" in the

---

[1] Jn vii 5

[2] If the sisters of Jesus had "not the thoughts of Jesus" (see p 111, quoting Origen on Mt xiii 56), that might account for their dropping out of view in all but very early Christian records

[3] Mk vi 3, Mt xiii 57 Luke differs

[4] Mk iv 17 εἶτα γενομένης θλίψεως ἢ διωγμοῦ διὰ τὸν λόγον εὐθὺς σκανδαλίζονται, Mt xiii 21 (sim) γενομένης δὲ.. σκανδαλίζεται, Lk viii 13 ἐν καιρῷ πειρασμοῦ ἀφίστανται

[5] Mk ix 42 (and sim Mt xviii 6, Lk xvii 2) σκανδαλίσῃ ἕνα τῶν μικρῶν τούτων.

JESUS IN HIS OWN COUNTRY

first of them and "cause to stumble" in the third. It will be convenient to retain "offend" for the most part, with the warning that it is used to mean "cause to stumble," so that "I am offended" means "I am caused to stumble." Luke agrees with Mark-Matthew in the warning not to "offend" a "little one," but never uses the word elsewhere except in the saying "Blessed is he that shall not *be offended* in me," where he agrees verbatim with Matthew[1]. He uses it, in all, twice. Yet the word is very freely used by Mark and the parallel Matthew, and also sometimes by Matthew independently.

What induced Luke to avoid this ancient Synoptic word? John, like Luke, uses it but twice. Do John's instances and abstinences throw any light on Luke's motive, and on the meaning, or meanings, of the Greek "offend"? How is it used, if at all, in Greek literature? How in LXX? If there is a Hebrew original, or originals, what are the renderings given by the Targumists and by the Greek translators of the second century? Such are the questions before us.

The Greek for "offend" does not occur in Greek literature. Nor does it occur in the LXX in the transitive ("cause to offend"). It occurs in the canonical LXX once, in the passive, "Many [countries] (R.V.) *shall be overthrown*[2]." There it represents the passive of a Hebrew word (*câshal*) meaning "stumble." But Theodotion's parallel rendering is "be weak," and the LXX itself has previously rendered *câshal* in the same context, no less than four times, by other words[3].

---

[1] Mt xi 6, Lk vii 23. This is in the Double Tradition, commonly called "Q." In the Double Tradition, Luke comparatively seldom differs from the Greek of Matthew.

[2] Dan xi 41.

[3] R.V. also varies. In Dan xi 14 "they shall *fall*," ib 19 "he shall *stumble*," ib 33 "they shall *fall*," Heb has כשל, LXX προσκόπτω. In ib 35 "some of them that be wise shall *fall*, to refine them," LXX has διανοηθήσονται (confusing כשל with שכל which it renders by διανοεῖσθαι in ix 13, 25). In xi 41 "many [countries] shall be

125 (Mark vi. 1—6)

JESUS IN HIS OWN COUNTRY

If we ask why such a recondite Greek word as *scandalizein*
—rather implying "snare" or "trap[1]"—should be used in this
single passage, we may perhaps find it in the conception of
conquered countries as being caught in the snare of the con-
queror. This view is confirmed by two instances in which the
Hebrew of Ben Sira gives, for the passive Greek "offended,"
a Hebrew original (*yâkash*) meaning "ensnared[2]" The Greek
noun *scandalon* mostly corresponds in LXX to two Hebrew
nouns, one of them derived from *câshal*, "stumble," but the
other from *yâkash*, "ensnare[3]." Both these Hebrew nouns are
rendered by one and the same Aramaic noun[4]. It follows that
the Aramaic word used by Jesus in His doctrine about "offending" might have a wide significance according to context,
sometimes implying a retrievable "stumbling," but sometimes
an "ensnaring" almost, or wholly, irretrievable

For example, in the Parable of the Sower, where Mark has

---

overthrown," LXX has σκανδαλισθήσονται Theod has always ἀσθενέω
For a connection between ὁ ἀσθενῶν, ὁ προσκόπτων, and σκάνδαλον,
see Rom xiv 1 τὸν δὲ ἀσθενοῦντα, ib 13 μὴ τιθέναι πρόσκομμα τῷ
ἀδελφῷ ἢ σκάνδαλον, ib 20—21 τῷ διὰ προσκόμματος ἐσθίοντι. .ἐν ᾧ ὁ
ἀδελφός σου προσκόπτει, xv 1 τὰ ἀσθενήματα τῶν ἀδυνάτων

[1] See Steph *Thes* vii 319—20 on σκανδάληθρον the "trigger" in
a mousetrap, and on σκάνδαλον explained by Hesychius as τὸ ἐν ταῖς
μυάγραις It is metaph in Aristoph *Ach* 687 "mousetraps (σκαν-
δάληθρα) of words "

[2] Sir ix 5 σκανδαλισθῇς (v r σκανδαλίσῃ σε) (תוקש from יקש),
xxxii (Gr xxxv) 15 σκανδαλισθήσεται (יוקש)

[3] Gesen 430 gives the verb יקש as "lay a bait," "lay snares,"
and the noun מוקש as a "bait in a fowler's net," and then "snare,"
but Job xl 24 (R V) "pierce through his nose with a *snare*" is
difficult A V. has "[his] nose pierceth through snares," Rashi
explains "snare" as "instrumenta artificialia piscatorum " Σκάνδαλον
= מכשול (from כשל) in Lev xix. 14, 1 S xxv. 31, Ps cxix 165, but
מוקש (from יקש) in Josh xxiii 13, Judg ii 3, viii 27, 1 S xviii 21,
Ps lxix 22, cvi 36 etc

[4] Onk has (Brederek) תקלא in Lev xix 14 "nor put a *stumbling-
block* before the blind," and also in Exod. x. 7 "a *snare* unto us,"
xxiii 33 etc.

126 (Mark vi 1—6)

JESUS IN HIS OWN COUNTRY

"they are offended," as quoted above, the parallel Luke has a word that would etymologically denote "apostasy[1]." Also Hermas—a writer often closely akin to Mark—says "These are they that have faith indeed, but, having also the riches of this world, when tribulation arises, by reason of their riches and their business-affairs *they deny their Lord*[2]" Something like entanglement in a snare is implied by the context, which speaks of "the deceitfulness of riches[3]."

Luke does not differ from Mark and Matthew as to the warning against "offending little ones." But he omits the sequel ("If thine eye *offend* thee") and the context—which imply that the flesh, as well as the deceitfulness of riches, can "offend[4]" Also he omits Christ's prediction to the disciples "All ye *shall be offended*," and Peter's protest that he, at all events, will not be "*offended*[5]" Apparently Luke thought *scandalizein*—which he perhaps connected with "ensnaring"—too strong a word to describe the temporary and unpremeditated lapse of Peter and the disciples.

We have now to ask what we can learn from the Johannine use, and non-use, of this word

---

[1] In Lk. viii. 13 οἳ πρὸς καιρὸν πιστεύουσιν καὶ ἐν καιρῷ πειρασμοῦ ἀφίστανται, the preceding πιστεύουσιν obliges us to supply ἀπὸ τῆς πίστεως after ἀφίστανται, so that it means "depart from [the faith]," i e apostatize Comp 1 Tim iv 1 ἀποστήσονται τῆς πίστεως

[2] Hermas *Vis* iii 6. 5 Comp Gesen 430 *b* on יקש, in Prov. vi 2, = "*ensnared*, in business entanglements"

[3] Mk iv 19, Mt. xiii 22, ἡ ἀπάτη τοῦ πλούτου, parall to Lk viii 14, which does not mention ἀπάτη

[4] Mk ix 43 foll, Mt xviii 8 foll Luke also omits Mk xiv. 38, Mt xxvi 41, "the flesh is weak (ἀσθενής)"

[5] Mk xiv 27, Mt xxvi 31 (adding "in me") The parallel Luke has in the context (xxii 31) Σίμων, Σίμων, ἰδοὺ ὁ Σατανᾶς ἐξῃτήσατο ὑμᾶς τοῦ σινιάσαι ὡς τὸν σῖτον Comp Dan xi 35 "Some of them that be wise *shall fall* (or, *be offended*) to refine them," quoted above (p 125, n. 3), where LXX has "*shall bethink themselves*"

JESUS IN HIS OWN COUNTRY

§ 10. *"Offended," in John*

"Offending" is not mentioned by John till he describes a "murmuring" of "disciples" against Christ's teaching in Capernaum[1]. The teaching begins by referring to "the living bread," and proceeds to the gift of Christ's "flesh" and "blood." At first, it is only the Jews that murmur, saying, "Is not this Jesus, the son of Joseph, whose father and mother we know[2]?" Then, as the doctrine rises in paradox, "The Jews strove with one another, saying, How can this man give us his flesh to eat[3]?" Still it is only "the Jews." But at last, when the climax is reached, "many of his disciples, when they heard [it], said, This is a hard saying, who can hear it[4]?" And now Jesus for the first time introduces the word in question, implying, not indeed that the disciples have already "been offended" but that they are on the brink of it "Jesus, knowing in himself that his disciples were murmuring about this, said unto them, Is this *offending* you[5]?"

This saying should be read with what comes early in the narrative, namely the purpose of the multitude to make Jesus a king, and also with what concludes the narrative—the saying of Jesus "Was it not I that chose you, the Twelve? And one of you is a devil," followed by the Evangelistic statement

---

[1] Mk ii 1 "Capernaum" is parall to Mt ix 1 "his own city" Some confusion might arise from various interpretations of a tradition that "they murmured against Jesus *in His own house*" meaning (*Son* 3460 c) "among His own disciples," but wrongly taken to mean "among His own folk," i e in Nazareth, Capernaum or Galilee

[2] Jn vi 42 This resembles the Synoptic comments assigned to Christ's hearers in "his own country" (Mk vi 3, Mt xiii 55, Lk iv 22) But John does not say that these Jews "were offended"

[3] Jn vi 52   [4] Jn vi 60.

[5] Jn vi 61 τοῦτο ὑμᾶς σκανδαλίζει, The present tense here seems to have an inceptive force, describing a process that is just, or almost, beginning and is to be arrested.

JESUS IN HIS OWN COUNTRY

"Now he spake of Judas[1]." Then it will be seen that the "offending" involves a stumbling at the Law of self-sacrifice, a falling back which Jesus regards as originating from "the ruler of this world," who is already acting on Judas, and, through Judas, attempting to cause the Twelve to "go away" from Him. This falling back is implied in the words "From this [time] many of his disciples *departed backward* and would no longer walk with him. Jesus therefore said to the Twelve, Can it be that even ye desire to *go away*[2]?" This means, in effect, that many of Christ's disciples "*were offended*," in a sense approaching to apostasy or denial of their Master, and the context suggests that Jesus regarded such apostasy not only as being a falling back from the Son of God but also as indicating a tendency to follow after, or worship, Satan, "the ruler of this world[3]."

In the same serious sense does Jesus repeat the word "offended" to His disciples, when He warns them, on the night before the crucifixion, of the persecution that awaits them. "These things have I spoken unto you that *ye may not be offended*...whosoever killeth you shall think that he doeth service to God[4]." In word, this almost amounts to a contradiction of the Mark-Matthew tradition "All ye shall *be offended*[5]." But it is not a contradiction in thought. Only John expresses the Synoptic thought differently, thus. "The

---

[1] Jn vi 15, ib 70—71

[2] Jn vi 66—7 ἀπῆλθον εἰς τὰ ὀπίσω ὑπάγειν implies that εἰς τὰ ὀπίσω should be repeated after ὑπάγειν. In the Parable of the Sower, where Mark iv 17 has "they *are offended*," the parall Luke viii 13 ἀφίστανται is rendered by Delitzsch "they *depart backward*"

[3] Such "following" is not mentioned here, but it seems to be implied by the context. Several passages of the Gospels and Epistles teach us that men must serve one of "two masters," and that Satan claims authority over all the kingdoms of the earth and offers it to those who worship him, and Jesus Himself recognises that, in some sense, Satan is "ruler of this world" for those who do not accept the Son of God as having "overcome the world."

[4] Jn xvi 1—2   [5] Mk xiv 27, Mt xxvi 31

hour cometh, yea, is come, that *ye shall be scattered, every man to his own, and shall leave me alone*[1]" That is to say, the "stumbling," or "being offended," of Peter and the Twelve was not to be a deliberate going backward from Christ, or a going after Satan, like the treachery of Judas. Against that Jesus took measures to secure them. But He could not secure them against a flight for safety, caused by temporary panic, like the temporary "stumbling," predicted in Daniel, which was to befall even some of "the wise," in order to "refine" them[2].

Concerning that other kind of "stumbling" in which a man causes others to "stumble" or "be offended" John says nothing in his Gospel, but he probably refers to it in the Epistle, as follows "He that saith he is in the light and hateth his brother is in the darkness even until now. He that loveth his brother abideth in the light, and there is no *scandalon*, i.e. *stumbling-block*, or *cause-of-offence, in him*[3]" This resembles the words of the Psalmist "Great peace have they that love thy law, and *there is no stumbling-block to them*[4]." But the Psalm, which has "*to them*," means simply (as A.V.) "Nothing shall offend them" The Epistle, which has "*in him*," enlarges the meaning. "In him there is no cause of stumbling [either for himself or for others]"

In the Epistle, "he that loveth his brother" is assumed also to love God as Father, so that there is a chain of causes and effects :—(1) "love of the Father," (2) "love of the brethren," (3) "light," (4) "no stumbling-block" Antithetical to this, there would be (1) "idolatry" or homage to "the ruler of this

---

[1] Jn xvi 32
[2] Dan xi 35 On the startling words peculiar to Matthew (xvi 23, addressed to Peter) σκάνδαλον εἶ ἐμοῦ, see *Joh Gr* **2566**c They are omitted by the parall Mk viii 33, which will be discussed later on
[3] 1 Jn ii 9—10 σκάνδαλον ἐν αὐτῷ οὐκ ἔστιν. "Is" is emphatic, "Cause-of-stumbling, in him, has no existence"
[4] Ps cxix 165 οὐκ ἔστιν αὐτοῖς σκάνδαλον

JESUS IN HIS OWN COUNTRY

world," (2) "hate of the brethren," (3) "darkness," (4) "stumbling." Similarly, in Ezekiel, stumbling is connected with idolatry· "Son of man, these men have *taken their idols into their heart, and put the stumbling-block of their iniquity* before their face[1]" Jewish tradition explains Ezekiel's peculiar doctrine connecting "stumbling-block" and "iniquity," as referring to the unmasking of "hypocrites[2]" Thus, although John never uses the Synoptic word "hypocrite," we perceive, through Ezekiel, that John expresses a condemnation of the *thing*, in words of his own that help us to realise what the thing is

John also helps us to think for ourselves in an intelligent and Christian spirit about the meaning of another important Biblical word, namely, "desire"—such "desire" as is the cause of "stumbling." Mark says, in the Parable of the Sower, somewhat obscurely, that the good seed is choked by "the desires concerning the remaining things[3]" This might be regarded as meaning that "desire," in itself, is evil. And Paul might be regarded as meaning the same thing when he (too briefly) quotes the Law as saying "Thou shalt not *desire*[4]"

---

[1] Ezek xiv 3.

[2] See *Son* 3553 i, quoting Ezek iii 20 ("if he commit *iniquity* and I lay a *stumbling-block* before him") with Rashi "He does his own deeds in secret, and shews himself off as just," and with *Joma* 87 a which infers that "*hypocrites* are to be *unmasked*" Comp Jn iii 19—20 "men loved the darkness rather than the light, for their deeds were evil For everyone that doeth ill hateth the light and cometh not to the light lest his deeds should be reproved"

[3] Mk iv 19 αἱ περὶ τὰ λοιπὰ (Delitzsch שְׁאָר הדברים) ἐπιθυμίαι There is perhaps some error In LXX, λοιπά is represented by שְׁאֵר, which also means "flesh," and by יתר which also means "superfluous" Either of these words would make better sense than λοιπά

[4] Rom vii 7, and xiii 9 where it is quoted after "thou shalt not steal," without any modifying words such as are given in Exod xx 17 "Thou shalt not desire *thy neighbour's house* ." The Targum uses the Heb in Exod, חמד, in a bad sense (as it is always used in Aram), but in Heb (Gesen 326) it is sometimes used in a good sense Paul uses ἐπιθυμέω, briefly, in a bad sense But in LXX and

JESUS IN HIS OWN COUNTRY

The Law did not forbid "desire." It merely forbade *desire of that which belongs to one's neighbour*. All God's fatherly gifts, the visible as well as the invisible, may rightly be "desired," and may come to a man with the divine blessing, increasing his love for the Giver and Father

The only Johannine mention of desire is in Christ's saying to the Jews, "Ye are from [your] father the devil, and *the desires* of your father it is your will to do[1]." The Jews had just protested, "We were not born of fornication[2], we have one Father, even God." Jesus is contradicting their protest. The many "desires" of Satan are here tacitly contrasted with the will of the "one Father." And love, as in the Epistle, so in the Gospel, is made the test that convicts the hypocritical idolater, who worships Satan in worshipping himself· "If God were your Father ye would love me."

Thus, in order to explain and reinforce the Synoptic negative doctrine, which warns us against "stumbling" or "being offended," or against "offending" others, the Fourth Gospel gives us a positive doctrine about love, and peace, and the unity of man with the Father through the Son—which make all stumbling impossible. Where the Psalmist says "*Great peace have they that love thy Law*, and there is no occasion of stumbling to (*or*, for) them," John, in effect, teaches us, in the place of "thy Law," to read "thy Son." Moreover, he leads us to substitute, for the negative "no occasion of stumbling," the positive "peace." For he brings Jesus before us as saying,

---

N T it often has a good sense. See Origen *Comm Joann* xx 20 (Lomm ii 246) κατὰ τὰς θείας γραφὰς ἡ ἐπιθυμία τῶν μέσων ἐστίν

[1] Jn viii 44

[2] See Ezek xvi 15, 26, etc on this metaphor. Comp Clem Alex 551—2 on πλεονεξία as being called πορνεία, and as being opposed to αὐτάρκεια. He adds καὶ ὡς εἰδωλολατρεία ἐκ τοῦ ἑνὸς εἰς τοὺς πολλοὺς ἐπινέμησίς ἐστι θεοῦ, οὕτως ἡ πορνεία ἐκ τοῦ ἑνὸς γάμου εἰς τοὺς πολλοὺς ἐστιν ἔκπτωσις. A thought of this kind is latent in Jn iv. 17—18 "thou hast had five husbands" and comp Philo i 131 on the "seducer (φθορεύς)" who acts through the five senses

JESUS IN HIS OWN COUNTRY

at first negatively, "These things have I spoken unto you *that ye may not be made to stumble*," but afterwards, positively, "These things have I spoken unto you *that in me ye may have peace*. In the world ye have tribulation, but be of good cheer; I have overcome the world[1]."

§ 11. *"Not without-honour," in Mark and Matthew*[2]

The Greek adjective, *atīmos*, here applied to a "prophet" and rendered by R V "without honour," was often applied to persons by Attic writers, but only in the sense of "disfranchised." And Greek writers in general used it to mean "dishonoured" rather than "without honour[3]." Origen explains the word as implying *"treating as an outlaw," "persecuting,"* and as referring to the treatment of Christ by the

---

[1] Jn xvi 1, 33

Space has not allowed us to discuss John's use of προσκόπτειν —which expresses "stumbling" without conveying any notion of "ensnaring." It is not used by the Synoptists except in Mt iv 6 and Lk iv 11 (both quoting Ps xci 12) and Mt vii 27 (*"smote upon* that house"). It occurs in Jn xi 9—10 "Are there not twelve hours in the day? If a man walk in the day he *stumbleth* not . . But if a man walk in the night he *stumbleth*"—uttered by Jesus when resolving to go into Judaea, at the peril of His life, in order to raise Lazarus from death

The Johannine passage seems to mean that even if a man dies while attempting to do God's work in God's appointed work-time of "twelve hours," he does not really "stumble (προσκόπτω)." As to the "twelve hours," see *Pesikt* (Wu p 173, a Midrash on Cant viii 1) where Joseph says to his brethren that he is bound to help them, for it would be against the course of nature to do otherwise "Ye represent the course of the world. The day hath twelve hours, the night hath twelve hours. can I alter the course of the world?" Another version (quoted in Wu *ib* p 173 n) adds "My father [*i e* Jacob] begot you, and shall I bury you?"

[2] Mk vi 4, Mt xiii 57 οὐκ ἄτιμος, Lk iv 24 οὐδεὶς δεκτός

[3] With a negative, and applied to things, *"not dishonourable"* may mean *"honourable,"* but the *Thesaurus*, which gives no instance of this applied to persons, quotes only (col 2377) Aesch *Sept.* 589 οὐκ ἄτιμον ἐλπίζω μόρον

Jews as a whole¹ In the LXX it represents Hebrew words thrice—once "without-name" and once "lightly-esteemed²." In the third instance, where Isaiah says, of the Suffering Servant, "*he was despised*," the LXX says "*his form was without-honour (atīmon)*³" This is a passage that has greatly influenced early Christian literature

Justin Martyr represents Trypho the Jew as saying "Your so-called Christ was *atīmos* and *without-glory (adoxos)*, so that he actually incurred the extreme curse [contained] in the Law of God, for he was crucified⁴" But this is, so to speak, a trap made for Trypho to fall into. For Justin replies at once that this argument might have held good, but for the prophecy that he, Justin, had previously quoted "If I had not explained from the scriptures that I quoted above that *His form would be without-glory* and *his generation inexpressible*... " Justin is referring to Isaiah's description of the Suffering Servant, which he has previously quoted in full, and which contains many references to the absence of "glory⁵" Justin does not on this occasion repeat the word "*atīmos*" Elsewhere *he repeatedly uses it with allusion to this prophecy, as referring to Christ's first Advent, but almost always inserts some phrase denoting that the "atīmia" was temporary and earthly, referring merely to outward "form," "appearance," or "presence"* Nowhere does he say—what he makes Trypho say—that Christ Himself was "*atīmos*⁶"

---

¹ Origen on Mt xiii 57 (Lomm iii 47—51) uses ἀτιμάζω and ἀτιμόω repeatedly Moses, he says (*ib* 49) ἠτιμώθη among his countrymen when they tried to stone him, "And his 'country' was not the stones of this or that place [*i e* city] but those following him, the people"

² Job xxx 8, Is iii 5

³ Is liii 3 נבזה (nif of בזה), LXX ἀλλὰ τὸ εἶδος αὐτοῦ ἄτιμον, Sym ἐξουδενωμένος

⁴ Justin Martyr *Tryph* § 32 ἄτιμος καὶ ἄδοξος γέγονεν . ἐσταυρώθη γάρ

⁵ *Tryph* § 13, quoting Is liii 14 foll (LXX) οὕτως ἀδοξήσει τὸ εἶδος καὶ ἡ δόξα σου. οὐκ ἔστιν εἶδος αὐτῷ οὐδὲ δόξα..

⁶ Justin quotes ἄτιμος in *Apol* § 50 and alludes to it in *ib* § 52 (with ὡς), *Tryph* §§ 14, 36, 49, 85, 100, 110, 121

JESUS IN HIS OWN COUNTRY

It has been shewn that the Hebrew in Isaiah, corresponding to LXX "*his form was without-honour (atīmon)*," is "he was despised," and is rendered by Symmachus "[he was] set at naught[1]." "Set at naught" is applied by Mark alone to the sufferings of Christ as predicted by Jesus[2], and by Luke alone to the contumelious treatment of Christ by Herod[3] When the Hebrew of Isaiah repeats "he was despised" in the same verse, the LXX renders it "he was dishonoured[4]" This word occurs in Christ's words—apart from parables—only once in the Gospels, "I honour my Father and ye dishonour me," uttered shortly before the attempt of the Jews to stone Him[5].

These facts give us glimpses into the reasons that might induce early Christians to use, or not use, the word *atīmos* in the description of Christ's reception by His own people. The use of it might seem to Mark (followed by Matthew) to point to a fulfilment of Isaiah's prophecy. But to the later Evangelists—conveying as it did to Greeks the sense of civic degradation—the word might seem inappropriate to the circumstances The circumstances might fairly be said to warrant no more than this—a complaint that a prophet, in his own neighbourhood, did not find (1) "*a favourable reception*" or (2) "*honour*" Of these two interpretations, Luke adopts the former, John the latter[6].

---

[1] Is liii 3 Sym ἐξουδενωμένος "He was despised" is repeated later in the same verse, and similarly rendered by Aq ἐξουδενωμένος.

[2] Mk ix 12 ἐξουδενηθῇ (om by parall Mt xvii 12, Lk omits the whole)

[3] Lk xxiii 11

[4] LXX Ἠτιμάσθη (not ἠτιμώθη), Aq ἐξουδενωμένος

[5] Jn viii 49 ἀτιμάζετε followed by (viii 59) "they took up stones" Ἀτιμάζω occurs nowhere else in the Gospels except in the Parable of the Vineyard, Mk xii 4 parall to Lk xx 11 in connection with "wounding in the head" or "scourging"

[6] Lk iv 24 "No prophet is *acceptable* (or [*favourably*] *received*) (δεκτός)," Jn iv 44 "a prophet.. hath not honour (τιμὴν οὐκ ἔχει)" Jn iv 45 "the Galilaeans *received* (ἐδέξαντο) him" seems, at first sight, a complete contradiction to Luke But John goes on to say

(Mark vi 1—6)

JESUS IN HIS OWN COUNTRY

No new spiritual truth emerges from these Lucan and Johannine corrections of the ancient Mark-Matthew tradition about *atīmos* as applied to the Saviour. But they exemplify the difficulties of rendering the Gospel into Greek in the earliest days of the Church They help us to realise cross-currents of Greek and Jewish thoughts, meeting and jostling each other in Christian interpretations of the Prophets, and especially of Isaiah, when prophecy became the basis—not avowed but latent—of Evangelistic expression[1]

Moreover the Fourfold Tradition at this point is also of special interest as an instance of Johannine Intervention, because John does not exactly support Mark against Luke, but rather explains Mark, and, as it were, apologizes for him Indeed, as to the meaning of the text, he seems to correct Mark in a Lucan direction, but he does it with the minimum of verbal alteration, as if saying· "Luke substitutes '*acceptable*' for

---

that the reason why they "*received*" Him was that they had been to Jerusalem and had seen the wonders that He had performed there This suggests the thought "If the Galilaeans 'received' Jesus, it was not as 'neighbours' receiving a prophet belonging to their 'neighbourhood,' but because some of their number had reported at home what He had done away from home, in Jerusalem"

Comp Lk iv 23 "Whatsoever we have heard done *at Capernaum*, do also here in thine own country" Luke's tradition resembles John's, but with important differences (1) In Luke, the Nazarenes are regarded as murmuring because the works reported to have been done elsewhere were not done in their presence, in John, the Galilaeans are regarded as receiving Jesus because of those works (2) In Luke, the "elsewhere" is Capernaum, in John, it is Jerusalem

[1] The word ἄτιμος (sing) does not occur in the Early Fathers except Clem Rom § 16, and there as a quotation from Isaiah liii 3 (LXX) [The pl ἄτιμοι occurs only in Clem Rom § 3 as a quotation from Is iii 5, where LXX has sing] In the early Apologists, it does not occur except as quoted above from Justin Martyr—where, with the exception of one pl instance (*Apol* § 9 ἀτίμων σκευῶν, comp Rom ix. 21 ὃ μὲν εἰς τιμὴν σκεῦος, ὃ δὲ εἰς ἀτιμίαν), it practically always alludes to Is liii 2—3 Clem Alex 252 explains Is liii 3 ἄτιμον εἶδος as referring merely to Christ's outward appearance.

(Mark vi 1—6)

JESUS IN HIS OWN COUNTRY

Mark's '*not-honourable*,' which, for Greeks, often means 'disfranchised.' Luke is quite right. But the same result may be effected by a less violent change, simply altering '*is not-honourable*' into '*has not...honour*'"

§ 12 "*And he was not able to do there any mighty work*," in Mark[1]

Origen in his commentary on the parallel Matthew ("and he did not many mighty works there") calls attention to Mark's words "He did not say '*was not willing*,' but '*was not able*', for there had to come toward the energizing mighty work a joint-action from the faith of him on whom the mighty work was energizing..."[2] Luke's context differs so widely from Mark's that we cannot attach much importance to his omission of "was not able." But Matthew's omission of the Marcan "*was not able*," in the midst of an otherwise Mark-following narrative, makes the passage conspicuously suitable for testing the Rule of Johannine Intervention.

John not only adopts the bold saying but also extends its application and places it in the mouth of Jesus Himself. "*The Son is not able to do anything from himself—[anything] except he see the Father doing something, for such things as he [i e the Father] is doing, these things also the Son likewise doeth*[3]" These words, though applicable to all action on the part of the Son, and though applied later on to the action of "judging[4],"

---

[1] Mk vi 5 καὶ οὐκ ἐδύνατο ἐκεῖ ποιῆσαι οὐδεμίαν δύναμιν , Mt xiii 58 καὶ οὐκ ἐποίησεν ἐκεῖ δυνάμεις πολλάς Lk omits the whole

[2] Origen on Mt xiii 58 ὡς ἐρχομένης μὲν ἐπὶ τὴν ἐνεργοῦσαν δύναμιν συμπράξεως ὑπὸ πίστεως ἐκείνου εἰς ὃν ἐνήργει ἡ δύναμις. . He adds that this is "hindered from energizing by the [man's] faithlessness (κωλυομένης δὲ ἐνεργεῖν ὑπὸ τῆς ἀπιστίας)" Thus the light may fall on our eyes, but it is "hindered from energizing" if we keep them closed There is a need of our σύμπραξις, i e opening our eyes

[3] Jn v 19

[4] Jn v 30 "I am not able from myself to do anything, as I hear, I judge"

refer primarily to the healing of a man on the sabbath. What Origen said about the necessity of a *"combined-action (sumpraxis)"* if a "mighty work" was to be performed, John also teaches—but with a difference. Origen spoke of the "combined-action" of the sick man and his Healer. John speaks of the simultaneous action of the Son and the Father, who gives to the Son insight into the condition of the diseased man and a power—or perhaps we should say a command—to heal his disease. The Father appears to be regarded as saying to the Son about this or that particular sufferer "This man has faith to be healed by thee, or this man has the germ or spark of faith ready to spring into flame at thy word. I give thee this man to heal." This is not inconsistent with Origen's view of *sumpraxis*. But it is wider, and deeper, and it helps us to understand the cure at the pool of Bethesda, where the sufferer was hardly capable of "combined action" in any degree at first, and only in a slight degree even after he had been healed, since he did not know who had healed him.

If we pursued this subject further, discussing the Marcan doctrine about what God or man was *"able"* to do, or about what was *"possible,"* we should be carried on to much later periods in the Gospel narrative. Suffice it to say, here, that Mark, in such sayings as "All things are *possible* to him that believeth" and "All things are *possible* unto thee[1]," has committed himself to traditions that are probably historically accurate and of great spiritual value, but at the same time liable to be misunderstood and perverted by opponents of the Christians. Epictetus declines to read the discussions of the Greek philosophers about "things-possible." On that subject, if any one asks him, "Which of these tenets do you hold?" he says he shall reply "I do not know[2]", he also ventures

---

[1] Mk ix. 23, xiv. 36, not in the parallel Matthew-Luke.
[2] Epict. ii. 19. 5—9. The words (*ib.* 9) "Chrysippus has written wonderfully [well] in the First Book on Things Possible (ἐν τῷ πρώτῳ περὶ δυνατῶν)" are uttered *to* Epictetus, not *by* Epictetus.

JESUS IN HIS OWN COUNTRY

to say that Zeus "*was not able*" to persuade all men to believe the truth, and even to introduce Zeus as saying "*If it had been practicable*, Epictetus, I would have done so-and-so for you[1]."

In taking this view, Epictetus is not so far removed from Hebrew thought as we might at first sight assume. The word "Almighty," so frequent in our English Versions of the Old Testament, represents, in Hebrew, "*Shaddai*," which would almost certainly be regarded by Jews in the first century as implying "the Giver of Good" In the LXX, "*Almighty*" (*Pantokratôr*)—besides rendering "*Shaddai*"—is also used to render "*of Hosts (Sabaoth)*" in "the Lord *of Hosts*." Neither of these Hebrew titles denotes "almightiness[2]"

John's method of dealing with this difficult, this insoluble, question[3]—of things "possible" and "impossible" for the Son of God—may be stated, first, in its negative, then in its positive, aspect Negatively, the Evangelist avoids the use of the words "*possible*," "*impossible*," and of the kindred word for miracle, which we render "*mighty-work*" (but which might also mean "*potentiality*," so that to a Greek it is connected with the thought of possibility[4]). Also, whereas all the Synoptists use the verb signifying ability or possibility, "to *be able*," without a negative, in the leper's petition to Jesus, "If thou

---

[1] Epict iv 6 5, 1 1 10, εἰ οἷόν τε ἦν
[2] See παντοκράτωρ in *Oxf Conc* , also *Notes* **2998** (xxvii) *f—m* on "Almighty," and *Son* **3120** *a—c*, **3123** *a*
[3] Note that the first use of ἀδυνατέω in LXX is in Gen xviii 14 (Heb) "Is any thing (*lit* word) too hard for (*lit* from) the Lord?" This refers to the promise of a son previously made to Sarah, so that the meaning of "word" might here be "*word* [*of promise*]" But the Targumists, both Onkelos and Jer Targ , have "Is any thing *concealed* from the Lord?" and Rashi adopts it (though *Gen r. ad loc* does not)
[4] That is to say, δύναμις John does not use δύναμις, "*mighty-work*," or δυνατός, "*possible*," or ἀδύνατος, "*impossible*" All the Synoptists, besides frequently using δύναμις, use ἀδύνατος and δυνατός in Mk x 27, Mt xix 26, Lk xviii 27

wilt, *thou art able* to cleanse me¹," John never uses the verb except with a negative, or an interrogative implying a negative With a negative, he applies it, as we have seen, to the Son "The Son is *not able* to do..," "I am *not able* to do²"

So much for the negative point of view. From the positive point of view, Christ's miracles in the Fourth Gospel are regarded as "*signs*" or as works "*given*" to the Son by the Father. John introduces them as "*signs*" without telling us, at the moment, what they are signs of "This beginning of *signs* did Jesus" But the following words, "and manifested his glory³," explain how they are "signs" The first Biblical mention of "signs" refers to the heavenly bodies They were created "for *signs*" as well as "for seasons," and part of their work, as "*signs*," was to make "the heavens declare the glory of God⁴" So the "signs" of Jesus declared the glory of the Father through the Son

These "signs" were also gifts, and Jesus calls them "the works that the Father *hath given me*⁵" He also repeatedly describes as "given" to Himself those whom He has spiritually healed, and brought into the circle of His disciples "All that which the Father *giveth* me will come unto me, and him that cometh to me I will in no wise cast out⁶." In effect, the Fourth Gospel may be said to substitute for "God Almighty" "God the Giver" The Father gives His Son to die for the world, He also gives the Church to the Son; and when the Son prays to the Father for the disciples "Keep them in *thy name that thou hast given me*⁷," it is implied that the relation between the Father and the Son is not only one of perfect unity, but also one in which God the Father is to be regarded as giving Himself

---

¹ Mk 1 40, Mt viii 2, Lk v 12, all having δύνασαι
² Jn v 19, 30   ³ Jn ii 11
⁴ Gen 1 14, Ps. xix 1   ⁵ Jn v. 36
⁶ Jn vi 37 See *Joh Gr* **2740** on πᾶν ὃ δέδωκας in Jn
⁷ Jn xvii 11

to the Son and the Son as giving Himself to the Father, and in both cases the gift is for the sake of man

Reviewing this Johannine doctrine we perceive that John does not attempt to reconcile the Creator's foreknowledge and almightiness with the existence of sin in His human creatures. He ventures to represent Jesus as saying *"Was it not I that chose you the Twelve?* And one of you is a devil"*,* and, later on, to the Twelve, *"*I speak not of you all, *I know whom I chose;* but—that the scripture might be fulfilled, 'He that eateth my bread lifted up his heel against me'"; and, later still—when Judas had gone out—"*I chose you,* and appointed you that ye should go and bear fruit...*I chose you out of the world*[1]*"* We are not told when Judas began to become "a devil" The Evangelist perhaps assumes that, when Judas was first "chosen," he was a sincere follower of Jesus, but that, when the doctrine of self-sacrifice was proclaimed, the "hard saying" repelled him, and he fell back into a darkness that became antagonism to his Master. All this, however, is not stated We are left to infer it from what we are told later on, that Christ's "choosing" was for a certain purpose, to be fulfilled by the person chosen, namely, to *"bear fruit"* If the chosen one, the branch in the Vine, does not "bear fruit," then the Husbandman "taketh it away[2]"

This might lead us to say, " Then the Evangelist commits himself to the view that God's 'election' is not absolute " But this, if true, would not be the whole truth or a fair statement of the truth. It would be truer to say that he leads his readers to refrain from committing themselves to any views about "election" that might interfere with their trust in divine love and righteousness, and their sense of a consequent responsibility and duty to make a return,—which their consciences

---

[1] Jn vi 70, xiii 18, xv 16—19
[2] Jn xv. 2 "Every branch in me that beareth not fruit, he taketh it away "

JESUS IN HIS OWN COUNTRY

tell them they can make—of human love and human righteousness. He uses the term "electing" in different senses—perhaps deliberately—now including, now excluding Judas

Not improbably John has Synoptic usage in mind Mark, alone of the Synoptists, uses the strong phrase "*the elect whom he* [i e *God*] *elected*¹", Luke, alone of the Synoptists, describes Jesus as "*having elected* twelve" out of the mass of the disciples². Mark's phrase would probably exclude Judas; Luke includes him. John, in two of the three passages in which he describes Jesus as avowing that He "chose" or "elected" disciples, represents Him as including Judas and as presaging evil ("one of you is a devil," "but—in order that the Scripture might be fulfilled³") The third passage drops all presage except of good ("I chose you...that ye should go and bear fruit...I chose you out of the world⁴") None the less, since they are still to be, locally and actively, "in the world," He prays for them to the Father "I pray not that thou shouldst take them from the world, but that thou shouldst keep them from the evil [one]⁵."

This doctrine teaches all of us—even those of us who are most confident that they belong to "the elect"—to feel that we need this prayer of the Saviour in our behalf We are to fix our thoughts not on His constraining "might" but on His constraining "love" Love cannot constrain by anything except by itself. Not even the Love of the Father in heaven

---

¹ Mk xiii. 20. Comp Mk xiii 22 "to deceive, if [it were] possible, *the elect*," where Mt xxiv 24 adds "*even*" before "*the elect*" (Luke omits the whole) Clem Alex 969 (*Fragm*) says that "the men of the calling (τοὺς μὲν τῆς κλήσεως ἀνθρώπους) will be led astray at the coming of Antichrist, but it is impossible for the elect, wherefore He says '*even, if* [*it were*] *possible, my elect*'"

² Lk vi 13, ἐκλεξάμενος The parall Mk iii 13—14, Mt. x 2 do not use ἐκλέγομαι

³ Jn vi 70, xiii 18.   ⁴ Jn xv 16—19

⁵ Jn xvii 15

JESUS IN HIS OWN COUNTRY

"is able to do any mighty work" in a heart that will not receive the Spirit of His Son

§ 13. *"And he marvelled because of their unbelief,"* in Mark[1]

Matthew (as well as Luke) omits this. The Greek word in canonical LXX, when meaning "marvel," often implies astonishment or dumb dismay[2]. In Greek literature its meaning varies. Pythagoras said that the fruit of philosophy was to *"wonder at* nothing," and Plutarch protests against the abuse of this maxim by "many[3]." It has probably influenced Horace, Epictetus, and Seneca, in their use of the word or its Latin equivalent[4]. In *Johannine Vocabulary* it is shewn that John mostly, if not always, uses the word in a bad sense[5]. That being so, we ought not to expect him to intervene verbally in behalf of Mark. And, as a fact, he nowhere describes Jesus, on any occasion, as "marvelling." Are we then to say that this is a case where, owing to special verbal circumstances, the rule of Johannine Intervention is broken?

Possibly it is so. But it is worth noting that, on the only other occasion (beside this Marcan one) where Synoptic writers describe Jesus as "marvelling," the "marvel" is represented by Matthew and Luke (not by Mark, who omits the narrative) as being caused, not by *"unbelief"* (as here in Mark) but by *"belief*[6]*."* This coincidence (or we may call it anticoincidence?) leads us to ask whether Hebrew Prophecy on any occasion represents the Lord Himself as "marvelling", and, if so, how the Greek translators rendered the Hebrew; and whether the

---

[1] Mk vi 6
[2] See *Oxf Conc* (excluding the phrase θαυμάζω πρόσωπον)
[3] Plutarch *Mor* 44 c (*De Audiendo*, § 13)
[4] See Schweig Epict 1 29 3, quoting Hor *Epist* 1 6 1 "Nil admirari," and Seneca *Epist* 45 praising "*mirabilia* calcantem"
[5] *Joh Voc* **1673** *a—b*
[6] Mt viii 10, Lk. vii 9. The marvel is caused by the "faith," or "belief," of a centurion

JESUS IN HIS OWN COUNTRY

context may have any bearing on our Marcan passage, and further, by what indirect means John might approximate to a representation of the Messiah as in some sense "marvelling" even though he could not bring himself to use the word

Isaiah twice uses the word concerning the Lord, the Redeemer of Israel, at the moment when the nation had gone astray from "judgment", "The Lord saw it, and it displeased him that there was no judgment, and he saw that there was no man, and *marvelled* that there was no intercessor," whereupon the Lord Himself "put on righteousness as a breastplate" to come to their help[1] The Septuagint (but not Aquila) misrenders this, so does the Targum, Jewish comment (such as there is) suggests a various reading for "*marvelled*," or explains it as meaning "*was silent*[2]"

John nowhere represents Jesus as being "silent," or as being silenced by "astonishment," in view of human "unbelief" On the contrary, in the Fourth Gospel, Jesus appears to regard inability to believe as necessary in some men—the men being what they are Emphasizing "*ye*" as if it were "ye of all people"—Jesus says to the Jews "How are *ye* able to believe, [ye] who receive glory one from another and seek not the glory that cometh from the only God[3]?" And John, in his own person, says about them "For this cause *they were not able to believe*," namely, because they were blinded to the glory and love of God by their love for the glory of men[4]. Having written about Jesus, early in the Gospel, "He knew what was in man[5]," John could not consistently describe Him as "astonished" by what He "knew"

---

[1] Is lix 15—17 (comp lxiii 5)

[2] Is lix 16 κατενόησε, Targ "notum est coram eo", Rashi, "conticuit", sée his context, and Ibn Ezra (who dissents from Menahem's connecting the passage with Numb xxiv 3 שׁתֻם) In Is lxiii 5, LXX προσενόησα, Aq has ἐξηπορήθην

[3] Jn v 44 πῶς δύνασθε ὑμεῖς πιστεῦσαι,

[4] Jn xii 39   [5] Jn ii 25

JESUS IN HIS OWN COUNTRY

This is true, and yet it is not the whole truth. Jesus is regarded in the Fourth Gospel as knowing at a very early date the future treachery of Judas. And yet, when it is close at hand, He is "troubled in spirit", and, just before that, as though brought face to face with the divine decree, not in collision, but in silent resignation, He says "I know whom I have chosen, but—that the scripture may be fulfilled.¹" The Saviour is not "astonished," but He is brought to a position where He recognises that He can do nothing as a Saviour for a soul that He desires to save, and this "troubles" Him

It is reasonable to conclude that John, though not intervening in any definite way in favour of Mark, might be said to intervene against a superficial interpretation of all the Synoptists, in order to point out that Jesus never "marvelled" and never encouraged others to "marvel," in the sense of mere amazement and astonishment. That conclusion is reasonable because those for whom John wrote, even if they did not discuss the superficial difference between Mark and the two later Synoptists, would be likely to talk about the "admiration," "wonder," or "marvel," ascribed to the Messiah by all the Synoptists alike in defiance of philosophic doctrine

Beyond that, we cannot speak with the same confidence. But we may also, though with less confidence, regard it as probable that John went further in his allusive thought, somewhat to this effect "I find Mark saying that the Messiah '*marvelled*' because of the '*unbelief*' of His neighbours at Nazareth, while Matthew and Luke say that He '*marvelled*' because of the '*belief*' of a centurion. Both sayings are correct in a certain sense. But in the Greek world they are likely to be misinterpreted. Of the two sayings, Mark's comes nearer to the general truth. Jesus said to a nobleman, 'Except ye, the dwellers at Capernaum, see signs and wonders, *ye will assuredly*

---

¹ Jn xiii 21, 18 (comp xvii 12).

A L 145 (Mark vi 1—6) 10

JESUS IN HIS OWN COUNTRY

not believe[1]'—increasing the man's own belief, but certainly not praising it, and rather suggesting a general dispraise. Before this, He said to Nicodemus 'If I told you [and your friends] earthly things and ye believe not, how shall ye believe if I tell you heavenly things?[2]' Also He said to the Jews 'How is it possible for you to believe—you who receive glory one from another?'

"These things I shall make clear in my Gospel, shewing how belief in God and in His glory was not possible in those who did not place the love of God and of God's glory above the love of themselves and their own glory, the glory that comes from this world, so that even the Lord's brethren said to Him 'If thou doest these things shew thyself unto the world.' For neither did His brethren believe on Him[3].

"It was a custom of Jesus, when He was brought face to face with a seeming triumph of the powers of darkness, a triumph for a time, darkness before dawn, to say '*But*—in order that the Scripture might be fulfilled.' Thus He left the disciples to ask '*But what?*' He Himself gave no answer to the question, but broke off from speech into silence. This He did at the moment when He was arrested. After saying to the Jews 'I was with you day by day in the Temple and ye did not seize me' He is recorded by the Evangelists to have spoken thus —

Mk xiv 49	Mt xxvi. 56	Lk. xxii. 53
'*but still, in order that* the Scripture might be fulfilled'	'*but all this is come to pass in order that* the Scriptures of the Prophets might be fulfilled'	'*but still* this is your hour and the power of darkness'

"Matthew and Luke have paraphrased the Saviour's words so

---

[1] Jn iv 48 [2] Jn iii 12
[3] Jn vii 4—5.

JESUS IN HIS OWN COUNTRY

as to explain them Mark alone has retained the Saviour's actual utterance and silence I also shall retain it, as shewing how the Lord sometimes kept silence not through blank astonishment but as recognising the unsearchable wisdom of the power by which things evil are permitted to come to pass in order that good may follow[1] "

---

[1] See *Joh Gr* **2105—11** quoting Mk xiv 49 ἀλλ' ἵνα, Mt xxvi 56 δέ, Lk xxii 53 ἀλλά.

CHAPTER VI

THE SENDING OF THE APOSTLES[1]
[Mark vi 6 b—13]

§ 1. *Johannine "sending of the apostles"*

BEFORE discussing the expressions peculiar to Mark in the Synoptic accounts of the sending of the Apostles by Jesus, it

---

[1] Mk vi 6b—13 (R V)

(6 b) And he went round about the villages teaching

(7) And he called unto him the twelve, and began to send them forth by two and two, and he gave them authority over the unclean spirits,

(8) And he charged them that they should take nothing for [their] journey, save a staff only, no bread, no wallet, no money (*lit* brass) in their purse (*lit* girdle),

(9) But [to go] shod with sandals and, [said he], put not on two coats

(10) And he said unto them, Wheresoever ye enter into a house, there abide till ye depart thence

(11) And whatsoever place shall not receive you, and they

Mt ix 35, x 1, 5—15 (R V)

(35) And Jesus went about all the cities and the villages, teaching in their synagogues, and preaching the gospel of the kingdom, and healing all manner of disease and all manner of sickness

(1) And he called unto him his twelve disciples, and gave them authority over unclean spirits, to cast them out, and to heal all manner of disease and all manner of sickness

(5) These twelve Jesus sent forth, and charged them, saying, Go not into [any] way of the Gentiles, and enter not into any city of the Samaritans

(6) But go rather to the lost sheep of the house of Israel

Lk xiii 22, ix 1—6, x 4 (R V)

(22) And he went on his way through cities and villages, teaching, and journeying on unto Jerusalem

(1) And he called the twelve together, and gave them power and authority over all devils, and to cure diseases.

(2) And he sent them forth to preach the kingdom of God, and to heal the sick (*some anc auth omit* the sick)

(3) And he said unto them, Take nothing for your journey, neither staff, nor wallet, nor bread, nor money, neither have two coats

(x 4) Carry no purse, no wallet, no shoes and salute no man on the way

THE SENDING OF THE APOSTLES

will be convenient to note the very few and brief Johannine mentions of such "sending"—that is to say, sending of disciples

Mk vi. 6b—13 (R.V.) contd.	Mt. ix 35, x 1, 5—15 (R.V.) contd	Lk. xiii. 22, ix. 1—6, x 4 (R.V.) contd.
hear you not, as ye go forth thence, shake off the dust that is under your feet for a testimony unto them (12) And they went out, and preached that [men] should repent (13) And they cast out many devils, and anointed with oil many that were sick, and healed them	(7) And as ye go, preach, saying, The kingdom of heaven is at hand (8) Heal the sick, raise the dead, cleanse the lepers, cast out devils freely ye received, freely give (9) Get you no gold, nor silver, nor brass in your purses (*lit* girdles), (10) No wallet for [your] journey, neither two coats, nor shoes, nor staff for the labourer is worthy of his food (11) And into whatsoever city or village ye shall enter, search out who in it is worthy, and there abide till ye go forth (12) And as ye enter into the house, salute it (13) And if the house be worthy, let your peace come upon it but if it be not worthy, let your peace return to you (14) And whosoever shall not receive you, nor hear your words, as ye go forth out of that house or that city, shake off the dust of your feet (15) Verily I say unto you, It shall be more tolerable for the land of Sodom and Gomorrah in the day of judgment, than for that city	(ix. 4) And into whatsoever house ye enter, there abide, and thence depart (5) And as many as receive you not, when ye depart from that city, shake off the dust from your feet for a testimony against them (6) And they departed, and went throughout the villages, preaching the gospel, and healing everywhere

149 (Mark vi 6—13)

THE SENDING OF THE APOSTLES

or apostles, described as a past act, not as future. Almost the only one that comes under this category is in an utterance of Jesus (following shortly after the last words of John the Baptist) "*I sent you* to reap that whereon ye have not laboured. Others have laboured and ye are entered into their labour[1]" The next—also an utterance of Jesus—saying that an apostle "is not greater than he that sent him," cannot be said (at most) to do more than imply past sending[2] The third ("I have sent them into the world") seems to hover between past and future, as if it meant "I made them messengers, bearers of a message that is destined to go forth to the world[3]" The last instance is in the present tense ("I send"), contemplating future result, and the verb for "sending" is varied "As the Father hath sent me, even so *send I you* [*severally on your several errands*][4]"

Returning to the first of these instances, we perceive that, if it refers to any past and literal sending, the reference is probably to the previously mentioned "baptizing" practised by Christ's disciples after they and their Master had passed into "the Judaean land," that is, the districts of Judaea round about Jerusalem[5]. Concerning this, it is said that "Jesus himself baptized not, but his disciples [did]," and their converts are described as "more" than those baptized by John the Baptist[6]. The context informs us that "John was not yet

---

[1] Jn iv 38 The last words of John the Baptist are (iii 30) "He must increase, but I must decrease" (see *Joh Gr* Pref p viii)

[2] Jn xiii 16 "A servant is not greater than his lord, nor *an apostle* (ἀπόστολος) greater than *he that sent him* (τοῦ πέμψαντος αὐτόν)" R V txt "*one that is sent,*" though it makes smooth reading, conceals two facts —(1) that John here, and only here, uses the word ἀπόστολος, (2) that he uses two different words to express "sending" But R V marg says "Gr *an apostle*"

[3] Jn xvii 18 "As thou didst send me into the world, even so sent I them into the world" See *Joh Voc* **1723** *g*

[4] Jn xx 21 ἀπέσταλκέν με πέμπω ὑμᾶς See *Joh Voc* **1723** *f—g*

[5] Jn iii 22 εἰς τὴν Ἰουδαίαν γῆν, see *Joh Gr.* **2670** *b*.

[6] Jn iii 22 foll, iv 1—2

THE SENDING OF THE APOSTLES

cast into prison," but we are led to infer from the tone of the Baptist's last words that his imprisonment and death followed shortly afterwards[1] If the first Johannine Mission of the Twelve referred to this circuit in "the Judaean land," it would seem to have been brief, unimportant, and limited in scope[2]. It appears to have hardly taken the disciples away from their Master's side, so that—in referring to the converts made as the result of their mission—the Evangelist hesitates between saying "Jesus baptized" and "the disciples baptized"

In this first mention of "sending," Jesus apparently desires to caution the disciples against self-conceit *"Others* have laboured," He says. Who are those *"others"*? Later on, when Jesus says "Nor is an apostle greater than he that sent him," there is no such perplexing plurality, but here the question arises whether "others" meant merely the Law and the Prophets, so that the meaning is, in effect, this, "Do not suppose you are inventing, or are following me as inventing, a new religion"

The meaning is probably more than this. "The Law and the Prophets" included John the Baptist, the greatest of all the prophets And the time was a crisis for John the Baptist and for Jesus The Jews were making comparisons between them and endeavouring to sow jealousies between their several disciples, the group that still adhered to John, and the larger group that was gathering round Jesus Andrew had been a disciple of the Baptist before he became a disciple of Jesus, and so had a companion of Andrew, unnamed[3]. When Jesus said

---

[1] Jn iii 24—30

[2] It is possible that some misunderstood tradition about this early mission to the villages, or village-cities, round Jerusalem may have originated the Tradition peculiar to Matthew x 5—6 "Depart not into the way of the Gentiles but go rather to the lost sheep of the house of Israel" A very early evangelist, explaining "the Judaean land," might say "This meant merely the Jews [not including Peraea, Samaria, or Galilee]" A later one might say "This meant that they were *not* to go to Samaritans or Gentiles"

[3] Jn i 40

THE SENDING OF THE APOSTLES

"Others have laboured," Andrew and his companion could hardly fail to remember that, if they had been lately baptizing and making converts more numerous than those of John the Baptist, it was to the Baptist that their success was partly due. Moses and Isaiah had "laboured," but so had John. John was soon to pass out of men's view, to prison, and then to death—perhaps was already in prison. The disciples of Christ were to take up the work, the Baptist's work and Christ's work, gathering in the harvest. Let them prepare themselves to discharge their task by reverence for the Lord of the Harvest, and for the unity that bound His workers to one another and to Himself, and for the continuity of their work, which was, in truth, His work. Such seems to be the meaning of the Johannine "I sent you" and its context.

§ 2. *Jesus "going round the villages in a circle," in Mark*[1]

The Diatessaron does not quote from Mark at this point, but from Matthew. Its quotation from Mark, with the addition

---

[1] Mk vi 6 (R V)

Mk vi 6 (R V)	Mt ix 35 (R V)	Lk xiii 22 (R.V)
And he went round about the villages (*lit* went about (περιῆγεν) the villages in a circle) teaching	And Jesus went about (περιῆγεν) all the cities and the villages, teaching in their synagogues, and preaching the gospel of the kingdom, and healing all manner of disease and all manner of sickness	And he went on his way through cities and villages, teaching, and journeying on unto Jerusalem

Matthew repeats the very rare intransitive περιῆγεν in a similar tradition placed much earlier, as follows —

Mk i 39 (R.V.)	Mt iv 23 (R V)	Lk iv 44
And he went into their synagogues throughout all Galilee, preaching and casting out devils	And Jesus went about (περιῆγεν) in all Galilee, teaching in their synagogues, and preaching the gospel of the kingdom, and healing all manner of disease and all manner of sickness among the people	And he was preaching in the synagogues of Judaea (so W H, and R V marg).

Here *Diatess* omits the first half of Mt iv 23, but quotes, in its

152 (Mark vi 6—13)

THE SENDING OF THE APOSTLES

of "Nazareth" and "in their synagogues" ("And he went about in the villages *that [were] around Nazareth,* and taught in their synagogues"), does not occur till later on[1], just before the story of the execution of John the Baptist. The parallel Matthew, "And Jesus *went about all the cities and the villages,* teaching in their synagogues," is placed by the Diatessaron in two positions, not only here[2], before the Sending of the Apostles, but also much earlier[3], when Jesus came out of Simon's house in Capernaum saying "Let us go into *the next village-cities.*" These, as has been shewn elsewhere[4], might mean *the villages round Jerusalem.* This somewhat favours the arrangement adopted in Rushbrooke's *Synopticon,* which places, as parallel to the Mark-Matthew tradition, the Lucan words "And he went on his way through cities and villages, teaching, and *journeying on to Jerusalem*[5]." The centre of the Marcan "circle" appears to be quite uncertain[6]. The Lucan tradition may have been one of several attempts to explain "the villages in a circle."

---

place, words from Mt ix 35 (*Diatess* vii 7) "And Jesus was going about all the cities and the villages, and teaching in their synagogues, and preaching the gospel of the kingdom, and healing all the diseases and all the sicknesses, and (Mk i 39 b) casting out the devils." It also quotes Mt. ix. 35 before the Sending of the Apostles, in *Diatess* xii 40. Its version of Mk vi 6 b "And he went about in the villages that [were] around Nazareth" it places much later (in *Diatess* xvii 53).

Lk iv 44 is read by *Diatess* as "in the synagogues of Galilee" and placed very early (*Diatess* vi 35), after the healing of the nobleman's son (Jn iv 46—54), and before Mt iv 13. On Lk iv 44 "the synagogues of Judaea," read by W H without alternative, see *Beginning* p 209 foll., *Proclam* pp 233, 241 foll.

[1] *Diatess* xvii 53   [2] *Diatess* xii 40   [3] *Diatess* vii 7
[4] See *Proclam* p 241 on (Mk i 38) κωμοπόλεις
[5] Lk xiii 22
[6] The interpretation of the Diatessaron (which transfers Mark's tradition to a later period) "Nazareth," although following naturally from Mark's context, is antecedently improbable since Nazareth had given to Jesus but a poor reception.

153 (Mark vi 6—13)

THE SENDING OF THE APOSTLES

Matthew at this point—between the mention of "the cities and villages" and the Sending of the Twelve—inserts a saying of Jesus about "the harvest" and the need of "labourers[1]." Luke also has this. And we have seen above that John has a saying about the harvest in his first use of the word "sending," as applied to the Apostles by Jesus ("I have sent you"). If, therefore, Matthew, Luke, and John agreed in prefixing this saying to an early Mission of the Twelve, about the time of the death of John the Baptist, we might feel some confidence that they all referred to the Mission described by Mark. But Luke has the following preface to his harvest-tradition "*Now after these things the Lord appointed seventy [two] others, and sent them, two and two, before his face into every city and place whither he himself was about to come*. And he said unto them, The harvest is plenteous ...[2]"

This, if taken with the Lucan context, makes it clear that Luke deviated from Matthew in his account of the Sending of the Apostles. Precepts that Matthew regarded as addressed to the Twelve, Luke regarded as additions erroneously made by Matthew to the brief tradition of Mark. They were really (in Luke's opinion) addressed to the Seventy [Two] who were sent later on[3]. In all these varying traditions, there is nothing to disprove the supposition that John accepted the Marcan Sending of the Twelve and referred to it in the words "I sent you to reap". Nor is there anything, so far, that calls for Johannine intervention.

---

[1] Mt ix 37—8. It prefixes a saying that Jesus (*ib* 36) had compassion on the multitudes, because they were "as sheep not having a shepherd".
[2] Lk x 1—2.
[3] See *Clue* 233—6, *From Letter* 922, 1015.

THE SENDING OF THE APOSTLES

§ 3 "*He began*[1] *to send them out by two and two,*"
    in Mark

Why does Matthew reject the Marcan "by two and two"? And why does Luke reject it in his Sending of the Twelve but retain it in his Sending of the Seventy?

Matthew may have omitted it because it might be felt by some to be out of harmony with his epithet of "first[2]," which he alone attaches to Peter in his account of the appointment of the Apostles, inserted by him here Also, as he alone mentions "Israel" in the context[3], he may have thought that the symmetry between the Twelve Tribes of Israel and the Twelve Apostles, one for each tribe, was disturbed by the insertion of "by two and two "

Luke may have rejected it for similar reasons, so far as concerned the Sending of the Twelve, but may have recognised that it was a historical fact referring to *some* Mission of Apostles, and that it ought to be inserted in connection with that Mission He accordingly inserted it in a Mission of Seventy (or Seventy Two) Apostles, which he described vaguely as occurring "after these things[4]." This Lucan insertion favours the view that "two," in Mark, is part of the original tradition. And, in itself, "two" is antecedently probable In certain circumstances, there are obvious advantages in sending Missionaries in pairs.

---

[1] Mk vi 7 "began" See *Corrections* **535** *a* on ἄρχομαι, which, in the course of some five and twenty instances in Mk, is never retained by Mt -Lk , jointly, except in the parallels to Mk xiv 19 It is used by John only once We can hardly expect Johannine intervention on a grammatical point of this kind But see *Joh Voc* **1674** *a* on the unique instance of ἄρχομαι in Jn xiii 5 "He *began* to wash," interpreted by Origen as meaning that Jesus "*began*" the purification then, and completed it afterwards Ἄρχομαι in Mark, here, may have been interpreted by some as implying "the first of several acts of sending "

[2] Mt x 2 πρῶτος Σίμων ὁ λεγόμενος Πέτρος.

[3] Mt x 6, 23   [4] Lk x 1

THE SENDING OF THE APOSTLES

But a question arises as to the nature of those "circumstances" What view would Luke and John, severally, be likely to take of them?

Luke's view is that the Apostles were to be *"witnesses"* of Christ's resurrection With an expression of this view, we may almost say, his Gospel terminates, and the Acts begins[1] Hence "two" becomes at once probable. For the Law said "In the mouth of *two witnesses*, or *three*, shall every word be established," and this saying is quoted both in Matthew and the Second Epistle to the Corinthians[2], as being familiar to those who heard it

John never uses the masculine noun, *"witness," martus*, so frequently employed by Luke in the Acts Even when he ought to have used it in the words of Jesus quoting from the Law about witnesses, he avoids it, thus. "Yea, even in your law it is written that the *witness (marturia)* of *two human beings* is true," and continues, "I am he that *witnesseth* concerning myself, and the Father that sent me *witnesseth* concerning me[3]" One reason perhaps why John never uses the masculine noun *martus*, *"witness,"* is that it is technically applied in the sense of "martyr" to Stephen and others[4] But another probably is, that he desires to take this *"witnessing"* out of the region of legal technicalities of the nature of an *affidavit*, and to raise it into the region of a spiritual "witnessing," in which there is a harmony or correspondence between the members of a human family and the members of the divine Family—divine and yet, in some sense, "human-beings"—the

---

[1] Lk xxiv 48 "Ye are *witnesses of these things*," Acts 1 8 "*witnesses of me*," ib 22 "a *witness of his resurrection*," comp ib 11 32 etc

[2] Mt xviii 16, 2 Cor xiii 1 quoting Deut xix 15

[3] Jn viii 17—18 δύο ἀνθρώπων ἡ μαρτυρία ἀληθής ἐστιν ἐγώ εἰμι ὁ μαρτυρῶν περὶ ἐμαυτοῦ καὶ μαρτυρεῖ περὶ ἐμοῦ ὁ πέμψας με πατήρ

[4] Acts xxii 20 "thy *martyr* (μάρτυρος) Stephen," Rev ii 13 "my *martyr*, Antipas" See *Joh Voc* **1696** *e*, and comp Rev xi 3, xvii 6. It is also applied to Jesus in Rev 1 5, iii 14

THE SENDING OF THE APOSTLES

Father and the Son, answering one another and testifying about the Spirit of Sonship The "human being" is not to merge himself in the *martus*, or "martyr"

Some thought of this kind may be implied in traditions recorded by Matthew about the "two or three" gathered together in the name of Christ, and about the "agreement" of even "two" in prayer[1]. R Jochanan interpreted the sayings "Two are better than one," and "A threefold cord is not quickly broken[2]," as referring to father, mother, and child; and the Fourth Gospel is pervaded, in spite of the lofty nature of its mysticism, with the belief that the nature of God in heaven is best revealed to men through the nature of the family on earth

As if to compensate for never using the masculine *martus*, John freely uses the verb *marturein*, "bear witness," and *marturia*, "witness [borne]," both in his Gospel and in his Epistle But the subject of the *marturia* is not Christ's resurrection alone, or even prominently It is Christ Himself, and His saving influence or personality[3]. John the Baptist, no doubt, is said to have "witnessed" concerning the descent of the Holy Spirit on Jesus[4]. But he can hardly be supposed to have seen this with the mere corporal eye And the same statement may apply to the Evangelist's vision of the water and the blood described in the Gospel and referred to in the Epistle[5]

Theophylact, illustrating the Marcan "by two and two," quotes from Ecclesiastes the saying "Two are better than one," and Jerome, commenting on the latter, says "It is better to have Christ abiding in oneself than to be alone and open to the assaults of the Adversary[6]" A similar thought is expressed in the Fourth Gospel where Jesus not only says about Himself

---

[1] Mt xviii 19—20.   [2] Eccles iv 9, 12
[3] Jn xv 27, 1 Jn 1 1—2   [4] Jn 1 32—4
[5] Jn xix 35 (comp 1 Jn v 6—7), see *Joh Gr* **2383—4**
[6] See Prof Swete on Mk vi 7, and Jerome on Eccles iv 9

THE SENDING OF THE APOSTLES

that He is never alone because the Father is with Him, but also declares that the true believer shall never be alone but shall have the helpful presence of Two in his heart "If a man love me he will keep my word, and my Father will love him, and we will come unto him and make our abode with him[1]" Victor of Antioch (on Mark) declares that Matthew, as well as Mark, divides (though "not clearly") the Apostles into pairs Luke, as we have seen, divides the Seventy thus, but not the Twelve It seems impossible that these textual differences should not attract the attention of Christians before the end of the first century, leading them to ask questions about the nature of apostolic testimony, and whether—and if so, why, and for how long a time—it was necessary that the Apostles should testify in pairs When we realise this we shall feel that it is not so wildly fanciful as it may have appeared at first sight, to suppose that John desired to suggest a spiritual and permanent rule in place of one that was becoming mechanical. The invariable need was that every Apostle, even when alone, should be able to say, "And yet I am not alone[2]," and that he should feel himself to be bearing witness on earth in the Spirit of the Two Witnesses in heaven, namely, the Father and the Son[3].

§ 4. *"Save a staff only," in Mark*[4]

The parallel Matthew and Luke say that the Apostles are *not* to take "a staff" while Mark says that it is the one thing

---

[1] Jn xiv 23, xvi 32   [2] Jn xvi 32
[3] Comp 1 Pet v. 1   On the allusions to twofold witness in Philo and Jewish literature, see *Joh Gr* **2588—90**, and on 1 Jn v 8 "Three are they that bear witness," see *Joh Gr* **2306**   There is an allusion to the Jewish doctrine about two witnesses in Heb vi 18 "two immutable things," namely, God's "promise," and God's "oath."

It is interesting to note the only Johannine mention of twofold apostolic action in bringing people to Christ   It is little more than passive   Philip and Andrew are (Jn xii 21—2) the agents by whom "certain Greeks" are introduced   But the Greeks take the initiative, "Sir, we would see Jesus"

[4] Mk vi 8, Mt x. 9—10, Lk. ix 3

THE SENDING OF THE APOSTLES

that they *may* take (or perhaps *must* take). Also, Mark and Luke include "*bread*" in the things that are not to be taken. But Matthew omits "*bread*[1]," perhaps following some tradition that identified it with "staff." For a sufficiency of bread might be metaphorically called in Hebrew "*the staff of bread*." And this might account for some of the Synoptic variations[2]. It has been shewn that the original precept might have bidden the disciples take "*nothing except* (מה) *the staff of bread*"—meaning, in a spiritual sense, the "daily bread" that comes from the Father—altered by Greek corruption into "nothing, *not* (מה) staff, bread," and then into "nothing, *not* staff, *not* bread[3]."

To internal evidence must be added external. The words of Jacob "*With my staff* I passed over this Jordan[4]," though (apparently) not much noticed in the Talmuds, are allegorized by Philo and the Midrash. Rashi paraphrases them thus: "I had with me *neither silver, nor gold, nor cattle, but only my staff*." Rashi adds "There is also an allegorical exposition; Jacob had cast his staff into the Jordan and the Jordan was parted asunder." Philo takes "staff" as meaning God's *paideia*, i.e. schooling, training, or chastening[5]. This recalls the words of the Psalmist "Thou art with me, thy *rod* and thy *staff*, they comfort me, thou preparest a table before me...." There the Targum has "Thy Word is for my *support* (or, *sustenance*), thy upright rod and thy law shall comfort me"; and the context, as well as the special word "*support* (or,

---

[1] "Bread" is mentioned in *Didach* xi 6 "Let the missionary receive *nothing except bread* [to suffice him] until he reach his lodging for the [next] night," but in such a way as to shew that the writer may have accepted "*nothing save a staff only*" as meaning "*nothing save the staff, or sustenance, of bread* [for the day]."

[2] See *Clue* **263**—7, which refers to "*staff of bread*" in Lev xxvi. 26, Ps cv 16 etc., and to Nehem v 14 "*the bread* of" לחם, perhaps confused by LXX with "belonging to them," להם, αὐτῶν.

[3] *Corrections* **390** (11) (a).   [4] Gen xxxii 10

[5] Philo i 82—3

THE SENDING OF THE APOSTLES

sustenance)," indicates that God is regarded, not only as guiding, but also as "sustaining" with food[1].

The Marcan tradition—after the words "save a staff only"—proceeds as follows, "no bread, no *wallet* (A V *scrip*)." Matthew altogether omits "bread," and changes the order, but also has "no *wallet* (A V *scrip*)." Luke has "neither staff, nor *wallet* (A V *scrip*), nor bread." Thus all mention "*wallet*" (or "*scrip*"). Now the word for this in Delitzsch's Hebrew, and also in the Syriac of the Gospels, is applied to a shepherd's "*scrip*" both in Hebrew and Aramaic, and occurs in the Targum of the only passage where "*scrip*" occurs in our English Version of the Old Testament "And he [David] took his *staff* in his hand, and chose him five smooth stones.. and put them in the shepherd's bag.. even (*lit* and) in his *scrip*[2]." Jewish tradition said that David's coinage had on one side "*a staff and a shepherd's scrip*[3]." A proselyte says, "If an Israelite approaching the holy things shall die, how much more an insignificant stranger who comes with *his staff and his scrip*[4]!" Shammai, when he believed that Jonathan ben Uzziel had committed an error, is said to have "come to him (*or*, against him) *with his staff and with his scrip*"—which suggests a metaphorical meaning[5]. In view of these passages, and others

---

[1] Ps xxiii. 4—5. See Levy *Ch* ii 177 on "*support*" as meaning "*food*." Jerome is in doubt whether "staff" means "chastisement" or "sustenance and future consolation." The Greek ῥάβδος represents (Hastings iv 291) (1) the shepherd's rod or club, (2) the shepherd's staff, (3) the common staff. Aramaic (Brederek) does not preserve these distinctions.

[2] 1 S xvii 40. [3] *Gen r* on Gen xii 2 (Wu p 178).

[4] See *Hor Heb* (on Mk vi 8, Mt x 10) quoting *Sabb* 31 a.

[5] *Baba Bathra* 133 b. Goldschmidt renders it "fiel mit Stab und Sack uber ihn (עליו) her," and explains it as "strove with him (zankte mit ihm)"—apparently taking it metaphorically. But *Hor. Heb* (on Mk vi 8) has "Shammai came *to* him with his staff and with his scrip," and adds "the Gloss saith, 'He came to contend with Jonathan, because he had violated the will of the dead.' Behold the vice-president of the Sanhedrin carrying a *scrip*,

THE SENDING OF THE APOSTLES

collected in Horae Hebraicae, two conclusions become certain, first, that every Jew would expect "staff" and "scrip" to go together, secondly, that if Jesus said "*staff, but not scrip,*" some paradox was intended.

In the dialogue between Goliath and David, when Goliath, jeering at the shepherd's "staff," says "Am I a dog that thou comest unto me with *staves?*" David replies, "Thou comest to me with a sword, and with a spear, and with a javelin, but I come unto thee *in the name of the Lord of Hosts*[1]" This suggests the thought that the shepherd's "*staff*" of David might be regarded as the emblem of the protecting presence of the Lord, like the staff of Jacob. And the question arises whether the Marcan tradition could be explained in the same way, as a combination of metaphorical with literal precept to the early preachers of the Gospel· "Take staff but not scrip, nor anything but the staff As for your support, after the day's journey, throw yourselves on the hospitality and kindness of those to whom you bring the Good News But not so for the journey itself For that, be like Jacob, and take 'the staff.'"

§ 5 *A parallel from the Essens*

Josephus says about the Essenes that when they journey they take nothing at all abroad with them "but go *in arms* (or, *in full armour*) on account of robbers[2]." This is absurd. It is also contradicted, in effect, by Philo's statement about the Essenes "Darts, or javelins, or daggers, or helmet, or breastplate, or shield—of all these you will find no craftsman among them, nor *maker-of-arms*, or maker-of-machines, or, to sum up,

---

in which he laid up victuals for his journey " Rodkinson translates it "came to rebuke him," omitting all mention of "*staff and scrip* "

[1] 1 S xvii 43, 45
[2] Joseph *Bell* ii 8 4 ποιοῦνται τὰς ἀποδημίας, οὐδὲν μὲν ὅλως ἐπικομιζόμενοι, διὰ δὲ τοὺς λῃστὰς ἔνοπλοι On ἔνοπλος, mostly meaning "in full armour," or "fully armed," see Steph *Thes*

THE SENDING OF THE APOSTLES

anyone practising things that have to do with war[1]." An explanation of Josephus' error is suggested by Hippolytus, who, instead of the adjective *enhoploi*, "in-arms," uses *hoplon*, in the singular, which means "*an implement [of any kind]*" The Essenes, he says, "go about, carrying nothing but an *implement*[2]" In Greek, *enhoplon* may mean either "*one implement*," or "*in-full-armour*[3]" It is a reasonable conjecture that Josephus has mistaken "one implement" for "in full armour" But the reasonableness will be converted to something like certainty if we can shew what the "one implement" was.

Now both Josephus and Hippolytus describe in detail the Essenes as giving "a little hatchet," along with "white linen raiment," to those who join their sect[4] Later on, this is identified with a "shovel[5]" This "shovel" is described as being used in fulfilment of the Deuteronomic precept to cover excrement that it may not pollute the camp in which the Lord

---

[1] Philo ii 457 "maker-of-arms (ὁπλοποιόν)"

[2] Hippol ix 15 (T and T Clark, p 353, but ed Duncker ix. 20, p 474) περιίασι δὲ τὴν πατρῴαν γῆν ἑκάστοτε ἀποδημοῦντες μηδὲν φέροντες πλὴν ὅπλου, Clark "nothing except arms," Duncker "nihil gestantes praeter *arma*" But Steph *Thes* gives no instance where the sing ὅπλον means "arms" It means an implement of any kind When meaning an instrument of war, it mostly means "shield" in LXX, *e g* Ps xxxv 2, lxxvi 3, xci 4 "his truth is a shield and a buckler," LXX ὅπλῳ κυκλώσει σε ἡ ἀλήθεια αὐτοῦ In Hippolytus, the sense requires "They go about [*as it were*, perh. ins ὡς] their native land whenever they travel abroad"

[3] That is to say, ENOΠΛON may mean (1) ἐν ὅπλον or (2) ἔνοπλον Hippolytus, adopting the former, might drop ἐν as being superfluous and unintelligible The clause in Josephus, "on account of robbers," might naturally be added to explain why peaceful folk like the Essenes travelled (as he thought) "*in-arms*"

[4] Joseph *Bell* ii 8 7 (simil Hippol *ed* Duncker ix 23) ἀξινάριον

[5] Joseph *Bell* ii 8 9 τῇ σκαλίδι, τοιοῦτον γάρ ἐστιν τὸ διδόμενον ὑπ' αὐτῶν ἀξινίδιον τοῖς νεοσυστάτοις (sim Hippol ix 25 but with ἀξινάριον (Duncker))

THE SENDING OF THE APOSTLES

God "walketh[1]." Our R V. says "Thou shalt have a *paddle* among thy weapons" (where A V. has "upon thy weapon"). But the margin gives "*shovel*" The Hebrew regularly means "[*wooden*] *nail*" or "*peg*" Also the literal Hebrew says that it is not "among" but "upon," or "above," the "implements" or "weapons" of the Israelites[2] The Jerusalem Targum has "A *nail* shall be fixed for you *upon the implements of your arms in the place where ye gird on your swords*"

The scriptural passage, and the varieties of rendering it, indicate that some may have regarded the "nail," or "peg," or "little hatchet," as an instrument of war, but others as one of peace, and may have severally adapted their descriptions to their views[3] It is important to note that Zechariah uses

---

[1] Deut xxiii 13 "paddle (יתד)," marg "shovel" Gesen 450 *a* gives only this instance of the meaning "spade" Elsewhere it mostly means "peg," or large pin, nail etc , and is rendered by LXX πάσσαλος, as here Metaphorically, it is applied to any leader on whom Israel depends, *e g* Zech x 4 "From him shall come forth the *corner stone*, from him the *nail*," Targ "*King Messiah*," comp Is xxii 23 and Ezr ix 8 The Patriarchs (Levy ii 277) were called "*nails*" In LXX, Heb "nail" = ἄνθρωπος (1), ἄρχων (1), πάσσαλος (11), στήριγμα (1), τάσσω (1).

[2] The word rendered "weapons" occurs only here (Gesen 24 *b*) Walton has "super tuam zonam," as LXX ἐπὶ τῆς ζώνης σου, Onk and Syr "super arma tua"

[3] Comp the description of the weapons of the Roman infantry in Josephus (*Bell* iii 5 5) ἡ δὲ λοιπὴ φάλαγξ [φέρει] ξυστόν τε καὶ θυρεὸν ἐπιμήκη, πρὸς οἷς πρίονα καὶ κόφινον ἄμην (V Γ ἄμην) τε καὶ πέλεκυν, πρὸς δὲ ἱμάντα καὶ δρέπανον καὶ ἅλυσιν, ἡμερῶν τε τριῶν ἐφόδιον ὡς ὀλίγον ἀποδεῖν τῶν ἀχθοφορούντων ὀρέων τὸν πεζόν Here the writer's object appears to be to shew that the Roman foot-soldier was so burdened that he "did not fall far short of a pack-mule" (Whiston, quaintly, "hath no great need of a mule to carry his burdens") Now a recognised part of this burden was the "vallus," or stake for palisading the camp, to which Virgil alludes (*Georg* iii. 347 "Romanus in armis injusto sub fasce") and which Horace mentions (*Epodes* ix 13 "fert *vallum* et arma miles") Why does Josephus, who gives so fully the details of the "injustus fascis" and the "arma," make no mention of the "vallus"? And what

THE SENDING OF THE APOSTLES

"*the Nail*" absolutely (along with "the Corner Stone") where the Targum has "*the Messiah*" (along with "the King") to describe one on whom Israel hangs or depends; and this metaphor was carried into the Midrash, so that Abraham, Isaac, and Jacob are called "the three *nails* of the world[1]." This favours the supposition that the Essenes attached to the term some emblematic significance. The language of Josephus also, in introducing the term, makes it difficult to believe that the Essenes regarded the implement merely as one for digging a small hole[2].

Philo describes the Deuteronomic "nail" as "meaning symbolically the *logos* that digs up the secrets of things done," and allegorizes the context at great length[3]. Neither there nor elsewhere does he give us a glimpse of Jewish tradition on the subject. Nor does he mention it in his short account of the Essenes. But in one passage referring to it he likens it to "a kind of defensive weapon," using the very word we are in need

---

precisely does he mean by ἄμη, which Hudson renders "rutrum," Whiston "pick-axe," L S (1) "shovel" or "mattock," (2) "water-bucket," (3) "harrow" or "rake"?

The passage is of importance because it shews that Josephus (or his secretary) is inadequate, if not inaccurate, in his description of the arms of the Roman legionary, with which he must have been well acquainted, and prepares us to believe that he was inaccurate in his mention of the "full armour" of the Essenes.

[1] *Gen r* on Gen xiv 20 (Wu p 200) See also *ib* on Gen xxv 11 (Wu p 295) "the *nails* of the earth," in bad sense (Wu "die Machtigen")

[2] See Joseph *Bell* ii 8 6 "To those who seek their sect admission is not immediate, but [the candidate] remains outside for a year, and they prescribe to him the same way of life [as their own], giving him both *a little hatchet* (ἀξινάριόν τε) and the above-mentioned girdle and white raiment." This is stated before we are informed of the use (or one of the uses) of the "little hatchet." And the passage suggests that the "little hatchet" (as well as the "white raiment") is regarded emblematically

[3] Philo i. 72.

164 (Mark vi 6—13)

THE SENDING OF THE APOSTLES

of (*hoplon*) to explain Josephus' mistake[1]. In conclusion, we can say certainly that the Essenes did not travel about "in arms," and, almost as certainly, that the statement to that effect in Josephus is an error rising out of an erroneous interpretation of the "peg" in Deuteronomy. But it is not so easy to put aside his statement that the Essenes gave their neophytes something that might be so termed. And, if they did—whether it was merely used as an emblem or not—their practice might influence the language of Jesus in sending forth the messengers of His Gospel. Instead of "the Nail," Jesus might speak of "the Staff," with the Psalmist's thought in His mind, "Thy rod and thy staff, they comfort me," and with the desire to impress that thought on His disciples. Every traveller naturally had a "staff." But His travellers were to have one spiritually as well as literally. Thus Jesus might utter a mixture of the metaphorical with the literal which might be misunderstood and altered by Matthew and Luke, but retained by Mark, who often records what was certainly obscure and what he himself possibly did not fully understand. "Take no scrip, take no bread, but a staff must needs be taken."

§ 6. What corresponds to "the staff" in John?

It would be an error to say that there is an allusion to the Psalmist's comfort of the "rod" and the "staff" of God—and hence perhaps to the Marcan tradition about the "staff"—in the Johannine reiterated mention of the Comforter[2]. For the Comforter does not mean the Sustainer or Supporter. It means "the Paraclete," "the friend called in to aid," the "alter ego" of Christ. Nevertheless, there is in the doctrine of the Paraclete an emphasizing of the truth of the Marcan

---

[1] Philo i 118 "θωρήξῃ," φησὶ γοῦν, "τῷ πασσάλῳ," is to be explained by the preceding (*ib* 117) σὺν λόγῳ παραγενώμεθα, ὥσπερ ὅπλῳ τινὶ ἀμυντηρίῳ. We are to "arm ourselves" with the Logos, or "nail," as being a defensive weapon like a breastplate.

[2] See *Joh Voc* **1720** *k*, *Joh Gr* **2793** foll.

THE SENDING OF THE APOSTLES

tradition "*save a staff only*" if we regard Mark as meaning that Christ's Missionaries are to depend on the *sustaining power of the Holy Spirit alone*, and not to trust to aids of their own, represented by the bread and the wallet and the silver and the gold that they may carry with them Such a doctrine is expressed later on in Mark's and Luke's versions of the Discourse on the Last Days, when the disciples are told not to "premeditate" their pleadings before the rulers of this world, but to trust to the Holy Spirit to give them utterance[1] But in the Mission of the Apostles the doctrine is not expressed by Luke.

In John this doctrine is everywhere It branches into so many metaphors that we are in danger of overlooking the one radical thought—that of "sustaining" The sustaining power raises, supports, and uplifts, from the moment of our spiritual birth It is the water that regenerates from above; it is the wind, or spirit, or breath that regenerates within, it is the living water that quenches the thirst of the soul led astray by sin; it is the living bread, it is the life of the vine that gives life and fruit to the branches; it is the flesh and the blood of the Son bestowed on the disciples, it is the Father, by whom the Son lives, it is the Son, who is the resurrection and the life of men, and lastly, it is the Son's Friend, the Other Self, who is to pass into the hearts of the disciples in the Son's place, when the Son has ascended to the Father. Under cover of all these metaphors John says to us, in effect, "The Lord does not impose on you a number of definite practices or definite abstinences He said to His Apostles that they need take nothing with them 'save a staff only' He meant, and He still means when He says the same thing to us, 'Take nothing with you save me only If you take my Spirit you will take me And, taking me, you will take your staff.'"

---

[1] Mk xiii 11, Lk xxi 14—15 It is not expressed there by Matthew (xxiv 11—12) who inserts it in the Mission of the Twelve (x. 19—20)

THE SENDING OF THE APOSTLES

§ 7 "*Shod* (R V) *with sandals,*" *in Mark*[1]

The word rendered "shod" is literally "fastened-below." When applied to persons, it means "*fastened-up* [as regards the shoe, or sandal]." In the case of a light shoe or slipper, a sloven, like Socrates, might go about *not* "fastened up[2]" But one who desired to be alert for action, as for example, a soldier, must be ready for the general's orders, as Epictetus says, "[with shoes] fastened, clothes on, armour on[3]" The Four Gospels all represent John the Baptist as using some metaphor about "*shoes*" in speaking of himself as God's messenger, and of Jesus, as his successor, and three of them mention the "loosing" of the "latchet," or "strap," with which the shoe was fastened[4] It is in accordance with this metaphor that Mark here mentions, as a positive precept for the messengers of the Gospel, that they must go forth on their mission "with sandals fastened."

But why does Mark speak of "sandals" instead of "shoes"? Probably because he meant "*not shoes but sandals.*" That is to say, the shoes were not to be heavy, such as (according to some interpreters) Matthew had in view when he wrote "whose shoes I am not able to carry[5]" They were to be light like the "sandals" of Mercury[6]. That is what the word would

---

[1] Mk vi 9

[2] Plato *Sympos* 174 A "He met Socrates, fresh from the bath, (lit.) *fastened up as to his shoes* (τὰς βλαύτας ὑποδεδεμένον)—a rare thing with him" Socrates explains that it is because he is going out to dinner Hesychius explains σανδάλια as σάνδαλα, γυναικεῖα ὑποδήματα, ἃ καὶ βλαύτια Comp *Gorg* 490 E, where it is ironically suggested that a shoemaker must "walk about fastened-up in very large shoes laced up fully (μέγιστα δεῖ ὑποδήματα καὶ πλεῖστα ὑποδεδεμένον περιπατεῖν)"

[3] Epict 1 16 4 ἕτοιμοί εἰσι τῷ στρατηγῷ ὑποδεδεμένοι, ἐνδεδυμένοι, ὡπλισμένοι

[4] See *Beginning* p 79 foll   [5] Mt iii 11

[6] See Steph *Thes* quoting *Hom H Merc* 79

THE SENDING OF THE APOSTLES

suggest to Greeks. Probably there was an original allusion to Isaiah's saying (quoted by Paul) concerning the "beautiful feet" of the preachers of glad tidings who "published peace[1]" The precept was metaphorical. The preachers of the Gospel were to be not only alert and unencumbered, but also joyful, as messengers inviting guests to a feast[2].

§ 8. *What corresponds to "sandals" in John?*

If we accept "sandals" in Mark as an emblem of messengers of peace and glad tidings, inviting the world to a feast of joy, we can hardly fail to be struck by the fact that toward the end of the Synoptic Gospels, and particularly in Christ's Discourse on the Last Days, there are very few indications of this aspect of the message. In that Discourse, Luke has "A hair of your heads shall assuredly not perish," and, later on, "But when these things are beginning to come to pass, look up and lift up your heads[3]"; but Mark and Matthew omit both these utterances. In Mark, the Greek "rejoice" is never used except in the "rejoicing" of the chief priests over the treachery of Judas, and in the ironical insult offered to Judas by the Roman soldiers, "*Rejoice* (i.e. *hail*), King of the Jews[4]"; nor does Jesus (in Mark) mention peace except in the phrase "Go in

---

[1] Is liii 7 quoted in Rom x 15. Comp Targ on Cant vii. 1 "How beautiful are the feet of Israelites going up to appear before God thrice in the year with *sandals* of sealskin," where "*sandal*" is the Greek σάνδαλον transliterated. Sealskin is Talmudically connected (Levy Ch ii 176—7) with "joy". It represents Heb (A V) "badgers' skin" used in the adornment of the Tabernacle (Gesen 1065 a) and applied to "sandals" in Ezek xvi 10

[2] See *Corrections* **390** (ii) (*e*) *a*. The meanings of the Hebraized word *sandalon* are various, and often different from Greek usage. Matthew and Luke might find difficulty in a word that generally meant, in Greek literature, a woman's shoe. But these considerations increase the probability that Mark represents the earliest tradition. In Goodspeed σάνδαλον does not occur

[3] Lk xxi 18, 28   [4] Mk xiv 11, xv 18

THE SENDING OF THE APOSTLES

peace," and in the precept "Be-at-peace with one another[1]." The other Synoptists are less silent, but none of them come up to the level of the joyfulness of Isaiah

In explanation of Mark, it may be argued that "joy" and "peace" are assumed in the first sentence that he records as coming from Jesus, which ends with the words "Believe in the *gospel*[2]," i e in the good tidings of Isaiah That is no doubt the case And the acts of exorcism and healing and forgiving, and the bringing of the "little ones" into Christ's circle of disciples, are fulfilments of the good tidings. But this joyful aspect fades away as we proceed If the conclusion of Mark's Gospel were extant it might have shewn the Saviour to us comforting His disciples with the assurance that joy and peace were henceforth theirs, and theirs to give to others But as it is, there is no such assurance And it is not very fully or directly expressed in Matthew's conclusion Luke is the only Synoptist who ends his Gospel with a note of "great joy" And the "joy" is merely described by Luke, not uttered by Jesus.

In contrast with the Synoptic Discourse on the Last Days, the Johannine Final Discourse represents Jesus as saying to the disciples, first about peace, "*Peace* I leave (*or* bequeath) unto you, *the peace that is my own* I give unto you," and, later on, "These things have I spoken unto you that in me ye may have *peace* In the world ye have tribulation But be of good cheer, I have been victorious over the world[3]" Then, as to "joy," it is mentioned no less than six times in the Discourse, beginning with the saying "These things have I spoken unto you that *the joy that is my own* may abide in you and that your *joy* may be fulfilled[4]"

There can be little doubt that these gifts of "*peace*" and

---

[1] Mk v 34, ix 50   [2] Mk i 15
[3] Jn xiv 27, xvi 33
[4] Jn xv 11 (*bis*), xvi 20, 21, 22, 24 See also Jn iv 36 "that he that soweth and he that reapeth may rejoice together," and *ib* xvi 22 "your heart shall rejoice"

THE SENDING OF THE APOSTLES

"*joy*," transmitted by Christ, who defines them as His "own," and testified to by all the Epistles, and by the history of the early Church, were historically much more important subjects in Christ's doctrine than would be inferred from the Synoptists alone What Mark has left us to infer—from little more than the mere mention of the "sandals" that are to be worn by the messengers of the Good Tidings or Gospel—John has expressed and expanded in Christ's promises of that which was the essence of the Gospel—namely, the "peace" and the "joy" that He alone could bestow

§ 9 "*Scrip*," "*girdle*," "*purse*[1]"

We now come to clauses of special importance in their bearing on the question, "Were the precepts to the Twelve literal, or metaphorical, or both?" It is largely through Luke that we perceive this bearing For Luke, who alone mentions "*purse*"—and that only in the Precepts to the Seventy, not in the Precepts to the Twelve—represents Jesus, later on, as saying to the Twelve "When I sent you without *purse* and scrip and shoes, lacked ye anything?. But now he that hath a *purse*, let him take it, and likewise a scrip And he that hath not [one] let him sell his cloak and buy a sword[2]" Also, where Matthew has "Treasure up for yourselves treasures in

---

[1] These words occur as follows in the Sending of the Twelve and the Sending of the Seventy "scrip," πήρα, in Mk, Mt, and Lk (the Twelve), and also in Lk x 4 (the Seventy), "girdle," ζώνη, only in Mk vi 8, Mt x 9, "purse," βαλλάντιον, only in Lk x 4 (the Seventy)

Πήρα occurs in 1 S xvii 40 (Sym) "even in his *scrip*," LXX συλλογήν R V has not altered "scrip" there, but in N T it has everywhere substituted "wallet" for "scrip " I have retained "scrip" so as to indicate the possibility of allusion in N T to O T Instead of "girdle" (the girdle being used as a purse) R V has txt "purse," marg. "Gr. girdle " I have retained "girdle," so as to distinguish Mk-Mt ζώνη, "girdle," from Lk βαλλάντιον "purse "

[2] Lk xxii 36 R V marg "and he that hath no sword and buy one "

THE SENDING OF THE APOSTLES

heaven," Luke has, in a metaphorical sense, "Make unto yourselves *purses* that wax not old, a treasure in the heavens...[1]"

These quotations, though they leave a great deal unexplained, demonstrate at all events the following facts about Luke. (1) He distinguishes between *"purse"* and *"scrip"* (2) He represents Jesus as speaking to the Twelve about a past prohibition to take *"purse" and "scrip,"* whereas the past prohibition to the Twelve, as he himself records it, mentioned *"scrip"* alone[2]. (3) He records a prohibition of *"purse" and "scrip"* as given to the Seventy (4) He represents Jesus, on the eve of the Crucifixion, as speaking to the Twelve and cancelling the past prohibition of *"purse"* and *"scrip*[3]*."* (5) He represents Jesus, at the same moment, as inculcating the "buying" of a "sword" (6) He represents Jesus, at an earlier period, as using *"purse"* in a metaphorical sense where the parallel Matthew ("treasure up treasures") does not mention it These facts point to the almost certain inference that Luke was dissatisfied with the Mark-Matthew traditions about *"scrip"* and *"girdle,"* and to the highly probable inference that he found difficulty in distinguishing between literal and metaphorical meanings in the Precepts to the Twelve and in the Precepts (that he supposed to be given) to the Seventy.

Before passing to the parallel Mark-Matthew, with its mention of *"girdle,"* we should note the following Mishna which can hardly fail to have been in force during the first half of the first century "Let no man enter into the mount of the Temple with his staff, nor with his shoes, nor with his *purse* (or, *pouch, ponditho*), nor with dust on his feet," where the Gemara has

---

[1] Mt vi 20, Lk xii 33

[2] But Luke mentions money, *lit* "silver" (ix 3 μήτε ἀργύριον) Wetstein on Lk x 4 quotes a Scholiast explaining Aristoph *Nub* 157 ἄνευ βαλαντίου as ἄνευ ἀργυρίου

[3] He does not record any cancelling of the prohibition of a "staff"

(Mark vi 6—13)

THE SENDING OF THE APOSTLES

"neither with his staff in his hand, nor with his shoes on his feet, *nor with money bound up with his linen, nor with a purse (pondîtho) hanging on his back*[1]" Horae Hebraicae, besides these passages, quotes another in which, while the Mishna has *tharmîl*, "*scrip*," the Gemara has *pondîtho*, explained by the Horae as "an inner garment with pockets to hold money etc ," but also defined by an early authority as "a hollow *girdle* (or *belt*) in which they put up their money[2]" Here, then, we have "*scrip*," interchanged with "*purse*," and also with "*girdle [for money]*"

Now, returning to the Synoptic accounts of the Sending of the Twelve and the Sending of the Seventy, we find in them these same utensils of a pilgrim mentioned with similar variations It does not seem likely that the coincidence is accidental. More probably Jesus alluded to ancient Jewish precepts—sometimes literally, but more often metaphorically—when He sent forth His disciples, or spoke of sending them If so, and if we take Mark as the closest approximation to His precepts, He bade the disciples go forth as to the mount of the Temple, observing the precepts of the Temple in some respects, but not in all They were *not* to lay aside their "staff," the staff of Jacob, they were *not* to discard "sandals," fit emblems of the "beautiful feet" of the messengers of the Gospel of Peace. But they were to discard the "scrip," inasmuch as they were to depend on the Father for their daily bread.

The next point is the "brass [money]" in the "girdle." An ancient Greek grammarian says that ignorant and common people used the word "brass" (equivalent to our "coppers"

---

[1] *Hor Heb* on Mt x 9 quoting *J Berach* ix 5 and *Bab Berach* 62 b

[2] *Hor Heb* ib pp 182—3 It also quotes two authorities defining the *tharmîl* as hung round the neck (one adds "of the shepherd") and carrying victuals Comp Levy iv 671 b quoting *Gen r* sect 39 "How was David's coinage stamped? 'With a staff and a *scrip* (*tharmîl*) on one side," and also *Kel* xxiv 11 "there are three kinds of *tharmîl*" The connection between the *tharmîl* and David favours the rendering "scrip"

172 (Mark vi 6—13)

THE SENDING OF THE APOSTLES

or "copper") about money in general[1]. Matthew and Luke, taking it thus, might naturally object to the term thus standing by itself Matthew uses it, but not standing by itself. He has "no gold, [no,] nor yet silver, [no,] nor yet *brass*," so as to give the word emphatically its proper meaning of "coppers" Luke substitutes the ordinary Greek word "silver [money]," meaning "money" in general

But it appears probable that "brass" was deliberately used in the earliest tradition to mean "cumbersome and vile coinage," with perhaps a suggestion also of liability to rust[2], and of the confining and restricting effect of a girdle full of brass money, hampering the limbs like a fetter This view is supported by Biblical instances of the Hebrew "brass" being used for "fetters[3]" The word in this sense is plural But it is exceptionally singular, and rendered "brass" by LXX, where Jeremiah says "He hath made *my brass* heavy[4]" The Hebrew "brass" is also used metaphorically to denote worthless people, who are as "dross[5]" Isaiah said about the Messiah that "righteousness" and "faithfulness" should be His "girdle" The "faithfulness" mentioned by Isaiah is, in fact, "truth," and is so rendered by LXX, and Revelation declared that it

---

[1] See *Corrections* 390 (11) (β) quoting Pollux ix 92

[2] See *Corrections* 390 (11) (γ)—(ε), and add Plutarch *Mor* 665 A describing how lightning rusted brass coinage belonging to "a man asleep, girt with a money-belt containing coppers," ζώνην χαλκοῦς ἔχουσαν ὑπεζωσμένον Pesikt sect 15 (Wu p 167) quoting Is 1 22 "dross," speaks of brass money silvered over by forgers In Mk xii 41 (contrary to *Corrections*) "brass" may be meant literally, besides conveying a suggestion of contempt "The multitude" gave as alms "brass," which they could very well spare, "the rich" gave "many things"—both classes "out of their superabundance"—but the poor widow's two mites surpassed all their gifts The parall Luke has (xxi 1) "the rich, casting into the Treasury their *gifts*"

[3] Gesen 639 *a*

[4] Lam iii 7 "He hath made *my* (R.V) *chain* heavy," LXX ἐβάρυνε χαλκόν μου (Targ "my fetters of *brass* on my feet")

[5] Ezek xxii 18 "all of them are *brass* they are the dross of silver"

THE SENDING OF THE APOSTLES

was "a golden girdle[1]" The Epistle to the Ephesians says to all Christians "Stand, having *girded* your loins with *truth*[2]" This "girdle" of truth, metaphorically represented by a "girdle" of "gold," would be the opposite of a "girdle" of falsehood, dross or "brass" Interpreted thus, Mark's peculiar tradition about "no brass in the girdle" falls into line with his peculiar tradition about being "shod with sandals" Both apply to the Apostles as messengers of the Gospel The latter means that their message is to be one of joy and divine beauty, the former means that the messengers are to be alert, active, and unencumbered, with consciences free from any hampering sense of untruthfulness

The Fourth Gospel does not intervene as to these negative precepts about "scrip," "purse," and "girdle." It gives us the impression that Jesus did not send His disciples away from Himself, or prepare them for being thus sent, till just before the Crucifixion Then, and not till then, the Last Discourse represents Jesus in the Fourth Gospel as saying and reiterating to His disciples "Do not suppose that I will desert you, when I am taken from you in the flesh, leaving you as unhelped, unguided wanderers in the wilderness of this world Ask what ye will, in my name, and I will give it you 'Without me ye can do nothing,' but with me, and 'in my name,' ye can do all things All shall be yours—scrip, purse, staff, sandals fit for the messengers of gladness, they shall all be given to you in the Peace and Joy that I will bestow Even the sword, where need is of the sword, shall not be wanting to you in the power of that Spirit of mine, that other Self, which shall comfort those that need comfort, while it convicts those that need conviction In the world ye shall have tribulation. But be of good cheer I have been victorious over the world[3]"

---

[1] Is xi. 5, Rev i 13   [2] Eph vi 14
[3] See *Light* **3829** on the "paradox" in N T contained in "the few mentions of 'victory,'" which are "mostly accompanied by mentions of what the world would call defeat"

THE SENDING OF THE APOSTLES

§ 10. *"Anointing with oil," in Mark[1] and James*

In N T —apart from a quotation from the Psalms and from a negative sentence in Luke ("my head with oil thou didst not anoint")[2]—the only mention of "anointing with oil," besides this of Mark, runs as follows "Is any among you suffering [hardship][3]? Let him pray Is any cheerful? Let him sing praise. Is any among you sick[4]? Let him call for the elders of the church, and let them pray over him, having anointed him with oil in the name [of the Lord][5] And the prayer of faith[6] shall

---

[1] Mk vi 13 ἤλειφον ἐλαίῳ πολλοὺς ἀρρώστους καὶ ἐθεράπευον The text is ambiguous because, after ἐθεράπευον, we might supply "them," or "sick folk in general " SS has "were anointing with oil many, and were healing the infirm," indicating two classes D, ἀλείψαντες ἐλαίῳ πολλοὺς ἀρρώστους ἐθεράπευον, makes it clear that there were *not* two classes So does the v r ἐθεραπεύοντο, in some inferior MSS, and in Pseudo-Jerome ("sanabantur") whose comment (on Mk vi 4—5) says "cum ungebant oleo aegros infirmitatem fidei [i e eorum] virtute corroborant," "they strengthen the infirmity of [their] faith by a mighty work " This suggests a moral as well as a physical strengthening

[2] Heb i 9 χρίω (quoting Ps xlv 7) and Lk vii 46 ἀλείφω

[3] Jas v 13 κακοπαθεῖ Comp Jas v 10—11 κακοπαθίας, instanced by the prophets and Job It would include, but not necessarily mean, persecution

[4] Ἀσθενεῖ, "weak" in body, or in mind, or in soul, or in resources, according to context

[5] Ἀλείψαντες, not literally "anointing" but "having anointed " "With oil" distinguishes the anointing from one with perfumed ointments for luxury "In the name of the Lord" distinguishes it from mere medical anointing

Ἀλείφω, in LXX, represents three distinct Hebrew words, (1) טוח = "daub," "whitewash," (2) סוך = "anoint [for health or comfort]," (3) משח = "anoint [priests, kings, and sometimes prophets] " Delitzsch uses סוך here

Heb סוך = (Tromm) ἀλείφω (6), χρίω (2) Heb משח (holy anointing) = ἀλείφω (4), χρίω (62) Thus, as a rule, holy anointing is distinguished by LXX from sanitary anointing The former, from which "Messiah" ("the Anointed") is derived, = χρίω, the latter = ἀλείφω

[6] "The prayer of faith" emphasizes the fact that the anointing is not merely medical

175 (Mark vi 6—13)

THE SENDING OF THE APOSTLES

save[1] the failing [man][2], and the Lord shall raise him up[3], and if he have committed sins it shall be forgiven him[4]"

The difficulties of this passage are obvious. If "sick" and "save" and "raise up" refer to physical health, then the writer

---

[1] "Save," σώσει. Σώζω, in N T, = A V "heal," R V txt "make whole," R V marg "save," in Mk v 23, Lk viii 36, Acts xiv 9, A V and R V txt "make whole," R V marg "save," in Mk v 34, Lk viii 48, 50, Acts iv 9 etc.
Διασώζω, in Mt xiv 36, = A V "make perfectly whole," R V "make whole", in Lk vii 3, = A V "heal," R V "save."

[2] Τὸν κάμνοντα "the failing [one]," is often used for "the patient," lit "him that is failing [in vital power]." The only other N T instance of κάμνω is Heb xii 3 ἵνα μὴ κάμητε ταῖς ψυχαῖς ὑμῶν ἐκλυόμενοι. Comp the only instance of κάμνω in canon LXX, Job x 1 κάμνων τῇ ψυχῇ μου, Heb "My soul is weary," and Hermas Mand viii 10 κάμνοντας τῇ ψυχῇ παρακαλεῖν, ἐσκανδαλισμένους. ἐπιστρέφειν. ἁμαρτάνοντας νουθετεῖν. These passages—and the frequent Biblical use of ἐκλύομαι absolutely (e g Heb xii 5 quoting Prov iii 11) meaning "fall to pieces," "collapse"—indicate that in Heb xii 3 ταῖς ψυχαῖς goes with κάμητε (not with ἐκλυόμενοι). In Tatian § 16 ὁ κάμνων θεραπεύεται and § 18 (δαίμονες) ἀποπτάμενοι τῶν καμνόντων, κάμνω refers to those possessed with devils. The passages, as a whole, suggest that κάμνω in Jas implies a spiritual breaking down, a failure in faith, as well as a failure in health. Comp Ps lxxvii 2—10 where the Psalmist, failing in faith and apparently in health at the same time, exclaims "Hath God forgotten to be gracious?" and then adds "This is my *infirmity* (Aq ἀρρωστία)" (see context in R V txt and marg.)

[3] "Shall raise him up (ἐγερεῖ αὐτόν)." This is ambiguous because ἐγείρω, when used transitively with a personal object, may mean (1) "raise [from a bed of sickness]" or (2) "raise [morally and spiritually]" (as in Clem Rom § 59 τοὺς πεπτωκότας ἔγειρον. ἐξανάστησον τοὺς ἀσθενοῦντας, παρακάλεσον τοὺς ὀλιγοψυχοῦντας), or (3) "raise [from the dead]." But in N T, though the third use is frequent when the word is applied to God "raising up" Jesus, i e from the dead, yet ἐγείρω without νεκρούς is not applied to God "raising up" men from the dead except in 2 Cor iv 14 "He that *raised up* the Lord Jesus *shall raise up* us also with Jesus"—where the antithesis explains the exceptional usage. The evidence of N T use favours the rendering (in James) "shall raise him up [from his sick bed]."

[4] Jas v 13—15

seems to promise Christians immortality on earth, for no Christian need die if he has time to "call for the elders." If the words refer to spiritual health, then they appear to promise forgiveness to the perpetrator of the most detestable sins if he can induce "the elders" to "pray over him" with "the prayer of faith." Origen, in a passage that does not quote James, but only a phrase from the Johannine Epistle ("a sin unto death"), yet indicates a danger that might arise from the language of James, when he describes "*certain men who claim even more than the priestly power*," and who profess to obtain forgiveness for everything, "*as though, through their prayer, even 'the sin unto death' was remitted*[1]." Also Irenaeus speaks of heretics who professed to "redeem" the dying, anointing them and teaching them invocations whereby they might evade the powers of evil after death[2]. Elsewhere Irenaeus testifies to the fact that, in his days, besides exorcism, and prophesying, some had the gift of healing (by the laying on of hands) "the *failing* [ones]"—where he uses the Jacobean word above noted[3]. He does not here mention "oil", but Tertullian says that the emperor Severus kept in his palace, till the day of his own death, a Christian named Proculus, out of gratitude "for having once *cured him by oil*[4]."

---

[1] Origen *De Orat* § 28 *ad fin*. ὡς διὰ τῆς εὐχῆς αὐτῶν. λυομένης καὶ τῆς πρὸς θάνατον ἁμαρτίας, an allusion to 1 Jn v 16, which he proceeds to quote

[2] Iren I 21 5 "Alii sunt qui *mortuos* redimunt ad finem defunctionis, mittentes eorum capitibus oleum et aquam ..et cum supradictis invocationibus ..et *praecipiunt eis*, venientibus ad potestates, haec dicere postquam mortui fuerint." The context proves Grabe to be right in saying that "mortuos" is an error (for "morientes") perhaps caused by a mistranslation of τελευτῶντας. Comp Epiphanius (borrowing from Irenaeus) *Haer* 36 (vol. II. p 263) τοὺς τελευτῶντας καὶ ἐπ' αὐτὴν τὴν ἔξοδον φθάνοντας, and especially τῇ κεφαλῇ τοῦ ἐξελθόντος, which ought to mean "of the departed," but which is rendered (as the sense seems to demand) "morientis"

[3] Iren II 32 4 τοὺς κάμνοντας . ἰῶνται καὶ ὑγιεῖς ἀποκαθιστᾶσιν

[4] Tertull *Ad Scap* § 4 "qui eum per oleum aliquando curaverat."

THE SENDING OF THE APOSTLES

These facts shew that in the second century there were much-discussed traditions about Christian anointing with oil, pointing back to a first-century practice, which has been left unmentioned by all the Gospels but Mark's, and by all the Epistles except that of James

§ 11. *"The sin unto death"*

Above, we have found Origen quoting the Johannine Epistle about "the sin unto death" in a warning against some who claimed for themselves, and for their prayers in behalf of the sinner, a more than priestly power[1]. There, he did not quote from James. Elsewhere, commenting on Leviticus ("If the anointed priest shall sin"), he does quote from James There, he lays main stress on the confession of the sinner, not on the prayer of the elders He is describing the seventh and last of the paths to the remission of sins It is through penitence, tears, and confession "Herein is fulfilled that which James the Apostle says, If anyone is infirm (infirmatur) let him call the elders of the church, and let them place their hands on him, anointing him with oil in the name of the Lord And the prayer of faith shall save the infirm (infirmum) [om '*and the Lord shall raise him up*'], and if he has been [entangled] in sins they shall be remitted to him[2]"

It is strange that so careful a quoter as Origen should here omit the words "*and the Lord shall raise him up.*" If the Latin expresses what Origen wrote in Greek, it may be that he thought the "raising up" an ambiguous phrase (meaning either "raise up from the sick bed," or "raise up after a spiritual fall[3]," or

---

[1] See p 177, quoting *De Orat* § 28

[2] Origen (on Lev iv 3 "if the anointed priest shall sin") *Lev Hom* 11 4 (Lomm ix 193).

[3] Comp Clem Rom § 59 above quoted τοὺς πεπτωκότας ἔγειρον and see πίπτω meaning "fall [through want of faith]" etc in Rom xi. 11, 22, xiv 4, 1 Cor x 12, xiii 8 "love never *falleth*," i e never utterly fails or breaks down

THE SENDING OF THE APOSTLES

"raise up at the last day") the insertion of which would obscure what he deemed to be certainly the drift of the whole passage, namely, the way open to forgiveness for the infirm soul entangled in sins.

In the same commentary, later on, speaking of the path to forgiveness through tears, Origen says "There are also those sins which are said to be '*unto death*[1].'" But he does not explain how far "the elders," in the Epistle, correspond to "the priest of the Lord" whom he describes as receiving the confession of sins under the Law, or why one "elder" would not (apparently) suffice[2]. In his Johannine commentary he says that John, while mentioning "a sin unto death," at the same time "points out a distinction, namely, that a certain sin is the soul's death and a certain sin is its sickness[3]" But elsewhere—about an apparent proof from the Gospels and Epistles that some sins are to the soul's loss but not to its death—he quotes the Johannine distinction between sins unto death and sins not unto death, and adds "What kinds of sins are unto death, and what are not unto death, but unto loss, I do not think can be distinguished easily by any human being[4]"

---

[1] Origen *Lev Hom* xi 2 (Lomm ix 380) "Dicimus enim et ad Deum quoniam (Ps lxxx 5) '*Dedisti nobis panem lacrimarum*' Sunt ergo ista peccata quae dicuntur '*ad mortem*'" (1 Jn v 16)

[2] *Lev Hom* ii 4 (Lomm ix 193) "Est adhuc et septima [*i e* via ad remissionem peccatorum]...cum lavat peccator in lacrimis stratum suum. .et cum non erubescit *sacerdoti Domini* indicare peccatum suum et quaerere medicinam, secundum eum qui ait (Ps xxxii 5) '*Dixi pronuntiabo adversum me injustitiam meam Domino, et tu remisisti impietatem cordis mei*' In quo impletur . (Jas v 14) vocet *presbyteros ecclesiae* . ." Comp *Luc Hom* xvii. (Lomm v 150) quoting Ps xxxii 5 and mentioning as a condition "Si revelaverimus peccata nostra non solum Deo *sed et his* (v r *iis*) *qui possunt mederi vulneribus nostris*" Rashi regards the "confession" in Ps xxxii 5 as made by David to Nathan (2 S xii 13)

[3] Origen *Comm Joann* xix 3 (Lomm ii 166)

[4] *Exod Hom* x 3 (Lomm ix 126) "Non puto facile a quoquam hominum posse discerni," after quoting 1 Cor iii 15, Mt xvi 26 and

THE SENDING OF THE APOSTLES

This frank expression of inability to explain the Johannine distinction justifies the conclusion that, in very early days, when faith-healing was frequent in the Christian Churches, and when anointing the sick was frequently used in the hope of a miraculous healing, the Marcan tradition in the Precepts to the Twelve would be a subject of much discussion. We cannot go so far as to say that John alludes to it in his Epistle. But we can say that such an allusion is by no means improbable.

§ 12 *"Anointing" among the Jews*

Anointing among the Jews for the sick was practised as a medicinal remedy. But the book of Job and very many passages in other books of the Bible testify to the belief that sickness was regarded as a divine punishment for sin. And all would admit that sickness does often come as the effect of intemperance, sensuality and other vices. It would therefore be natural

---

1 Jn v 16. He adds "Scriptum namque est (Ps xix 12) Delicta quis intelligit?" A connection between "sin unto death" under the Law and "sin unto death" under the Gospel is traceable—though the phrase is not used—in Heb x 28—31 "A man that [is found to have] set at naught *Moses' law* (Deut xvii 2—6) *dieth without compassion.* Of *how much sorer punishment,* think ye, shall he be counted worthy who hath *trodden under foot the Son of God!"* i e more particularly, by apostatizing and publicly "blaspheming Christ." Comp. Acts xxvi. 11 "I strove to compel them *to blaspheme,"* and Pliny's letter to Trajan (§ 96) which says that he acquitted those who *"male dicerent Christo."*

See Schottgen (on 1 Jn v 16) on the Talmudic distinction between a sin that makes the sinner liable to death, and one that makes him liable to excommunication. *Numb r* Wu p 268 quotes 1 S ii 25 "They [i e Eli's sons] hearkened not unto the voice of their father, because the Lord was minded to slay them," in a recognition of sins so persisted in that a "decree of death" goes forth. Jewish expressions of this kind, referring to literal as well as spiritual death, if retained by Jewish Christians in the first century, might explain several apparent instances of confusion between the literal and the spiritual. For the meaning perhaps attached by John to "the sin unto death," see below, p 188.

180 (Mark vi 6—13)

THE SENDING OF THE APOSTLES

that among the Jews this anointing should be accompanied by prayer. Ben Sira, in a passage printed below, instructively indicates that the prayer might proceed from the physician as well as from the patient, and shews how naturally a promise of healing ("pray unto God for God will heal") might be made with confidence, because, even if the patient was not physically healed, his sins might be forgiven and he might receive spiritual healing[1]

A Jewish tradition about the celebrated Rabbi Meir shews how anointing of this kind, no doubt accompanied by prayer, might be practised by a patient's friends whose presence might correspond to that of "the elders" mentioned by James. "R. Simeon Ben Eliezer saith, R. Meir permitted the mingling of wine and oil, and to anoint the sick on the sabbath. But

---

[1] Ben Sira (*ed.* Schechter and Taylor) begins (xxxvii. 30—31) by warning his readers against "luxury" that brings "sickness," against "surfeit" that is followed by "loathing," and against "intemperance" that ends in "perishing." Then, after declaring that God appointed the physician for men, and brought medicines out of the earth, he proceeds as follows (xxxviii. 7—14) "By them doth the physician assuage pain, and likewise the apothecary maketh a confection that his work may not fail, nor health from among the sons of men. My son, in sickness be not negligent; pray unto God, for He will heal. Flee from iniquity, and from respect of persons, and from all transgressions cleanse thy heart. Offer a sweet savour as a memorial, and fatness estimated according to thy substance. And to the physician also give a place, and he shall not remove, for there is need of him likewise. For there is a time when in his hand is good success: for he too will supplicate unto God, that He will prosper to him the treatment (*or*, draught), and the healing, for the sake of his living."

The LXX differs somewhat from the Hebrew, and concludes thus "There is a time when also in *their hands* [i.e. *the hands of the physicians*] there is good success, for *they too* will supplicate the Lord that He may prosper to them [the] relief [of the sufferer] and healing for the sake of continuance in life." The plural appears to refer to physicians, but it might represent also the sufferer's friends administering the ointment prescribed by the physician.

181 (Mark vi. 6—13)

THE SENDING OF THE APOSTLES

when he once was sick, *and we would do the same to him*, he permitted it not[1]."

Quoting this, the author of Horae Hebraicae prefixes to it the remark, "The Jews say, and that truly, such an *anointing* was physical, although it did not always obtain its end But this *anointing* of the apostles ever obtained its end" The first of these statements may be accepted But the second is hazardous. When Ben Sira writes (as quoted above) "My son, in sickness be not negligent, pray unto God, *for He will heal*," we may say, "This means '*He will sometimes heal*' or '*He will give thee, if not bodily healing, something corresponding to it*'" May we not also say the same thing about the anointing described by Mark and that described by James? It seems probable that, when the Jewish practice of medical anointing passed into the hands of Christian elders—who anointed in the name of Christ, and who often effected marvellous results of physical healing[2]—the old words "sickness," "healing," and "raising up" might be used sometimes physically, but sometimes spiritually, so that in the course of a few years, after faith-healing had become comparatively rare in the Christian

---

[1] See *Hor Heb* (on Mk vi 13) quoting *J Berach* iii 1 The story is repeated in *J Sabb* xiv 3 (also in *B Sabb* 134 a)

[2] Of these, the most remarkable is Peter's raising Tabitha to life But there is a difficulty in believing that Tabitha's friends could have sent for Peter almost as if reckoning upon his power to raise the dead (Acts ix 37—8) "Now it came to pass in those days that she fell sick and died (ἀσθενήσασαν ἀποθανεῖν), and they washed her and placed her in an upper chamber Now, as Lydda was nigh unto Joppa, the disciples, having heard that Peter was there, *sent* (ἀπέστειλαν) *two men to him with entreaty, Delay not to come on to us*" The difficulty will be diminished if we suppose that the aorist, ἀπέστειλαν, here means "[*previously*] *sent*," i e *when she fell sick or reached such a stage that death seemed imminent* See *Joh Gr.* **2460** quoting Jn v 13 "Jesus [*previously*] *conveyed himself away*" (R V and A V "*had conveyed himself away*") It is noteworthy that the Acts and the Epistles (except that of James) make no mention of "anointing with oil"

182 (Mark vi 6—13)

THE SENDING OF THE APOSTLES

Church, the traditions about past faith-healing and those about past spiritual healing were often not easy to distinguish.

§ 13 "*Anointing [with oil]*" *metaphorical*

Eusebius quotes Philo as saying about the Essenes that they were "anointed for fellowship[1]," and this, not using the word *chrīein*, which denotes spiritual anointing, but using the word we have been all this time discussing, *aleiphein*, "*anoint [for health, or comfort]*[2]" The explanation is this. The Greeks used *aleiphein* to mean "anoint for gymnastic exercise." Hence they applied it literally to the Master of a gymnasium, training the young gymnasts for their exercises But hence they also applied it metaphorically to any kind of training for action[3]. Philo here thus applies it metaphorically to Moses of whom he says "*Our Lawgiver anointed* myriads of his disciples *for fellowship*" Clement of Alexandria does the same thing, saying that the Logos "*anoints*," not meaning "holy anointing" or "consecration," but preparation for a wrestling against evil—such a wrestling as befell Jacob, the wrestler at Peniel, when the Logos trained and anointed him for his conflict[4].

In the only passage where the Apostolic Fathers mention this "anointing (*aleiphein*)," it is connected with "teaching," where Ignatius writes "Be not *anointed* with the evil savour of the *teaching* of the ruler of this world," contrasting this with the "ointment" that "the Lord received on His head that He might breathe incorruptibility to the Church[5]" Its only instance in Epictetus is literal, but yet such as to shew how

---

[1] Euseb *Praepar Evang* viii 11 μυρίους δὲ τῶν γνωρίμων ὁ ἡμέτερος νομοθέτης ἤλειψεν ἐπὶ κοινωνίαν, οἳ καλοῦνται μὲν Ἐσσαῖοι οἰκοῦσι δὲ πολλὰς μὲν πόλεις τῆς Ἰουδαίας

[2] See above, p 175, n 5   [3] Steph *Thes* ἀλείφω

[4] Clem Alex 132 ὁ συγγυμναζόμενος καὶ ἀλείφων κατὰ τοῦ πονηροῦ τὸν ἀσκητὴν Ἰακώβ. The context calls the Logos ὁ ἀλείπτης. τῷ Ἰακώβ See Mayor's Index (ἀλείφω)

[5] Ign *Eph* § 17

THE SENDING OF THE APOSTLES

a Christian writer might apply the word metaphorically to a catechist, or recently baptized Christian still "under training[1]" Some traditions of this kind, applied to converts or catechists, may have been intelligible enough in Rome (or other Western Churches) to Christians familiar with vernacular Greek, but may not have seemed to Matthew and Luke adapted for Eastern Churches or for educated Greeks

§ 14 *"Many that were infirm," in Mark[2]*

Returning to the word "infirm" in the Marcan passage under discussion, we note that it is never used by Luke   In Attic Greek it implies mostly "slackness"; it is hardly ever used in canonical LXX, and never by any of the early Fathers or Apologists[3]   Matthew uses it but once—where the parallel Mark describes Jesus not as healing but as "teaching," but Luke mentions both[4]   Origen explains the word in Matthew metaphorically, and, in the same context, he explains the only N T instance of the word outside the Gospels   "For this cause among you many are weak and *infirm*, and not a few are falling-asleep," that is to say (according to Origen) many are weak in faith, or, as it were, chronic invalids, and not a few are falling into a slumber that will make them dead to all faith[5]

---

[1] Epict 1 2 26 ὡς ἀνήρ, ἔφη, ἀνὴρ δ' Ὀλύμπια κεκηρυγμένος καὶ ἠγωνισμένος   οὐχὶ παρὰ τῷ Βάτωνι ἀλειφόμενος, i e a crowned veteran, whose name has been proclaimed in the Olympian games, "no longer *under training in the school of Bato*"

[2] Mk vi. 13

[3] See ἄρρωστος in Steph Thes , Oxf Conc , and Goodspeed   LXX has more frequently ἀρρωστέω and ἀρρωστία

[4]
Mk vi 34	Mt xiv 14	Lk ix 11
And he began to *teach them many things*	And he (lit) tended (ἐθεράπευσεν) their *infirm* [ones]	And he spake to them of the kingdom of God and *them that had need of* (lit) tending (θεραπείας) he proceeded to heal (ἰᾶτο)

[5] Origen on Mt xiv 14 quoting and fully explaining 1 Cor xi 30 πολλοὶ ἀσθενεῖς καὶ ἄρρωστοι καὶ κοιμῶνται ἱκανοί   Apparently Origen regards the loss of spiritual strength and spiritual health, and the

THE SENDING OF THE APOSTLES

By Mark himself the word is obviously taken in a literal sense when he says that Jesus, in His own "country," *was not able to do any "mighty work,"* except that He "*laid his hands on a few infirm [folk] and healed them*[1]" The Mark-Appendix makes the unqualified promise "These signs shall follow them that believe in my name...they shall lay hands on *the infirm* and they shall recover[2]." This, like the similar passage in the Epistle of James, must mean "they shall *sometimes* lay hands," or perhaps "they shall *sometimes* recover" Or "*sometimes*" must be inserted in both cases No "oil" is mentioned in the Mark-Appendix.

The result of these traditions about the "infirm," as also of those about "anointing," and "raising them up," is to confirm the impression that the followers of Jesus did actually heal in a physical sense, but that the accounts of physical and those of spiritual healing were so expressed, and so mingled,

---

access of spiritual slumber, as being God's judgments on those who partake unworthily of the Lord's Supper Origen explains κοιμῶνται by νυστάζοντες τὴν προαίρεσιν and ὑπνώσσοντες τοῖς λογισμοῖς, and ἐνυπνιαζόμενοι as if it referred to fleshly dreamers who, he says, (comp. 2 Pet. ii. 10) "blaspheme glories." But we must have regard to the fact that Paul is alluding to some who made a feast, or even a drunken feast, of the Lord's Supper Isaiah—after frequent rebukes of those that (Is v 11, 22) "follow strong drink," and after predicting that (*ib* xxiv 9) "strong drink shall be bitter to them," and declaring that (*ib* xxviii 7) "the priest and the prophet have gone astray through strong drink," at last bids the drunkards go on their own wilful course and endure a "deep sleep" as the consequent judgment, a sleep caused not by wine but by retribution (*ib* xxix 9—10) "Take your pleasure and be blind.. for the Lord hath poured out upon you the spirit of deep sleep . .." Comp Jerem li 39 "I will make them *drunken* that they may rejoice, and *sleep a perpetual sleep, and not wake*" Such a "sleep" is a "judgment," but it is not a dreaming so much as a deadly torpor Comp Ps xiii 3 "Lighten my eyes lest I *sleep death*"

[1] Mk vi 5 "healed," *lit* "tended," ἐθεράπευσεν, on which see *Proclam* pp 208—20
[2] [Mk xvi 17—18]

THE SENDING OF THE APOSTLES

that the enemies of Christians might sometimes shew good reason for impugning their veracity[1].

Another point to be noted is that Mark's statement of the manner in which the Twelve carried out the precepts of the Lord ("and they went forth and preached...and healed them[2]") *makes no mention of their baptizing.* We should have expected "baptizing" to follow "preaching," thus: "And they went forth and preached that men should repent, *and they baptized many.*" According to the Fourth Gospel, this was the one thing that the Twelve did, namely, "baptized" many—and so "many" that the Evangelist calls them "more disciples than John baptized." And that this was in the name of Jesus, that is to say, under the authority of Jesus, we learn from the fact that at first the Gospel says that Jesus baptized, though afterwards it adds "Jesus himself baptized not, but his disciples did[3]." It is difficult to believe that Mark's original omitted "baptizing." Perhaps, however, "baptizing"—expressed by "enlightening," or by "raising up from darkness," or by "anointing with the Spirit," or by "anointing in the NAME" —is latent in the Marcan "anointing."

This is compatible with the hypothesis that the tradition (which is omitted by Matthew) is antedated by Mark and belongs

---

[1] See Lightf on Clem Rom § 59 (quoted in part above, p 176) "Raise up the fallen , *heal the ungodly* . , feed the hungry, release our prisoners ($\delta\epsilon\sigma\mu\acute{\iota}ovs$), lift up the weak ($\tau o\grave{v}s\ \grave{a}\sigma\theta\epsilon\nu o\hat{v}\nu\tau as$), comfort the faint-hearted." Here "prisoners" is (doubtless) literal, but "the ungodly" is, in Syr , "*aegrotos*." This might represent $\grave{a}\sigma\theta\epsilon\nu\epsilon\hat{\iota}s$, *i e* "the sick." Against this, however, is the subsequent $\grave{a}\sigma\theta\epsilon\nu o\hat{v}\nu\tau as$, which would come superfluously after a preceding $\grave{a}\sigma\theta\epsilon\nu\epsilon\hat{\iota}s$. Harnack says "$\grave{a}\sigma\theta\epsilon\nu o\hat{v}\nu\tau\epsilon s$ animo, $\grave{a}\sigma\theta\epsilon\nu\epsilon\hat{\iota}s$ corpore imbecilles sunt." But Lightf replies "Both words are used indifferently either of physical or of moral weakness." This remark gives us an insight into many possibilities of error in the first century permeating Christian accounts of healing—error not arising from dishonesty, but from the blending of the literal with the metaphorical and from consequent ambiguity

[2] Mk vi 12—13   [3] Jn iv 1—2.

THE SENDING OF THE APOSTLES

to precepts given after the Resurrection. But, if the Marcan tradition refers to a period before the Resurrection, we may suppose that the Fourth Gospel intervenes, perhaps moved by a thought of this kind: "Mark says that the Twelve, when they were sent out by Jesus before the Resurrection, '*anointed with oil*' Matthew and Luke reject this. But it means that they *baptized*, not indeed with that complete baptism which brings the *chrism* with it, but with the baptism of John administered in the name of Jesus."

§ 15. *Johannine tradition*

Passing now to Johannine tradition, we find that, although John makes no mention of the "infirm" or of "anointing with oil" either in his Gospel or in the Epistle, yet in the latter he does mention that higher kind of "anointing," a spiritual one, or *chrism*, which kept those whom he calls "little children" from the doctrine of "antichrists," and from every "lie," so that they might "abide in" the Lord and "have boldness at his coming[1]" But the *chrism* does not, of itself, suffice to save them. They must "abide in" the Giver of the *chrism*[2]. This strikes at the root of some above-mentioned heresies, which inculcated material anointings, with incantations, as a means of evading the clutches of such demons as might lie in wait for a dying soul to intercept its passage to the region of blessedness[3]. Toward the end of the Epistle, the writer goes even further in his discouragement of any mechanical doctrine of saving by prayer and anointing. If we ask anything according to God's will, he tells us that God "heareth us," and "if any man see

---

[1] 1 Jn ii 18—28 "Little children . at his coming." "Anointing" here is (*ib* 20, 27) χρίσμα, *i e* holy anointing, not ἄλειμμα (from the Marcan word ἀλείφω).

[2] 1 Jn ii 27 μένετε ἐν αὐτῷ, followed by καὶ νῦν, τεκνία, μένετε ἐν αὐτῷ—whether the first μένετε is indicative or imperative—in any case expresses, as a whole, a very emphatic warning.

[3] See above, p 177 n 2.

THE SENDING OF THE APOSTLES

his brother sinning a sin not unto death, he shall ask." But it is added "There is a sin unto death, not concerning this do I say that he should make request[1]." In this, and in the context, there is a vagueness, and a reticence, that are very perplexing; but the words become less obscure if regarded as a protest against immoral formalism and in behalf of instinctive and spiritual morality. They appear to illustrate, and to be illustrated by, the saying peculiar to the Fourth Gospel, "Whose soever sins ye retain they are retained." There are circumstances where we are to be quiet and to believe in God, but not to pray. "A man is not to pray, even for 'his brother,' in such terms as go against his conscience, and against the testimony of the Holy Spirit within him"—this appears to be the meaning of the Johannine warning. The necessity of such a warning throws light on the degeneracy of many Christians at the time when the Epistle was written, and on the probability that "the anointing of the infirm with oil," mentioned by Mark alone of the Evangelists, had been gravely abused. John does not say this, nor does he say anything definitely negative to forbid such abuse. But he directs our attention to that higher kind of anointing, the *chrism*, the anointing with the Holy Spirit, which we received from the Lord, and which will abide in us if we abide in Him[2]

---

[1] 1 Jn v 14—16

[2] No attempt has been made in this chapter to answer the very natural question, "Why does Mark omit—what James inserts—that the anointing with oil was '*in the name of the Lord*'?" On this see *Son* **3534** *d*. The Hebrew for "*oil*" is easily confused, and is once (Prov xxvii 16) actually confused by LXX, with the Hebrew for "*name*." If the original said, "They anointed many (*a*) *with oil* (*b*) *in the NAME*," i e "name of the Lord," the similarity of (*a*) and (*b*) might induce Mark to omit the latter, thus reducing the tradition to the level of a mere sanitary or medical anointing. This Matthew and Luke might naturally reject.

Also, the ambiguity of expressions bearing on the Resurrection has been merely touched on. It will be more fitly discussed when we come (Mk xii 18—27) to the controversy between Jesus and the

THE SENDING OF THE APOSTLES

Sadducees on that subject. The Pauline Epistles recognise that even in the Church of Corinth (1 Cor xv 12, comp 2 Tim ii 18) some said that there was no resurrection, perhaps meaning that they had already "risen" in baptism, according to the words of the Christian song (Eph v 14) "*Awake* (or, *arise*) (ἔγειρε) thou that sleepest, and *rise up* (ἀνάστα) from the dead, and Christ shall dawn on thee." John exhibits Jesus Himself as twice using such ambiguous language on subjects of this kind that His disciples were deceived. He said "Lazarus is fallen asleep" (Jn xi 11) and they thought He meant it literally, but He meant "Lazarus is dead." He also said to Martha (*ib.* xi. 23) "Thy brother shall rise up (ἀναστήσεται)" and Martha replied (*ib* xi 24) "I know that he will rise up in the rising up in the last day", but He meant more than that.

Some critics may say that John describes Jesus as deliberately and gratuitously mystifying the disciples. But perhaps they might change their minds if they realised the variety of Christian thought in the first century as to the time, place, and manner of the general resurrection. It is manifest in the Epistles. It is manifest also in Revelation (xx 5—6) which speaks of "the first resurrection," to be followed by a "second death." Realising this, many may feel that the Fourth Evangelist wrote with wisdom as well as with a deep love of fundamental truth. It is probable that Jesus did, as a fact, use ambiguous terms, feeling that death was "a sleep" and that resurrection was a spiritual union with the Father. On both sides, and in opposite directions, Christian extremists hardened Christ's metaphorical and prophetic language into materialistic dogmas. John pointed out, between the two extremes, a midway path of spiritual faith, faith in One who said—or rather meant and taught in substance, for He did not probably (*Proclam* Pref p. xii) use the exact words— (Jn xi 25) "I am the resurrection and the life."

CHAPTER VII

JOHN THE BAPTIST'S DEATH
[Mark vi. 14—29]

§ 1. *What was said after the Baptist's death*

THE parallel texts given below, relating what was said after the Baptist's death about Jesus, differ in such a way as to shew early confusion of traditional phrases, assigned to different speakers, or placed in different contexts[1].

For example, the saying that John was "*risen from the dead*" is attributed by Mark (probably) to the people first, and

---

[1]

Mk vi 14—16 (R V)	Mt. xiv 1—2 (R V)	Lk ix 7—9 (R V)
(14) And king Herod heard [thereof], for his name had become known and he (*some anc auth they*) said, John the Baptist (*lit* the Baptizer) is risen (ἐγήγερ-ται) from the dead, and therefore do these powers work in him (15) But others said, It is Elijah And others said, [It is] a prophet, [even] as one of the prophets (16) But Herod, when he heard [thereof], said, John, whom I beheaded, he (οὗτος) is risen (ἠγέρθη)	(1) At that season Herod the tetrarch heard the report concerning Jesus, (2) And said unto his servants, This is John the Baptist, he (αὐτὸς) is risen (ἠγέρθη) from the dead, and therefore do these powers work in him	(7) Now Herod the tetrarch heard of all that was done and he was much perplexed, because that it was said by some, that John was risen (ἠγέρθη) from the dead, (8) And by some, that Elijah had appeared, and by others, that one of the old prophets was risen again (ἀνέστη) (9) And Herod said, John I beheaded but who is this, about whom I hear such things? And he sought to see him

190 (Mark vi 14—16)

JOHN THE BAPTIST'S DEATH

secondly to Herod[1]. Matthew mentions it only once, and then assigns it to Herod, adding that he said it "to his servants[2]" Luke mentions it only once, but assigns it, not to Herod but to "some" ("he was much perplexed because that it was said by *some*[3]")—whom presumably Herod heard saying it. Luke adds, as one of the popular rumours, "that one of the old prophets was *risen-again*"—where the sense seems to demand that "*risen-again*" should mean "*risen from the dead*[4]." Mark concludes with Herod's own words "*The John whom I beheaded —this [same John] is risen*," where he does not say "risen from

---

[1] Mk vi 14—16 reading ἔλεγον with W H txt ⌜ἔλεγον⌝. So Field *Ot Nori.* ad loc. "And king Herod heard [thereof], (for his name had become known and they" [*i e* folk] "said, John...But others said..., and others said..) But Herod, when he heard [thereof], said, John, whom I beheaded, the same (οὗτος, see Mt xxi 42, Jn iii 26) is risen." Field says "The sentence is suspended, in order to introduce the opinions of the people, and taken up again at vi 16."

[2] Mt xiv 2 εἶπεν τοῖς παισὶν αὐτοῦ. This would explain how it came to be known. It was not a soliloquy. Herod's guilty conscience forced him to say it aloud to those about him.

[3] If εἶπεν τοῖς παισὶν were written εἶπον ἐν τοῖς παισὶν, "*they said*, among his servants," this would correspond to the Marcan ἔλεγον, "*they said*," and ἐν τοῖς παισὶν would be a way of adding "in Herod's own palace."

[4] Lk ix 8 προφήτης τις τῶν ἀρχαίων ἀνέστη (not ἠγέρθη). But it may mean "one of [the rank of] the old prophets has arisen." The parall Mk vi 15 has προφήτης ὡς εἷς τῶν προφητῶν, "a [new] prophet as [*great as*] one of the [old] prophets." Mark's insertion of ὡς avoids the suggestion of a resurrection from the dead.

The preceding Ἠλείας ἐφάνη in Lk ix 8 is not the same as Ἠλείας ὤφθη or ἀνέστη. It is perhaps used with allusion to Sir xlviii 1 "Then stood up Elias the prophet *as fire, and his word burned like a lamp*." Comp Jn v 35 "he [*i e* John the Baptist] was the lamp that burneth [*i e* is burned] and shineth," ὁ λύχνος ὁ καιόμενος καὶ φαίνων. Even when Luke is describing idle popular talk, he perhaps prefers not to write that Jesus "*is* Elias," but rather to use a phrase that suggests "*shone forth*" as well as "*appeared*" (comp Lk i 17 "in the spirit and power of Elias") so as to imply, not identity of person, but similarity of glory.

JOHN THE BAPTIST'S DEATH

the dead" as above, but "risen", and the parallel Luke has "*John I beheaded but who is this...*¹?"

It will be found in the next section that the Lucan word "*much-perplexed*," applied here to Herod's perplexity *after John's death*, recurs in Mark in a shorter form, "*perplexed*" —but applied to Herod's relations *with his living prisoner*, John, and probably in quite a different sense². It will also be found that, whereas Mark describes Herod as "*fearing John*" (that is, as respecting him) and as "keeping him safe," the parallel Matthew says that Herod would have put John to death, but "*he feared the multitude*" These confusions, and the fact that in all the Synoptists prominence is given to Herod—a name never mentioned in the Fourth Gospel—might lead us to anticipate that John would not intervene here in any way, directly or indirectly He generally intervenes where Luke differs from Mark But here Luke agrees with Mark more closely than Matthew does That is another reason for not expecting Johannine intervention

There are two sentences, however, one in Mark, and one in Mark and Matthew, as to which we might expect Johannine intervention because Luke omits them. The first is "for his name had become manifest" This seems to mean that the name of Jesus had been unknown to Herod, or obscure, up to this time, but that now—after the death of John the Baptist, and after Jesus had sent out the Twelve to preach and heal— it became, or had become, so far manifest that Herod heard of

---

¹ If Mark's original had some brief expression like "Whom I beheaded, John—this [is] he," it might branch out into the present Marcan and Lucan texts For clearness, (1) Mark might supply "is risen" (shortened as a repetition of the previous "risen from the dead"), (2) Luke, taking the sentence interrogatively, and regarding the relative as an error for the interrogative, might read "Who— [for] I have beheaded John—is this?" Then he might supply "about whom I hear such things"

² Lk ix 7 διηπόρει, Mk vi 20 ἠπόρει See p. 199 foll.

JOHN THE BAPTIST'S DEATH

it[1] This is altered by Matthew into "Herod...had heard the report about Jesus[2]," without any previous contextual mention of the works of the Twelve Luke substitutes a perfectly neutral phrase "heard all the things that were being done," that is, done by the Apostles, who are described in the previous verse as "healing everywhere[3]"

The second sentence is, in Mark and Matthew, "*For this cause the [miraculous] powers work-inwardly in him* [i e *in Jesus*][4]," where the "cause" has been previously expressed, in Mark by "John the baptizer is raised from the dead," but in Matthew by "This is John the Baptist, he [himself] is raised from the dead"

In both these cases the Fourth Gospel appears to intervene. As to the former, it tells us that even before the arrest of the Baptist, Jesus was making more converts than those made by John, and that this fact was known to the Pharisees[5], so that

---

[1] Mk vi 14 ἤκουσεν ὁ βασιλεὺς Ἡρῴδης, φανερὸν γὰρ ἐγένετο τὸ ὄνομα αὐτοῦ We are not told *what* Herod "heard," but Mark's text suggests that it was the previously mentioned wonders worked by the apostles (Mk vi 13) If they were worked (comp Jas v. 14) "in the name" of their Master, then the meaning would be "For by reason of the works performed *in His name, the name of Jesus* became manifest"

"*He*" (meaning Jesus) has not been mentioned since Mk vi 10 "*and he* said unto them" Hence "*for his name* had become known" presents itself very abruptly to the reader It is likely to have been altered by Matthew and Luke on that account, apart from other reasons.

[2] Mt xiv I ἤκουσεν...τὴν ἀκοὴν Ἰησοῦ R V "*report*," but A V "*fame*," both here and in Mt. iv 24 ἀπῆλθεν ἡ ἀκοὴ αὐτοῦ εἰς ὅλην τὴν Συρίαν Some word between "*report*" and "*fame*" is needed to express ἀκοή in this context

[3] Lk ix 7 ἤκουσεν τὰ γινόμενα πάντα, referring to *ib* ix 6 . θεραπεύοντες πανταχοῦ

[4] Mk vi 14 (sim Mt xiv 2) καὶ διὰ τοῦτο ἐνεργοῦσιν αἱ δυνάμεις ἐν αὐτῷ

[5] Jn iv 1 Comp iii 22, which implies that the disciples of Christ, at that time, when baptizing in Christ's name, or under Christ's direction, remained in His neighbourhood

JOHN THE BAPTIST'S DEATH

some time before the Baptist's death, the "name" of Jesus would probably be "manifest" to all those who knew the name of the Baptist. As to the latter—the notion that Christ's miracles were in some way the result of the Baptist's rising from the dead—the Fourth Gospel puts into the mouth of "many" of the people words that expose its absurdity "And many came unto him [*i e* Jesus] and they said, *John indeed did no sign*, but all things whatsoever John spake of this man were true[1]."

Luke, in this description of idle sayings about the Baptist and Jesus, inserts a saying that Jesus was Elijah, and another that He was an ancient prophet risen again Herein he resembles or follows Mark The Fourth Gospel represents the Baptist as being expressly questioned whether he was "Elijah," and whether he was "the prophet," and as returning to both questions an express negative[2]. It also indirectly meets the absurd notion that "power" passed out of the Baptist into Jesus by teaching, in effect, that the power, or nature, of Jesus was of a different kind from the Baptist's The Baptist's last words (it says) were that Jesus "must increase" while he himself "must decrease[3]." But this, the Evangelist implies, did not mean that Jesus was to receive, in larger measure, similar power to the Baptist's The power was to be of a different kind. The Baptist, though the friend of the Bridegroom, was "of the earth" whereas Jesus was "from above[4]." The same thing is said later on by Jesus Himself in a different metaphor, describing John as "the lamp that burneth and shineth" whereas Jesus is "the light of the world[5]."

---

[1] Jn x 41.
[2] Jn i 21
[3] Jn iii 30.
[4] Jn iii 31.
[5] Jn v. 35 καιόμενος (*Joh. Gr.* **2275** *b*), viii 12

JOHN THE BAPTIST'S DEATH

§ 2   *The cause of the Baptist's death*[1]

The part alleged to have been played by Herodias and her daughter in bringing about the Baptist's death is not mentioned

---

[1] Mk vi 17—29 (R V)

(17) For Herod himself had sent forth and laid hold upon John, and bound him in prison for the sake of Herodias, his brother Philip's wife for he had married her
(18) For John said unto Herod, It is not lawful for thee to have thy brother's wife
(19) And Herodias set herself against him, and desired to kill him, and she could not,
(20) For Herod feared John, knowing that he was a righteous man and a holy, and kept him safe And when he heard him, he was much perplexed (*many anc auth* did many things), and he heard him gladly
(21) And when a convenient day was come, that Herod on his birthday made a supper to his lords, and the high captains (*lit* chiliarchs), and the chief men of Galilee,
(22) And when the daughter of Herodias (*some anc auth* his daughter Herodias) herself came in and danced, she (*or,*

Mt xiv 3—12 (R V)

(3) For Herod had laid hold on John, and bound him, and put him in prison for the sake of Herodias, his brother Philip's wife

(4) For John said unto him, It is not lawful for thee to have her

(5) And when he would have put him to death, he feared the multitude, because they counted him as a prophet

(6) But when Herod's birthday came,

the daughter of Herodias danced in the midst, and pleased Herod.
(7) Whereupon he promised with

Lk iii 18—20 (R V)

(18) With many other exhortations therefore preached he good tidings (*or*, the gospel) unto the people,
(19) But Herod the tetrarch, being reproved by him for Herodias his brother's wife, and for all the evil things which Herod had done,
(20) Added yet this above all, that he shut up John in prison

JOHN THE BAPTIST'S DEATH

by Josephus. He says merely that Herod Antipas imprisoned and executed the prophet because he was too influential with

Mk vi. 17—29 (R.V.) *contd*	Mt. xiv 3—12 (R V.) *contd*.	Lk. iii. 18—20 (R.V.)
it) pleased Herod and them that sat at meat with him, and the king said unto the damsel, Ask of me whatsoever thou wilt, and I will give it thee (23) And he sware unto her, whatsoever thou shalt ask of me, I will give it thee, unto the half of my kingdom (24) And she went out, and said unto her mother, What shall I ask? And she said, The head of John the Baptist (*lit* the Baptizer) (25) And she came in straightway with haste unto the king, and asked, saying, I will that thou forthwith give me in a charger the head of John the Baptist (*lit* the Baptizer) (26) And the king was exceeding sorry, but for the sake of his oaths, and of them that sat at meat, he would not reject her (27) And straightway the king sent forth a soldier of his guard, and commanded to bring his head and he went and beheaded him in the prison, (28) And brought his head in a charger,	an oath to give her whatsoever she should ask (8) And she, being put forward by her mother, saith, Give me here in a charger the head of John the Baptist (9) And the king was grieved, but for the sake of his oaths, and of them which sat at meat with him, he commanded it to be given, (10) And he sent, and beheaded John in the prison (11) And his head was brought in a charger, and given to the damsel and she brought it to her mother (12) And his dis-	

JOHN THE BAPTIST'S DEATH

the people¹ But we cannot doubt that Mark's story about Herod's oath—possibly a prearranged "oath"—represents what people in Galilee believed to have been (and what probably was) the historical fact—that the life of the last of the Jewish prophets was openly and publicly sacrificed for a dance². This belief must have powerfully influenced the multitude in their feelings and expectations about Jesus. Many patriotic Jews among His admirers would be alienated from Him when His tacit refusal to make any effort at a rescue resulted in the prophet's brutal and ignominious execution. As soon as Christ's own disciples heard of the news of the murder, the first impulse of many of them would be to exclaim "Surely our Master must do something now. Surely He will avenge the Prophet on this false king, this 'king Herod³.' Why do we not make the Son of David king?"

Mk vi 17—29 (R.V.) contd.	Mt xiv. 3—12 (R.V.) contd.	Lk. iii. 18—20 (R.V.)
and gave it to the damsel, and the damsel gave it to her mother (29) And when his disciples heard [thereof], they came and took up his corpse, and laid it in a tomb	ciples came, and took up the corpse, and buried him, and they went and told Jesus	

¹ See *Son* **3338**b quoting Josephus *Ant* xviii 5 2, and adding "Very likely there was an 'oath,' but a prearranged 'oath'"

² It has been urged that the daughter of Herodias could not have been young enough to be a κοράσιον at the time of the dancing But see Schurer I ii 28 for the facts that induce him to conclude "Just the weakest point in the Gospel story is proved on more careful examination to be not improbable"

³ Why does Mk vi 14 foll call Herod Antipas "king"—and that, too, five times? Everyone knew that he was never "king," except in a will made by his father (Joseph *Bell* 1 32 7) and afterwards (*ib* 1 33. 7) cancelled When Antipas, persuaded by Herodias, came to Rome with a petition to be made "king" (*ib* ii 9 6) he was deprived of his tetrarchy and banished to Spain In his own palace, he was perhaps called "king" by his courtiers If so,

This would accord with the project—recorded in the Fourth Gospel alone as occurring about this time—to make Jesus a "king[1]." Jesus frustrated it by withdrawing. Soon afterwards we hear that many of His disciples abandoned Him. The Gospel says it was because of Christ's "hard saying"— the doctrine of the giving of His flesh and blood for the world[2]. But that does not exclude other, and perhaps more powerful causes. If Jesus had put Himself at the head of a band of Galilaeans bent on avenging the Baptist, the mass of His followers would not have been deterred from following Him by any "hard sayings." They would abandon Jesus (we may feel sure) not only because He seemed to talk dreams like Ezekiel the prophet of parables[3], but also because He did not do deeds, such as they expected from the Messianic Son of David.

These Marcan details, though historically true and dramatically interesting, tend to divert attention from Jesus to the Baptist. Mark may most accurately represent the contemporary gossip of Galilee laying the blame for the prophet's death rather on Herodias than on Herod; yet we cannot be surprised that in subsequent Gospels his early narrative was condensed or omitted as not being history. Luke, the historian, wholly omits it. Yet there remains one faint trace of Luke's recognition of Mark's narrative in one tell-tale similarity of phrase. It lies in Luke's and Mark's accounts of Herod's "perplexity," touched on above, but worthy of a little more notice here, because it may give us insight into the original form of the narrative.

Mark speaks of frequent interviews between Herod and the Baptist in language that recalls the interviews between Paul

---

there may be a tinge of irony in Mark's fivefold mention of the title. Comp Paul's speech to a real "king" in Acts xxvi 2—27 and note how he repeats "king" six times. Jews in the first century were keenly alive to the distinction between a "king" and a "tetrarch."

[1] Jn vi. 15   [2] Jn vi 60
[3] Ezek xx 49 "They say of me, Doth he not speak parables?'

(Mark vi 17—29)

JOHN THE BAPTIST'S DEATH

and Felix in the Acts, and also conversations between Rabbis and Roman Emperors mentioned in the Talmuds[1] In Paul's case, though Felix was at first "terrified," the result was that he kept Paul in prison for two years and left him there, after repeatedly trying to get money out of him His conscience does not appear to have been touched The Rabbis are often described as being subjected in interviews to searching questions, of the nature of a "dilemma," "poser," "puzzle," or "perplexity," from which they emerge triumphant.

Now the verb (*aporein*) here used by Mark about Herod is used, from Aristotle downwards, to mean "*raise a difficulty* (or, *objection*)" in a philosophic discussion[2] It is used transitively by Irenaeus to describe how Jesus (according to certain heretics) "*posed*" the Pharisees by a question[3] Clement of Alexandria says that an Indian Gymnosophist was "*posed*" by Alexander with the query "How shall a man best attain love[4]?" The Clementine Homilies use the word (along with "shouting down") as meaning "*bring to a standstill*[5]"

This interpretation of *aporein* is consistent with Mark's addition of "*many things*," which he often uses with verbs of teaching, exhorting, etc , to imply repeated utterances, and not to mean "much" in the sense of "*deeply*[6]" The difficulty

---

[1] See Acts xxiv 24—7 and Levy 1 33, and 107—8 (on Hadrian and Antoninus)

[2] See L S and the Index to Plutarch which gives ἀπορεῖν as "disputare" (as well as "dubitare") Ἀπόρημα means an "objection" thus raised

[3] Iren 1 20 2

Clem Alex 759 ἀπορηθείς (Clark "*posed* with the query"), comp ib 788 τὸ πρὸς τῶν αἱρετικῶν ἀπορούμενον "*the dilemma* put by heretics"

[5] *Clem Hom.* 1 11 κατασιωπᾶν καὶ ἀπορεῖν αὐτὸν...ὡς βάρβαρόν τινα δαιμονῶντα

[6] Comp πολλά with verbs of speech in Mk 1 45, iv 2, vi 34, xv 3 Perhaps also we should render Mk ix 26 πολλὰ σπαράξας "having *repeatedly* convulsed him" In Mk v 10, παρεκάλει αὐτὸν πολλά implies both repetition and urgency

JOHN THE BAPTIST'S DEATH

presented by the Marcan *aporein* has probably caused Matthew to omit it and has certainly caused many authorities to read it as *poiein* ("he *did* many things," i e did good deeds at the Baptist's suggestion)[1] And the same difficulty has probably caused Luke to prefix *dia* to *aporein*, so as to mean "*much-perplexed*," and to transfer it to another context where Herod is said to have been "*much perplexed*," not by what the living prophet said to him, but by what people said about the dead prophet and his apparent successor, Jesus of Nazareth[2]

Mark's narrative bears the stamp of consistent truth, not necessarily historical truth, but popular truth, noised about, first in Galilee and then in the Church at Rome In Rome, the death of the Baptist by the orders of Herod but at the instigation of Herodias, could not but remind Roman Christians of the death of Cicero by the orders of Mark Antony but (as people said) at the instigation of his wife Fulvia[3] According to Mark and Mark alone, Herod exclaimed "The John whom I beheaded is risen[4]" This was the same John whom he had kept as an interesting prisoner, "hearing him with pleasure," though

---

[1] So R V marg and inferior Gk MSS with Syr and Lat versions So Daniel (iv 27), in effect, suggests to Nebuchadnezzar that he will be wise to do "many things," especially almsgiving

[2] Lk ix 7 διηπόρει Comp Acts v 24, x 17 διηπόρουν (-ει), and *ib* 11 12 διηπορούντο denoting perplexity about marvels apparently supernatural Διαπορέω (Steph *Thes*) has the same meanings as ἀπορέω but is not so often used as ἀπορέω to denote a philosophic and dispassionate "objection"

[3] See Mayor's Notes on Juvenal x 120 "'It is said that Antony set Cicero's head before the table at his meal, till he had glutted himself with the sight' Fulvia, another Herodias [Hieron in Rufin iii 42], spat upon the head, took it on her knees, and stabbed the tongue with her hair pin, D Cass xlvii 8 §§ 3—4" Cicero had alluded (2 Philipp. v 11) to Fulvia as the "fate" of her three husbands, Antony being the third This makes Fulvia's act probable, though Plutarch omits it

[4] Mk vi 16 ἠγέρθη 'Ἐκ νεκρῶν has to be supplied from vi 14 ἐγεγήγερται ἐκ νεκρῶν and is inserted in the text by A V following some MSS.

JOHN THE BAPTIST'S DEATH

"raising many objections" to his doctrines. There is an antecedent probability in such a cry of the conscience as Mark seems to attribute to Herod "I took pleasure in arguing against his doctrine, and against the doctrine of the rising of the dead, and now God has raised him up to punish me for his death[1]"

Among minute indications of the early and popular character of Mark's whole narrative, there is (as has been noted above) his repeated use of "king," applied to Herod[2]—a title altered by Matthew and Luke into "tetrarch," though Matthew subsequently falls (once) into the use of the Marcan title. But it is to the internal evidence of the narrative as a whole that we must mainly look for the demonstration of its early date—to its disordered sentences, its digressiveness, and its disproportionate diffuseness, natural in some Petrine story—especially if Peter had been one of the Baptist's disciples—but unsuited for Luke the historian, and for John the Evangelist of the Word of God compared with whom the Baptist was but "a voice"

Luke deals very freely with such Marcan fragments as he selects. As for Herodias, he merely makes mention of her marriage in connection with "all the evil things that Herod had done" and places it before the baptism of Jesus and at the end of his account of John the Baptist, whom, he says, Herod "shut up in prison[3]." As for the Baptist's death, the only Lucan mention of it is in "John have I beheaded," discussed above. There is no suggestion that Herod said anything about a resurrection from the dead. Indeed the notion that he said this and that his conscience was stricken is inconsistent with

---

[1] In Matthew, Herod says "he is risen from the dead" but not "whom I beheaded." In Luke, Herod says "John I beheaded" but not "he is risen from the dead." Mark has both.

[2] Mk vi 14, 22, 25, 26, 27 βασιλεύς, Mt xiv 1 and Lk ix 7 τετραάρχης, Mt xiv 9 βασιλεύς. See above, p 197, n 3

[3] Lk iii 18—20

201 (Mark vi. 17—29)

JOHN THE BAPTIST'S DEATH

what follows "But who is this about whom I hear such things? And he sought to see him." These words prepare the way for a tradition peculiar to Luke, and inserted by him much later on, that Herod did actually see Jesus and "mocked him with his men of war"—a story probably resulting from a misunderstanding[1], but still affording evidence as to Luke's view, namely, that Herod Antipas had not been touched by any remorse for the execution of the Baptist

The Johannine method resembles the Lucan in the brevity of its only allusion to the Baptist's imprisonment ("John was not yet cast into prison[2]") But it differs in this respect, that it makes no mention at all of "beheading" or of execution in any form. If the works of Josephus and the Synoptists had perished we should never have known from the Fourth Gospel how or when the Baptist died We should have known only that his last recorded words were about Jesus "He must increase, but I must decrease[3]"

---

[1] See *Clue* 55—60, and *Son* 3183 *c—d* on "Luke's attitude to Herod Antipas"

[2] Jn iii. 24

[3] Jn iii 30 [Jn iii 31—6 is probably the Evangelist's comment, and not the words of the Baptist, see *Joh Gr* Pref p viii] In Luke, the last recorded words of the Baptist are (Lk vii 19) "Art thou he that is to come, or look we for another?"

CHAPTER VIII

CHRIST'S MIRACLES OF FEEDING

[Mark vi. 29—44, viii. 1—9, viii. 14—21]

[See p 208, n. 1]

§ 1. *The complexity of the evidence*

THE study of Christ's miracles of feeding is complicated by Jewish peculiarities not only of thought but also of expression. For example, the Feeding of the Five Thousand challenges some kind of comparison (such as we find in the Fourth Gospel) with the giving of the manna in the wilderness[1]. Now concerning the latter it is said in Exodus "The people shall go out and gather (lit) the word of the day in its day[2]." That is to say, the amount necessary for the day was to be gathered on that same day. It was also to be eaten on that same day. None of it was to be left till next morning[3].

According to the texts of our English Versions, the Lord's Prayer, instead of saying "Give us *the bread of the day in its day*," says "Give us *this day our daily bread*," or "Give us *day by day our daily bread*[4]" But these appear to be Christian

---

[1] Jn vi 31

[2] Exod xvi 4   The Heb for "word" often means "thing" or "matter"   LXX omits it, τὸ τῆς ἡμέρας εἰς ἡμέραν, Vulg "quae sufficiunt per singulos dies "   Aq inserts αὐτῆς after ἡμέραν

[3] Exod xvi 19

[4] Mt vi 11 τὸν ἄρτον ἡμῶν τὸν ἐπιούσιον δὸς ἡμῖν σήμερον, Lk xi 3 τὸν ἄρτον ἡμῶν τὸν ἐπιούσιον δίδου ἡμῖν τὸ καθ' ἡμέραν   The pres imperat denotes continuous action. A.V. marg in Lk has "for the day" instead of "day by day "   R V. marg in both has "*Gr.* our bread for the coming day" instead of "our daily bread "

203   (Mark vi 29—44)

attempts to render in Greek some Aramaic expression corresponding to the Hebrew of Exodus For Origen tells us that the Greek for "daily," *epiousios*, did not exist till it came into use in the Lord's Prayer. It is a word of irregular formation and doubtful meaning of which he gives two interpretations, (1) "sufficient for our existence," (2) "fit for future [time]," that is, "fit for the next world[1]" Matthew makes the prayer one for a special giving and for a special day, "*Give* (aorist) us *to-day*"; Luke makes it a prayer for continuous giving for every day, "*Give* (pres.) us [*continually*] *day by day*[2]."

The Jews themselves differed in their interpretations of the passage in Exodus. R. Joshua said that they were to collect from one day to the next as one does from the sabbath-preparation-day to the sabbath itself, R. Eleazar denied this[3] In a prayer of this kind, "the bread of the day" might have meanings varying with the time of day when it was uttered and with the time from which one reckoned "the day" as beginning, whether at sunrise as in nature, or at midnight as among the moderns, or at sunset as among the Jews. There are good reasons for concluding that, in the Lord's Prayer, the Greek word that we render "*daily*" meant "*belonging to the day that is now coming on*," which would be specially appropriate to a prayer uttered in the early morning. But the conclusion could not easily be reached without studying the ancient precept in Exodus[4].

---

[1] See Origen *De Orat* § 27

[2] Comp Lk ix 23 "take up his cross *daily*," where the parall. Mk viii 34, Mt xvi 24 omit "daily"

[3] See *Mechilt* on Exod xvi 4

[4] In Exodus (xvi 13, 14) the manna comes with "the morning" and "the dew" See Steph *Thes* iii 1460 for passages shewing that ἡ ἐπιοῦσα, sometimes without ἡμέρα, means the day that is "coming on" and will arrive in a few hours or minutes, where αὔριον, "the morrow," would sound too formal Also comp Prov xxvii 1 (Heb) "Boast not thyself of (lit) [the] day [that is] to-morrow (LXX τὰ εἰς αὔριον), for thou knowest not what *a day* (LXX ἡ ἐπιοῦσα) may bring forth" Here, and here alone, the LXX has

CHRIST'S MIRACLES OF FEEDING

Passing to the Gospels we find that whereas in Mark (followed by Luke) Jesus is described as sending out the

ἡ ἐπιοῦσα with Heb equiv (in Prov iii 28 it is corrupt) and the meaning is declared by Rashi to be "*to-day*" ("forsitan *hodie* accidet aliquid mali quod aboleat cogitationes de die crastino"), Walton also renders the Targ יומא as "hodierna dies" R Eleazar said (*Mechilt* on Exod xvi 4) "He that hath what he shall eat to-day, and saith, 'What shall I eat to-morrow?' is of little faith" From ἐπιοῦσα there appears to have been constructed an irregular adj ἐπιούσιος meaning "belonging to the coming day" In ἐπιοῦσα, "on-coming," ἐπὶ means "on", but in many compound words it means "*fit*," as in ἐπιτερπής, "*fit* to please," and ἐπιούσιος may possibly have conveyed to those who first used it a duplicated meaning, "*fit* (or, *sufficient*), for the *on-coming* day"

'Επιέναι occurs in LXX elsewhere only in Deut xxxii 29 εἰς τὸν ἐπιόντα χρόνον, Heb "their latter-end (אחריתם)," Aq εἰς ἐσχάτην αὐτῶν, and 1 Chr xx 1 ἐν τῷ ἐπιόντι ἔτει, Heb. "at the time of the return of the year," Vulg "post anni circulum," Syr "anno sequenti," A V. "after the year was expired"

These variations may be illustrated from Jas ii. 15 τῆς ἐφημέρου τροφῆς, R V "*of daily food*," on which Field says "More correctly, '*of the day's supply of food*,' as distinguished from τῆς καθ' ἡμέραν τροφῆς" These two renderings, in effect, correspond to Matthew's and Luke's renderings of the petition for bread in the Lord's Prayer And it is probable that the original Aramaic of that petition is best represented by Matthew, and is based on the precept about the manna "the word *of the day in its day*," that is, "the day's supply in the same day"

Field (on Jas ii 15) quotes from Menander a line contrasting the life that is ἐφήμερος, i e "*dependent on the day's supply*," with the life that has περιουσία, i e "*superabundance*" From this it follows that ἐπιούσιος, when meaning ἐφήμερος, might suggest a popular contrast with περιούσιος, so that, as the latter implied "*above* sufficiency," the former might mean "*fit for* sufficiency"

Some confusion of this kind might be facilitated by the Hebraized use of οὐσία to mean (Levy i 43 *b*) "*property*" in various senses

But minor causes of varying interpretation must not divert us from the main and almost sufficient cause, namely, that the petition originally referred to the saying in the Law, "the word of the day in its day" The same ambiguity that varied the interpretation of the clause in the Law might also vary its interpretation in the Gospel. That the "bread" was (at all events primarily) spiritual may be inferred from the context in the Prayer and from Christ's doctrine as a whole

CHRIST'S MIRACLES OF FEEDING

Apostles with the precept "take no bread," Matthew omits the prohibition, and the Didaché limits it ("no bread except [to suffice] till a lodging is found for the night")[1]. The only other Marcan instance of "bread" in words of Christ is in the saying "It is not fit to take the children's bread and cast it to the dogs[2]." Reasons have been given for thinking that these words may have belonged, in the original tradition, to the disciples, and that they have been assigned to Jesus by error[3]. But in any case they are metaphorical and do not clearly shew what is beneath the metaphor[4].

We may fairly say that we do not find in Mark a single instance where Jesus is described as inculcating a doctrine of Bread And yet we know, not only from the Lord's Prayer, but also from other passages in Matthew and Luke, as well as from copious discourses in John, that such a doctrine must have existed Mark seems to hint at some hidden truth or mystery when he says concerning the disciples, shortly after the Feeding of the Five Thousand and the Walking on the Sea, "For they understood not in the matter of the loaves, but their heart had been hardened (*or*, made callous[5]) " But he does not tell us what the mystery was.

---

[1] These passages, which have been discussed above (p. 159) under Mk vi 8, are mentioned here merely in order to shew the necessity of discussing verbal detail in Mark

[2] Mk vii 27 This statement refers only to ἄρτος sing Mk viii. 17 has the pl , and the literal rendering is "ye have not *loaves* "

[3] See *Son* **3353** (iv) *a* foll.

[4] The woman's desire was that Jesus should heal her daughter. How this healing could "take the bread of the children" away from the children is not clear, unless the meaning was that Christ's energy was limited, and that, if part of it were bestowed on Syrophoenicians. less would remain for Jews More probably "*take and cast*" is rhetorically used for "*cast*," i e give it to the dogs as well This is not the sort of saying that one would assign to Jesus even as a beneficent trial of the woman's faith

[5] Mk vi 52 οὐ γὰρ συνῆκαν ἐπὶ τοῖς ἄρτοις, ἀλλ' ἦν αὐτῶν ἡ καρδία πεπωρωμένη On πώρωσις, "callousness," see *Proclamation* p. 362 foll

CHRIST'S MIRACLES OF FEEDING

These considerations should prepare us for a more than usually patient and laborious investigation of Mark's words and phrases in connection with Christ's feeding of the multitudes, while we attempt to ascertain what was the nature of this "callousness of the heart" and what was the nature of the truth "in the matter of the loaves," which truth, in consequence of the "callousness," the disciples "understood not[1]."

There will be the usual temptation to explain everything from one cause And the cause to which many facts appear to point will be found to be poetic metaphor But there is also the possibility of error arising from antedating post-resurrectional acts and words of Christ[2] And we shall have to remember that even in pre-Christian days there was already established the homely but sacred meal connected with the *Kiddûsh*, or Sanctification of the Sabbath[3]. It may be taken as certain that Jesus, in some form, celebrated the *Kiddûsh* on many occasions with His disciples; and it is probable that on some occasions He extended it to the sanctification of other days, and admitted strangers to the meal. Such celebrations, when related in the language of poetic metaphor—and with allusions to such admissions of thousands at a time into the Church as are described in the Acts of the Apostles—might account for much that could not be explained as the result of metaphor alone

---

[1] I dismiss, as unworthy of consideration, the notion that it meant that the disciples ought to have learned from the multiplication of the loaves that Jesus could do whatever He liked, and therefore that they were culpably foolish and faithless in being astonished that He could walk upon water

[2] See "Post-resurrectional" in Indices of *Son* and *Proclamation* and the present volume, and see *Proclam* pp 1, 56–7 concerning a miraculous draught of fishes, placed by Luke before, but by John after, Christ's resurrection See also above, pp. 52–3

[3] On the *Kiddûsh*, see *The Religion and Worship of the Synagogue* (Oesterley and Box) p 346 foll

CHRIST'S MIRACLES OF FEEDING

There are no less than seven accounts of miraculous feeding in the Gospels —(1) the Feeding of the Five Thousand, related by four evangelists, (2) that of the Four Thousand, related by two, (3) that of the seven disciples (after Christ's resurrection) related by one Mark (followed by Matthew) besides giving two of these accounts, adds a comment[1]. He represents Jesus as referring to two of the miracles thus· "When I brake the five loaves among the five thousand, how many baskets (*cophinoi*) full of broken pieces took ye up?....And when the seven among the four thousand, how many full baskets (*sphurides*) of broken pieces took ye up?[2]" Here Jesus is described as distinguishing, not only the two actions and the numbers affected by them, but even the two kinds of "*baskets*" used on the two occasions.

Philo, in his treatise on the Feast of the Baskets—meaning the baskets of the firstfruits mentioned in Deuteronomy—says that it extended over about half the year, being "at two seasons[3]." He appears to mean the "season" of the corn harvest (including the barley harvest which came first in late spring) and the "season" of "fruits," strictly so called, which extended to the autumn The Hebrew for the "basket" mentioned in Deuteronomy is different from that used by

---

[1] Mk vi 29—44, after describing (*a*) what immediately followed the death of John the Baptist, describes (*b*) the Feeding of the Five Thousand, Mk viii 1—9 describes (*c*) the Feeding of the Four Thousand; Mk viii 14—21 describes (*d*) Jesus as reproaching the disciples for not learning what they ought to have learned from these two actions These Marcan passages, with their parallels, will be found below, (*a*) p 216, (*b*) pp 269, 283, 297, 315, 336, 348, (*c*) pp 263, 269, 283, 297, 315, 336, 348, (*d*) pp 210-11

[2] Mk viii 19—20, Mt xvi 9—10, omitted by Luke

[3] See Philo ii 298 foll *De Fest Coph* § 3 where he says that the song of the baskets (καρτάλλων) is sung δυσὶ καιροῖς ὁλοκλήρῳ μέρει ἡμίσει τοῦ ἐνιαυτοῦ He is referring to Deut xxvi 2—4 καὶ ἐμβαλεῖς εἰς κάρταλλον λήψεται ὁ ἱερεὺς τὸν κάρταλλον The LXX omits "*all*" in "*all* the fruits of the land," but Philo seems to assume that its inclusion is implied

CHRIST'S MIRACLES OF FEEDING

Jeremiah, speaking of the vintage, "as a grape-gatherer into the *baskets*[1]" This suggests that something more than a mere literal difference between two kinds of *"baskets"* may be intended in the two Marcan narratives of feeding—possibly some allusion to the firstfruits of the cornfields and to those of the vineyards and orchards, taken metaphorically as applicable to the ingathering of converts into the Church of Christ

§ 2 Traces of metaphor underlying the narratives about the "baskets"

The last-quoted words of Jesus about the two kinds of "baskets" follow a warning in Mark (and a similar one in Matthew) addressed by Jesus to the disciples, "And he charged them, saying, Take heed, beware of the leaven of the Pharisees and the leaven of Herod." This the disciples take literally, saying "We have no loaves." Jesus rebukes them for their literalism, reminding them of the *cophinoi* and the *sphurides* and saying "Do ye not yet understand?" In Mark the connection is obscure. But it is made clearer by Matthew, who represents Jesus as saying "How is it that ye do not perceive that I spake *not to you concerning loaves? But beware of the leaven of the Pharisees and Sadducees.*" Afterwards Matthew adds "Then understood they how that he bade them *not beware of the leaven of loaves, but of the teaching of the Pharisees and Sadducees."*

This, though clear, leads us to think of metaphorical loaves as well as metaphorical leaven. If the "leaven" is the formal teaching by which the Pharisees vitiated the Law, then it would seem that the "loaves," metaphorically regarded, are the Law itself. In that case, might not the "five loaves" be the five books of the Law "broken up" and explained to the multitude, piece by piece?

---

[1] Jer vi 9, so R V. txt, Targ , LXX, Rashi, and Jerome In Deut xxvi 3, Jer Targ has (Etheridge) "baskets, hampers, and paper cases"

CHRIST'S MIRACLES OF FEEDING

This will be considered later on Meanwhile we must add that there is a difficulty in the mention of a perplexity about "leaven" at a time of the year when, according to Synoptic chronology, no question of leavened or unleavened bread could arise The Passover and the Feast of Unleavened Bread were not then at hand. Why should the disciples suppose that their Master warned them against literal "leaven," at a season when literal leaven was quite lawful? It is not surprising that Luke omits all the Mark-Matthew tradition about "loaves." He retains merely a warning against "leaven" as given below[1].

---

[1] In the parallel passages printed below, and for the most part in others printed in footnotes, R V text is followed (with a very few occasional deviations indicated by brackets) as being convenient for rapid reference enabling the reader to take a broad view of the subject under consideration But in the detailed study of the Greek text, R V text is frequently departed from.

Mk viii 14—21 (R V)
(14) And they forgot to take bread (*lit* loaves), and they had not in the boat with them more than one loaf
(15) And he charged them, saying, Take heed, beware of the leaven of the Pharisees and the leaven of Herod
(16) And they reasoned one with another, saying, We have no bread (*lit* loaves).
(17) And Jesus perceiving it saith unto them, Why reason ye, because ye have no bread (*lit* loaves)? do ye not yet perceive, neither understand? have ye your heart hardened?
(18) Having eyes,

Mt xvi 5—12 (R.V)
(5) And the disciples came to the other side and forgot to take bread (*lit* loaves).
(6) And Jesus said unto them, Take heed and beware of the leaven of the Pharisees and Sadducees
(7) And they reasoned among themselves, saying, We took no bread (*lit* loaves)
(8) And Jesus perceiving it said, O ye of little faith, why reason ye among yourselves, because ye have no bread (*lit.* loaves)?
(9) Do ye not yet perceive, neither remember the five loaves of the five thousand, and how

Lk xii. 1 (R V)
In the meantime, when the many thousands of the multitude were gathered together, insomuch that they trode one upon another, he began to say unto his disciples first of all, Beware ye of the leaven of the Pharisees, which is hypocrisy.

210 (Mark vi. 29—44)

CHRIST'S MIRACLES OF FEEDING

Besides the Lucan omission of all that part of Mark which connects "leaven" with the feeding of the two multitudes, it will be seen below that there is a remarkable lacuna in Matthew. He omits "they had not in the boat with them more than one loaf." The omission is not surprising. Though Mark often deals in picturesque superfluities, few of his details are so apparently superfluous as this—if taken literally. But, if we can regard it as an ancient symbolical tradition, inserted here as if it were literally true, then it may become both intelligible and interesting. Paul speaks of *"one loaf, one body"* in connection with *"the loaf that we break"* in the Christian Eucharist[1]. John also describes Jesus, after the Resurrection, as feeding seven disciples on a fish and *"a loaf*[2]*."* It seems a reasonable supposition that Mark has here preserved, out of

Mk viii. 14—21 (R.V.) contd	Mt. xvi. 5—12 (R.V.) contd	Lk. xii. 1 (R.V.)
see ye not? and having ears, hear ye not? and do ye not remember? (19) When I brake the five loaves among the five thousand, how many baskets † full of broken pieces took ye up? They say unto him, Twelve. (20) And when the seven among the four thousand, how many basketfuls † of broken pieces took ye up? And they say unto him, Seven. (21) And he said unto them, Do ye not yet understand?	many baskets † ye took up? (10) Neither the seven loaves of the four thousand, and how many baskets † ye took up? (11) How is it that ye do not perceive that I spake not to you concerning bread (*lit* loaves)? But beware of the leaven of the Pharisees and Sadducees. (12) Then understood they how that he bade them not beware of the leaven of bread (*lit* loaves), but of the teaching of the Pharisees and Sadducees	

† N B "Baskets," when first mentioned = *cophinoi*, when next mentioned = *sphurides*

[1] 1 Cor. x 16—17.
[2] Jn xxi. 9, 13. On the sing. "*loaf*," see *Son* 3422*i*.

place, a symbolical tradition of weighty and solemn meaning, of which he has misunderstood the weight and importance. This hypothesis is at all events more probable than to suppose that Mark has preserved, in its place, a literal detail that never had any importance at all. Matthew's rejection of it may then be explained because he believed it to be out of its right place, and so wrongly placed as to give a false impression which he could not correct. If this hypothesis is accepted, the Marcan detail of the "one loaf" may fairly be regarded along with its Johannine counterpart, as an instance of Johannine Intervention, where John has given the right place and the right interpretation to a tradition misplaced and misunderstood by Mark.

Now let us return to Luke's omission of the connection of "leaven"—called by him "the leaven of the Pharisees, which is hypocrisy"—with the miraculous feeding. Does John fail to intervene? It might be assumed that he does fail since he nowhere mentions either "leaven" or "unleavened." But he mentions "Passover," that is, in effect, the Feast of Unleavened Bread. And, what is more, he speaks of "the Passover *of the Jews*," and "the Passover, *the feast [so called] of the Jews*," in such a way as to suggest that he contrasts "the Passover of the Jews" with "the Passover of Christians." This he does repeatedly[1]. He does not indeed expressly contrast the material "leaven" cast out by the Pharisees with the spiritual "leaven" that they retained, but he does imply this distinction.

This we shall see if we put ourselves in the position of Christians of the first century. They would certainly apply Pauline language to the Lord's last Passover. "He kept it," they would say, "on the Cross, or rather He was our Passover on the Cross, so that we might '*keep the feast not with old leaven but with the unleavened bread of sincerity and truth*'; but the rulers

---

[1] Jn ii. 13, xi. 55 τὸ πάσχα τῶν Ἰουδαίων, vi. 4 (W.H.) ⌜τὸ πάσχα⌝, ἡ ἑορτὴ τῶν Ἰουδαίων

of the Jews, His murderers, they kept it in what the Apostle Paul called *'the leaven of malice and wickedness*[1]*.'"* Now John, toward the conclusion of his Gospel, expresses the same thought, not indeed in words, but (as often) in dramatic action His Gospel lays ironical stress on the scrupulousness with which the rulers of the Jews, on the morning of the Crucifixion, at the very time when they were constraining Pilate to destroy Jesus by judicial murder, "entered not into the palace." Their reason was "*that they might not be defiled*, but might eat the passover[2]." They duly "*ate*" their "*passover*," but it was "the passover of the Jews." They cast out their leaven. But they *were* "*defiled*"—with the leaven of malice and wickedness.

In the light of these later Johannine utterances let us consider whether John perhaps desired to express something more than a mere chronological fact, when he prefixed to his account of the Feeding of the Five Thousand the words "Now *the Passover, the feast of the Jews*, was at hand. Jesus, therefore, lifting up his eyes, and seeing that a great multitude cometh unto him, saith unto Philip, Whence are we to buy bread, that these may eat[3]?" This was immediately after the murder of John the Baptist. Many a Galilaean in those days would regard John as a shepherd of Israel; and Mark tells us that Jesus had compassion on the multitude because they were "as sheep

---

[1] 1 Cor. v 8
[2] Jn xviii 28 See also Jn xi 55 "Now *the passover of the Jews* was at hand and many went up...*to purify themselves*," on which Origen says (Lomm ii 372) "The multitude did not know how to purify themselves Wherefore, while fancying that they were offering '*their own Passover*' as a service to God, they were so far from 'purifying themselves' that they became more accursed than they were before ..." Origen says, and quotes passages to shew, that (*ib* 371) "We must not suppose the Passover of the Lord to be also *the Passover of the Jews*, for the Passover according to the Law [of God] is that of the Lord, but the Passover of those who break the Law (τῶν παρανόμων) is *that of the Jews*."
[3] Jn vi. 4—5, "bread," *lit*. "loaves"

without a shepherd[1]." The Pharisees, as far as we know, had made no such protest as John the Baptist made against Herod Antipas, nor had they directly or indirectly supported the prophet. They were also plotting the death of Jesus, while professing to be the teachers of the Law, the Word of Life.

Such conduct—combined with a severe enforcement of precepts of purification—was called by Jesus in the Synoptic Gospels "hypocrisy." It was, in effect, "the leaven of malice and wickedness." The Law, as taught by such teachers, was a false parody of "bread." In the Fourth Gospel, Jesus, before the Feeding of the Five Thousand, says, "Whence shall we buy *loaves* that these may eat?" and, later on, in terms of reproach or warning, "Ye ate of the *loaves* and were satisfied[2]." But these are the only Johannine passages where Jesus uses the plural "loaves." A little later He uses the singular, which He frequently repeats, "My Father giveth you *the true bread* out of heaven[3]" It is John's custom to dwell on positives rather than negatives, and on truths rather than falsehoods. In the Synoptic Gospels, Jesus warns His disciples negatively against "the leaven of the Pharisees" (Luke adding "which is hypocrisy"). This is the false leaven, and implies the false bread. In John, a similar warning to the multitude is included in His positive doctrine concerning "the true bread." And the words "Whence shall we buy loaves?" addressed to Philip, may convey the same warning to the disciples, a warning against those many kinds of false foods which one buys at the cost of spiritual health and life, whereas the true bread, the living bread, is bought "without money and without price[4]," coming as a gift to those who are taught by the Giver of all Good to give themselves to Him even as He gives Himself to them.

---

[1] Mk. vi. 34. Luke (ix 11 foll) omits this Matthew (xiv 14 foll) omits it here, but places it earlier (ix 36).
[2] Jn vi 5, 26. [3] Jn vi. 32.
[4] Is lv. 1, see below, p. 272.

CHRIST'S MIRACLES OF FEEDING

As regards the word "buy," in connection with food or bread, we may note here that the Synoptists use it nowhere except in the Feeding of the Five Thousand[1]. There all the Evangelists have it, but with this important difference, that while the Three ascribe it in various forms ("are we to buy," "that they may buy") to the disciples, the Fourth ascribes it *to Jesus, associating Himself with the disciples*—"*Whence are we to buy loaves?*" Mark, alone of the Synoptists, has "*buy loaves*" It is highly probable that this Johannine repetition of the Marcan "*buy loaves*" in what seems[2] an entirely different context is deliberate. The probability is increased by the fact that, in the same context, John agrees with Mark, against Matthew and Luke, in mentioning "two hundred pennyworth of loaves," as uttered by a disciple or disciples. These two details, even if they stood alone, would suffice to prove that John had in view Marcan traditions. But they do not stand alone. They are parts of a web of traditions, indicating an unusual abundance of complex evidence, bearing on the Rule of Johannine Intervention, and, ultimately, on the historical fact at the bottom of all these narratives

---

[1] Ἀγοράζω occurs in Mk vi 36 with τί φάγωσιν and *ib* 37 with ἄρτους, in Mt xiv 15, Lk ix 13 with βρώματα It occurs also in Jn iv 8 with τροφάς and vi 5 with ἄρτους

[2] "Seems," because it is conceivable that John does not reject, but supplements, the Synoptic traditions about buying Perhaps he regards Jesus as first overhearing, and then receiving, complaints from His disciples ("How are we to buy?") These He repeats in a kindly "tempting" of Philip "Yes, truly, how are we to buy?"

CHRIST'S MIRACLES OF FEEDING

§ 3. *The immediate sequel of John the Baptist's death*[1]

According to Matthew, the Baptist's disciples, after burying their Master, came and *"brought word"* of his death to Jesus,

[1] Mk vi 29—34 (R V)

(29) And when his disciples heard [thereof], they came and took up his corpse, and laid it in a tomb
(30) And the apostles gather themselves together unto Jesus, and they told him all things, whatsoever they had done, and whatsoever they had taught
(31) And he saith unto them, Come ye yourselves apart into a desert place, and rest a while For there were many coming and going, and they had no leisure so much as to eat
(32) And they went away in the boat to a desert place apart
(33) And [the people] saw them going, and many knew [them], and they ran there together on foot (*or*, by land) from all the cities, and outwent them

(34) And he came forth and saw a great multitude, and he had compassion on them,

Mt xiv 12—14 (R V)

(12) And his disciples came, and took up the corpse, and buried him, and they went and told Jesus

(13) Now when Jesus heard [it], he withdrew from thence in a boat, to a desert place apart and when the multitudes heard [thereof], they followed him on foot (*or*, by land) from the cities.
(14) And he came forth, and saw a great multitude, and he had compassion on them, and healed their sick.

Comp Mt ix 36
But when he saw the multitudes, he was moved with compassion for them, because they were dis-

Lk ix 10—11 (R V)

(10) And the apostles, when they were returned, declared unto him what things they had done And he took them, and withdrew apart to a city called Bethsaida
(11) But the multitudes perceiving it followed him and he welcomed them, and spake to them of the kingdom of God, and them that had need of healing he healed.

CHRIST'S MIRACLES OF FEEDING

who, on "hearing [of it]," withdrew into a desert place. But according to Mark, the Baptist's disciples, "on hearing [of it]," buried him; and the apostles gathered to Jesus and *"brought word"* to Him of all that they had done and taught. Matthew's use of *"bring word"* accords better than Mark's with the usage of N.T. and of Greek in general The Greek verb *"bring word,"* literally, *"bring-message-from,"* implies etymologically, and for the most part practically, bringing word from a certain person or place about what the bringers have heard (as a message) from that person, or have seen or heard at that place. It does not often mean simply describe what the describers have themselves done. In that sense, *"declare"* or *"relate"* would be a better word than *"bring word"* Luke, who follows Mark in inserting a coming of "the apostles" to Jesus, says that they *"declared"* to Him "all that they had done[1]."

The text of Mark is liable to suspicion. We do not know whether this is the first or the second instance in which he uses the word "apostles[2]" If it is the first, it comes here with

Mk vi 29—34 (R V) contd	Mt xiv 12—14 (R V) contd	Lk ix 10—11 (R V)
because they were as sheep not having a shepherd and he began to teach them many things.	tressed and scattered, as sheep not having a shepherd	

Jn vi 1—5 a (R.V) (1) After these things Jesus went away to the other side of the sea of Galilee, which is [the sea] of Tiberias. (2) And a great multitude followed him, because they beheld the signs which he did on them that were sick. (3) And Jesus went up into the mountain, and there he sat with his disciples. (4) Now the passover, the feast of the Jews, was at hand (5) Jesus therefore lifting up his eyes, and seeing that a great multitude cometh unto him,. .

[1] Mk vi 30 (and Mt. xiv. 12) "brought word (ἀπήγγειλαν)," Lk ix 10 "declared (διηγήσαντο)" Luke omits "all that they had taught"

[2] See *Proclamation* p. 394 on Mk iii 14 (R.V. marg. "some anc. auth. add *whom also he named apostles*").

CHRIST'S MIRACLES OF FEEDING

extreme abruptness; and, even if it is the second and refers to those mentioned by Mark above, "whom also he [*i e.* Jesus] named apostles," we should expect Mark to say, not that "they *gather* themselves together" to Jesus, but that "they *returned*" —which Luke actually says[1]. In his parallel to Mark's expression "and *when* his disciples *heard thereof,*" Matthew omits the "hearing[2]," which Mark may have added (as LXX often adds it) to imply "consequently[3]." But Matthew also omits all mention of the "apostles." This seems best explained from an original and ambiguous "they." This Matthew may have taken as meaning *the persons last mentioned*, namely, the disciples of the Baptist, but Mark as *the persons last mentioned before the digression concerning the death of the Baptist*, namely, the Twelve Apostles. Luke's omission of the Marcan phrase "whatsoever things they had taught" can be best explained by supposing it to be a Marcan amplification for clearness, the original being simply "they brought word of *everything*." This, if "they" were the disciples of the Baptist, would mean "they brought word of the whole story of the Baptist's death[4]." But Mark took it

---

[1] Mk vi. 30 συνάγονται, Lk ix. 10 ὑποστρέψαντες Συνάγω, which occurs five times in Mark, is used thrice of multitudes, and once (Mk vii 1) of Pharisees and scribes, "gathering together" to Jesus It is not the word we should expect for the return of so small a number as twelve persons, unless it was intended to suggest that they had been sent in different directions (comp Lk ix 6 "everywhere")

[2] Mk vi. 29 καὶ ἀκούσαντες οἱ μαθηταὶ αὐτοῦ ἦλθαν καὶ ἦραν..., Mt. xiv. 12 καὶ προσελθόντες οἱ μαθηταὶ αὐτοῦ ἦραν... Matthew applies "hearing" to Jesus in the next verse, Mt xiv 13 ἀκούσας δὲ ὁ Ἰησοῦς. See next note

[3] Comp Josh ix 11, 2 K ix 13, Esth. iv. 4, Job i 20 (A), where Heb has "and [consequently]," and LXX (or v r) inserts ἀκούσας.

[4] SS has "they declared to him all that *he did* and *he taught*" Prof Burkitt says that this is "probably a mere error" of SS, the pronunciation for this being the same as that for "they did and taught." If the scribe of SS attached any meaning to the text it would seem to be this, "the disciples of John recounted to Jesus

CHRIST'S MIRACLES OF FEEDING

as referring to the Twelve. The notion that the Apostles at this critical and busy moment found leisure to bring word to Jesus about "*whatsoever things* they had taught," as well as "*whatsoever things* they had done," is antecedently improbable —at least in this hyperbolical form—and the rejection of it by Luke increases the improbability.

Since these details refer mainly to the Baptist, we cannot expect the Fourth Gospel to intervene although Luke deviates from, or omits, what is in Mark[1].

§ 4. "*And he saith unto them, Come ye...and rest a little,*" *in Mark*[2]

Matthew and Luke omit these words But, whereas Luke nowhere has any words of Jesus resembling them, Matthew has an invitation at least so far resembling Mark's that it contains similar words for "come" and "rest": "*Come* unto me...and *I will give-you-rest*...ye shall find *rest* for your souls[3]." The context in Matthew is a paradox, namely, that by taking on oneself a new "yoke," one may find "rest" from a heavy "burden." Ben Sira writes to the same effect about "discipline" or "instruction," saying "Incline thy shoulder and carry her, and loathe not her cords..., for afterward thou shalt find her *rest*[4]." A different aspect of "*rest*," namely, rest from wanderings, is presented by Jeremiah, "Ask for the

---

all their Master's last actions and utterances," including those mentioned in Mk vi 20.

[1] See *Beginning* pp. 66, 68—71, "Non-intervention in matters affecting John the Baptist"

[2] Mk vi 31 Δεῦτε ὑμεῖς αὐτοὶ κατ᾽ ἰδίαν εἰς ἔρημον τόπον καὶ ἀναπαύσασθε ὀλίγον. SS has here "Come, let us go to *the wilderness*...," but in vi. 32, "they went to *a desert place*" The "desert place" will be discussed in a later section, p 223 foll

[3] Mt xi 28—9 Δεῦτε πρός με πάντες...κἀγὼ ἀναπαύσω ὑμᾶς...εὑρήσετε ἀνάπαυσιν ταῖς ψυχαῖς ὑμῶν The words δεῦτε and ἀναπαύω are common to Mark and Matthew.

[4] Sir vi 28 (ed Schechter and Taylor), "rest," ἀνάπαυσιν, מנוח.

219 (Mark vi 29—44)

old paths... and walk therein, and ye shall find *rest*, 1 e *repose*, for your souls[1]" Again another aspect is presented where Isaiah says "This is the *rest*, give ye *rest* to him that is weary" There "weary" corresponds to a Hebrew word meaning faintness caused by hunger, or by thirst, or by wandering, and the LXX has "this is the rest for *him that is hungry*[2]" The Greek words used by Mark and Matthew for "rest" may also mean "refresh" in general, and "refresh with food" in particular. But in the latter sense, "with food" would have to be inserted. Mark does not insert it, and therefore we have no right to assume that he means "refresh yourselves a little [with food]." That interpretation however—besides being suggested by Mark's following words, "for those that were coming and those that were going were many, and *they* (1 e. *the disciples*) *had no leisure so much as to eat*"—appears to be favoured by Origen, who, after quoting Mark and Luke (about the "rows" or "companies" of the Five Thousand), speaks of "*those who were about to refresh-themselves on the nourishment of Jesus*[3]."

If Mark and Matthew took different views of the "rest," or "refreshment," to which Jesus invited His disciples, we can understand why Luke omitted the invitation Mark places it immediately after the return of the Apostles from their mission; Matthew places it not long after Jesus had "made an end of

---

[1] Jerem vi 16, מרגוע, LXX ἁγνισμόν, Aq [ἀνάψυξιν], Sym. ἠρεμίαν

[2] Is xxviii 12 τοῦτο τὸ ἀνάπαυμα τῷ πεινῶντι The word rendered πεινᾶν, עיף=διψάω (5), πεινάω (4), ἐκλύω (3)—for which comp Mk viii. 3, Mt xv 32 in the Feeding of the Four Thousand.

[3] Origen *Comm Matth* xi. 3 (Lomm. iii 73) τοὺς ἀναπαυσομένους ἐπὶ ταῖς Ἰησοῦ τροφαῖς I have not found such an instance in Steph *Thes*, nor one parall to Mt xi 28 ἀναπαύσω ὑμᾶς, but there "from your burdens" may be supplied from what precedes In Aesch *fragm* 178, ἀναπαύει, with καματὸν ἵππων, prob. does not mean (as L S) "refresh," but (as Steph *Thes*) "pausare," "make to cease "

CHRIST'S MIRACLES OF FEEDING

commanding his twelve disciples[1]" Luke in a quasi-parallel passage mentions the return of the Seventy to Jesus with a report about their mission; but he appends no invitation—only a promise, such as the Mark-Appendix places after Christ's resurrection[2]. Later on, in his Gospel, Luke represents Jesus as eating *in the presence of* His disciples, and later still, in the Acts—according to an ancient interpretation of a very difficult passage—as "*eating with them*"; but even there, no invitation on the part of Jesus to the disciples is mentioned in the context[3].

---

[1] Mt xi 1 Mt xi 2—24 contains digressions about John the Baptist, Chorazin and Bethsaida Then *ib* 25—7 contains an acknowledgment of the Father's purpose to reveal His mysteries to "babes" Then follows (xi 28—30) the promise of "rest" to the weary.

[2] Luke, after the woe pronounced (x 13 foll) on Chorazin and Bethsaida, and the return of the Seventy, represents Jesus as saying (x 19) "I have given you authority . and nothing shall in any wise hurt you" (comp Mk [xvi 18] a promise made after Christ's resurrection)

[3] Acts 1 4 συναλιζόμενος, R V and A V txt "being assembled together with them," marg "eating (A V + together) with them" See *Notes* **2892—5**, to which should be added references to the "covenant of *salt*" in Numb xviii 19 (comp Lev ii 13) and to the prominence given by Philo (ii 477, 483—4) to "*salt* (ἅλες)" in his description of the meals taken by the Essenes in common Aquila used the word συναλίζομαι to mean "take a friendly meal with" in Ps cxli 4 "let me not *eat of* their dainties" There LXX has συνδοιάζω, *i e* "make one out of two," "be in close companionship" (comp 1 S xxvi 19 "cleave to," Sym συνδυάζεσθαι) Aquila's instance does not conclusively shew whether he regarded συναλίζομαι as derived (1) from ἁλίζω "collect [a crowd into a small space]" or (2) from ἁλίζομαι "be salted," *i e* "fed on salt"—salt being, both for Greeks and for Jews, the symbol of close, friendly, and festive intercourse (Steph. *Thes* 1 1580 ἅλες "convictus et communio et sodalitatis necessitudo"). Against (1), there is the fact that ἁλίζω appears to be never used with a personal object in the singular, but always of a crowd, army, etc This important word will come before us again when we discuss the Marcan (ix 49) doctrine of being "salted with fire" (which Matthew and Luke omit)

(Mark vi 29—44)

CHRIST'S MIRACLES OF FEEDING

This passage in the Acts brings before us, as a possibility worth considering, the hypothesis that Mark, among a number of detached traditions about Eucharistic feeding which he has included in his narrative of the Five Thousand, may have antedated a tradition (about Jesus as inviting His disciples to a sacred meal) which may have been placed after the Resurrection by other Evangelists, and, in particular, by John. In any case, since "Come and rest" is a saying of Jesus mentioned by Mark and omitted by Luke, we are bound to look for something like it in John. And something like it—much more like it than appears at first sight—occurs in the Johannine account of the post-resurrectional feeding of the seven disciples on the one loaf, where Jesus is represented in our Revised Version as saying to the disciples, "Come, break your fast[1]."

Instead of "break your fast," some such phrase as "take-your-morning-meal" would have been a better rendering of the verb *aristân*. It is nowhere used in N.T. except (twice) in this Johannine passage, and in one passage of Luke, where a Pharisee invites Jesus to a morning meal[2]. There, the texts of our English Versions render it "dine." But the Greek word never means "dine." It is constantly distinguished from "dine," and contrasted with "dine[3]."

Returning to John, and rendering the invitation literally,

---

[1] Jn xxi 12 δεῦτε, ἀριστήσατε. On δεῦτε, "Come!" never used by Luke, but used by Mk-Mt in the "invitation" now under consideration (and elsewhere), see *Proclam* pp 48—9.

[2] Lk. xi 37 ἀριστήσῃ. R V text "dine," marg. "*Gr* breakfast." The context speaks of the washing of hands. Possibly, among the common people, though not among the Pharisees, the rule was not so strictly observed before "breakfast" as before the later meal.

[3] See Steph *Thes*. It can no more mean "dine" than our "breakfasted" could mean "dined." Luke uses the words "*dine*" and "*dinner*" (δειπνεῖν, δεῖπνον) about six or seven times, and the verb "to *breakfast*" only here. In one passage (xiv. 12) "a breakfast or a dinner," he distinguishes the two.

"*[Come] hither! Take-your-morning-meal!*" we perceive that it accords not only with the literal time—the dawn that brought success to the fishermen after the laborious night of failure—but also with the metaphorical or spiritual time, the dawn that was to bring success to the apostolic fishermen casting the net of the Gospel. The meal was their "morning-meal" preparing them to carry forth the Gospel to the world[1]. It appears to correspond both literally and spiritually to the Marcan tradition "Come ye...and rest," omitted by Luke, of which perhaps a version is given by Matthew. As in Mark, so in John, the invitation precedes a meal on bread and fish; but, as in Matthew, the "rest" or "refreshment" is not of the body but of the spirit. Matthew expresses it by "Take my yoke upon you" and "Learn from me"; John expresses it by the words addressed to Peter, and through Peter to the whole assembly of Christians, commanding each in his appointed way to carry the cross, and to serve Christ by serving those for whom Christ died: "Feed my sheep," and "Follow thou me[2]"

§ 5. "*Come ye, [by] yourselves, apart, into a desert place,*" *in Mark*[3]

The words "into a desert place" appear to imply, not a desert place meaning a dry and barren waste, but simply "a lonely, quiet, or retired, place" But they are omitted (with the rest of the sentence) by Matthew and Luke, perhaps as being liable to misunderstanding. The words "by yourselves" and "apart" go some way to make the meaning clear, but not quite far enough. The meaning seems to be that in

---

[1] In canonical LXX, ἀριστᾷν occurs only twice as representing Hebrew correctly, (*a*) Gen xliii 25 Heb "eat bread," (*b*) 1 K xiii. 7 Heb "support [thyself with food]," R V and A.V. "refresh thyself," Heb סעד and sim. in Targum. The Clementine Heb rendering of Jn xxi 12 ἀριστήσατε is עדנו.

[2] Mt. xi. 28—9, Jn xxi. 15—22.

[3] Mk vi 31.

CHRIST'S MIRACLES OF FEEDING

the general excitement and consternation consequent on the murder of John the Baptist, Jesus perceived that it would be good for the disciples to be alone with Him for a while. To be alone with Him would not be to be really "alone," or "desolate," or "abandoned in a wilderness." Being with the Son, they would be with the Father. Epictetus has a discourse entitled "What is *desertedness* (or, *a desert* (erēmia)) and what kind of person is *deserted* (erēmos)?" It begins thus: "*Deserted*[*ness*] is a kind of unbefriended state. For he that is *alone* is not necessarily *deserted*, as also he that is in a crowd is not necessarily *undeserted*[1]."

That John recognised this truth is shewn later on when he represents Jesus as saying "Ye shall leave me alone; and [yet] I am not alone, because the Father is with me[2]." He could not indeed represent Jesus as saying to the seven disciples for whom He has prepared the fish and the loaf "Come ye, by yourselves, apart, into a quiet place"—for they were in a quiet place already. But he does succeed in giving us the impression that, before the Feeding of the Five Thousand, Jesus had invited the disciples to accompany Him away from the multitude into a place of quiet. In the description of the man seeking the one sheep that has strayed, where Matthew has "*the mountains*," Luke has "*the desert*." So here, John does not call the place of retirement "*a desert place*" but "*the mountain*," thus: "And a great multitude followed him... and Jesus went up into *the mountain*, and there he sat with his disciples[3]."

In this way John, in effect, reproduces the Marcan "desert place," but without the notion of desertedness. By "sat with

---

[1] Epict. iii. 13. 1
[2] Jn xvi 32.
[3] Jn vi 2—3, comp. Mt xviii 12 "the mountains," Lk xv 4 "the desert." The "loneliness" of "the mountain" comes before us afterwards (Jn vi 15) "Jesus withdrew again into the mountain *himself alone*."

his disciples" he implies that Jesus was not only with them but also was with them in quiet converse. As regards the term "desert place" or "wilderness" used by all the Synoptists in their narratives of feeding[1], it is noteworthy that John does not use any form of it in the narrative itself. But afterwards, in the subsequent comment of the Jews, and in Christ's reply, he twice has "ate the manna *in the wilderness*," that is, *in the wilderness of Sinai*. The Jews seem to say this with unmixed satisfaction, "*our fathers ate*" Jesus adds a note of warning, "*your fathers ate...and died*[2]."

Before passing from the words of Jesus ("come ye...into *a desert place*") we must note that the Syriac Versions have, not "*a desert place*," but "*the wilderness*," *midbar*[3]. This has quite a different meaning. *Midbar* might be applied to a wilderness or open country near any town or district, named in the context; but where no such place is named it always means (in the Bible) the wilderness of Sinai, as, for example, where the Lord bids Moses say to Pharaoh "Let us go...three days' journey into *the wilderness* that we may sacrifice to the Lord our God[4]." Among the reasons why Matthew and Luke omit these words, one may have been a doubt whether they were correctly used. In early poetic accounts of Christ's miracles of feeding, the language of Scripture about the manna in the Midbar of Sinai might be applied to the Christian "table in the wilderness" in expressions sometimes not strictly correct if taken literally. These might naturally be rejected by later Evangelists.

---

[1] Mk vi 35, Mt. xiv. 15 (sim Lk ix 12) ἔρημός ἐστιν ὁ τόπος, Mk viii 4, Mt xv. 33 ἐρημία

[2] Jn vi 31, 49

[3] Mk vi 31 (SS) "let us go into *the wilderness* (midbar)," but vi. 32 "they went to *a desert place*" and vi 35 "the *place* is *desert*"

[4] Exod iii 18, rep. viii 27. It is worth noting here that a mention of "three days" (which will be discussed later on, p. 263 foll.) occurs at the beginning of the Feeding of the Four Thousand

CHRIST'S MIRACLES OF FEEDING

§ 6. *The concourse of "many," in Mark*

Mark four times uses the word "many" here, thrice in connection with the concourse of *"many"* or "the *great* [lit. *much*] multitude," and once about the *"many* [things]" that Jesus began to teach them[1] There are several variations in the MSS and Versions. A specimen of these is given below from the Syro-Sinaitic[2], which avoids one or two difficult questions raised by the received text.

It is not difficult perhaps to realise that the disciples might feel not only overcrowded by people continually coming to Jesus, but also harassed by people continually going away. But it is difficult to believe that the multitude, which (according to Matthew) included women and children, "outwent" the boat that contained Jesus—the multitude going round the lake, a distance of about ten miles, and the boat going across the lake, a distance of about four[3].

---

[1] Mk vi 31—4 "For those that were coming and those that were going (ὑπάγοντες) were *many*, .and *many* saw (εἶδαν) them (αὐτούς) going (ὑπάγοντας) and recognised (ἔγνωσαν, marg ἐπέγνωσαν) [them] (*or*, and they [*i e* people] saw them going, and *many* recognised [them]), and on foot from all the cities they ran-together there and outwent them (συνέδραμον ἐκεῖ καὶ προῆλθον αὐτούς). And having come forth [from the boat] he saw a *great* (πολὺν) multitude.. and he began to teach them *many* [*things*] (πολλά) "

[2] Mk vi. 31 foll (SS) "Many were going and coming unto him .. and many saw them and recognised them and went by land after him from all the cities And when they came and he saw a great multitude...and he had begun to teach them" SS alters "those coming and those going" into "going and coming unto him," thus emphasizing the arrivals rather than the departures, or perhaps using "going and" pleonastically (as it is often used in English); it substitutes "went after him" for "ran-together", it omits "outwent them", it substitutes "they came and he saw" for "he came forth [from the vessel] and saw "

This important version had not been discovered when W H discussed the variations of Mk vi 33 in W H. Intr p. 95 foll

[3] Prof. Swete says *ad loc* "Across the Lake from *Tell Hum* or *Khan Minyeh* is scarcely more than four miles, by land the distance

Luke seems to imply, by omitting all these Marcan details, that they seemed to him either unimportant, or difficult, or both, and that the one important fact was that "the multitudes followed" Jesus—how "they followed" being a matter of detail that might be neglected. Perhaps Luke, in this respect, is imitating Matthew, who also accepts "the multitudes followed" as a convenient summary of Mark's diffuse statements[1]. But Luke deviates from Matthew as well as from Mark by omitting the words "And, having gone forth [from the boat] he saw a great multitude[2]." They do not seem very important, and, even if John had nothing whatever corresponding to them, though we should have to confess that the law of Johannine Intervention failed here, it would not seem a very serious failure But John has in the context something that appears to correspond to them, only modified by a suggestion of symbolism, as follows "After these things Jesus went away beyond the sea of Galilee [the sea] of Tiberias. Now a great multitude was following him, because they were [constantly] seeing the signs that he was doing on the sick. But Jesus went up to the mountain, and there sat with his disciples Now the passover was near—the feast of the Jews

---

to the upper part of Batîhah could hardly be above ten (Sanday, *Fourth Gospel*, p 120) unless they went by road and crossed the Jordan by the bridge " He adds "If there was little wind, it would be easy to get to the place before a sailing boat " But if there was so "little wind" that they could not cover "more than four miles" while a crowd including women and children covered "ten," would they not have at once used their oars, which Mark (vi 48) and John (vi 19) describe them as using on their return?

[1] Mt xiv. 13 καὶ ἀκούσαντες οἱ ὄχλοι ἠκολούθησαν αὐτῷ, Lk. ix. 11 οἱ δὲ ὄχλοι γνόντες ἠκολούθησαν αὐτῷ Mark does not use ἀκολουθέω here. His view is that the multitude went round the lake before Jesus so as to meet Him when He landed—which would not naturally be described as "following."

[2] Mk vi 34, Mt. xiv. 14 (identical in order as well as in words) καὶ ἐξελθὼν εἶδεν πολὺν ὄχλον.

CHRIST'S MIRACLES OF FEEDING

[so called]. Jesus therefore, *lifting up his eyes and beholding that a great multitude was coming to him*, saith unto Philip...[1]."

It will be noted that here, while first accepting the Matthew-Luke prosaic summarizing word, "*followed*," John adds a form of the Mark-Matthew tradition that Jesus "*beheld*" this "*great multitude*." That this is symbolical is indicated by the contextual "lifting up of the eyes"—an act thrice attributed to Jesus by John and always as a symbol[2]. It is also attributed thrice in Scripture to Abraham The first Abrahamic instance is where the Patriarch "lifted up his eyes" and beheld the three divine Persons to whom he ministered and gave bread; the second is where he saw the mountain on which he was to offer up his son; the third is where he saw the ram that was to be Isaac's substitute[3] It is a commonplace in Jewish tradition that whatever Abraham did in service to God, God has done, or will do, in return, to Abraham's seed. It would therefore be appropriate that before the Feeding of the Five Thousand, who represented the congregation of Israel, the Son of God should "go up into the mountain" and "*lift up his eyes*," and "behold that a great multitude was coming unto him."

---

[1] Jn vi 1—5 This implies that Jesus was on the spot and receiving the multitude (as Lk ix 11 "he welcomed them"), not that the multitude was on the spot awaiting Jesus whom they "outwent" (as Mk vi 33) In Mk vi 33 προῆλθον αὐτούς, "they outwent them," "*they*" may mean (1) Jesus and the disciples, or (2) the multitude (and "*them*" is similarly ambiguous) The former meaning of "*they*" is the more consistent with the circumstances; taking the short cut across the lake, Jesus and the disciples easily "outwent" the multitude Then, some hours afterwards, Jesus received and welcomed those who persistently followed Him Mark's use of προέρχομαι with accus is noteworthy (see Steph *Thes*) In Lk xxii. 47 it is used of Judas "*going before*" the soldiers as their guide.

[2] See *Joh Voc* **1608** (quoting Philo) and *Joh. Gr.* **2616—7** on Jn vi 3—5. The other instances are xi 41 (at the tomb of Lazarus), xvii 1 (before "Father, the hour hath come"). Once Jesus uses the phrase as a precept, iv. 35 "Lift up your eyes," *i.e* to the harvest in the heavens.   [3] Gen xviii. 2, xxii. 4, 13.

CHRIST'S MIRACLES OF FEEDING

Whatever may have been the historical reality, the Evangelist contemplates it as including a vision The Son, the Sacrifice, the Bread of Life, who in old days came to Abraham and received Abraham's bread, now "beholds" the children of Abraham coming to Him in need of bread Visibly, they are five thousand Jews from northern Palestine; but invisibly they are the seed of Abraham as a whole, invited to enter the circle of that large family of nations which was to be blessed with the blessing pronounced on Abraham. As Abraham gave bread to the Son, so the Son gives bread to Abraham's children. And as Abraham offered up Isaac to God, so the Son of God, in the sign of the bread that followed, signified that He Himself was purposing to offer Himself up for Abraham's children in accordance with the will of the Father in heaven.

If this instance stood alone, the hypothesis of Johannine Intervention here would not be a very probable one; but when taken with many other instances of which some few are certain and many others are highly probable, it acquires considerable probability And this is greatly increased by the drift of Jewish traditions concerning Abraham and his relation to the Messiah. In a Gospel that assigns to Jesus the words "Abraham rejoiced to see my day, and he saw it and was glad[1]," it is obvious that we must expect to find thoughts about Abraham latent under many of the acts and utterances of Him to whom these words are assigned. We may safely assert that the actual words are John's, not Christ's, but we shall not be so safe in making such an assertion about the thoughts.

This proof of intervention is quite irrespective of the correctness of the Marcan or the Johannine tradition. Even if Mark is quite wrong, it will still be true that John, believing Mark to be right in a certain sense, has intervened to shew that sense. What that "sense" might naturally be will be perceived from such a prophecy as that of Amos, "I will send a

---

[1] Jn viii. 56 See *Joh Gr.* 2097, 2688—9

famine in the land, not a famine of bread, nor a thirst of water, but of hearing the words of the Lord; and they shall wander from sea to sea, and from the north even to the east; they shall run to and fro to seek the word of the Lord[1]." Jesus Himself seems to allude to this prophecy in the words "Many shall come from the east and the west"—where Luke adds "and from the north and the south"—" and shall sit down with Abraham and Isaac and Jacob in the kingdom of heaven[2]." Also a prophecy of Daniel, interpreted by Irenaeus as referring to Christ, says "Many shall run to and fro and knowledge shall be increased[3]." This, when combined with the prophecy of Amos, might originate just such traditions as Mark has thrown together about the concourse of "many" to Christ's teaching, and to the banquet that He provided for those who suffered from a "famine" for "hearing the words of the Lord." The hypothesis of such an origin would give a satisfactory explanation of Mark's diffuse traditions and Luke's omissions. "Mark,"

---

[1] Amos viii 11—12

[2] Mt viii 11, Lk xiii 29 The occasions on which these parallel sayings were uttered are quite different Origen, quoting the Gospels, has (*Comm Rom* ii 14, Lomm vi 148) "ab oriente et occidente *et a quatuor ventis terrae*" Does this mean "and [indeed, not only from east and west, but also, as Luke says] from the four winds of the world"? The Targum on Amos viii 12 has "from the sea to *the west* (מערבא) and from the north to the east" *Sabbath* p 138 b (ed Goldschmidt) quotes Amos "From sea to sea from east (ממזרח) and from west (וממערב)" with no note On Zech ix 10 "from sea to sea," the Targ says "from the sea even to the west," but Kimchi "from the South Sea which is called Red, to the North Sea which is called Ocean " These variations may have influenced Christian traditions about the concourse to Jesus. Some might take "from sea to sea" as "from the sea of Galilee to the Mediterranean," *i e* the parts about Tyre and Sidon Luke would not interpret "sea" as referring to the sea of Galilee since he always calls it "lake "

[3] Dan. xii 4 LXX ἕως ἂν ἀπομανῶσιν οἱ πολλοὶ καὶ πλησθῇ ἡ γῆ ἀδικίας But Theod ἕως διδαχθῶσιν πολλοὶ καὶ πληθυνθῇ ἡ γνῶσις (הדעת) (see *Clue* **7, 90—1**), and so Iren iv 26 i "quoadusque discant multi et adimpleatur agnitio "

we may say, "recorded a historical fact (that is, the Concourse) in the language of poetry based on prophecy—not knowing the nature either of the language or of its basis—and left the old traditions just as they were without making them fit together; Luke omitted them; John penetrated to the old poetical purpose underlying Mark and expressed it in a new symbolism."

In a comment on Mark's narrative of the first concourse to Jesus attention was drawn to the apparent allusiveness of the Marcan "great number," as pointing to expressions in Genesis concerning the seed of Abraham[1]. But in that Marcan narrative we may trace also the influence of Amos (variously interpreted) in suggesting the regions of the world from which believers were to draw near to the Messiah[2]. The same influences may be traced in Mark's narrative of a second concourse The Hebrew use of the somewhat rare verb "*run-to-and-fro*," applied to those hungering and thirsting after truth by Amos, and to "*many*" by Daniel[3], may very well explain Mark's perplexing accumulation of verbs of motion, commented on above—"*coming and going*," "*running together*," and "*outstripping*"—all omitted by Matthew and Luke.

This recognition of Mark's allusiveness, in connection with a prophecy about "*many*," will come before us again when we consider such Marcan words of Jesus as "to give his life a ransom for *many*," and, "this is my blood which...is shed for *many*[4]." Both of these sayings appear to be based on words of Isaiah: "By his knowledge shall my righteous servant justify

---

[1] *Proclamation* p 376, quoting Mk iii 7—8 πολὺ πλῆθος. .πλῆθος πολύ

[2] Amos viii 12, mentioning the "north," may explain why Mark (*Proclamation* p 375) followed by Matthew, inserts "Galilee," as representing the "north" (besides being the "Galilee of the Gentiles" mentioned by Isaiah) Luke vi 17 omits "Galilee"

[3] Amos viii 12, Dan. xii 4 "run-to-and-fro" (Gesen 1001—2)

[4] Mk x 45, xiv 24 parall to Mt xx 28, xxvi. 28, omitted in parall. Lk. xxii 27 and *ib*. 20 (see W H)

CHRIST'S MIRACLES OF FEEDING

many...he bare the sin of *many*¹" Both are adopted by the parallel Matthew but omitted by the parallel Luke.

Are we to infer that in both these passages Mark has been induced by the influence of prophecy to attribute to Jesus sayings that He did not really utter, which Luke has consequently omitted? Without anticipating the discussion of these Marcan traditions in their order, we may note here, as to the first of them, that the parallel Luke introduces, as words of Jesus, "he that sitteth at meat" and "he that serveth," and represents Jesus as saying "I am among you as he that serveth²." Now John represents Jesus as actually "serving" while the disciples sit at meat—and serving in such a way as to suggest a picture of the Saviour of the world wiping off the stains of sinful men upon Himself³. This points to a Johannine intervention between Mark and Luke, as if John said: "It is true that Mark has added, to the actual words that Jesus uttered, words that He did not utter. But he added

---

¹ Is liii 11—12 Of רבים, freq = "*many* [*men*]," Gesen 913 *a* gives, as the first instance, Exod xxiii 2 (*bis*) "Thou shalt not follow *a multitude* (so R V and A V) to do evil, neither shalt thou speak in a cause to turn aside after *a multitude* (A V *many*) to wrest [judgment]," LXX οὐκ ἔσῃ μετὰ πλειόνων ἐν κακίᾳ οὐ προσθήσῃ μετὰ πλήθους ἐκκλῖναι μετὰ πλειόνων ὥστε ἐκκλεῖσαι κρίσιν On this, Rashi says "Sunt hujus textus expositiones sapientum Israelis, sed sermo Scripturae eis non convenit ..." But it does not appear to be disputed that the Heb. "*many*," in a suitable context, may mean "*the many*," or "*the majority*."

² Lk. xxii 27 τίς γὰρ μείζων, ὁ ἀνακείμενος ἢ ὁ διακονῶν,...ἐγὼ δὲ ἐν μέσῳ ὑμῶν εἰμι ὡς ὁ διακονῶν

³ Jn xiii 4 foll. See *Notes* **2963—4** shewing that Origen (on Jn xiii 5) quotes Luke xxii 27 with a reminiscence of Mk x 45 "He who said 'I came not as the guest but as the attendant'...He Himself puts water in the basin." Origen also (Lomm. ii 401) connects the Saviour's "wiping off" on Himself the filth from the feet of the disciples with Is liii. 4 (comp Mt viii 17) "He beareth our infirmities." See *Son* **3276** *a* where the belief is expressed that this representation was not a dramatic fiction, but was based on tradition.

them to explain what Jesus *meant* by 'ministering'. Luke, rejecting those additional words, has left the saying of Jesus in such a context as to lead his readers into a misunderstanding of His 'ministering.' It was not waiting at table, handing this dish or that. It might rather be described as a washing of the feet before the repast. And indeed the Saviour did this kind of service for His disciples, wiping off on Himself the defilements that could not but from time to time befall them in the course of their pilgrimage through the impurities of this present world[1]."

§ 7 *"They had no leisure so much as to eat," in Mark*[2]

It is of course possible that this Marcan tradition meant, from the first, nothing more than this, that the disciples had literally "no leisure" to eat enough for their simple wants, that Mark inserted it in this sense; and that Matthew and Luke omitted it—influenced perhaps in part by the fact that Jesus seemed to have summoned them at an early hour of the morning[3], before the time had come for a regular meal—because they thought it hyperbolical. Or Matthew and Luke may have omitted it as being unimportant from a spiritual point of view.

---

[1] On Gen xviii 4 "let a little water be fetched and wash your feet," Rashi says that as the water is fetched by Abraham's "servant" "per aliquem qui mittitur," i e. *Sheliach*, or *Apostle* (*Proclamation* pp 391, 395), so God recompenses Abraham's children by a messenger ("legatum"), namely, Moses. But *Gen. r.* ad loc sees a divine recompense of water proceeding not only from Moses (Numb xxi. 17) who gives water to drink, but also from God (Is iv 4, Ezek xvi 9) who Himself purifies Israel with water (sim more fully in *Numb r.*, on Numb. vii 48, Wü pp 348—9).

[2] Mk vi 31 οὐδὲ φαγεῖν εὐκαίρουν, D ουδε φαγειν ευκαιρος (i e. εὐκαίρως) ειχον, a "nec cibum poterant capere," SS (lit.) "and there was not for them place even bread to eat."

[3] Mk vi 30—35 shews that a great deal took place between the summons of Jesus and the advent of evening, so that the summons must have been early

CHRIST'S MIRACLES OF FEEDING

But there are so many instances where Mark's apparently unimportant little phrases about certain subjects, and particularly about the Doctrine of Bread, are much more important than they seem, that this phrase invites investigation Its insertion in an early Gospel would become intelligible if it originally described the disciples as being unable to "eat their bread" at a common meal with such "gladness and singleness of heart[1]" as characterized the meals taken by them in company with Jesus. Such meals would partake of the nature of a religious service The omission of the phrase by Matthew and Luke would, by itself, oblige us to discuss it; and the fact that it refers to bread (not indeed here mentioned but certainly implied by the word "eat") makes the discussion all the more necessary.

The Marcan verb "*have-leisure*," literally "*have-good-season*," occurs nowhere else in the Gospels nor in LXX. Codex D substitutes a phrase with a corresponding adverb meaning "*in-good-season*." This adverb occurs in Ben Sira "Be not thou hindered from paying a vow *in-good-season*[2]"; and the corresponding adjective occurs in the Psalms "These wait upon thee that thou mayest give them their meat *in-due-season*[3]." These passages vaguely suggest that in the beginnings of the Christian Church forms of the word might be associated by some with the Eucharist, or with Christ's "breaking of bread" before the Eucharist was formally instituted. But the verb, though proscribed by the Grammarians as a barbarous equivalent of the legitimate phrase "have leisure[4]," is used by Luke (in the

---

[1] Acts ii 46 "breaking bread at home they did take their food with gladness and singleness of heart"

[2] Sir xviii. 22 μὴ ἐμποδισθῇς τοῦ ἀποδοῦναι εὐχὴν εὐκαίρως. It occurs nowhere else in LXX

[3] Ps civ 27 τὴν τροφὴν αὐτοῖς εὔκαιρον (V Γ εις καιρον, εν ευκαιρια, εις ευκαιρον) This is the only instance in canon LXX, but in 2 and 3 Macc εὔκαιρος occurs five times.

[4] "Have leisure," σχολὴν ἄγω, or σχολάζω. See Steph *Thes.*

CHRIST'S MIRACLES OF FEEDING

Acts) concerning the Athenians: "Now all the Athenians and the strangers sojourning there (lit) *were-wont-to-have-good-season* for nothing else except to say or hear something of more than usual novelty[1]." Luke obviously means, by his use of the imperfect tense in such a context, not that the Athenians really *had* no leisure, but that they *would habitually make* no leisure. They habitually said "*We have no leisure* for this or that." But if they had spoken the truth they would have said "We are not disposed to do this or that[2]." Mark, like Luke, uses the verb in the imperfect tense. Is it not possible, then, that Luke rejected the word here in his Gospel because it seemed to him to suggest that the disciples were like the Athenians, restlessly *refusing to "find leisure"* for something for which they ought to have "found leisure"?

This supposition Luke might deem incredible. But the Fourth Gospel indicates that there was a spirit of restlessness among the Five Thousand, which extended to the disciples, including ultimately almost all but the Twelve; and if we consider these indications along with the recent execution of John the Baptist by Herod, we shall perceive that there may be nothing absurd in the supposition that the Twelve themselves were restless and unsettled and not disposed to "find leisure" for "eating bread" in the presence of their Master with the "gladness and singleness of heart" to which He was gradually accustoming them[3]

---

and (preferably) Wetstein on Mk vi 31, quoting *Etymol*, *Moeris*, *Thomas*, and *Phrynichus*

[1] Acts xvii 21 εἰς οὐδὲν ἕτερον ηὐκαίρουν ἢ λέγειν τι ἢ ἀκούειν τι καινότερον It was not only to be "new" but "newer [than usual]" And their first object was to "say" something of this kind, their second, to "hear" it

[2] Comp Acts xxiv 25, where Felix *says*—in answer to Paul's "reasoning" about "righteousness" and "the judgment to come"—"When I get a [suitable] season (καιρὸν) I will call thee unto me"; but he *means* "I am not disposed to listen to reasoning about 'righteousness,' I want money "

[3] Acts ii. 46

The first intimation of this is in the exclamation of those who have fed on the loaves and fishes, "This is of a truth the prophet that cometh into the world," where it is added that Jesus perceived that they proposed "to take him by force to make him a king[1]." Jesus reproaches them thus, "Ye seek me, not because ye saw signs, but because ye ate of the loaves[2]." They prefer "the meat that perisheth" to "the meat that abideth unto eternal life[3]." Jesus does not reproach the Twelve thus. But He implies that one of them (Judas Iscariot) deserved such a reproach ("one of you is a devil"); and to all of them He says "Will ye also depart[4]?" These would-be king-makers might be called—in the language of Matthew and Luke describing Christ's Temptation—instruments of the Tempter, tempting Jesus to pay Satan homage; and perhaps that thought underlies the Johannine saying "one of you is a devil."

If the disciples, amid the political excitement and concourse consequent on the death of John the Baptist, shewed some disposition to favour the views of the multitude, who wished to make their Master a king, that would explain not only Mark's brief and obscure mention of "want of leisure to eat," but also John's long and emphatic comment on the necessity of "eating," and on the impossibility of doing God's work without the sustenance of God's Bread, the "living" Bread, God's Word, God's Son.

Summing up the evidence as to the Marcan phrase about "leisure to eat," we find that the conclusion is doubtful as to its precise allusion and as to the reasons why Luke omits it. But there is a fair probability that it contains, or might be regarded in early times as containing, some allusion to the Hebrew thought of food as God's "seasonable" gift and to the expression of this by the LXX in the Psalmist's

---

[1] Jn vi 14—15 [2] Jn vi 26.
[3] Jn vi. 27.   [4] Jn vi. 67—70

language about God as giving food to His creatures "in its season[1]." Further, there is evidence enough to justify our accepting, as a working hypothesis, the supposition that under Mark's original there was latent an obscure Eucharistic meaning. This, if existent, is wholly lost by Matthew and Luke, who omit the Marcan phrase, but not by John, who attempts to elicit and to expound it[2].

§ 8. *"To a desert place apart,"* in Mark and Matthew

It will be observed below that instead of "to a desert place" —where we should rather expect a "solitary" or "retired" place—Luke has *"to a city called Bethsaida*[3]*."* Mark himself mentions Bethsaida later on, immediately after the Feeding of the Five Thousand and before the Walking on the Sea. There, however, he describes the disciples, not as coming back *from* Bethsaida (as we should have expected from Luke's account) but as coming *to* Bethsaida, and the parallel Matthew

---

[1] See Ps. civ. 27, cxlv. 15, and the comment (in *Gen. r.*, on Gen. 1. 3, Wu p. 11) on Prov. xv 23 "a word *in its season*, how good it is!" where it is maintained that the "word" is "*Light*," which God uttered "in its season" when He said, "Let there be *Light*!" and He saw that the Light was "good." The Lord's Prayer, and the Sermon on the Mount, and the Temptation, all point to the conclusion that Jesus taught that the Father in heaven is the Giver of every good thing, and of each in "its season," which is also "His season." The Eucharist includes this lesson.

[2] Comp. 1 Cor xi. 20 συνερχομένων οὖν ὑμῶν ἐπὶ τὸ αὐτὸ οὐκ ἔστιν κυριακὸν δεῖπνον φαγεῖν. The various renderings of these words, and the interpretations of modern commentators, shew how other early Eucharistic traditions might be misunderstood.

[3]

Mk vi 32	Mt. xiv 13	Lk ix. 10
And they went away in the boat to a desert place apart.	Now when Jesus heard it he withdrew (ἀνεχώρησεν) from thence in a boat to a desert place apart...	And he took them and retired (ὑπεχώρησεν) apart to a city called Bethsaida.

(Mark vi 29—44)

CHRIST'S MIRACLES OF FEEDING

omits "Bethsaida," while the parallel Luke omits both "Bethsaida" and the whole of the narrative that follows[1].

These facts indicate some early confusion about "Bethsaida." Instead of this name the Curetonian Syriac in Luke has "a desert place," while the Sinaitic Syrian has "to the gate of a city called Bethsaida[2]." Codex D has "village" instead of "city." The Latin and other versions mostly omit "city" and insert "desert place." One way of explaining not only these variations, but also Luke's inconsistency in "came *to Bethsaida*" and "we are here *in a desert place*," would be to suppose that Luke has mistaken *Beth Saida*, a poetic phrase meaning House of Provisioning, for the "city" of that name. The same Psalm that represents Israel as exclaiming "Can God prepare a table in the wilderness[3]?" says "He rained

---

[1] Mk vi. 45
And straightway he constrained his disciples to enter into the boat, and to go before [him] unto the other side *to Bethsaida* ..

Mt xiv. 22
And straightway he constrained the disciples to enter into the [*or*, a] boat, and to go before him unto the other side ...

Lk ix. 18
And it came to pass, as he was praying alone (καταμόνας) ....

Lk ix. 18, which follows Luke's Feeding of the Five Thousand, is printed here to shew Luke's divergence at this stage from Mark and Matthew.

Mk vi. 47, Mt xiv. 23, and Jn vi. 15 agree with Luke ix. 18 in representing Jesus as "alone (μόνος)" after the Feeding of the Five Thousand, but they mention it in their preface to the Walking on the Waters, which Luke omits.

[2] In Lk ix. 10 (Curet.) "and he *took* (דבר) them apart-by-themselves and went to a place [that was] desert," the verb "*took*" in the form מדבר (*e.g.* 1 S. xix 14 (Targ. and Syr.) "to *take*" (מדבר) David") might be regarded as meaning (א)מדבר, *midbar*, the regular word for "*wilderness*" in Hebrew and Aramaic. Walton's Syr. has "in locum desertum Bethsaidae," and *a, b, e* and *Brix* all insert "locum desertum" without "urbs" or "vicus."

[3] Ps. lxxviii. 19 Heb. "in the wilderness," but LXX, here and *ib.* 15, quite contrary to rule, has ἐν ἐρήμῳ, omitting the article. Contrast Exod. v. 1, vii. 16, viii. 20, 28 etc., and perhaps a hundred more instances, all ἐν τῇ ἐρήμῳ. The Heb., when unpointed, might mean "the" or "a" wilderness. Israelites, when described in poetry as

down manna upon them to eat, and gave them of the corn of heaven..., he sent them *provision* to the full[1]." Now the Hebrew for "*provision*" is there *Saida*. Poetically therefore it might be said that God in bringing Israel into the wilderness where He rained manna on them, brought them to "a *house, or place, of provision*," that is, "*Bethsaida.*"

This view is confirmed from Greek sources The Greek for "*provision*" is literally "*supplying with corn,*" *episitismos*. This word applies exactly to the supply of manna. For manna was, as the same Psalm says, "*corn* from heaven," not "bread," but of the nature of "*corn*," since it had to be ground and seethed to make it eatable[2]. *Episitismos* in LXX always corresponds to the Hebrew "Saida" It is used, in Genesis, of Joseph supplying "*provision*" from Egypt to his brethren, and, in Exodus, of the inability of Israel to supply themselves with "*provision*" for their journey into the wilderness[3]. The instance in Exodus would make the word peculiarly appropriate in the Psalm which represents God as making for Israel in the wilderness that "*provision*" which Israel could not make for themselves in Egypt. Similarly, we shall presently find Luke, alone among the Evangelists, representing the disciples as saying to Jesus, "Send away the multitude...that they may find *provision (episitismos)*[4], because we are here *in a desert*

---

being new to the wilderness of Sinai, might speak of it as "a" wilderness, but afterwards as "the" wilderness.

[1] Ps lxxviii 25 "provision," צֵידָה, ἐπισιτισμός (R V. "meat")

[2] Ps lxxviii 24 "corn (דָּגָן)" LXX renders this word elsewhere 37 times (Tromm) by σῖτος, but ἄρτος only here—a mistranslation. On the grinding and seething of the manna see Numb. xi 8. The mistranslation ("bread") is repeated by unbelieving Jews in Jn vi 31. Jesus implies in His answer that it was *not* (ib 32) "the true bread out of heaven" It should be noted however that "*the bread* of the mighty" is mentioned in Ps lxxviii 25.

[3] Gen. xlii. 25, xlv 21, Exod. xii 39, ἐπισιτισμός here and elsewhere (11 times in Heb. LXX and alw. = צֵידָה, Saida).

[4] Lk ix 12 ἐπισιτισμός (R V. 'victuals"). It does not occur elsewhere in N T.

place." The coincidence is not likely to be accidental, especially since *episitismos* does not occur anywhere else in N.T. It is reasonable to believe that there is an allusion to Exodus, and to the "provision" of manna in the wilderness

According to this view, Luke is right in retaining this word *episitismos*, unique in N.T., but wrong in duplicating it as "Bethsaida," and in placing "Bethsaida" at the beginning of the narrative. It should have come at the end. The disciples say, in effect, as the representatives of Israel, "We are in the wilderness. We are unable to *make provision* for the people. Send them away that they may *make provision* for themselves." Jesus replies by "*making provision*" Accordingly, after the gathering of the fragments, the conclusion of the narrative should have been: "Thus did the Lord lead His people that were in the wilderness into *a place of provision*, i.e. *into Bethsaida.*" As a fact, Mark places a mention of Bethsaida in that position, though not in suitable context[1]. Matthew omits "Bethsaida," and it is very probable that it is an error of Mark If so, it is similar, and yet dissimilar, to that of Luke. Mark, like Luke, has perhaps confused a poetic phrase with a proper name. But unlike Luke, Mark has placed the name at the end of the narrative, whereas Luke (less correctly) has placed it at the beginning.

The Johannine equivalents to "desert place" or "wilderness" in the Feeding of the Five Thousand have been touched on above. As to Bethsaida John cannot be expected to intervene As a rule, he avoids Synoptic names, being the only Evangelist that does not use the name "Gennesaret," and that does use "Tiberias" Bethsaida he mentions only in connection with Philip, who is "from Bethsaida[2]."

---

[1] Mk vi 45 "unto the other side *to Bethsaida*," Mt. xiv 22 om. "*to Bethsaida*"

[2] Jn i 44, xii 21 W.H. marg has Bethsaida in Jn v. 2, but that is the name of a pool.

CHRIST'S MIRACLES OF FEEDING

§ 9 *"In the boat," in Mark*[1]

Mark, having previously told us that Jesus ordered that a boat should be constantly ready[2], now calls it naturally *"the boat."* Matthew, not having made this statement, calls it *"a boat*[3]*."* Luke does not mention it here, and rather implies that Jesus quietly withdrew on foot, and that the multitudes followed Him on foot afterwards, when they became aware of His departure[4]. John suggests the same thing at the beginning of his narrative, and afterwards suggests it again, or indirectly affirms it, with curious detail. First he says that Jesus (R V.) *"went away to the other side of* (A.V. *went over*) the sea of Galilee*[5]*"; then he says that, after the Feeding, when the disciples came down to the sea for the purpose of going to Capernaum, they *"entered into a boat"* He does not here say *"the boat,"* which would have clearly meant the boat in which they had come. And yet afterwards he says that "the multitude saw...that there was *no other boat* there, *save* [*only there had been*] *one*, and that Jesus entered not with his disciples into *the boat*, but that his disciples had gone away alone—howbeit there came (*or*, had come) [*other*] *boats* from Tiberias...[6]" These

---

[1] Mk vi. 32

[2] Mk iii 9 See *Proclamation* p 377 suggesting that in the early Galilaean Church there may have been sometimes a play on the two words—almost identical in Aramaic and Syriac—*"boat"* and *"teaching"*

[3] Mt xiv 13

[4] Lk ix 10—11 ὑπεχώρησεν . οἱ δὲ ὄχλοι γνόντες ἠκολούθησαν αὐτῷ One would not infer from these words that Jesus "withdrew" by sea and the multitudes "followed" by land

[5] Jn vi 1 ἀπῆλθεν πέραν Nonnus adds "in a ship (νηὶ πολυκλήιδι ταμὼν ἀντώπιον ὕδωρ)." If that had been the meaning, it would have been easy to make it clear by substituting διεπέρασεν or διῆλθεν for ἀπῆλθεν Διαπερᾶν is used in Mk v 21, vi 53, Mt ix 1, xiv 34 about crossing the Lake, and διέρχεσθαι in Mk iv 35, Lk viii 22 The text of Jn suggests that Jesus passed into the translacustrian region without going across the Lake

[6] Jn vi 16, 22. R.V "save one," though literal, is misleading.

A L   241 (Mark vi 29—44)   16

statements—which can hardly be explained as originating from Johannine symbolism or dramatic picturesqueness—may perhaps be explained by supposing that there were very early differences of tradition about the manner in which Jesus and the disciples passed to, and returned from, the translacustrian scene of the Feeding of the Five Thousand[1]. Later on, at the conclusion of the Feeding of the Four Thousand, we shall find Mark saying that Jesus crossed to "the parts of Dalmanutha," whereas Matthew says that He crossed to "the borders of Magadan," and there are reasons for thinking that both of these names are not real place-names but phrases mistaken for place-names, such as *"their haven"* or *"the parts [of the] opposite [coast]*[2]." If that is probable it strengthens the probability that, in the present Lucan passage, "Bethsaida" is not a place-name, but a phrase mistaken for a place-name, *"House of Provision*[3]*"*

---

[1] In John, some mention of these details might seem necessary to explain how it came to pass that many of the Five Thousand, immediately after the miracle on the eastern side of the Lake, were addressed by Jesus in Capernaum, on the western side

[2] Mk viii 10, Mt xv 39 As regards "Dalmanutha," see *Corrections* **498** *g, h*, which gives as alternatives (1) the emphatic form of the Talmudic word for "harbour"—a Hebraized form of λιμήν—preceded by the relative *d*-, so as to mean "belonging to the harbour," (2) a transliteration, in Mark, of the preceding word "parts" (μέρη, מנותא) But it should have been added that, against the second explanation, Prof Dalman says (and gives evidence to shew) that (*Words* p 66) "τὰ μέρη with the meaning of 'district' is a pure Graecism, quite incapable of being literally reproduced in Aramaic" In Ps cvii 30 "the *haven* of their desire," the Syr has, for "haven," a form of λιμήν (*Thes Syr* 1952, comp. 1941) common in Syriac This favours the hypothesis called (1) above. For R V. "haven," Gesen 562 *b* has "city" See below, p 243, n 4

[3] Comp Macar p 85 "For He satisfied five thousand, having caused them to lie down *in the desert as if it were a Megalopolis* (ὡς εἰς μεγαλόπολιν κατακλίνας τὴν ἔρημον)"

CHRIST'S MIRACLES OF FEEDING

§ 10. *Signs of conflation in Mark*

Writing of Christ's eastward passage together with the disciples across the Lake, Mark describes the people as *"knowing"* them and as *"running together* from all the cities." In the following verse he omits the Matthew-Luke tradition that Jesus "healed" the people, but inserts—what Matthew and Luke do not contain—that He "taught" them[1]. Later on, writing of Christ's westward return across the Lake, Mark—as we shall presently find—says again that people at Gennesaret *"knew"* Him, and that they *"ran about"* or *"ran round"*[2]. And there he adds, at great length, that the sick were healed by Jesus in the "market-places[3]" Later still, after the Feeding of the Four Thousand, Mark describes Jesus as coming to "Dalmanutha." This name—non-occurrent elsewhere inside, or outside, the Bible—has been shewn to be explicable as an allusion to the Psalmist's *"haven"* in *"the haven* of their desire[4]," a Hebrew word that occurs nowhere else in the Bible but is frequent in Aramaic, meaning "open place," "street," "market-place." Something of the nature of a *harbour* is suggested in the tradition peculiar to Mark "they moored-to-the-shore[5]."

---

[1] Mk vi 33—4

[2] Mk vi 54—5 περιέδραμον, "ran about," occurs nowhere else in N T. In LXX it occurs twice and in both cases = Heb שׁוּט (the word quoted above, pp 230—31, from Amos and Daniel) The second instance of LXX περιτρέχω is Jerem v 1 *"Run ye to and fro through the streets of Jerusalem .and seek in the broad places thereof if ye can find a man, if there be any that doeth justly...and I will pardon her."*

[3] Mk vi 56 ἀγοραῖς Mt xiv 35 ("they brought to him all the sick") omits "market-places"

[4] See note above, p 242, on Ps cvii 30 "haven (מָחוֹז) " Levy iii 70 gives the word as = (1) "city," (2) *Machos*, the name of a place, (3) any enclosed place Levy Ch ii 23 gives it as freq = *"town with market-place,"* and also *"market-place,"* as in Lam ii 19 (Targ)

[5] Mk vi. 53 "...unto Gennesaret *and moored-to-the-shore* (καὶ

CHRIST'S MIRACLES OF FEEDING

It is necessary to look forward here to these later Marcan passages in order to take a collective view of Mark's whole narrative. For if we find clear signs of reiteration in the employment of one word of prophetic use, such as "*run-to-and-fro*," we ought to be prepared to find them in other words. And if they are found, then we must recognise that all this Marcan account of the sequel of the Baptist's death must be regarded as coming from sources quite different from those of the narrative of the death itself. In that narrative there is diffuseness but little or no room for prophetic allusion, and there are few or no signs of Marcan "conflation" But here we seem to be in an altogether different atmosphere, so that we may expect continuous conflations such as might be exemplified in many LXX renderings, and especially in Daniel[1]. The influence of this consideration extends beyond the Feeding of the Five Thousand to its sequel. This, in all the Evangelists but Luke, contains a description of Christ appearing to the disciples in their boat while, as Matthew says, it was being "*sorely tried* (literally, *tormented*) *by the waves*", but Mark, besides saying that the disciples themselves were being "*sorely tried* (literally, *tormented*)" adds that they were "*in the act of rowing*"; and John, too, describes the disciples as "*rowing*[2]." Now the regular Hebrew and Aramaic word for "*row*" is the same as that which we have been commenting on above, as meaning "*run-to-and-fro*"

προσωρμίσθησαν)," Mt xiv 34 "unto Gennesaret" Προσορμίζω does not occur in LXX nor again in N T Delitzsch renders Mark "*and they drew near to the dry land*," the Clementine transl has "*and they drew near the shore of the sea.*" D, SS, *a*, *b*, and Corb omit it. Steph *Thes* vi 1974 quotes figurative uses of it from Demosth p 795, 14 πρὸς οὓς αὐτὸς ἔχωσας λιμένας (misericordiae) .πρὸς τούτους μὴ προσορμίζου, and from Philostr p 717

[1] See *Clue* **127** on Dan iv 19, also **105—111** on 2 S. xxiv 19—20 compared with 1 Chr xxi 19—20, and **95** foll on "Longer Conflations"

[2] Mk vi 48, Mt. xiv 24, Jn vi. 19.

244 (Mark vi 29—44)

in Amos and Daniel[1]. And the question will come before us whether John is here deliberately intervening in favour of Mark—against Matthew, who omits the word *"rowing,"* and still more against Luke, who omits the whole of the story about *"rowing"*—and, if so, in what sense, whether symbolical or otherwise.

§ 11 *"On foot," in Mark and Matthew*[2]

Why does Luke omit *"on foot"*? One reason may be that in Hebrew, "a multitude following [a leader] *at his feet*" may be confused with "a multitude following *on their feet*[3]." But another reason may be that Luke did not perceive a latent allusion in the Marcan phrase, which he consequently deemed superfluous.

Mark is describing a miracle akin to that of the Manna, which speedily followed the departure of Israel from Egypt. And the description of that departure contains the first mention of the phrase *"on foot"* to be found in our English Version of the Bible: "about six hundred thousand [that were] *on foot*[4]." There the Hebrew adds "the men [of military age], besides children[5]" Rabbi Ishmael explains that "children" includes

---

[1] Jon i 13 (Heb.) has the exceptional word חתר "dug [into the sea]," but the Targ. has שוט, which is used of "rowing" in Heb. of Is xxxiii 21, Ezek xxvii 8, 26

[2] Mk vi 33, Mt xiv 13 R.V. marg *"by land"* Delitzsch *"on their feet."*

[3] *Clue* 75—6 contains an attempt to explain Mk vi 33, Mt xiv 13 thus See 2 S xv 16—18 (*bis*) ברגליו, Walton "in pedibus suis," (*semel*) ברגלו, Walton "in pede suo," R.V (*ter*) "after him," Targ. (*ter*) "cum illo," LXX (1) τοῖς ποσὶν αὐτῶν, (2) πεζῇ v r πεζοί, (3) τοῖς ποσὶν αὐτῶν Comp Jer xii 5 "thou hast run with the *footmen*," LXX "thy *feet* run "

[4] "On foot," so R V here (Exod. xii 37), but the same Heb is rendered "*footmen*" in Numb xi 21 "Six hundred thousand *footmen* (רגלי) [are] the people...." See below, pp. 349—50.

[5] Exod xii 37 "the men [of military age]" *ha-gebârîm*, Rashi "men above 20 years old" The first instance of *geber* is in Exod. x. 11 "Go now, *the men* [among you]...," where Moses has

CHRIST'S MIRACLES OF FEEDING

"women," and Rabbi Jonathan adds "the aged[1]"—additions that may illustrate the words added by Matthew alone at the conclusion of both the Miracles of Feeding, "besides women and children[2]."

In the Fourth Gospel there is nothing on the surface to indicate Johannine intervention in favour of Mark here. On the contrary John rather seems to favour Matthew-Luke by himself saying, as they do, that the multitude "followed" Jesus[3]. He does not add *"on their feet"*; although, later on, he certainly implies that they did not come by boat and leaves us to infer that they came on foot[4]. The picture he gives us is of Jesus on a mountain, first looking down and seeing that the multitude that had been following Him is now approaching, and then descending to give them food. If therefore "foot" is to enter at all into the Johannine picture, it would seem that we are to think of the crowd as down below at the feet of Jesus, somewhat as the Song of Moses says concerning Israel at Sinai, "They sat down *at thy feet*, [everyone] shall receive (*marg.* received) of thy words[5]."

But John goes on to say "Now the passover, *the feast of the Jews*, was nigh[6]." And it is at all events worth noting that both in New Hebrew and in Aramaic the word *"foot"* is very frequently used to denote *"a feast,"* and especially one of the three great feasts. Possibly therefore John may be following a tradition that explained *"on foot"* as *"at the feast,"* to which

---

asked (x 9) that "young" and "old" may go, Rashi explains that Pharaoh is refusing to let the children go

[1] See *Mechilt.* on Exod xii 37. Jer Targ on Exod xii 37 adds *"none riding on horses* except the children"—apparently intended to explain antithetically the phrase *"on foot"* applied to the men

[2] This addition is contained in Mt xv 38 as well as Mt xiv 21. See below on Mk vi. 44, p. 348 foll.

[3] Jn vi 2, Mt xiv 13, Lk ix 11 "followed"

[4] See above, p 241

[5] Deut xxxiii 3 LXX ὑπὸ σέ, Aq. τοῖς ποσί σου.

[6] Jn vi. 4

CHRIST'S MIRACLES OF FEEDING

John added an explanatory context indicating that it was "*the passover*[1]."

It is not contended that the Johannine "passover" is proved to represent the Marcan "on foot." The evidence is not sufficient for that. But, in view of the multitude of positive proofs of the rule of Johannine Intervention, the evidence is sufficient here for at least a negative conclusion—it is not proved that the rule fails, and there is nothing unreasonable in the supposition that the rule holds[2].

§ 12. "*He had compassion*," *in Mark and Matthew*[3]

The verb here rendered "*had compassion*" means literally "*had* [*the*] *bowels* [*of his compassion opened*]*[4]*." In the Healing of the Leper Mark alone used this word[5]. Here Matthew follows Mark in using it, but Luke does not[6]. It is therefore a case where we should expect Johannine intervention.

If we ask why Luke omitted it here, we shall find that it cannot well be because the word is unknown in the LXX and in literary Greek; for Luke uses it elsewhere thrice, and once

---

[1] See Levy iv 424—5, which shews that this meaning of "*foot*" was very common, and that the double meaning of the term was sometimes played upon The phrase "*in the foot of*" also meant (1b) "*on account of*," so that "they followed *on account of* Jesus [and His signs]" (comp Jn vi 2) might be expressed by "*at the feet of* Jesus" "*Foot*" is also thus used in Aramaic (Levy Ch ii 406 a) Gesen. 290 b renders חגן (LXX ἑορτάζω) not "feast," but "make-pilgrimage," "keep a pilgrim-feast"

[2] It is not contended that John is right Further reasons will be given below (pp. 348—51) for thinking that Mark's tradition alluded to the phrase "*on foot*," or "footmen," connected with the exodus of Israel from Egypt   [3] Mk vi 34, Mt xiv 14

[4] Comp the use of the noun in 1 Jn iii 17 A V "shut up *his bowels* [*of compassion*]," R V "*his compassion*," τὰ σπλάγχνα αὐτοῦ.

[5] Mk i 41, σπλαγχνίζομαι, "a new verb in the Greek language," see *Proclam* pp 251—2.

[6] Mk vi 34, Mt xiv 14 ἐσπλαγχνίσθη, Lk. ix. 11 ἀποδεξάμενος.

CHRIST'S MIRACLES OF FEEDING

about Jesus[1]. But it may be explained by his other contextual variations from Mark. Mark states, as the reason for compassion, "They were as sheep that had no shepherd," and then "He began to teach them many things"—as though the whole multitude were spiritually shepherdless and pitiably ignorant of spiritual things. Later on, Mark says about the disciples, "They understood not [the truth] about the loaves, but their heart was callous[2]"—as though, even by the disciples, some latent spiritual truth, underlying the sign of the Feeding, had been overlooked. All this is omitted by Luke. It would not suit his comparatively prosaic and passionless representation: "Having received (or, welcomed) them, He proceeded to speak to them about the kingdom of God, and to heal those that needed tendance[3]." Apparently Luke did not see that the occasion was one that called for a feeling so strong as to need the Marcan word to describe it.

Passing to John, we perceive that in accordance with Mark's brief observation—but at much greater length, and not in his own words but in words attributed to Jesus—he lays stress on the spiritual meaning of the Feeding, which not only the multitude but also almost all the disciples misunderstood. But neither here nor elsewhere in his Gospel does he mention "bowels of compassion." Can we say, then, that he implies it either here or elsewhere?

It will seem probable that he does, if we bear in mind the Johannine habit of dramatizing and ask ourselves how John would dramatically represent Jesus as "*having-bowels-of-compassion*." The Johannine Epistle says, about Him, "Hereby know we love, because *he laid down his life for us*, and we

---

[1] Lk vii. 13 (of Jesus at Nain), x. 33, xv. 20 (all peculiar to Luke)

[2] Mk vi 52, not in the parall Mt xiv 33. Luke omits the whole narrative (the Walking on the Sea).

[3] Lk ix 11 ἀποδεξάμενος αὐτοὺς ἐλάλει αὐτοῖς περὶ τῆς βασιλείας τοῦ θεοῦ καὶ τοὺς χρείαν ἔχοντας θεραπείας ἰᾶτο

ought to *lay down our lives* for the brethren. But whoso hath the world's goods, and beholdeth his brother in need and *shutteth up his bowels* from him, how doth the love of God abide in him[1]?" The "*shutting up of the bowels*" of compassion, then, is the Johannine opposite of Christ's sacrifice, or "laying down life" for others. It follows that the "opening, or free action, of *the bowels of compassion*" would be the Johannine equivalent of Christ's "*laying down His life for the brethren.*" Now though the word "*bowels*" is not mentioned in the whole of the Fourth Gospel, yet the thing—*that is to say, a yearning compassion for the hunger and the thirst of the sinful world*, and a longing to lay down life that the world may live—is implied, not only in the words "The bread that I will give is my flesh, for the life of the world," but in the whole of the doctrine of the gift of His flesh and blood, enunciated "in synagogue, as he taught in Capernaum[2]."

If this view is correct, John is expressing dramatically and symbolically a moral and sacrificial view of the Feeding of the Five Thousand of which there is no trace in Luke. Mark and Matthew suggest it twice, first, by saying that Jesus "*had compassion*," and later on, in the Feeding of the Four Thousand, by representing Jesus Himself as saying "*I have compassion.*" John seems to attempt to make us feel that in this "sign" Jesus is (so to speak) "*doing compassion*," i.e. symbolically offering up Himself, as a sacrifice for men. In the Epistle to Philemon Paul calls Onesimus first his "*child*" and then his "*bowels*," and *The Testaments of the Patriarchs* represents Joseph as saying to his brethren "Pity the *bowels* of Jacob our father," meaning "Pity his *beloved son*[3]." Philo also represents

---

[1] 1 Jn iii 16—17.
[2] Jn vi 51—9.
[3] Philem 10, 12, *Test XII Patr Zab* ii 2. Comp *ib Neph* iv. 5 "until there shall come the *bowels* (σπλάγχνον) of the Lord, a man doing righteousness."

CHRIST'S MIRACLES OF FEEDING

Jacob as calling Joseph *"my bowels*[1].*"* Thus there was a connection, for Jews in the first century, not at first perceptible to us, between *"compassion"* and *"a son,"* or rather *"a dear son," "a son specially beloved."*

If this connection is obscure to us it must have been much more obscure to Greeks in the first century. For to them the word "bowels," though conveying often the notion of some strong inward feeling, more often implied depth of resentment than depth of love[2]. It was therefore an appropriate task for the Fourth Evangelist to make this connection clear. He himself certainly believed that the Sign of the Five Thousand was a sign of God's love in sending down His Compassion incarnate in Jesus Christ to give Himself as the living bread for the life of men. This he found hinted at in the Marcan tradition about "bowels of compassion," but only hinted at—and so obscurely that Luke passed it over in word and neglected it in thought. To remedy this defect John may have adopted *"Son"*—meaning *"*a Son uniquely beloved, or only-begotten*"* —as a Hellenic paraphrase for the Hebrew *"bowels of compassion*[3].*"* At all events he represents Jesus as teaching in the synagogue at Capernaum a consistent doctrine such as might be based on this paraphrase.

In conclusion we may naturally ask what induced Mark to use—if not to invent—this unprecedented Greek verb (unprecedented at least so far as researches of modern commentators go) to express Christ's compassion. Might he not have used

---

[1] Philo II 45 rhetorically represents Jacob as saying that the wild beasts, in devouring Joseph, devour τῶν ἐμῶν σπλάγχνων

[2] See Steph. *Thes.* which alleges, as exceptional uses, σπλάγχνον "de utero," of fatherhood in Soph *Oed T.* 1066, and of motherhood in Pind *Ol* VI 43 and Aesch *Sept* 1031

[3] Comp *Test XII Patr* Lev. IV. 4, where the text has "The Lord shall visit all the Gentiles *in His bowels [of compassion],"* but several versions have, as a Christian modification, *"in the bowels [of compassion] of His Son."*

CHRIST'S MIRACLES OF FEEDING

the verb "pitied," frequent in LXX and thrice used by himself[1]? It is hardly enough to say Mark wanted to express abundant or extreme pity, for he could have added adverbs (as he adds them elsewhere) to express this[2].

It is reasonable therefore to look back to O.T. for some Biblical instance of a phrase implying "bowels of compassion." A notable one—almost the only one outside the prophets—occurs in Genesis, where it is said of Joseph that "*his bowels did yearn upon his brother*[3]." The context describes Joseph's brethren as coming to buy corn from him. Jewish Christians from a very early date would naturally accept Joseph as a type of Christ; and Joseph, giving food to his brethren in Egypt, might represent one aspect (a rudimentary one) of Jesus giving food to His brethren in the wilderness[4]. Then the compassion of Jesus for the multitude, whom He fed as His little ones, might be likened in early Christian poetry to the "bowels of compassion" of Joseph—who was himself called "the bowels of Jacob," as we have seen above—"yearning" for his beloved brother Benjamin, "the little one" among the Twelve. Thoughts of this kind may well have been in the mind of those who originated early Christian songs and poetic traditions concerning Christ's acts of compassion for the hunger and thirst of the multitudes.

---

[1] Ἐλεεῖν, of which there are about 150 instances in O T

[2] E g σφόδρα, λίαν, περισσῶς

[3] Gen xliii 30 (where the marg gives only 1 K iii 26 (apart from prophecy)) I have found no ancient comment on the rather curious use of "lift up the eyes" in the context (*ib* 28—9) "And they [*i e* Joseph's brethren] .made obeisance And he [*i e* Joseph] *lifted up his eyes*, and saw Benjamin his brother"

[4] See Jerome on Ps. cv. 21 "He made him [Joseph] lord of his house" Jerome explains "house" as "the Church acquired by [His] blood"

CHRIST'S MIRACLES OF FEEDING

§ 13. *"They were as sheep not having a shepherd," in Mark and Matthew*[1]

The mention of a shepherdless flock comes appropriately here in Mark, because it follows the account of the execution of John the Baptist whom many Jews had been regarding as their "shepherd." Matthew places it earlier, between what may be called a Circuit of Healing and the Mission of the Twelve[2] Luke nowhere inserts it Textual grounds may suffice perhaps for a partial explanation of his omitting it here[3]. But Luke will be found also to omit, much later on, another Mark-Matthew tradition about "the shepherd"—the quotation, attributed to Jesus, "I will smite the shepherd and the sheep shall be scattered[4]." We must therefore not ignore the possibility that Luke may have been influenced by some doubt as to the utility of this tradition for his readers The conception of a king as a shepherd is both Hebrew and Homeric. Yet it was liable to philosophic scoffing such as Epictetus addresses to Homer's Agamemnon· "What then are you? A *'shepherd'* in truth. For you weep like *the shepherds* when a wolf snatches one of their sheep[5]."

---

[1] Mk vi 34, comp Mt ix 36
[2] Mt ix 35 "And Jesus went about all the cities and the villages, teaching.. and preaching...and healing all...sickness" This is parall to Mk vi 6 "And he went about the villages round about, teaching" Neither Mk vi 6 nor the parall Lk xiii 22 (which adds "journeying to Jerusalem") makes any mention of "healing" Mt ix 36 proceeds "When he saw the multitudes, he was moved with compassion ($\dot{\epsilon}\sigma\pi\lambda\alpha\gamma\chi\nu\acute{\iota}\sigma\theta\eta$) for them because they were.. as sheep not having a shepherd " Then follows (Mt ix 37, x 1) the injunction to pray for "labourers" for "the harvest," and the Mission of the Twelve
[3] See below, p. 256 foll.
[4] Mk xiv 27, Mt xxvi 31, om. by Lk xxii 39 foll The quotation in the Gospels differs from the Heb of Zech xiii 7. There are special reasons why Luke might omit it. See *Son* (Index "Shepherd")
[5] Epict iii 22 35 "*snatches* ($\dot{\alpha}\rho\pi\acute{\alpha}\sigma\eta$)," comp Jn x 12 "the

CHRIST'S MIRACLES OF FEEDING

The Fourth Gospel, whether consciously alluding to such jibes or unconsciously using language that meets them, vindicates at all events the character of the ideal shepherd. It admits that the ideal has not been reached, and that all who have come forward hitherto, representing themselves as true shepherds, have been, as compared with the true Shepherd, "thieves and robbers[1]." But it claims for the Good Shepherd a very different part. The thief (it says) comes to "steal" and to "destroy"; the wolf comes to "snatch"; the hireling "fleeth"; but the Good Shepherd comes, not only to give food to the sheep, but also, by "laying down his life" in conflict with "the wolf," to save them from being "snatched."

John has in mind the thought of the false king, the king of Babel, the hunter or "snatcher" of the souls of men, the wolf[2]. The true king is He who, as Paul says, "being in the form of God, counted it not *a [prize-for-]snatching* to be on an equality with God, but emptied himself, taking the form of a servant[3]." Yet the Jews in Jerusalem accused Jesus, in effect, of doing this very thing, "making himself equal with God[4]," that is to say, "*snatching*" at it as a "*prize*." And what are we to say to the fact that the only other Johannine mention of "*snatching*" comes at the conclusion of the Feeding of the Five Thousand, in a passage implying the complete failure of the multitude to understand the spiritual meaning of the sign. "They were about to come and *snatch him [away]* to make him king[5]"? Is it a mere accident that the sheep of Israel, whom Jesus

---

wolf *snatcheth* (ἁρπάζει) them." Perhaps one of Luke's reasons for omitting the tradition of Mk vi 34 was that he thought it attached too great importance to the recent death of John the Baptist.

[1] Jn x. 8, see *Joh. Gr.* 2361—2
[2] Philo ii 41—42, 90 contrasts "shepherding" which is the fit training for a king, with "hunting" which is the training for war
[3] Philipp. ii. 6 "a [prize-for-]snatching (ἁρπαγμόν)"
[4] Jn v. 18
[5] Jn vi 15. Ἁρπάζω occurs in Jn, elsewhere, only in x 12, 28, 29 (the Good Shepherd and the comment on it)

came to save from *"the snatcher,"* are here described as themselves desiring to *"snatch [away]"* their Shepherd that they may convert Him into a "king" after their own hearts—a veritable wolf? In imputing to John a deliberate choice of a peculiar phrase to describe a fact we do not impugn the fact itself. The fact in the present instance—the attempt to make Jesus a king—may be accepted as historical because of its antecedent probability, although no other Evangelist mentions it, but the choice of the word to express the fact may not improbably have been suggested by the Johannine sense of irony.

§ 14   *"Shepherd"* (sing) *nowhere mentioned by Luke*

Both Matthew and Luke mention an owner of sheep as follows:

Mt. xviii 12 (R V.)	Lk. xv. 4 (R.V.)
How think ye? if any man have a hundred sheep, and one of them be gone astray, doth he not leave the ninety and nine, and go. [1], and seek that which goeth astray?	What man of you, having a hundred sheep, and having lost one of them, doth not leave the ninety and nine... , and go after that which is lost, until he find it?

The man's conduct seems open to censure—especially in Luke's version, which represents him as "leaving to themselves" or "abandoning[2]," the ninety-nine sheep. At all events opponents of Christianity might object to such a human shepherd as the type of the divine Shepherd. Perhaps some might say he was no true shepherd. Readers of Philo would know that he distinguishes the "cattle-feeder" from the "shepherd" as follows, "Now to those who allow their beasts to fill themselves with what they desire in a promiscuous mass we must

---

[1] R V. "leave the ninety and nine and go unto the mountains," W H "leave the ninety and nine on the mountains and go."
[2] Lk xv. 4 καταλείπει, comp Mt. xviii 12 ἀφήσει

CHRIST'S MIRACLES OF FEEDING

give the name of 'cattle-feeders,' but that of 'shepherds' on the other hand to those who give them what is needful and only what is exactly suitable[1]." The man who "abandoned" his ninety-nine sheep (it might be urged) did not discharge the duty of a shepherd and was not worthy of the name.

Jerome gives two explanations of the parable. Some think (he says) that the Shepherd is the incarnate Son descending to save the one wandering sheep below, the human race (in which case the ninety-nine would be, presumably, the angels in heaven); others think that the ninety-nine are those whom He called "just persons that need no repentance[2]." In the latter case, the parable is still open to the jibe of Celsus, who asked "what evil" these just persons had done to incur the punishment of being abandoned[3]. It is only a prosaic or captious spirit that would take literally this "abandonment" of the safe and unwandering sheep, but still the Fourth Evangelist might naturally feel that there was room for another exposition of the tasks of the Good Shepherd in which He might be described as performing one task without neglecting another[4].

Luke, in his only mention of "flock," calls it a "little one" and connects it with "kingdom," "Fear not, little *flock*; for it is your Father's good pleasure to give you the *kingdom*[5]"; and again, in his parallel to the Marcan passage that speaks of "teaching" and "sheep without a shepherd," Luke mentions

---

[1] Philo i. 306 "cattle-feeders," κτηνοτρόφους.
[2] Lk xv. 7 [3] Orig *Cels* iii 62
[4] Philo, besides quoting Numb xxvii 16 foll. from LXX "sheep that have no shepherd," with the paraphrase (i 307) χωρὶς ἐπιστάτου καὶ ἡγεμόνος, also alludes to it (i 170) δίχα ἐπιστάτου καὶ ἡγεμόνος, without quoting it. Such a condition he calls (*ib*) ὀρφανίαν (comp Jn xiv 18).
[5] Lk xii 32 τὸ μικρὸν ποίμνιον, on which see *Son* **3440** *b* quoting Clem Alex 953, who uses Lk and Mt xviii 10 μικρῶν to illustrate Christ's doctrine of "little ones" This would make good sense, "*flock of the little-ones*," i e flock of the children of the New Kingdom.

CHRIST'S MIRACLES OF FEEDING

"*kingdom*[1]." Somewhat similarly in one of the Psalms, where the Hebrew has "he *shepherded* them," and the R.V. "he *fed* them," the Targum has "he *reigned* over them[2]." Such variations of rendering are all justifiable. But they imply preferences of this or that aspect of "*shepherding.*"

Luke seems to like the royal aspect. John, if he does not dislike, at all events avoids it. He represents Jesus as using the word "*kingdom*" on only two occasions, namely, in dialogues with Nicodemus and Pilate, both of whom misunderstand it[3]. Also, in John, the flock is not called "little," though it is divided, at the close of his Gospel, into three classes, one of which consists of "little-sheep[4]." In the Parable of the Good Shepherd we are told that the sheep are of more than one fold, though they will all be brought together so as to make "one flock, one shepherd[5]."

§ 15. "*And he began to teach them many things,*" *in Mark*

The parallel Matthew-Luke makes no mention of "teaching," but Matthew mentions "curing," and Luke has "welcoming" and "speaking about the kingdom of God" and "healing[6]." An explanation of these variations is afforded by the hypothesis of an original Hebrew verb "*to shepherd.*" Mark has given us a hint of this in his negative phrase above discussed ("sheep not having a *shepherd*"). But we have now to note that the Hebrew verb "*to shepherd*" occurs more frequently in the Bible than might be supposed. The English Version does not reveal it, because "shepherding" includes various actions such as feeding and tending, which may be expressed in English

---

[1] Mk vi 34, Lk ix 11   [2] Ps lxxviii. 72
[3] See *Joh Voc.* 1685 *a* quoting Jn iii 3, 5, xviii 36.
[4] Jn xxi 15—17 (txt doubtful)
[5] Jn x. 16.
[6] Mk vi 34 ἤρξατο διδάσκειν αὐτοὺς πολλά, Mt xiv 14 ἐθεράπευσεν τοὺς ἀρρώστους αὐτῶν, Lk. ix. 11 ἀποδεξάμενος αὐτοὺς ἐλάλει αὐτοῖς περὶ τῆς βασιλείας τοῦ θεοῦ, καὶ τοὺς χρείαν ἔχοντας θεραπείας ἰᾶτο

256 (Mark vi 29—44)

CHRIST'S MIRACLES OF FEEDING

by their several verbs "feed," "tend," etc This is the first and probably the principal cause of variation A second cause is the accidental similarity of the Hebrew verb "*shepherd*" to forms of the verb meaning "*know*" or "*cause to know*" (i e "*teach*")

This second cause has been discussed in a previous treatise[1]. One of the instances there given deserves to be repeated here because it illustrates both causes at the same time "The lips of the righteous [man] *shepherd* many[2]" Here "to *shepherd*" may mean "to *guide*," or "*tend*," as well as "*feed*," but LXX has confused it with "*know*," meaning "[*come to*] *know*," i e "*learn*" Moreover the LXX renders "many" (the Hebrew *rab*) as though it meant "great" or "lofty," and renders the whole sentence "The lips of the righteous [*come to*] *know* lofty [things]" This suggests an explanation of the phrase in our Marcan context "*and many knew* [*them,* or *him*]," as being an error for "*and he caused-to-know many*," i e either "*he taught many* [*persons*]," or "*he taught* [*them*] *many* [*things*]"—which is, in substance, the phrase at the heading of this section

More important than this verbal cause is the cause placed first above—namely, the Hebrew thought and stream of tradition about God's "*shepherding*" Jacob illustrates it when he begins his career at Bethel, praying that the Lord would guide him, guard him, and feed him[3], and he expressly mentions the word when he closes his career in Egypt, invoking

---

[1] See *Son* **3437** *c*—*d*, which refers to *Clue* **5, 7**, and **90**, and deals with Mk vi 34 and the parall Mt -Lk from the verbal point of view

[2] Prov x 21 (R V) "*feed* (ירעו)," LXX ἐπίσταται, "*learn*," or, "[*come to*] *know*," leg ידעו Targ retains the Heb in רעין (Aram), but in the sense "*treat-as-friends*" (Walton, "*placiunt*"), Aq ποιμαίνουσι "*they shepherd*," Field "*pascunt* (i e *erudiunt*)" In Job xxxii 7, the causative "*make to know*" ידיעו, i e "*teach*," is rendered by LXX "*know*"

[3] Gen xxviii 20 "If God will be with me, and will keep me in this way that I go and will give me bread to eat .."

CHRIST'S MIRACLES OF FEEDING

"the God that *shepherded* me all my life long unto this day[1]." Moses implied "*shepherding*" when he besought the Lord to appoint a successor to himself "that the congregation of the Lord be not as sheep that have no shepherd[2]." And all his life testified that he too, like Jacob, recognised that the good shepherd on earth was the type of the Shepherd in heaven, the God that had guided Israel out of Egypt and guarded and fed them in the wilderness, to whom the Psalmist appealed as Shepherd of Israel and of whom the Psalmist said "The Lord is *my shepherd*, I shall not want[3]"

This last sentence is one of the very few quoted from the Psalms by Philo, who speaks of it ecstatically as a song that should be sung by every man that loves God, and above all by the Cosmos, or Universe, which is the "flock" of the living God who governs all things like a shepherd and a king[4]. Poets, he says, are wont to give to kings the title of shepherds of the people; but the Lawgiver (that is, Moses) gives this title only to the wise, who are real kings[5]. Elsewhere Philo declares that— however men may laugh at the notion—the only way of becoming a perfect king is to become an adept in the science of shepherding[6].

---

[1] Gen xlviii 15—16 "The God that hath *shepherded* me all my life long unto this day, the Angel that hath redeemed me from all evil..." *Gen r ad loc*, assuming that "*shepherding*" means nourishing, says that it is a greater work (as in Ps cxlv 16) to "*shepherd*" than to "*redeem*," the former being the act of "God," the latter of "the angel," and that the "shepherding" is as difficult as the cleaving of the Red Sea.

[2] Numb. xxvii. 17.

[3] Ps lxxx 1, xxiii 1   Comp Hos iv 16 "The Lord will *shepherd them*, i e. Israel," R V "*feed*," Targ "deducet," LXX νεμήσει, Is xl. 11 "Like a shepherd his flock shall he *shepherd*," and sim Targ, LXX ποιμανεῖ

[4] Philo 1. 308

[5] Philo 1. 306

[6] Philo 11. 90 καί μοι δοκεῖ ..μόνος ἂν γενέσθαι βασιλεὺς τέλειος ὁ τὴν ποιμενικὴν ἐπιστήμην ἀγαθός

In a very different strain, yet to the same effect, the Jewish comment on "The Lord is my shepherd" declares that the "shepherd" includes the three characters of Father, Shepherd (as Guide and Guardian), and Brother, and it adds a very early tradition that, although the occupation of the shepherd with his staff and scrip is commonly believed to be one of the meanest on earth, David "knew better." David argued thus: "Jacob called the Lord a Shepherd, saying 'The God that *shepherded* me all my life long', therefore I, too, will call Him a *Shepherd* and will say 'The Lord is my *Shepherd*[1].'"

The longest of the historical Psalms leads up to the shepherding of Israel as its climax. It tells us how Israel wandered in the wilderness, "led" by God's "cloud" and "fire," and receiving from Him "manna," or "corn of heaven," and "bread" and "meat to the full," and "flesh." All these gifts—which imply guidance and food such as a shepherd gives—were yet to no purpose for Israel because "their heart was not right with him[2]" But the last three verses describe how Israel was finally "*shepherded*" by God's chosen representative· "He chose David also his servant and took him from the sheepfolds...to *shepherd* Jacob his people and Israel his inheritance; so he *shepherded* them according to the integrity of his heart and guided them by the skilfulness of his hands[3]."

---

[1] See *Tehill* on Ps xxiii 1 (Wu pp 209—10) giving several traditions on "my shepherd" The first tradition of all is a comment on "*my*" (in "*my* shepherd") It begins from Cant ii 16 "My beloved is *mine* and I am *his*," and passes to Exod. xx. 2 "I am Jehovah, *thy* God," Is li. 4 "*my* nation"

[2] Ps lxxviii 14—37 In *ib.* 52 "he led forth his people *like sheep* and guided them in the wilderness *like a flock*," we are brought to the thought of the sheep, but not to the word "shepherd"

[3] Ps lxxviii. 70—72 This is quoted in *Exod r.* on Exod iii 1 "And Moses was *shepherding* the flock," where it is said that Moses (as also David afterwards) divided the sheep into three classes (comp Jn xxi 15 foll) according to age, so that he might feed them suitably. We are also told that Moses, finding a lamb that had

CHRIST'S MIRACLES OF FEEDING

Returning to the Synoptic tradition under consideration, we see that Mark's "began to teach them many things," though cold and inadequate in itself, becomes less inadequate if regarded in the light of the Marcan context, which depicts Jesus as compassionating the multitude because they were "as sheep without a shepherd." Luke's text, which mentions "welcoming" and "healing" as well as "speaking about the kingdom of God," is more adequate than the tradition of Mark ("to teach them many things") taken by itself, but misses the thought of "compassion" and all the deep pathos implied in Hebrew traditions about the divine Shepherd to whom Israel says, "My beloved is mine and I am his[1]."

John may be said to combine the Marcan "teaching" with the Lucan "welcoming" and "healing"—only expressing the latter in a more vivid and passionate way. As to "teaching," he says—at the end of Christ's long discourse about the meaning of the Feeding of the Five Thousand—"These things said Jesus...as he *taught* in Capernaum[2]." But in the discourse itself, he declares in effect that, under this sign, the Shepherd of Israel was revealing Himself as purposing to give His own "flesh" and "blood," to be "living bread," food and life for the flock. This doctrine Jesus sets forth in such a form that Peter, despairing of finding any other shepherd like Him, exclaims, "Lord, to whom shall we go? Thou hast words of eternal life[3]." Thus John places before us two characters, briefly hinted at in Mark—the character of the Teacher and the character of the Compassionate Shepherd. The latter—which in Luke is limited to the Seeker after one lost sheep—

---

strayed away through thirst, took it on his shoulder to bring it back to the flock. Whereupon God said "Thou hast shewn compassion in leading sheep of flesh and blood. By thy life! thou shalt also shepherd my sheep, the flock of Israel."

[1] Cant. ii. 16.
[2] Jn vi 59. Διδάσκω, in Johannine narrative, occurs elsewhere only in vii. 14, 28, viii 20.
[3] Jn vi 68.

John does not intend to describe or even to mention till later on[1]. But he suggests it here, in anticipation, to the minds of those who meditated on the goodness of God towards Israel in preparing a table for them in the wilderness.

§ 16. *"When the day was now far spent," in Mark*

At this point the Four Gospels diverge[2] The difference resembles one already discussed in the narrative of Christ's first public acts of healing, where Mark says that "it had become late" and the sun "[had] set," Matthew that "it had become late," but Luke that the sun was still "setting[3]" Here Mark's expression is "an advanced hour," a comparatively rare phrase[4] Matthew uses the more ordinary Greek expression "*evening.*" This however does not seem applicable to a time before the miracle but to one after it And such an application John seems to give it when he says further on "When *evening* came his disciples went down to the sea[5]"; Mark also himself says that "when *evening* had come," the disciples were rowing "in the midst of the sea[6]."

Luke says, "*The day began to incline* (or, *decline*)," an expression that does not recur in N.T. except in his Gospel after the Resurrection, where he uses the perfect "Abide with us, for it is toward evening and *the day has now inclined*[7]."

---

[1] Lk xv 4—6, Jn x 11 foll.
[2] Mk vi 35 καὶ ἤδη ὥρας πολλῆς γενομένης (marg. γινομένης), Mt xiv. 15 ὀψίας δὲ γενομένης, Lk ix 12 ἡ δὲ ἡμέρα ἤρξατο κλίνειν
[3] *Proclamation* p 213 foll on Mk i 32, Mt. viii 16, Lk iv 40.
[4] Wetstein on Mk vi 35 quotes Dion Hal *Ant* ii 54 ἐμάχοντο καὶ διέμενον ἄχρι πολλῆς ὥρας ἀγωνιζόμενοι ἕως ἡ νὺξ ἐπιλαβοῦσα διέκρινεν αὐτούς Steph *Thes* quotes Polyb. v. 8 3, and Joseph *Ant* viii 4 3 Thucydides uses πολλή with νύξ.
[5] Jn vi 16 ὡς δὲ ὀψία ἐγένετο
[6] Mk vi 47 καὶ ὀψίας γενομένης ἦν τὸ πλοῖον ἐν μέσῳ τῆς θαλάσσης. The context implies a time subsequent to that implied by John.
[7] Lk xxiv. 29 πρὸς ἑσπέραν ἐστὶν καὶ κέκλικεν ἤδη ἡ ἡμέρα.

The "day," or the sun, is said to "incline" not only in Greek and Latin but also once in Hebrew[1], and it may "incline" toward "afternoon" as well as toward "evening." Luke, by saying *"began to incline"* here and *"has inclined"* elsewhere, seems to intend to emphasize *"began"* here, so as to mean *"incline toward afternoon."* In the story of Emmaus there are reasons for thinking that Luke is imitating the language of the LXX[2]. But there are no such reasons here. It seems probable that Luke is here using an expression, frequent in Greek and Latin, and capable of meaning with slight modifications "afternoon" or "evening," by which he corrects an error of Mark's in such a way that a Greek reader of the Gospels might say: "Mark has taken '*when the day was inclining*' for '*when the day had inclined*' and has paraphrased it in the latter sense. Luke has restored the original phrase, leaving his readers to give it its correct sense."

Some Hebrew original like "between the two evenings"— used about the sacrifice of the Paschal Lamb—might explain the Synoptic variations Such an original has already been suggested as capable of explaining the Synoptic variations in the accounts of Christ's first public healing[3] Still more appropriately would it explain them here. For in that earlier narrative there was nothing that pointed to the Passover. But there is much of that nature here. It is antecedently probable that the Galilaean Church would use expressions likening the Feeding of the Five Thousand to the Eucharist or to a prophetic sign of the Eucharist, a preliminary type of a Christian Passover.

---

[1] Judg xix. 8 (R V) "tarry ye *until the day declineth*," (A V) "they tarried *until afternoon* (marg *till the day declined*)." Κλίνει ἡμέρα (sing.) recurs only *ib* xix. 9—11 (A) and Jerem. vi. 4 Steph. *Thes* iv 1651 gives instances from Greek and Latin. The "declining" may be toward "evening" or toward "afternoon"

[2] Comp in Judg xix 7 ἐβιάσατο, and in Lk xxiv 29 παρεβιάσαντο, as well as the rare κλίνει ἡμέρα

[3] See *Proclamation* p 213 foll.

CHRIST'S MIRACLES OF FEEDING

John himself tells us that "the Passover of the Jews" was "near[1]" No doubt he means us to take this literally. But it would be characteristic of him to intend us also to take it as suggesting something more: "And another 'passover' was also 'near,' the Passover of the Christians" As the sacred Lamb of the Jewish Passover was slain for the sins of Israel "between the two evenings," so the same hour might be regarded in early Galilaean traditions as appropriate for Christ's announcement of the sign of the Eucharistic Sacrifice which He was destined to offer up as the Passover for the sins of the whole world.

§ 17. "*They continue with me now three days*," *in Mark and Matthew*[2]

The Feeding of the Four Thousand, in several of its expressions, gives to Christ's act a more personal note than is found in the Feeding of the Five Thousand[3]. It is more like Isaiah's description of the considerate Shepherd of Israel gently leading the flock[4]. Moreover Mark's preceding context

---

[1] Jn vi 4

[2] Mk viii 2, Mt xv 32 It will be convenient to discuss the Feeding of the Four Thousand here, as a parallel to the Feeding of the Five Thousand, in order to compare and contrast the two

[3] Mk viii 1—3 (R.V.)   Mt xv 32 (R.V.)

(1) In those days, when there was again a great multitude, and they had nothing to eat, he called unto him his disciples, and saith unto them,
(2) I have compassion on the multitude, because they continue with me now three days, and have nothing to eat
(3) And if I send them away fasting to their home, they will faint in the way, and some of them are come from far

And Jesus called unto him his disciples, and said, I have compassion on the multitude, because they continue with me now three days and have nothing to eat and I would not send them away fasting, lest haply they faint in the way

[4] Is xl 11 Comp Mk viii 2 foll "I have compassion" as compared with vi 34 "he had compassion." And see Mk viii 3 "If I send them away fasting...they will faint in the way; and

263 (Mark vi 29—44)

CHRIST'S MIRACLES OF FEEDING

appears to be influenced by the language of Isaiah, describing the healing and safe guidance of ransomed Israel, returning to Jerusalem across the wilderness¹ This should prepare us to find traces of prophetic and poetic influence in the narrative that follows. Accordingly we find Jesus describing the multitude as "fasting," or "hungry," and as likely to "faint in the way," very much as the Psalmist says of the redeemed of Israel, "gathered" from the four quarters of the world, "They wandered in the wilderness in a desert *way...hungry* and thirsty, *their soul fainted in them*²." "Gathering" is not so easily applicable to the Exodus from Egypt³ as it is to the gathering of the scattered captives of Israel predicted by Isaiah, or to the gathering of the spiritual Israel contemplated in early Christian traditions⁴. To the latter there would apply the words in Mark (but not in Matthew) "*and some of*

---

some of them are come from far" There is nothing like this in the earlier narrative

¹ Mk vii 37 "He maketh even the deaf (τοὺς κωφοὺς) to hear and dumb [folk] (ἀλάλους) to speak," Mt xv 31 "They saw dumb [folk] (κωφοὺς) speaking . and blind [folk] (τυφλοὺς) seeing, and they glorified the God of Israel" In Mark, the preceding context describes the healing of (Mk vii 32) κωφὸν καὶ μογιλάλον, i e "deaf and *stammering*" Μογιλάλος, "*stammering*," occurs nowhere in the Greek Bible except here and Is xxxv 6 τρανὴ δὲ ἔσται γλῶσσα μογιλάλων, Heb "and the tongue of *the dumb* shall sing" Ibn Ezra reduces this to prosaic and non-miraculous fact by calling it "a figurative expression for '*they shall find water everywhere*,'" and contrasting Lam iv 4 "the tongue of the suckling cleaveth to the roof of his mouth for thirst" But Mark apparently takes the prophecy as predicting miraculous fact about the healing of a "*stammerer*"

² Ps. cvii 2—5

³ See however *Tehill ad loc* (Wu ii 134) "The Holy One said to the Israelites, 'In Egypt ye were scattered, *and I gathered you in one little hour to Ramses*, and now also are ye scattered into all lands, and as I *gathered* you in ancient days so will I *gather* you in the future,' as it is said... (Is xi 12) 'He *shall gather* the dispersed of Judah from the four corners of the earth'"

⁴ Comp Jn xi 52 "that he might gather into one (εἰς ἕν) the scattered children of God"

CHRIST'S MIRACLES OF FEEDING

them are come from far," applicable to the old remoteness of the Gentiles, illustrated by the language of Isaiah[1].

But we must be on our guard against confining Mark to one Prophecy or one Psalm as his source. The Psalm above quoted does not mention *"three days."* But the account in Exodus on which the Psalm is based, does contain a mention of "three days" ("And they went *three days* in the wilderness and found no water") previously mentioned as the time necessary for a journey to be taken for the purpose of offering a sacrifice to Jehovah[2]. Then, further, if we examine other Hebrew texts, or Jewish traditions about *"three days,"* or *"the third day,"* beginning from the sacrifice of Isaac on Mount Moriah, we shall find that, both in the Bible and in the Midrash and in Philo, as also in the words of Jesus about Himself, a mystical meaning is attached to the phrase[3]. In Philo, the sacrifice of Isaac is connected with that perfect tribute which will be duly paid by the mind, when "perfected," to the "perfecting" God· "When therefore does it duly pay? When it arrives *on the third day* at the place whereof God spoke to it[4]." He goes on to speak of the mind at this stage as passing

---

[1] Eph ii 17 "And he came and preached peace *to you that were far off* and peace to them that were nigh," comp Is lvii 19 "Peace, peace, to *him that is far off* and to him that is near"

[2] Exod xv 22, comp *ib.* iii 18, v 3, viii 27

[3] Gen xxii 3—5 "And Abraham rose up early in the morning and saddled his ass, and took two of his young men with him and Isaac his son.... *On the third day* Abraham lifted up his eyes and saw the place afar off And Abraham said unto his young men, Abide ye here with the ass . ." The context implies, but does not mention, *"two days,"* preceding. Josephus mentions it, as follows *Ant* 1 13 2 "Now the two servants went along with him *two days*; but on *the third day*, as soon as he saw the mountain, he left those servants that were with him till then in the plain ..."

[4] Philo 1 457 (playing on τέλος and its compounds) τελειωθεὶς ὁ νοῦς ἀποδώσει τὸ τέλος τῷ τελεσφόρῳ θεῷ Πότε οὖν ἀποδίδωσιν, Ὅταν (Gen. xxii 4) ἐπὶ τὸν τόπον. τῇ ἡμέρᾳ τῇ τρίτῃ παραγένηται .

CHRIST'S MIRACLES OF FEEDING

by distinctions of time and migrating into "the timeless nature[1]"

The very great difference of Philo's language from the simple style of the Gospels must not altogether hide the underlying resemblance of thought between this and the saying of Jesus about being "*perfected on the third day*[2]." The Midrash on the story of Abraham takes as its first illustration the words of Hosea "After *two days* will he cause us to live [again]; *on the third day* he will raise us up and we shall live before him[3]." Then, after enumerating other instances of the phrase, it introduces into the story of Abraham (what Josephus perhaps also implies in his mention of "two days") a distinction between the "servants" who do not accompany Abraham "*on the third day*," and the son who does. Abraham sees the Shechinah over the mountain, and asks his son and his two servants whether they see what he sees The son says "Yes" The two servants say "No[4]," being only (so to speak) in the second-day stage. To them accordingly it is said "Abide ye here with the ass." But the son (it is implied) having entered the third-day stage, is allowed to go on and to be perfected on the Mount of Sacrifice.

The frequency with which Jesus is recorded in all the Gospels to have used the phrase "on the third day," or some similar expression, about His own resurrection, or about the restoration of the Temple, or about the approach of the Passover, makes it probable that here, in the Feeding of the Four Thousand, it is used in some allusive sense. Perhaps it

---

[1] Philo *ib.* παρελθὼν τὰς πλείους μοίρας τῶν χρονικῶν διαστημάτων καὶ ἤδη πρὸς τὴν ἄχρονον μεταβαίνων φύσιν

[2] Lk xiii 32—3 "I cast out devils and perform cures to-day and to-morrow and *on the third* [*day*] *I am* [*to be*] *perfected* (τελειοῦμαι). Howbeit I must go on my way to-day and to-morrow and *the next* [*day*], for it cannot be that a prophet perish out of Jerusalem"

[3] Hos vi 2

[4] This resembles (I think) something in Wagner's *Parsifal*.

CHRIST'S MIRACLES OF FEEDING

alludes to the precept twice enjoined on Israel at the Giving of the Law, "Be ready *against the third day*[1]" Origen speaks of the Four Thousand as being "*testified to*," in respect of their "*abiding by the Lord for three days*[2]" Clement of Alexandria, writing of Abraham's "seeing *on the third day*," says that '*the three days* are the mystery of the seal[3]." In view of the extracts given above from Scripture, Midrash, Philo, and the Gospels, it would be unwise to dismiss these Christian comments as baseless Christian allegorizing[4]. They all point back to a widespread Hebrew conception of "*the third day*," as being not only a phrase of time but also a phrase of accomplishment, what Philo calls "the timeless nature[5]."

Passing to the Fourth Evangelist we have to consider his attitude, first, toward the Mark-Matthew tradition about a supplementary miracle of Eucharistic Feeding, and secondly, toward this mystical tradition about "three days." As to the first, while nowhere denying that there were, even before the Resurrection, other similar miracles such as the Feeding of the Four Thousand, he turns our attention to something that

---

[1] Exod. xix. 11, 15.
[2] Origen *Comm Matth* xi 19 (Lomm iii 123)
[3] Clem Alex 690 Comp Clem Alex *Excerpt Theod* 988—9 where "baptism" is called ἡ σφραγίς and τὸ τῆς ἀληθείας σφράγισμα. and see Euseb iii 23 8 (quoting from Clem Alex) τὴν σφραγῖδα τοῦ κυρίου
[4] Jerome, however (on Mt xv 32), affords an instructive instance of the excesses of the Christian transmutation of Jewish tradition, "Misereretur turbae quia *in trium numero*, Patri, Filio, Spirituique Sancto credebant"
[5] See p 266, n 1 Mark (iv 28) speaks of (1) "the blade," (2) "the ear," (3) "the full corn" John (xii 24) speaks of the grain of corn (1) falling, (2) dying, (3) producing fruit Revelation (1 4) speaks of the IS and the WAS and the COMING Underlying the whole of the Fourth Gospel there seems to be the conception of (1) the Thought, (2) the uttered Thought, or Word, (3) the influencing Thought, or Spirit All these are forms of the *thought* of "the third day"

CHRIST'S MIRACLES OF FEEDING

happened after the Resurrection, supplementary, but dissimilar in important details—a quiet and homely little meal, the relation of which to the Synoptic narratives will be discussed as we proceed. As to the second point, the doctrine of "three days," John teaches that it referred to the raising up of what Jesus and the Jews called "this temple," but that it meant "the temple of his body[1]" No doubt, this included (in the Evangelist's judgment) the manifestation of Christ in the body to the disciples after death. But it certainly included also the rising up of Christ's Body in the sense of the Church, the New Temple. In that connection, we should have to use the Philonian phrase again and say that the "three days" had "a timeless nature[2]."

---

[1] Jn ii 19—21

[2] On the difficulty of making any confident assertion about the number of Christ's visits to the Temple, see *Introd* pp 90—6 John may have desired to impress on his readers, at the very outset of his Gospel, that Jesus regarded the Temple as being a Congregation of human beings, that is to say "sons of men," built up on, and into, one ideal Son of Man, who was also Son of God. As John expounds the Doctrine of Bread before its chronological place, in connection with the Feeding of the Five Thousand, so he may have briefly expressed the Doctrine of the New Temple before its chronological place, in connection with what he believed to be Christ's first public visit to the Temple

CHRIST'S MIRACLES OF FEEDING

§ 18. *"Buying" or "Whence?"*

In the texts printed below[1] the following are the most remarkable agreements and disagreements (1) The four narratives of the Five Thousand speak of *"buying,"* though in varying contexts. (2) The two narratives of the Four Thousand omit *"buying"* and ask *"whence?"* (3) John combines *"buying"* with *"whence?"* (4) Mark repeats *"buying"* twice (*"that they may buy," "are we to buy?"*). (5) Matthew has merely *"that they may buy."* (6) Luke has merely *"unless we are to buy."* (7) In the Synoptists, *"buying"* (or *"whence"*)

---

[1] Mk vi 35—7 (R V)

(35) And when the day was now far spent, his disciples came unto him, and said, The place is desert, and the day is now far spent;
(36) Send them away, that they may go (ἀπελθόντες) into the country and villages round about, and buy themselves somewhat to eat
(37) But he answered and said unto them, Give ye them to eat And they say unto him, Shall we go (ἀπελθόντες) and buy two hundred pennyworth of bread (*lit* loaves), and give them to eat?

Mt xiv 15—16 (R V)

(15) And when even was come, the disciples came to him, saying, The place is desert, and the time is already past, send the multitudes away, that they may go (ἀπελθόντες) into the villages, and buy themselves food
(16) But Jesus said unto them, They have no need to go away (ἀπελθεῖν), give ye them to eat

Lk ix 12—13 (R V)

(12) And the day began to wear away, and the twelve came, and said unto him, Send the multitude away, that they may go (πορευθέντες) into the villages and country round about, and lodge, and get (εὕρωσιν) victuals for we are here in a desert place
(13) But he said unto them, Give ye them to eat And they said, We have no more than five loaves and two fishes; except we should go (πορευθέντες) and buy food for all this people

Jn vi 5—7 (R V)

(5) Jesus therefore lifting up his eyes saith unto Philip, Whence are we to buy bread (*lit* loaves), that these may eat?
(6) Now this he said tempting (*or*, trying) him, for he himself knew what he purposed (*or*, was destined) (ἔμελλε) to do
(7) Philip answered him, Two hundred pennyworth of bread (*lit* loaves) is not sufficient for them, that each may take a little

Lk ix. 14 *a* adds here "For they were about five thousand men," which is parall. to Mk vi 44, Mt. xiv. 21.

Mk viii 4 (R V.)

And his disciples answered him, Whence shall one be able to fill these men with bread (*lit* loaves) here in a desert place?

Mt xv. 33 (R V)

And the disciples say unto him, Whence should we have so many loaves in a desert place, as to fill so great a multitude?

is uttered by the disciples; in the Fourth Gospel, "*whence*" and "*buy*" are uttered by Jesus identifying Himself with the disciples ("*whence are we to buy?*").

In these passages, "whence" means "from what possible source," with an assumption that there is no possible source. "Whence," in any sense, is rare in LXX; but in this sense it does not occur more than thrice[1]. The Pentateuch has but one instance. That occurs in a remonstrance of Moses, somewhat similar to the remonstrance of the disciples. Moses pleads that he cannot feed Israel in the wilderness. "*Whence to me flesh,*" he asks, "to give to all this people[2]?" "Whence to me flesh?" means, of course, "Whence could I *get* flesh?" But we might supply other verbs such as "*find,*" or even "*buy.*"

Moses adds "Shall flocks and herds be slain for them to *suffice* them? Or shall all the fish of the sea be gathered...to *suffice* them[3]?" "*Suffice*"—a rare word both in LXX and in Gospels—occurs in the Johannine answer to the question "*Whence?*" asked by Jesus. "Two hundred pennyworth of loaves does not *suffice* for them," says Philip, "that each may take a little[4]." This combination of the rare words '*whence*" and "*suffice,*" together with the similarity of circumstances, leads to the conclusion that John has in view, not only the Gospel traditions about the Feeding, but also the remonstrance of Moses. There is also a fair, though slighter, probability that the same remonstrance underlies the Mark-Matthew tradition.

---

[1] "Whence?" in "Whence ($\pi \acute{o} \theta \epsilon \nu$) comest thou?" etc. occurs in Gen xvi 8, xxix. 4, etc But, in the sense "from what possible source?" (implying "there is no possible source") it occurs (in A.V.) only in Numb xi 13, 2 K vi. 27, Nahum iii. 7.

[2] Numb xi. 13

[3] Numb xi 22, see below, p. 271, n. 3.

[4] Jn vi 7 '$A \rho \kappa \acute{\epsilon} \omega$ occurs only eight or nine times in canon. LXX and four times in the Gospels.

CHRIST'S MIRACLES OF FEEDING

This hypothesis—of a brief original like that in Numbers "*Whence [should there accrue]* to me flesh?" or, still better, one in which "to me" was omitted—might explain the extraordinary Gospel variations as to "*buying*" No verb being in the original, evangelists would have to supply one—such as "*get*," "*find*," or "*buy*" Compare the Mark-Matthew "that they may *buy* food," parallel to the Lucan "that they may *find* provision (R.V. get victuals)" This may be illustrated from Proverbs "A scorner seeketh wisdom and [*doth*] *not* [*find it*]," where "*find*" is supplied by the LXX and English Versions[1].

In the Feeding of the Four Thousand, Mark's parallel to Matthew's (lit.) "*Whence to us so many loaves as to fill* so great a multitude?" is "*Whence shall one be* (SS *art thou*) *able to fill with loaves* these men[2]?" This indicates that the original had no definite personal pronoun. Also the Syro-Sinaitic of Mark has "*find*" for "be able" These small links of verbal evidence connect the Gospel narratives both with one another and with that in Numbers which represents Moses as twice asking, in the Hebrew text, "shall it be *found* for them[3]?"

From "finding" to "buying" is a transition of thought that may be illustrated from Job and Isaiah Job asks "Where shall wisdom *be found?*" and proceeds to speak of "*the price*"

---

[1] Prov xiv 6 Comp 1 S. xxvi 18 (A V) "What evil [*is*] in my hand?" LXX εὑρέθη ἐν ἐμοί, Job xii 12 (A V) "With the ancient [*is*] wisdom," (A) εὑρίσκεται, Prov v. 4 (Heb.) "Her end [*is*] bitter," LXX εὑρήσεις, 1 e. "*thou wilt find* it bitter"

[2] In Mk viii. 4 πόθεν δυνήσεταί τις, SS has literally "*Whence dost thou find* [power]?" Thes Syr. 4147—8 shews that the radical meaning of the word is "find," and it is easy to see that "*I find* [*how*] to do" may mean "*I am able* to do"

[3] Numb xi 22 (Heb.) "Shall flocks and herds be slain...and *shall it be found* (LXX ἀρκέσει) for them... (rep) and *shall it be found* (LXX ἀρκέσει) for them?" i e "shall sufficient food be found for them?" No persons are indicated as the finders See Gesen 593 *b* and 594 *a* indicating that the literal translation is "and so *one find* [enough] for them," i e shall it be found

CHRIST'S MIRACLES OF FEEDING

as being beyond all silver, gold, and jewels[1]. Isaiah says "Ho, every one that thirsteth, come ye to the waters; and he that hath no money, come ye, *buy* (*shâbar*) and eat; yea, come, *buy* (*shâbar*), without money and without price, wine and milk[2]" The word *shâbar* is not often used for "*buy*" It means "*buy-corn*" Rashi, on Isaiah, says that it is used here as in the words "*to buy corn*"—alluding to the first Biblical use of the word in the description of "all countries" coming "into Egypt to Joseph *to buy-corn*[3]."

This allusion brings out the prophet's meaning· "Egypt sells its corn for a price. But God sells you His corn, the corn of heaven, the Law of Righteousness, without money and without price[4]." The Greek word used in the Gospels for "buying" is used by the LXX about the buying of corn in Genesis and about the buying of wine and milk in Isaiah. Consequently, in any Christian narrative that described the feeding of the multitudes by Christ in a form intended to symbolize the spiritual food of the Eucharist, it would be appropriate to use the word "*buy*" by way of contrast, in such a way as to make it clear that Christ's bread could *not* be "bought"—or, at all events, not bought in the ordinary sense of the word.

But the Synoptic Tradition does not make this clear. It speaks about the Five Thousand as (possibly) (Mark-Matthew)

---

[1] Job xxviii 12—19
[2] Is lv 1, Targ "Come, hearken and learn, without price and without money, doctrine that is better than wine and milk"
[3] Gen xli. 56—7 contains the first Biblical instances of *shâbar* The causative means "*sell [corn]*" and the active "*buy [corn]*" A V "*sold* unto the Egyptians...all countries came. .to *buy [corn]*" LXX ἐπώλει... ἀγοράζειν.
[4] Ibn Ezra, on Is. lv. 1, says that wine and milk "serve both for food and drink" He seems to anticipate the objection that *shâbar* ought not to be applied except to that which is eaten Rashi, on Genesis, says (if the text is genuine) "You must not say that *shâbar* is used only of corn, for it is used also of *wine* and *milk* (Is lv. 1)."

272 (Mark vi 29—44)

CHRIST'S MIRACLES OF FEEDING

"going away and buying" or (Luke) "going and finding," and also about the impossibility that the disciples should (Mark) "go away and buy" or (Luke) "go and buy[1]"; but it so distracts us with verbal variations that we are in danger of learning nothing from the words[2]. "They were uttered by the disciples," we may say, "not by Jesus, and the disciples were in the dark, and did not know what they were speaking about"

John, without denying that the disciples used these expressions about "*buying*," and also about the impossibility of finding "*whence*" they might procure food in any way, declares that Jesus Himself used expressions of this nature, and that He did it in a kindly and gentle (we may almost say playful) spirit, "tempting (*or*, trying)" Philip. The Evangelist's view is that Jesus had reasons for choosing this particular disciple—a little slow perhaps, but sure and straightforward—in order to lead him, and through him the rest of the Apostles, towards a higher stage of revelation. It was not the highest but only a higher. "He himself"—John says, in a kind of aside—"knew what he would do," but He did not at present say "what he would do." He merely prepared Philip for expecting at once, and for receiving later on, some mystical

---

[1] "Going away" = ἀπελθόντες "Going" = πορευθέντες RV makes no distinction here, though rendering the infin ἀπελθεῖν "go away" in Mt xiv. 16

[2] The key to the original is perhaps to be found in the deliberative subjunctive ἀγοράσωμεν, found in Mk, Lk, and Jn, and meaning "*ought we*, or, *are we*, or, *we are*, to buy" "Ought" is expressed in Heb by (1) the future ("Thou *shalt*, i e *oughtest to*, do"), (2) the infin after "it is" ("*It is* [*fit*] to do," "*it is* [*fit*] for thee to do") Confusion might arise between "*Is it* [*fit*] to go away and buy?" and "*It is* [*fit*] to go away and buy" The former would be taken as "*Is it* [*fit*] *for us* [i e the disciples]?" the latter, as "*It is* [*fit*] *for them* [i e. the five thousand]" See *Oxf Conc* LXX δεῖν, and e g. Ezek xxxiv. 2 Heb "Shall [*i e* should] they not feed?" LXX οὐ βόσκουσιν (interrogative) The ambiguity might be increased by two datives "[fit] *for us* to buy *for them*"

CHRIST'S MIRACLES OF FEEDING

doctrine about the spiritual Bread. "He himself knew what he would do" means "He knew what He was destined to do on the Cross, buying the Bread of Life for the world at the cost of His blood[1]."

§ 19. *"Two hundred pennyworth," in Mark and John*[2]

Why was this precise sum mentioned by the disciples, or recorded by Mark to have been mentioned by them? Why did Matthew and Luke omit Mark's tradition? Why did John insert it? The question here is, not *whether* John intervenes for Mark, but *why* he intervenes.

"Two hundred pence (*or*, denars)" is a sum frequently specified in Talmudic enactments about fines, damages, marriage portions, etc.[3] Also, if a man had an income of less than two hundred denars, he could claim certain exemptions and allowances. It was legally recognised as being, so to speak,

---

[1] For this mystical meaning of the word "buy," ἀγοράζω, John has previously prepared the way by representing the disciples (Jn iv 8, 32) as leaving their Master alone and going *"to buy"* food in Sychar (which He rejects, telling them that He has food to eat that they know not of) The third and last instance of ἀγοράζω is where Judas Iscariot, going forth to betray the Master whom he has sold, is regarded by some of the disciples (Jn xiii 29) as being instructed by Jesus to *"buy"* something needed for "the feast [of the Passover]" For Jn vi 6 "destined (ἔμελλε) to do," see *Son* **3402**a

But what are we to say as to the plural *"loaves"* ("whence are we to buy *loaves*?") assigned by John to Jesus here and nowhere else except in the reproach (Jn vi 26) "ye ate of *the loaves*"? Does the Evangelist represent Jesus as speaking, as it were, down to the level of Philip, about the rudimentary food to be provided on this occasion? If so, we may illustrate from the plural (Jn iv 8) "buy *food(s)* (τροφάς)," unique in N T , where the "foods" are called by Origen *ad loc* "suitable foods (τροφὰς) *with the heterodox* (παρὰ τοῖς ἑτεροδόξοις)," and Ammonius (*ad loc* Cramer p 216) sees a warning against "various *foods of luxury* (ἐδεσμάτων)" Τροφαί is used of "forbidden foods" in 4 Macc 1 33, iv 26 (comp 3 Macc. iii 7)

[2] Mk vi 37, Jn vi 7

[3] See *Hor Heb* on Mk vi 37 Wetstein is silent

"a poor man's income[1]." Christ's disciples were poor men. Hence, when exhorted by Jesus to give bread to the multitude, one of them might be supposed to reply "Even if we had the whole of our year's income in our hands, should we go away and spend it all in a single meal—and that, too, insufficient—for this multitude?"

Thus explained, the Marcan tradition becomes intelligible. But, outside Palestine, who would know the explanation? Moreover, even with this explanation, it is not clear, because Mark at this stage has not yet told us the number of the multitude, and does not mention it till the very end of the narrative[2] This omission may be contrasted with the orderly insertion in the O T narrative of the meal given by Elisha to the sons of the prophets Elisha's servant, receiving "*twenty loaves* of barley," says at once, "What! Shall I set this before *an hundred* men[3]?" Similarly Luke, in his parallel to Mark, lets us know at once the number of the multitude thus "Unless we are to go and buy food for all this people—*for they were about five thousand* men[4]." Without this knowledge, the inadequacy of two hundred denarii is by no means obvious. For a denarius was a labourer's daily wage[5] and could presumably suffice for one simple meal for several labourers. Two hundred denarii might therefore well provide for a single meal for a considerable number, quite large enough to be called a "multitude."

Again, "two hundred denarii" might possibly imply *gold*

---

[1] *J Pea* viii 8 (Mishna) and *Sota* 21 b. *Hor. Heb.* omits this. So also does Schlatter on Jn vi 7.

[2] Mk vi 44

[3] *Hor Heb.* on Jn vi 9 refers to 2 K. iv 42 and *Chetub.* 105. 2, 106 9, where "the masters enhance the number of men fed by Elisha to two thousand two hundred" from the Scriptural "one hundred"

[4] Comp Numb xi 13 "Whence should I have flesh to give to *all this people*?" ib 21—2 "The people. .are *six hundred thousand* ...shall flocks and herds be slain for them to suffice them...?"

[5] Mt xx. 2—13

CHRIST'S MIRACLES OF FEEDING

denarii In that case—since a gold denarius was worth twenty-five silver denarii—the sum would amount to five thousand silver denarii, that is to say, the daily wage for five thousand men[1]. Then the meaning of the expostulating disciples would be "Are we [so rich that we are] to go and buy bread for two hundred [gold] denarii and to give them to eat [a meal worth a day's wage for each man]?"

This is an improbable supposition. For "denarii," without the epithet "gold," would be taken by all to mean "silver denarii." But difficulties like these may explain, not only why Matthew and Luke omitted Mark's tradition about the denarii, but also why Matthew modified the context by transferring "go away" from the disciples to the multitude ("they have no need to go away"), as indicated above[2], and why Luke inserted at this stage the number of the multitude[3].

John retains Mark's "two hundred pence," but assigns the expression to Philip instead of to the disciples collectively. He does not follow Luke in inserting the number of the multitude

---

[1] See *Son* 3420 g referring to Levy 1 399 b Wagenseil's *Sota* p 552 has an obscure remark about a dower of 200 denarii "ut ita ducenti isti denarii efficiant omnino (?) xxv denarios argenteos, quorum cujusque pondus xxvi grana hordacea." If "each" were written for "altogether (omnino)," this would seem to be a confused statement about denarii of gold, as being each worth twenty-five denarii of silver The mention of a grain of barley as a standard of weight for denarii is perhaps worth noting, in view of the Johannine mention of denarii and barley loaves in the same context

[2] See p. 269, comp. p. 273, n 2

[3] Another possible cause of corruption can be but briefly indicated In Greek, the sign of "5000" is ͵Ε and the sign of "200" is C′, and Ε and C are frequently confused Schlatter (on Jn vi 7) quotes *Siphr* Deut. 355 "Oil *for* (ב) *a hundred myriads* do I need"—where ב seems to mean "*for the sake of*," somewhat like Gen xviii. 28 (Gesen 90 b) "on account of five," but it usually means "*at the price of*" Perhaps "for 200 denarii," in Greek, when "denarii" was denoted by a sign, might be confused with "for five thousand [men]" Or ἀγοράσωμεν δηναρίων with C′ might be corrupted into ἀγοράσωμεν δὴ ἀνδρῶν with ͵Ε

276 (Mark vi 29—44)

CHRIST'S MIRACLES OF FEEDING

here to shew the inadequacy of the sum. But he represents Philip as saying that it would be quite inadequate As to the "pence," he makes no effort to shew what may have been in Philip's mind, but he seems to suggest, as being in Christ's mind, a very different kind of "buying"—namely, what might be called a "ransoming" of the souls of men at a price above visible "denarii"

The first Biblical mention of "ransoming" the "soul" occurs in connection with the numbering of the Israelites. They are to give "every man a ransom for his soul[1]" The Law proceeds "*This* shall they give...half a shekel." The Jerusalem Targum explains "*this*" by adding "This valuation was shewn to Moses in the mountain as with a *denarius* of fire[2]." In one of the many forms in which this tradition is repeated, it is said that God's words so terrified Moses that he replied "Who can give a ransom for his soul?" It was then (said R. Meir) that God shewed Moses a coin of fire and said "*This* shalt thou give[3]."

The three Synoptists agree that on one memorable occasion Jesus called for a denarius and said to the Pharisees "Whose is this image and inscription[4]?" To this they replied "Caesar's." He then bade them give "to Caesar that which is Caesar's." Presumably that which was "*Caesar's*" meant the denarius. And it was "*Caesar's*" because it was stamped

---

[1] Exod xxx. 12 In Exod xxi 30 (A V) "*ransom of his life* (*lit* soul)," R V. has "*redemption*" (see context)

[2] Similarly Rashi says "God shewed Moses a coin of fire of which the weight was half a shekel, and said, *This* (istiusmodi) shall the Israelites give"

[3] See *Numb r* Wu pp 275—6, also *Pesikt* (Piska II) Wu pp 10—21, and *ib* Wu. p. 76. In some forms of the tradition, it is explained that "this" means "Not what thou didst suppose but what I shew thee," or that the coin was under the throne of God. In *Pesikt* p. 76, one tradition says that the coin is the sacrificial lamb of Numb xxviii 3.

[4] Mk xii 16 foll, Mt xxii 18 foll., Lk xx. 24.

with Caesar's image and name. But, if so, what is the meaning of "*God's*" in the following words, "And to God that which is "*God's*"? Does it imply merely this, "If you give the Roman denarius to pay tribute to Caesar, you are equally bound to give the Jewish shekel—that is, the temple shekel, the shekel with its sacred symbols stamped upon it—to God"?

That is, at first sight, an attractive explanation because it is so simple, and lays down so definite a rule. But, on second thoughts, does it seem like Jesus to lay down definite rules (except in hyperbole such as "turning the cheek" and "walking two miles") without regard to motive? Does not Christ's phrase, "that which is God's," imply a heavenly denarius, so to speak, stamped with God's image and name? And what is this stamp but the impress of the Spirit of the divine Love? This love best represents the divine nature in its relation to men. This love God gives to men that they may pay it back to Him, thereby ransoming themselves from selfishness and sin, and making themselves free for a life of sonship toward the Father in heaven and of brotherhood toward His children on earth.

The Jews, in many of their comments on the "ransom of a man's soul," or on other texts that speak of the soul's "ransom," say, or imply, that the ransom is "almsgiving," which they call technically "righteousness[1]." Sometimes they are careful to add that such almsgiving must be disinterested, or at all events not ostentatious; but frequently they use unguarded hyperbole, such as that "*a farthing given to a poor man* bestows on the giver a vision of the Shechinah," and that "I shall behold thy face in righteousness," in the Psalms, means "I shall behold thy face" after the Resurrection "*because*

---

[1] Prov. xiii 8 "The ransom of a man's soul is his riches" is often associated with Exod. xxx 12—13, and is explained by Rashi as being true "because he *distributes alms*" from his riches.

(Mark vi 29—44)

of alms[1]" Against the identification of "righteousness" with "alms"—which resembles the occasional identification of "charity" with "alms" in modern English—Jesus vehemently protested But He did not deny, and indeed He emphasized, the helpful and purifying influence of singlehearted almsgiving. Alms rightly given on earth (He taught) reproduced themselves in heaven, so that the perishable coin from "the treasure on earth" procured for the giver an eternal "treasure in heaven[2]."

It is only the Double Tradition of Matthew and Luke that speaks thus of this "treasure in heaven." And there the context contains no mention or implication of the negative aspect, "ransoming," but only of the positive aspect, reward. But both aspects are hinted at in the Threefold Tradition about the rich young ruler to whom Jesus says "Sell whatsoever thou hast, and give to the poor, and thou shalt have *treasure in heaven*[3]." According to Matthew, the man needed to be ransomed from himself He was so fettered in self-satisfaction that he believed he had fulfilled not only the commands of the Decalogue but also the precept "Thou shalt love thy neighbour as thyself[4]." He seems to have been what the Pastoral

---

[1] See *Bab Bathr* 10 a, and *Tehill* on Ps xvii 15, where Rashi, however, does not thus limit righteousness. Comp *Hor Heb* (on Mt vi. 1) "They called alms by the name of righteousness," and the passages there alleged to prove this See also the Heb of Sir iii 30, and xl. 24 In the latter, the editors give an alternative, "*righteousness* (or, *almsgiving*) delivereth above them both"

[2] Comp Mt vi 20 "treasure up treasures...," parall. to Lk xii. 33 "Make to yourselves purses that wax not old, a treasure in the heavens that faileth not" To this Luke (but not Matthew) prefixes "Sell your goods and give alms"

[3] Mk x 21 on which see *Beginning* p 263 There it is pointed out that Mark may have confused "*deceived himself,*" ΗΠΑΤΗCΕΝ ΑΥΤΟΝ, with "*loved him,*" ΗΓΑΠΗCΕΝΑΥΤΟΝ, or that Hebrew confusion may have produced the false impression that Jesus "loved him"

[4] Mt xix. 19

Epistles call "a lover of self" as well as "a lover of money[1]." If Jesus perceived that he was "in love with himself[2]," we can understand why He imposed on him a condition that He knew the man would fail to fulfil. Through the failure the man would be at least benefited at once to the extent of having his self-love disturbed. Hereafter, he might attain to the vision of the true love, the denarius of fire, the ransom of the soul.

The "denarius" will come before us again when we discuss the Anointing at Bethany, where Mark—again followed by John, but not by Matthew—mentions "three hundred denarii" as the price of the ointment[3]. The above-mentioned "denar" of the Jerusalem Targum is also latent in Matthew's description of the *stater*, i.e "*shekel*," taken by Peter from a fish's mouth in order to satisfy the claims of the collectors of the *didrachm*, i.e "half-shekel[4]." That narrative, whatever may be the full explanation of its details, adds to the cumulative evidence that metaphors or allegories based upon the payment of coin as a "ransom for the soul" would be prominent in the doctrine of early Evangelists, and that literal statements made about denarii in Mark would be allegorized by John. Such allegorizing is comparatively rare in the Talmud, but frequent in the Midrash and poetic Targums, which may often throw light on the imagery underlying Christ's doctrine. In the present instance, quite apart from its value as an exemplification of Johannine Intervention, John's retention of the Marcan "denarii"—taken with the new Johannine context, which

---

[1] 2 Tim iii. 2 φίλαυτοι, φιλάργυροι.

[2] I have not found an instance of ἀγαπᾶν ἑαυτόν though φιλεῖν ἑαυτόν is very common. But Mark might use ἠγάπησεν αὐτόν, "he was in love with himself," to denote an excess of the habit expressed by φιλεῖν

[3] Mk xiv 5.

[4] Mt xvii 24—27 A V. "*tribute* [*money*]...*a piece of money*," R V "*the half-shekel...a shekel*," W H τὰ δίδραχμα...στατῆρα. On this, and on Philo's allegorizing of "the half of the shekel," which LXX calls "the half of the didrachm," see *Notes* **2999** (x)

CHRIST'S MIRACLES OF FEEDING

allows us to regard it as part of a reply to a mystical utterance of Christ about "buying"—appears to accord with the Johannine doctrine that God is Love. Man, God's coin, restamped by the redeeming Son of Man with the divine image that has been wellnigh obliterated by sin, is to present himself wholly, in the Spirit of Sonship, to the Father. This sacrifice, and not the partial and formal sacrifice of almsgiving, constitutes the real and spiritual ransom by which the sinner is redeemed from his lower self[1]

If we reject the view that John gave a mystical application to the Marcan "two hundred denarii," what other view are we prepared to take of his retention of it? Are we to say that he retained it simply because it was in Mark, and because he saw no reason why Matthew and Luke should reject it? In that case, we must suppose him to have argued to this effect: "It is desirable to retain as much of Mark's detail as possible. I do not explain what was Mark's reason for mentioning this precise sum, but I am able to add that it was *not* (as Mark supposes) 'the disciples' that mentioned it. It was only Philip."

This would suggest that Philip's utterances were not held in much account by the Evangelist. But is that so? Philip loves the concrete and substantial, perhaps. When Nathanael argues, in the abstract, that no one can be the Messiah if he is from Nazareth, Philip appeals to the concrete and substantial: "Come"—that is, "come to Jesus"—and "see[2]." When Jesus speaks spiritually about "seeing" the Father, Philip

---

[1] At the same time the Fourth Gospel contains evidence shewing that its author felt the metaphors of "ransoming" and "buying" to be inadequate, and desired to supplement them by another metaphor or (x 6) "proverb," in which the Good Shepherd is described as rescuing His sheep from the Wolf at the cost of His life—yet not by ransoming, but by conquering See *Son*, Index "Ransom"

[2] Jn 1. 46.

CHRIST'S MIRACLES OF FEEDING

asks for a substantial object of vision, "Shew us the Father[1]" Nevertheless it is to Philip that Providence directs the Greeks to come, saying "We would see Jesus[2]." And it is Philip's materialistic utterance, "Shew us the Father," that draws forth from Jesus the words "He that hath seen me hath seen the Father." The Evangelist seems to suggest that this particular Apostle, even though he did not "see" things like a Rabbi or a Philosopher, was more than once made the instrument of Providence for helping others to "see" things as they are. For that reason (it would seem) Jesus "tempts" him—not for Philip's harm but for the world's good. He was worth "tempting." It was destined that through Philip's reply to Christ's question "*Whence are we to buy?*" the world should be led to reflect on the paradoxical nature of that purchase-money with which the Son of God was to buy for them the unpurchasable Bread[3].

---

[1] Jn xiv. 8. Comp. Exod. xxiv. 10 "and they saw the God of Israel."

[2] Jn xii. 21.

[3] Some may reply "Philip and Andrew are mere *dramatis personae* introduced by the Fourth Evangelist, here as elsewhere, in order to present his own thoughts about Jesus in a dramatic setting." But note what Papias says about the pains that he took to inquire not so much about books as about sayings, and in particular (Euseb. iii. 39. 4) "what had been said by *Andrew* or what by *Peter*, or what by *Philip*, or what by *Thomas*...." Is it not very rash to deny that in the Evangelist's days there were current many things alleged to have been "said by *Andrew*, *Philip*, and *Thomas*," not contained in the Synoptic Gospels, and that he made it part of his business to find a place for them in his Gospel wherever they illustrated the Teaching of Christ? No one disputes that Papias did this. Why should we deny the possibility that the Fourth Evangelist did the same thing?

CHRIST'S MIRACLES OF FEEDING

§ 20. *"How many loaves have ye? Go [and] see," in Mark*[1]

These words are in Mark alone. Their omission by Matthew and Luke may be explained by the difficulty of giving them

[1] Mk vi 37—38 (R V)

(37) But he answered and said unto them, Give ye them to eat And they say unto him, Shall we go and buy two hundred pennyworth of bread (*lit* loaves), and give them to eat?
(38) And he saith unto them, How many loaves have ye? Go [and] see And when they knew (γνόντες), they say, Five, and two fishes

Mt xiv 16—18 (R V)

(16) But Jesus said unto them, They have no need to go away, give ye them to eat
(17) And they say unto him, We have here but five loaves, and two fishes
(18) And he said, Bring them hither to me.

Lk ix 13—14 a (R V)

(13) But he said unto them, Give ye them to eat And they said, We have no more than five loaves and two fishes, except we should go and buy food for all this people
(14a) For they were about five thousand men

Jn vi 5—9 (R V)

(5) Jesus therefore . saith unto Philip, Whence are we to buy bread (*lit* loaves), that these may eat?
(6) And this he said to(?) prove him, for he himself knew what he would do.
(7) Philip answered him, Two hundred pennyworth of bread (*lit* loaves) is not sufficient for them, that every one may take a little
(8) One of his disciples, Andrew, Simon Peter's brother, saith unto him,
(9) There is a lad here, which hath five barley loaves, and two fishes but what are these among so many?

Mk viii 2 b—5 (R.V.)

they.. have nothing to eat
(3) And if I send them away fasting to their home, they will faint in the way, and some of them are come from far
(4) And his disciples answered him, Whence shall one be able to fill these men with bread (*lit* loaves) here in a desert place?
(5) And he asked them, How many loaves have ye? And they said, Seven.

Mt xv. 32 b—34 (R.V.)

they.. have nothing to eat: and I would not send them away fasting, lest haply they faint in the way
(33) And the disciples say unto him, Whence should we have so many loaves in a desert place, as to fill so great a multitude?
(34) And Jesus saith unto them, How many loaves have ye? And they said, Seven, and a few small fishes

For the purpose of clearness, texts partially given above are repeated here It will be noted that the six accounts all begin with some words of Jesus about the giving of food, or the need of food,

(Mark vi 29—44)

any sense that seems in harmony with the narrative of a stupendous miracle. They seem to imply that Jesus was at some distance from the little store of food carried by the disciples. Finding them ignorant of its amount He sends them away to ascertain it. "Having ascertained it[1]"—for that is what the Greek means—they report "five, and two fishes." All this is very simple. But is it not too simple? Why record it? Matthew and Luke—possibly because it is too simple—do not record it. They represent the disciples as replying at once to Christ's "Give ye them to eat"—without any mention or indication of an interval—that they have only "five loaves and two fishes." In the miracle of the Four Thousand, there is the same absence of interval—"How many loaves have ye? And they said, Seven...."

John differs from all the Synoptists in that he does not represent Jesus as saying to the disciples "Give ye them to eat." On the contrary, Jesus says to Philip "Whence are we to buy loaves that these may eat?" It is added "This he said tempting (*or*, trying) him, for he himself knew what he would do." This seems to imply "He knew that, in truth, He did not purpose to buy loaves; He intended to prepare Philip to learn a lesson about *bread that could not be bought*." But on the other hand it might imply "He knew what Philip would say about denarii, and He purposed to teach Philip a lesson about *bread that could indeed be bought*—only for a very different price, the invisible 'denarius' of Redemption." In either case we are made to feel that we must look below the surface for some allusive meaning, indicating the doctrine of sacrifice, that is, of "buying," or "redeeming." Philip is to be taught this by being *"tried"* or *"tempted."* The Evangelist has probably some latent meaning in this mention of "tempting."

---

for the multitude to *"eat"*. But John connects his mention of "loaves that these may eat" with "buying"—as a prospective act for Jesus and the disciples ("are we to buy?")

[1] Mk vi 38 γνόντες, on which see *Proclam* p. 268 n

CHRIST'S MIRACLES OF FEEDING

He never uses the word again. In NT it mostly implies the malignity of an adversary—and especially the Adversary called Satan—who tries us that we may fall And though the Synoptists use it abundantly, and often of Jesus being tempted, they never describe Jesus as tempting others

These considerations lead us to the story of God's "tempting" Abraham before the sacrifice of Isaac on Mount Moriah—the first Biblical instance of the word "tempt," and the only one in the whole of Genesis[1]. We have seen above, in the Johannine description of Jesus as "lifting up his eyes and beholding a great multitude coming to him," an allusion to Abraham seeing the vision of the Seed of the Promise Here it should be added that "lift up the eyes" is applied to the Patriarch when he hospitably entertains the Three, who come to make the Promise[2]. In the Dialogue that follows the Feeding of the Five Thousand in the Fourth Gospel, Jews speak of the Giving of the Manna[3]; and Jewish Christians in the first century could not but connect the Manna with the Loaves and Fishes, both in comparison and in contrast. Now it was a

---

[1] Gen xxii 1 ἐπείραζεν. The Heb is נסה, which also occurs in Syr and Palest of Jn vi 6, and in Delitzsch's Hebrew This must be distinguished from δοκιμάζω, "test," "prove," which mostly = בחן in LXX, but never נסה. There is perhaps a touch of irony when Paul tells the Corinthians—who "seek a *proof* (δοκιμὴν)" of the Christ that "speaks in" him—that they had better "*tempt*, or *make trial of*" themselves (2 Cor xiii 5) "*Make-trial-of* (πειράζετε) yourselves whether ye are in the faith, *prove* (δοκιμάζετε) yourselves" Πειράζω, applied to persons in NT, almost always means trial proceeding from adversaries, and Rev ii 2 ἐπείρασας τοὺς λέγοντας ἑαυτοὺς ἀποστόλους is hardly an exception But John perhaps felt that, if he had used δοκιμάζω, as in 1 Jn iv 1 "*prove* (δοκιμάζετε) the spirits whether they be of God," he would have misled his readers Jesus did not wish to "*prove*" Philip to see "whether" he would answer this or that, He wished to "tempt" him, as God "tempted" Abraham, as a preparation for a blessing that was to follow

[2] Gen xviii 2 "He lifted up his eyes, and looked, and lo ."
[3] Jn vi 31 foll

CHRIST'S MIRACLES OF FEEDING

recognised tradition among the Jews that whatever hospitality Abraham gave to the Three, God gave to the Israelites in the wilderness: "R Jehudah said in the name of Rab: All that Abraham did for the angels by himself, the Holy One, blessed be He, did for his children by Himself; and what Abraham did for them through a messenger, the Holy One did the same for his children through a messenger[1]." What "messenger" is here meant? And is there anything in any of the Gospel narratives of Christ's miracles of feeding that includes something corresponding to Abraham's "messenger"? This will be considered in the next section, in the hope that it may throw some light on the Marcan tradition, at present unexplained, "*Go [and] see.*"

§ 21. "*There is a lad here,*" *in John*[2]

In the five Synoptic accounts of feeding it is stated by the disciples, or assumed by Jesus, that the loaves belong to the disciples ("we have no more than," "how many have ye?"). The Fourth Gospel alone, after Christ's question "How shall we buy bread?" and after Philip's reply about the insufficiency of two hundred pennyworth, represents Andrew as saying "There is a *lad* (*paidarion*) here that has five barley loaves and two fishes." About this Chrysostom says, "I think that he [*i.e.* Andrew] did not say this in simple ignorance, but because he had heard the wonders of the prophets and how Elisha worked the sign over the loaves[3]." The loaves brought to Elisha were an offering from a stranger; and Chrysostom seems

---

[1] *B Metzia* 86 *b* The context enters into detail, *e g.* "Abraham's "butter" and "milk" are rewarded with "manna" Comp *Numb r.* on Numb vii 48 (Wu p 348) sect 14, repeating the same doctrine of the reward of Abraham's hospitality

[2] Jn vi. 9.

[3] Chrys on Jn vi 9, referring to 2 K iv. 42 "And there came a man ..and brought the man of God bread of the firstfruits, twenty loaves of barley...."

to assume that the loaves of the "lad" came also from some stranger, that is to say, they did not belong to the disciples or to any "lad" in their service. And this is the natural interpretation of the words in John.

It is not unlikely that John was influenced by the miracle of Elisha and the barley loaves, in conjunction with other causes. But the first cause might be Hebrew corruption. The first Biblical mention of "barley" in LXX arises from a misreading of a word meaning "measure" or "estimation[1]." "*Loaves estimated* at two hundred denarii" might be confused with "*loaves of barley* for two hundred denarii." Thus a tradition might arise about the loaves that they were "loaves of *barley*." This might naturally be added to the story, partly in view of Elisha's miraculous multiplication of barley loaves, and partly because "barley loaves" might seem to accord with the time of the year[2], and also with a symbolic application of Christ's act. But this hypothesis does not explain John's introduction of the word "*lad*," *paidarion*. For that is not used in the story of Elisha[3] Moreover *paidarion* occurs nowhere else in N.T. and (with one exception) nowhere in Christian writers of the first century and a half[4]. We are therefore led to ask, outside Greek writings, for something corresponding to the Johannine *paidarion* in Hebrew Scripture, or in Jewish traditions about Scripture.

Now, *paidarion* in LXX regularly corresponds to a Hebrew word frequently rendered in Genesis "lad[5]." And the first Biblical mention of the Hebrew word corresponding to "*lad*"

---

[1] See *Son* **3420** *f—g*, quoting Gen xxvi 12.
[2] Jn vi 4 "the passover was nigh" (see above, p. 246).
[3] 2 K iv. 43 (A V) "his servitor" is explained (Gesen. 1058 *a*) as Elisha's "chief servant," LXX λειτουργός, superior to παιδάριον.
[4] Goodspeed gives it as occurring only in *Polyc. Mart.* §§ 6—7, where it refers to two servants of Polycarp, one of whom, under torture, betrays his master's hiding place
[5] In A V, "lad" sing. = נַעַר, *naar*, 17 times in Genesis (but not again till Judg xvi 26) and 12 times in 1 Samuel.

is in the story of Abraham's hospitality to the Three Persons: "And Abraham ran unto the herd and fetched a calf...and gave it unto *the lad*, and he hasted to dress it[1]." Here A V. has "*a young man*," and R.V. "*the servant.*" But the exact rendering is "*the lad [in attendance]*," "*the young [servant].*" It might be applied to "the youthful [son of the house]" if the context suited such an application, and accordingly some Jewish authorities interpret it here as Ishmael[2]. The LXX does not here render the word by *paidarion*, but that is its regular rendering of the word[3]. The "lad" mentioned in the story about Abraham's hospitality appears to be the person contemplated by R. Jehudah in the words above quoted "What Abraham did [for the Three] through a *messenger*, the Holy One did the same for his children through a *messenger*[4]"

The title of "messenger" or "apostle" would seem here to apply to Moses. Through him God gave the manna to Israel; and it has been shewn that Moses and Aaron are called God's "*apostles*" or "*messengers*[5]." It is said about Moses in the cradle, according to our English versions, that the daughter of Pharaoh "saw *the child* and behold *the babe* wept[6]." But the Hebrew text has, for "*babe*," the word regularly corresponding to *paidarion*; and Rashi seems to render it by "*lad*," expressly saying "His voice was deep (gravis) like that of a *lad* (pueri), not like that of a very little infant (parvuli infantis)"— apparently attaching a mystical or prophetic significance to

---

[1] Gen xviii 7 LXX τῷ παιδί
[2] So *Gen r* and Rashi (on Gen. xviii 7), and *Aboth R Nathan* (on *Aboth* 1 16)
[3] Heb נער =(Tromm) παιδάριον about 140 times, παιδίον (23), παῖς (14), νεανίσκος (21), νεώτερος (10), νέος (7) etc
[4] See p 286
[5] See *Proclam* p. 392, quoting Jerem 11 2 (Targ) "my two apostles Moses and Aaron in the wilderness"
[6] Exod 11 6 (A V and R V.) "child" = ילד, "babe" = נער, LXX ὁρᾷ παιδίον κλαῖον, merging the two words in one

CHRIST'S MIRACLES OF FEEDING

the fact that the babe Moses in his cradle (like the babe Herakles in Greek story) was already more than an infant[1].

All this, however, though it may explain John's application of the tradition about the "lad" when it had arisen, does not explain how it arose. If such a "lad" existed, why was the fact omitted by the Synoptists? If there was not, how came John to suppose his existence[2]? To these questions there is at present no answer based on definite evidence. But there are reasonable (though conjectural) answers—derived from what we know about Mark and John in general, and about these Marcan and Johannine narratives in particular—namely, that John is attempting to explain Mark's "*Go, see*"

One explanation may be conjecturally given to the following effect. "The disciples had no food of their own at hand. But, as Jesus bade them '*go*' and '*see*,' they '*went*' and '*saw*.' They found some one with five loaves and two fishes. These they brought to Jesus saying that they had no more. In reality, they had not even these. But as the owner was willing to give them, they brought them as their own. All this is obscurely suggested in the Marcan '*Go, see*,' and is altogether omitted by Matthew and Luke. But in fact this stranger with the 'five loaves and two fishes' whom the disciples '*went*' and '*saw*,' may have been a person not to be left out. He may have been

---

[1] See *Numb r.* (on Numb iii 14, Wu p 42) quoting Exod ii 6 and *ib* 23 and saying that the "sighing" of Israel and the "weeping" of Moses in the cradle were the preparation of the nation for fulfilling the purpose of God On Zech ii 4 (8) "*this young man*," Kimchi, who assumes the prophet to be meant, says that he is so called, either as being literally "young" (like Jeremiah) or as being subordinate to a superior as Joshua was to Moses (Exod xxxiii. 11 "Joshua the son of Nun *a young man*")

[2] To a third question, "If there was not, how came John to invent it?" my reply would be that repeated investigations in previous parts of *Diatessarica* have shewn that John does not "invent"—though he may have received visions that some would call "inventions" This tradition may have been one of "the sayings of Andrew" inquired into by Papias (s above, p. 282, n 3)

CHRIST'S MIRACLES OF FEEDING

like the stranger in Genesis ('a certain man') who met Joseph wandering in the field and said to him 'What seekest thou[1]?' That 'man,' they say, was Gabriel. But Gabriel would not be appropriate here For in this action the Lord is recompensing to Abraham's children the hospitality that He Himself received from Abraham, in which Abraham was helped, not by a 'man' but by a *'lad.'* Let us say, then, that this unknown stranger was a *'lad.'* And as the *'lad'* assisted Abraham in preparing food for the Lord, so let us now see a *'lad'* assisting the Lord in preparing food for Abraham's descendants. The 'lad' then received 'a calf' from Abraham and 'prepared' it. The 'lad' now gives 'five loaves and two fishes' to the Lord Jesus, and He prepares them by letting them pass through His hands as He distributes the food to all the people. This *'lad'* was Moses, who wrote the five books of the Law, containing also songs and predictions[2]. As the five loaves are symbolic of the Law, so the fishes might be symbolic of psalms and prophecies, whether called 'a few,' or, as some might say, 'two fishes,' that is, 'the Psalms and the Prophets' considered as two books. This was the food that Moses, the servant of God, offered to the Messiah, the Son of God, who distributed it to the people. And as Joshua, the first Jesus, is called a

---

[1] Gen xxxvii 15, on which see *Joh Gr* **2649** b

[2] Jerome, on Mt xiv 17, says "In another Evangelist we read (Jn vi 9) *There is a lad here who has five loaves*—who seems to me to signify Moses" The text continues "Duos autem pisces vel utrumque intelligimus Testamentum, vel quia par numerus refertur *ad legem*" But one MS adds "*et prophetas*," which seems necessary to the sense ("the even number refers to the Law and the Prophets"). Later on he says "*The Law with the Prophets* is broken and divided into fragments (in frusta discerpitur) and its mysteries are brought forth to view, so that what did not nourish, as long as it was whole and abiding in its pristine state, might, by being divided into parts, nourish the multitude of the Gentiles (gentium)"

Origen, on Mt xiv 17, says that "perhaps" the five loaves contained a veiled reference to "the sensible (αἰσθητοὺς) words of the Scriptures corresponding in number on this account to the five senses," and the two fishes to the λόγος προφορικός and the λόγος

'*lad*' when ministering to Moses[1], so is Moses himself called a '*lad*' when ministering to the second Jesus."

The second explanation, though similar to the first in detail, would differ in this respect, that it would base itself in part on apostolic tradition It would go back to one of those "sayings of Andrew" about which Papias tells us that he used to make inquiry, something to this effect·—"Andrew, the Apostle, said (*or*, used to say) that *the Five Loaves and the Two Fishes did not appertain to the Twelve, but to a Servant* [meaning Moses] Also Andrew said (*or*, used to say)—speaking of the Law and the Prophets in themselves and before they were broken up like bread and expounded by the Lord—'*What could they avail for the multitudes* [*seeking the Bread of Life*][2]?'"

The second of these explanations seems to me decidedly more probable than the first, but if either of them is even partially correct we find ourselves in an atmosphere of

---

ἐνδιάθετος ("which are a relish, so to speak, to the sensible things contained in the Scriptures") or, perhaps, to the word that had "already come (φθάσαντα)" to the disciples "about the Father and the Son", but he adds that others may be able to give a fuller and better interpretation

Clement of Alexandria 665—6, while implying that the "five pillars" of Exod xxvi. 37 are less sacred than the "four pillars" of Exod xxvi 32, simply mentions "the five loaves" in connection with "the things of sense"

Thus, the further back we go, the less proof we find that "*five*" was regarded by Greek commentators as referring to the five books of the Law They may be wrong They may have failed to catch the poetic allusions of the Galilaean tradition But still we have to keep our minds open to the possibility that "*five*" may have originally had some other reference (*e g* meaning "*a few*") and that the explanation of the "five loaves" as the five books of the Law came later It certainly is not entirely satisfactory, because it is difficult to find a corresponding explanation of the "two fishes"

[1] Exod xxxiii. 11 "His [*i e* Moses's] minister Joshua, the son of Nun, *a lad*," R.V "*a young man*" Perhaps the Heb *naar* is intended to convey the double notion of youth and service.

[2] On the ambiguous "said" or "used to say"—ambiguous in Hebrew as well as in Greek (ἔλεγε), see *Joh Gr* **2470 a**.

Jewish symbolism and mystical tradition through which we must look at the whole of the context. It is easy to realise this about the "two hundred denarii" discussed above. But the reader may feel it absurd that he should be asked to extend this hypothesis to the Marcan phrase *"Go, see!"* to which we now return These words he may declare to be not only simple in themselves, but also in accord with another Marcan tradition about the disciples as having "forgotten" to bring "loaves with them[1]."

But the literal truth of that other tradition itself is very doubtful. It is omitted by Luke. And the Marcan context, saying "Save one loaf, they had not [any loaves] in the boat with them," is omitted by Matthew and is suggestive of metaphor literalised We ought therefore to give a patient consideration to the suggestion that, in the present passage, *"Go, see!"* may be a Marcan misinterpretation of *"Come and see,"* a phrase used in Jewish tradition to call attention to weighty sayings, especially about the ways of God as superior to those of man. John uses a form of it thrice in passages where it is susceptible of a mystical meaning[2]. Also, in particular, *"See"* is applied to numbers when rabbinically interpreted For example, Horae Hebraicae illustrates the "barley loaves" in John by quoting a fanciful exaggeration about the feeding of the sons of the prophets with "loaves of barley" by Elisha, in which *"See!"* occurs thrice; and the formula is sometimes repeated much more frequently[3]. Somewhat similarly,

---

[1] Mk viii 14, parall Mt. xvi 5, om Lk xii 1.

[2] See Schlatter, on Jn 1 39 "come and ye shall see," referring to *ib* 46 and xi 34 and quoting from *Mechilt* (on Exod xii 1, xx 12) "*Come and see* what God replies to him" and "*Come and see* their reward " See also Wetstein, *Hor Heb* , and Schottgen, on Jn 1 39

[3] *Hor Heb.* on Jn vi 9 quoting *Chetub* 105 2, 106. 9 on 2 K iv 42 "Twenty loaves, and the loaf of the firstfruits, *see,* one and twenty; the green ear, *see,* two and twenty.. and so, *see,* there were two thousand and two hundred fed " I substitute "see" for "behold," as Wunsche habitually does, *e g* on Numb vii 66 foll p 372 "*siehe,*

in an early Galilaean tradition about the Feeding of the Five Thousand, attention may have been called to the number of the loaves "*See* (or, *Go and see*) *there are five loaves*[1]." This was misunderstood by Gentile interpretation (adopted by Mark) as though the first half of the sentence came from Jesus, who said "*Go and see* [*how many loaves there are*]," and the second half from the disciples, who said "*There are five loaves*"

It is perhaps worth noting that the phrase "five loaves" occurs in the narrative of an incident in the life of David to which Jesus Himself called attention—the eating of the sacred shewbread by laymen contrary to the Law. All the Gospels mention this But they do not quote the exact words of David, which are "Give me *five loaves of bread* in mine hand or whatsoever is present[2]." No other passage in the Bible mentions "*five loaves*" The meaning appears to be (as the Vulgate renders it) "*even* five [if you can give no more]." "Five" therefore may be regarded as typical of a small number[3]. In the Feeding of the Five Thousand, the Son of David restores and consecrates the "five loaves" that David might be said, in some sort, to have taken away and desecrated. It ought not to be surprising if, apart from other mystical views of the number "five," this allusion in itself caused a Jewish Christian Evangelist to call attention to the coincidence by means of the formula "*Come and see.*" It ought to be less surprising that the formula was misunderstood by Gentiles.

---

das sind zwei,...*siehe*, das sind vier..." where it occurs seven times, *ib* p 374 it occurs six times

[1] The Heb בא, which regularly means "come," is frequently used for "go," e g Gen xxxi 18 R V "go," LXX ἀπελθεῖν

[2] 1 S xxi 3 referred to in Mk ii 26, Mt xii. 4, Lk vi 4.

[3] See Lev xxvi 8 "*Five* of you shall chase an hundred," and Is xxx. 17 "at the rebuke of *five*" The attempt to explain it otherwise (*J. Succa* vi 8 (Schwab p. 50)) is unsatisfactory

CHRIST'S MIRACLES OF FEEDING

§ 22. "*Here*," *in all the Gospels*

The Johannine phrase discussed in the last section, "*there is a lad*" is followed by "*here*." "*Here*" is also inserted by Matthew as follows —

Mk vi. 38	Mt xiv. 17	Lk ix 13
They say (D and SS add "to him"), Five	But they say to him, We have not *here* save five…	But they said (*lit*) There are not to us more than five

In *Corrections* it was suggested that "*here*" might be added by Matthew for emphasis, or that there might be some confusion between "*here*" and "*bread*" which are very similar in Hebrew[1]. The latter suggestion is favoured by a passage in the Psalms where Gesenius accepts an emendation based on this similarity[2] But of course both causes might be at work Matthew repeats the Greek "*here*" in the next verse after a verb of motion in words of Jesus that he alone records, "Bring them *here* to me[3]." Luke also, in a parallel to Mark-Matthew "the place is desert," has "We are *here* in a desert place[4]." Lastly, in the Feeding of the Four Thousand, "here" is inserted by Mark who has "Whence shall one be able *here* to satisfy these with loaves in a wilderness[5]?" but omitted by the parallel Matthew, "Whence [can come] to us in a wilderness so many loaves as to satisfy so great a multitude?". The recurrences of the same word meaning "here" or "hither" in the narratives of miraculous feeding suggest the examination of the Biblical use of the word above mentioned, meaning "*hither*" but confusable with "bread."

It occurs for the first time in the words of the fugitive Hagar whom "the angel of the Lord found by a fountain of

---

[1] See *Corrections* **403** (1), where it is also pointed out that "to him" and "not" are often confused in Hebrew (see Gesen 520 *b*)

[2] See Gesen pp 240—1 on Ps lxxiii. 10 adopting לֶחֶם "bread" for הֲלֹם "hither"

[3] Mt xiv. 18 φέρετέ μοι ὧδε αὐτούς, not in parall Mk-Lk.

[4] Lk ix 12 [5] Mk viii 4

water in the wilderness of Shur." Hagar exclaims "Have I even *here* looked after him that seeth me[1]?" Rashi explains "*even here*" as meaning "*even here in the desert*," and that makes good sense, recognising that God sees everywhere; but the Jerusalem Targums confused the word with an almost identical one meaning "dream" or "vision," and the LXX renders it "face to face[2]." As a rule, the word means "hither," not "here," and it will be observed that Matthew repeats it (in Greek) in the sense of "hither" on the second occasion.

In the sense of "*here*," it would be appropriate to the disciples, ignorant of their Master's design and saying "*Here [in this lonely place]* we have no bread worth mentioning, or, we can do nothing for the multitude." But, if "here" has this meaning, then "*in this lonely place*" is a desirable addition; for, without it, "*here*" might mean simply "*on the spot*" Accordingly Mark (in the narrative of the Four Thousand) and Luke, who both use "*here*," add "in a desert, or lonely place[3]." Matthew, in the narrative of the Four Thousand, does not follow Mark in inserting "*here*" along with "*in a desert*", but, in the narrative of the Five Thousand, he inserts "*here*" twice, apparently taking it to mean, not "*here in a lonely place*," but "*here on the spot*";—"We have no bread worth mentioning *here on the spot*," to which Jesus replies "Bring it to me *here on the spot*" Mark, in the Feeding of the Five Thousand, omits "*here*," but apparently implies, like Matthew, that, if inserted, it would have meant "*on the*

---

[1] Gen xvi. 13

[2] In Daniel, חלם repeatedly means (Theod) ἐνύπνιον, (LXX) ὅραμα In Gen xvi 13 Onk has "I have begun to see" (? confusing הלם with some form of חלל) LXX has ἐνώπιον (? corr for ενυπνιον) In Gen. xvi. 14 LXX has ἐνώπιον again for לחי =viventis. Elsewhere LXX has ἐνταῦθα (4), ὧδε (4), etc These facts indicate that ancient interpretation did not (as Gesen does) limit the word to the sense of "*hither*."

[3] Mk viii 4 (the Four Thousand) πόθεν . ὧδε...ἐπ' ἐρημίας, Lk. ix 12 (the Five Thousand) ὧδε ἐν ἐρήμῳ τόπῳ ἐσμέν

CHRIST'S MIRACLES OF FEEDING

spot"; although the disciples had no bread "*on the spot*," they had some a little way off, as to which Jesus sent to inquire how much there was

Coming to John's phrase "There is a lad *here*" we have to confess at once that, but for all these variations and apparent allusions in the Synoptists, we should take it to mean simply "*on the spot*" or "*at hand.*" But if the "*lad*" is to be regarded as the representative of Moses, and if John had before him various traditions likening the Five Thousand in the Desert to Israel in the Wilderness of Sinai, then we shall not reject as improbable the hypothesis that this saying of Andrew about "a lad here," besides having its literal meaning, might also mystically allude to "Moses *in the wilderness*[1]"

§ 23. "*By companies*[2]," "*by ranks*[3]," *in Mark*

The Greek for "company," *symposion*, means literally "drinking-party." The Greek for "rank," *prasia*, means perhaps literally "greenery," and in practice a rectangular "garden-bed[4]." Neither of these words is adopted by the

---

[1] In examining this hypothesis of allusion to the story of Hagar, or of confusion arising from Hebrew corruption, we must not ignore the fact that elsewhere Matthew and Luke appear to insert "hither" simply for emphasis. (See *Corrections* 425 on Mk ix 19, Mt xvii 17, Lk ix 41) And the LXX does sometimes insert it for this reason where it is not in the Hebrew, besides omitting it sometimes where it is in the Hebrew (See *Corrections* 425 (1) *a* and *b*) But the recurrence of "here" in these narratives of feeding is rather too frequent to be explained thus

[2] Mk vi. 39 συμπόσια συμπόσια.   [3] Mk vi 40 πρασιαὶ πρασιαί.

[4] Hesych says that πράσα=τὰ βρύα κ τὰ φυκία, and πρασιαί=αἱ ἐν τοῖς κήποις τετράγωνοι λαχανιαί The facts suggest that the word originally denoted "*green*" and was then applied to any very common green vegetable, *e g* the leek (comp in English, "*greens*") L S. gives πράσιον="horehound," and πράσον=(1) leek, (2) a leek-like sea-weed Hesych suggests πέρας "boundary" as the origin of the word —οἷον περασιοὶ διὰ τὸ ἐπὶ πέρασι τῶν κήπων. The word πρασιά is frequent in Homer Field (on Mk vi 40) shews that the word was *not* (as has been maintained) associated with the thought of "flower-beds" or "parterres" implying variety of colour

CHRIST'S MIRACLES OF FEEDING

parallel Matthew, Luke, or John[1] The question therefore arises whether John has, or has not, in his context, something that expresses the thought underlying Mark's peculiar expressions. If he has not, this passage will have to be recognised as an instance of the failure of the Rule of Johannine Intervention.

Symposion occurs only once in canonical LXX. There it represents the Hebrew phrase "*drinking-party of wine*[2]." Philo, it is true, repeatedly uses it in describing the sacred meals of the Therapeutae. But he expressly uses it as a paradox, "*contrasting their symposia with the symposia of other*

---

[1] Mk vi 39—40 (R V)

(39) And he commanded them that all should sit down (*lit* recline) by companies upon the green grass (40) And they sat down in ranks, by hundreds, and by fifties

Mt xiv 19 *a* (R V)

And he commanded the multitudes to sit down (*lit* recline) on the grass

Lk ix 14—15 (R V)

(14) For they were about five thousand men And he said unto his disciples, Make them sit down (*lit* recline) in companies (κλισίας), about fifty each (15) And they did so, and made them all sit down (*lit* recline)

Jn vi 10 (R V)

Jesus said, Make the people sit down Now there was much grass in the place So the men sat down, in number about five thousand.

In the Feeding of the Four Thousand the reclining is mentioned merely as a command thus —

Mk viii 6 *a* (R V.)
And he commandeth the multitude to sit down on the ground

Mt xv 35 (R.V)
And he commanded the multitude to sit down on the ground

R V in these six columns does not represent several differences in the Greek For example, R V "command"=ἐπιτάσσω, κελεύω, and παραγγέλλω

[2] Esth. vii 7 συμπόσιον="*drinking-party* (משתה) *of wine* (היין)" Συμπόσιον οἴνου=the same Heb in Sir xxxv (xxxii.) 5, xlix 1 In Is i 22 (Aq) and Hos iv 18 (Sym and Quint) συμπόσιον represents Heb סבא (Gesen. 685 *a*) "drink," "liquor," (?) "drunken-revelling" The parallel Lk. ix 14 has κλισίας Κλισία, in literary Greek (Steph *Thes*) means a "booth" (comp. 3 Macc vi 31, the single instance in LXX) But Luke appears to mean "sitting-place" as in Joseph *Ant* xii 2 12.

CHRIST'S MIRACLES OF FEEDING

folk," for the Therapeutae, he says, drink nothing but "running water[1]" In Mark there is no such contrast. Mark's choice of the word therefore requires explanation. It seems singularly unsuitable in a narrative about feeding with bread and fish where there appears no suggestion, and certainly no mention, of wine, or of anything to drink.

But in fact there *is* such a suggestion, though a most obscure one, in the Marcan word *prasiai*. For this, though literally meaning only "garden-beds," can be shewn to have practically meant *garden-beds that need irrigation*, that is to say, metaphorically "*drinking.*" Aquila assumes this in his rendering of the words "As the hart *thirsteth* (R V. *panteth*) after the water brooks, so *thirsteth* (R.V. *panteth*) my soul after thee, O God[2]." Here Aquila uses a verb formed from *prasia*, "garden-bed," to signify "thirsting [like a garden-bed that thirsts for water from heaven]." Ben Sira, too, after representing Wisdom as saying "They that eat me shall yet be hungry and they that drink me shall yet be thirsty," *i.e.* athirst for heavenly knowledge, uses the word *prasia* as follows: "I will water my best garden, and will water abundantly my *garden-bed*[3]." The thought is of the irrigating trenches of a garden or vineyard, opening their mouths like panting animals, and crying to heaven for water to feed the rows of vegetation. The word occurs in a papyrus of the first century in such a

---

[1] Philo ii 477 ἀντιτάξας τὰ τῶν ἄλλων συμπόσια (the word is mentioned about a dozen times in the context) The Therapeutae drink (*ib.* 477) ὕδωρ ναματιαῖον

[2] Ps xlii 1, see Gesen 788, עָרַג, "long for," עֲרוּגָה "garden terrace or bed " Rashi gives various explanations, and says that "Menachem" illustrates from Cant. v. 12 (R V 13) where Aq has πρασιαί Aq. also has πρασιοῦσθαι in Joel i 20 "the beasts of the field pant (A V. *cry*) unto thee," where Jerome says "*like a garden-bed thirsting for rain* For this is what Aquila means, in one word, saying ἐπρασιώθη"

[3] Sir xxiv 21, 31 ποτιῶ μου τὸν κῆπον, καὶ μεθύσω μου τὴν πρασιάν, where μεθύσω, "I will *satisfy as if with wine*," harmonizes with a hypothesis connecting πρασιαί with συμπόσια

298 (Mark vi 29—44)

context as to shew that it would be naturally connected with irrigation[1].

The Targum on a passage in Ezekiel mentioning what Aquila calls "*garden-beds*" has a slightly different form of the word, meaning "*trenches*," and especially trenches for the irrigation of vines[2]. And the metaphorical name "the vineyard in Jabneh" (some indeed call it no metaphor but a name based on fact) was applied to "the university in that place," the reason being that "the scholars sat *rows* [*and*] *rows* like a vineyard that is planted *rows* [*and*] *rows*[3]."

These facts, taken together, explain Mark's two peculiar traditions. The original appeared to him to describe the multitude as placed "[*in*] *rows* [*and*] *rows*," meaning either "like vines," or "like vineyard trenches," waiting for water, the living water of the Word[4] This was at first expressed by *prasiai*. But as this did not convey clearly to Greeks the notion of thirst, Mark prefaced it by *symposia*[5]. Matthew and Luke omitted both these terms—*symposia*, "drinking-parties," because it might convey the notion of carousing, and *prasiai*, "garden-beds," because it did not convey to them the

---

[1] *Berlin Urkunde* 530. 27 "The water scarcely gives drink enough for one *row*" μόλις γὰρ μίαν πρασεὰν (sic) ποτίζει τὸ ὕδωρ. Comp 1 Cor xii 13 ἐν πνεῦμα ἐποτίσθημεν and iii 2 γάλα ὑμᾶς ἐπότισα, also iii 6 Ἀπολλὼς ἐπότισεν, "watered" (after "I planted")

[2] Ezek. xvii. 7, 10 Heb עֲרֻגוֹת, A.V. "furrows," R V. "beds," Aq. πρασιαί, Targ. עוּנִית, which = "trenches," see Levy iii 625 *b* and Levy *Ch* ii 205 *b*

[3] *Hor Heb* on Mk vi 40 quoting *Jevamoth* cap 8. For a similar explanation see *Jer. Berach* iv. 1 fol 7 *d*, and elsewhere (Levy ii. 408 *b*) The word for "*rows*" is rare in O T. (Gesen 1004 *b*, quite diff from the one meaning "garden-bed") but freq in later Heb. (Levy iv 525—6)

[4] This is the aspect of "rows" that commended itself to Mark. But there is also the military aspect in which the "rows" would be regarded as "files," see below, p 309, n. 3, and pp. 309—14.

[5] See *Clue* 31 shewing that "the correct rendering in a conflation mostly follows the incorrect one."

suggestion of spiritual thirst, and they did not see any reason for such an out-of-the-way metaphor

What course does John adopt? In the narrative of the actual miracle, it must be admitted, he says nothing that in the remotest degree implies a *symposium*. But in Christ's comment we are taught that the "loaves" with which the Five Thousand have been "filled" are but types of a "bread from heaven"; then we learn that this "bread" is Christ Himself; then we are told that He—not the bread but Christ Himself—satisfies *"thirst" at the same time as hunger*: "He that cometh unto me shall never hunger, and he that believeth on me shall never *thirst*[1]." Subsequently the epithet "living"—familiar to the Jews as an epithet of running water—is applied to this "bread" as being a source of spiritual life[2] And thus we are finally led to a new and astonishing revelation of the nature of this new "food" that is to be "bought" by Jesus—namely that it is to be His own "flesh." The literalising Jews ask "How can this man give us his flesh to eat?" Jesus, in His answer, increases (for literalisers) the impossibility. He abruptly implies that the "flesh" will not be separated from "blood" Thus at last we are brought to the actual mention of the word "*drink*," for which we have been gradually prepared · "Except ye eat the flesh of the Son of man and *drink* his blood, ye have no life in yourselves[3]." This, once mentioned, is reiterated "He that eateth my flesh and *drinketh* my blood," "My blood is *drink* indeed," "He that eateth my flesh and *drinketh* my blood abideth in me and I in him[4]" Such is the Johannine expansion of the Marcan *symposia*

It has not been maintained above that *symposia* was a part of Mark's original, or that Matthew and Luke were wrong in omitting it The question for us has been, not as to Mark's

---

[1] Jn vi 35 This is in response to the prayer "Lord, evermore give us this bread "
[2] Jn vi 51 [3] Jn vi 52—3 [4] Jn vi 54—6

correctness, but as to whether John intervenes in order to bring out some spiritual doctrine latent under Mark's text, even when Mark is incorrect or (as in this case) inappropriate in expression. The result has been to reveal, apparently, not a failure but an instance, of Johannine Intervention And it is a peculiarly interesting one. For here Mark's error appears to have been a Greek husk, so to speak, containing a kernel of Jewish doctrine. This kernel John has extracted, amplifying the exposition of its doctrine so that it illuminates the whole of his conception of Christ's character and action.

As regards *prasiai*, or "garden-beds," it cannot be conclusively shewn that John has similarly intervened If he regarded the *prasiai* as the Jewish equivalent of the Gentile *symposia*, he may have decided that he had done enough when he had expounded the doctrine implied for Greeks in the Greek word *symposia*[1].

---

[1] The thought of πρασιαί as "rows of vines," thirsting for water, would be very distinct from John's conception of the one Vine The latter (not "vine-rows" but "vine") may have been in his mind when he writes, as words of Jesus, (vi 56) "He that ..drinketh my blood abideth in me and I in him "

If we drink His blood, it follows that, in some sense, He is in us, but how does it follow that we "abide" in Him? An explanation is not given in the doctrine that follows the Feeding, but one is suggested later on, when it is said (Jn xv 4) that we abide in Christ as branches in the Vine This means that we are in the Christ-Nature or Vine-Nature, in the Nature that produces the sap and the fruit and that juice of the Vine which is called in Scripture (Gen xlix 11) "the blood of grapes " It is *in us*, but we are also *in it* because it is *in us* This metaphor of the single Vine is more accordant with the ancient Hebrew imagery than is the later Jewish tradition about "vine-rows [and] vine-rows" describing the array of disciples in "the vineyard" of "the university of Jabneh "

If there is any Johannine equivalent of the Marcan *prasiai*— regarded as "rows of vines," thirsting for rain—it is to be looked for in passages describing the "living water," which John alone mentions

CHRIST'S MIRACLES OF FEEDING

§ 24. *"On the green grass*[1]*," in Mark*

Barely stated, the facts bearing on this Marcan phrase might be summed up as a case of Johannine Intervention thus: "Mark has 'on the *green grass*,' Matthew 'on the *grass*,' Luke no mention of '*grass*' at all, John '*There was much grass in the place*'; John obviously intervenes. The Greek *chortos*, '*grass*,' mostly means 'hay' in literary Greek, and may have that meaning here But that does not affect either the fact that Luke omits and John inserts the Marcan *chortos*, or the inference—that it is a case of Johannine Intervention."

All this is true But if we passed on, content with this, we should pass over a great deal that will be found interesting and illuminative for those who are prepared to recognise truth under metaphor, and to accept guidance toward some parts of the truth from ancient Christian commentaries that must be admitted to be, as to other parts, fanciful and extravagant. Such a comment is that of Jerome (on Matthew): "They are commanded to '*lie down on grass* (or, *hay*) (foenum)*'* and, according to another (alium) Evangelist, '*on the earth*[2],' in fifties or hundreds, in order that, after they have trampled (calcaverint)[3] on their '*flesh*' and all its '*flowers*,' and placed

---

[1] Mk vi 39—40 ἐπέταξεν αὐτοῖς ἀνακλιθῆναι πάντας...ἐπὶ τῷ χλωρῷ χόρτῳ, καὶ ἀνέπεσαν.., Mt xiv 19 κελεύσας τοὺς ὄχλους ἀνακλιθῆναι ἐπὶ τοῦ χόρτου, Lk ix 14—15 Κατακλίνατε αὐτοὺς κλισίας..., καὶ κατέκλιναν ἅπαντας, Jn vi 10 Ποιήσατε τοὺς ἀνθρώπους ἀναπεσεῖν. ἦν δὲ χόρτος πολὺς ἐν τῷ τόπῳ ἀνέπεσαν οὖν οἱ ἄνδρες....

[2] "*On the earth*" is not said by any Evangelist here Did Jerome suppose it to be implied by Luke ("make them lie down")? Luke omits "*on the grass.*" On the Feeding of the Four Thousand Jerome (on Matthew) remarks "Ibi *super foenum* discumbunt, hic *super terram.*" If Jerome is referring to that we must read here "another [place of the] Evangelist (Mt. xv 35)"

[3] "Trampled," comp the expostulation in Ezekiel (xxxiv 18) to the "rams" and "he-goats," which not only eat up the pasture of the weaker cattle but also "*tread down*" the "*residue.*" What they do in a bad sense, Jerome here supposes to be done in a good sense

CHRIST'S MIRACLES OF FEEDING

under [their feet] the pleasures of the world as being merely *drying grass* (or, *hay*) (arens foenum)[1], they may then ascend through the penitence denoted by '*fifty*' to the perfect height denoted by '*a hundred*[2].'"

In his interpretation of "grass," Jerome is here following Origen, who says "I think He bade the multitude *lie down in the grass* by reason of that which is said in Isaiah 'All flesh is grass'—that is to say, place beneath [their feet] '*the flesh*' and subjugate the disposition of '*the flesh*[3].'"

This passage of Isaiah is quoted also in the Petrine Epistle as contrasting "*flesh*," which is "*as grass*," with the utterance of the everlasting God; and it is alluded to in the Epistle of James[4]. Jesus Himself did not command His disciples to "trample" on "the flowers"; but He bade them "consider the lilies" and ask themselves whether they might not trust their heavenly Father to clothe them, since He "so clothed the *grass* (*chortos*) of the field[5]."

It is important to recognise that this word *chortos*, when connected with a mention of men and not cattle or agriculture, is likely to have a depreciative meaning. Paul uses it to describe a false and flimsy structure (of "*hay*") built by some

---

[1] Comp Is. xl 6—8 "All flesh is grass (χόρτος), and all the goodliness thereof is as the *flower* of the field.... Surely the people is *grass* The *grass* withereth (ἐξηράνθη = arens), the *flower* fadeth but the word of our God shall stand for ever"

[2] "Fifty" is mentioned by Mark and Luke, but not by Matthew; "a hundred" is mentioned by Mark alone

[3] Origen (on Mt xiv 19) τοὺς ὄχλους ἐκέλευσεν ἀνακλιθῆναι ἐν (sic) τῷ χόρτῳ ..τουτέστιν ὑποκάτω ποιῆσαι τὴν σάρκα καὶ ὑποτάξαι τὸ φρόνημα τῆς σαρκός.

[4] 1 Pet 1. 24, Jas 1 10, 11

[5] Mt vi 30 εἰ δὲ τὸν χόρτον τοῦ ἀγροῦ... Note the difference in Lk xii 28 εἰ δὲ ἐν ἀγρῷ τὸν χόρτον... Luke rejects the phrase "grass of the field" used by Matthew and frequent in LXX. He substitutes "*But if [while it is still] in the field* [or, *in a field*] *the grass*—living (*lit* existing) to-day and [to be] thrown into the oven to-morrow—is so clothed by God" His object is to shew Greek readers that χόρτος, in this passage, does *not* have its ordinary meaning "*hay*"

Christians who profess to accept Christ as their "foundation[1]." Also in literary Greek the noun *chortos* is regularly used to mean food for beasts, as distinct from corn or wheat that is food for men; and hence the verb *chortazein* is used to mean, not only when applied to cattle "fill with hay (*or*, with fodder)," but also when applied to men, "cram, or stuff, oneself with food," after the manner of swine[2].

In LXX, *chortos* is represented mainly by two Hebrew words. Both of these signify "herbage," but one signifies more definitely "green grass" and is once rendered by LXX "green[3]." It seldom has any such opprobrious sense as in literary Greek[4]. In O.T., where A V. has "*hay*" R.V. has "*grass*" in text or margin[5], and it is said that people in Palestine do not dry grass as we do for winter fodder, and that there is no evidence that the Hebrews had such a custom[6].

---

[1] 1 Cor iii 12

[2] See Steph *Thes* χόρτος, and add Epictet ii 14 24 "most men value nothing more than *fodder*—for wealth is *fodder*" (comp. *ib* 29) Epictetus uses χορτάζω similarly (ii 16 43) and once in a passage that resembles a bitter version of a saying of Christ's (i 9 19) "You are [as good as] dead When you are *crammed* (χορτασθῆτε) for the day, you sit weeping about the [fodder of the] morrow" Ast's two instances in Plato are *Pol* ii. 372 D, IX 586 A in which men are likened to "swine," or to creatures "stooping down to dinner-tables," εἰς τραπέζας [κεκυφότες] βόσκονται χορταζόμενοι καὶ ὀχεύοντες.

[3] See Gesen 348 חָצִיר "green grass, herbage," 793 עֵשֶׂב "herb, herbage." Χόρτος = the former about 12 times, the latter about 25 times (besides other Heb words much more rarely) In Prov xxvii 25, חָצִיר = LXX "green [things]" χλωρῶν, R V "*the hay* (marg *grass*) is carried and the tender grass sheweth itself"

[4] The Hebrew "grass" denotes transience but not degradation except in special contexts such as Ps cvi 20 "the similitude of an ox that eateth *grass*," on which see *Tehill* and Rashi *ad loc*, also *Mechilt* (on Exod xiv 29, Wu p 108) and Dan iv 25—33 (of Nebuchadnezzar).

[5] Prov xxvii 25, Is xv 6, the only instances of "hay" in A V. (O.T).

[6] See Hastings' *Dict*. "Hay," which says "The winter is the season

Mark has previously used *chortos* in a sense unprecedented (so far as is known at present) to mean the shooting blade of corn (perhaps taking it to mean the early green shoot of corn which the eye cannot distinguish from grass)[1]. Here Mark goes further and inserts "green." Perhaps he wishes to make it clear to his readers that he means, not "hay," but "grass[2]."

Are we then to infer that in the present passage Mark is simply stating a literal fact in the language of the LXX without any allusion to Hebrew Scripture or Jewish tradition? It would be safer to say that he stated what he believed to be a literal fact and to leave it an open question whether his original had an allusive character. For we are dealing with a Gospel narrative about a miraculous giving of "bread," or literally "loaves"; and it is certainly a coincidence to be noted that, in the LXX, the first mention of *"bread"* (or *"loaf," artos*)—"In the sweat of thy face wilt thou eat *bread*"—immediately follows the words, pronounced as a curse, "Thou shalt eat the *grass* (*chortos*) of the field[3]."

The question was asked by ancient Jewish teachers "Was there really a change in the doom pronounced by God on Adam? If so, how explain it?" The Jerusalem Targums say it was changed because of Adam's piteous expostulation, and Talmudic tradition supports them: "Lord of the world," cried Adam, "shall I and my ass eat out of one crib[4]?" These

---

of green grass here " The ignorance of this fact might lead to early misunderstandings.

[1] Mk iv 28.

[2] Wetstein, on Mt. vi 30, says that χόρτος is "hay (foenum)," but that here and elsewhere in the Gospels it is used of grass still green, and he quotes Plutarch *Q. N.* p 25 C χόρτος ὑόμενος, κόπτεται γὰρ οὐ ξηρὸς ἀλλὰ χλωρός

[3] Gen iii 18—19

[4] *Pesach* 118 *a*, and sim *Aboth R. Nathan* on *Aboth* 1 1 "Said the Holy One, Blessed be He 'As thou hast trembled, therefore in the sweat of thy face thou shalt eat *bread*'" (where Rodkinson italicises "*bread*"). See *Son* 3422 *a*, which quotes the fuller dialogue

traditions are not of the first century. But even in the first century we find Philo making a distinction between the symbolism of "grass" and "green [grass]"[1]. This, though perhaps derived from Greek influences, indicates that discussions about "grass," and "fodder," and also about the relation of these to that "bread" which is "the word of God," were likely to be current in the first century, among Jews as well as among Christians[2]. On the whole we may say that there is nothing so absurd as there appears to be at first sight in the hypothesis that *"on the green grass"* in the Marcan narrative had, from the first, a poetic and allusive as well as a literal meaning

Before passing to the Johannine equivalent (in the phrase "now there was much grass in the place") we must note, as a part of John's consistent treatment of the whole subject, his way of dealing with the verb *chortazein* derived from *chortos* "grass," and meaning *"to fill with grass"* It is applied by all the Synoptists to the multitudes, meaning "they were filled" in the sense of "satisfied[3]." For this, they have some authority in the LXX, but hardly any except in the Psalms[4].

in the Targums, where God is regarded not as altering, but as interpreting, "the herb," עשׂב   This = χόρτος seven times in Genesis, beginning with 1 11 βοτάνην (אשׂר) χόρτου (עשׂ)

[1] Philo 1 48 (on Gen 11 4 foll.) "Grass" = χόρτος, "green [grass]" = χλωρόν.

[2] Χόρτος occurs in early Christian writers (s Goodspeed) only in Justin's *Dialogue* § 20 *passim* (apart from quotations in *ib*. §§ 34 and 50) There Justin, after saying that God (Gen ix 3) gave Noah the right to eat of every animal, represents the Jew as on the point of interrupting him "And as he was ready to say '*as the herbs of green-vegetation* (λάχανα χόρτου)' I anticipated him." This shews that *chortos* was a recognised topic of discussion

[3] Mk vi 42, Mt xiv 20, Lk ix 17. Comp Mk viii 4—8, Mt xv 33—7 (about the Four Thousand)

[4] The Heb שׂבע meaning "satisfy" or "sate" = (Tromm) ἐμπλήθω or ἐμπίμπλημι 50 times, and πλήθω 19 times, but χορτάζω only 13 times (Tromm , by error, 12), and, of these 13 instances, 9 are in the Psalms

CHRIST'S MIRACLES OF FEEDING

It must be admitted that Paul once uses it about himself. And his language might be rendered (somewhat tamely) "I have been initiated into the secret both of *having-my-fill* (*chortazein*) and hungering[1]." But it is better to regard it as Pauline hyperbole (almost equivalent to "stuffing and starving"). And to most Greeks, unacquainted with the LXX, the Synoptic statement would certainly sound like a reproach—as if it meant that the Five Thousand were "filled like swine" without thanks to the giver and without sense of the nature of the gift[2] By John the word is thus reproachfully used, not in his own words but (which is more weighty) in the words of Jesus to condemn their unintelligent greediness "Ye seek me, not because ye saw signs, but because ye ate of the loaves and *were filled [like cattle with fodder]*[3]." The words that follow enjoin "*labour*"— and labour like that of the husbandman, which distinguishes

---

[1] Philipp iv 12 μεμύημαι καὶ χορτάζεσθαι καὶ πεινᾶν On this, Lightfoot, while admitting that it was originally not applied to men except in a depreciatory sense, adds that "in the later language it has lost this sense.. being applied commonly to men and directly opposed to πεινᾶν, e g. Matth. v. 6 On χορτάζειν see Sturz *de Dial. Mac.* p 200 "

But Sturz *does not give a single instance where a serious writer of literary Greek, uninfluenced by the Gospels, applies it to men without depreciation* The Synoptic Gospels prove nothing except that they were influenced by the usage of the Psalms. Epictetus always uses it of men in a bad sense and so does Plutarch (II 616 A) in the single instance given in the Index The first eleven volumes of the *Oxyrhynchan Papyri* and the first four volumes of the *Berlin Urkunde* do not contain the word in any sense

[2] Goodspeed shews that the only Christian instance of χορτάζω up to A D. 150 is Clem Rom § 59 τοὺς πλανωμένους τοῦ λαοῦ σου ἐπίστρεψον, χόρτασον τοὺς πεινῶντας But this (like Polyc *Phil.* § 6) alludes to Ezek xxxiv. 16 πεπλανημένον ἐπιστρέψω καὶ βοσκήσω, which follows *ib.* 15 "I myself will feed my sheep " This indicates that Clement uses the word metaphorically in a prayer to God to "satisfy" His hungering "sheep "

[3] Jn vi 26. This is Jn's only instance of χορτάζω.

man from cattle: "Labour not for the food that perisheth, but for the food that abideth unto eternal life[1]."

In conclusion, the apparent attitude of the other Evangelists to Mark's peculiar tradition "on the green grass," may be roughly described as follows. Matthew omits "green," possibly regarding it as a mere picturesque epithet. Luke omits the whole phrase, perhaps as being of doubtful meaning, and perhaps because, looking at Mark's picture from a western point of view as an expanse of long grass not yet cut, he thought that five thousand men, lying down on it, would do mischief such as Jesus would not have sanctioned. John, omitting "green," suggests that it may have been "hay," not "grass." Also he suggests the same thing by slightly altering the context. For he does not speak of "*the* grass" as a natural element in the scene (like "*the* trees," "*the* forest," etc.). He suggests that there *happened to be a great quantity of hay lying about in swaths in that district*[2] If that was, or was supposed to be, the case, it would be an occasion on which Jesus might naturally be supposed to say to the multitude, somewhat as in the Sermon on the Mount, "*consider the grass of the field* how God provideth it with clothing." This, in Hebrew or Aramaic, might be expressed by "*set [your minds] on the grass of the field*." But this is liable to be confused with "*set yourselves on*, i.e. *lie down on, the grass of the field*[3]."

---

[1] Jn vi 27, on which (and on ἐργάζεσθε, meaning agricultural labour) see *Son* 3017, 3421 *f*. The words accord with the above-mentioned prayer of Adam to God that he might be allowed to work for bread instead of browsing on grass

[2] If the Passover was (Jn vi 4) "at hand," some might suppose hay-making to be going on (but see p 304, n 6) Nonnus seems to imply "happened to be" by τις in his paraphrase of Jn vi 10 ἦν δέ τις αὐτόθι χόρτος ἀπείριτος The multitude (he says) took their meal "*on the top of the hay*," ὑψόθι χόρτου. "Each man was leaning as it were against a party-wall all of them reclining in rows," ἕκαστος ἐρείδετο γείτονι τοίχῳ κεκλιμένοι στοιχηδόν That is, they leaned against the "swaths" covering a widely extended space.

[3] See Gesen p 963 on Judg xix 30 where the Heb has "*Set ye for yourselves* (לכם) *upon it*" = R V "*consider of it*," LXX (Swete) θέσθε

CHRIST'S MIRACLES OF FEEDING

This would give, as the original, a tradition somewhat resembling the spiritual interpretation of Origen and Jerome, but with an important difference. It would be, not "Set yourselves *above*, or *against*, the grass of the field, as if it were an enemy to be conquered," but "*Set yourselves [to think] over it* in order to learn the lesson that it teaches[1]."

§ 25 "*By hundreds and by fifties*," *in Mark*[2]

Mark is the only one of the Evangelists that mentions "hundreds" in this connection. What he has in view is five thousand men in a hundred parallel rows, each row containing fifty men[3]. If he had previously mentioned five thousand as

ὑμῖν αὐτοὶ ἐπ' αὐτήν.., Targ "set your hearts upon it." The Gk varies greatly. Field reads αὐτοῖς And θέσθε ὑμῖν αὐτοῖς ἐπ' αὐτήν might be supposed to be an error for θέσθε ὑμᾶς αὐτοὺς ἐπὶ αὐτήν

[1] Comp 4 Esdr ix 24—27 "'Ibis in campum florum, ubi domus non est aedificata, et manduces (*sic*) solummodo de floribus campi . . .' Et sedi ibi in floribus et de herbis agri manducavi...in saturitatem... et *ego discumbebam supra foenum*" The meaning is obscure, but it is probable that "*reclining on the hay*" has a metaphorical meaning. The thought in the context (ix 29—37) does not appear to be Christian It speaks of the "sowing" of "the Law" in "the wilderness" A receptacle (it says) remains as a rule when its contents perish But Israel, the receptacle of the Law, perishes while the Law abides This is (in word at all events) opposed to Jn xii 24 "except a grain of wheat. .die, it abideth by itself alone"

[2] Mk vi 40	Mt om	Lk ix 15	Jn vi 10
καὶ ἀνέπεσαν πρασιαὶ πρασιαί, κατὰ ἑκατὸν καὶ κατὰ πεντήκοντα.		καὶ ἐποίησαν οὕτως καὶ κατέκλιναν ἅπαντας	ἀνέπεσαν οὖν οἱ ἄνδρες (or, ἀνέπεσαν οὖν, ἄνδρες) τὸν ἀριθμὸν ὡς πεντακισχίλιοι.

In the preceding verse, Luke (ix 14), after stating the total number himself, has represented Jesus as dictating to His disciples the number *in each group*, κατακλίνατε αὐτοὺς κλισίας ὡσεὶ ἀνὰ πεντήκοντα The total number is not specified by Mark and Matthew till the conclusion of the narrative (Mk vi 44, Mt. xiv. 21)

[3] "Rows" This is the word suggested by Mark's "garden-borders" But the reader must be prepared to substitute "files" for "rows," if it appears later on that the original contemplated a military arrangement in which each "row" or "file" was composed

309 (Mark vi. 29—44)

the total (as Luke has done) he need not have mentioned "hundreds," for "five thousand [arranged] *by fifties*" (which, in effect, is what Luke says) implies "fifty *hundreds*." But Mark has not yet mentioned "five thousand." Moreover he desires his readers to see the multitude in regular array—geometrically, so to speak—in oblong "garden-borders," as has been pointed out above. Hence his peculiar tradition—in effect, "a hundred by fifty."

It is not surprising that Matthew omits the Marcan phrase, for it would interfere with Matthew's addition of "women and children[1]." But it is, if not surprising, at least worth considering, that Luke, desiring perhaps to condense Mark, chooses to omit "hundred" rather than "*fifty*." Is there any indication that he may have been influenced by Jewish traditions about companies of "*fifty*," in connection with Israel—either Israel in the wilderness receiving the Law of God, or Israel as God's army marshalled for war?

For poetic or prophetic Jewish traditions about companies of fifty we naturally turn to comments on the words of Isaiah about "the judge and the prophet...*the captain of fifty*[2]." Jerome dilates on the mystical significance of "*fifty*," in connection with "repentance," "Pentecost," etc. He does this (he says) because the "captain (princeps)" of repentance is Christ, and he quotes the words of the Jews to Jesus "thou

---

of 50 men See L S on στοῖχος, "esp of persons standing one behind another," and "of soldiers, *a file*"

[1] Also it might mean "a hundred at a time and fifty at a time" Comp 1 K xviii 4 "a hundred...and hid them *fifty* [*at a time*] (κατὰ πεντήκοντα)," or "*fifty in one place and fifty in another*" See *Sanhedr* 39 b Rashi says that there were "two caves" Origen (*Comm Matth* xi 3) says that the ranks were hundreds and fifties "*since there are different ranks* (τάγματα) *of those who need the nourishment* [*that comes*] *from Jesus, because not all are nourished by equal logoi* (τοῖς ἴσοις λόγοις)"—an explanation of which the chief value is that it proves that he considered some explanation of Mark's twofold numbering to be necessary.

[2] Is iii 2—3.

art not yet *fifty years old*," as indicating their refusal to accept Him as their "*captain of fifty*¹." Whence did Jerome receive this explanation of "*captain of fifty*"? Rashi and Ibn Ezra say nothing about it. One of the most poetic treatises of the Talmud says "Do not read '*captain of fifty*,' but '*captain of fifths*².' This is he who knows how to handle matters in the *five sections* of the Law." But it adds another explanation "An interpreter is not appointed over the congregation who is less than *fifty years old*³." This accords with Jerome's above-quoted application of "*captain of fifty*."

Another Jewish tradition, also highly poetic and mystical, after quoting Zechariah and Jeremiah on "The Branch" and adding "This is the Messiah," represents God as saying "I will set up a '*captain over fifty*,'" implying that this "*captain*," too, is the Messiah. Then it numbers the books of the Bible, and the divisions of some of the books, and makes out the total to be "*fifty*." Thus "*captain of fifty*," without any change of "*fifty*" to "*fifths*," is made to mean the same thing as "*captain of fifths*" above, that is, "Master of Scripture⁴."

These Jewish variations of interpretation are partly caused by the fact that, in Hebrew, "*fifty*" is the plural of "*five*" and easily confused with "*five*," and partly by the fact that the word, when used as the plural participle of a verb, means "*arranged in battle array*⁵." A notorious instance of such

---

¹ In some of these remarks Jerome resembles Origen (on Numb iv 3, 47, Lomm x 35, 41), but Origen does not there quote Is iii 3 (nor Jn viii 57, perhaps, anywhere).
² "*Fifths*" (Levy ii. 78 *b*) a name given to the five books of the Pentateuch, and the five books of the Psalms
³ *Chag* 14 *a*
⁴ *Numb r* on Numb xvi 35 (Wu p 451)
⁵ See Gesen 332 *b* An explanation suggests itself from "quincunx," e g Caes *Bell Gall* vii 73 "obliquis ordinibus *in quincuncem dispositis*" Gesen, however, does not offer this explanation, but suggests doubtfully (1) "Ar *army*," and (2) "army as composed of *five parts*" (not explaining what the "*five parts*" are). The

CHRIST'S MIRACLES OF FEEDING

confusion occurs in the description of the going forth of Israel from Egypt, "And the children of Israel went up *arranged-in-battle-array* out of the land of Egypt[1]." Here R.V has "*armed*"; A V. "*harnessed*" (i.e. "*in armour*") in text, but "*by five in a rank*" in margin; LXX "*in the fifth generation*"; Aquila "*in armour*"; Symmachus "*hoplites*," i e "*heavy-armed soldiers*"; Theodotion "*on the fifth day*[2]." Besides these variations, there are others in Jewish tradition. Onkelos adopts "*armed*," and the second Jerusalem Targum "*armed with good works.*" But the first Targum has "every one *with five children.*" Rashi, who accepts "*armed*," adds "Others say '*the fifth part*,' because four-fifths died in the darkness of Egypt." There are other interpretations of all kinds, some of which take the word as meaning "*fifty*," or even "*five hundred*[3]"

---

quincunx is so called from its resemblance to the arrangement of the five spots on dice ⁙ The Heb occurs only in Exod xiii 18, Josh i 14, iv 12, Judg vii 11 (but perhaps it should be read also in Numb xxxii 17)

[1] Exod xiii 18

[2] Exod xiii 18, Field agmine instructo, LXX πέμπτῃ γενεᾷ, Aq ἐνωπλισμένοι, Sym ὁπλῖται, Theod πεμπταίζοντες—which Field illustrates from the medical use of τριταιαίζω and τεταρταίζω, to suffer from a "tertian" or a "quartan" fever Does Theod regard the Israelites as being delivered from disease (comp Deut xxviii 60 "the diseases of Egypt")?

Jerome, quoted by Field, defends Aquila's rendering, but says "Licet pro eo quod nos *armati* diximus...*instructi*, sive *muniti*, propter supellectilem qua Ægyptios spoliaverunt, possit intelligi" He seems to see the difficulty of supposing that the Israelites had "armour" before they took it from the Egyptians who were drowned in the Red Sea (as Josephus says *Ant* ii 16 6)

[3] *J. Sabb* vi 4 has "*with five kinds of arms*," *Mechilt* ad loc also has this, but adds (2) "*ready*" or "*alert*," (3) "*one out of five*," (4) "*one out of fifty*," (5) "*one out of five hundred*" Pesikt (Piska x. Wü p 110) gives, as the last of five explanations, "R Jose said that they went forth '*to five generations* (*zu funf Geschlechtern*)'"— apparently including great-great-grandparents with the babes descended from them (not, as LXX, "in the fifth generation [from the Coming of Israel into Egypt]")

CHRIST'S MIRACLES OF FEEDING

It is reasonable to suppose that poetic Jewish Christian traditions describing one of Christ's Eucharists, or Common Meals of Thanksgiving, accompanying the Giving of the Word of God, might lay stress (as Philo repeatedly does in describing the meals of the Therapeutae) on the order and harmonious regularity pervading the assembly[1], and that this might be expressed in language that alluded to the Going Forth of Israel from Egypt to receive the Bread of the Law, as well as to narratives about the actual giving of bread by Elisha, or about the giving of manna. The language of Paul—like the language of Exodus—often takes a military aspect. Mostly he connects it with the single Christian warrior But he appears to be thinking of Christians "in the ranks," when he tells the Colossians that, though he is absent from them, he rejoices to call to view the "[soldier-like] order and solid-formation" that characterize them as believers in Christ[2].

If at one or more of what we may call Christ's camp-meetings He commanded the people to be arranged in groups for the purpose of order, it would be natural that the group should be "fifty" (rather than the Latin military unit of a hundred) This would of course not imply military intention or anything except Jewish custom. But when the story afterwards came to be told in Christian traditions, Greeks would not be able to see any reason for grouping "according to fifty" It might be explained to them that it meant "in military order"—for example, *"according to the pattern of the quincunx"*—and that, as there were five thousand men, and fifty centuries, the division might be indifferently described as into a hundred fifties or fifty centuries. Mark thus inserts both numbers. But to some it might occur that vines also

---

[1] See Philo ii 481 "before the lying down (κατακλίσεως), standing consecutively, [row by row], *in order* (ἑξῆς κατὰ στοῖχον ἐν κόσμῳ)," ib 483 ἐν αἷς ἐδήλωσα τάξεσι ἐν κόσμῳ, ib 484 κατὰ τάξεις ἐν κόσμῳ.

[2] Coloss ii 5 τάξιν καὶ στερέωμα, comp. Philo on τάξεις above quoted

were habitually planted "*according to the quincunx*," and that groups of that kind (*prasiai* or *symposia*) were better suited to the scene of a Christian love-feast than companies of soldiers. Hence might spring the other details in Mark's version. To Matthew all these detailed illustrations, especially those based on the military meaning of "fifty," would naturally seem doubtful in view of the presence of "women and children" whom he (alone of the Evangelists) adds to the five thousand[1]. Luke follows Mark as to the traditional "*fifty*," but appears to regard all the rest of Mark's context as superfluous.

Since Luke does not reject the Marcan "*fifty*" and can hardly be said to reject the Marcan "hundred"—because he virtually implies it by his context—there is no ground for expecting, as to these numerical details, any Johannine Intervention. But it has been pointed out above that John does appear to intervene as to the Marcan *symposia*, so as to emphasize an interpretation of these "companies" alien from military thought. Consistently with this non-military aspect, John also rejects the Mark-Luke numbers of the "companies." We cannot say that he does it for Matthew's reason—because "women and children" are to be added. For John does not mention them. Perhaps he does it because this division of the five thousand into small companies of men—as a Roman army might be divided into centuries under centurions, or a Jewish army into fifties under "captains of fifty"—introduces a kind of intermediate agency between each of the five thousand and the One Lord This intermediation John ignores. In his Gospel, Jesus alone distributes the bread to each—as we shall see later on—not through the instrumentality of His disciples, but with His own hands.

---

[1] Mt xiv 21, also xv. 38

CHRIST'S MIRACLES OF FEEDING

§ 26. *"Taking," "blessing," and "looking up to heaven*[1]*"*

(1) "Taking" occurs in all the six narratives, with the same Greek verb, and mostly as a participle[2]. Its meaning will depend on the place or person whence the loaves are "taken." If they are on the spot, "taking" would appear to mean a solemn and emblematic taking up in the hands, such as might denote a "taking up," or "offering," to God, or an appropriation of the food to God, as though the breaker of bread said to God in the name of the company "We bless thee for *this*, which we lift up[3]."

---

[1]
Mk vi 41 (R V)	Mt xiv 19 (R V)	Lk ix 16 (R V)	Jn vi 11 (R V)
And he took (λαβὼν) the five loaves and the two fishes, and looking up to heaven, he blessed, and brake the loaves, and he gave to the disciples to set before them, and the two fishes divided he among them all	. And he took (λαβὼν) the five loaves, and the two fishes, and looking up to heaven, he blessed, and brake and gave the loaves to the disciples, and the disciples to the multitudes	And he took (λαβὼν) the five loaves and the two fishes, and looking up to heaven, he blessed them, and brake, and gave to the disciples to set before the multitude	Jesus therefore took the loaves, and having given thanks, he distributed to them that were set down ; likewise also of the fishes as much as they would

"Brake" in Mk vi 41, Lk ix 16 is κατέκλασεν, see p 321 foll.
In the Four Thousand, as in the Johannine Five Thousand, "give thanks (εὐχαριστεῖν)" is substituted for "bless (εὐλογεῖν)"

Mk viii 6—7 (R.V)
(6) ...And he took (λαβὼν) the seven loaves, and having given thanks, he brake, and gave to his disciples, to set before them, and they set them before the multitude.
(7) And they had a few small fishes and having blessed them, he commanded to set these also before them.

Mt xv 36 (R V)
And he took the seven loaves and the fishes, and he gave thanks and brake, and gave to the disciples, and the disciples to the multitudes

[2] John in the Five Thousand, and Matthew in the Four Thousand, have ἔλαβεν, not λαβών

[3] Schottgen on Mt xiv. 19 says "*Sumptio* ista, quae hic et alibi memoratur, actus est peculiaris patris familias," and quotes *Sabb* 117 *b* נקט (Goldschmidt "hielt") But Schlatter on Jn vi 11

The first Biblical instance of "take," in connection with sacrifice, is where God says to Abraham "*Take for me* a heifer," and other creatures, and it is added that Abraham "*took for him* all these...[1]." Philo comments on the pregnancy of "*Take for me*," which implies, he says, first, that we have nothing good of our own except that which we "*take*" from God; secondly, that we are to "*take*" it *for Him*, as being the loan or deposit that He has placed with us, for which we must give account[2]. He also comments on the paradox implied in human "giving," since, "strictly speaking, we merely *take* (or, *receive*) but are only popularly said to give[3]."

In doctrine of this kind there is sometimes difficulty in passing from a Greek translation back to a Hebrew original because the same Hebrew word, as a rule, represents both "take" and "receive[4]." But we find Paul, as well as Philo,

---

quotes *Siphri* נטל on Numb. vii 6 "Mose nimmt sie (נוטלם)." *Hor Heb* (on Mt xxvi 26) quotes, from the Passover Service, "He *takes up* the unleavened bread in his hand, and saith, 'We eat this unleavened bread ..'. .then.. *taking* two loaves, he breaks one," and (p 352, from *Berach* 51 a) "he *takes up* (נוטלו) the cup in both hands, but puts it into his right hand, he *lifts it* from the table a hand's breadth and .fixes his eyes upon it, etc."

Λαβών, or ἔλαβεν, also occurs in the Synoptic and Pauline accounts of the Lord's Supper Lk xxii 17 δεξάμενος ποτήριον εὐχαριστήσας εἶπεν is exceptional Λαμβάνει occurs in Jn xxi 13 "Jesus cometh and *taketh* the loaf and giveth to them...."

[1] Gen xv 9—10. Λάβε μοι (A V. and R V. "take me")....ἔλαβεν δὲ αὐτῷ (A V "took unto him," R.V. "took him") Onkelos has "offer *coram me*," Jer. Targ. "accipe *mihi* oblationes et offer *coram me*"

[2] Philo 1. 487 λάβε, μὴ σεαυτῷ, δανεῖον δὲ ἢ παρακαταθήκην νομίσας τὸ δοθέν

[3] Philo 1 490 κυρίως μὲν λαμβάνομεν, καταχρηστικῶς δὲ διδόναι λεγόμεθα. In *Quaest ad Genes* it is said, ad loc "Pro illo *Ferto mihi*, optime dictum est *Accipe mihi*."

[4] Heb לקח = λαμβάνω more than 800 times, δέχομαι 26 times. The total number of instances of δέχομαι in *Oxf Conc* correctly representing a Heb original is only 42 The LXX throws too great a burden on λαμβάνω and too little on δέχομαι. Luke alone

inculcating that we have nothing that we did not "*take*," that is, "*receive*," and, in the Acts, reminding the Ephesians of "the words of the Lord Jesus, how he said that it was more blessed to give than to *take*[1]" The testimony of these two early writers, when combined with the use of the Greek "*take*" in the Pentateuch and in the Synoptic and Pauline accounts of the Eucharist, makes it probable that "take" has a ritual meaning also in the Gospel miracles of feeding, and that the Evangelists regarded its meaning there as akin to its meaning later on in the Last Supper

Passing to the Fourth Gospel we find that the "taking" is the one point—out of the three mentioned at the beginning of this section—in which it verbally agrees with the Synoptists. But, by introducing "a lad" on the spot as "having" the loaves and fishes, it introduces a possible difference as to the nature of the "taking"—leaving us in doubt whether Jesus receives them as an offering from the "lad," or takes them from the "lad" as the property of the disciples. There is an indefiniteness here like that in the Feeding of the Seven Disciples who "when they got out upon the land, see a fire of coals there and a fish laid thereon and a loaf[2]." The "loaf" that they "see" reminds us of what Elijah "looked" at when he "looked, and behold, there was at his head a cake baken on the coals." Elijah is bidden by "an angel" to "arise and eat[3]." In the Feeding of the Seven, no "angel" is mentioned, but a supernatural origin of the food is clearly indicated; and then the "taking" of it

---

uses δέχομαι in Eucharistic narrative (xxii 17) δεξάμενος ποτήριον (Mk-Mt λαβών). Delitzsch renders it by the same word (לקח) as he uses to represent the Eucharistic λαμβάνω

[1] 1 Cor iv 7, Acts xx 35
[2] Jn xxi 9
[3] 1 K. xix 5 (Heb) "Behold an angel (LXX 'some one (τις)')' touched him, and said unto him, Arise and eat" This Hebrew word "coals" occurs only in 1 K xix 6 and Is. vi 6 of Isaiah's preparation for the work of prophecy (Gesen. 954 *a*).

by Jesus is described thus: "Jesus *cometh* and *taketh* the loaf and giveth to them—and the fish likewise[1]."

It has been shewn (p. 290) that the "lad" might well correspond to Moses. Now the Prologue of the Fourth Gospel, after saying that the Word, or Only Begotten, was full of grace and truth, and that "from his *fulness* we all received," explains the reception thus: "For the Law was given through Moses; the grace and the truth" [of God, whether latent and included in the Law of Israel, or latent and included in the laws of conscience and human nature] "came into being through Jesus Christ[2]." If the Law, illustrated by the Psalms and the Prophets, corresponds to the five loaves and the fishes, and "Moses" to "the lad," then the "fulness" that brings forth "the grace and the truth" is expressed by that multiplying power of the Saviour which results in food for five thousand souls with a superabundance of "the fulnesses of twelve baskets."

(2) "Blessing" is not used by John, who substitutes "giving thanks," expressed by the Greek *eucharistein*, familiar to us in "Eucharist." One reason for this is indicated by the variations in the versions of Mark and Luke where "blessed *them*" is altered to "blesses *over them*[3]." Jews regarded food as God's gift, *over* which, or *for* which, men were bound to bless the Giver; but they did not bless the food[4]. On the other

---

[1] Jn xxi 13 ἔρχεται Ἰησοῦς καὶ λαμβάνει τὸν ἄρτον καὶ δίδωσιν αὐτοῖς The impression left on the reader is that Jesus "comes" to each disciple separately, and "takes" and "gives" the loaf to each separately, and that there is no "breaking." The whole loaf is perhaps regarded as given to each, being miraculously reproduced *Acts of John* § 8 uses "distributed" or "divided" of a single loaf, thus, τὸν δὲ αὐτοῦ [ἄρτον] εὐλογῶν διεμέριζεν ἡμῖν

[2] Jn 1 14—17, on which see *Joh Gr* Index

[3] In Mk viii 7 εὐλογήσας αὐτὰ εἶπεν καὶ ταῦτα παρατιθέναι, Delitzsch omits "*them*," SS has "and *upon them* also *having blessed*," D has εὐχαριστήσας εἶπεν καὶ αὐτοὺς ἐκέλευσεν παρατεθέναι (sic)   In Lk ix 16 εὐλόγησεν αὐτούς, Delitzsch, D, *a*, and *b* have "*blessed upon them*," and SS has "*blessed upon them* (or, *upon it*)."

[4] Gesen. 139 gives only 1 S. ix. 13 as instance of a priest "blessing"

CHRIST'S MIRACLES OF FEEDING

hand, when God Himself is said for the first time in Scripture to "bless," He blesses the fishes and the birds and bids them "multiply." Also when He blesses "bread," or "fruit," or other articles of food, it signifies that He gives increase as well as wholesomeness[1]. Hence in Christ's Feeding of the Multitudes, where loaves and fishes were assumed to be multiplied, it is readily intelligible that some Evangelists would regard the word "blessing" as being used in a special and divine sense, so that it implied multiplying, while others would regard it as meaning the usual "blessing" before a meal in the ordinary way.

One way of avoiding ambiguity would be to substitute "give thanks" for "bless." In the Feeding of the Four Thousand Matthew does this, while Mark has, first, "*gave thanks* and brake" about the loaves, and secondly, "*blessed them* [i e *the fishes*]." It is not surprising that John almost entirely avoids the word "bless," as being a technical Jewish term[2]. Origen says that "when men '*bless*' God it stands for '*praising*' or '*thanking*' God[3]." In Leviticus and elsewhere, where LXX has "*praise*," Aquila has *eucharistia*, or "*thanksgiving*[4]." The latter includes a sense of gratefulness and

---

a sacrificial meal, and here Rashi says that the Targum has "*over* the food" But Breithaupt points out that in the extant text of the Targum, "*over*" is omitted See Levy *Ch* 11 293, taking פרם as "spread out [the hands]," but Breithaupt takes it as "break"

[1] Gen 1 22, Exod xxiii 25, Deut vii 13

[2] John uses no form of εὐλογέω except in xii 13 εὐλογημένος—the cry of the multitude, perhaps regarded as the fickle multitude Philo (1. 453), quoting Gen xii 2 (on which see Rashi), says that εὐλογημένος "is reckoned along with (παραριθμεῖται) *the* [*vain*] *opinions and reports of the multitude* (ταῖς τῶν πολλῶν δόξαις τε καὶ φήμαις)," but that εὐλογητός is reckoned "along with *that which is in truth praiseworthy* (τῷ πρὸς ἀλήθειαν εὐλογητῷ)"

[3] Origen (Lat) *Comm Rom* ix 14 (on Rom xii 14).

[4] Lev vii 12 "If he offer it for (עַל) a *thanksgiving* (תודה)," περὶ αἰνέσεως, Aq ἐπὶ εὐχαριστίας. Εὐχαριστία recurs several times in Aquila, especially in the Psalms. But neither Aquila nor canon. LXX uses εὐχαριστέω.

319 (Mark vi 29—44)

CHRIST'S MIRACLES OF FEEDING

spontaneousness, not so manifest in "praise", and the latter, *eucharistein*, is the term adopted by John in the Feeding of the Five Thousand as a substitute for the Synoptic "bless[1]"

(3) "Looking up to heaven" is expressed in the Synoptists by a word that often means *"recovering sight*[2]." John substitutes "lifting up his eyes[3]"; but places it, not where the Synoptists do, before the breaking and distribution, but at the outset of the narrative, where Jesus "seeth that a great multitude is coming to him," that is, sees the vision of the coming of the spiritual seed of Abraham which was to constitute the Church. The action, both here and in the two other Johannine instances of it, seems to imply a looking up to heaven, not so much to bring down a blessing as rather to behold, and to exult in, and to fulfil, the glory of God. At the grave of Lazarus, when Jesus "lifted his eyes above," He utters, not prayer but thanks, "Father, I give thanks to thee

---

[1] *"Bless"* might be substituted for *"give thanks"* in translating from Hebrew. The Heb. ידה, *"acknowledge [God's greatness, glory, kindness,* etc]" is rendered εὐλογέω in Isaiah xii 1 (LXX) εὐλογῶ σε, κύριε, xxxviii. 19 οἱ ζῶντες εὐλογήσουσίν σε (and in effect a third instance occurs in Is xxv 3 εὐλογήσουσίν σε (ירא mistaken for ידה)). The Heb ידה is given by Delitzsch in Mt xi 25, Lk x 21 ἐξομολογοῦμαί σοι, πάτερ, R V "I thank (marg or, *praise*) thee, O Father," where John would probably have written, as in the words uttered at the grave of Lazarus, (xi 41) εὐχαριστῶ σοι. In wrestling with death for the sake of Lazarus there was an act of sacrifice which some would have called the subject of prayer rather than of a thankoffering. But Jesus "thanks" God for the power to perform it. In the Johannine Feeding of the Five Thousand, Jesus is regarded not merely as breaking bread and blessing God over it as at a meal, but also as offering up a thankoffering to the Father for giving power to the Son to offer Himself to, and for, the multitude. They do not accept Him, nevertheless Jesus, looking into the future, might see cause for *eucharistia* as in Mt -Lk referred to above, "I thank thee, O Father .. that thou didst hide these things from the wise and understanding and didst reveal them unto babes."

[2] Ἀναβλέπω, used in no other sense by John (ix 11, 15, 18, comp Mk viii 24, x 51, etc)

[3] Jn vi 5 ἐπάρας οὖν τοὺς ὀφθαλμοὺς...

CHRIST'S MIRACLES OF FEEDING

that thou hast heard me[1]." Before the Last Discourse, though there is prayer, there is also a vision of "the hour" of glory: "Lifting up his eyes to heaven he said, Father, the hour is come. Glorify thy Son that the Son may glorify thee[2]."

§ 27. *"Breaking in pieces" or "breaking"*

We now approach a subject of unusual difficulty and complexity—complicated partly by verbal ambiguities, partly by early Christian custom arising out of Jewish custom, and partly by Christian doctrinal considerations and applications of Hebrew prophecy—the "breaking" of bread in the miracles of Feeding.

In the Feeding of the Five Thousand (but not in that of the Four Thousand) Mark emphasizes this act by using a compound verb that means literally "break down," "snap off," or (metaphorically) "break down in spirit[3]." But it is apparently used by him to mean "break in pieces." It occurs but once in LXX and is non-existent in Christian writers of the first century and a half. Yet Luke follows Mark in using it here, though it occurs nowhere else in N T., and though the uncompounded verb is quite frequent (as also is the noun) to denote Christian "breaking of bread." Mark may have desired to shew that this was *not* an ordinary "breaking of bread," but that Jesus broke a loaf into minute parts each one of which was magnified Luke may have followed Mark for the same reason.

At all events Luke does follow Mark, and this is one of

---

[1] Jn xi 41   [2] Jn xvii 1.
[3] Mk vi 41, Lk ix 16 κατέκλασεν   The word is not in Goodspeed's Concordances   In LXX, it occurs only in Ezek xix 12 (Heb) "she was *plucked up* in fury," κατεκλάσθη ἐν θυμῷ   It occurs also in Job v 4 (Symm) Heb *"they are crushed* in the gate " Steph *Thes* does not give any instance where the word must necessarily be interpreted "break in pieces," but a great number where it has a different meaning.

several cases where, when Luke agrees with Mark, John appears to disagree, or at all events tacitly dissents. For John omits all mention of any kind of "breaking." By this course he avoids such a question as "Were the fishes broken as well as the loaves?" Mark implies that they were not. For he (and he alone) specially inserts "*the loaves*" after the mention of "*breaking*," and then he (alone) adds "he divided the two fishes to all," apparently implying that, although they were "divided" in the sense of "distributed," the fishes were *not* "broken[1]."

It may be suggested that John had also another reason, based on the axiom that the Bread, or the Fish, is to be regarded as One and as diffusing unity among those who partake of it. In accordance with this thought, he (and he alone of the Evangelists) quotes, as a prophecy about the Crucifixion, the precept concerning the Paschal Lamb, "A bone of him shall not be broken[2]." Later on, in the presence of the Seven Disciples, Jesus "cometh, and taketh the loaf and giveth to them, and the fish likewise"; but no mention is made of "*breaking*[3]." The hypothesis that John was influenced by a mystical view of the unity of the Eucharistic food is confirmed by what Philo says concerning the dividing, and the reuniting, of the parts of the whole burnt offering which "from one, becomes many, and from many becomes one[4]." It is also favoured by the fact that John

---

[1] See the next section, where it will appear that Matthew obscures this difference, and Luke omits it altogether. The distinction is also clear in Mk viii. 6—7 καὶ λαβὼν τοὺς ἑπτὰ ἄρτους εὐχαριστήσας ἔκλασεν...καὶ εἶχαν ἰχθύδια ὀλίγα· καὶ εὐλογήσας αὐτὰ (without any mention of breaking in the case of the fishes)....

[2] Jn xix 36, quoting Exod xii. 46, Numb. ix 12 (συντρίβω)

[3] Jn xxi. 13 Contrast with this Lk xxiv 30—35 "Having taken the loaf he blessed [God] (εὐλόγησεν) and having broken [it] he offered [freely] (ἐπεδίδου) to them...how he was known by them in the breaking (τῇ κλάσει) of the loaf"

[4] Philo ii. 241. This is preceded (*ib* 240), and followed, by

CHRIST'S MIRACLES OF FEEDING

(alone) tells us that in the parting of Christ's garments by the soldiers, His "coat"—a type of the Church—escaped "rending," and that in the miraculous draught of fishes, the "net"—another type of the Church—"was not rent[1]."

That John would have been influenced by motives of this kind is very probable. But it is not probable (according to our experience of his Gospel hitherto) that he would have omitted this ancient tradition of "breaking" if he had not believed it to be either erroneous or, at all events, likely to give a wrong spiritual impression. There are reasons for thinking that confusion arose in early times from various interpretations of Isaiah's precept rendered by our Versions "*Deal* (Heb *pâras*) thy bread to the hungry[2]." *Pâras* is nowhere rendered "deal" except in this passage. It means "*break in half*," and here, "*break in half* thy loaf for the hungry[3]." Ibn Ezra takes it thus. But the Talmud records a tradition that the word ought to be written as *pâras(h)*[4]. Then it might mean "separate"

---

mentions of εὐχαριστία, e g 1b 243 ὅταν βουληθῇς σῇ διανοίᾳ εὐχαριστῆσαι θεῷ περὶ γενέσεως κόσμου τὴν εὐχαριστίαν ...

[1] Jn xix 24. xxi 11 using σχίζω in both cases. Luke in his narrative of the Draught of Fishes says (v 6) "the nets began to be torn asunder (διερήσσετο)"

[2] Is lviii 7 פרס (but Targ פרנס "*sustentabis* pane tuo") Ibn Ezra says "it means here to break a loaf of bread" (and he compares Lam iv 4 "no man *breaketh* (פרש not פרס) to them"). Jerome *ad loc* says "frange . non plures panes sed unum panem." "*Deal*" means "distribute"—but does not give the full Hebrew sense.

Modern emendations and modern suggestions as to what the text of Isaiah originally was, however interesting and valuable they may be, do not concern us when we are endeavouring to approximate to Jewish interpretations of the passage in the first century.

[3] Gesen 828 *a* "break in two," "divide" (of the divided hoof) (Lev xi 3 etc.). On Jerem xvi 7 "neither shall men *break* [bread] for them (להם)," Gesen suggests לחם "bread," instead of להם.

[4] *Baba Bathra* 9 *a*, Goldschmidt renders this "forsche nach und dann gib ihm." He adds in a note that many MSS have פרש, but that the Masora on Numb iv 7 expressly says that פרס is the right reading. Gesen. 831 gives פרש = "spread out, spread," but פרש

CHRIST'S MIRACLES OF FEEDING

or "spread out". In this form it might be applied to the "spreading out" of the hands in blessing, or to the "separation" of Scripture into sections, or to its "explanation" in plain words, or to any technical "separation" in Jewish ritual[1].

The Hebrew *pâras* (used by Delitzsch in Christ's Miracles of Feeding) is particularly appropriate to meals given willingly

---

"make distinct, declare, New Heb separate oneself, separate, explain"

[1] The authorities, and even the texts, so differ as to the terms פרס, פרש, and פרש that it is impossible here to do more than refer to what is said about them by Levy, Levy *Ch sub voc*, by *Hor Heb* on κλάσας in the Gospels, and by Schottgen (in the Gospels and on 2 Tim ii 15) Wetstein says practically nothing The Targumists avoid פרס in Is lviii 7, and פרש in Lam iv 4, but they retain פרס in Jerem xvi 7 "Neither shall men *break* [*bread*] for them in mourning," A.V. "*tear* [*themselves*] for them in mourning"

On this last passage Rashi has a note obscure, but most instructive, indicating the possibility of confusing פרס in Heb "breaking a loaf in half" with some technical use of פרס in Aramaic, perhaps "spreading out the hands," referring to a benediction He says that *pâras*, in Jeremiah, "significat fractionem" as in Dan v 25, 28 "*u-pharsin*," i e "*and divided*" (*pharsin* being a form of *pâras*) Then he adds "For with food did they refresh the mourners in the street, and they did *spread out for them that Benediction* [which is called] 'He that bringeth forth' (eisque explicabant benedictionem illam, המוציא)" This refers to the words of the Benediction pronounced by the father of the family, or the principal Rabbi, over the breaking of bread at a meal "Blessed art thou, O Lord our God, Lord of the world, '*Thou that bringest forth* [*food from the earth*]'"

Rashi proceeds, "Jonathan istud 'nam ipse יברך,' id est, 'benedicet convivio,' Chaldaice vertit 'nam ipse פריס,' id est, 'frangit cibum'" This mention of "Jonathan" refers to the Targum of "Jonathan" on 1 S ix 13 "he [i e Samuel] *doth bless* (יברך) the sacrifice," where the Targum has (lit) "*doth break* (פריס) the food," which Rashi renders freely "benedicit super cibum, id est, benedictionem facit super cibo" "Bless [God] *over* (or break [? bread] *over*) the sacrifice," would be more regular, but Breithaupt rejects the insertion of "over" as erroneous These passages establish the conclusion that the Hebrew "*bless*," in connection with food, might be expressed in Aramaic by a word that in Hebrew means "*break*."

out of a small store to the hungry. There is another word mostly used in New Hebrew for the literal breaking of bread; but that, in the Bible, has a bad sense[1]. The Talmud uses *pâras* to remind a master of a house that, at a meal in his house, he must not "pronounce the benediction" (*lit* "divide the dividing") for "travellers," his guests, unless he eats with them, but he may do it for his family in order to accustom them to the fulfilment of the precept[2]. Another passage— but one of doubtful meaning—uses the word *pâras* concerning a distribution of fishes to the citizens of Jerusalem[3].

There is no clear indication in the Gospels that the "breaking (*pâras*)" of bread by Jesus was connected with the thought of the "explanation (*pârash*)" of the Law[4]. It is true that the Lucan narrative of the manifestation of Jesus "in the *breaking of the bread*," at Emmaus, at all events prepares the way for that manifestation by a mention of His "*interpretation*" of the sayings in the Scriptures concerning the Messiah, which is

---

[1] See Levy i 251 b on בצע which, as a Heb verb, means (Gesen 130) "cut off, break off, *gain by violence*," and, as a noun, "*gain made by violence*." That is the word used by Delitzsch about breaking bread in the narratives of the Eucharist, though he uses פרס in the miracles of feeding. See p 327, n 1

[2] See Levy *Ch* ii 294 a quoting *R haschana* 29 b, and adding, as a common phrase, "the time needed to eat a פרס, i e *half [of a loaf]*"

[3] *Sanhedr* 49 a, on I Chr xi 8, Joab "merely tasted" them and then "*distributed* (פרים) to them." This suggests that, in the Feeding of the Five Thousand, "*breaking*," which John omits, might have been regarded by him as an error for "*distributing*," which he inserts. The food is called by Goldschmidt "Fischtunke (*sic*) (מוניני) und kleine Fische (צחנתא)." But the latter (Gesen. 850 a, and Levy *Ch* ii 320 a) would seem to mean stinking fish. Hence the interpretation is doubtful. "Joab" is the distributer, and there may be irony in the description of him as attempting to feed Jerusalem with "fishes" not only "stinking," but also broken in pieces.

[4] Onkelos uses פרש in Deut i 5 (R V.) "Moses began to *declare* this law," where Heb באר (Gesen 91) = "make plain," "explain."

CHRIST'S MIRACLES OF FEEDING

subsequently called His "*opening* of the Scriptures," and the result is that "their eyes were opened and they knew him[1]." But such a scriptural "opening" is connected with a word that means the opening of a door, rather than the opening or spreading out of the hand. It is frequently called "opening [with] an opening," and in that form occurs repeatedly in the Talmud where a Rabbi "*opens*" his discussion of some passage of Scripture by quoting another[2]. Nevertheless Luke helps us to perceive a very real sense in which it may be maintained that beneath the narratives of miraculous feeding, and of Christ's meals with disciples before and after the Resurrection, there was originally and historically (whether we easily perceive it or not) a connection between the "breaking" of the bread of the Law, and the "opening," or "spreading out," of

---

[1] Lk xxiv 27 διερμήνευσεν, comp *ib.* 32 διήνοιγεν ἡμῖν τὰς γραφάς. In LXX, פרשׂ = ἀνοίγω in Is xxxvii 14, describing a literal "spreading out" of a letter before the Lord, and = διανοίγω in Prov xxxi. 20 "she *spreadeth out* (A V. stretcheth out) her hand (*lit.* palm) to the poor." The contextual repetition of διανοίγω in Lk xxiv 31 διηνοίχθησαν οἱ ὀφθαλμοί suggests a kind of play on the thought of "*opening*." It is repeated again, after Jesus has partaken of the broiled fish, in Lk xxiv 45 "then he *opened* (διήνοιξεν) their mind." Διανοίγω occurs elsewhere in N T only in Mk vii 34 "Be thou *opened*," Lk ii 23 (quoting Exod xiii 2 "that *openeth* the womb"), Acts vii 56 "the heavens *opened*," xvi 14 "whose heart the Lord *opened*," xvii 3 "reasoned with them from the scriptures, *opening* and alleging that it behoved the Christ to suffer."

[2] Comp *Megill* 10 *b* "R Jonathan *opened the opening* (פתח לה פתחא) for this section (פרשׂתא, from פרשׂ, *separate*) from the following [text]"—a phrase repeated about a dozen times in 10 *b*—11. Delitzsch uses פתח in Lk xxiv 32 and Acts xvii 3 "Paul. .reasoned with them from the scriptures, *opening* and alleging that it behoved the Christ to suffer, and to rise again from the dead... " *Hor Heb*, Wetstein, and Schottgen are silent as to any Hebrew authority for this use of "opening," and no satisfactory Greek authority is alleged. It might mean "opening" the discussion of, for example, the "section" in Isaiah about the Suffering Servant by quoting such passages as Hos vi 2 "After two days he will revive us."

the meaning of the Law, and the "opening" of the minds of the disciples to that meaning, and, at the same time, the "opening" of their hearts to the divine character of their Master and Saviour, the Bread of Life. We may illustrate this connection from a Talmudic passage that speaks of the material "breaking" of bread (*bâtsa* as distinguished from Isaiah's *pâras*) and defines its spiritual object· "The Master of the House *breaks [the bread]* that he may *break it with a good eye*[1]"

Now it was one of Christ's fundamental doctrines that the "*eye*" of His disciples must not be "*evil*," but must be "*single*," *i.e.* straightforwardly and lovingly fixed on God, and on Man regarded as in God, being made in God's image. It was to be an "eye" of kindness and goodness, recognising as the two great commandments of the Law, the love of God and the love of the neighbour. These two precepts, taken up and expressed in the Psalms and the Prophets, might be regarded as the relish, or flavour, of the Law, which, without them, was what we should call "dry bread." In the Sermon on the Mount Jesus might be described as taking and breaking the dry bread of the five loaves of the Law, and flavouring it, so to speak, with the *opson* of these two fishes, and distributing it to the multitudes[2].

It would be a fanciful but brief and not inaccurate summary of many of the charges brought by Jesus against the formalists who in His days constituted the majority of

---

[1] *Berach* 46 *a*, a tradition of R. Jochanan in the name of Simeon ben Jochai

[2] Some "breaking," or "spreading out," or "interpretation," of the Law in this sense would be included in Mark's (vi 34) statement that Jesus "taught" the Five Thousand "many things" before feeding them with the five loaves and the two fishes. Not much importance can be attached to the traditions in *Sabb* 116 *a* and *Gen r* (on Gen xxvi 17, Wu p 307) where it is said by Samuel Bar Nachman and by Ben Kaphra that there are seven books of the Law (see contexts).

the Pharisees, to take as our text Isaiah's ancient word, in its ancient Hebrew meaning, and to say that they modernised it by their Jewish traditions. They thought of it as inculcating the religious duty of *"spreading out"* the hands in prayer to God in heaven, but Jesus thought of it as inculcating the duty—moral and spiritual rather than religious—of *"breaking one's loaf in half,"* even our single loaf, in order to give it to the spiritually, as well as the materially, "hungry."

Returning to the Fourth Gospel we may say that a great deal of evidence converges to the conclusion that John's omission of the "breaking" was due in part to various and perplexing inferences as to the nature and results of the act, though in part also to a Johannine motive, namely, the desire to avoid everything that could give rise to the notion that Christ was so "divided" as not to be always One[1].

§ 28. *"And the two fishes he divided among [them] all," in Mark*[2]

Mark, in both his narratives, makes a distinction, not made by Matthew or Luke, between the loaves and the fishes.

---

[1] Comp 1 Cor 1 13 "Is Christ divided (μεμέρισται)?"

[2] In the accounts of the Distribution, Mark (four times) and Luke use παρατίθημι of the food "set before" the multitude Matthew never uses it except previously about (xiii 24, 31) *"parables"* which Jesus *"set before"* the disciples John here uses ὀψάριον instead of ἰχθύς for "fish"

The R.V. does not express all the shades of difference which will be found in the Greek text printed below

(The Five Thousand)

Mk vi 41	Mt xiv 19	Lk. ix 16	Jn vi 11
καὶ λαβὼν τοὺς πέντε ἄρτους καὶ τοὺς δύο ἰχθύας ἀναβλέψας εἰς τὸν οὐρανὸν εὐλόγησεν καὶ κατέκλασεν τοὺς ἄρτους καὶ ἐδίδου τοῖς μαθηταῖς ἵνα παρατιθῶσιν αὐτοῖς, καὶ τοὺς δύο ἰχθύας ἐμέρισεν πᾶσιν.	καὶ λαβὼν τοὺς πέντε ἄρτους καὶ τοὺς δύο ἰχθύας, ἀναβλέψας εἰς τὸν οὐρανὸν εὐλόγησεν καὶ κλάσας ἔδωκεν τοῖς μαθηταῖς τοὺς ἄρτους οἱ δὲ μαθηταὶ τοῖς ὄχλοις	λαβὼν δὲ τοὺς πέντε ἄρτους καὶ τοὺς δύο ἰχθύας ἀναβλέψας εἰς τὸν οὐρανὸν εὐλόγησεν αὐτοὺς καὶ κατέκλασεν καὶ ἐδίδου τοῖς μαθηταῖς παραθεῖναι τῷ ὄχλῳ	ἔλαβεν οὖν τοὺς ἄρτους ὁ Ἰησοῦς καὶ εὐχαριστήσας διέδωκεν τοῖς ἀνακειμένοις ὁμοίως καὶ ἐκ τῶν ὀψαρίων ὅσον ἤθελον

CHRIST'S MIRACLES OF FEEDING

In the Five Thousand, he says that Jesus (not the disciples) "divided" the fishes. In the Four Thousand, he seems to introduce the fishes as a kind of after-thought or addition ("that they were to set *these, too,* before [the multitude]").

Moreover Mark distinguishes between "setting-before" and "dividing." "Set-before" he uses four times, and always of the action of the disciples. Jesus Himself is described by Mark as (1) "giving" to the disciples, and as (2) ordering the disciples to "set before" the people. These clauses contain no difficulty. But there is difficulty in "he divided the two fishes to all." Perhaps we may explain it from the precedent of David, who

(The Four Thousand)

Mk viii 6—7	Mt xv. 36
καὶ λαβὼν τοὺς ἑπτὰ ἄρτους εὐχαριστήσας ἔκλασεν καὶ ἐδίδου τοῖς μαθηταῖς αὐτοῦ ἵνα παρατιθῶσιν καὶ παρέθηκαν τῷ ὄχλῳ καὶ εἶχαν ἰχθύδια ὀλίγα καὶ εὐλογήσας αὐτὰ εἶπεν καὶ ταῦτα παρατιθέναι	ἔλαβεν τοὺς ἑπτὰ ἄρτους καὶ τοὺς ἰχθύας καὶ εὐχαριστήσας ἔκλασεν καὶ ἐδίδου τοῖς μαθηταῖς οἱ δὲ μαθηταὶ τοῖς ὄχλοις.

In Mk vi 41, SS and Walton Syr have "*they divided*" (for "*he divided*"), and in Mk viii 7, codex ℵ has *prima manu* παρέθηκεν, corrected into εἶπεν καὶ ταῦτα παρατιθέναι. These variations do not appear in Swete (ed 1898).

The Diatessaron, in the Four Thousand, omits the whole of Mk viii 7 "*and they had* a few little fishes, *and having blessed them he said [to them] that they should set these also before [the multitude]*"—except "a few little fishes," which it places earlier (as Matthew does) Thus it omits one of the Marcan mentions of παρατίθημι. On the other hand, in the Five Thousand, it mentions παρατίθημι twice (where Mark has it only once) thus "Then Jesus said unto them, 'Bring hither those five loaves and the two fishes' And when they brought him that, Jesus took the bread and the fish, and looked to heaven, and blessed and divided"—substituting "dividing" for "breaking-in-pieces" (κατέκλασεν) or "breaking" (κλάσας)—"and gave to the disciples to *set before them*, and the disciples *set for the multitudes* the bread and the fish" This last clause ("set   fish") appears to come from Mk viii 6 *b* "and they set [them] before the multitude," and to be a substitute for Mk vi 41 *b* "and the two fishes he divided unto all"

CHRIST'S MIRACLES OF FEEDING

"*divided* to every man of Israel" food specified in the context[1]. It is not meant that David himself "set the food before" Israel, but that he specified the portion to be "divided" to each and caused it to be set before each. In Mark, the meaning may be that, whereas the loaves were broken and set before the people, "*the two fishes*" were *not* "broken," but "*divided to all,*" that is, "*distributed to all, the two fishes being given to each person.*" This miraculous reproduction of the two fishes for each person Mark may intend to describe as a separate act of Jesus.

In the Four Thousand, the fishes are called "little" and "few"—terms that might easily be interchanged[2]. Also the number "two" is dropped, so that any suggestion of "two for each person" is avoided, and we may suppose them to have been multiplied not in pairs but indefinitely by Jesus who commanded that the disciples should set an indefinite number of them before the people. This hypothesis would help us to see why Mark here calls them "little-fishes"—a word not elsewhere used in N.T. or LXX. It might also explain John's peculiar addition "and of the fishes *as much as they desired*"—that is, they were not restricted to "*the two*[3]."

But there is another way of explaining this Greek diminutive, as well as the use of "two." We find corresponding peculiarities in the LXX where the widow in Zarephath says to Elijah "I have...but an handful of meal...and, behold, I am gathering *two sticks*...that I may...dress it and die[4]" "*Two*

---

[1] 2 S vi 19 καὶ διεμέρισεν παντὶ τῷ λαῷ εἰς πᾶσαν τὴν δύναμιν τοῦ Ἰσραὴλ..., 1 Chr. xvi. 3 καὶ διεμέρισεν παντὶ ἀνδρὶ Ἰσραὴλ ...

[2] In Mt xv 34, SS and Curet. have different words for "few" (Burk "a few fishes," Walton "aliquot pisces minutos"), and in Mk viii 7, Burk. and Walton have "a few fishes "

[3] Some reasons for John's preference of ὀψάριον to ἰχθύς here are given in *Proclam* p 86 Also, if John had used ἰχθύς, he would have seemed to prefer it to ἰχθύδιον As it is, he puts both the Synoptic terms aside, introducing one of his own

[4] 1 K xvii 12 "two (שְׁנַיִם) sticks (עֵצִים)," δύο ξυλάρια. This is

is here uniquely used in O T. for "*a very few*[1]." The Greek translators, feeling in a confused way that scantiness—not small number—is implied by "*two*," and yet not liking to suppress the literal meaning, compromise by rendering the Hebrew "*sticks*" into a Greek diminutive ("two little-sticks") nowhere else found in LXX.

Mark seems to have done something of the same kind but not so accurately as the LXX. In the Five Thousand he takes "two" literally, and explains it as the literal answer to a question of Jesus "How many loaves have ye?" They answer "five, and two fishes," though nothing was asked about the fishes[2] In the Four Thousand, writing in his own person, Mark does not venture to say "*They had two fishes.*" This would have been as inappropriate as it would have been for the narrator of the story of the Widow to write in his own person that "*she was gathering two sticks*" Such hyperbole, allowable in a complainant, is not allowable in a historian. So Mark paraphrases "two" by "a few." Yet he might well feel that this was unsatisfactory. "A few fish" might naturally mean more, not less, than "two fish," and thus the wonder of the miracle would be impaired. So Mark compromises by changing "fishes" into "little fishes"

John shews us dramatically how the "two" and the "five" might have originated in the expostulation of a single disciple like Andrew, who exclaims "There is a lad here with five

---

the only instance of ξυλάριον in LXX, but ץע = ξύλον nearly 250 times The translators felt that "*two*," like "*handful*," implied some kind of minuteness, and this they expressed by the diminutive ξυλάρια while retaining "*two*"

[1] Gesen 1041 *a* gives no other instance but this where "*two*" is thus used (without the juxtaposition of "three" (or "one") as in "two or three")

[2] Matthew and Luke go back more closely to the original by representing the "five" and the "two" to be part of a remonstrance on the part of the disciples, somewhat like that of the widow of Zarephath

CHRIST'S MIRACLES OF FEEDING

barley loaves and *two opsaria*, but what are these among so many?" It should be noted that John never mentions the fishes as "two" when writing in his own person, as the Synoptists do. He mentions "the five barley loaves" thus[1], but not "the two fishes"

As to the Synoptic distinction—expressed in various ways—between the giving by Christ to the disciples, and the giving by the disciples to the multitudes, John puts this aside He represents Jesus as Himself "distributing"—like David, who in an instance above mentioned[2], is said to have "distributed" to all Israel[3] John rejects the Synoptic word "*set-before [the people]*" although it is associated in LXX with the thought of Abraham "setting before" the Three his hospitable food[4], a hospitality for which (according to Jewish tradition) requital was made by God, in every detail, to Abraham's descendants.

Lastly—when describing Jesus as "distributing"—John does not use Mark's word "divide" Perhaps he felt that, for Greeks, it might suggest the thought of "divided in dissension," as when Paul says to the Corinthians "Is Christ *divided*[5]?" At

---

[1] Jn vi 13   [2] See above, pp 329—30
[3] Mk vi 41, Lk ix 16 ἐδίδου (Mt xiv 19 ἔδωκεν) τοῖς μαθηταῖς followed by Mk *ib* ἐμέρισεν πᾶσιν, compared with Jn vi 11 διέδωκεν τοῖς ἀνακειμένοις, may be illustrated by Gen xlix 27 יְחַלֵּק (Field) "dividet, LXX δίδωσι (potior scriptura διαδώσει), Aq μερίσει" This exhibits the same three variations that we find in N T. (1) "*give* (δίδωμι)," (2) "*give separately* (διαδίδωμι)," (3) "*divide* (μερίζω)"

[4] Gen xviii 8 παρέθηκεν. There it = Heb "*gave before their faces*" In Exod xix. 7 παρέθηκεν αὐτοῖς πάντας τοὺς λόγους (and *ib*. xxi. 1), it=Heb. "*set before their faces*" See Gesen. 817 *b* which says that both "give" and "set" are thus used of food, but that "give before the face" usually means "propound," and is applied to laws Matthew (see above, p 328, n 2) uses παρατίθημι only about parables.

Comp 2 K iv 43 "Am I to *set this before* an hundred men?"— which is the exclamation of Elisha's servant—and *ib* 44 "so he *set it before them*" John passes over this intermediate act of service

[5] 1 Cor 1 13 μεμέρισται ὁ Χριστός, Μερίζω denotes "divided by conflict" in Mk iii 24 etc

all events he chooses an ambiguous word that may mean either
(1) "give in turn what one has received" or (2) "give to
separate persons[1]." The word is hardly used in LXX, but
may very well represent the Hebrew "*apportion*," while at the
same time the Greek reader receives from it the suggestion that
the Son is here giving in turn to men something that He has
Himself received from the Father. This is confirmed by
Christ's subsequent words "My Father *giveth you* the true
bread out of heaven" and "*I am the bread of life*"—when taken
with a previous utterance "As the Father hath life in himself,
even so *gave he to the Son* also to have life in himself[2]." The
Son, giving Himself utterly to the Giver of eternal life, the
Father in heaven, receives from Him power to become the
Bread of Life for the Father's children on earth.

In connection with the multiplication of the fishes, the
following facts indicate that it might have a Messianic allusiveness in the Galilaean Church. The New Hebrew and Aramaic
for "fish," *nun*, though non-existent in the Bible as a noun,
occurs once as a verb (*yinnon* or *jinnon*), meaning literally
"*shall abound with offspring*," thus, "His name *shall-abound-
with-offspring* (Field *sobolescet*, Walton *filiabitur*) before the
sun[3]." On the Hebrew "*shall abound*," *Jinnon*, Schottgen
says "It means 'shall be multiplied like fishes' But the

---

[1] Διαδίδωμι (= Heb word) occurs only in Gen xlix 20, 27
(A), and Josh. xiii 6 (LXX) In Genesis it = נתן and חלק, and
B has (*bis*) δίδωμι. For διαδίδωμι = "give in succession" see Steph.
Thes ii 1139 Goodspeed gives διαδίδωμι only in Hermas *Sim* v.
2 9 where the faithful servant, having received ἐδέσματα from his
Master, "distributes" some of them to his fellow-servants

[2] Jn vi 32, 35, v 26

[3] Ps. lxxii 17 RV. txt "*shall be continued*," marg "*shall have
issue*" The Biblical Heb for "fish" is דג (Aram נון) The
verb דנה occurs but once (Gesen 185 *b*), Gen xlviii 16 RV.
"*grow-into-a-multitude*," where AV marg says "(Heb) *as fishes do
increase*," and Onkelos has "increase like *the fishes* (נוני) of the sea."

Jews *took it as a proper name*[1]." This, though over-stated, is confirmed by several passages in Midrash and Talmud, which indicate that in poetic traditions the Jews regarded *Jinnon*, in this Psalm, as one of the names of the Messiah existent before the Creation[2]. Now the preceding verse says "There shall be *abundance* (marg. *an handful*) of corn in the earth on the top of the mountains[3]"; and on the word rendered "abundance" Rashi says "Our rabbis expound it as meaning *cakes in the days of the Messiah, and the whole of this Psalm they explain as being about the King Messiah*[4]."

The Jewish Commentary on the Psalms quotes a tradition of this kind as going back to R. Jochanan: "The land of Israel will *bring forth little round cakes*[5]." The commentary does not quote any corresponding tradition about "*Jinnon*," that the waters of Israel "will bring forth a multitude of little fishes," or that the Messiah "will multiply fishes." But it is not difficult to see that such a tradition would be likely to find favour in the first century among the Jews and especially among the fishermen and others who dwelt round the sea of Galilee. The commentary on Numbers called *Siphri* says "There went with Israel in the wilderness a well, and supplied fat fishes more than their need required[6]." The "well" was believed to flow from a "rock" that "followed" Israel; and

---

[1] Schottgen ii 20 This is not universally true, for the Targum has "*was prepared* before the sun," perhaps (like the LXX) having a different reading, and Rashi takes it as meaning "kingdom" and "empire" Gesen 630 *b* suggests that the original may have been יכון "be established," "endure," LXX has διαμενεῖ

[2] See Levy ii 246 *a* quoting three passages, and Schottg ii 240 quoting others

[3] Ps lxxii 16, see Gesen 821 *a*

[4] Rashi himself explains the word as meaning either "additionem et multitudinem" or "beneplacitum"

[5] *Tehill* ad loc mentions R Chija bar Asi as uttering it "in the name of R Jochanan" (who lived in the time of Vespasian)

[6] *Siphri* on Numb. xi 22

CHRIST'S MIRACLES OF FEEDING

according to Paul, "the rock was Christ[1]." In proportion as Christianity advanced, such traditions about "fishes," or "loaves," or "round cakes" of the Messiah, would fall into disrepute among the Jews, as having a Christian sound. I have not found Jochanan's tradition quoted elsewhere, although many passages in Midrash and Talmud refer to the verse in the Psalms. But, if it was avoided because of its resemblance to Christian traditions, the same motive may explain the silence of Jewish tradition about multiplication of fishes in Messianic times[2].

---

[1] 1 Cor x 4

[2] In view of the very early use of the Greek *ichthus*, "fish," to denote by means of the letters *i, ch, th, u, s,* "Jesus Christ, Son of God, Saviour (or, Crucified)"—see *Orac. Sibyll.* viii. 217 foll —it may be of interest to note the very different use made by the Jews of *n*, the initial letter of "*nun*," "fish." They called attention to the fact that *n* and the two next letters of the alphabet (נ, ס, ע) were initial letters of (1) נון "fish," (2) סמא "remedy," (3) עין "eye," thus indicating that "fish" was a "remedy" for the "eye" (as it is in Tobit xi 4—11)

Also the Jewish dependence on fish for a sumptuous meal in which they were to "*honour*" the [Friday] evening preceding the Great Sabbath is illustrated by a story (Levy iii 360, Gen *r*, Wu p 47) about a Jewish tailor, who ventured to outbid the servant of "a ruler" in Rome by buying a fish, the only one in the shop, for twelve denarii The ruler called the tailor before him to explain his conduct "My lord," said the tailor, "it is a day on which all our sins, which we have committed during the whole year, are to be forgiven When such a day comes *ought we not to honour it?*"

It is worth noting that in the Double Tradition of Matthew (vii 9—11) and Luke (xi 11—13) where Jesus wishes to describe the willingness of the Father in heaven to give (Mt) "good [things]" or (Lk) "the Holy Spirit," to those that ask Him, the one metaphor in which Matthew and Luke agree (according to the text of W H) is that in which the good gift is represented by "a fish" (as the opposite of "a serpent"). For the rest (Mt. "bread...stone," Lk. "egg...scorpion") they disagree.

CHRIST'S MIRACLES OF FEEDING

§ 29 *"Twelve basketfuls"* (R.V.), *in Mark*[1]

Of the differences between the parallel columns printed below, one has been discussed incidentally above, namely, the Synoptic use of the verb "satisfied" (literally "foddered") where John has "filled[2]." Mark's phrase "and *of* [Gk *from*] the fishes" may either be taken with "broken pieces" so as to mean "and [*broken pieces*] of the fishes," or with "some," understood, so as to mean "and [some] of the fishes[3]." The frequent use of the Hebrew *"from"* to mean *"some of"* decidedly favours the latter interpretation here; and so does the Johannine use of "from" in the saying of Jesus to the

[1] Mk vi 42—3 (R V)	Mt xiv 20 (R V)	Lk ix 17 (R V)	Jn vi 12—13 (R V)
(42) And they did all eat, and were filled (ἐχορ-τάσθησαν) (43) And they took up broken pieces, twelve basketfuls (κοφίνων πληρώματα), and also of the fishes.	(20) And they did all eat, and were filled (ἐχορ-τάσθησαν) and they took up that which remained over of the broken pieces, twelve baskets full (κοφίνους πλήρεις).	(17) And they did eat, and were all filled (ἐχορ-τάσθησαν) and there was taken up that which re-mained over to them of broken pieces, twelve baskets (κόφινοι).	(12) And wh⋯ they were fill⋯ (ἐνεπλήσθησαν), saith unto his d⋯ ciples, Gather ⋯ the broken piec⋯ which remain ov⋯ that nothing ⋯ lost (13) So th⋯ gathered them u⋯ and filled twel⋯ baskets (κοφίνο⋯ with broken piec⋯ from the five barl⋯ loaves, which ⋯ mained over un⋯ them that h⋯ eaten

Mk viii. 8 (R.V.)
And they did eat, and were filled (ἐχορτάσθησαν), and they took up, of broken pieces that remained over, seven baskets (σφυρίδας).

Mt. xv. 37 (R.V)
And they did all eat, and were filled (ἐχορτάσθησαν) and they took up that which remained over of the broken pieces, seven baskets full (σφυρίδας πλήρεις).

[2] See above, p. 306 foll.

[3] Gesen 580 *b*, *inter alia*, quotes Exod xvi 27 "there went out [*some*] *from the people*" (where LXX inserts τινὲς), Lev xxv 49 "[*some one*] *from the kinsfolk* may redeem it," LXX ἡ ἀπὸ τῶν οἰκείων. .λυτρώσεται, which would naturally be rendered "redeem *from the kinsfolk*."

seven fishermen after Christ's resurrection "Bring [*some*] *of* (lit. *from*) *the fish* that ye have now caught[1]."

A more important point is the ambiguity of the Marcan "they took up," referring to the broken pieces. Grammatically, "*they*" would mean the previously mentioned "*all*," that is to say, the multitude. Luke—in accordance with Mark's vague use of "they" in such phrases as "*they say*" to mean a passive ("*it is said*")—substitutes a passive "*there was taken up*." John defines the agents with remarkable distinctness, not only assigning the act to the disciples but adding that Jesus gave express commandment to them to perform it: "Gather ye the broken-pieces that have superabounded that nothing may be lost[2]."

Here, if "crumbs" falling from the food had been meant, the Greek word for "crumbs" used in Christ's Dialogue with the Syrophoenician woman might have been employed[3]. Nor would any form of the word "superabundant" (in Greek, *perissos*) have been needed[4]. On the other hand, to suppose that the meaning is "portions deliberately broken off," and that Jesus broke them off, raises the question, "Is it likely that John would represent Jesus as breaking off 'superabundant' pieces, so as to cause waste?" The difficulty might lead us to conclude

---

[1] Jn xxi 10 Ἐνέγκατε ἀπὸ τῶν ὀψαρίων ὧν ἐπιάσατε νῦν Chrys retains "from," κελεύει ἐκ τῶν ὃ ἐνεγκεῖν, but Nonnus (ἄξατε νεπόδων ἄγρην) drops it. The context does not shew why "*the fishes*" might not have been mentioned instead of "*some of the fishes*," nor why the latter is expressed in an idiom unusual except in Hebraic Greek After Christ's command, Peter "went on board and drew the net to land full of great fishes " It may be implied, but it is not stated, that he "brought [*some*] *of them*" to Jesus as specimens and proofs of success

[2] Jn vi. 12 Συναγάγετε τὰ περισσεύσαντα κλάσματα

[3] Mk vii 28, Mt xv 27 ψιχία, on which see Levy iv 140 *a* and *Pes* 10 *b* describing a "child" as "crumbling his bread "

[4] Some form of περισσεύειν is used by Mt , Lk , and Jn in the Five Thousand, and by Mt in the Four Thousand, but περισσεύματα by Mk in the Four Thousand.

—especially as John has not described Jesus as "breaking" the bread—that the multitude are to be regarded as wastefully breaking off from their portions large "pieces" too big to be called "crumbs," and that John meant such "pieces" as these. This would accord with Origen's view that it is the unworthiness of the multitude that prevents them from consuming all the nourishment provided for them[1].

But these arguments may be misleading unless supplemented by the probability (we may almost say the certainty) that John is influenced by the words of Elisha over the barley loaves, "Thus saith the Lord, They shall eat and *they shall cause to superabound* or *leave thereof*," that is to say, "*They shall be satisfied and shall have a superfluity*[2]." This saying about the barley loaves of Elisha, if applied to the Johannine barley loaves of Jesus, might meet the objection "The Lord could not have broken more pieces than were needed." The mystical answer might be, in John's words, "He knew what he would do," that is to say, "He knew that what was apparent waste would not be waste, because it would come back as in a future 'gathering together,' so that 'nothing should be lost[3]'" In this sense, the pieces that were broken were *not* "more than were needed," if the lesson of the sign was to be fully taught It was intended that some of the food should be "*left*," or that there should be a "*superabundance.*"

These remarks may explain why Mark (alone of the Evangelists) omits, in his Feeding of the Five Thousand, all mention

---

[1] Origen *Comm Matt* xi 19 (Lomm iii 125) The four thousand are superior to the five thousand, and "more receptive ($\chi\omega\rho\eta\tau\iota\kappa\omega\tau\epsilon\rho\sigma\iota$)" (comp Jn viii 37 οὐ χωρεῖ) so that they leave less unconsumed

[2] 2 K. iv 43—44 The verb יתר, "leave," may mean "leave as a remnant saved from destruction," but it may also mean "leave as superfluous", and forms of יתר = περισσεία about 13 times, and περισσός more than 20 times

[3] Jn vi 12 What the Jews rejected might be regarded as coming back to the Apostles in the form of a "gathering" of the Gentiles (see Rom xi 15—32)

CHRIST'S MIRACLES OF FEEDING

of "*superabundance,*" and substitutes, literally, "*fillings,*" in a curious phrase rendered by R.V. "*basketfuls,*" but by A V. "*baskets full*[1]"; Matthew has the latter, "*baskets full,*" but retains "*superabundant*[2]"; Luke makes no mention of "*full*" in any form, but has "*superabundant*[3]." The explanation suggested is, that the Hebrew "*left,*" or "*superabounding,*" twice repeated in the miracle of Elisha, was taken by Mark in the Feeding of the Five Thousand as meaning "*running over*" or "*quite full*[4]." By taking it thus, the charge of imputing to Jesus a superfluous multiplication of food would be somewhat softened[5]

Luke inserts the dative "*to them*" after "superabounded." John inserts a similar dative, but one of a much more special kind—"*to those who had consumed* [*the food*][6]." This Greek word "*consume* [*food*]"—meaning in literary Greek "*gnaw,*" "*eat up,*" and often applied to eating raw flesh, etc.— occurs in LXX fairly often to represent the ordinary Hebrew

---

[1] Mk vi 43 κλάσματα δώδεκα κοφίνων πληρώματα καὶ ἀπὸ τῶν ἰχθύων, A V. "twelve baskets full of the fragments, and of the fishes" "*The* fragments" suggests "*the* fragments that would naturally fall from such a meal." But there is no "the" The literal rendering is "broken pieces, fillings of twelve baskets, and of (*lit.* from) the fishes"

[2] Mt xiv 20 τὸ περισσεῦον τῶν κλασμάτων δώδεκα κοφίνους πλήρεις, "that which was [found] superabounding of the broken pieces, twelve baskets [quite] full," where "full" is emphasized by its position

[3] Lk ix 17 τὸ περισσεῦσαν αὐτοῖς κλασμάτων κόφινοι δώδεκα, "that which was [found] superabounding by them (*or*, for them) of broken pieces, baskets [precisely] twelve," where "twelve" is emphasized by its position

[4] Πλήρωμα occurs rather rarely (15 times) in LXX It corresponds to Heb "full" Cant v 12 "*channels* of waters" is paraphrased as "*fillings* (πληρώματα) of waters" to express full-flowing streams Much more defensibly might the Heb "*left,*" יתר, be thus paraphrased

[5] Note however that Mark does not avoid περισσεύματα in Mk viii. 8 (the Four Thousand)

[6] Jn vi 13 τοῖς βεβρωκόσιν.

"eat," but mostly in a bad sense. In the Prophets it refers to the devouring effect of fire, rust, or blight, or the eating of food defiled or offered to idols. In Genesis it does not occur once. But in Exodus and Leviticus it is frequent, occurring about ten times in prohibitions ("this shall not be eaten") (as well as positively). For our purposes, however, the two points of special importance are that (1) it occurs for the first time in connection with the Paschal Lamb, of which it is said "It shall be *consumed* in one house," and that (2) this follows the precept "Ye shall cause none of it to *superabound* (lit. *be left over and above*) till the morning[1]."

Do not these facts go some way toward justifying what at first sight seems the wild imagination of Origen—namely, that a fault of non-receptiveness is implied in those who "leave broken pieces"? May it not be that John had in view both *dicta*—(1) that of the Law "Ye *shall cause none of it to superabound*," and (2) that of Elisha "They *shall cause to superabound*"? At all events John would probably regard the "superabounding" as divinely ordained in order that remnants from the Bread of the Gospel, rejected by the unbelievers among the Jews, might pass to the Gentiles; and yet, as in the Epistle to the Romans, the rejection would be regarded as a fault in the Jews, who did not discern, and receive in its entirety, the Living Bread, which was also the Paschal Lamb

Jerome calls Christ's distribution of bread "a sowing of food," and implies, somewhat obscurely, that the food was "divided into (*or* with a view to) a manifold harvest[2]." About the distribution, the following comment has been preserved as coming from Ammonius· "He [*i e.* Jesus] did not give

---

[1] Exod xii 10 "ye shall let none of it remain," Exod xii 46 "it shall be eaten ($\beta\rho\omega\theta\acute{\eta}\sigma\epsilon\tau\alpha\iota$) " The word for "superabound" is יתר, the same as that in 2 K iv 43—44

[2] Jerome, on Mt xiv 19, "Frangente Domino, *seminarium fit ciborum*. Si enim fuissent integri.. nec divisi in *multiplicem segetem....*"

[the food] to the multitudes to carry (?), but to the disciples, since He above all things desired to train these—the destined teachers of the world. For the multitude was not destined to receive any great fruit from the miracle (*lit.* wonder) For they straightway forgot it and began to ask for another miracle (*lit.* wonder). But these [*i.e.* the disciples] were destined to receive no common gain[1]." This appears to express at all events an important part of John's meaning The first harvest was, so to speak, a failure—the harvest for the multitude, the Five Thousand, that is, for Israel after the flesh. The second harvest—the gathering of the fragments by the Apostles, regarded as their harvest by Ammonius—was not a failure. It was the harvest of souls to be subsequently gathered by the Twelve, who (in spite of Judas) were typical of the Twelve Tribes of Israel after the Spirit The key to the Johannine meaning lies in the words of Jesus "that nothing may be lost"—a phrase peculiar (with slight variations) to the Fourth

---

[1] Cramer p 243 on Jn vi 13 The words οὐκ ἔδωκε δὲ τοῖς ὄχλοις βαστάζειν ἀλλὰ τοῖς μαθηταῖς somewhat resemble a passage from Origen's commentary on Mt. xiv 16 (quoted below, p 356) where Origen applies φέρειν to the disciples And Origen there, like Ammonius here, uses παιδεύω to describe Jesus as "training" the disciples through the miracle of the Five Thousand But Origen represents Jesus as saying, in effect, to the disciples, "I *have trained* you to give the Bread Now give it" Ammonius—much more accordantly with Johannine doctrine—regards the "*training*" *as now going on* in the course of this miracle ("since he especially desired to train these (ἐπειδὴ μάλιστα τούτους παιδεῦσαι ἐβούλετο)") And Ammonius speaks of the disciples, not as "teaching" but as "*destined to be teachers* (τοὺς μέλλοντας ἔσεσθαι διδασκάλους)" Ammonius meets the objection that Judas received a basketful by saying that, as the rest of the Twelve received "no ordinary *gain*," so Judas received "no ordinary *condemnation* when he carried the basket (ἦν δὲ καὶ τῷ Ἰούδα κατάκριμα τὸ γινόμενον οὐ τὸ τυχὸν, βαστάζοντι τὸν κόφινον)" Does Ammonius mean, in his first sentence, "He did not give to the multitudes [the right] to *carry* (βαστάζειν) [*the baskets of fragments*] but to the disciples," and does he, in the last, allude to Jn xii 6 "[Judas] (R.V. marg.) *carried* (ἐβάσταζεν)..."?

CHRIST'S MIRACLES OF FEEDING

Gospel, and used to describe something corresponding to what the Prophets call the "remnant" of Israel[1].

As regards Mark's ambiguous words "and from the fishes" John intervenes, at least negatively, so far as to indicate that there were no fishes or fragments of fishes in the twelve baskets. The baskets were "filled [to the top] from the five barley-loaves[2]." According to his view, the fishes that Mark described as being "taken up" were not placed in the twelve baskets. They must have been brought to Jesus, if at all, separately.

As to the difference between the "twelve *cophinoi*" filled in the earlier miracle, and the "seven *sphurides*" filled in the later one, we have seen above[3] that a distinction between kinds of "baskets" is recognised by Jewish Tradition in connection with the "basket" of firstfruits which is made the subject of a kind of votive hymn in Deuteronomy[4]. Philo paraphrases this hymn in a fragment of a treatise on the Feast of Baskets in which he says that it was celebrated "*on two seasons*" of the year[5]. But Rashi says expressly "*once in the year, not twice*[6]." In this, he is following the Talmud, which says "Firstfruits

---

[1] Comp Jn iii 16 ἵνα μὴ ἀπόληται, vi 12 ἵνα μή τι ἀπόληται, vi 39 ἵνα. μὴ ἀπολέσω, x 28 οὐ μὴ ἀπόλωνται, xvii 12 οὐδεὶς .ἀπώλετο εἰ μὴ ., xviii 9 οὐκ ἀπώλεσα

[2] John expresses Mark's πληρώματα, Mt πλήρεις, Lk om, by (vi 13) ἐγέμισαν, using the same word that he used before (ii 7 *bis*) in the miracle of Cana, to describe the waterpots as "filled to the top"

[3] See above, pp. 208—9.

[4] Deut xxvi 2—4 "Thou shalt put it in a basket...the priest shall take the basket," LXX κάρταλλον, Aq ἀγγεῖον. The Heb occurs (Gesen. 380 *b*) only there and *ib*. xxviii 5, 17 LXX ἀποθῆκαι

[5] See Philo *post* ii 298 ἔστι δέ τις παρὰ ταῦτα ἑορτὴ μὲν θεοῦ, ἑορτῆς δὲ πανήγυρις ἦν καλοῦσι Κάρταλλον... § 3 τὸ ᾆσμα τοῦτο (*i e* Deut. xxvi 5—15) ᾄδεται δυσὶ καιροῖς.

[6] On Deut xxvi 3 Rashi says "una vice in anno, non vero bis," and (on *ib* 10) "non.. nisi a fine septem septimanarum," *i e* from the end of the week of weeks which introduced the Feast of Pentecost

are *not to be offered before Pentecost*[1]" The Targum on Deuteronomy paraphrases "basket" by three words, and the LXX renders "basket" in a later passage of Deuteronomy by "receptacles[2]." Also a Jewish distinction is made between these "*baskets*" when made of metal and when made of twigs or similar material[3].

Pseudo-Jerome says "The seven *sportae* (i e *sphurides*) are the first seven Churches. The broken pieces of bread are the mystical perceptions belonging to *the first Pentecost*[4]." This mention of "Pentecost" connects the Christian narrative with the "baskets" in Deuteronomy, according to the Rabbinical view adopted by Rashi ("*not before Pentecost*"), and with the Symposion of the Therapeutae described by Philo as honouring not only the seventh day but also the square of seven, *i e.* the eve of Pentecost[5] On the other hand, Philo's mention of "*two seasons*" indicates another view in accordance with which there might be "*two*" Symposia, one of a rudimentary character. Such a rudimentariness would be symbolized by "barley," which, as we have seen, John alone mentions in connection with the Feeding of the Five Thousand

---

[1] *Biccurim* (Mishna) 1 3 quoted by Wagenseil (*Sota* p 661)

[2] On Deut. xxvi 3 the three words of Targ Jer I are rendered by Walton (1) "canistra," (2) "sportulas," (3) "cophinos papyraceos" In Deut xxviii 5, 17, LXX has ἀποθῆκαι

[3] So *Tosephoth* quoted by Wagenseil (*Sota* p 662) *J Biccurim* (Mishna) iii. 8 says "The rich offered their firstfruits in κάλαθοι plated with gold and silver" Levy ii 168 *a* gives טנא (the Deuteronomic "basket") as "ein grosses, metallenes Gefass" and quotes *j. Sota* ix 24 *b* "a leaden *receptacle* full of barley bran "

[4] On Mk viii 1 foll "Septem panes dona sunt septem Spiritus Sancti Quatuor millia annus est Novi Testamenti cum quatuor temporibus Septem sportae primae septem Ecclesiae. Fragmenta panum *mystici intellectus primae septimanae sunt*," i e they are the outpourings of "*mystical understanding* (or, *perception*)," with the gift of tongues, recorded in Acts ii 1 foll

[5] Philo ii 481 οὐ μόνον τὴν ἁπλῆν ἑβδομάδα ἀλλὰ καὶ τὴν δύναμιν [*i.e* the power or square of the hebdomad] τεθηπότες...ἔστι δὲ προεόρτιος μεγίστης ἑορτῆς, ἣν πεντηκοντὰς ἔλαχεν.

At this stage, the following objection may be raised: "John is supposed to regard the Feeding of the Five Thousand as rudimentary. Mark is supposed to relate the Feeding of the Four Thousand as a miracle of an advanced character. Luke omits the latter. According to the rule of Johannine Intervention, John ought to insert it. But he does not. Is not the rule broken?"

We reply that the rule is not broken because John does insert a second miracle of feeding, and that, too, "of an advanced character." Only John, as often, does not repeat what is in Mark but adds something corresponding to what is in Mark. This John places after the Resurrection. Whereas Mark symbolizes the advance by a change from the Jewish *cophinos*[1] to the Gentile *sphuris* or *sporta*, John symbolizes it in a different way by representing Jesus as feeding seven disciples from one loaf (*artos*) and one fish after they have caught and presented to Him an offering of "a hundred and fifty-three" fishes. Through that mystic number, representing the Law merged in the Spirit[2], and through the context as a whole, John leads us to see, in that final meal after the Resurrection, a type of divine Unity working through human multitudinousness, so as to lift mankind above Jewish and Gentile distinctions, bringing about for all alike the fulfilment of Christ's promise about the one "bread" or "loaf": "The *bread* (*artos*) that I will give is my flesh, for the life of the world[3]."

§ 30. *"They that ate the loaves," in Mark*[4]

Instead of the past participle Matthew has the present participle of a different verb (*esthiein*) never used by John,

---

[1] The connection of *cophinus* with *Judaeus* twice by Juvenal III 14, VI. 542, justifies our regarding it as being thus connected in the minds of Gentile readers of the Gospels in the first century
[2] See *Joh Gr* 2283 c
[3] Jn vi 51
[4] Mk vi 44 οἱ φαγόντες τοὺς ἄρτους, Mt xiv 21 οἱ δὲ ἐσθίοντες.

CHRIST'S MIRACLES OF FEEDING

but used by the Synoptists in discussions about eating and in the narratives of the Eucharist where a past tense is not required[1]. We have seen above that John here uses about the eaters a word ("*consume*") that seemed to allude to the eating of the Paschal Lamb[2]. This hypothesis of allusion will be confirmed if we can shew that John had some reason, or at all events some consistent method, in his avoidance of *esthiein*.

This is shewn by a passage where John represents Jesus as quoting from the Psalms "He that *eateth* my bread lifted up his heel against me[3]." Here the LXX uses *esthiein*. But John uses a word signifying "*chew* (*trōgein*)," which occurs nowhere in the LXX and only once in N.T. outside the Fourth Gospel[4]. In that single instance—which occurs in Matthew's description of the luxurious feeding (lit. "*chewing* and drinking") in the days of Noah—the parallel Luke has the ordinary *esthiein*[5]. This is easily intelligible, but why should John—

The latter might be rendered "the eaters," the former "those that had eaten the loaves." For the parallels, see below, p. 348, n. 3.

[1] See *Joh Voc* **1680 b**. Φαγεῖν is freq. in the Synoptists and fairly freq. in Jn, but Jn never uses ἐσθίειν. The difference between ἐσθίειν and φαγεῖν is often simply a difference of tense, i.e. of time, ἐσθίειν having no aorist, and φαγεῖν no present or imperfect.

[2] See pp. 339—40.

[3] Jn xiii. 18 ὁ τρώγων μου τὸν ἄρτον. Nonnus has ἔρεπτων, a word applied to horses, geese, fishes, feeding in multitudes, but applicable to men with a notion of greediness.

[4] Τρώγω is mostly used with an object. But it is frequently used without an object where the juxtaposition of "drinking" makes the meaning clear. Steph *Thes* quotes πίνειν καὶ τρώγειν from Demosth p. 402, 21, and Plutarch *Mor* 716 E, and τρώγειν καὶ πίνειν from *ib* 613 B.

[5] Mt xxiv. 38 τρώγοντες καὶ πίνοντες (Lk xvii. 27 ἤσθιον, ἔπινον) describing the revels of those on whom the deluge came. Τρώγω, "chew," is applied in various contexts to feeding on uncooked food. In Mt., it means "chewing" delicacies that might be called "dessert," where "eat for pleasure" would express the meaning, as in Hermas *Sim.* v. 3 "Take only bread and water, and give in alms from your *delicacies* that you were intending (lit.) *to chew* (τρώγειν)."

CHRIST'S MIRACLES OF FEEDING

without any justification derivable from the Hebrew text of Scripture—represent Jesus as quoting from the Psalms the words "He that *cheweth* my bread"?

The following explanation is obscurely suggested by Jerome's commentary on the Psalm, and (more clearly) by Origen's commentary on earlier passages in the Gospel where John represents Jesus as using the word "chew[1]." Jerome says that Judas "was receiving celestial food...and distributing it to others[2]." Origen, when commenting on what he calls the "paraphrase" of the Psalm as quoted by Jesus, says that the bread referred to was "most nourishing[3]." Elsewhere, in his treatise on the daily bread in the Lord's Prayer, he takes in order the passages in which Jesus speaks of the need of His disciples to "*chew*" His flesh and "*drink*" His blood, and not only repeats the epithet "nourishing" again, but adds to it others such as "solid," and "athletic[4]." Taken together, Origen's remarks confirm the view that the language of Christians about the Eucharist might give rise, even as early as the days of Nero, to a popular belief that they practised in their "mysteries" the eating of human flesh[5].

---

i.e to eat for pleasure In other contexts it might mean "*chew (a crust)*" and be applied to a beggar See Steph *Thes* τρώγω, which shews that the grammarians expressly distinguish τρώγω, as having a more particular meaning than ἐσθίω, and as being applied to the eating of τραγήματα, "sweetmeats "

[1] Jn vi 54, 56, 57, 58 In all these, Jesus is speaking John never uses τρώγω in his own person

[2] Jerome on Ps xli 9

[3] Origen on Jn xiii 18 (Lomm ii 419) παραπέφρασται, (*ib* 420) τροφιμωτάτων.

[4] Origen *De Orat* § 27 (Lomm xvii 205 foll) leads us from ὁ τρόφιμος λόγος to the thought of its στερρότης and εὐτονία, as being ἀθλητικὴ τροφή distinguishing it from "manna" and "milk."

[5] See p. 398 foll. If this was so, John might indirectly vindicate the Christians, and also teach the true doctrine of Christ, by representing Him as using spiritual language about His flesh and blood, which was misunderstood at first even by His own disciples.

A close examination of the Greek justifies Origen. Neither the Latin, nor the Syriac, nor the English Versions represent the abruptness with which the word *"chewing"* is as it were thrown in the faces of the Jews by the Fourth Gospel after they have said "How can this [man] give us his flesh to *eat* (*phagein*)?" It is true that Jesus is made to reply at first with a repetition of their word ("Except ye *eat* (*phagein*) the flesh of the Son of man and drink his blood, ye have not life in yourselves"). But He immediately adds "He that *cheweth* (*trōgein*) my flesh and drinketh my blood hath life eternal.... He that *cheweth* (*trōgein*) my flesh and drinketh my blood abideth in me, and I in him. As the living Father sent me and I live because of the Father, [so] also he that *cheweth* (*trōgein*) me—he too shall live because of me. This is the bread that came down from Heaven. Not as the fathers *ate* (*phagein*) [manna] and died[1]—[not so is it now]; he that *cheweth* (*trōgein*) this bread shall live for ever[2]."

These last words, contrasting the death that came after Israel "*ate*" the manna with the life that will belong to him that "*cheweth*" the "bread" that "came down from heaven," should be illustrated from Israel's complaint about the manna that it had no sustaining moisture for them. "Our soul is *dried away*," they cried, and "who shall give us *flesh* to eat[3]?" The Fourth Gospel represents Jesus as affording to the spiritual Israel a food of spiritual nature that should satisfy both hunger and thirst. It was to be the "*flesh*" of the living Son, which

---

[1] "Died" See Numb. xiv 30 "save Caleb . and Joshua"

[2] Jn vi 52—8 Our English Versions have "*eat*" throughout, and so have the Syriac The Latin Versions vary somewhat strangely, *d* renders φαγεῖν by "manducare" in 52 and 58 (where *d* has "non sicut manducaverunt (ἔφαγον). .qui manducat (ὁ τρώγων)" Chrysostom, commenting on this passage, makes no comment on the transition in Jn from φαγεῖν to τρώγειν.

[3] Numb. xi. 4—6 בשר. Comp Ps lxxviii 20 "Will he provide *flesh* (שאר)," LXX τράπεζαν, where Rashi says that שאר (which rather suggests flesh with blood in it, Gesen 984—5) stands for בשר.

CHRIST'S MIRACLES OF FEEDING

could not possibly be received apart from the reception of His blood. Isaiah invites the soul to "eat" the food of heaven as being "wine" and "milk," not mentioning, but assuming, that it included "bread[1]" So John connects the life and being of the Son with "bread" and with "flesh," and even with "blood," not mentioning, but assuming, that this included "wine[2]"

§ 31. *"Five thousand men" or "about five thousand [men]"*[3]

The following questions arise out of the Marcan phrases. Why does Mark insert "men (*viri*, not *homines*[4])" in one narrative and omit it in the other? Why does Mark insert "*about*" in one narrative and omit it in the other? Why does John insert "*in number*" before "about five thousand"? Why does Matthew in both narratives insert "apart from women and

---

[1] Is lv 1 "buy and *eat*," where Ibn Ezra remarks of "wine" and "milk" that each serves for food as well as for drink

[2] John's above-noted application of τρώγειν to Judas in an altered quotation from LXX is perhaps part of a consistent tradition (not mentioned by the Synoptists) concerning the bread dipped in wine and given to Judas alone

[3]
Mk vi 44 (R V)	Mt xiv. 21 (R V)	Lk. ix. 14 (R V)	Jn vi. 10 (R.V.)
And they that ate the loaves were five thousand men.	And they that did eat were about five thousand men, beside women and children	For they were about five thousand men.	So the men sa down, in numbe about five thou sand.

Mk viii 9 (R.V)	Mt xv. 38 (R.V.)
And they were about four thousand	And they that did eat were four thousand men, beside women and children

Note that ἄνδρες is inserted except in Mk viii 9 The Greek phrases are as follows In the Five Thousand, Mk vi 44 πεντακισχίλιοι ἄνδρες, Mt xiv 21 ἄνδρες ὡσεὶ π., χωρὶς γυναικῶν καὶ παιδίων, Lk. ix 14 ὡσεὶ ἄνδρες π., Jn vi 10 οἱ ἄνδρες (or, ἄνδρες) τὸν ἀριθμὸν ὡς π In the Four Thousand, Mk viii 9 ὡς τετρακισχίλιοι, Mt xv 38 τετρακισχίλιοι (marg ὡς τετρακισχίλιοι) ἄνδρες, χωρὶς γυναικῶν καὶ παιδίων (marg παιδίων καὶ γυναικῶν).

[4] "Men," ἄνδρες 'Ανήρ occurs in Mk elsewhere, only in the sing vi 20 "a righteous *man*," x 2, 12 "husband"

348 (Mark vi. 29—44)

CHRIST'S MIRACLES OF FEEDING

children"? And why do Luke and John omit Matthew's clause?

If we look for illustrations from Scripture to answer these questions, we find that the first Hebrew instance of *"about" with numbers of men* occurs in the description of Israel going forth from Egypt[1]. The same passage contains almost the first instance of the plural of "man of military age[2]," as distinguished from women and children: "And the children of Israel departed... *about* six hundred thousand *on-foot* (or, *footmen*)—*the men [of military age]*, apart from children[3]." This looks back to the first Biblical use of the plural of the word, uttered by Pharaoh, who refuses to let the *"children"* go, but will let the *"men"* (Heb. *geber*) go. In the LXX, these two passages are the first where we find Mark's Greek word for "men" representing the Hebrew *geber*[4] Later on, the Pentateuch omits both *"about"* and "men of military age" in the passionate exclamation of Moses *"Six hundred thousand footmen (or, travellers on foot)* are the people amid whom I am[5]." Jewish tradition notes the apparent discrepancy between this and the preceding mention of the same number; for, during

---

[1] Exod xii 37 Heb כ "like," *i e.* about LXX εἰς "amounting to" This is the first instance mentioned in Gesen. 453 *a*. Strong's Concordance, which is generally very accurate, omits it.

[2] Heb גבר, *geber* See Gesen 149—50

[3] Exod xii 37 "apart from *children* (טף)," LXX πλὴν τῆς ἀποσκευῆς 'Αποσκευή, outside LXX, would mean "baggage," the Latin "impedimenta," but in LXX it freq represents טף, *"children"* Here Aq has χωρὶς ἀπὸ νηπίου, Sym ...τοῦ ὄχλου. Comp Exod x 10—11, where Pharaoh says to Moses that he will not let go the "children (טף)" (LXX, Aq. and Sym as here) but "Go ye, now, *the men [of military age]*," Aq πορεύεσθε δή, οἱ ἄνδρες, LXX πορευέσθωσαν δὲ οἱ ἄνδρες (a variation that somewhat resembles the variation in the punctuation of Jn vi 10). Steph. *Thes* does not mention this meaning of ἀποσκευή, but see Gen. xxxiv. 29, xliii 8, etc

[4] 'Ανήρ in Pentateuch occurs about 180 times, but not as representing *geber* except in these two passages and Deut. xxii 5 (forbidding an adult male to put on woman's clothing, and *vice versa*)

[5] Numb. xi 21.

349 (Mark vi 29—44)

the interval, the number is stated elsewhere to have increased. Accordingly Rashi says "Moses was not solicitous" about including additions[1]. Many passages in Midrash comment on the numbering of Israel on or before the night of the Exodus as one of ten occasions on which Israel was numbered[2].

Passing to the Gospels we see that some of their variations correspond to variations in Hebrew Scripture or Jewish tradition. Mark's omission in one narrative, and insertion in another, of "*about*" and "*men [of military age]*," corresponds to the omission of these words in Numbers and the insertion of them in Exodus Matthew's insertion of "*men*" in both narratives indicates that he regarded "*men*" as emphatic, meaning "*men, not to speak of women and children*" This followed the precedent of Exodus, where "apart from *children*" was interpreted by R. Ishmael as "apart from *the women and the little ones*," and by R. Jonathan as "apart from *the women, the children, and the aged*[3]."

---

[1] See Exod xxxviii 26, Numb. 1. 45—6 "all that were able to go forth to war ..603,550" (comp. Numb 11 32) Rashi, on Numb xi 21, says "Non solicitus fuit [Moses] ut singulatim numeraret," and tells us of a Rabbi who suggested that the additional 3550 (called by him 3000) were not included because they did not murmur—so that they did not belong to the sixty myriads destined to die in the wilderness

This view is confirmed by Sir xvi 8 "So were 600,000 רגלי, edd *footmen, that were taken away in the arrogancy of their heart*," Sir xlvi 8 "two alone were reserved, *out of* 600,000 רגלי, edd *men on foot*" Clem. Rom § 43 calls them "*the* 600,000," although at the time mentioned (Numb xvii 1 foll) the number would have been increased, συνεκάλεσεν πάντα τὸν Ἰσραὴλ, τὰς ἑξακοσίας χιλιάδας τῶν ἀνδρῶν

Sota 12 b gives a quaint interpretation of רגלי, "footmen," in the utterance of Moses It meant "*on my account*," and implied a presumption for which Moses was punished!

[2] Ten occasions are mentioned in *Numb. r* on Numb 11 32, and *Pesikta* sect 2, Wu p 18 etc In *Numb r* on Numb xxvi 2 it is said that whenever Israel went wrong it needed to be numbered

[3] See *Mechilt* on Exod xii 37.

It is more difficult to say why John inserts *"in number,"* before "about five thousand." It is apparently superfluous. Yet in his subtle, mystical, and allusive Gospel cautious critics will very seldom confidently commit themselves to a statement that they have found superfluities Can it be that John is affected by Jewish traditions above referred to concerning the "numbering" of Israel as being connected with imperfection or evil?

That, perhaps, is the Johannine view When Luke in the Acts mentions "number" in passage after passage describing the growth of the Church, he does it with obvious satisfaction[1]. But it is doubtful whether John has any such satisfaction in the numbering of the Five Thousand. Regarded mystically, the number "five" is of the flesh, like the "five husbands" of the woman of Samaria, and "the five barley loaves" are typical of rudimentary revelation. Regarded historically (according to John's view), the Five Thousand so completely fail to understand the nature of Christ's sign that they are described as purposing "to snatch him away that they may make him a king[2]." We can at least say that this explanation is more probable than the hypothesis that John inserted *"in number"*—and this in a narrative so familiar to the Church in various forms and so obviously typical—without attaching to the insertion some meaning, or at all events some allusive significance.

---

[1] Ἀριθμός occurs in the Acts (iv 4, etc), four times out of five, about the growth of the Church But in the Epistles it occurs only in Rom ix. 27 "If the *number* of the children of Israel be as the sand of the sea *it shall be the remnant that shall be saved*" This appears to depreciate the value of "numbering." The other N.T. instances of ἀριθμός (except Lk xxii 3 "Judas...of the number of the twelve") are all (10) in Revelation This book also (vii 9) speaks of "a great multitude which no one could number, standing before the throne" The first mention of "counting" and "numbering" in the Bible is in Gen. xiii 16 (comp xvi 10) and declares that the seed of Abraham *cannot* be numbered.

[2] Jn vi 15.

CHRIST'S MIRACLES OF FEEDING

§ 32. *Irenaeus and Origen on the "five thousand" in the Acts, and Clement of Alexandria on the "five loaves"*

The narratives of the Feeding of the Five Thousand are likely to have been influenced not only by allusions to the events in the history of Israel, and particularly the giving of the manna, but also by prospective allusions to the growth of the Christian Church, more particularly during the period when thousands at a time were converted, according to the Acts, by the preaching of Peter. This influence is not likely to have been so great as that of Eucharistic allusion, but still it is not to be passed by.

Irenaeus says that the convincing effect of prophecy in bringing souls into the Church explains the success of the apostolic preaching, whereby "on one day there were baptized *three thousand men, and four, and five*[1]." The Acts mentions the "baptizing" of "three thousand," and subsequently speaks of "five thousand," but nowhere *"four thousand"*; and such language, however it may be explained, shews that early variations might arise about the details of the growth of the Church, some of which might bear on the Gospel narratives of miraculous Feeding[2]. Origen, if his text is not corrupt,

---

[1] Iren iv 23. 2 "et una die baptizati sunt hominum tria millia, et quatuor, et quinque"

[2] Acts II 41 οἱ μὲν οὖν ἐβαπτίσθησαν, καὶ προσετέθησαν ἐν τῇ ἡμέρᾳ ἐκείνῃ ψυχαὶ ὡσεὶ τρισχίλιαι, iv 4 πολλοὶ δὲ τῶν ἀκουσάντων τὸν λόγον ἐπίστευσαν καὶ ἐγενήθη ἀριθμὸς τῶν ἀνδρῶν ὡς χιλιάδες πέντε Grabe on Irenaeus points to Acts II 47 ὁ δὲ κύριος προσετίθει τοὺς σωζομένους καθ' ἡμέραν as a possible explanation The tradition from which Irenaeus borrowed may have stated that the number of the baptized *"became* on one day 3000, and then 4000, and then 5000" "The [total] number *became"* might easily be confused with "the number [added on this or that occasion] *was.*" Comp. Acts iv 4 ἐγενήθη, A V *"was,"* R V. *"came to be."* This may be illustrated by a difference between Lk ix 13—14 Curet "'But let us go ourselves [and] buy food for all this multitude,' *for they were become five thousand men,"* and SS "'Except we go and buy ourselves food for all this multitude, *for*

appears to combine the Feeding of the Five Thousand by our Lord with the conversion of the Three Thousand in the Acts, and to regard both as fulfilments of the exclamation of Isaiah, "Shall a nation be brought forth at once[1]?" Jerome, commenting fully on the same prophecy, says "It also refers to that time when, on one day, there believed three thousand, and five thousand, of the Jewish people[2]." But Origen's text, as it stands, by inserting a mention of *the Saviour's "Incarnation,"* and also by placing the Five Thousand before the Three Thousand, makes it difficult to suppose that he is referring merely to the Acts. Possibly "three," in Origen's text, is an error for "four." His view certainly was that the miracle of the Four Thousand typified the inclusion of the Gentiles. This "inclusion," if Origen wrote "four thousand," he may have described (in the language of the Acts) as "adding," just as he describes the miracle of the Five Thousand (in the language of the Acts) as "believing":—"When the Saviour

---

they are five thousand men'" Possibly Acts iv 4 ἐγενήθη ἀριθμὸς τῶν ἀνδρῶν is a corruption of some tradition that "there was made a numbering (ἀρίθμησις) of the men." Something is needed (but Hebrew origination might suffice) to explain the omission of ὁ before ἀριθμός (comp Acts vi 7 ὁ ἀριθμὸς τῶν μαθητῶν).

[1] Origen *Jerem Hom* ix 3 (on Is lxvi 8) "But 'a nation was brought forth (ἐτέχθη) at once' *when the Saviour (?) had been with us on earth* (ὅτε ἐπιδεδήμηκεν ὁ Σωτήρ) and in one day five thousand believed (ἐπίστευσαν) and on another day there were added (προσετέθησαν) three thousand." I do not understand the force of the perfect ἐπιδεδήμηκεν contrasted with the aorists. Is it possible that we should read the pluperf ἐπεδεδημήκει, i e "when the Saviour had [*recently*] *been incarnate*"? Comp the earliest instance of ἐπιδημέω quoted in Euseb *H E* iv 3 2 (from Quadratus) οὐδὲ ἐπιδημοῦντος μόνον τοῦ Σωτῆρος ἀλλὰ καὶ ἀπαλλαγέντος. In that case we must suppose that Origen is quoting from the Acts but reverses the order of the Acts in order to put the larger number first. "There 'believed,' as the Acts says, five thousand men, and on another [and earlier] day there were added [to the Church], as the Acts says, three thousand."

[2] "Et ad illud tempus referre quando una die tria millia et quinque millia de Judaico populo crediderunt."

was on earth and there *'believed'* (Acts iv. 4) in one day Five Thousand, and in another day there were *'added'* (Acts ii. 41) Four Thousand[1]."

Other early Christian literature throws little light on distinctions between the Synoptic "five thousand" and "four thousand," or the "five loaves" and the "seven loaves." The plural "loaves" is not used by the Apostolic Fathers and Apologists[2]. The only mention of the "five loaves" by Irenaeus is in an attempt to shew that the number "five" is of frequent occurrence in Scripture and need not have the mystical meaning attributed to it by heretics. In doing this, he asserts that "*five*" is the number of the pillars that support the veil of the Holy of Holies. But in fact there were "*four*[3]." His error is the less excusable because Philo had taught that the "*four*" pillars before the Holy of Holies were spiritually superior to the "*five*" pillars before the screen of the Tabernacle[4]. Clement of Alexandria adopts Philo's interpretation of the "*five* pillars" as referring to the things of the senses and applies it depreciatively to "the *five* loaves," which, he says, "are most mystically broken by the Saviour, and supply fulness (?) to the crowd of those hearing Him; for great [indeed is] *the [crowd] that gives heed to the things of sense as being alone realities*[5]." Clement then mentions "the four pillars" that

---

[1] That is to say, the *order* of the two miracles is that of the Gospels, but the *language* is that of the Acts, because Origen regards the miracle placed second in the Gospels as being of the nature of an "addition" such as the Acts connects with "three thousand." If Origen wrote thus, it would be very natural for scribes to alter his "four" into "three" (Δ into Γ)

[2] Goodspeed gives it, however, as a v r of Cod A in Justin Martyr *Apol* lxvii 3 ὡς προέφημεν . ἄρτος προσφέρεται, where προέφημεν refers to ch lxv and ch lxvi mentioning the sing ἄρτος.

[3] Iren ii 24 4

[4] Philo on Exod xxvi 32—37 Irenaeus (see Grabe's note which should have been added in Clark's translation) has confused the two verses

[5] Clem. Alex 665 ταύτῃ τοὶ μυστικώτατα πέντε ἄρτοι πρὸς τοῦ Σωτῆρος

stand at the entrance of the Holy of Holies, as being typical of a more inward and spiritual knowledge Then he passes to the number "seven," as being that of the planets and of the branches of the sacred lamp, and of "the seven eyes of the Lord" which ("they say") are "the seven spirits resting on the rod that flowers from the root of Jesse[1]." Although Clement does not, in this connection, make mention of the "seven loaves" that were broken for the "four thousand," the transition suggests that he had that thought in his mind. If he had, it would be consistent with Origen's view that the miracle of the Four Thousand was higher in the spiritual scale than the earlier miracle of the Five Thousand.

§ 33. *"Give ye them to eat," why omitted by John*

This omission has not been commented on above because our first business has been to discuss Marcan passages omitted or altered by Luke, and this is not one of them. All the Synoptists have the words "Give ye them to eat," and all of them, especially Luke, emphasize the pronoun "*ye*[2]." Origen explains the emphasis, allegorizing the "eating," as if Jesus meant "*Ye*, my disciples, *ye* whom I have trained to give the Bread of Life to others, give *ye* them to eat, and do not think of sending away the hungry multitude unfed[3]." Origen also, in his own person, declares that Jesus "said *Give ye them to*

κατακλῶνται καὶ πληθύνουσι τῷ ὄχλῳ τῶν ἀκροωμένων, πολὺς γὰρ ὁ τοῖς αἰσθητοῖς ὡς μόνοις οὖσι προσανέχων Πληθύνω is perhaps used as a mild paraphrase of χορτάζω.

[1] Rev v 6, Is. xi 1.

[2] In Mk vi 37, Mt xiv 16 δότε αὐτοῖς ὑμεῖς φαγεῖν, the addition of ὑμεῖς to δότε shews that the pronoun in "give *ye*" is emphasized, but in Lk ix 13 (W H txt) δότε αὐτοῖς φαγεῖν ὑμεῖς, "*ye*" is extraordinarily emphatic, coming at the end of the sentence

[3] Origen on Mt xiv 16 (Lomm iii 68) Ἐπεὶ οὖν παιδεύσας ὑμᾶς ἱκανοὺς ἐποίησα πρὸς τὸ διδόναι τοῖς δεομένοις λογικὴν τροφὴν, ὑμεῖς δότε...

eat because of that power to feed others besides themselves which He had bestowed on the disciples[1]."

It may be taken as certain that John did not believe that the disciples had received at this time the "power to feed others" in the full spiritual sense. Origen adds "So long as these five loaves and two fishes were not *borne* (or, *brought*) by the disciples of Jesus, they did not increase[2]." But John represents Jesus as Himself distributing the bread to the multitude[3], and excludes the disciples from any part in the miracle except the collecting of the broken pieces. The Johannine view of the miracle is quite different from that of the Synoptists. In John, Jesus cannot say to the disciples "Give *ye* them to eat," for they have nothing to give. The loaves do not belong to them. Origen himself points out this, though he quaintly connects it with the inferior nature of the "barley" loaves. "John alone says that the loaves were 'barley loaves.' Wherefore, perhaps, in the Gospel of John, the disciples *do not acknowledge that the loaves are with them,* but say, in John, 'There is a lad here who has five barley loaves and two fishes[4].'"

It must be admitted that John, by omitting Christ's precept to the Twelve, not only greatly lowers the spiritual character of the Feeding of the Five Thousand, but also departs from what appears to be the earliest and most faithful traditions about it. In the Synoptists, the miracle is a kind of firstfruits of the Eucharist, illustrating the Christian Law of Giving. In the Fourth Gospel, it is a kind of last repetition of the old

---

[1] Origen (Lomm. III 69) δι' ἣν ἔδωκε δύναμιν καὶ ἑτέρων θρεπτικὴν τοῖς μαθηταῖς.
[2] Origen (Lomm. III 70) ὅσον μὲν οὐκ ἐφέροντο. Is it possible that he is referring to Mt xiv 18 φέρετέ μοι ὧδε αὐτούς, "bring them hither to me," so that the meaning is "Until they were *brought by the disciples of Jesus* [*to their Master*]"? Ἐφέροντο does not seem a suitable word to mean "*distributed*" by the disciples to the multitudes.
[3] Jn vi 11, omitted in the Arabic Diatessaron.
[4] Origen (Lomm. III 70).

CHRIST'S MIRACLES OF FEEDING

gift of Manna, and the old gift of the Law, exemplifying the failure of both to satisfy and redeem mankind, and demonstrating the need of a new source of spiritual life[1].

§ 34 *"Eating" in the presence of the Lord*

We have spoken above of the meal provided by Elisha for a hundred of the sons of the prophets; but some mention should also be made of an earlier Scriptural precedent, when Aaron and two of Aaron's sons and seventy of the elders of Israel went up with Moses, "and they saw the God of Israel...and they beheld God *and did eat and drink."* The latter part of this is paraphrased by Onkelos, "They saw the Glory of the Lord, and *rejoiced in their sacrifices, which were accepted with favour, as though they had eaten and drunk,"* but by the Jerusalem Targum, "They saw the Glory of the Shekinah of the Lord, and *rejoiced that their oblations were received with favour, and so did eat and drink*[2]." The passage is frequently referred to in Midrash, where it is mostly implied that Aaron's sons were led into error, perhaps an error of familiarity, in eating and drinking, and were punished for it[3]. But other passages

---

[1] If many versions or MSS followed Lk ix 13 (codex *a*) "date eis manducare" (omitting *"vos"*) we might suppose that textual variations induced John to omit a phrase that meant no more than "give them something to eat" But the omission in codex *a* is so exceptional that nothing can be based on it And the conclusion seems necessary that John's omission was dictated almost entirely by the feeling that the real Eucharistic "giving" was not understood, and indeed was not fully instituted, till after the Resurrection, when Jesus gave the command "Feed my sheep"

[2] Exod xxiv 9—11 The Targums are quoted from Etheridge

[3] See *Exod r* (Wu pp 38, 317), *Lev. r* (Wu p 136), *Numb r.* (Wu. p 411), *Pesikt* (Wu p 252) Rashi says *ad loc* "contemplati erant illum curiose (*or*, animo elato) etiam inter edendum ac bibendum, sic interpretatio Tanchumae habet, sed Onkelos non ita interpretatus est" Comp Lev x 8 (Jer Targ) "Drink neither wine nor anything that maketh drunk, ..as thy sons did, who have died by the burning of fire"

connect the "eating and drinking" with a "banquet" on "the glory of the Shechinah," quoting from Proverbs "In the light of the King's countenance is life[1]." This "banquet," and the "sitting down" with Abraham and Isaac and Jacob in the aeon that is to come, are referred to in the tradition of Matthew and Luke[2]. Luke also once connects "table" and "covenant" and "thrones" in such a way as to constitute a parallelism between his words and those of the Pentateuch describing the "eating and drinking" of the "nobles" of Israel[3]; but the parallel Matthew has nothing that suggests a banquet. Nor has Matthew any mention of eating in his parallel to an earlier passage where Luke has "We ate before thee and drank, and in our streets didst thou teach[4]."

In the passage last quoted from Luke, Cyril paraphrases "*ate*" as the imperfect "*used to eat*," supposing that the words were uttered as an appeal to the Father (not to the Son) and that the words "*ate before thee*" referred to sacrifices eaten in the Temple. But if that had been the meaning, the imperfect

---

[1] See Taylor's note on *Aboth* iii 25 "Everything is prepared for the banquet," quoting *Berach* 17 a, and *Numb r* xxi, which says that the ministering angels "are fed on the splendour of the Shechinah, for it is said (Prov. xvi 15) '*In the light* etc'" On Prov xvi 15 see *Pesikt* Wu pp 70, 140, 252, etc

[2] Mt viii 11, Lk xiii 29

[3] Lk xxii 29—30 Comp Exod xxiv 11 "nobles," a noticeable word, LXX ἐπιλέκτων (one of 13 deviations of LXX discussed in the Talmud, see Levy 1 508 a). The parall Mt xix 28 mentions "thrones" and "judging," but has nothing that suggests a banquet

[4] Lk xiii 26 ἐφάγομεν ἐνώπιόν σου καὶ ἐπίομεν The parall. Mt vii 22 οὐ τῷ σῷ ὀνόματι ἐπροφητεύσαμεν is blended by Origen repeatedly with Lk so as to drop the difficult phrase ἐνώπιόν σου. Cyril (see Cramer *ad loc*) explains "*thee*" as "*God*," thus "How then used they to eat and to drink (ἤσθιον καὶ ἔπινον) in the presence of *God*? By performing the sacrificial-service (λατρείαν) of the Law" And he explains "thou didst teach" as referring to the Scriptures, the word of God, heard by the Jews in the synagogues.

might have been used by Luke here as elsewhere[1]. Nevertheless Cyril is right in supposing that "*ate before thee*" is not the same as "*ate with thee*," and that it suggests some act of a disciple of Christ corresponding to the eating of a sacrifice by an Israelite "in the presence of" Jehovah to whom it is offered. But what act, what "eating," could be meant? The least unsatisfactory explanation, perhaps, is that Luke has placed the words in such a position that they may refer to the "eating" of the Five Thousand, which, according to Mark and Luke, was preceded by "teaching" or something corresponding to teaching (so as to fulfil the saying "*thou hast taught* in our streets[2]"). That would bring the Lucan tradition into harmony with the Johannine view, that the Five Thousand, for the most part, though they "*ate in the presence of*" Jesus, never truly knew Him or believed in Him. He "taught" in their "streets," but they did not accept the teaching

We are not, however, on safe ground in attempting to build positive conclusions as to fact on this Lucan passage[3]. For there may have been other occasions to which "we ate" might definitely refer, e g the Feeding of the Four Thousand. That Luke does not mention this miraculous act does not exclude the possibility that he collected traditions referring to it although he did not know the reference And if there were two such miraculous acts why should there not have been three or more—believed to have occurred before the Resurrection? It does not follow that there were only two because Mark has recorded only two, any more than it follows that there was only

---

[1] Lk xvii 27, 28 ἤσθιον, ἔπινον, followed by ἐγάμουν and ἠγόραζον. Ἐσθίω is freq used for habitual or uncompleted eating

[2] Mk vi 34 διδάσκειν, Lk ix 11 ἐλάλει περὶ τῆς βασιλείας τοῦ θεοῦ

[3] The fact that Matthew deviates from Luke, and the nature of Matthew's deviation, indicate that we have not here actual words of Christ, but early evangelistic paraphrases of them, indicating how extremists, on either side, whether anti-judaizers or judaizers, would be rejected by Jesus if they rejected His Spirit.

CHRIST'S MIRACLES OF FEEDING

one because Luke and John have recorded only one—that is to say, only one before the Resurrection. The Acts of John boldly declares that every meal of the disciples with Jesus, even at a Pharisee's table, was miraculous: "Now if ever, having been invited by one of the Pharisees, He went in compliance with such an invitation, we used to go with Him. And one loaf used to be set by the inviter for each [of the guests], among whom He also used to receive one [and no more]. But He, blessing His [own] loaf, would distribute [it] to us. And from the little [thus distributed] each [of us] used to be filled-to-repletion, and our loaves were kept whole and sound, so that amazement fell on those who invited Him[1]."

§ 35. *"That he should give something to the poor," in John*

John tells us that after the Last Supper, when Jesus said, "That thou doest, do (R.V.) quickly," some supposed that Jesus meant "Buy what things we have need of for the feast, or, that he should give something to the poor[2]." Either supposition implies that Judas had been tardy about performing one of two duties that ought seemingly to have been performed before the Supper. We can understand this about the things needed "for the feast"; but how does it apply to the words "that he should give something to the poor"? Was that a duty calling for immediate performance? Only if the duty was connected in the minds of the disciples with the meal at

---

[1] *Acts of John* § 8 "One loaf (ἄρτος εἷς)" appears to be meant to be more emphatic than ἄρτος would have been (without εἷς) "One" is emphasized by its position in "among whom He also used to receive *one* [*and no more*] (ἐν οἷς καὶ αὐτὸς ἐλάμβανεν ἕνα)" "Filled to repletion," ἐχορτάζετο is here used as in the Synoptists, and not in a bad sense (as in Jn vi 26) Incidentally the mention of "one loaf" is important as shewing the smallness of such "loaves" as we read of in the Bible.

[2] Jn xiii 29.

which they were seated. If their Master had habituated them to the practice of giving something to the poor from their common purse on any special occasion when He sat down to a meal with them, in that case—and only in that case—could they suppose that Jesus sent out Judas, the purse-bearer, with something of the nature of a reproach for neglecting the duty to the poor, "That which thou art bound to do, do more quickly[1]"

On another occasion, Luke represents Jesus as saying "Now do ye, the Pharisees, cleanse the outside of the cup... but your inner part is full of ravening....Only *give ye the things that are inside [the vessel] as alms*, and behold, all things are pure unto you[2]." Here the meaning might be taken to be, literally, "send out some of the food in the dish to the poor and then all that is in the dish is pure." The parallel Matthew has "*Cleanse first the inward part of the cup*," shewing that this literalism ("send out to the poor") would not represent the meaning[3]. Yet it may represent a part of the meaning. Luke's version may represent a fact, namely, that Jesus was in the habit of giving to the poor either a portion of the meal at which He presided, or else a gift of money in lieu of that portion where the poor were not present in person. This would be a way of teaching the duty inculcated by Isaiah "Draw out thy soul to the hungry, and satisfy the afflicted soul[4]."

In view of these passages and of what Philo tells us about the common meal of the Therapeutae, we ought not perhaps to put aside the above-quoted grotesque extract from the Acts of John with a mere negation: "Of course there was nothing like this." Of course there was nothing "like this" literally. But

---

[1] Jn xiii 27 τάχιον "more quickly" See *Joh Gr* **1918** and Index

[2] Lk xi 39—41, see *Son* **3362** (iv) *a*, and below, p 455 foll

[3] Mt xxiii 26

[4] Is lviii 10, on the interpretations of which see *Proclam.* p. 312 "It is not to exclude, but to accompany, material giving."

CHRIST'S MIRACLES OF FEEDING

are we not in danger of failing to realise that there may have been something "like this" spiritually, even before the Eucharist was instituted? Even at the house of a Pharisee where Jesus was but a guest, the disciples might be made by Him to feel that He was still their King, and that "in the light of the king's countenance there was life[1]," and that in His doctrine there was the living bread[2]. Much more would this be the case where Jesus was Himself the host and the breaker of the bread. It seems antecedently probable that Jesus would have put into the breaking of the bread, and into the blessing of God over the bread, something beyond the formal Jewish meaning, something that was of the nature of a sacrifice.

In one of the Psalms, what is called by our Revised Version "*the sacrifice of thanksgiving*," is called by the Authorised Version, more simply and more literally, "*thanksgiving*"; and Aquila, too, renders the precept "Sacrifice unto God *eucharist*[3]." The next Psalm says "The sacrifices of God are a broken spirit; a broken and a contrite heart, O God, thou wilt not despise[4]." To such a sacrifice Jesus seems to have pointed in His story of the publican who would not so much as lift up his face to heaven but stood afar off saying "God be merciful to me a sinner[5]."

Sorrow for wrong done to one's neighbour goes hand in hand with love and sympathy for one's neighbour; and the awaking consciousness of one's own sins awakens kindness towards others. Jesus is represented by Matthew as twice quoting from Hosea the words "I desire kindness and not

---

[1] Prov. xvi 15. See above, p. 358, and Addendum on p. 402.
[2] See Addendum on p. 402.
[3] Ps l 14 Aq θῦσον (זבח) τῷ θεῷ εὐχαριστίαν (תודה) (LXX θῦσον τῷ θεῷ θυσίαν αἰνέσεως) See Gesen 393 a. "*Acknowledgment*" would be, in many respects, a good rendering of the Hebrew word תודה, since it could include "confession" and (Gesen 392 b) "thanksgiving."
[4] Ps li. 17.
[5] Lk. xviii. 13, peculiar to Luke.

sacrifice[1]," and by Mark as endorsing the saying of a scribe—that to love God and one's neighbour is "better" than sacrifices[2]. Some early Evangelists may have argued. "We, too, we Christians, have a sacrifice. Jesus did not mean that God really desired no sacrifice The words 'I desire kindness and not sacrifice' are misleading if interpreted apart from the doctrine of Christ as a whole." This may be the reason (or one of the reasons) why Mark and Luke omit the quotation from Hosea, and why Matthew and Luke omit the Marcan tradition. Nevertheless it may be taken as certain that the omitted passages represent Christ's fundamental thought.

§ 36. *"We all partake of the one loaf*[3]*"*

One more remains to be added to the allusions inherent in early traditions about Christ's Doctrine of Bread, and about the acts accompanying it. It comes to us stamped with Pauline authority, but very difficult (one would suppose) for Greeks to understand without some knowledge of Jewish customs[4]. Speaking to his Corinthian converts about the Christian Eucharist Paul says "We all partake of *the one loaf.*"

This assumes that "the one loaf" was the emblem of unity and that the Corinthians understood the assumption. There is nothing in Greek literature that points to, or explains, any such notion. But we learn from Maimonides and from a Talmudic tract called *Erubin,* that is, *Communions* or *Mixings,* that the Jews had such a notion and a practice based upon it. The scribes carried it back to Solomon, and the language used by Paul indicates that it was at all events an established practice of the Synagogue in Corinth during the first century.

---

[1] Mt ix 13, xii. 7 quoting Hos vi 6
[2] Mk xii 33   [3] 1 Cor. x 17.
[4] Acts xviii 7—17 shews the important part played by the Corinthian Synagogue in connection with the foundation of the Corinthian Church.

CHRIST'S MIRACLES OF FEEDING

Maimonides tells us, in effect, that it is forbidden to neighbours to go [on the sabbath day] from one house to another "unless all the neighbours on the sabbath eve enter into communion (*lit.* make an *Erub* or Mixing).... But how is that communion made? They communicate in one food, which they prepare on the eve of the sabbath, as though they would say, We all communicate, and we have all one food[1]" Then he adds that this communion must be made with a whole loaf. Portions, however large they may be, of large loaves, cannot replace the one small loaf however small it may be: "They do not consort together in courts save with a whole loaf[2]."

The Teaching of the Twelve Apostles contains a brief Eucharistic ritual in which what Paul calls "*the loaf that we break*" is briefly called "*the broken [thing]*," or "this which we are breaking[3]" This is said to be a unique use of the word *clasma*, which in the Gospels and elsewhere means "fragment" Certainly it does not mean "fragment" here. For the ritual continues "As this *clasma* existed [once as seed] scattered abroad (*or*, widely sown) on the hills, and having been gathered together, became one, so let thy Church be gathered together

---

[1] See *Hor Heb* on 1 Cor x 17

[2] The quotation continues "Although the bread of the batch be a whole *seah*, if it be not a whole loaf, they do not enter into consortship with it But if it be whole, if it be no more than an *assarius* only, they enter into *consortship* with it"

"How do they enter into κοινωνίαν, *communion*, in the courts? They demand of every house which is in the court one whole cake or loaf, which they lay up in one vessel, and in some house which is in the court, although it be a barn, or a stable etc And one of the company blesseth, and so all eat together," etc

The phrase for "a whole loaf" is פת שלימה בלבד "a loaf complete by itself" Apparently the blessing and breaking would take place over one of these "whole loaves," one representing the whole number

[3] *Didach* ix 3 περὶ δὲ τοῦ κλάσματος· Εὐχαριστοῦμέν σοι . follows πρῶτον περὶ τοῦ ποτηρίου· Εὐχαριστοῦμέν σοι, implying that "the broken" was a Eucharistic term as familiar to the readers as "the cup"

from the ends of the earth into thy kingdom[1]." This passage, and the Jewish practice of "communion by means of the one loaf," indicate that the word "bread (*or* loaf)" conveyed to Jews suggestions of unity that would be unintelligible to Greeks without explanation.

In the first passage where "bread" is mentioned in the Bible the LXX represents God as saying to Adam "In the sweat of thy brow shalt thou eat thy bread[2]" But the Hebrew omits "thy," and the Targum takes the meaning to be, in effect, "Thou shalt be permitted to eat bread, the food of man, instead of eating the herb of the field, the food of beasts—which was at first the sentence pronounced on thee." The Jews appear to have discerned in a loaf—prepared by the hand of man out of many particles through many processes, sowing, reaping, threshing, grinding, kneading and baking—a unity not apparent in a heap of grass or herbs. This unity seemed a fit symbol of the unifying power that converts individuals into a community, congregation, or church When and whence this notion came into their literature is perhaps not ascertainable, but that it was current among the Christians of the first century is certain. We ought therefore to be prepared to find a trace of it in the Fourth Gospel.

§ 37. "*Jesus...taketh the loaf and giveth to them*[3]," *in John*

The Fourth Gospel concludes with a description of Jesus giving a meal in the morning to seven of His disciples who

---

[1] *Didach* IX. 4 ὥσπερ ἦν τοῦτο τὸ κλάσμα διεσκορπισμένον ἐπάνω τῶν ὀρέων καὶ συναχθὲν ἐγένετο ἕν, οὕτω συναχθήτω σου ἡ ἐκκλησία ἀπὸ τῶν περάτων τῆς γῆς εἰς τὴν σὴν βασιλείαν The position of ἦν shews that it is best taken by itself and not as part of a pluperf "had been scattered" See p 340, n. 2, for Jerome's saying "seminarium fit ciborum," and see *Son* **3606** *a* for the metaphor of "sowing" Israel

[2] Gen. III. 19.

[3] Jn XXI 13 ἔρχεται Ἰησοῦς καὶ λαμβάνει τὸν ἄρτον καὶ δίδωσιν αὐτοῖς. On Jn XXI 9 A V. "fish.. bread," Westcott says "Rather, *a fish* . *a loaf*.... Compare *ib* 13 *the fish...the loaf* The thought of unity

have been fishing The food is first spoken of thus, as being seen by the fishermen disciples who have been fishing: "So when they got out upon the land they see a fire of coals laid and a fish laid thereon and a loaf[1]." No mention is made of the source whence the food came. Nor are the fishermen at once invited to partake of it First they are bidden to draw in the net They had caught nothing all through the night But at the dawn, having been instructed to cast the net "on the right side," they have at last caught a draught, and the "*at last*" is emphasized in the command "Bring of the fish that ye have *now* taken." When this duty is performed they are invited to the morning meal, and then it is said that Jesus "cometh and taketh the loaf and giveth to them and the fish likewise"

Why and whence is Jesus described as "coming"? Is He to be regarded as now coming from a distance although at the beginning of the story He "stood on the beach" and the disciples have now "got out upon the land"? This seems impossible. "Coming" seems superfluous, if taken literally. But it may be taken as the act of "Him that Cometh[2]," like the Light that "cometh into the world," coming to all the seven collectively and to each individually. Then it becomes intelligible.

Similarly as regards the "taking," we are not to regard the word literally as signifying that He went to the fire and

---

seems to be distinctly presented" In Jn vi 11, W. H read διέδωκεν (Tisch. ἔδωκεν) but here δίδωσιν (D εὐχαριστήσας ἔδωκεν). In Jn xxi. 13, SS has "and Jesus took [the] bread and [the] fish and blessed [God] over them and gave to them"

[1] Jn xxi 9 βλέπουσιν ἀνθρακιὰν κειμένην καὶ ὀψάριον ἐπικείμενον R V omits κειμένην, or paraphrases it by "there" But in view of John's use of κεῖμαι elsewhere and the contextual ἐπικείμενον here, it seems desirable to render the two participles "*laid*" and "*laid thereon*" See below, p. 368 foll

[2] On "Him that Cometh" as a name of the Messiah, see *Joh Voc* 1633, *Son* 3239—41.

CHRIST'S MIRACLES OF FEEDING

took off the loaf[1], either once for all the disciples, or seven times for each of them He "takes" it as the father of any Jewish family might "take" bread in his hands before blessing God and breaking it In the Feeding of the Five Thousand Jesus is described as "giving separately" or "distributing." Here He simply "gives." What He "gives," whether a part of the loaf or the whole, is not made clear. It would have been easy to make it clear. But the writer leaves it in doubt—with what looks like deliberate purpose—as if to lead us to say "After all, what does it matter? Jesus comes. This must mean He comes to each He gives. This must mean He gives to each. And what else can He give to us as our bread except Himself? We had a foretaste of this truth in the sign of the barley loaves; and the truth itself is now set forth in this homely farewell breakfast given by the Lord to prepare the disciples to labour for Him after His departure."

If words that at first appear superfluous in this narrative are to be regarded as symbolical or allusive, what symbolical meaning are we to attach to the *"fire of coals laid"*? Why is the word *"laid"* inserted—a word so superfluous (seemingly) that it is left untranslated by our English Versions? And what allusion, if any, exists in the rare word "fire-of-coals"? The Greek for "fire of coals" occurs nowhere else in N.T. except in the Johannine account of Peter's denials. There it is said that the servants of the High Priest had "made" the *"fire of coals,"* but here no "maker" or "layer" is mentioned. A supernatural origin is however suggested, like that of the "coals" by the side of Elijah whom "an angel touched," and "he looked, and behold, there was at his head a cake *baken on the coals*[2]." The Hebrew there rendered "coals" occurs nowhere else except in Isaiah "Then flew one of the seraphim

---

[1] Apparently the loaf is on the embers. So Nonnus takes it, calling the loaf νέον, "new," and the fire μαραινομένην, *i e* dying down

[2] 1 K xix 6 *"coals,"* marg. *"hot stones."*

unto me having *a live coal* in his hand," where the touch of the coal purifies the prophet's lips and prepares him to deliver his message[1] An ancient Christian commentary calls attention to the coincidence that Peter "denied and confessed near a coal fire[2]" Are we to suppose that it is more than a coincidence, and that the coal fire represents trial or temptation of two kinds.—first, in the High Priest's palace, temptation, for evil, proceeding from men, secondly, by the Sea of Tiberias, temptation, for good[3]. proceeding from God?

There is more to be said for such a view than at first sight appears. For if such a representation were intended we could the better understand that this fire is regarded as "laid," "set," or "appointed." The Greek word is the same as that used in the sayings "The axe is *laid* to the root of the trees[4]," and "This [child] is (lit) *laid* (R V *set*) for the falling and rising up of many in Israel[5]." It is also used by John in connection with the sign of the wine at Cana: "Now there were there stone water-vessels, six [in number], in accordance with the purifying of the Jews, *laid [ready]*," that is, *prepared for use, or for Christ's sign*[6]. And the same apparent superfluity and latent mysticism is to be found in the account of the vinegar at the Cross: "After this, Jesus,...that the scripture might be accomplished, saith, I thirst A vessel lay [ready for

---

[1] Is vi 6 "*live coal*," marg "*hot stone*"

[2] See *Son* **3369** *a* foll

[3] Yet where is the "temptation for good"? May we see it in the question "Lovest thou me *more than these?*" as if it meant "Wilt thou still *set thyself up above the others*, and say, *Though all should stumble yet not I?*" In his reply, Peter does not now give prominence to "I" but to "Thou" That is to say he makes no profession directly about himself, but appeals to Christ's knowledge ("thou knowest that I love thee")

[4] Mt iii. 10, Lk. iii 9   [5] Lk ii 34

[6] Jn ii 6 ἦσαν δὲ ἐκεῖ λίθιναι ὑδρίαι ἓξ κατὰ τὸν καθαρισμὸν τῶν Ἰουδαίων κείμεναι The *Philocalia* of Origen § 12 (Lomm xxv 14) paraphrases this as αἱ ἐπὶ καθαρισμῷ τῶν Ἰουδαίων ὑδρίαι κεῖσθαι λεγόμεναι, but that is only a paraphrase

CHRIST'S MIRACLES OF FEEDING

the soldiers, or for the fulfilment of scripture] full of vinegar[1]." Similarly here the meaning may be that the "coal fire" was "laid" by the hand of God, the sign of that fiery trial through which the soul is to pass into communion with Him This is a new revelation not given to the Five Thousand. They took the bread of the barley loaves and were filled with it as cattle with fodder. But this bread, or rather this one loaf, comes *"laid above"* fire; and the fire itself is no ordinary one, but fire as from the altar in heaven, *"laid"* by the hand of God

It should be noted that after Peter and the rest have partaken of this food baked on the coal fire, Peter is warned that he himself will "follow" Jesus on the way of the Cross, dying by crucifixion. If that is to be his fiery trial, the question arises whether in early Christian literature there are any traces of a comparison between martyrdom and the baking of bread baked on the coals There is something of the kind in the account of the martyrdom of Polycarp. He was burned alive, and the martyr's body is said to have emitted a fragrant odour like that of *"bread that is being baked*[2]*"* Eusebius omits this; but there can hardly be a doubt that he omits it, not as a corrupt reading but in fear that the detail might shock his readers The fear was (doubtless) well grounded in the days of Constantine. But when the Church was not yet established, and while it was still being watered with the blood of martyrs, passionate metaphor was natural and necessary Clement of Alexandria not only uses language resembling that rejected by Eusebius, but also applies it to Christ Himself Commenting on the words of Jesus "The bread that I will give is my flesh, which I will give for the life of the world," Clement implies that the *"flesh"* must be prepared by *"fire"* to become the food of the world Then, playing on the double meaning of

---

[1] Jn xix 29 σκεῦος ἔκειτο ὄξους μεστόν Nonnus "there was ready (ἑτοῖμον ἔην)"

[2] *Polyc Mart* § 15 ὡς ἄρτος ὀπτώμενος (v r ὀπτόμενος) is omitted (Lightf) by Eusebius

the Greek *puros*, i.e. "fire" or "wheat," he introduces the thought of the wheat rising up in a kind of resurrection, and likens it at the same time to "*bread that is being baked*[1]" Aesthetically such language may be repellent, but it will be of use if it leads us to think how very much is implied by the author of the Fourth Gospel, for himself and for those who are in sympathy with him, by the vision of "the fire of coals" and that which was "laid thereon."

§ 38. *Christ's "leaven"*

This loaf that is seen, along with the fish, on "the coal fire[2]," is it to be supposed to be leavened or unleavened? The same question applies to the "one loaf" that the disciples had with them when they were told to "beware of leaven[3]." Tertullian implies a connection of "leaven" with fire through the "oven" in which bread is baked[4]. He is referring to Christ's saying that the Kingdom of God "is like unto leaven, which a woman took and hid in three measures of meal till it was all leavened[5]", but he does not explain to us the nature of this "leaven," or its relation to "the leaven of the Pharisees." Ignatius recognises a "*new leaven*" as appertaining to Christ[6].

---

[1] Clem. Alex 125 ἐνταῦθα τὸ μυστικὸν τοῦ ἄρτου παρασημειωτέον, ὅτι σάρκα αὐτὸν λέγει καὶ ὡς ἀνισταμένην δῆθεν διὰ πυρός, καθάπερ ἐκ φθορᾶς καὶ σπορᾶς ὁ πυρὸς ἀνίσταται, καὶ μέντοι διὰ πυρὸς συνισταμένην εἰς εὐφροσύνην ἐκκλησίας ὡς ἄρτον πεπτόμενον

[2] Jn xxi 9   [3] Mk viii 15

[4] Tertullian *Adv Marc.* (on Lk xiii 21) "fermentationem quoque congruere..regno Creatoris quia post illam clibanus vel furnus gehennae sequatur." See context. Is he referring to Hosea vii 4?

[5] Mt. xiii 33 ὁμοία ἐστὶν ἡ βασιλεία τῶν οὐρανῶν ζύμῃ ἣν λαβοῦσα γυνὴ ἐνέκρυψεν εἰς ἀλεύρου σάτα τρία ἕως οὗ ἐζυμώθη ὅλον, sim. Lk xiii 21

[6] Ign *Magn* § 10 ὑπέρθεσθε οὖν τὴν κακὴν ζύμην τὴν παλαιωθεῖσαν καὶ ἐνοξίσασαν, καὶ μεταβάλεσθε εἰς νέαν ζύμην, ὅς ἐστιν Ἰησοῦς Χριστός. On this, Lightf quotes 1 Cor v 7 "purge out *the old leaven*," but gives no instance of "*new leaven*." He adds "On the metaphor generally see the note *Galatians* v 9." In that note, he says "The

CHRIST'S MIRACLES OF FEEDING

Justin Martyr recognises a "*new leaven*" as the opposite of the "*old*" Egyptian "*leaven*," which was to be superseded by the "new," after the brief interval of the week of unleavened bread[1]. It is possible that this aspect of Christ's doctrine—implying an antithesis between "old leaven" and "new leaven," between "bad leaven" and "good leaven"—was overshadowed by the Pauline antithesis between "leaven" and "the unleavened[2]." At all events it is a significant fact that in the writings of the early Christian Fathers and Apologists the words "leaven" and "unleavened" do not occur except in

---

leaven of Scripture is always a symbol of evil, with the single exception of the parable (Matt xiii 33, Luke xiii 20, 21), as it is for the most part also in rabbinical writers see Lightfoot on Matt xvi. 6 and Schottgen on 1 Cor v 6."

But "for the most part" would be misleading if it led the reader to suppose that either Lightfoot (*i e* the author of *Horae Hebraicae*) or Schottgen quotes, from "rabbinical writers," a single instance of "leaven" in a good sense Nor does Wetstein quote one Nor is any alleged in the Biblical Dictionaries of Black and Hastings ("Leaven") Dr A Buchler informs me that he has been unable to find any such instance

[1] Justin (*Tryph* § 14) is bold enough to say to the Jews "Wherefore also, *after the seven days of eating unleavened bread*, God commanded you to knead for yourselves *new leaven*, that is to say, the doing of other works and not the imitation of those that were old and vile " He has previously said (*ib*) "For this is the symbol of the unleavened, [being intended] in order that ye may not do the old deeds of *the evil leaven* "

[2] 1 Cor v 6 foll "Know ye not that a little *leaven* leaveneth the whole lump? Purge out *the old leaven*, that ye may be a new lump, even as ye are *unleavened* For our passover also hath been sacrificed, [even] Christ, wherefore let us keep the feast, not with *old leaven*, neither with *the leaven of malice and wickedness*, but with the *unleavened bread* of sincerity and truth "

If Paul had been asked "But what are we to do during the rest of the Christian Year, after keeping the Christian Passover? Are we never to partake of the bread described by our Lord as 'wholly leavened'?" he would doubtless have replied "Yes" But he deals with a different aspect of the metaphor, as if Christians were always keeping their Passover.

the two passages quoted above from Ignatius and Justin Martyr, and in one other instance where Justin says to the Jews "If ye eat *unleavened* bread ye say that ye have fulfilled the will of God[1]." Perhaps one reason why the doctrine of Christ's leaven fell into the background was that among Gentiles, as well as among Jews, there was a feeling that leaven was corrupt and impure[2]. Another reason may have been that Christ's doctrine was obscured· by superabundant allegorism[3]

---

[1] Justin Martyr *Tryph* § 12.

[2] See Lightf on Gal v 9, "Plutarch, *Quaest Rom* 109 (p 289 E), in answer to the question why the Flamen Dialis was not allowed to touch leaven, explains it, ἡ ζύμη καὶ γέγονεν ἐκ φθορᾶς αὐτὴ καὶ φθείρει τὸ φύραμα μιγνυμένη " Comp. Tertull *Adv Marc* iv 30 "post illam [i e fermentationem] clibanus vel furnus gehennae "

[3] Jerome, on Mt xiii 33, gives three explanations of it, and says that he has not space for others Many of them might deal with the allegorical meaning of the "three measures of meal," on which see Clem Alex 694 The N.T. ἐνέκρυψεν εἰς ἀλεύρου σάτα τρία might invite comparison with Gen xviii 6 (Aq. Sym) τρία σάτα σεμιδάλεως (al exempl τρία μέτρα ἀλεύρου σεμιδάλεως) καὶ ποίησον ἐγκρυφίας, on which Philo has much to say Clem Alex 693—4 (following Philo) connects Gen xviii 6 ἐγκρυφίας, "cakes hidden [in the embers]" with a mystical "hiding," and subsequently quotes Mt xiii 33 ἐνέκρυψεν, referring to the threefold nature of man

The doctrine of "good leaven" and "bad leaven" seems to imply the pre-existence of a food that can be assimilated to good or evil Elsewhere Jesus speaks of a "good eye" and an "evil eye," and of an antagonism, or want of harmony, between "the flesh" and "the spirit," and implies (Mk xiv 38, Mt xxvi 41, but not Lk) that man can control the evil or the weakness. Some of these expressions may be illustrated by a very ancient Jewish doctrine about a "good" and a "bad" *nature* in man See *Aboth* iv. 2 "Who is mighty ? He that subdues *his nature* (יצרו) " (Taylor's note). The Heb *yetser* (Gesen 428) meant "*form, framing, purpose,*" occurring for the first time in Gen vi 5 "every *imagination* of the thoughts of his [man's] heart was only evil " It means, in New Heb , "*impulse*" or "*tendency*" (Gesen "good or bad tendency in man") Levy gives abundant instances of the New Heb use, and (ii 258) of the fem יצירה meaning the earthly and the heavenly shaping ("Bildung") of man Inter alia it quotes j. *Jeb.* iv. 5ᶜ "zwei Bildungen

And yet is it not in accordance with the simple homeliness and restfulness of Christ's doctrines that He should have raised a protest for leaven as an emblem of quiet and unobtrusive growth, and for leavened bread as a homely and pleasant gift of God? Luke places the parables of leaven and mustard seed after the sabbath cure of the "daughter of Abraham." The ruler of the synagogue reproved the act. Jesus said to him and his abettors, "Ye hypocrites[1]!" He implies that they were defiled with "the leaven of the Pharisees,"—a hypocritical zeal, a sin against the light, in placing the literal prohibitions of the Law of Leviticus above the dictates of natural humanity God, in Nature, works not so much by repressing as by developing. And this Jesus proceeded to shew by the parables of the mustard seed, and of the leaven fermenting in the loaf. The leaven was kindness, divine kindness, passing from the Father in heaven to His children and from His children to one another

An instance of what Paul might have called "*the leaven of the Pharisees*" may be found in the record of the proceedings

---

des Menschen, naml zuerst innerhalb dreier Tage nach Empfang des Samens, und dann nach 40wochiger Schwangerschaft"

Ign *Magn* § 10, after the words "*new leaven* which is Jesus Christ," continues, "*Be salted* (ἁλίσθητε) in Him, lest any one among you grow putrid (διαφθαρῇ) since from your savour ye will be detected (ἐλεγχθήσεσθε)"—which alludes to Mk ix 49—50 (comp Mt v 13, Lk xiv 34) "for everyone shall be salted with fire " On the other hand Justin Martyr (*Tryph* § 14) before mentioning "*new leaven*," discourses on "*baptism*," and "*the water of life*"—not the "living water" that satisfies spiritual thirst, but the "water of life" regarded as washing away spiritual defilement Both writers illustrate the variety of metaphor with which early Christians, following the earliest traditions of their Master's words, inculcated the doctrine of spiritual regeneration, and they lead to the conclusion that this doctrine was very much more in His thoughts than we might have inferred from the Synoptic Gospels, and from the absence of any continuous discourse about it in the Double Tradition of Matthew and Luke (commonly called "Q").

[1] Lk xiii 15

CHRIST'S MIRACLES OF FEEDING

of the Council of Jerusalem. After the admission of uncircumcised Gentiles to the Church by Peter, in accordance with a revelation from the Lord, "There arose up certain of the sect of the Pharisees who believed, saying, It is needful to circumcise them, and to charge them to keep the law of Moses[1]." Paul did not speak on this occasion. But, had he spoken, it would probably have been to this effect: "In Christ Jesus neither circumcision availeth anything nor uncircumcision, but faith working through love.... This persuasion [cometh] not from him that calleth you. *A little leaven leaveneth the whole lump*[2]" This "little leaven" is leaven in a bad sense. Why cannot we point to mentions of "*a little leaven*" in a good sense? Perhaps because this metaphor was too cosmopolitan for many Jews and too homely and original for many Gentiles But these very reasons are reasons for believing that it originated from Jesus Himself—more alive than His disciples to the quiet and unobtrusive influences of beneficent Nature.

These considerations indicate that the whole of the Mark-Matthew comparison between the Feeding of the Five Thousand and that of the Four Thousand may have been omitted by Luke, not because he disbelieved that there had been such a comparison, but because he believed that it referred to a period after Christ's resurrection The disciples may have received at that time some revelation about the admission of the Gentile element into the Church, such a revelation as Peter received at Joppa. A voice may have come to them from Jesus, warning them against the "leaven" of "the Pharisees," the leaven of exclusiveness and unkindness, and reminding them that all alike, Jews and Gentiles, must feed on a bread that was not unleavened but was leavened with the "new leaven" of "faith working through love" The circumstances of the two acts of feeding were different, but the

---

[1] Acts xv 5   [2] Gal v 6—9.

principle was the same. As the Apostles, when ministering to the twelve tribes of Israel, received correspondently twelve *cophinoi* of fragments, so, when ministering to the multitude of the Gentiles, who came from the four quarters of the world, they received seven *sphurides*, a number that would correspond to "the seven Spirits of God" and "the seven Churches," mentioned in Revelation. The "five loaves" of the Law were broken for the former; the "seven" loaves of the Spirit for the latter. But the loaves were broken by one and the same Lord. The difference did not prevent the recognition of the fact that all alike, Jews and Gentiles, partook of the "one loaf."

§ 39   *The passionateness of the Eucharist*

In the foregoing investigation the main object has been to ascertain, not what was the fact, but what was believed to be the fact by the Evangelists, and especially in those narratives where Luke omitted or altered something that was in Mark. And we have been led to the conclusion that Mark contains traces—not found in Luke and rarely found in Matthew—of early Eucharistic doctrine taught by Christ before the institution of the Eucharist John appears to have cleared away what obscured those traces so that they shew something like a path, which he has broadened and lengthened into a highway running right through his Gospel. But this path or highway may guide us to the actual and historical fact.

Among the Jews it was customary for the father of the family, at the commencement of a family meal, to take up a loaf and to bless God over it and break it. This practice Jesus appears to have adopted, breathing into it a new spiritual meaning and a passionateness of His own. It was not enough, He might say, to lift up and break the loaf We must, as Jeremiah said, "lift up our heart with our hands unto God in the heavens[1]," and the best way to lift up the heart to God

---

[1] Lam. iii 41.

the Father in the breaking of bread was to do something from one's heart for His children that had no bread This something was not to be the mere giving of alms for the sake of reward. Such alms (Jesus declared) the Pharisaean formalists gave. They allowed a conventional religion of rules to drive out the natural morality of the conscience. They encouraged a son to withhold a *Corban* from his needy parents in order to give it to God But Christ's religion was to be of the heart, and His almsgiving was to be a "drawing out" of the "soul" to the hungry[1], a suffering with their sufferings, an action that partook of the nature of sacrifice

It is not definitely recorded that Jesus ever carried out these precepts in a literal way by summoning the poor to His table and giving them food, or by sending them food or money before sitting down to table[2]. Jesus had no house, no "table," that He could call His own But all the Evangelists agree that on one occasion, out in "the wilderness," He (so to speak) extemporised a "table" for a hungry multitude. Mark and Matthew add that He did this on a second occasion. John relates that He did this, after the Resurrection, on a third occasion. In the apocryphal Acts of John it is said that He did this habitually for His disciples even when He and they were in the house of a stranger.

There is a striking difference between Mark and Luke in one of these traditions about Jesus and His disciples at their common meal. Whereas Luke represents Jesus as saying to His disciples "Who is greater, he that sitteth at meat or he that serveth [at table]?....But I am in the midst of you as he that serveth [at table]," Mark represents Him as saying "The Son of man came not to be served [at table] but to serve [at table], and to give his life (*or*, soul) a ransom for many."

---

[1] Is. lviii 10.
[2] See, however, p 360 foll., on Jn xiii 29 "that he should give something to the poor"

Also the occasions differ. Luke places the words much later than Mark, as being actually uttered at table, during the Last Supper[1].

John deals with these traditions in a simple, concrete, and dramatic way. Perhaps he knew that Mark's noun "servant [at table]," *diaconos*, or "deacon"—omitted by Luke—was liable to be confused with the Christian official "deacon[2]." At all events he first uses the noun concerning the "*servants [at table]*" in Cana who draw the water that becomes wine[3]. Then he uses the verb concerning Martha's literal, homely, waiting at table "Martha *was serving [at table]*[4]" Then, in the Temple on the morrow, when Jesus has heard that "certain Greeks" desire to see Him, there is a noteworthy change in the use of the word. The Law of the spiritual Harvest, and of Life through Death, is proclaimed as if it were also the Law of the Feast, or Joy, or Table, in Heaven, at which Table no soul is admitted to feast until it has first "*waited*," or "*served*," and he that desires thus to "*serve*" must be willing to lose his life: "He that loveth his life loseth (*or*, destroyeth) it, and he that hateth his life in this world shall keep it unto life eternal. If any one *is bent on serving me [at my table]* let him follow me, and where I am there also shall be *my servant [that serves at my table]*. If any one *is bent on serving me [at my table]*, him will my Father honour[5]."

This is the last Johannine instance of the *word* "serve [at table]" either as noun or as verb, but John proceeds to dramatize the *thing* by representing Jesus as actually "serving [at table]," during the Last Supper, girding Himself with a towel and washing the feet of the disciples. This no other Evangelist has related. In previous parts of this series the

---

[1] Mk x. 45, Lk. xxii 27. [2] *Proclam* p 404
[3] Jn ii 5, 9
[4] Jn xii 2. Comp Lk x 40 "Martha was distracted (περιεσπᾶτο) about much *serving [at table]* (διακονίαν)"
[5] Jn xii 25—6. See *Joh Gr* **2552** *c*.

question has been discussed whether John's narrative of this particular act of "serving at table" can be accepted as literally true in spite of its omission by the Synoptists, and the opinion was expressed that the event was probably historical even if it did not occur on that particular occasion[1]. This opinion has been confirmed by further study revealing, through many sources, but especially through Mark and John, traces of early passionate feeling, expressed in passionate words, concerning the Sacrifice of the Eucharist and details connected with it. Some of these expressions might be omitted or softened in later days.

§ 40. *The "kiss of love"*

It is of the utmost importance that we, Christians, should recall as far as possible this Christian passionateness, so far as it came from Christ Himself The details of the Miracles of Feeding—the "taking" and "blessing" and "breaking," and the question whether the "breaking" may be metaphorical as well as literal, meaning the dividing and distribution of the word of God—are all subordinate to the realisation of the spirit of the common meal which we call the Eucharist, and to the question of the origin of that spirit Hence, in conclusion, a few words of apparent digression from the Miracles of Feeding in the Gospels to the thought of the Eucharist as it is discerned in the Epistles, may really be no digression at all, but a return to the essence of our subject. Now among the accompaniments of the Eucharist (or of Christian gatherings) most frequently mentioned in the Epistles is the "kiss." Paul speaks of "a holy kiss," Peter of "a kiss of love" wherewith Christians are to salute one another[2] Whence did this spring?

---

[1] See *Son* **3276 a** (and Index, "Washing") and the references there given

[2] Rom xvi 16, 1 Cor xvi. 20, 2 Cor xiii 12, 1 Thess v 26, ἐν φιλήματι ἁγίῳ (and comp 1 Pet v 14 ἐν φιλήματι ἀγάπης) The meaning might be "with *the* holy kiss," or "*the* kiss of love" The long article on "Kiss" in Smith's *Dict Antiq* ii. 902—6 contains

CHRIST'S MIRACLES OF FEEDING

We find nothing alleged from Jewish or Gentile practice that explains it[1]. It is true that Jesus is represented as saying reproachfully to a Pharisee at whose table He is sitting as a guest "Thou gavest me no kiss[2]"; but no commentator (so far as I know) shews that the kiss was a mere courtesy among the Jews—a courtesy expected by guests from their host as a matter of course. Has Luke been misled by the special practice of Christians? Did Jesus introduce it among His disciples as a sign that they belonged to the Family of God?

It was a practice open to obvious abuse Only the earlier Pauline Epistles and the first Epistle of Peter contain the precept to salute after this fashion. Clement of Alexandria complains of the abuse of it between the sexes[3]. Athenagoras is said to quote an apocryphal precept of caution about it[4].

---

no mention or suggestion of any Jewish or Gentile origin or precedent for the Christian rite

[1] On Rom xvi 16 (on which Wetstein and Schottgen give no help) Fritzsche has a long note, and Lightfoot has one on 1 Thess v 26 But they give no illustration from Jewish usage Nor is there any light thrown by Hamburger 1 685, or Levy III 453—4 where different kinds of kisses are distinguished

[2] Lk vii 45 On this *Hor Heb* is silent, as also on 1 Cor xvi 20 "a holy kiss"

[3] Clem Alex 301 "The shameless use of the kiss, which ought to be mystic, occasions foul suspicions and evil reports"

[4] Athenagoras *Legat* § 32 This is important because if (as the translator in Clark's translation suggests) Athenagoras is quoting "probably from some apocryphal writing," the testimony takes us back to a period even earlier, and perhaps much earlier, than A D 177 "For the Logos again says to us 'If anyone kiss a second time because it has given him pleasure, [he sins],' adding, 'Therefore *the kiss, or rather the salutation, should be given with the greatest care* (οὕτως οὖν ἀκριβώσασθαι τὸ φίλημα μᾶλλον δὲ τὸ προσκύνημα δεῖ) ..'." Here the correction of "kiss" into προσκύνημα, implying an act of homage or "worship" (in the old English sense), and the precept to "be precise about it (ἀκριβώσασθαι)," prove that the author of this early saying is referring to what Paul and Peter call "the holy kiss" or "kiss of love" He seems to regard it as almost equivalent to an act of homage or love to Christ, as the Lord and the Beloved,

Athenagoras is defending the Christians against the charge of practising promiscuous intercourse, and he declares that, so far from doing this, they recognise fellow-believers as being spiritually blood relations according to age, sons or daughters, brothers or sisters, fathers or mothers; and he bids us recognise "the kiss or rather the obeisance" as the symbol of family affection Similarly the Jews, excusing the "kiss" given by Jacob to Rachel, added to the three lawful kinds of kissing a fourth, namely, the kiss between blood relations[1]. Now the Synoptic Gospels tell us that Jesus introduced as it were a relationship of blood between all His disciples, including them in His own relations when He said "Who is my mother and my brethren? And looking round on them that sat round about him, he saith, Behold, my mother and my brethren! For whosoever shall do the will of God, the same is my brother, and sister, and mother[2]"

The parallel Luke—which has been discussed elsewhere[3]—omits this last phrase where "sister" is added to "brother." John has nothing of the kind verbally. But if, by "brother" and "sister," we mean "beloved as a brother" and "beloved as a sister," then we may say that by implication John did not shrink from including sisters as well as brothers in the newly instituted Family of Christ. He does this as usual in a dramatic and concrete form The sisters of Lazarus, he says, "sent to Jesus, saying, Lord, behold, he whom thou lovest is

---

paid invisibly to Him when paid visibly to the brethren and sisters who are members of His Body

[1] See Gen xxix 11 and *Gen. r ad loc*, also *Exod r.* on Exod iv 27, and Levy iii 453 *b*. The other three lawful kinds were (1) "the kiss of magnifying (נדולה) or glorifying," given by Samuel to Saul (1 S. x. 1), (2) "the kiss of meeting [after long absence]" (Exod iv. 27), (3) "the kiss of separation" (Ruth 1. 14).

[2] Mk iii 33—5, Mt xii 48—50, comp. Lk. viii 21.

[3] The exact details of the parallelism are somewhat complicated. See *Proclamation* p 470 foll.

CHRIST'S MIRACLES OF FEEDING

sick[1]" Then he adds, "Now Jesus loved Martha and her sister and Lazarus"; and he represents the tears of Martha's sister as preceding, and in part causing, tears from Jesus, and thus as preceding (and perhaps preparing for) the raising of Lazarus[2].

Lucian is the only writer of literary Greek quoted in the Thesaurus as using the expression "salute with a kiss," and the context shews how bad an impression the connection of such a phrase with Christian worship might produce on Gentiles[3] Philo would certainly not have approved of it, for he expatiates on the frequent falseness of this "superficial welcoming," and is at great pains to distinguish the Greek, *philēma*, "kiss," literally "act of love," from *philia*, "love" (or "friendship")[4]. Thus no Greek source presents itself for this Christian custom. And we have seen above that no Jewish source presents itself either, except in special conditions. We are driven to the conclusion that in some way one or more of those "special conditions" was fulfilled. Now one of these "special conditions" was blood-relationship. That, as we have seen, Christ might be said to have introduced among

---

[1] Jn xi. 3
[2] Jn xi 5, 33 foll.
[3] See Lucian ii 248 *Alex* § 41 φιλήματι ἀσπάζεσθαι, and οἱ ἐντὸς τοῦ φιλήματος, *i e* "those who were included in [the circle of those honoured with] a kiss," about a monster of sensuality, named Alexander Possibly Lucian regarded Alexander as having borrowed from the Christians (though Alexander was opposed to them) this detail of their worship, and as having perverted it A preceding chapter (*ib.* § 38) says that Alexander began his "mysteries" by proclaiming "Out with the Christians!"

Reasons of seemliness may have combined with textual reasons to induce John to omit the Synoptic tradition that Judas "betrayed with a *kiss* (נשק)" See *Son* 3326 c, and add Ps cxl 7 "day of battle (נשק)," explained (Levy iii 453 a) by some as "*arming*" against the Messiah. This is more probable than the Greek corruption suggested in *Paradosis* 1365.

[4] Philo i 478—9 φίλημα δὲ διαφέρει τοῦ φιλεῖν. A "kiss" he calls ἐπιπόλαιον δεξίωσιν.

His disciples. Another condition was consecration. This, too, might be regarded as proceeding from Christ's lips when He was present in the Eucharist. Another was either parting or return after absence. This would be fulfilled with special reality when Jesus, after the Resurrection, fulfilled His promise, "I will see you again, and your joy no man taketh from you." When He came thus to "see" them "again," it is said by John that He "breathed into them" and said "Receive ye the Holy Spirit[1]." Perhaps this might be regarded as, in some sense, the "kiss" of Christ According to Jewish tradition, God "kissed" Moses when He drew forth his soul in a peaceful death[2] That might be called a kiss of parting, the work of life on earth being over But the name might also be given to the kiss of return, when the Lord prepared His disciples for the work of the Gospel, touching their lips and comforting their hearts with the kiss of the Holy Spirit. And the disciples, having once received this kiss from their Master at their first Eucharist after the Resurrection, may have henceforth passed on the salutation from one to another at every Eucharist, as being the kiss "of love" and "holy[3]."

---

[1] See *Son* 3623 g—j on Jn xx 22 ἐνεφύσησε

[2] Deut xxxiv 5 Jer Targ Miriam also (*M. Kat* 28 a) died by "God's kiss," Abraham (*Test Abr.* § 20) by kissing the hand of the Angel of Death

[3] The thought of the *philēma*, or "kiss," as proceeding from Jesus leads us to the thought of the title *philoi*, or "friends," used by Jesus about His disciples Luke is the only one of the Synoptists who represents Jesus as using it thus —

Mt x 27—8	Lk. xii 3—4
"What ye hear in the ear, proclaim upon the housetops, and be not afraid of them that kill the body… "	"What ye have spoken in the ear in the inner chambers shall be proclaimed upon the housetops, and *I say unto you my friends*, Be not afraid of them that kill the body.…"

In the Fourth Gospel, Jesus explains (Jn xv. 13—15) what He means when He says to the disciples "Ye are *my friends*" Friendship may imply dying for one's friend ("Greater love hath no man

CHRIST'S MIRACLES OF FEEDING

Even if we reject this explanation some of us may be benefited by being compelled to confess that there is beneath this ancient Christian rite something that needs to be explained. The explanation, whatever it may be, appears to involve the recognition of a personality in Jesus even more marvellous than we had supposed. Many believe easily enough in Christ's material miracles who do not realise His spiritual, social, and (so to speak) revolutionary miracles wrought on human nature. This "holy kiss" seems to represent a kind of high-water mark, reached at one rush by the religion of Christ during the period that followed His death, and perhaps to be reached again, after an interval of many centuries hereafter, but in a different way. Then it was reached by a visible Presence and an audible Voice. Hereafter the Presence may be not visible, and the Voice not audible, to the bodily sense. But in either case the Spirit will be the same, human yet divine, cosmopolitan yet homely, the Spirit of the Family of God breathed into God's children by God's Son[1].

---

than this") but such death is not a condition "Ye are *my friends* if ye do the things that I command you." The term "*Caesar's friend*" was known to the mob (Jn xix 12) in Jerusalem Epictetus uses it repeatedly in his lecture on Freedom (iv 1 8—95) bidding his pupils not to seek freedom by gaining admission to the circle of "*Caesar's friends*" but (*ib* 98) to "attach themselves to God." Luke's tradition, taken with the context ("kill the body") enables us to understand that there would be a tendency in the Christian Church to call the martyrs "*Christ's friends*" in a special sense

The conclusion of the Fourth Gospel (Jn xxi. 15—22) neutralises such a tendency It shews that Peter, the future Martyr on the Cross, had no precedence in the matter of friendship, over the silent disciple "whom Jesus loved." The proof of Peter's affection demanded by Jesus is not expressed in an imperative "Then die for me," but in "Feed my sheep." In 3 Jn 14 (15), the expressions "*The friends* salute thee," and "salute *the friends*," are probably to be explained (from Jn xv. 14) as meaning "*the friends of the Lord* [*with me*]" and "*the friends of the Lord* [*with thee*]" (not "my friends" and "thy friends")

[1] Attention has been called (*Joh Voc.* **1697**, and Index) to the

CHRIST'S MIRACLES OF FEEDING

§ 41. *"Testament" or "Covenant"*

The last two sections bear less directly on the miracles of feeding than on what appears to be their outcome. What follows will depart still further from the miracles and will turn itself toward the Eucharist Not that we must permit ourselves to discuss so important a subject here out of its place. But in fact all the preceding forty sections have been leading us up, through the words "Give ye them to eat," to the question "What was Jesus Himself preparing to give us to eat?" Consequently, in taking our leave of the miracles of feeding, some reply to this question seems demanded

---

fact that Mark never uses the word ἀγάπη Hermas, who frequently resembles Mark, mentions ἀγάπη as a virtue thrice, twice connecting it with "understanding (φρόνησις)" —(*Sim* ιx 17) "Having therefore received the seal, they had *one understanding*, and one mind, and their faith became one, and their *love one*," (*ib*. 18) "the church of God shall be one body, *one understanding*, one mind, one faith, *one love*" But he also uses it as a proper noun to denote the last of the Angels that build up the Church (*Vis* ιιι 8 (*bis*), comp. *Sim* ιx 15) And here he regards it as proceeding "from Understanding," called 'Επιστήμη 'Αγάπη is called by the Greek Thesaurus "a mere Biblical word (vox mere biblica)" In LXX it is almost confined to Cant and almost always has a sexual significance, but the Wisdom of Solomon applies it to man's love of God (ιιι 9) and says that the beginning of wisdom is the desire of discipline, and (vι 18) "the care (φροντὶς) of discipline is *love*, and *love* is the keeping of her laws (ἀγάπη δὲ τήρησις νόμων αὐτῆς)" Comp Jn xιv 23 "if a man love me he will keep (τηρήσει) my word"

The Fourth Evangelist does not mention the noun "love" (Jn v 42 "I know you, how that ye have not *the love of God* within you") till he has prepared his readers for it by connecting the verb with God as loving (ιιι. 16, 35) "the world" and "the Son" After that one mention of the noun, it is not mentioned again till the night before the Crucifixion where it is, in effect, defined (xιιι 34—5, xv 9 foll.) as a unique love personified by Christ The Gospel manifests not only a spiritual struggle to express an inexpressibly divine emotion, but also an intellectual attempt to rescue the word ἀγάπη from its Old Testament associations.

We have seen above that John omits the words "Give ye them to eat." But we have been led to the conclusion that they were part of the earliest form of the narrative. If that is so, Jesus (we may suppose) was, even in those early days, training the disciples to "give" to the multitude, as, later on, He Himself was destined to "give" to the disciples in the Eucharist. What was that "gift"? As to part of it, all the Synoptists are agreed They all tell us that He "gave" it with the words "This is my body." About this we shall say nothing here, since there is no disagreement. But as to another part there is a difference. Mark and Matthew indisputably represent Jesus as connecting the words "my blood" with a word (*diathēkè*) variously translated by our English Versions "covenant" or "testament," so that Jesus says "This is the blood of my *covenant* (or, *testament*)[1]." Luke, in one version of his text, the one adopted by our Revised Version, has "This cup is the new *covenant* (or, *testament*) in my blood." But Westcott and Hort place this (and some of the context) in double brackets, as not being a part of the original text[2] Thus we are led to narrow down our question about the "gift" to a question, in the first place, as to the meaning attached by Jesus to the word *diathēkè*.

In LXX, the word *diathēkè* occurs for the first time in connection with the deluge by which God purposed to destroy mankind but to spare Noah "Everything that is in the earth shall die, but I will establish my *covenant* with thee[3]" The

---

[1] Mk xiv 24, Mt xxvi 28 Or the meaning may be (as R V) "This is my blood of the *covenant* (or, *testament*) " The Greek is τὸ αἷμά μου τῆς διαθήκης.

[2] Lk xxii 20 Curet omits this SS combines xxii 17, 20 thus " ..divide it among you; this is my blood, the new *testament* " For "*testament*," SS uses דיאתיקא, a Syriac form of the Greek διαθήκη, which is regularly used for "testamentary disposition," "will" (*Thes Syr* 873) The word for "covenant," e g with Noah, Abraham, Israel, etc , is represented by Syr קימא = Heb ברית (*Thes. Syr.* 3534)

[3] Gen. vi 17—18.

Hebrew for "covenant" is *berîth*, meaning "compact," "alliance," "league," "agreement," "pledge of friendship." This is often well expressed by "covenant"—as when Joshua made a "covenant" with the Gibeonites at the time when he was purposing to destroy the Canaanites[1]. But in the case of Noah's *berîth*, as also often elsewhere, Aquila and Symmachus both substitute *sunthēkè* for *diathēkè*[2]. And they appear to be justified. For *sunthēkè*, in Greek, regularly has the meanings of the Hebrew *berîth*, that is, "compact," "agreement," etc.; *diathēkè* has not. The regular meaning of *diathēkè*—outside LXX and outside writings influenced by LXX—is "*last will and testament*"[3].

---

[1] Josh ix. 6—16, see Gesen 136.

[2] They also substitute συνθήκη for LXX διαθήκη in Gen xvii. 2 (the BERÎTH with Abraham) There Jerome says "Notandum quod ubicumque in Graeco *testamentum* legimus, ibi in Hebraeo sermone sit *foedus*, sive *pactum*, id est BERÎTH." Field, on Is lvi 6 (one of the very few instances where Aq. and Sym are recorded to have used διαθήκη), says " Pro διαθήκην juxta usum binorum interpretum requiritur συνθήκην "

[3] The only instance known to me of διαθήκη meaning "*agreement*," in Greek outside the sphere of LXX influence, is one quoted by Wetstein (on Mt xxvi 28) from Aristophanes (*Av* 439) This is mentioned by Lightfoot (on Gal iii 15) as one of "some few exceptions " Westcott, who writes later, does not add any of these "exceptions" in his very long note on *Diathēkè* in *The Epistle to the Hebrews*. He says merely (p 301) "The more general sense of 'arrangement,' 'agreement' is also found (Arist. *Av* 440) " But Steph. *Thes* gives no instance of "the more general sense" except the one from Aristophanes.

Josephus (*Ant* xvii 3 2, xvii. 9 7, *Bell* ii 2 3) not only uses *diathēkè* several times for a "will," but also avoids using it in the phrase "the ark of *the covenant*," as, for example, in describing the passage of the Jordan by Joshua, and the capture of Jericho, where the phrase recurs frequently in Scripture Justin Martyr, in his Dialogue with the Jew, where he frequently quotes LXX, uses διαθήκη more than thirty times, but in his Apology, addressed to Greeks, he does not use it once, *De Monarch*. ii 3 quotes from the *Diathēkai* of Orpheus, apparently regarded as meaning "*last instructions*"—a testamentary recantation. Hermas never uses *diathēkè*.

CHRIST'S MIRACLES OF FEEDING

Philo affords conclusive evidence that the LXX application of the Greek *diathēkè* to the "covenants" of God with Noah and Abraham caused difficulty to students of the Greek text. Unfortunately his Greek comment on the *berîth* with Noah is lost. When referring, however, to the *berîth* with Abraham, he says "*Diathēkai* are written for the sake of those who are worthy of a free gift, so that a *diathēkè* is a symbol of grace[1]" Then he says "About the whole subject of *diathēkai* I have written fully in two lectures, and I pass over the subject to avoid repeating myself" But he adds something that indicates (although briefly and obscurely) a connection in his mind between the *diathēkè* with Abraham and the "*inheritance*" promised to Abraham[2]. "To one class of men," he says, "God holds forth benefits through earth, water, air, sun, moon, sky, [and] other incorporeal powers[3],

---

[1] Philo 1 586 "a free gift (δωρεᾶς)" This appears directed against the view that the *diathēkè* was a "compact," or "agreement" As a fact, the Hebrew, *berîth*, does mean "compact" But the Greek διαθήκη does not

[2] It should be noted that the Hebrew verb "*inherit* (ירש)" occurs for the first time in the Bible where God establishes His *berîth* with Abraham · Gen xv. 3—8 "One born in my house shall *inherit* me. shall not *inherit* thee...he that shall come forth out of thine own bowels shall *inherit* thee.. to give thee this land to *inherit* it ... Whereby shall I know that I shall *inherit* it?" In the preceding context, according to our R V text, God has promised Himself to Abraham (xv 1) "I am...thy exceeding great reward" All this is above the level of "compacts" and "agreements" in the ordinary sense of the terms

There is however no Hebrew noun—whether derived from ירש or otherwise—that represents the "bequeathing," or "testamentary disposition," of an inheritance The Heb verb צוה, "give [testamentary] instructions," is represented in Targ by the Aram verb פקד in 2 S xvii 23, 2 K xx 1, Is xxxviii 1, but the noun from פקד is not known to occur in Palestinian Aramaic, see below, p 390, n

[3] Philo 1 587. Comp Gal iv 3 "We were in bondage under the elements (στοιχεῖα) of the world," where however στοιχεῖα probably means "elements" in a metaphorical as well as in a literal sense.

but to another class through Himself alone, *making Himself the inheritance of those who receive Him.*" All this is based on the utterance of God to Abraham, which Philo reads thus· "And I, behold, [am] my *diathēkē* with thee¹." He adds, as comment, "Now this suggests the following meaning. Though there are very many kinds of *diathēkē*, bestowing kindnesses (*lit* graces) and free gifts on those who are worthy, yet the highest kind of *diathēkai* I MYSELF AM."

What Philo means—and especially what he means by "free gift" and "grace"—can hardly be understood unless we realise that by *diathēkē* he means, not "covenant" but "testament." By a "testament" a man may leave gifts and legacies to friends, servants, and dependants, but the highest form of it is that by which a father leaves "his real estate" to his son, who is to succeed him after the testator's death. God cannot die. Nevertheless God makes Abraham His "heir," and bequeaths to him, so to speak, His "real estate," His own personal presence, Himself This conclusion as to Philo's meaning is confirmed by a Latin fragment of a comment of his on God's *diathēkē* with Noah "In the case of men an inheritance transmitted by them is possessed [by the heir then, and only then] when the men themselves exist no longer but are dead But on the other hand God, since He is everlasting, *concedes to the wise a joint participation in the inheritance that He transmits [to them while He is still living]*, and He rejoices at their entering into possession of it²"

---

¹ Gen xvii 4 καὶ ἐγὼ ἰδοὺ ἡ διαθήκη μου μετὰ σοῦ This may be variously punctuated Clem Alex 427 quotes ἰδοὺ ἐγὼ (sic) ἡ διαθήκη μου μετὰ σοῦ as a proof that "Moses manifestly calls the Lord a *diathēkē*."

² Philo *Quaest in Gen* (on Gen vi. 18 "I will establish my covenant with thee"). The comment concludes as follows "Secundo ampliorem quandam largitur sapienti haereditatem. Non enim dixit *Ponam foedus meum tibi*, sed *te*. id est, Tu es justum verumque foedus, quod statuam generi rationali pro possessione ac decore quibus opus est virtutis" I am unable to explain this The

In this last passage, about the *diathēkè* with Noah, we see Philo apparently influenced, partly by the natural meaning of the Greek word (namely, "testament"), and partly by the thought of the subsequent *diathēkè* with Abraham, so that he imports into the transaction with Noah a meaning that the Hebrew can hardly justify. As to the motives of the LXX in using *diathēkè* to render *berîth* we cannot speak confidently. It is possible that they avoided *sunthēkè*, the correct rendering, because the thought of God as making a "compact" or "treaty" with man seemed too anthropomorphic. In the illustrious instances of Noah and Abraham, the LXX may have felt justified in attempting to force into the Hebrew word some higher thought—taking *diathēkè* to mean not exactly a "*will*" but a "*deed of gift.*" Then this precedent may have been followed by them in subsequent instances, for consistency's sake, where the Hebrew could not have that meaning.

At this stage, after these repeated mentions of "*testament*" in Greek, before we pass to the Gospels, it will be well to ask, "How would a Jew of the first century in Palestine express himself in Aramaic, if he wished to say 'This is my *last will and testament*'?" The answer is important and to some it may be surprising. The Jew could not possibly express this by "This is my *berîth*" any more than we in English could express it by "This is my *treaty.*" He would have to say "This is my *diathēkè*," using a Hebraized form of the Greek word. Abundant instances of this use are given by Levy and Krauss. Babylonian Jews might have used another word (apparently of rare occurrence); but Palestinian Jews appear to have had practically no other[1].

---

heading of the comment is "Quid est *Statuam foedus meum tecum*?" The expression "I will give [i.e. appoint] thee for a covenant" occurs in Isaiah xlii 6, xlix 8, but Philo hardly ever quotes prophecy, and there is no various reading of *te* for *tecum* (or *tibi*) in renderings of Gen vi 18.

[1] See Levy, Levy *Ch*, Krauss, and *Thes Syr* on דייתיקי or

CHRIST'S MIRACLES OF FEEDING

Now coming to the Epistles we perceive that the Epistle to the Hebrews definitely says "For wherever there is a *diathēkè* there *the death of the maker-of-the-diathēkè must of necessity have its course* (lit *be brought*), for a *diathēkè* [*is as it were*] *based on dead persons*[1]" The Epistle to the Galatians takes the *diathēkè* with Abraham expressly out of the region of "law," and by implication out of the region of "compact," into the region of "heirs" and "promise" and "faith," when, after insisting on the unalterableness of a human *diathēkè*[2], it goes on to say " A *diathēkè* [such as that with Abraham] confirmed beforehand by God, *the law*, which came four hundred and thirty years after, doth not disannul, so as to make the *promise* of no effect ...But before *faith* came we were kept in ward under the law....And if ye are Christ's, then are ye Abraham's seed, *heirs* according to *promise*[3]." In the light of these two passages we perceive that elsewhere, when Paul speaks of God's *diathēkè* with Abraham he not only does not include the thought of "compact," but excludes it and implies God's "free gift" (as

---

דיאתיקי used *passim* for "a will." Levy iv 88 *a* gives one instance of the phrase "a writing of פקדתא," *i e* "a writing of last instructions," "a will," in *Git* 50 *b* But I am informed by Dr A. Buchler that this is in a discussion of Babylonian scholars and that he knows no instance of it in Palestinian Aramaic. Levy i 404 quotes, *inter alia*, *J Berach.* v. 9 *b*, where God is represented as saying that He gave the dew to Abraham "in a *diathēkè*," where Schwab has (p 101) "C'est *à titre immuable* que j'en ai fait don à Abraham" (comp Gal iii 15 foll. on the unalterableness of the *diathēkè* with Abraham) But it means "deed of gift" in *Gen* r , on Gen. xxiv 10 "All the good[s] of his master was in his hand," where the comment is "This means a *diathēkè*," *i e* a deed of disposition by which Abraham, while still living, made over his property to his servant in trust for Isaac This is exceptional Neither here nor elsewhere do Levy's instances indicate that the Hebrew *diathēkè* was used to mean "bargain," "treaty," or "compact"

[1] Heb ix 16—17
[2] Gal iii 15
[3] Gal iii 17—29

Philo does) and the thought of a Father bequeathing an inheritance to sons[1].

In dealing with the Law of Moses Paul labours under great difficulties The LXX so frequently calls it a *diathēkè* that Paul is obliged to do the same. But he explains it as a testamentary disposition of an inferior character given to Israel for a time—almost as if he were Ishmael not Isaac—for "So long as the heir is a child, he differeth nothing from a bondservant[2]" This *diathēkè* is both old and new. Relatively to the Christian *diathēkè*, it is old and ready to be superseded. Relatively to the Promise, it is "new," but not in a good sense—being the *diathēkè* of Sinai, which "beareth children unto bondage," a novel though necessary makeshift It cannot invalidate the ancient and unalterable *diathēkè* of God bequeathing Himself to Abraham His son and heir[3].

---

[1] Comp Rom ix 4 "Whose is the adoption and the glory and the *diathēkai*," ib xi 27 "this is the *diathēkè* from me to them (comp Is lix 21) when I shall take away their sins" The Epistle to the Hebrews (viii 8—10) quotes Jeremiah (xxxi 31—3) as predicting that God will make "a new *diathēkè*" for Israel, "I will put my law in their inward parts and in their heart will I write it, and I will be their God, and they shall be my people" This is in Paul's mind as the true *diathēkè*, the fulfilment of the *diathēkè* with Abraham and Isaac "the heir" The *diathēkè* of Sinai (Gal iv 24) "bearing children unto bondage" is represented by Hagar That, too, is a legacy of a kind, since Ishmael is Abraham's child, but it is of an inferior kind

[2] Gal. iv. 1.

[3] See 2 Cor iii 6—14 ἡμᾶς διακόνους καινῆς διαθήκης. ἐπὶ τῇ ἀναγνώσει τῆς παλαιᾶς διαθήκης. Eph ii 12 ξένοι τῶν διαθηκῶν τῆς ἐπαγγελίας, appears to mean "strangers to the *diathēkè* of the promise to Abraham in all the forms in which it was given to him and confirmed to his successors" For the remaining Pauline instance "this is the new *diathēkè* in my blood" see below, § 42. The instances in the Epistle to the Hebrews—where both meanings are intermixed—are too frequent to be quoted.

CHRIST'S MIRACLES OF FEEDING

§ 42. *"Testament" in the Gospels*

Passing now to the Gospels we find that, apart from the narratives of the Eucharist, their evidence is almost entirely negative, since the word occurs but once, namely, in the Song of Zacharias "To remember his holy *diathēkè*, the oath that he sware unto our father Abraham[1]" Jesus repeatedly speaks of "the law," but never of the *diathēkè* of God, either with Abraham, or with Israel at Mount Sinai. Nor does any evangelist use the word, when writing in his own person

In the accounts of the Eucharist the texts vary greatly. The Revised Version gives a longer Lucan text including a phrase that contains the word *diathēkè*, and closely agreeing with a Pauline passage that includes the same phrase[2]. Westcott and Hort give a shorter Lucan text omitting the phrase and containing no mention of *diathēkè*[3]. Also, in Mark and Matthew, Westcott and Hort reject "new" as applied to *diathēkè* The Revised Version, although it says that "some ancient authorities" insert *new* in Mark, and that "many" insert it in Matthew, nevertheless does not itself insert *new* in either Gospel.

This omission of "new" makes all the difference in the interpretation of *diathēkè* If "new" had been part of the text, we might have supposed the meaning to be "This is my blood of the New Covenant, or the blood of my New Covenant, as distinguished from the blood of the Old Covenant which was given to Israel on Mount Sinai." Even with the addition of "new," such a doctrine would seem abrupt and almost startling—especially in view of the fact that Jesus is not

---

[1] Lk 1 72—3
[2] Lk xxii 20 "This cup is the new *diathēkè* in my blood," comp. 1 Cor xi 25
[3] W H pass from Lk. xxii 19 "This is my body" to Lk xxii 21 "But behold, the hand... ," bracketing "that is given for you... that is shed for you"

recorded in any Gospel to have ever previously mentioned the word thus interpreted "covenant," either to the multitude or to the disciples. But, without the addition of "new," the meaning "covenant" seems quite impossible.

That being the case, we are led to accept, as probable, an explanation based on the demonstrated meaning of the Palestinian Aramaic word *diathēkè*, namely, "last will and testament." There may possibly have been some allusion to the *diathēkè* in Sinai[1] But much more probably there was no allusion at all to that or to anything else in the Old Testament. It was an utterance of personal affection and of divine conviction. Using the language habitual in Palestine, Jesus said to His disciples, "This is the blood that signifies my death and yet not my severance from you. This is the blood of my last will and testament in which, though dying, I bequeath to you my life and presence in perpetuity[2]"

Here we must add that although Mark and Matthew do not represent Jesus as speaking of a *"new diathēkè"* in connection with "cup" or "blood," they do represent Him as using the word *"new"* in connection with the act of drinking

---

[1] Comp Exod xxiv 8 ἰδοῦ τὸ αἷμα τῆς διαθήκης ἧς διέθετο Κύριος πρὸς ὑμᾶς περὶ πάντων τῶν λόγων τούτων These words Christians would naturally connect with Christ in after times, as they are connected in Heb ix 19, 20 etc And the tradition peculiar to Luke and added by him a little later on (xxii 29) κἀγὼ διατίθεμαι ὑμῖν .βασιλείαν (perhaps referring to the crown to be gained by the blood of martyrdom) may be an allusion to the διαθήκη of Sinai But the words of Institution seem best interpreted as a simple, direct, non-allusive and personal utterance in which Jesus bequeathed Himself to His disciples.

[2] This conclusion—rejecting the word "new"—is compatible with a grateful acknowledgment of the value of the Pauline tradition (1 Cor. xi. 23 "received from the Lord") concerning the *meaning* of the Eucharist, as being something that was to be "done in remembrance" of the Lord, and also concerning the relation of it, as a "new" and higher "testament," to the old and inferior one. But the Pauline tradition has no claim to be regarded as more faithful than that of Mark and Matthew to Christ's original words.

CHRIST'S MIRACLES OF FEEDING

from a "cup" at the Eucharist[1]. The parallel Luke, though in other respects closely similar to Mark and Matthew, omits "new[2]." John therefore is bound (according to the Rule of Johannine Intervention) to insert something about "newness," equivalent—from a Johannine point of view—to what Mark and Matthew have about "not drinking from *the offspring of the vine*" until Jesus shall "drink it *new*" in "the kingdom of God" (or, as Matthew has it, "the kingdom of my Father").

Starting, then, from the Synoptic "*offspring of the vine*," we ask for some equivalent in John. Origen, when commenting on "*the offspring of the vine*," in Matthew, asks "What vine?" He replies (from John) "That vine of which He Himself [i e. Jesus] was the figure, saying *I am the Vine, ye the branches*. Whence He says again *My blood is truly*

---

[1]
Mk xiv 25	Mt xxvi 29	Lk xxii 18
Verily I say unto you, I will no more drink of the offspring of the vine, until that day when I drink it new in the kingdom of God	But I say unto you, I will not drink henceforth of this offspring of the vine, until that day when I drink it new with you in my Father's kingdom	For I say unto you, I will not drink from henceforth of the offspring of the vine, until the kingdom of God shall come

The columns follow R V, except in rendering γένημα "offspring" instead of "fruit" The formula for "blessing over the wine" was *Berach* 35 a (Mishna) "Blessed [is] He that created *the fruit* (פְּרִי) of the vine," and the usual Greek for פְּרִי is καρπός But in Deut and Isaiah it is sometimes rendered γένημα

[2] Luke has also a corresponding utterance of Jesus about "eating," peculiar to his Gospel (xxii 16) "I will assuredly not eat it [where "it" refers to (xxii 15) "this Passover"] until it be fulfilled in the kingdom of God " There, too, Luke omits "*new*"

The importance attached to "*the cup*" may be illustrated by the tradition in *Pesach* 106 a "The Rabbis said that (Exod xx 8) *Remember the Sabbath* meant *Remember it over the wine*" This "remembering" was a part of the "Hallowing of the Sabbath," a domestic rite known to have been practised before, and probably long before, the days of Hillel and Shammai

drink ...For truly He '*washed His robe in the blood of the grape*[1].'"

Now all would agree that the blood of Jesus represents His "love" ("greater *love* hath no man than this, that a man lay down his life for his friends[2]") And the love of Jesus is regarded in the Fourth Gospel as a new kind of love At the conclusion of His prayer to the Father for the disciples, Jesus says that He will make the Father's name known to them, "that *the love wherewith thou lovedst* me may be in them, and I in them[3]"; and He has previously defined this love in "a new commandment" to the disciples. Their love is to be like His love· "*A new commandment* give I unto you, that ye love one another—*even as I have loved* you, that ye also love one another[4]."

Does not this "new commandment," in John, correspond to the "new wine," in Mark and Matthew? That the epithet "new" is emphatic is confirmed, not only by the context, but also by the play on "new" and "old" in the Johannine Epistle[5], and by the fact that, apart from narrative, this is the only instance of the epithet in the whole of the Fourth Gospel[6]. Some may object that "commandment" implies constraint. "Love," they may say, "must not be commanded." That is not an objection that would be felt to be a serious one by John or by any spiritually-minded Jew, who would accept as God's gifts the two "great" commandments of the Law. God's

---

[1] Origen *Levit Hom* vii 2 (Lomm ix 292—3) quoting Mt xxvi. 29, Jn xv 5, vi 55, Gen xlix 11 Comp *Didach* § 9 "First, about the *cup* —We give thanks to thee, our Father, for the holy *Vine* of David thy servant (παιδός), which thou madest known to us through Jesus thy servant (παιδός)"

[2] Jn xv 13   [3] Jn xvii 26

[4] Jn xiii. 34   There would be nothing "new" in the commandment "love your neighbours," or "love one another," but there was something "new" in the kind of love

[5] The commandment was (1 Jn ii 7) "not new" and yet (*ib* 8) "on the other hand new"

[6] Jn xix 4 "a new tomb" is the only other instance.

commandments are affectionate imperatives, like the Pauline paraphrase "Be ye reconciled unto God[1]." They come to us appealing for love—love toward God the Father, and love toward men the brethren. And, coming to us through the Son, they convey to us, if we will receive them in the Spirit of the Son, a power to respond to the appeal. Hence, in the Fourth Gospel, a "commandment" is regarded as something "given" by the Father to the Son, and even as being "eternal life[2]." The final mention of the word by Jesus indicates, so to speak, an appropriation of the Commandment of Love by the Son. "This is my very own commandment, that ye love one another[3]." By using "commandment" and not the ambiguous *diathēkè*, John avoids all notion of "covenanting" or "bargaining," And yet he also avoids any expressions that imply unconditional "giving" to those who are incapable of "receiving" the gift

No Gospel inculcates more consistently than the Fourth the necessity of something real at heart and spiritually solid, incompatible with nebulous mysticism or inflated bubbles of profession. Conditions—of act as well as thought—are not only expressed but also reiterated. "If ye have love one to another," and "If ye do that which I command you," are but two out of many specimens[4] Our expectation, then, that John would intervene—so far as concerns the Marcan tradition, certainly omitted by Luke, about the "newness" of the wine that was to be drunk by Jesus after His death—appears to be justified. We have no right to push our expectation further and to claim that John should intervene about the Marcan *diathēkè* to tell us whether it meant "testament" or

---

[1] 2 Cor. v 20
[2] Jn xii 49, 50
[3] Jn xv. 12 On the emphasis of ἡ ἐντολὴ ἡ ἐμή see *Joh Gr.*, Index ἐμή
[4] See ἐάν in Jn xiii 17, 35, xiv 15, 23, xv 7, 10, 14.

CHRIST'S MIRACLES OF FEEDING

"covenant." For, as we have seen, it is not certain that Luke omits this word.

Nevertheless we may say with confidence that, all through Christ's Last Discourse and Last Prayer, John is endeavouring to set before us the Son as playing (so to speak) the part of a Testator in behalf of the Father. In the Father's name, He is bequeathing Himself to mankind. The difficulty pointed out by Philo—that God the Father cannot die, so as to make a "testament" in the ordinary way—disappears in the Person of the incarnate Son. The Son could die. Since He could die He could make a "testament" as Mark and Matthew apparently say that He did. The difficulty for John, therefore, consisted, not in the actual words of Jesus, but in the interpretations of them by Christians, who might confuse "testament" with "covenant," or might give to both terms formal and unspiritual significations

In the Fourth Gospel this danger is avoided partly by negative means—by avoiding the word "testament." But far more importance attaches to the positive means—the introduction of a substitute that could not possibly be reduced to the level of a technical term. This substitute—which reminds us of the promise to Abraham as interpreted above, "And I, behold, [am] my *diathēkè* with thee"—is a personal Testament, a Paraclete, an Alter Ego, or Second Self, who is to represent the Son after His departure and to recall the Son's acts and words and strengthening presence, with increased power Thus, without hearing from His lips any such words as "This is my testament," we see Jesus revealed to us in this Gospel as standing in the midst of His troubled followers on the eve of His departure from them, and bestowing on them a Testament of a new kind, no less "new" than His love. It is a Testament indeed yet not a writing. It is a spiritual Friend sent to take His place in their orphaned hearts, and to breathe into them the assurance that although absent He is present and that they are not orphans in the

CHRIST'S MIRACLES OF FEEDING

comfort of His perpetual presence: "Peace I leave unto you, my own peace I give unto you, not as the world giveth give I unto you." "I will not leave you orphans; I come unto you[1]"

In the preceding remarks about the language of the Eucharist nothing has been said about the fact that this language was misunderstood as early as the days of Nero, and gave rise to accusations against the Christian religion that were credited by all classes, educated as well as uneducated. Tacitus, writing about Nero's persecution of the Christians, calls them "hateful because of their shameful crimes," guilty of "hatred of the human race," practising "a deadly superstition," and deserving of "the severest punishments"—and this even in Rome, "the resort of all things abominable and shameful[2]." Suetonius perhaps assumes all this when he more briefly says that Nero, along with other measures of wholesome reform, "punished Christians, a class of men given up to a new and maleficent superstition[3]"

We have evidence as to the nature of the "shameful crimes (*flagitia*)" imputed to the Christians by everybody and believed in by Tacitus In large measure, they sprang out of distorted reports of the Christian Eucharist, which was regarded as a "Thyestean banquet[4]" Thyestes fed on the flesh of his own son. The language of Christians describing the Father as giving the flesh and blood of the Son for the life of the world, could easily be taken literally even by honest pagans, and still more

---

[1] Jn xiv. 27, 18.
[2] Tac. *Ann* xv 44
[3] Suet *Ner* § 16.
[4] See Athenagoras (before 177 A D) § 3 "Three things are alleged against us, atheism, Thyestean feasts, Œdipodean intercourse " Atheism would be inferred from the refusal of Christians to worship the Greek and Roman gods, Œdipodean intercourse might be inferred from mystical language about the Church as the Bride of the Son

easily by enemies and spies. The Second Apology of Justin Martyr mentions the charge of feasting on human flesh in connection with "mysteries of Cronos[1]." "Thyestean banquets" are mentioned both by Athenagoras and by the Elders of the Church of Lyons (writing about the persecution under Verus) in such a way as to shew that they were accusations of long standing[2] Such "banquets" are almost certainly included in the "shameful crimes" mentioned by Tacitus

How could the Fourth Evangelist deal with falsehoods of this kind, while still preserving unimpaired the spiritual reality expressed in the passionate language of the Eucharist as proceeding from Christ "This is my body," "This is my blood"? To an educated Greek, like Plutarch, such language might suggest the ὠμοφαγίαι—that is, the "eatings of raw flesh (or, living creatures)"—practised in their "mysteries" by some of the worshippers of Bacchus[3] No doubt a Bacchic dance seems to us a thing that could not conceivably be connected even by the bitterest foes of the Christians with the celebration of the Eucharist But the Acts of John takes a different view. On the night before the crucifixion, it tells us, Jesus bade the disciples form a circle, Himself standing in the centre, and they "danced" round Him in response to His "dancing[4]." If a Christian

---

[1] Justin Mart 2 *Apol* § 12, mentioning Κρόνου μυστήρια, *i e*. sacrifices of children (connected in the Bible with Moloch).

[2] Euseb v. 1 14, and see Iren *Fragm* 13

[3] Plutarch, *De Defect Orac* § 14 (*Mor* 417 c) ἑορτὰς δὲ καὶ θυσίας . . ἐν αἷς ὠμοφαγίαι καὶ διασπασμοὶ . . . θεῶν μὲν οὐδενὶ δαιμόνων δὲ φαύλων ἀποτροπῆς ἕνεκα φήσαιμ᾽ ἂν τελεῖσθαι This is the earliest mention of ὠμοφαγία given by Steph *Thes* The next is from Clem Alex 12 "The bacchanals hold their orgies in honour of the frenzied Dionysus, celebrating their sacred frenzy by *the eating of raw flesh*, and go through the distribution of the parts of butchered victims .." Plutarch does not mention "Dionysus" as Clement does, but says, in effect. that such rites, even if nominally consecrated to a god, were really addressed to demons

[4] *Acts of John*, §§ 11—12 mentions χορεύω and χορεία seven times, besides ὀρχοῦμαι and σκιρτάω

Gnostic could write thus about the Christian Eucharist, might not a Roman historian like Tacitus, or a literary Greek like Plutarch, be excused for going a little further and for supposing that the Christians practised a "mystery" in which they actually tore to pieces and devoured human flesh?

Until we realise the fact that from the days of Luke to those of Tertullian Christians in the arena were scoffed at in torture and death, as being monsters who butchered little children and "left a bite in their bloodstained bread[1]," we shall not realise the task set before the author of the Fourth Gospel. Luke had greatly altered the language of Eucharistic Institution— perhaps by paraphrase, or perhaps, if the longer text is altogether rejected, by omission; but he had written nothing bearing on the Eucharist in a positive way so as to vindicate the Christians from an accusation that seemed no less true to the accusers than it seems absurd to us.

What was needed was some expansion and full explanation of that which Jesus actually did say, something that might compel a dispassionate and educated Greek or Roman reader like Plutarch or Pliny, to confess. "After all, it seems that this man Christus did not mean 'flesh' literally. He was not speaking calmly; he was not speaking like a philosopher; he did not preserve a calm tranquillity as Socrates did up to the very moment of drinking the hemlock; he seems to have lost his presence of mind when face to face with death; but at all events he did not encourage his followers to tear and devour human flesh."

John, on the other hand, does seem to have included in his Gospel some such vindication of the Christians. He places it, however, not on the night preceding the Crucifixion but long before. And he does it in an indirect and unexpected way. He represents Jesus as *actually using language that Gentiles might naturally take in a literal sense* as referring to ōmophagia—and this, in an atmosphere of calm when there was no thought of

---

[1] Tertull *Apol* §7, *Ad Nat* 1. §7

impending death Later on, when death does actually impend, he represents Jesus as using no such language; for then, on the night before His death, His thoughts turn not on Himself, nor on the immortality of His own soul (like the thoughts of Socrates) but on the future welfare of the disciples to whom He is bequeathing His legacy of love But here, at this earlier stage, Jesus utters fervent and strange language—strange to Jews as well as to Greeks and Romans—about "feeding" on His "flesh" and "blood," to express in metaphor the transference from Himself to others of a vital and vitalising personality. "Flesh and blood," among the Jews, was a phrase representing human weakness as contrasted with divine strength. The Son of God had taken upon Himself, or into Himself, human weakness—human "flesh" and human "blood"—in order to transmit it to the sons of men as divine strength, according to the word of God "My strength is made perfect in weakness."

At the same time John does not conceal from us the fact that this metaphor was misunderstood even from the first, not only by Jews in general but also by Christ's own disciples. Jesus Himself perceives this misunderstanding but will not on that account soften or attenuate the truth His disciples must rise up to it He will not draw it down to them· "It is the spirit that quickeneth The flesh profiteth nothing The words that I have spoken unto you are [indeed] spirit and are [indeed] life[1]"

Coming as they do after the exclamation "How can this man give us *his flesh* to eat?" and after the explanation given by Jesus which the disciples still find difficult, the words "*the flesh* profiteth nothing" seem intended to have a twofold meaning. Jesus seems to mean, not only, "*the fleshly or material view of things* is unprofitable," but also "*the flesh about which I spoke to you* when I said 'Except ye eat *the flesh of the Son of*

---

[1] Jn vi 63

CHRIST'S MIRACLES OF FEEDING

man'—this, in a literal sense, and regarded materially, is of no profit." But this must be admitted to be doubtful. What is hardly doubtful—or at all events cannot be dismissed as improbable—is the conclusion that the Johannine version of Christ's discourse, taken in its context, and with an appreciation of the circumstances, was adapted to open the eyes of any educated Greek or Roman to the falsity of the popular charge against the Christians that they celebrated in their mysteries "Thyestean feasts" and fed on the "raw flesh" of human beings

ADDENDUM

The connection between the Synoptic doctrine of the Sacrifice on the Cross and the Johannine doctrine of the Living Bread is illustrated by the following hymn

> To sacrifice, to share,
>   To give as Jesus gave,
> For others' wants to care,
>   Not our own lives to save,—
>
> This is the Living Bread
>   Which cometh down from heaven,
> Wherewith our souls are fed,
>   The pure, immortal leaven
>
> The hidden Manna this,
>   Whereof who eateth, he
> Grows up in perfectness
>   Of Christlike symmetry.
>
> Who seeks this bread shall be
>   Nor stinted nor denied
> Our hungry souls in thee
>   O Christ, are satisfied!

From *The St Olave's Hymnal*, p 379 (LUCY LARCOM).

CHAPTER IX

JESUS WALKING ON THE SEA
[Mark vi. 45—52]

§ 1. *The sequel of the Feeding of the Five Thousand*[1]

CHRIST'S Walking on the Sea is not related by Luke. Consequently, so far as concerns the Rule of Johannine Intervention,

---

[1] For convenience of reference, R V is given at full length below, as usual, but in detailed comment it is frequently departed from. In Mt xiv 24, R V marg "many furlongs" etc (which is W H txt) is accepted as probably correct.

Mk vi 45—52	Mt xiv 22—33	Jn vi 15—21
(45) And straightway he constrained his disciples to enter into the boat, and to go before [him] unto the other side to Bethsaida, while he himself sendeth the multitude away.	(22) And straightway he constrained the disciples to enter into the boat, and to go before him unto the other side, till he should send the multitudes away.	(15) Jesus therefore perceiving that they were about to come and take him by force, to make him king, withdrew again into the mountain himself alone
(46) And after he had taken leave of them, he departed into the mountain to pray	(23) And after he had sent the multitudes away, he went up into the mountain apart to pray and when even was come, he was there alone	(16) And when evening came, his disciples went down unto the sea,
(47) And when even was come, the boat was in the midst of the sea, and he alone on the land	(24) But the boat was now in the midst of the sea (*some anc auth* was many furlongs distant from the land), distressed by the waves, for the wind was contrary.	(17) And they entered into a boat, and were going over the sea unto Capernaum And it was now dark, and Jesus had not yet come to them
(48) And seeing them distressed in rowing, for the wind was contrary unto them, about the fourth watch of the night he cometh unto them, walking on the sea, and he would have passed by them	(25) And in the fourth watch of the night he came unto them, walking upon the sea	(18) And the sea was rising by reason of a great wind that blew.
(49) But they,	(26) And when	(19) When therefore they had rowed about five and twenty or thirty furlongs, they behold Jesus walking on the

JESUS WALKING ON THE SEA

we are spared the necessity of examining Mark's text, phrase

Mk vi. 45—52 contd.	Mt. xiv. 22—33 contd.	Jn vi. 15—21 contd.
when they saw him walking on the sea, supposed that it was an apparition, and cried out (50) For they all saw him, and were troubled But he straightway spake with them, and saith unto them, Be of good cheer it is I, be not afraid.	the disciples saw him walking on the sea, they were troubled, saying, It is an apparition, and they cried out for fear (27) But straightway Jesus spake unto them, saying, Be of good cheer, it is I; be not afraid (28) And Peter answered him and said, Lord, if it be thou, bid me come unto thee upon the waters (29) And he said, Come And Peter went down from the boat, and walked upon the waters, to come (*some anc auth.* and came) to Jesus. (30) But when he saw the wind (*many anc auth. add* strong), he was afraid, and beginning to sink, he cried out, Lord, save me. (31) And immediately Jesus stretched forth his hand, and took hold of him, and saith unto him, O thou of little faith, wherefore didst thou doubt?	sea, and drawing nigh unto the boat. and they were afraid (20) But he saith unto them, It is I; be not afraid.
(51) And he went up unto them into the boat, and the wind ceased and they were sore amazed in themselves, (52) For they understood not concerning the loaves, but their heart was hardened.	(32) And when they were gone up into the boat, the wind ceased (33) And they that were in the boat worshipped him, saying, Of a truth thou art the Son of God.	(21) They were willing therefore to receive him into the boat and straightway the boat was at the land whither they were going.

JESUS WALKING ON THE SEA

by phrase, to note what Luke alters or omits. There are, however, reasons why Marcan details should not be passed over In particular, the introduction to the Walking on the Sea, that is to say, the sequel of the Feeding of the Five Thousand, claims attention, because it marks a line where Luke breaks away from Mark and Matthew and leaves them altogether for a considerable interval.

This interval may be called the Period of Suspense It begins shortly after the execution of John the Baptist and lasts till the Confession of Peter and the Transfiguration, when Jesus definitely resolves to go up and meet the end in Jerusalem During this interval Jesus seems to have become an object of suspicion to Herod Antipas, who feared that Jesus might attempt to avenge the Baptist's death; unpopular with the multitude, because He did not attempt to avenge it; and disappointing to many of His own disciples, who found Him unpractical and fanciful, departing from all the precedents of the ancient Deliverers of Israel, and failing to satisfy their Messianic expectations This part of His life He spent (according to Mark and Matthew) moving about from place to place in North Palestine, reaching Tyre and Sidon on the West, and finally Caesarea on the East, a city in the tetrarchy of Philip, which was called distinctively Caesarea Philippi. Here he was not under the jurisdiction of Herod Antipas, nor under that of Pilate, and here it was that He received the confession of Peter and, shortly afterwards, resolved to go up to Jerusalem[1].

---

[1] Luke (ix 51—3) represents Christ's resolution to go up to Jerusalem as a reason why Samaritans rejected Him But this would call forth the zeal of Jewish disciples and followers (comp *ib* 57), and some one, not a follower, is described (*ib* 49—50) as casting out devils in His name and as being "not against" Jesus The preceding disputes of the disciples about supremacy (*ib* 46) shew that they believed Him to be about to assert the claims of the Son of David The appeal "thou Son of David" is recorded by all the Synoptists as uttered when Jesus passed through Jericho on His way to Jerusalem (Mk x. 46) "with his disciples and a great multitude" All this

Then He appears to have regained His popularity with the multitude, but the rulers of the Jews feared and hated Him more than ever.

Luke tells us nothing of all these wanderings in North Palestine. But he gives us glimpses of reasons that might cause them. When rumours arose about Jesus as the Baptist's successor, Luke tells us significantly that Herod "sought to see" Him[1]. The Pharisees also, in Luke, warn Jesus, "Get thee out"—presumably from Galilee or Peraea—"and go hence, for Herod would fain kill thee[2]." And Luke has previously said "There were some present at that very time who brought word to him [i e Jesus] about the Galilaeans whose blood Pilate had mingled with their sacrifices[3]." This implies a warning against going into Pilate's jurisdiction. But Luke describes Jesus as rejecting both warnings, and as persevering in His resolution to go up to the City, "because it is not possible that a prophet should perish out of Jerusalem[4]."

None of these details, whether those peculiar to Mark and Matthew or those peculiar to Luke, are mentioned by John[5]. But he throws light on the period as a whole by telling us that the multitude sought to make Jesus "king" and that Jesus "withdrew" from them[6]. Thus he makes us see both why Herod Antipas would suspect Jesus and why the multitude would be disappointed in Him At the same time we receive the impression that the radical cause of Christ's unpopularity

---

indicates that from the time when Jesus decided to go to Jerusalem He regained popularity

[1] Lk ix 9   [2] Lk. xiii 31
[3] Lk xiii 1   [4] Lk xiii 33
[5] In almost all the passages where John mentions Judaea it is as a region from which Jesus departs to avoid the jealousy of the Jews (iv. 3, rep 47, 54), or to avoid persecution (vii 1), or to which He proposes to return at the peril of His life (xi 7) The only exception (and a very strange one) is where His brethren say (vii 3) "go to Judaea."
[6] Jn vi. 15.

JESUS WALKING ON THE SEA

and of the withdrawal of almost all His disciples was the mysterious and personal character of His teaching. To spiritual incompatibility John attributes the attempts to kill Jesus, which all emanate from "the Jews," that is, in effect, the rulers of the people, to whom Christ's "word" was not a "seed" but "a stone of stumbling[1]."

As regards the details of the narrative of the Walking on the Sea, although there is no parallel Luke to occupy us, there are important deviations of Matthew and John from Mark which (besides being interesting in themselves) may explain why Luke omitted the whole. The narrative seems to suggest a spiritual storm of doubt and temptation besetting the disciples, besides describing a material storm of wind and waves. And we shall find Matthew intensifying this aspect of doubt and temptation by introducing a story (not mentioned by Mark) of Peter attempting to walk on the waves and failing because he doubted. But before discussing these matters it will be well to have before us a summary of all the Mark-Matthew traditions from which Luke, at this point, breaks away. They constitute what may be entitled "Christ's journeying in North Palestine."

§ 2. *Christ's journeying in North Palestine*

After the Feeding of the Five Thousand, Mark, Matthew and John agree that Jesus went up *"into the mountain,"* and that He was there *"alone."* Mark and Matthew add (but John does not) that He went thither *"to pray."* Luke's next words do indeed mention *"praying"* and *"alone,"* but not

---

[1] Jn v 18, vii 1—35. Incompatibility is implied in viii 37 "Ye seek to kill me because my word hath not free course in you." Comp Wisd ii 13—14 "He professeth to have the knowledge of God and he calleth himself the child of the Lord. He was made to reprove our thoughts."

JESUS WALKING ON THE SEA

"mountain," and they are parallel, not to the Marcan tradition under consideration, but to one that comes much later —

Mk viii. 27	Mt. xvi 13	Lk. ix. 18
And Jesus came-forth and his disciples into the *villages of Caesarea Philippi,* and on the way .	But Jesus having come into *the parts of Caesarea Philippi.*	And it came to pass when he was *praying alone* .

Before this mention of "Caesarea Philippi," and after the Feeding of the Five Thousand, Mark mentions other places which it will be convenient to enumerate here —

Mk vi. 45	Mt xiv 22	Jn vi. 16—17
He constrained his disciples to enter into the boat and to go before [him] unto *the other side to Bethsaida* .	He constrained the disciples to enter into the boat and to go before him *unto the other side.* .	His disciples went down unto the sea and they entered into a boat and were going over the sea unto *Capernaum*

There are no parallels to the following:—

Mk vi. 53	Mt. xiv 34	Lk. om.
They came to *the land, unto Gennesaret* .	They came to *the land, unto Gennesaret.*	

This is closely followed, in Mark, by a mention of Jesus as going into "villages and cities," and healing, and subsequently rebuking the Pharisees and teaching the multitude. Then, it is said, more definitely —

Mk vii. 24	Mt. xv. 21	Lk. om.
But from thence he arose and went away into the borders of *Tyre [and Sidon]*[1]	And Jesus came out thence, and withdrew into the parts of *Tyre and Sidon.*	

---

[1] "And Sidon" is bracketed by W H

JESUS WALKING ON THE SEA

Jesus is here in the region entered by Elijah when the Lord said to him "Arise, get thee to Zarephath, which belongeth to Zidon...behold, I have commanded a widow woman there to sustain thee", but whereas Elijah was sustained by the woman, Jesus, metaphorically, feeds a woman with what are described as "*the children's* crumbs[1]" Then Jesus returns to the sea of Galilee.

Mk vii. 31	Mt. xv. 29	Lk. om.
And again having come forth from the borders of Tyre he came *through Sidon*[2] *to the sea of Galilee through the midst of the borders of Decapolis.*	And having departed thence Jesus came *by*[3] *the sea of Galilee*, and having gone up to *the mountain* he sat there.	

Mark next relates the healing of "one that was deaf," and the Feeding of the Four Thousand, after which it is said:—

Mk viii. 10	Mt. xv. 39	Lk. om.
And straightway he entered into the boat with his disciples and came into *the parts of Dalmanutha*	And he...entered into the boat and came into *the borders of Magadan.*	

---

[1] See 1 K xvii 9 and Lk iv. 25—6 Commenting on Lk , Origen says that the famine was a famine for the word of God, and that the widow was the same that is called by Isaiah (liv 1) "deserted," meaning the type of the Gentile Church Then he adds, "Thou wast a widow in Sarepta of Sidonia, from whose borders there cometh forth the Canaanitish woman and desireth to have her daughter healed, and, on account of [her] faith, earned that which she sought," thus alluding to Mt xv 22, parall to Mk vii. 26

[2] "Through Sidon" A V has "And again, departing from the coasts of Tyre and Sidon, he came ."

[3] "By (παρὰ) the sea"

JESUS WALKING ON THE SEA

In the next parallels, a journey on water—presumably across the sea of Galilee—is implied by Mark but not by Matthew:—

Mk viii. 13—14 (*lit.*)	Mt. xvi. 4—5 (*lit.*)	Lk. om.
And having left them, having again *gone on board*, he departed *to the other side*. And they had forgotten to take loaves...[1].	And having [finally] left them he departed. And the disciples, having come *to the other side*, had forgotten to take loaves.	

Then follows, in Mark alone (viii. 22—6) "And they come *to Bethsaida*, and they bring to him a blind man..." Him Jesus "brought out of the village" and healed, and sent away, saying, "Do not even enter into the village." And now comes the tradition above quoted, where Mark and Matthew say that Jesus came into the neighbourhood of "*Caesarea Philippi*," but Luke that He was "*praying alone.*"

It will be seen that, if we ask whence Jesus came to Caesarea, Mark answers "from Bethsaida." And it was to "Bethsaida" (again, according to Mark) that Jesus "constrained the disciples to go" immediately after the miracle of the Five Thousand, although they were in fact carried to "Gennesaret." Thus it may be said briefly that Mark, in relating the movements of Jesus, makes two mentions of Bethsaida or its neighbourhood, and that Luke omits practically everything that Mark places between these two mentions. The omitted passages include the Walking on the Sea, the Healing of the Syrophoenician woman's daughter, and the Feeding of the Four Thousand, all of which occur in the north of Palestine. Luke himself mentions

---

[1] Mk viii 13—14 καὶ ἀφεὶς αὐτοὺς πάλιν ἐμβὰς ἀπῆλθεν εἰς τὸ πέραν Καὶ ἐπελάθοντο λαβεῖν ἄρτους, Mt. xvi. 4 καὶ καταλιπὼν αὐτοὺς ἀπῆλθεν Καὶ ἐλθόντες οἱ μαθηταὶ εἰς τὸ πέραν ἐπελάθοντο ἄρτους λαβεῖν.

a coming to Bethsaida, but it is before, not after, the Feeding of the Five Thousand[1]

The Mark-Matthew passages covering this interval between the Feeding of the Five Thousand and the Confession of Peter will be discussed in their order. Meantime it may be noted that, although John gives no details of such journeyings, he tells us, in a general way, that when Jesus had set forth the doctrine of bread in Capernaum, "many of his disciples *went back and walked no more with him*[2]" Hereupon Jesus said to the Twelve "Will ye also go away?" and Peter protested his unshaken belief in Him as "the Holy One of God" This is consistent with the view that there was an interval—passed over by Luke without any indication and by John with nothing but this brief indication—between the Feeding of the Five Thousand and Peter's protestation, followed by Christ's resolution to go up to Jerusalem During this interval, although Jesus occasionally attracted multitudes around Him by His power of working wonders, He would seem (according to the Fourth Gospel) to have been gradually deserted by almost all disciples except the Twelve

Something of this kind Mark seemingly assumes to have happened by the time Jesus reached Caesarea. From the midst of the Pharisees (whom He had "offended" by His doctrine)[3], Jesus comes (desiring that no man should know of it) first to Tyre and the Syrophoenician woman[4]; then to the sea of Galilee where He heals the deaf man, then to a desert place where He feeds the Four Thousand; then to Dalmanutha where the Pharisees again "tempt" Him[5]; then to Bethsaida

---

[1] Lk ix. 10. [2] Jn vi 66.

[3] Mk vii 1 συνάγονται πρὸς αὐτὸν οἱ Φαρισαῖοι, Mt xv 12 (parall to Mk vii 17) οἶδας ὅτι οἱ Φαρισαῖοι... ἐσκανδαλίσθησαν,

[4] Mk vii 24 "He desired that none should know" indicates that few of His disciples accompanied Him There is a similar avoidance of publicity in Mk vii 33—6

[5] Mk viii 10—11

JESUS WALKING ON THE SEA

where the blind man is taken out of the village and not allowed to re-enter it[1], and lastly to Caesarea Philippi[2]. Here, according to Luke, "as he was praying alone, the disciples were with him, and he asked them saying, Who do the multitudes say that I am[3]?" Not one of them could reply "The multitudes confess thee to be the Christ." That confession was reserved for Peter when Jesus appealed from the multitudes to the disciples themselves. "But who say *ye* that I am? *Peter* answereth and saith unto him, Thou art the Christ[4]."

Among many notable sayings in this Marcan section the most important perhaps for us, in our attempt to explain Luke's deviation from Mark, is the saying "There is nothing from without the man that going into him can defile the man," or rather, to render the Greek literally, "*make the man common*[5]" These words are not easy to reconcile with Peter's apparent ignorance of the doctrine in the Acts, where the Apostle refuses to eat of certain food until he hears a voice from heaven saying "What God hath cleansed *make not thou common*[6]."

Perhaps Luke's knowledge of Peter's vision, as being required to remove his ignorance, was one of several causes that induced him to omit the Marcan section containing this exposition of Christ's doctrine of non-defilement. But we shall have to note, in its order, that Mark (but not the parallel Matthew) calls this saying "*a parable*[7]" Now John represents

---

[1] Mk viii 22—6

[2] Mk viii 27

[3] Lk ix 18. Luke does not mention Caesarea. Instead of οἱ ὄχλοι, Mk viii 27, Mt xvi 13 have οἱ ἄνθρωποι, i e "*men in general*, as distinct from *you*"

[4] Mk viii 29 "the Christ," Mt xvi 16 "the Christ, the Son of the living God," Lk ix 20 "the Christ of God"

[5] Mk vii 15, Mt. xv. 11 both use κοινοῦν, lit "make common" The word is quite different from that in Jn xviii 28 "that they might not be defiled (ἵνα μὴ μιανθῶσιν)" Κοινοῦν will be discussed in its place

[6] Acts x 15

[7] Mk vii. 17 "...his disciples asked of him the parable," parall

JESUS WALKING ON THE SEA

Jesus as telling the disciples that all His utterances were of the nature of proverbs, parables, or dark sayings, and would remain so until the Holy Spirit came to illuminate them. It is a reasonable hypothesis that this sweeping utterance of Jesus (about non-defilement) by which the Pharisees were alienated and Christ's own disciples astonished, was one of a number of such dark sayings. They reached out so far into the future that they might well seem to Luke to be erroneous anachronisms. But in fact they may have been the genuine utterances of Jesus cast into the minds of His disciples like seeds that needed time (and perhaps tribulation) before they could spring up and grow and bear fruit. This hypothesis is at all events so far probable as to make it worth while to include in our study of the Fourfold Gospel this Mark-Matthew narrative of journeyings in northern Palestine though Luke omits them all

§ 3   "*Having* (?) *bidden them farewell," in Mark*[1]

Mark and Matthew agree, with very slight differences, in saying that Jesus constrained the disciples to go on board and precede Him, with a view to returning across the water, while He was dismissing, or until He should have dismissed, the multitude[2]. Mark however has "*to Bethsaida*" as well as "*unto the other side*" Now Bethsaida could not be said to be "on the other side" According to Luke, it was close to the scene of the miracle[3]. In any case, it was on the North-East side of the Lake—not on the West with Gennesaret and Capernaum,

---

Mt xv 12 "...the disciples said unto him, Knowest thou that the Pharisees were offended when they heard this saying?"

[1] Mk vi 46 καὶ ἀποταξάμενος αὐτοῖς, Mt xiv 23 καὶ ἀπολύσας τοὺς ὄχλους.

[2] Mk vi 45 καὶ εὐθὺς ἠνάγκασεν τοὺς μαθητὰς αὐτοῦ ἐμβῆναι εἰς τὸ πλοῖον καὶ προάγειν εἰς τὸ πέραν πρὸς Βηθσαιδάν, ἕως αὐτὸς ἀπολύει τὸν ὄχλον, Mt xiv 22 καὶ [εὐθέως] ἠνάγκασεν τοὺς μαθητὰς ἐμβῆναι εἰς [marg. + τὸ] πλοῖον καὶ προάγειν αὐτὸν εἰς τὸ πέραν, ἕως οὗ ἀπολύσῃ τοὺς ὄχλους.

[3] Lk. ix. 10.

JESUS WALKING ON THE SEA

to which the disciples actually came[1]. Mark may perhaps be explained as meaning that the disciples were to row first of all to Bethsaida, where Jesus would meet them and come on board with a view to returning to Capernaum. At Bethsaida they might wait till He had disengaged Himself from the multitudes who flocked round Him[2]. A similar meaning—though with "*until*" instead of "*while*," and without "Bethsaida"—may be extracted from Matthew; the disciples were "to go on board and precede Jesus [with a view to crossing] to the other side [waiting] *until* Jesus had dismissed the multitudes."

So far, the statement of Mark as to the "preceding" of the disciples, and its correction by Matthew (to whom "Bethsaida" may well have seemed obscure and, in any case, superfluous) present no very great difficulty. And the statement, made by both, that Jesus "*constrained*" the disciples to precede Him may also be reasonably explained. John says that the multitude purposed to snatch Jesus away and to make Him "king." To leave their Master at nightfall in a lonely place and in the midst of an excited multitude who thus claimed Him as their own, may well have been distasteful to some of the Twelve. Others, including Judas Iscariot, may have sympathized too much with the excitement, and may have desired Jesus to take advantage of it. Jesus said to them not long afterwards "One of you is a devil." He referred to Judas Iscariot. But others of the disciples may have needed to be delivered from the temptation to join the multitudes in putting pressure upon Him to become a king of this world. If so, for their own sakes, they might need to be "constrained" to depart from Him for a season.

---

[1] Mk vi 53, Mt xiv 34 "Gennesaret," Jn vi 17 "Capernaum."
[2] Cramer (on Mk vi 45) has "Having therefore dismissed (ἀπολύσας) the multitudes (ὄχλους)—because men kept coming to Him, some of them probably to receive His blessing, and others for some kind of service (τῶν δὲ καὶ ἐπὶ θεραπείᾳ τινί)." Ἀπολύσας and ὄχλους are the forms used in Mt not in Mk. Θεραπεία might mean (1) homage *to* Jesus, (2) medical service *from* Jesus (comp Lk. ix 11)

JESUS WALKING ON THE SEA

But this explanation of "constraint" does not include an explanation of Mark's next words, which are ambiguous, "Having bidden them farewell" Does "*them*" mean "the disciples," or "the multitude" just mentioned ("*while he was dismissing the multitude*")? If it means "the multitude," why does not Mark repeat "*dismiss*" ("*having dismissed* them") as Matthew does? It is not like Mark to vary words, introducing a new and rare word "bid farewell" for the sake of mere variety without any difference of meaning. On the other hand, if "*them*" means "the disciples," the mention of "farewell" here seems to come too late, since Jesus has already "constrained" them to enter the boat and to precede Him across the sea

Examining the versions of Mark, we find that A.V., Vulgate, and Syriac render the two Greek words "*dismiss*" and "*bid farewell*" by one and the same word[1] But two of the principal Latin codices render the latter "*depart from*[2]" This affords an additional reason for investigating the meaning of the latter (which it will be convenient to transliterate as *apotassomai*) and its applicability here If it could mean that Jesus, though He at first proposed to "*send away*" the multitude as usual, found it necessary to disengage Himself from them with unusual abruptness, that would meet the objection above stated. It would shew that Mark changed his words because Jesus changed His procedure

Apotassomai is used by Philo, Josephus, Epictetus, and by Luke in his Gospel and in the Acts, to mean "*bid farewell*," literally and metaphorically[3]. But earlier than these is a

---

[1] "Dismiss" ἀπολύω, "bid farewell" ἀποτάσσομαι

[2] Mk vi 46 ἀποτάσσομαι, b "proficiscor," *Brix.* "discedo," as distinct from *ib* 45 ἀπολύω, "dimitto" A.V has "send away" twice, R V "send away" and "take leave"

[3] Ἀποτάσσομαι, in Philo ii 593 "Lest thine own Agrippa *bid farewell to life*," a letter from Agrippa to the Emperor, conveys a gentle threat to commit suicide. Josephus *Ant* viii. 13. 7 says that Elisha

passage where Paul says to the Corinthians that, at Troas, although "a door was opened" unto him "in the Lord," he could not stay there: "I had no relief for my spirit because I found not Titus my brother, but *bidding them farewell* I went forth into Macedonia[1]." Here an ancient Scholiast says "'*Bidding them farewell*' does not mean 'he *chose* not to preach the Gospel.' Far from it. It means that he could not stay as long as they wished"

A reason can be found for this apparently superfluous warning against "*chose*" in the fact that *apotassomai* had come to mean during the second century, among Christian writers, "*bid deliberate farewell*" *in the sense of discarding an old Master while choosing a new one.* Antithetically, the Christian was said to "bid farewell to," or "renounce," "the Angel of Wickedness," or "the things in the world," or "life," or "the wisdom of the Greeks," in order to devote himself to the service of God[2]. Paul, of course, had no such meaning when he described in passionate language how he left the Church at Troas against his own desire and theirs, under stress of a call not to be refused[3]. But the antithetical meaning of "renounce,"

---

begged to be allowed to "salute (ἀσπάσασθαι)" his parents before following Elijah, and that he accordingly "*bade them [final] farewell* (ἀποταξάμενος)," and was with Elijah as long as the latter lived Epictetus *Ench* xxxiii 6 (Stobaeus) says "As for dining out in private houses, for the most part *give it up* (τὸ πολὺ ἀπόταξαι) (but txt διακρούου "thrust it away"). In Joseph *Ant* xi 8 6 (345) ἀπετάξατο describes a ruler "dismissing" petitioners with the answer that he will look into the matter In Acts xviii 18, 21 it seems to imply an affectionate farewell for a long period, though with hope of return

[1] 2 Cor 11 13, on which see Cramer

[2] Hermas *Mand* vi 2 9, Justin Martyr *Apol* § 49, *Tryph.* § 119, Tatian § 1. In Ign *Philad* 11 ἀποταξάμενος τῷ βίῳ is taken by Lightf. metaphorically, but it is perhaps literal hyperbole, the meaning being "he has [virtually] renounced life [by perilling it for my sake]" It occurs in 2 Clem Rom vi. 4 and 5, and xvi. 2

[3] In Acts xviii 18 "take leave" is a poor rendering (instead of "bid farewell") in view of Paul's long and intimate relations with

JESUS WALKING ON THE SEA

or "not choose," had become so common in the second and third centuries that the Scholiast above quoted thought it necessary to explain that Paul *did not* use the word to mean "renounce[1]."

Returning to the Marcan *apotassomai*, we have to ask whether John *did* take the word in this sense—or at least a sense approximating to it. The supposition that he did is favoured by the fact that he represents Jesus as "withdrawing" from the multitude and that two Latin codices render *apotassomai* by "depart[2]." Such a departure might be regarded as a kind of "renunciation." Jesus had fed the multitude and had offered them the bread of heaven. They rewarded Him by acting as the agents of "the ruler of this world," purposing to "snatch him away" that they might make Him one of the

---

the Church of Corinth, and so it is in *ib.* 21, where he adds, to the Ephesians, "I will return to you if God will." An affectionate farewell is implied in Lk. ix. 61 "to those in my household," and a disruption of old ties in Lk. xiv. 33 "bid farewell to, or give up, all his [old] belongings (πᾶσι τοῖς ἑαυτοῦ ὑπάρχουσιν)."

Phrynichus (under ἀποτάσσομαι) says "'*I bid you farewell*' (ἀποτάσσομαί σοι) is quite outlandish (ἔκφυλον). For one ought to say '*I salute you*.' For this is what we find the ancients saying whenever they are parting from one another (ἐπειδὰν ἀπαλλάττωνται ἀλλήλων)." Probably he intends to censure the indiscriminate use of the phrase in the first person, and on slight occasions, not its use in narrative and on special occasions.

[1] On Mk. vi. 45 Cramer prints a scholium not explaining ἀποταξάμενος but contrasting the dismissal or "letting go," applied to the multitudes, with the "constraining" applied to the disciples — Ἐπὶ (read ἐπεὶ) τὸ πρότερον ἀπολῦσαι (read ἀπέλυσε) τὰ πλήθη ἠνάγκασεν δὲ αὐτοὺς—οὐκ ἀνεχομένους ἀποστῆναι ῥᾳδίως (τοῦτο μὲν διὰ τὴν διάθεσιν, τοῦτο δὲ καὶ ἀποροῦντας ὅπως ἂν ἔλθοι πρὸς αὐτούς, οὐκ εἰδότας ὅτι.)— ἀπολύσας οὖν τοὺς ὄχλους.. ἀνῆλθεν εἰς τὸ ὄρος... The sentence is broken by parentheses, so that ἐπεὶ...ἀπέλυσε is taken up by ἀπολύσας with resumptive οὖν. Then we have an antithesis between the "*crowds* (πλήθη)" and "*them*," i.e. the disciples. The former were "dismissed," the latter needed to be "constrained," partly because of their "[personal] disposition (διάθεσιν)" toward Jesus, and partly because they were at a loss to see how He could come to them.

[2] Mk. vi. 46, *b* "profectus ab eis," *Brix* "cum discessisset ab eis."

JESUS WALKING ON THE SEA

kings of the earth, after their type of kingship, which Jesus would have described as a worship of Satan. "Turning away from," or "renouncing," the agents of Satan, Jesus "went up into the mountain," into the presence of God. It is conceivable that John discerned an antithesis of this kind in Mark's words or at all events in one of the interpretations of them, suggested, but not adequately represented, by Matthew.

Why does John say nothing about the "constraint" put on the disciples by Jesus to leave Him? It is possible that John regarded the "constraint" as proceeding from the multitude to Jesus: "*They were [for] constraining Him to go before them,*" that is, to become their leader or king[1] If that is so, John does not omit, but re-interprets the Marcan "constraint" Mark may have been right as to the "constraint," which seems to fit all the circumstances. John may have been right about the desire to compel Jesus to become a "king," but wrong in supporting it from a tradition that mentioned "constraint" in an altogether different context Mark and John, together, help us to approximate to what was probably the historical fact

§ 4. *"Distressed" and "the fourth watch of the night," in Mark and Matthew*[2]

These words are omitted by John, who, instead of mentioning the time at which Jesus came to the disciples, mentions the distance over which the disciples had rowed: "*When therefore they had rowed about five and twenty or thirty furlongs*[3]." Macarius has preserved an ancient attack on

---

[1] See Gesen. 817 b
[2] Mk vi 48 (Mk inserts "about" before "the fourth watch," Mt. does not), Mt. xiv. 24—5, see p 403 It will be convenient to discuss "distressed," applied by Mark to the disciples but by Matthew to the boat, in the next section.
[3] Jn vi. 19 The parall Mt xiv. 24 (W H txt) "many furlongs from the shore" should be contrasted with this more definite statement Mt xiv 24 (R V txt) "in the midst of the sea" seems likely to be a corrupt assimilation to Mk vi 47 Codex D has, in Mk, ἦν

418 (Mark vi 45—52)

JESUS WALKING ON THE SEA

the Marcan phrase by a hostile critic, who says that the Lake is so narrow that even a canoe can cross it in two hours[1], and that the Lake is too small to have room for waves and tempests. Although this last statement is quite untrue, the critic hits a weak point in Mark, who tells us that "when even was come"—that is to say, roughly, during the first watch of the night, which lasted from 6 to 9 P.M.—"the boat was in the midst of the sea," and that Jesus did not come till "about the fourth watch," which lasted from 3 to 6 A.M. It is hardly credible that two watches of the night, or six hours, were spent in rowing on a small lake, without progress, and yet without drifting somewhere into the shore We have therefore to ask whether Mark may have been misled by some tradition connecting some trial of the faith of the disciples with "*about the fourth watch of the night*," which he has recorded here, out of place.

The indefiniteness implied by "*about*" indicates that the time might be taken by some as the beginning of the fourth watch, by others as the end[2]. If taken as the beginning, it would practically synchronize with the end of the third watch. Now the third watch is, by implication, called "cockcrowing" in Mark, later on, "Watch therefore; for ye know not when the

---

πάλαι τὸ πλοῖον ἐν μέσῃ τῇ θαλάσσῃ—which seems an attempt to meet objections as to time and space by suggesting that the vessel, having "long ago" reached the middle of the Lake, could make no further headway owing to the opposing wind. D, in Mt., has ἦν εἰς μέσον τῆς θαλάσσης.

[1] Macar. III 6 (ed Blondel, p. 60).

[2] See Macar III 13, p 84 Τετάρτῃ δὲ οὐκ ἀπὸ τέλους φυλακῇ τῆς νυκτὸς αὐτοῖς ἐνεφάνισεν, ἀλλ᾽ ἀπ᾽ ἀρχῆς, τουτέστιν ὥρᾳ τετάρτῃ τῆς νυκτός ᾽Εὰν δέ, ὡς σὺ φῇς, βιασθῶμεν εἰπεῖν τὴν ἀπὸ τέλους.... The Apologist appears to misrepresent his critic, who implies the same time in his phrase (*ib* III 6, p. 60) "tenth hour of the night" that the Apologist implies in his phrase "fourth hour of the night" (namely 3 A.M., reckoned, severally, from average sunset or from midnight) But the discussion, though confused, is instructive, as shewing that a night-watch might be reckoned from its beginning or from its end

JESUS WALKING ON THE SEA

lord of the house cometh, whether at even, or at midnight, or at *cockcrowing*, or in the morning[1]." It is probable that this tradition of Mark—not followed by the parallel Matthew, and altered by the parallel Luke—is very early, and that it contains a reference to Peter's denial, which took place *about the time of "cockcrowing,"* after he and the rest had received the warning "Watch and pray lest ye enter into temptation." This is all the more probable because the word *alectorophōnia*, "cockcrowing," is not alleged to have existed in the Greek language before this Marcan use of it. It would seem to be a Greek rendering of the Latin *gallicinium*, which passed into Mark's Gospel from Peter's indelible recollection of Christ's prediction "before the cock crow"

According to this view, "about the fourth watch of the night" in Mark's account of the Walking on the Sea must not be taken literally. There may have been, literally, some storm on the sea of Tiberias where Jesus appeared to the disciples as their Saviour guiding them to safety. But, if there was, we are not to assume that the details are here literally and exactly described as to time and place. The time described as "about the fourth watch" is to be regarded as "the hour of trial," corresponding to the "cockcrowing" in the darkness of the early morning before the Crucifixion when Peter denied his Master.

---

[1] Mk xiii 35. Mark assumes that "even" is 6—9 P M (1st watch), "midnight" 9—12 P M (2nd watch), "cockcrowing" 12—3 A M (3rd watch), "morning" 3—6 A M (4th watch) Comp Lk xii 38 "And if he shall come in the second watch, and if in the third," sim SS (and *Brix.*), but Curet has "If in the first watch he come ..happy is it for them...or if in the second watch or the third he come, " D has "and if he shall come in the evening watch ..and if in the second and the third" (and sim *Corb.* and *e, b* has simply "the evening watch") No particular "watch" is mentioned in Mt. xxiv 43 "if the master of the house had known in what watch the thief was coming"

Mark does not say that this warning was addressed specially to Peter, but the parallel Luke suggests it (xii. 41) "And Peter said Lord speakest thou this parable to us or also to all?"

JESUS WALKING ON THE SEA

In Mark, it is true, there is no special mention here of Peter connected with "the fourth watch." But there is in the parallel Matthew. Matthew inserts an attempt of the Apostle to walk on the waters, and relates how he began to sink and the Lord took hold of him and said "O thou of little faith, wherefore didst thou doubt[1]?" It is incredible that Mark knew of this miracle, as occurring at this point, and yet omitted it But we can understand how this phrase, "about the fourth watch of the night," the period that followed "cockcrowing," connected with the coming of the Lord in some trial or temptation of the faith of Peter and his companions, may have induced an early Evangelist—Matthew, or some authority followed by him—to place at this point a tradition about Peter's temptation, and fall, and restoration.

This leads us to ask whether the word "distressed," in the preceding context, might have originally referred to some temptation, or trial of faith, endured by all the disciples, but most notably by Peter.

§ 5   "Distressed," differently applied in Mark and Matthew[2]

The word rendered by R.V. "distressed" is applied by Mark to the disciples, but by Matthew to the boat The Greek Thesaurus gives no instance of the application of the word to an inanimate object of this kind, and we may safely infer that Matthew transferred it from the disciples in the boat to the boat itself because, when applied to persons, the Greek verb *basanīzein* often implied "torment" or "torture," and he thought it desirable to avoid such a suggestion.

But in fact *basanīzein*, though sometimes loosely used to mean tormenting for the mere purpose of causing pain—and

---

[1] Mt xiv. 31
[2] Mk vi 48 ἰδὼν αὐτοὺς βασανιζομένους ἐν τῷ ἐλαύνειν, Mt. xiv. 24 τὸ δὲ πλοῖον...ἀπεῖχεν βασανιζόμενον ὑπὸ τῶν κυμάτων.

JESUS WALKING ON THE SEA

in that sense loosely applied by Matthew to the torture of disease[1]—meant etymologically "test, or try, as one tests gold with a touchstone[2]." When applied to persons it meant "test" them (and this sometimes by torture) to ascertain whether they were speaking the truth. But this might easily pass into the meaning "test so as to bring out the truth," "test so as to refine, and purify, and make a man his true self." Hence Plato speaks of a righteous man stripped of all the rewards of righteousness as being "*tested [as it were by torment]* with a view to righteousness[3]" The first Epistle of Peter, though not using this word for "test," implies something very much like it when it speaks of "proof" in the words "Wherein ye greatly rejoice, though now for a little while, if need be, ye have been put to grief in manifold temptations, that the *proof* of your faith, [being] more precious than gold that perisheth though it is *proved* by fire, might be found unto praise...[4]."

A passage in Ben Sira rather favours the view that there was some early tradition, verbally followed by Mark, describing Jesus, personally, as looking down in pity on the disciples as they were "tested" by being tossed in the waves of temptation[5]. It is the only one where *basanīzein*, in the LXX, has

---

[1] Mt viii 6 δεινῶς βασανιζόμενος an expression not used in the parallel Lk vii 2 foll.

[2] See Steph *Thes*

[3] Plato *Polit* 361 C βεβασανισμένος εἰς δικαιοσύνην.

[4] 1 Pet i 6—7 ἐν ᾧ ἀγαλλιᾶσθε, ὀλίγον ἄρτι εἰ δέον λυπηθέντες ἐν ποικίλοις πειρασμοῖς, ἵνα τὸ ⌜δοκίμιον⌝ ὑμῶν τῆς πίστεως πολυτιμότερον χρυσίου τοῦ ἀπολλυμένου διὰ πυρὸς δὲ δοκιμαζομένου εὑρεθῇ εἰς ἔπαινον.... The words δοκίμιον and δοκιμαζομένου, R V "*proof.. proved,*" Hort "*test* (v 1 *approvedness*)...*tried* (*purified*)," suggest aspects of βασανίζω, though the Epistle does not mention the word itself Comp *ib* iv 12 τῇ ἐν ὑμῖν πυρώσει πρὸς πειρασμὸν ὑμῖν γινομένῃ The two tests of fire and water are mentioned in Ps lxvi 10, 12 "thou hast tried us as silver is tried," "we went through fire and through water."

[5] Comp Ps lxxxviii. 7 (and sim xlii 7) "thou hast afflicted me with all *thy waves*," and Chrys on Mt xiv 23—4 "He suffers them

JESUS WALKING ON THE SEA

a Hebrew equivalent. It says that Wisdom "goes in a strange form at first and will bring fear and fright upon him [*i.e.* on the pupil whom she is training] and will *test him* [*by torment*] in her training until he has [firm] faith in his soul [*i.e.* truly, in his heart, and not in mere *profession*]¹." Such a tradition would not exclude—indeed it would rather favour—the supposition that the "test," or "trial," was caused by some impurity, or imperfection, which needed to be refined away². Hermas, whose resemblance to Mark we have had frequent occasion to note, is almost the only early Christian writer that uses and repeatedly uses the verb "test" or "torment," and describes the tormenting as being used sometimes to produce amendment and not always to torment for the sake of mere punishment³.

In Hermas, the Angel of Punishment is described as "*driving about*" the sheep that need to be "*tested* [*by torment*]" for their good, in order that they may repent⁴. Here it may be noted that "*drive about*" is a compound of "*drive*," the word

---

all the night long to be *tossed on the waves* (κλυδωνίζεσθαι), rousing (I take it) their hardened heart." Mark describes Jesus as "seeing" the disciples in their trouble, Matthew does not

[1] Sir iv 17 quoted from the Hebrew in *Son* **3499** (iv) in a note on "Torments." Ἐμπιστεύειν, "have [firm] faith," is probably used absolutely here, as in Sir ii 13 (v r), iv 16, xix 4 (see Steph. *Thes*.).

[2] Comp. Lk xxii 31 "Simon, Simon, behold, Satan hath begged you [*i.e.* thee and thy companions] to sift as wheat, but I have made supplication for thee that thy faith fail not utterly, and do thou, hereafter, when thou hast returned, strengthen thy brethren."

[3] Goodspeed gives βασανίζω as occurring in Hermas about fifteen times, in Ign. only once, in *Polyc. Mart.* twice. In the early Apologists it is used only once, and then (Justin Martyr) in the sense of "scrutinise."

[4] Hermas *Sim.* vi 2 7 "driving about" περιήλαυνεν. Comp. Clem. Alex. 458 "The same [*i.e.* the Pastor of Hermas] says that repentance is high intelligence. For [a man] repenting of what he did no longer does it or says [it], but *tormenting* (βασανίζων) his own soul for his past sins he benefits [it]." Comp. 2 Pet. ii 8 which says that Lot "*tormented* [his] righteous soul" with the unrighteous works of the men of Sodom

JESUS WALKING ON THE SEA

used by Mark and John, in the Walking on the Sea, to mean "*rowing*." "Drive" occurs only once elsewhere in the Gospels, where Luke describes the man possessed with the Legion as "*driven* by the devil into the deserts[1]." The word that means in Hebrew "*row*" (literally "move to and fro") may mean in Aramaic "madman" or "fool"—as in the Targum on the Psalm "*Fools* because of the way of their transgression...are afflicted ...then they cry unto the Lord...and he delivereth them out of their distress[2]." In Greek, too, "to be driven in one's mind" is said to be "a more graceful phrase" than "to be mad[3]." The supposition that Mark's "rowing" conceals some obscure reference to mental or spiritual "driving," or at all events something more complex than the literal meaning, is confirmed not only by Matthew's omission of "rowing," but also by the fact that SS in Mark, instead of "tormented *in rowing*," has "tormented *from fear of the waves*[4]."

Origen consistently assumes that what our Versions render "distress" meant really a searching "test," "trial," or "temptation with a view to purification." The multitudes, he says, were not able to endure this test, so Jesus "dismissed" them. But He separated from them the disciples, whom He constrained to enter the boat, that is to say "the conflict of temptations and difficulties into which any one is constrained by the Word,

---

[1] Lk viii. 29 ἠλαύνετο. It occurs in N T elsewhere only in Jas iii 4 τὰ πλοῖα. ὑπὸ ἀνέμων σκληρῶν ἐλαυνόμενα, 2 Pet ii 17 ὁμίχλαι ὑπὸ λαίλαπος ἐλαυνόμεναι. It would be sometimes impossible to tell whether ἐλαύνεσθαι ὑπὸ πνεύματος meant "driven by a wind" or "driven by a spirit," and the same ambiguity would exist in Hebrew.

[2] Ps cvii 17—19 "fools," Heb אֱוִילִים, Targ שטין. See Gesen 1001—2 on שׁוט "row," "swim," "run to and fro" (n "scourge"), Dan xii 4 "run to and fro," LXX "become quite mad" or "be driven to madness," ἀπομανῶσιν.

[3] Steph *Thes* iii 679 quotes Thomas p 293, ἐλαύνεται τὴν γνώμην κάλλιον λέγειν ἢ μαίνεται.

[4] Mk vi. 48 D has "tormented *and* rowing," d "remigantes et laborantes (*i e* hard pressed)" (and similarly other Latin codices).

JESUS WALKING ON THE SEA

and goes unwillingly, as it were, when the Saviour wishes to train by exercise the disciples in this boat which is *tested [and tormented]* by the waves and the contrary wind[1]" Later on, without mentioning Peter as thus "tormented," he prepares the way for it by saying "Then when we see that we are encompassed by many grievous troubles, and when by toil we succeed passably in swimming through them[2], let us consider that our boat is in the midst of the sea, being at that moment *tormented* by the waves which wish us to make shipwreck of the faith or some one of the virtues[3]." Lastly he includes Peter in those who are thus "tormented," saying "If any Peter be found among us...having come down from the boat as if coming out of that temptation in which he *was being tested [and tormented]*...[4]"

This mention of Peter as being "tormented" for his good suggests the question, How, if in any way, does the Fourth Gospel represent Peter as being thus "tormented"? Want of space compels us to pass over many differences between the Synoptists and John at this point, as, for example, the reception of Jesus into the boat related by the former but omitted by the latter[5] But what Origen says about "swimming through"

---

[1] Origen on Mt xiv 22 foll (*Comm Matth* xi 5, Lomm iii. p 77 foll). He calls it (*ib* p 79) "the boat of temptations," and speaks of the disciples as (*ib* p 80) "having come into the midst of the sea and of the waves [that are] in temptations" and of (*ib* p 81) "enduring the *test [and torment]* from the waves until they become worthy of the divine assistance "

[2] Origen (Lomm iii. p 81) "swimming through," διανηξώμεθα, see *Proclam* Index "swim " Comp Plutarch *Mor* 1063 B "Those who are progressing (προκόπτοντες) are like. .swimmers (νηχομένοις) "

[3] Comp 1 Tim 1 19 περὶ τὴν πίστιν ἐναυάγησαν Lk xxii 31 σινιάσαι expresses Peter's trial in a different metaphor

[4] Origen *Comm Matth* xi 6, Lomm. iii. p. 82

[5] Chrysostom, on Mt xiv 29—31, has a perplexing comment that is instructive as shewing the difficulties of those who attempted to harmonize the narratives while taking them literally Quoting Jn vi 21, he says that Jesus did not go on board the boat till the disciples "were on the point of being near the land (μελλόντων αὐτῶν

JESUS WALKING ON THE SEA

troubles, and what he calls the "tormenting" of Peter, demands special attention Related by Matthew in the Walking on the Sea, it recalls to our mind, by contrast, the Johannine account of Peter's swimming to Jesus, connected by John with a miraculous draught of fishes, and placed by him after Christ's resurrection. Luke, who also (alone of the Synoptists) relates a miraculous draught of fishes, places the event long before Christ's resurrection, and connects it with the Call of the Fishermen And it has been shewn that Luke has probably done this under a misunderstanding, apparently confusing a Greek word that meant "he swam to shore" with another that meant "he made signs[1]." Luke appeared to be wrong and John right in the interpretation of the Petrine story We shall now ask whether there is any indication that Matthew is similarly wrong and John similarly right, in the interpretation of another Petrine story of the same kind.

§ 6. *How Peter "was grieved" by Jesus*[2]

At first sight it may seem something like bathos to pass from the thought of Peter "tormented" to the thought of Peter "grieved." Spiritually regarded, however, the transition may be climax rather than bathos. The Suffering Servant in Isaiah is "a man of sorrows and acquainted with *grief*," and it pleased God "to put him to *grief*[3]" Jesus, at Gethsemane, says "My soul is exceedingly *grieved*," and Paul speaks of the

---

πρὸς τῇ γῇ γίνεσθαι) " And he adds, about Peter, "Having overcome the greater [difficulty] he [Peter] was on the point of being harmed by the less, I mean, by the violence of the wind, not the sea " The Commentary on Jn attributed to Chrys says "Why did not Jesus ascend the vessel ?...He did not go on board the vessel in order that the wonder He was working might be greater " See *Joh Gr.* 2716—7

[1] See *Proclamation* pp 1 foll , 35 foll , 91 foll
[2] Jn xxi 17 "Peter was grieved (ἐλυπήθη) because he [Jesus] said unto him the third time, Lovest thou me?"
[3] Is liii. 3, 10.

JESUS WALKING ON THE SEA

purifying influence of *"grief according to God*[1]*."* When therefore we read in the Fourth Gospel that Peter was *"grieved"* by a question of Jesus, and bear in mind how often in this Gospel very deep thoughts are expressed in very simple language, we ought not to pass over the words without serious thought. Paul says to the Corinthians "For if I [I of all men] *grieve* you, why, who is he that is to gladden me—except the very same person that is *being grieved* by me[2]?" Much more (we may be sure) might Jesus say the same thing about Peter; He would not, without deep purpose, thus have "grieved" the disciple who was hereafter to "gladden" His heart.

The scene of this "grieving" of Peter is also the scene of what Origen calls the "tormenting" of Peter—the sea of Tiberias The time also may be said to be the same In Matthew it occurs "in the fourth watch of the night"; in John it occurs near the conclusion of that watch, when dawn was coming on[3] Both in Matthew and John the night has been spent in toil (differently, yet in both cases fruitlessly) In Matthew, Jesus came over the sea, walking to the vessel containing Peter and his companions; in John, Jesus "stood on the shore" In both, the disciples at first fail to recognise Jesus.

At this point, John's narrative of the fishing diverges into symbolism intended to prepare the way for the "grieving" that is to be caused by Jesus to the foremost and most strenuous of His faithful Apostles There is no "torment" of furious winds or waves to shake Peter's faith. He swims—the distance is not great—to his Master on the shore. There they see a

---

[1] Mk xiv 34, Mt xxvi. 38 περίλυπος, 2 Cor. vii 10 ἡ κατὰ θεὸν λύπη

[2] 2 Cor 11 2 εἰ γὰρ ἐγὼ λυπῶ ὑμᾶς, καὶ τίς ὁ εὐφραίνων με εἰ μὴ ὁ λυπούμενος ἐξ ἐμοῦ, The advantage of rendering λύπη "grief" (and not "sorrow") is that the similarity between noun and verb ("*grief*" and "*grieve*") can be briefly expressed.

[3] Jn xxi 4 πρωίας δὲ ἤδη γινομένης, A V wrongly, "when the morning was now come," R V "when day was now breaking"

427 (Mark vi 45—52)

JESUS WALKING ON THE SEA

meal prepared, baked on a fire of coals. This has been shewn above[1] to be a symbol of purifying trial, and sometimes of martyrdom. The swimming and the fire, taken together, suggest a double purification like the one in the Psalms ("we went through *fire and water*[2]") But still the purifying process is not complete

Therefore, although Peter has received, along with the rest of the seven, the *viaticum* that is to prepare him for the work of the Gospel, there comes from Jesus a heart-searching test, torment, or trial in the form of a question that seems to throw doubt on the present genuineness of his love because in a past hour of weakness he had denied his Master At first he replies meekly. To the question "Lovest thou me more than these?" he will not say *now* that he loves "*more*" He says, simply, "Yea, Lord, thou knowest that I love thee" But the question is thrice repeated Then, at last, turning on Jesus with a mixture of passionate adoration and something like passionate reproach for thus "tormenting" him, the deeply wounded disciple exclaims against such a question proceeding from one who knows all things "Lord, *thou knowest all things, thou knowest* that I love thee."

It needs some sympathetic effort on our part to enter into the mind of the Apostle thus enduring a chastening all the more grievous because it was so kind and so quiet. But, the more we think over it, the more clearly shall we perceive that the Evangelist regards it as a final trial of faith, a touchstone or test of the Petrine gold from which the Apostle comes forth recognised by our Lord as being not only a shepherd of His sheep but also a follower of Himself in a special way He is the only Apostle whose "manner of death" is specially predicted by Jesus as destined to be like His own, so that he might be said to follow his Master literally on the path of the Cross The very last words of Jesus on earth, as recorded in

---

[1] See above, pp. 367—9. [2] Ps lxvi 12.

JESUS WALKING ON THE SEA

the Fourth Gospel, contain a precept of special honour and privilege ("Follow thou me") addressed to the disciple whom He had recently "grieved[1]."

§ 7. "For they all saw him," in Mark[2]

In attempting to explain why Mark, after saying "when they saw him," adds "for they all saw him," we have to note that Matthew appears to recognise two classes of people in the boat, first "the disciples," and secondly, "the [men] in the boat," that is, the sailors. It is true that Origen, commenting on Matthew's peculiar addition at the end of the narrative, "*but those who were in the boat* worshipped him saying, Truly thou art God's Son," says "This *the disciples* in the boat say, for I do not think *that others than the disciples said it*[3]" But if Matthew had meant "the disciples," why should he not have said "*the disciples*," as he has said before[4]? According to Jerome, Matthew makes the same distinction here—namely,

---

[1] Comp Plutarch *Mor* 452 E where Diogenes condemns Plato for never having "grieved" a single one of his disciples, τοσοῦτον χρόνον φιλοσοφῶν οὐδένα λελύπηκεν.

[2] Mk vi 49—50 "But they, having seen him . thought that it was a phantasm, and cried out loudly, for they all saw him and were troubled," Οἱ δὲ ἰδόντες αὐτὸν.. ἔδοξαν ὅτι φάντασμά ἐστιν καὶ ἀνέκραξαν Πάντες γὰρ αὐτὸν εἶδαν καὶ ἐταράχθησαν, Mt xiv 26 "But the disciples, having seen him...were troubled, saying 'It is a phantasm,' and cried out from fear," Οἱ δὲ μαθηταὶ ἰδόντες αὐτὸν ..ἐταράχθησαν λέγοντες ὅτι φάντασμά ἐστιν, καὶ ἀπὸ τοῦ φόβου ἔκραξαν In Mark, D and the best Latin MSS ("and cried out loudly all [of them] and were troubled") omit γὰρ αὐτὸν εἶδαν, SS has "When they saw him...they supposed it was a devil (Walton, visionem fallacem), and when they all saw him they gave a cry "

To render Mk vi. 49 "but those who saw him," though allowable in literary Greek, would not be in accord with the style of Mark Bruder (*ed* 1888, pp. 587—8) gives no other instances of ὁ δὲ with particip used relatively in Mark except in Mk v. 14, xiii 13 [xvi 16].

[3] Origen on Mt xiv 33 οἱ δὲ ἐν τῷ πλοίῳ, says ὅπερ λέγουσιν οἱ ἐν τῷ πλοίῳ μαθηταί· οὐ γὰρ ἄλλους τῶν μαθητῶν νομίζω τοῦτο εἰρηκέναι.

[4] Mt xiv 26 οἱ δὲ μαθηταὶ ἰδόντες....

JESUS WALKING ON THE SEA

between "those who were in the boat," *i e* the sailors, and "the disciples"—that he made before, in the Stilling of the Storm, where he alone mentions "men" at the conclusion of the narrative "But the men marvelled[1]." The question is one of more than verbal importance, for it bears on the moral and spiritual value of the confession, in Matthew, "Truly, thou art God's Son" This confession, coming at the conclusion of Matthew's narrative, is in strange contrast with Mark's conclusion "they understood not." Also the contextual mention of the Greek *phantasma*—unique in N.T. and rendered by A.V. "*spirit*" but by R V more correctly "*apparition*"—demands careful consideration as being one of many details in this narrative that point to the thought of the risen Saviour, Christ, returning to the disciples across the waters of Sheol, no "phantasm," but reality. It is connected with the distinction between "seeing Jesus" and yet not "knowing" Him, or not "believing" Him to be "the Lord."

§ 8. "*An apparition*," *in Mark and Matthew*[2]

Instead of "an apparition," SS has "*a devil*," the Peshitta has "*a false apparition* (or, *vision*)," Delitzsch has "*the appearance of a spirit*" The Greek word here rendered "apparition,"

---

[1] Mt viii 27 (parall to Mk iv 41 "and they [*i e* the disciples] feared [with] a great fear," Lk viii 25 "but they [*i e* the disciples] feared and marvelled") On this Jerome says "Not the disciples, but *the sailors and the rest that were in the ship* 'marvelled' But if anyone contentiously wishes [to maintain] that those who 'marvelled' were disciples, we shall reply that they were rightly called 'the men (*homines*)'—those who knew not as yet the power of the Saviour (qui necdum noverant potentiam Salvatoris)" He says also on Mt xiv 33 "*Nautae atque vectores* vere Filium Dei confitentur," that is, "*the sailors and the passengers*"

In Mt xiv 33 "*those who were in the boat*" might be intended to mean "the disciples that were in the boat" as distinct from Peter, who had gone out of the boat and was now returning to it with Jesus. But this would not explain Mt viii 27 "*the men* marvelled"

[2] Mk vi 49, Mt xiv 26

JESUS WALKING ON THE SEA

phantasma, occurs nowhere else in the Gospels except in D's version of a passage in Luke "They thought they saw *a phantasm*," where the text has "*a spirit*[1]." Ignatius, apparently referring to Luke, says "For I know and believe that also after the resurrection He was in the flesh, and when He came to Peter and his friends, He said unto them, 'Take, handle me, and see that I am not *a bodiless demon*[2]'" In LXX and early Christian writers, *phantasma* hardly occurs[3]; but we may gather from its use in Euripides, Plato, Plutarch, and Pliny (who uses it as a Latin word), that when applied to the appearance of a human form it would mostly mean the "apparition" of one dead, and that it would convey a notion of unreality and sometimes of sinister influence[4]. It would seem that Mark used the word to mean "ghost," probably implying that the disciples, in their panic, thought that their Master had died, and that they beheld a mere "apparition" of Him, perhaps

---

[1] Lk. xxiv 37 See *Notes* **2824*** (1) *b—e*. Tertullian *Adv. Marc.* iv 43 *ad fin*, while quoting Christ's words as "*spiritus* ossa non habet," quotes, or paraphrases, the context as "quum haesitantibus eis ne *phantasma* esset, immo *phantasma* credentibus..."

[2] Ign *Smyrn.* § 3 Ἐγὼ γὰρ καὶ μετὰ τὴν ἀνάστασιν ἐν σαρκὶ αὐτὸν οἶδα καὶ πιστεύω ὄντα καὶ ὅτε πρὸς τοὺς περὶ Πέτρον ἦλθεν ἔφη αὐτοῖς· Λάβετε, ψηλαφήσατέ με, καὶ ἴδετε ὅτι οὐκ εἰμὶ δαιμόνιον ἀσώματον.

[3] In LXX it occurs only in Job xx 8 (A) (v r θαῦμα and φάσμα), Is xxviii 7 (A) (v r φάσμα), and Wisd xvii 15 Goodspeed gives it only in Tatian *Contr Graec* § 7 where the context mentions "an army of demons (δαιμόνων στρατόπεδον)"

[4] See Plutarch *Mor* 900 F quoting from Chrysippus, Φάντασμα δέ ἐστιν ἐφ' ὃ ἑλκόμεθα κατὰ τὸν φανταστικὸν ἑλκυσμόν· ταῦτα δὲ γίνεται ἐπὶ τῶν μελαγχολώντων καὶ μεμηνότων, and Plin *Epist*. vii. 27 (as quoted in Steph. *Thes.* but the text varies) asking a friend whether he thinks that "apparitions" "are really something (esse aliquid)," and have "a figure of their own and some kind of divine nature (propriam figuram numenque aliquod)," or whether they "receive a vain and variable image [born] from our fear (inanem et variam ex metu nostro imaginem accipere)" This shews that "phantasma," meaning "ghost," had passed from Greek into Latin early in the second century and probably in the first.

JESUS WALKING ON THE SEA

sent from some evil source, or portending evil, like the apparition of Samuel to Saul.

Luke omits the whole of the Marcan narrative of the Walking on the Sea, including the clause "*they thought* that it was a *phantasm*"; but his use of a similar clause later on (with the same rather rare word for "thought," "They *thought* they beheld *a spirit*, D *a phantasm*[1]") favours the inference that he did not really omit this clause, but only transposed it to what he believed to be its right place, namely, after Christ's resurrection. If he did transpose it he might naturally alter "*phantasm*" into "*spirit*" in order to suggest that the word merely meant "a bodiless spirit," without any such suggestion of baneful influence as would often be conveyed by the Greek and Latin word *phantasma* to educated readers. But the evidence of the Lucan context, and the paraphrase of Ignatius, indicate that the original word was not simply "spirit," but some word meaning "demon," or some phrase suggesting unreality or evil origin[2].

John, in the Walking on the Sea, agrees with Mark and

---

[1] "Thought," Mk vi 49 ἔδοξαν (non-occurrent in Mk elsewhere except Mk x. 42 οἱ δοκοῦντες ἄρχειν), Lk xxiv 37 ἐδόκουν

[2] The fact that Delitzsch renders φάντασμα by "appearance of a spirit" indicates that no single Hebrew word exactly represents the Greek, and favours the view that in Lk xxiv 37, as well as in Mk vi. 49, the original was שֵׁד, "demon," which has been euphemistically translated by Mark. Comp *Megill* 3 *a* warning a man not to salute "[even] *his neighbour* (חבירו)" at night, lest he should prove to be "a demon (שֵׁד)," sim *Sanhedr.* 44 *a*

The Mark-Appendix (xvi 12) says that Jesus was manifested to two of the disciples "*in another form* (μορφῇ) (Delitzsch, דמות)." Luke says about the two disciples (xxiv 16) "*their eyes were holden* that they should not recognise (ἐπιγνῶναι) him." Μορφή is represented in LXX by five words, but never by Delitzsch's word (which = ὁμοίωμα, or -ωσις, twenty-one times). Another word for "form," σχῆμα, occurs in LXX, only in Is iii 17 "the secret-parts [of the daughters of Sion]." Luke avoids the difficult questions, What precisely is meant by "form"? And what precisely is implied by "other"?

JESUS WALKING ON THE SEA

Matthew that the disciples feared and that Jesus said "fear not," but he makes no mention of a *phantasma* Also he gives us the impression that Jesus may have been walking, not actually on the sea but by the edge of the sea on the shore, drawing the boat toward the shore, so that He does not come to the boat (though the disciples "were willing to receive Him into the boat") but the boat comes to Him[1] If that is his meaning, he seems to regard Jesus as fulfilling the words "He drew me out of many waters[2]," not by drawing Peter (as Matthew says) out of the waves but by drawing all the disciples across the waves to Himself

To us, of course, the thought of a *phantasma* and the thought of "drawing" seem to have nothing whatever to do with one another But we have to consider, not what seems to us, but what would seem to Greeks in the first century Now Chrysippus uses, and Plutarch quotes, this word "draw," in what may be called a definition of *phantasma*. "*Phantasma* is that to which *we are drawn* in accordance with the absolutely vain and phantastic *drawing* These are the things that befall the melancholy and the mad[3]" In the next place, Epictetus, accepting man as the "logical creature," that is, the creature endowed with Logos, Reason (or Word in the Johannine sense), declares "that he is not *drawn* to anything so effectively as to *that which is according to the right logos*[4]" Elsewhere, he implies that the strongest thing in the world of humanity "is Nature, *drawing* [men] toward her will and purpose[5]" He nowhere mentions *phantasma*, but he mentions *phantasy* often, and once

---

[1] Jn vi 21. They (*ib* 19) "see Jesus nearing (ἐγγὺς.. γινόμενον)" just as sailors "see a coast receding" though the "coast" does not "recede" See *Joh Gr* **2346***a* (quoting Philo on Gen. iii 8) and **2716—7** etc

[2] 2 S xxii 17 εἵλκυσε, Ps xviii 16 προσέλαβε, where the Heb. (in both) is מָשָׁה, the word used (as Rashi remarks) about "drawing out" Moses from the water (Exod ii 10)

[3] Plutarch *Mor* 900 F quoted above, p 431, n. 4
[4] Epict i 2 4 ἕλκω   [5] Epict ii 20 15 ἕλκω

in a passage where he bids us go and look at Socrates and weigh his example against the temptations of pleasure· "By setting these [thoughts] against [those], you will conquer the *phantasy* and not be *drawn-and-dragged by it*[1]" Lastly, John, alone of the Evangelists, not only describes Jesus as the Logos but also represents Him as twice referring to the attractive "*drawing*" of the Father and of the Son: "No man can come unto me except the Father that sent me *draw* him," "I, if I be lifted up from the earth, will *draw* all men unto myself[2]."

With these facts before us, it does not seem improbable that John, in his version of the Walking on the Sea, was influenced by the Stoic doctrine about *phantasma* as being the result of "fear." He does not mention—perhaps he dislikes the very thought of mentioning—a *phantasma*, in connection with Jesus and His disciples, even though the context is to shew that there was no *phantasma*. He prefers to shew us that the fault rested with the disciples, not in anything outside them. The disciples, he says, "beheld" Jesus and yet "feared"! He leaves us to imagine what a *phantasma* they were creating for themselves when they recoiled from their own Saviour. Afterwards he shews us the Saviour drawing them toward Himself

Later on, in the Johannine narrative of Christ's last appearance to the disciples, though there is no mention either of a "phantasma" or of "drawing," there is a clear recognition of the fact that Jesus, at first, standing on the shore of Tiberias, appeared to be other than Himself, and that, by some means not mentioned, He caused them to "know" that He was "the Lord" Jesus, we are told, "stood on the beach, howbeit the disciples *knew not that it was Jesus*[3]" The day was breaking so that they could see Him. He spoke to them and they heard and did what He bade them. But not till after something more than mere words had passed, not till after the disciples

---

[1] Epict II 18 23, "drawn-and-dragged," ἑλκύω
[2] Jn vi 44, xii 32 ἑλκύω Jn never uses ἕλκω.
[3] Jn xxi 4 οὐ μέντοι ᾔδεισαν οἱ μαθηταὶ ὅτι Ἰησοῦς ἐστίν.

JESUS WALKING ON THE SEA

had done something in their Lord's service was it said "It is the Lord," and then by only one of the seven, "the disciple whom Jesus loved" Then, after a brief interval, the narrative passes into abrupt and irregular paradox: "Jesus saith unto them '[Come] hither, break your fast.' Not one of the disciples would dare to examine him [saying] 'Who art thou?'—[all of them] knowing that it was the Lord[1]"

The commentary of Chrysostom and the paraphrase of Nonnus given below indicate their feeling that the text needs explanation. But Nonnus does not really explain it at all. For he says that "*not even*" *Peter* ventured to say "Who art thou?" Why should Peter wish to ask it? The beloved disciple had told him it was the Lord, and he had swum to

---

[1] Jn xxi 12 λέγει αὐτοῖς [ὁ] Ἰησοῦς Δεῦτε ἀριστήσατε οὐδεὶς ἐτόλμα τῶν μαθητῶν ἐξετάσαι αὐτὸν Σὺ τίς εἶ, εἰδότες ὅτι ὁ κύριός ἐστιν. For ἐξετάζω here, comp Judith viii 13 "And now ye would fain *cross-examine* (or, *search out*) God and ye will know nothing to all eternity" The Arab Diatess has "for they knew that it was our Lord, *but he did not appear to them in his [own] form*," SS "Not one of his disciples was daring to ask him who it was because *they were believing* that it was he"

Chrysostom paraphrases thus "For they knew on the one hand (ᾔδεισαν μὲν γὰρ) that it was the Lord, and for this cause they did not ask (οὐκ ἠρώτων) Who art thou? But seeing His form *more* (or, *somewhat*) *altered* (τὴν δὲ μορφὴν ἀλλοιοτέραν ὁρῶντες) and full of awe-inspiring majesty (καὶ πολλῆς ἐκπλήξεως γέμουσαν) they were exceedingly amazed, and desired to ask something about it (ἐβούλοντό τι περὶ αὐτῆς ἐρωτᾶν) But the [feeling of] awe (τὸ δέος) and the fact of their knowing that it was no other but Himself, stopped their asking, and they merely went on eating the food that He framed for them with more authority" [than in the Feeding of the Five Thousand]

Nonnus paraphrases with more than his usual freedom After "the net was not rent"—deferring the invitation "Jesus saith, 'Come and break your fast'"—he proceeds, "Not then with daring did any man of that band of companions, watching with close-fronting eyes God present (ἀντωποῖς βλεφάροισι θεὸν παρεόντα δοκεύων) ask 'Who art thou?' And not [even] bold Simon asked [this], recognising near at hand (ἐγγύθι γινώσκων) that it was [the] Lord Jesus" Thus he applies "knowing" to Peter only, and this on the ground of his being "near at hand"

Him. Nonnus himself says that Peter was "near at hand" and "recognised" Jesus Chrysostom comes much nearer to an explanation The disciples (he says) knew that it was Jesus, but Jesus in an *"altered"* form, and they wished to ask Him, not really "Who art thou?" but *"something about it,"* i.e. about the alteration

What was this alteration? This above all things, it would seem, that there were no longer manifest the wounds in His hands which He had shewn them at His first appearance after death, and about which He had said to Thomas "See my hands" On the present occasion, when He gave them the bread and the fish, if the wounds had been still there, they could not have failed to see them In that case, they could have had no desire to ask Him anything But apparently the wounds were no longer there. Their absence would seem to be one of the points in which, as Chrysostom says, "His form was more altered and full of awe-inspiring majesty."

Then how did they "know" Him? If the "wounds" were not in the hands and if the "form" generally was altered, whence came their "knowing" that it was the Lord? The difficulty raised by this question seems to have induced the Syro-Sinaitic translator to substitute *"believed"* for *"knew"*, and the substitution, though erroneous, leads us to the right meaning. For *"knew"* means here *"knew in their heart of hearts"*—not by means of visible "proofs[1]," such as the wounds in the hands, but by invisible proof, by the sense of the presence of the Lord's Spirit. This kind of "knowledge" might be described by some as no knowledge at all but *mere "belief."* But others would say that this kind of "belief" is more than mere "knowledge" It may be illustrated by what Ignatius says to the Smyrnaeans, "I *know and believe* that also after the Resurrection He existed in the flesh; and when He came to Peter and his companions

---

[1] Comp Acts 1 3 τεκμηρίοις (Thucydidean "proofs") on which see *Introd* p 115

He said unto them, Take, handle me, and see that I am not a demon without body[1]." By this Ignatius apparently means "I know, yes, and I more than know, I have a belief [breathing in me from Christ and testifying to Christ][2]"

Perhaps we ought not to conclude our thoughts about the Johannine phrase "*knowing* that it was the Lord" without a word of reference to the Johannine "*seeing*" mentioned in the preceding manifestation, in which Jesus had said to Thomas "Because thou hast *seen* me thou hast believed; blessed are those that have not seen and have believed[3]" Thomas was now present again The things that he had "seen"—the wounds in the hands and side—were apparently now *not* to be "seen." Visibly, it was a different Jesus. Yet it differed in being, so to speak, more truly Jesus than before, a Jesus or Saviour independent of mere external or logical proofs, a Jesus not seen in the same way as in old days, but seen in the heart and received into the soul.

---

[1] Ign *Smyrn* § 3 Ἐγὼ γὰρ καὶ μετὰ τὴν ἀνάστασιν ἐν σαρκὶ αὐτὸν οἶδα καὶ πιστεύω ὄντα καὶ ὅτε πρὸς τοὺς περὶ Πέτρον ἦλθεν, ἔφη αὐτοῖς Λάβετε, ψηλαφήσατέ με, καὶ ἴδετε ὅτι οὐκ εἰμὶ δαιμόνιον ἀσώματον. On this, Lightf quotes Jerome as rendering οἶδα, "I know," by "vidi," "I have seen," and as inferring that Ignatius had seen our Lord in the flesh after the Resurrection It does not seem likely that Jerome would have made this mistake if he had not been led to it by feeling that there is bathos in saying "I know and believe that this is so"

[2] Comp Rom xiv 14 "I know and am persuaded *in the Lord Jesus* that nothing is unclean of itself (δι' ἑαυτοῦ)" A V. has "*by the Lord Jesus*" But "*in*" describes the region, so to speak, in which the persuasion dominates the apostle In one aspect, it is deep down, in a man's heart of hearts, the region of absolute conviction, in another, it is high up, in the heaven of heavens, the region of absolute reality The words "*in the Lord Jesus*" make all the difference

[3] Jn xx. 29 on which see *Joh Gr* **2499** *b*

JESUS WALKING ON THE SEA

§ 9. *"But their heart was hardened," in Mark*[1]

There is nothing, in the parallel Matthew, like this Marcan tradition about the "hardening of the heart," nor like the preceding words, "they were sore amazed in themselves." SS has "And they were wondering among themselves, for they had not perceived from the bread, because their heart was blind" The Arabic Diatessaron, besides resembling SS in meaning, transposes the words to a later position, "And when they came out of the ship to the land they marvelled greatly and were perplexed in themselves, and they had not understood from that bread, because their heart was gross[2]" If Mark is recording an early and genuine tradition, how can we explain Matthew's conduct in not only omitting it but also substituting a statement that they that were in the boat "worshipped" Jesus? The probable explanation is that the Marcan tradition —although early and genuine, for no one would invent so discouraging a recognition of the failure of Christ's miracle to produce conviction in the minds of His disciples—seemed to Matthew ambiguous and capable of an interpretation less harsh than the obvious one It might mean "They *had not* [*previously*] *understood*...but their heart *had* [*up till now*] *been hardened*[3]." This *implied* that the state of things was now

---

[1] Mk vi 51 b, 52 καὶ λίαν (Tisch λίαν ἐκ περισσοῦ) ἐν ἑαυτοῖς ἐξίσταντο, οὐ γὰρ συνῆκαν ἐπὶ τοῖς ἄρτοις, ἀλλ' ἦν αὐτῶν ἡ καρδία πεπωρωμένη Here b, Brix, SS and *Diatess* render συνῆκαν as pluperfect, so that the meaning might be "had not understood...but their heart had been hardened" Then the question would arise "But did they understand *now*? And was their heart hardened *still*?"

On "hardening" or "being made callous," see below, p 441, n 1

[2] Thus *Diatess* places Mt xiv 33 ("Thou art the Son of God"), Jn vi 21 b, and Mk vi 54 a, before Mk vi 51 b, 52 In combining "marvelled" and "were perplexed" it resembles several MSS, both Greek and Latin "Gross," comp Mt xiii 15, Is vi 10

[3] On the absence of a Heb pluperfect, and on consequent ambiguities, see *Joh Gr* **2480** and *Beginning* p 210, also above, p 182, n 2, quoting *Joh Gr* **2460**

JESUS WALKING ON THE SEA

changed. Now they understood and were amazed at Christ's divine power, recognising Him to be more than man. Matthew may be paraphrasing what he regards as Mark's *implied* meaning in a sentence expressing this recognition. This sentence he puts into the mouths of the men in the boat along with a statement of their worship, "They worshipped him saying, Truly thou art God's Son"

It is remarkable that even Origen—who occasionally quotes Mark while commenting on Matthew, and who comments fully on the parallel Matthew here—says not a word about this extraordinary divergence of Mark from Matthew. His silence illustrates the complaint of Victor of Antioch—which the student of the Gospels needs constantly to keep in mind—concerning the neglect from which Mark has suffered Writing certainly not earlier than the fifth century, Victor complains that he has failed to discover a single commentary on Mark, and says that he has consequently tried to collect scattered observations about his Gospel "that it may not seem the one book that has been overlooked in the whole of the New Testament[1]." Quoting this, Professor Swete observes "There was little in St Mark which was not to be found in St Matthew, or St Luke, or in both[2]"

This is true if "little" means "what takes up little space." But it would not be true if "little" meant "of little importance." And the Marcan tradition before us gives us a glimpse into other reasons for "overlooking" Mark—reasons quite distinct from the *prestige* attaching to Matthew's Gospel and the greater fulness of both Matthew and Luke There are many passages in Mark where we see him revealed to us as a writer inconveniently prone to insert brief, obscure, abrupt, and sometimes apparently unedifying traditions that require a great deal of explaining. This appears to be one of them.

---

[1] Cramer 1 263 ὅπως μὴ μόνον ἀπὸ τῶν τῆς καινῆς διαθήκης βιβλίων δόξῃ παρεωρᾶσθαι

[2] See Mark *ed.* Swete p. xxix

JESUS WALKING ON THE SEA

But these traditions are as a rule of great value, and the present one is no exception Victor himself apparently explains Mark's *"were hardened"* as meaning *"had been hardened."* He says that the miracle of the Walking on the Sea was intended "for the profit of the disciples." But in order to shew how they were "profited," he finds it convenient to pass into the text of the parallel Matthew: "Having been profited, therefore, they confessed Him to be God's Son, and He did not rebuke them when they said it. Nay, on the contrary[1], He confirmed what they said, by healing with greater authority, and not [merely] as before, those who came to Him."

Turning to the Fourth Gospel for a better explanation of the "hardening," we find that although it does not mention the *word* here, it implies the spiritual *thing*, and it mentions the *word* elsewhere—not indeed as applied to the disciples, but as applied to the Jews at large. Here, it spends nearly forty verses in shewing how completely the Jews misunderstood the doctrine of the living Bread[2], and how the disciples themselves were in danger of being "offended" by it This appears to be an explanatory amplification of Mark's obscure tradition "they understood not concerning the loaves" It shews that the misunderstanding was radical, implying a rejection of Christ's true personality and doctrine Elsewhere John uses the word *"harden"* in summing up the results of Christ's preaching to the Jews, which might popularly be called a failure "For this cause they could not believe, for that Isaiah said again, 'He hath blinded their eyes and he *hardened their heart...*'"; and at the close, he says that this divine "hardening" went hand in hand with human self-love and self-exaltation, "for they loved the glory of men more than the glory of God[3]."

---

[1] Cramer, on Mk p 332, has txt τοὐναντίον μὲν ὁ θεὸς, but in n, μὲν οὖν (ὁ θεὸς om) P Victor assumes that Mt xiv 33 "they that were in the boat" means "the disciples"

[2] Jn vi 26—65 [3] Jn xii 39—43

JESUS WALKING ON THE SEA

In a previous treatise it was pointed out that Mark and John are the only Evangelists that use this word, *pōroun*, *pōrōsis*, "hardening," or "callousness," applied (either as a noun or as a verb) to the "heart[1]" It is to be taken here as a key-word It was applied by Paul, in his Epistles to the Romans and the Corinthians, to describe the "callousness" of Israel (all except the remnant) in rejecting the Gospel which passed to the Gentiles[2] Mark's original appears to be regarded by John as having a similar meaning, overlooked by Matthew (and not contemplated by Luke who omits the narrative) If so, John's intervention means, in effect, "Note how much is implied in this Marcan word '*hardening*.' It was from this moment that Jesus began to manifest His sense that 'a *hardening* in part had befallen Israel,' so that they could not receive the doctrine of the living Bread"

If we regard "the loaves" as a type of the Eucharist, and the Walking on the Sea as a type of the return of Jesus to the disciples after His resurrection, then we may say that the conclusion of Mark's narrative, with a slight alteration, might have a post-resurrectional meaning: "And Jesus went up [from Sheol] into the midst of the disciples, and the tempest of their souls abated, and they were amazed with a great amazement, for they had not believed that this would come to pass, because they had not understood concerning the bread, that the Lord was to die and give His body to be the food of the Church, but their heart was still hardened when He went up to them on the third day, being raised from the dead[3]."

---

[1] See *Proclam* pp 362—4 Jn uses only the verb, *pōroun*

[2] Rom xi 7—25 "The rest of Israel *were made callous*...a *callousness* in part hath befallen Israel," 2 Cor iii 14—15 "their minds *were made callous* . a veil lieth upon their heart"

[3] Something of the nature of unbelief, but not amounting to "hardness of heart," is tacitly hinted at in Jn xx 8—9 "Then entered in therefore the other disciple also and he saw and believed, for *as yet they knew not the scripture, that he must rise from the dead*"

CHAPTER X

THE NEW LAW OF PURIFICATION
[Mark vi. 53—vii. 23]

§ 1. *Jesus is followed at first by the multitudes*

FROM this point Jesus begins a course of journeying in northern Palestine about which Mark is diffuse while Luke is silent and John rarely intervenes. Space will not allow of the full discussion of these journeys (summarised above) which begin here at Gennesaret and end at Caesarea Philippi Two details, in a short passage printed below, are discussed as specimens of the way in which Matthew deals with Mark[1].

---

[1] Mk vi 53—6 (R V)

(53) And when they had crossed over, they came to the land unto Gennesaret, (or, and when they had crossed over to the land, they came unto Gennesaret) and moored to the shore

(54) And when they were come out of the boat, straightway [the people] knew (ἐπιγνόντες) him,

(55) And ran round about that whole region, and began to carry about on their beds those that were sick, where they heard he was

(56) And wheresoever he entered, into villages, or into cities, or into the country, they laid the sick in the market-places, and besought him that they might touch if it were but the border of his garment and as many as touched him (or, it) were made whole (ἐσώζοντο)

Mt xiv 34—6 (R V)

(34) And when they had crossed over, they came to the land, unto Gennesaret

(35) And when the men of that place knew (ἐπιγνόντες) him, they sent into all that region round about, and brought unto him all that were sick,

(36) And they besought him that they might only touch the border of his garment and as many as touched were made whole (διεσώθησαν)

THE NEW LAW OF PURIFICATION

But the greater part is left undiscussed and is printed merely that the reader may not feel that there is concealed from him a large field where the rule of Johannine Intervention does not hold good.

Matthew omits the Marcan clause "and moored to the shore." Here it seems superfluous, but it would not be so if it were a poetic tradition based on the Psalmist's description of the vessel saved from the storm, "And so he bringeth them unto the haven of their desire[1]"

Again, Mark says indefinitely, "when they were come out of the boat (lit) *they* [i e. people] knew him" But Matthew supplies a definite subject, "*the men of that place*, knowing him, sent ..." This makes all the difference in what follows, for whereas Mark, speaking of people in general, says that they ran about that whole region and began to carry the sick to Jesus "wherever they [from time to time] heard (imperf.) he was," implying that Jesus was moving from place to place, Matthew omits all this and implies that the sick were brought to Jesus who was Himself stationary, "They sent into all that region round about and brought unto him all that were sick." Possibly Matthew was impelled to condensation by the difficulty of supposing the existence of "market-places" that were "in hamlets" (literally "in fields" or "in farms") which has induced many MSS and Versions to alter the text[2] All this testifies

---

[1] Ps cvii 30 The Heb מחוז (R V "*haven*") occurs only here. Gesen 562 *b* renders it "*city*," and notes that the Targum word, which is similar, means "*market-place, province*, Syr *small town*" This deserves attention in view of Mk vi 56 "*villages, cities.. market-places*," all of which Matthew omits The parall Jn vi 21 has "*the land* whither they were going" On the return from the Feeding of the Four Thousand the parall Mk viii 10, Mt xv 39 have severally "*Dalmanutha*" and "*Magadan*," on which see *Corrections* **498** *g, h*. To the instances of corruption there given add 1 Chr vii 29 "*Megiddo*," conflated as "*Balad. .Mageddi*"

On Mk vi 53 προσωρμίσθησαν, omitted by many good authorities, see above, p 243, n 5

[2] In Mk vi 56 many Lat codd, with D and SS, substitute

THE NEW LAW OF PURIFICATION

to the existence of "market-place" as the original word, to which other synonyms were added afterwards.

On this Victor of Antioch has a curious comment, implying that the miracle of the Walking on the Sea had increased men's faith in Jesus. He implies that "a long time" had elapsed since Jesus had set foot in that region, but that "the interval had not only not dissolved their faith but had even made it greater and kept it at its height[1]"

The Fourth Evangelist represents the multitude as seeking Jesus immediately after the miracle, but with no worthy object. "Ye seek me, not because ye saw signs, but because ye ate of the loaves and were filled[2]" That is to say, they did not understand the inner meaning of that which Jesus had said and done; and self-will and worldliness reigned in their hearts leaving no room for the living Bread[3] This rejection of Jesus as their spiritual Life and Saviour is compatible with their acceptance of Him as a marvellously successful Healer and with their desire to compel Him to become their king and to lead them against Herod Antipas to avenge the death of John the Baptist.

"*streets*" for "*market-places*," *a* has "in the *market-place* (*foro*) and in *streets*"

[1] Cramer *ad loc* p 333, Διὰ πολλοῦ χρόνου ἐπέβη. .ἀλλ' ὅμως ὁ χρόνος οὐ μόνον οὐκ ἐξέλυσε τὴν πίστιν ἀλλὰ καὶ μείζονα εἰργάσατο καὶ ἀκμάζουσαν διετήρησεν

[2] Jn vi 26

[3] Comp Jn viii 37 "My word hath *no free course* (or, *no room*) (οὐ χωρεῖ) in you"

THE NEW LAW OF PURIFICATION

§ 2 *Jesus is attacked by the Pharisees concerning the washing of hands*[1]

The diffuse detail in which Mark describes the various purifications practised by the Pharisees helps us to understand

---

[1] Mk vii 1—23 (R V)

(1) And there are gathered together unto him the Pharisees, and certain of the scribes, which had come from Jerusalem,

(2) And had seen that some of his disciples ate their bread with defiled (*or*, common), that is, unwashen, hands

(3) For the Pharisees, and all the Jews, except they wash their hands diligently (*or*, up to the elbow, *Gr* with the fist), eat not, holding the tradition of the elders

(4) And [when they come] from the marketplace, except they wash themselves (*lit* baptize themselves, *some anc auth read* sprinkle themselves), they eat not   and many other things there be, which they have received to hold, washings (*lit* baptizings) of cups, and pots, and brasen vessels (*many anc. auth add* and couches)

(5) And the Pharisees and the scribes ask him, Why walk not thy disciples according to the tradition of the elders, but eat their bread with defiled (*or*, common) hands?

(6) And he said unto them, Well did Isaiah prophesy of you hypocrites, as it is written, This people honoureth me with their lips, but their heart is far from me

(7) But in vain do they worship me, teaching [as their] doctrines the precepts of men

(8) Ye leave the commandment of God, and hold fast the tradition of men

(9) And he said unto them, Full well do ye reject the com-

Mt xv 1—20 (R V)

(1) Then there come to Jesus from Jerusalem Pharisees and scribes, saying,

(2) Why do thy disciples transgress the tradition of the elders? For they wash not their hands when they eat bread

(7) Ye hypocrites, well did Isaiah prophesy of you, saying,

(8) This people honoureth me with their lips, but their heart is far from me

(9) But in vain do they worship me, teaching [as their] doctrines the precepts of men

(3) And he answered and said unto them, Why do ye also transgress the commandment of God because of your tradition?

(4) For God said, Honour thy father and thy mother   and, He

445 (Mark vii 1—23)

THE NEW LAW OF PURIFICATION

that during the life of Christ a section of the Pharisees attached to some of these lustrations a sanctity almost like that of daily

Mk vii. 1—23 (R.V.) *contd.*
mandment of God, that ye may keep your tradition
(10) For Moses said, Honour thy father and thy mother, and, He that speaketh evil of father or mother, let him die the death (*or*, surely die)
(11) But ye say, If a man shall say to his father or his mother, That wherewith thou mightest have been profited by me is Corban, that is to say, Given [to God],
(12) Ye no longer suffer him to do aught for his father or his mother,
(13) Making void the word of God by your tradition, which ye have delivered and many such like things ye do
(14) And he called to him the multitude again, and said unto them, Hear me all of you, and understand
(15) There is nothing from without the man, that going into him can defile him but the things which proceed out of the man are those that defile the man
[(16) *Many anc auth insert* If any man hath ears to hear, let him hear]
(17) And when he was entered into the house from the multitude, his disciples asked of him the parable

Mt. xv. 1—20 (R.V) *contd.*
that speaketh evil of father or mother, let him die the death (*or*, surely die)
(5) But ye say, Whosoever shall say to his father or his mother, That wherewith thou mightest have been profited by me is given [to God],
(6) He shall not honour his father (*some anc auth add* or his mother) And ye have made void the word (*some anc auth* law) of God because of your tradition

(10) And he called to him the multitude, and said unto them, Hear, and understand
(11) Not that which entereth into the mouth defileth the man, but that which proceedeth out of the mouth, this defileth the man

(12) Then came the disciples, and said unto him, Knowest thou that the Pharisees were offended (*lit* caused to stumble), when they heard this saying?
(13) But he answered and said, Every plant (*lit* planting) which my heavenly Father planted not, shall be rooted up
(14) Let them alone they are blind guides And if the blind guide the blind, both shall fall into a pit
(15) And Peter answered and said unto him, Declare unto us the parable.

THE NEW LAW OF PURIFICATION

baptism[1] In particular, the importance attached early in the first century to the washing of hands before a meal may be inferred from a Talmudic tradition that it was instituted as a rite by the two famous Rabbis—often opposed to one another—Hillel and Shammai[2]. R Eleazar Ben Hazar is said to have been excommunicated because he "undervalued the purification of hands," and when he was dead, by the command of the Sanhedrin, a great stone was laid on his bier[3].

Examining Mark's text we find several terms that may be almost called technical. (1) Some of the disciples are said to

Mk vii. 1—23 (R.V.) contd.	Mt. xv. 1—20 (R.V.) contd.
(18) And he saith unto them, Are ye so without understanding also? Perceive ye not, that whatsoever from without goeth into the man, [it] cannot defile him, (19) Because it goeth not into his heart, but into his belly, and goeth out into the draught? [This he said], making all meats clean (20) And he said, That which proceedeth out of the man, that defileth the man. (21) For from within, out of the heart of men, evil thoughts proceed, fornications, (22) Thefts, murders, adulteries, covetings, wickednesses, deceit, lasciviousness, an evil eye, railing, pride, foolishness (23) All these evil things proceed from within, and defile the man	(16) And he said, Are ye also even yet without understanding? (17) Perceive ye not, that whatsoever goeth into the mouth passeth into the belly, and is cast out into the draught? (18) But the things which proceed out of the mouth come forth out of the heart, and they defile the man (19) For out of the mouth come forth evil thoughts, murders, adulteries, fornications, thefts, false witness, railings (20) These are the things which defile the man but to eat with unwashen hands defileth not the man

[1] On the *Hemerobaptists*, see Schurer II. ii 210, Levy iv. 538 a, and Lightf *Coloss* p 402.

[2] See *Hor Heb* on Mt. xv. 2 quoting *J Sabb* fol 3 4. Others said that Hillel and Shammai merely revived and emphasized the ancient rite

[3] *B. Berach* 19 a mentioning נטילת, and see Levy iv. 93 b, quoting the same tradition from *Ediy* 5, 6 but with טהרת Wetstein on Mt. xv 2 quotes from *Mischle* ix 2 a story how R Akiba in prison refused to refrain from the washing of hands even though he might have died of thirst

THE NEW LAW OF PURIFICATION

eat their bread "with *common hands*, that is, unwashed[1]." (2) It is said that the Pharisees do not eat unless they wash their hands *with the fist*, or *diligently*, where R.V marg gives as an alternative "*up to the elbow*[2]" (3) It is said that the Pharisees from the market-place will not eat "unless they *sprinkle themselves* (so W.H.)," but with a various reading "*baptize themselves*[3]." To discuss this passage adequately would require a treatise We must select what is of most importance, namely, the adjective "*common*," subsequently taken up as a verb (in Matthew as well as Mark) by Jesus Himself declaring that "there is nothing from without the man that going into him can *make him common*[4]."

The Hebrew word "common" is applied in the Bible to food where Ahimelech says to David "There is no *common* bread under mine hand, but there is *holy* bread[5]." It is natural to connect with this the Marcan use of "*common*," as if it meant simply "unconsecrated." But the Greek *koinos* has no such

---

[1] Mk vii 2 κοιναῖς χερσίν, τοῦτ' ἔστιν ἀνίπτοις.
[2] Mk vii 3 ἐὰν μὴ πυγμῇ νίψωνται τὰς χεῖρας, Tisch πυκνὰ for πυγμῇ
[3] Mk vii 4 ἐὰν μὴ ῥαντίσωνται, but W H marg and Tisch txt have βαπτίσωνται
[4] Mk vii 15, Mt xv 11, rep Mk vii 20, 23, Mt xv 18, 20
[5] 1 S xxi 4, *lit* "bread of commonness" The same word occurs in Lev x 10 "that ye may put a difference between the *holy* and the (R V) *common* (A V *unholy*)" R V also has "common," where A V has "profane," in Ezek xxii 26, xliv 23 (comp Ezek xlii 20) The Talmudic treatise *Chullin* meant a "*common*, or *unconsecrated*, food" Comp *Chag* ii 5 (Mishna) "For [the partaking of] *chullin* .. the hands must be washed (*lit* poured upon), for [the partaking of] *holy things* the hands must be immersed" In this sense, "*common*," חל is derived (Gesen 320) from חלל "pollute, defile, profane " It does not however mean "polluted" or "desecrated" but simply "unconsecrated"

Hor Heb on Mt xv 2 speaks of a "definition of a Pharisee" in the words "The Pharisees eat their *common food* (*chullin*) in cleanness (טהרה)," apparently meaning that they "immerse" where less strict Jews would simply "wash "

448 (Mark vii. 1—23)

THE NEW LAW OF PURIFICATION

meaning *Koinos* occurs but thrice in LXX as representing a Hebrew word, and then only as a paraphrase meaning community of property[1]. It may mean "popular"—and possibly "vulgar"—but it never conveys, in non-hebraic Greek, a notion of defilement.

We must therefore seek elsewhere some explanation of the Marcan *koinos* The most probable is one springing from a use of the word, such as we find in Josephus, applied to the Gentile way of life regarded as the "common" life of the Roman Empire, somewhat as the *koiné dialectos*, or vernacular Greek, was its "common" language. Jews would probably describe apostates from Judaism as turning to "the life of dogs" or "the life of defilement"; but Josephus speaks of them as "revolting from their national customs and preferring *the common life*[2]" Elsewhere Josephus describes some as going over from Judaism to the Samaritans because they were accused of "*common eating* (or, *community of eating*) or sabbath-breaking, or any other such fault[3]" This appears to be a polite way of expressing what the Fourth Book of Maccabees repeatedly calls "foul (*or*, polluted) eating[4]."

In the Marcan passage under consideration, Mark apparently intends to throw on the Pharisees the responsibility of using the word "common" without explanation ("eat their bread with *common hands*") whereas he himself has previously explained the sense in which he supposes Jews to have used

---

[1] See Prov 1 14 LXX "a *common* purse, *one* pouch," a conflation for Heb "*one* purse," xxi 9 οἴκῳ κοινῷ, Heb "domo *societatis*" (see R V marg) rep xxv. 24 οἰκίᾳ κοινῇ

[2] Joseph *Ant* xiii 1. 1 τῶν Ἰουδαίων τοὺς ἀποστάντας τῆς πατρίου συνηθείας καὶ τὸν κοινὸν βίον προῃρημένους.

[3] Joseph *Ant* xi 8 7 εἰ δέ τις αἰτίαν ἔσχεν παρὰ τοῖς Ἱεροσολυμίταις κοινοφαγίας, ἢ τῆς ἐν σαββάτοις παρανομίας, ἤ τινος ἄλλου τοιούτου ἁμαρτήματος

[4] 4 Macc vii 6 "Thou didst not defile (ἐκοινώνησας, v r ἐκοίνωσας) with *polluted-eating* (μιαροφαγίᾳ)..." (of a martyr) Μιαροφαγία recurs in 4 Macc v 27, vi 19, xi 25 Μιαροφαγεῖν also occurs in 4 Macc. v 3, 19 etc. (about ten times)

THE NEW LAW OF PURIFICATION

it ("with *common, that is, unwashen,* hands"). But no instance is alleged where "*common*" is thus applied[1]. The versions mostly omit or paraphrase it[2]. No doubt Paul says that "nothing is *common* of itself"—meaning "defiled"—except through the mind of him who thinks it to be "common[3]." But he applies it to that which is eaten, not to the hand of the eater. So also does Peter at first, though afterwards he says that he has learned to apply to human beings what God taught him about food[4]. Moreover, when Peter says "I have never eaten anything *common* or unclean," he clearly uses "common" to mean, not "unconsecrated," but what might be called "desecrated," in the sense of being forbidden by the Levitical Law.

It is not surprising that Luke has put all these details aside in the one brief reference that he makes to the Pharisaean habit of "immersing." He tells us that, when Jesus was invited by a Pharisee to breakfast, the host "marvelled that he (lit) *was not immersed* before the breakfast[5]." Probably "immersed" refers, not to the whole body but to the hands, which a strict Pharisee might "immerse" before a meal instead of merely "washing," *i.e.* having water poured over them[6]. But even Luke's phrase might give rise to misunderstanding, as though the Pharisee expected Jesus to have immersed His

---

[1] Wetstein, on Mt xv 11 κοινοῖ, quotes Joseph. *Ant* xi 8 7 κοινοφαγίας and says "non autem ista appellatio ex stylo Hellenistico, sed ex re ipsa ortum videtur habuisse" No commentator, as far as I know, gives an instance of "common" applied to "hands" by Jews or Greeks

[2] In Mk vii 2 the Syr. versions omit "common," *a* has "immundis," *b* om.; Delitzsch has "with uncleanness of hands"

[3] Rom. xiv. 14.

[4] Acts x 14, 28. Delitzsch renders κοινός in x 14 פִּגּוּל, but in x 28 חוּל

[5] Lk xi 38 "was immersed," ἐβαπτίσθη, SS "*baptized himself*," Lat. codd "*baptizatus est* (or *esset*)," *e* "*baptizavit*," Tertull. ad loc. "*tinctus esset*"

[6] See the distinction in the Mishna quoted above, p 448, n. 5

THE NEW LAW OF PURIFICATION

whole body. In these circumstances we might fairly expect John to intervene in order to teach the spiritual doctrine of washing, and it will be maintained that he does so, but this will be more conveniently discussed after considering the Mark-Matthew account of the reply of Jesus to the Pharisees, and also a Matthew-Luke account of a similar reply.

§ 3. *The reply of Jesus to the Pharisees, in Mark and Matthew*

The reply of Jesus goes far beyond the doctrine of impure hands, and passes into a doctrine of impure food. This is not unnatural, since the charge of the Pharisees mentioned "hands," not in a general way, but in connection with the act of touching food. Jesus first attacks the Pharisees for laying so much stress on the washing of hands, an act not enjoined by the Law, and so little stress on the duty of children to parents, a duty enjoined by the Law but relaxed by some Pharisees if a child could put in a plea of Corban[1]. In this connection there occurs the only mention of "hypocrites" in Mark's Gospel. "But he said

---

[1] This charge, as against all Pharisees, is not proved by *Horae Hebraicae*, Wetstein, or Schottgen, and it is contrary to the spirit of the Talmud. *Nedarim* ix 1 shews that "the sages" agreed with R Eliezer, against R Zadok, that a vow injurious to parents might be retracted. It has been suggested that the real attack of Jesus must have been directed against the Priests (who often derived profit from rash vows) The same suggestion would apply to Mt. xxiii 16 "whosoever shall swear by the gold of the Temple"—a passage not illustrated from the Talmud by *Horae Hebraicae*, which says "The gold here meant is that which was offered up in the *Corban*" While the Temple was standing, there may have been a section of Pharisees, especially in Jerusalem, who supported the Priests, as R Zadok did, in such views as Jesus condemned. Luke, writing after the fall of the Temple, would refrain from recording discussions about things that were becoming obsolete.

R Eliezer (*Aboth* ii 10—11) was a strong conservative, adhering to tradition, and this confirms the view that the charge brought by Jesus did not include the Pharisees as a whole

THE NEW LAW OF PURIFICATION

unto them, Well did Isaiah prophesy of you *the [great] hypocrites* ...This people honoureth me with their lips, but their heart is far from me. But in vain do they worship me, teaching [as divine] teachings commandments of men[1]."

This is intelligible. But it is added "And having called the multitude to him again, he said unto them, Hear me all of you and understand There is nothing from without the man that going into him can *defile* him (lit. *make him common*); but the things that proceed out of the man are those that *defile* (lit. *make common*) the man[2]" These words may have referred, at the moment, not to food absolutely forbidden by the Law, e g. the flesh of swine, but to food condemned as defiling by Jewish tradition owing to defects in the preparation of it, or in the partaking of it; and this view is confirmed by the context, which does not set aside the Law of Moses but only the traditions of the Elders. Thus we can understand that Jesus might have Himself condemned, at this time, any disciple venturing to eat swine's flesh. Not that it was defiling in itself, but it was forbidden by the Law, and to eat it was also an offence to the national feeling, being sometimes a sign of apostasy Many Jews had died as martyrs rather than eat it under constraint[3]. Thus, too, we can understand that there was need of a special vision for Peter, before he could believe

---

[1] Mk vii 6—7 where περὶ ὑμῶν τῶν ὑποκριτῶν is parall to Mt xv 7 ὑποκριταί ..περὶ ὑμῶν See *Proclam* p 368 (on Christ's application of the term *chânêph* to the Pharisees) quoting Bacon's *Essays* xvi 60 "*The great atheists* indeed are *hypocrites*" "[As] teachings" (*Son* 3347 (vi)) appears better interpreted "[as] teachings [of the Law, or of God]" than (R V) "[as their] doctrines" But the duplication might possibly imply mere emphasis, "teaching [as solemn] teachings."

[2] Mk vii 14 καὶ προσκαλεσάμενος πάλιν τὸν ὄχλον Mt xv 10 omits πάλιν. There is no previously mentioned "calling" of the multitude in Mark to which "again" could refer

[3] On the attempts to compel Jews to sacrifice, or eat, the flesh of swine see 1 Macc 1 47, 2 Macc vi 18, vii 1, 4 Macc v 2 etc.

THE NEW LAW OF PURIFICATION

that even "the creeping things of the earth" might be killed for food by a disciple of Christ[1].

Nevertheless Mark (or the writer followed by Mark) indicates his own belief that, in effect, neither swine's flesh nor any other food could, *in itself*, defile a man, because such meat (Jesus said) "*goeth not into his heart but into his belly*[2]." It would be the self-will of the eater, or perhaps his fear of torture and love of life, that would "defile the man" by "going into his heart." Accordingly, to the statement of what Jesus said, Mark adds, from himself, the words "[This he said] making all meats clean[3]." That is to say, this universal and permanent rule ("all food is pure") was to be reasonably inferred from, or was involved in, Christ's utterance.

Stated as it is, without limitation, this utterance might well offend any pious follower of Jesus who had hitherto believed that He had not come "to destroy the Law or the Prophets but to fulfil[4]." A comment recorded by Victor of Antioch recognises the epoch-making character of the utterance: "From this point," it says, "begins the New Law, the [Law] according to the Spirit, the [Law] that no longer seeks [its object] in bodily purifications nor in distinction of foods but in the virtue of the Spirit[5]." The commentator admits that the Law and the Gospel now diverged: "For the [teaching] of the Law looked rather to the outer man, but the [teaching] of the Lord to the inner, since indeed the season was now present when the Cross was destined to put an end to the [dispensation of]

---

[1] Acts x 12 "all manner of fourfooted beasts and creeping things of the earth"

[2] Mk vii 19

[3] Καθαρίζων πάντα τὰ βρώματα, not in the parall. Mt xv. 17.

[4] Mt v 17

[5] Cramer p 335, where read ζητῶν ἐν σωματικαῖς [for -οῖς] καθάρσεσι Victor (*ib* p 263) records the scattered comments of others, not being able to find any ancient continuous commentary on Mark. This commentator is therefore earlier (and from internal evidence probably very much earlier) than Victor himself

THE NEW LAW OF PURIFICATION

bodily things " This frankly admits, not only the novelty of Christ's doctrine, but also its anticipatory nature. It was not to be fulfilled till "the Cross" came to fulfil it[1].

[1] See *Son* 3493 *j*, "Jesus protests that 'nothing that [*thus*] goeth into the mouth' defileth the man," where "*thus*" means "in the manner and circumstances assumed by the rabbinical traditions " It is added "The implied '*thus*'...might easily be forgotten when the sentence was taken out of its context Mark appears to have forgotten it "

The fact that the saying is called "a parable" by the disciples and Peter indicates that, even at the time, they did not believe it was to be taken in a literal sense For this Jerome blames Peter: "Quod aperte dictum fuerat, et patebat auditui, Apostolus Petrus per parabolam dictum putat, et in re manifesta mysticam quaerit intelligentiam Corripiturque a Domino . " Jerome goes on to draw a moral from this practice of "seeking a mystical meaning in a plain matter " He says that it betokens "a faulty hearer" when a man desires "either to understand dark sayings as if they were clear or clear as if they were dark "

Perhaps Jerome is referring to Origen, who says that here, as in the Sermon on the Mount, Jesus again spoke to the multitude in parables (*Comm Matth* xi 13 *ad fin*) "But here [also] He [virtually] stretches out His hand to the multitude—calling it to Him and detaching [it] from the verbal acceptation of the questionings that relate to the Law—when He in the first place began to say to them 'Hear ye and understand' (though they did not yet understand what they heard) and in the next place, *as* [*if speaking*] *in parables*, began to say to them, 'Not that which entereth into the mouth ...'" Origen has previously said (*Comm. Matth* xi 12, Lomm iii 97) that we learn from the Gospels that the "obvious (πρόχειρος)" meaning of the Levitical precepts is not to be regarded as "the scope appointed for the Scripture (τὸν σκοπὸν εἶναι τῇ γραφῇ) "

These two ancient interpretations are in direct opposition. According to Origen all the Levitical precepts were of the nature of parables, and Jesus interpreted them in His parable. According to Jerome, Leviticus enjoined plain precepts and Jesus plainly revoked them, so that there was no parable at all Neither interpretation appears to represent the exact truth

Chrysostom (on Matthew) sides with Jerome, but is even less respectful to Peter, who, he says, was afraid to say to Jesus "Why hast thou spoken against the Law (διατί παράνομον εἶπας,) ?" Peter pleaded "obscurity," but "there was no obscurity " He concludes his comment by quoting Mark· "But Mark says that He uttered

(Mark vii 1—23)

THE NEW LAW OF PURIFICATION

§ 4 *The doctrine of Jesus on "purifying," in Matthew and Luke*[1]

The doctrine of Jesus, as given by Luke, on purifying, or cleansing[2]—in connection with the metaphor of a vessel—differs from the form of it given by Matthew. Luke mentions the literal giving of "alms," Matthew adheres to metaphor,

these words 'purifying [all] foods.' However, He did not make this clear (οὐ μὴν ἐνέφηνεν), nor did He say '*But to eat such foods defileth not the man* (τὸ δὲ βρώματα τοιάδε φαγεῖν οὐ κοινοῖ τὸν ἄνθρωπον).' For they could not yet [read οὔπω for οὔτε] endure to hear that clearly [stated] [*or*, to hear Him clearly speaking thus] (σαφῶς οὕτως αὐτοῦ ἀκοῦσαι). Wherefore also He added [in Matthew], 'But to eat with unwashen hands doth not defile the man.'" This comment, though (doubtless) wrong in attributing reticence to Jesus, is useful because it shews us how easy it would have been to say "A man may eat anything," if that had been the meaning, and because it leads consequently to the inference "That was *not* the meaning."

[1] Mt xxiii 25—6 (R V.)

(25) Woe unto you, scribes and Pharisees, hypocrites! for ye cleanse the outside (τὸ ἔξωθεν) of the cup and of the platter, but within (ἔσωθεν) they are full from extortion and excess
(26) Thou blind Pharisee, cleanse first the inside (τὸ ἐντὸς) of the cup and of the platter, that the outside (τὸ ἐκτὸς) thereof may become clean also.

Lk xi 39—41 (R V.)

(39) Now do ye Pharisees cleanse the outside (τὸ ἔξωθεν) of the cup and of the platter; but your inward part (τὸ ἔσωθεν ὑμῶν) is full of extortion and wickedness
(40) Ye foolish ones, did not he that made the outside (τὸ ἔξωθεν) make the inside (τὸ ἔσωθεν) also?
(41) Howbeit give for alms those things which are within (*or*, which ye can) (τὰ ἐνόντα), and behold, all things are clean unto you.

A V. has, in Mt xxiii 26, "Cleanse first that [which is] within the cup and platter," and in Lk xi 40—1 "Did not he that made that which is without make that which is within also? But rather give alms of such things as ye have (*marg.* as you are able), and, behold, all things are clean unto you."

[2] R.V. follows A.V. in rendering καθαρός by "clean" in this tradition, but there is an advantage in rendering it by "pure," so as to connect it with passages where R.V. and A.V. render it by "pure," *e.g.* Mt. v. 8 "blessed are the pure in heart," Tit. i. 15 "to the pure all things are pure" etc.

THE NEW LAW OF PURIFICATION

and makes no mention of alms. The Greek text in Matthew is ambiguous since it might denote (1) "the inside [surface], or interior, of a vessel," (2) "the contents of a vessel." Luke seems to oscillate between the two meanings. He also intermixes metaphor ("cup and platter") with non-metaphor ("you") Hence he writes first "the outside [surface] of the cup and of the platter...but the inside [surface] *of you.*" Then, after repeating an antithesis between "the outside" and "the inside," he proceeds to paraphrase freely And now he takes "the inside" as meaning *"that which is inside,"* i e. *"the contents."* And, in the same sentence, as if answering the question "How are the *'contents'* to be 'cleansed'?" he replies "By giving the contents as alms" (*"alms"* being, in Jewish thought, often interchangeable with *"righteousness"*). This is equivalent to "Give *the contents* as *alms.*" The next step is to find a corresponding antithetical meaning for *"the outside."* And this forces him, again mixing metaphor, to depart still further from Matthew. For the antithesis to "that which is *within the human vessel"* is "that which is *outside the human vessel,"* namely, *the whole external world of outward action* ("all things") as opposed to the internal source of action[1] So he concludes "and behold *all things* are pure to you" The thought is clear enough ("to the pure all things are pure[2]"). But it departs from Matthew in form. And Matthew seems closer to the original[3].

---

[1] If "the vessel" is taken literally, then "that which is inside" is the food, part of which is given to the poor, and "all things" would seem to mean all kinds of food But the confusion of the literal and the metaphorical makes it impossible to interpret each detail with confidence.

[2] Tit 1 15

[3] It is possible that Luke, on occasions where Matthew's Greek presented difficulties, may have corrected it by recourse to other traditions based on a Semitic original. In this particular original the same word might mean "give alms" and "cleanse" But Luke may have *started from* the Greek text (see Dalman's *Words* p 63)

THE NEW LAW OF PURIFICATION

We may be quite sure that Jesus did not enjoin, as a means of self-purification, the literal giving of the contents of a vessel in the form of alms *irrespective of motive*. His doctrine would be based on that of the Psalm concerning cleansing, which says "Thou desirest truth *in the inward parts*...purge me with hyssop...create in me *a pure heart*, O God[1]." And the kind of "alms" that He desired—altogether differing from the alms given by Pharisaean formalists—is implied by Isaiah "If thou *draw out thy soul* to the hungry." This inculcates, not self-affliction for self-affliction's sake (or for the sake of propitiating God for one's sins), but such affliction as must be felt by the kind-hearted, who will not shrink from sympathizing with sorrow while attempting to relieve it[2].

That this was the meaning of Luke's word—"contents" or "that which is inside"—is indicated by the rendering of SS "*That which is inside of you* give [as] alms, and lo, everything is pure unto you." This means "Give from your soul when you give alms." Such "alms" cannot be confused with formal almsgiving. But Luke has been misinterpreted by many, who have rendered "that which is inside" as if it were "*that which is in your power*" or "*as much as you can afford*[3]." Moreover the question would arise for many early readers of Matthew and Luke "How am I to 'cleanse the inside'? Does not the Psalmist call upon God to cleanse him?" Others, if they were familiar with the language of the Stoics, would know that the precept "*Cleanse the vessel*[4]" was

---

[1] Ps li. 6—10

[2] *Proclam* pp 312—3, quoting and commenting on Is lviii 10.

[3] The Latin codd vary, *a* and Corb render τὰ ἐνόντα "quod superest," *b* "quae sunt," *e* om, Brix "ex his quae *habetis*" (comp. Tertull. *Adv Marc* iv 27) etc For ἐνεῖναι particip = "that which is within," see 2 Clem Rom xix 2 τὴν ἀπιστίαν τὴν ἐνοῦσαν ἐν τοῖς στήθεσιν ἡμῶν, Just Mart 2 *Apol* xiii 5 διὰ τῆς ἐνούσης ἐμφύτου τοῦ λόγου σπορᾶς These are the only participial instances in Goodspeed.

[4] See Epictet. *Fragm* x (Schw 179) Schenkl p 410 σκέψαι εἰ κεκάθαρται τὸ ἀγγεῖον (comp iv 13 15 δεῖξόν σου τὸ ἀγγεῖον) where he

THE NEW LAW OF PURIFICATION

a common one, meaning, more especially, "Cast away self-conceit from your soul if you want to take knowledge into it." But still they would say "That is only the first step, what must the second be? To cast out self-conceit does not bring knowledge."

These differences between Matthew and Luke, and their metaphorical or verbal difficulties, somewhat obscure the plain doctrine taught in Mark, that what is spiritually impure comes out of a man—not into a man. Also there are warnings in the Pauline Epistles that, in some circumstances, knowledge does not suffice to purify. "Knowledge puffeth up," we are told, "but love buildeth up"; and this is connected with discussions as to what food is to be eaten or not to be eaten[1]. Thus, from several quarters, there would come appeals to the Fourth Evangelist to help believers to realise what was Christ's fundamental distinction between things "pure" and "impure" and what were the means by which He instructed His disciples to attain "purity."

§ 5. *Johannine Intervention*

We have seen that Christ's doctrine of purifying the vessel, as set forth in Matthew and Luke, was not only liable to misunderstanding but also, in very early times, actually misunderstood, and that the somewhat similar doctrine in Mark and

---

says that if one casts instruction into self-conceit (οἴησιν) all turns sour See iii 14 8, "Two things are to be cast out from men, self-conceit (οἴησις) and faithlessness (ἀπιστία)"

On ἀγγεῖον meaning the body, as the vessel of the soul, see Steph *Thes* i 233—4 But Plato *Gorgias* pp 493—4 (comp Lucret vi 17, and Horace *Epist* i 2. 54 ("sincerum est nisi vas")) indicates that it was commonly used to mean the soul as the receptacle of thought

[1] 1 Cor viii. 1 foll Comp Rom xiv 15 foll "If because of *meat* thy brother is grieved, thou walkest no longer in love ...Let us follow after things whereby we may *build up one another*;...all things indeed are pure, howbeit it is evil for that man who *eateth with offence*"

THE NEW LAW OF PURIFICATION

Matthew was mainly negative, teaching us that external things do *not*, in themselves, render a man impure. Though, however, Mark did not tell us how to become pure, he mentioned, in his list of the impurities that come "out of the heart of men," one that claims notice here—"an evil eye[1]."

We note this, not because of the condensed mixture of metaphor, but because it is perhaps the only Marcan instance of "eye" used in a metaphorical sense. The parallel Matthew does not mention it. Elsewhere, however, Matthew-Luke Tradition has a section about the "eye" as being the source of moral light or moral darkness to man according to its nature[2]. Mark nowhere mentions "the good eye," as opposed to "the evil eye." Matthew and Luke call it "the single, or simple, eye." But the Jews also spoke of a good eye[3]. A man with "a good eye" looks with good will both on what he gives and on him to whom he gives it; a man with an evil eye looks grudgingly on the gift though he may try to look kindly on the recipient. The former alone has the single, or simple, eye. But this metaphor might not be very clear to Gentiles[4]. Moreover, the Jews used it mainly about bountifulness or niggardliness. Yet, when rightly viewed, this doctrine of a good or evil eye extended to all man's relations with his neighbour. The doctrine of Jesus concerning "the good eye" implied that His disciples were to have a way of looking at things from God's impartial point of view, not a one-sided way varying with *meum* or *tuum*. It was to be "a single eye," God's eye—in so far as God gives it to man, that man may see things to some extent as God sees them—a fountain of spiritual light and life in man's heart.

---

[1] Mk vii. 22, om. in parall. Mt. xv. 19.
[2] Mt. vi. 22 foll., Lk. xi. 34.
[3] See *Hor. Heb.* on Mt. vi. 22 foll., and comp. Mt. xx. 15 "Is thine eye evil because I am good?"
[4] Steph. *Thes.* ii. 178 gives frequent instances of $\beta\acute{\alpha}\sigma\kappa\alpha\nu\sigma\varsigma$ $\dot{\sigma}\phi\theta\alpha\lambda\mu\acute{\sigma}\varsigma$, but I have not found one of $\dot{\alpha}\gamma\alpha\theta\dot{\sigma}\varsigma$ $\dot{\sigma}\phi\theta\alpha\lambda\mu\acute{\sigma}\varsigma$.

THE NEW LAW OF PURIFICATION

In Hebrew, among many words that mean "fountain," one also means "eye." The metaphor of a fountain of life is to be found in Jeremiah and the Psalms and Proverbs (although not there called "eye") Jeremiah says "My people have committed two evils; they have forsaken me, the fountain of living waters, and hewed them out cisterns, broken cisterns, that can hold no water[1]." Such a metaphor answers questions raised above by other less satisfactory metaphors about the purifying of various vessels. It declares that we must *not* be content with purifying any *vessel of our own*, whether called "cup," or "platter," or "dish," or "cistern" (not even though the "cistern" be not "broken") We must be content with nothing less than the Purifier Himself, who described Himself to Jeremiah as "the fountain of living waters[2]."

This metaphor of the fountain John accordingly employs, at an early period in his Gospel, not as yet mentioning the word "cleanse" or "purify[3]," but introducing one who assuredly needed to be purified—the woman of Samaria, who had had "five husbands" Sitting beside a "well" or "fountain"— for, in LXX, "fountain" and "well" are often represented by the same word—Jesus teaches the woman the doctrine of "living water" which alone can satisfy thirst. It has been said above that the same Hebrew word *En* (or *Ain*) that means "eye" means also often "fountain[4]" The first mention

---

[1] In Jer ii. 13, Ps xxxvi. 9 "with thee is the fountain of life, in thy light shall we see light," Prov xiii 14, xiv 27, Heb "fountain" is not the same as Heb "eye," see below, n 4

[2] See *Proclam* p 346 "Philo (i 575) quotes Jer ii 13, as proving that God 'is the most ancient of all fountains,' just before commenting on the story of Hagar at the fountain "

[3] John nowhere uses καθαρίζω, but he has καθαρισμός in ii 6, iii 25— both times with Ἰουδαῖος in the context Καθαίρω "cleanse," in Jn xv. 2, unique in NT, is perhaps antithetical to (*ib*) αἴρω "take away" Origen (on Jerem xxiv. 6) quotes it after a mention of καθαιρέω as if in contrast

[4] See Gesen and Levy on עין and comp Prov. iv 21 "from thine eyes (מעיניך)," LXX "thy *fountains* (αἱ πηγαί σου)," probably

THE NEW LAW OF PURIFICATION

of *En* in Scripture with the latter meaning is where Hagar, "by a *fountain*[1]," said "Thou art a God of *seeing*" John seems to draw a parallel between Hagar and the Samaritan woman. Hagar says "Have I...looked after him that seeth me?" (LXX "I have seen face to face one that appeared to me"); and the Samaritan woman is made to "behold" at all events that Jesus is "a prophet[2]," and through her the Samaritans are led to a knowledge that He is the Saviour of the world. Later on, while inviting everyone that thirsts to come to Him, Jesus says, not only "Let him come unto me and drink," but also "Out of his belly shall flow rivers of living water[3]." That is to say, he shall not only be filled with water but shall also be constantly flowing forth to others—no "cistern," but a "fountain"

We pass now to the first instance in the Fourth Gospel of any doctrine of Jesus about purifying[4] It occurs in what may

---

confusing it with (Gesen 745 *b*) מעין, a form of עין that also means "spring," "fountain" But in Jer ii 13, Ps xxxvi. 9, Prov xiii 14, xiv 27, πηγή = מקור (see p 460, n 1).

[1] Gen xvi 7

[2] Jn iv. 19 θεωρῶ ὅτι προφήτης εἶ σύ According to Onkelos, Hagar says (Gen xvi 13) "Thou art Eloah seeing all," and "I also have begun to see after that He hath been revealed to me" The Samaritan woman, who says (Jn iv. 29) "Come, see a man that told me all that [ever] I did," may be regarded as having "begun to see" See *Proclam* pp 345—6

[3] Jn vii 37—8

[4] Jn xiii 10—11, xv 3 Previously we have been prepared by John to suppose that Jewish "purifications" would play a great part in Jewish life Note the mention of "the Jews" in Jn ii 6 "water-pots of stone according to *the purification* (καθαρισμὸν) *of the Jews.*" Taken with other Johannine mentions of "the Jews," the term, as in Jn ii 13 ("the Passover of the Jews"), perhaps implies disparagement. Purification is connected with "disputation," or "questioning," and "a Jew," in iii 25 "a *questioning* on the part of John's disciples *with a Jew* about *purification*" Another word is used in Jn xi 55 "There was near at hand the Passover *of the Jews,* and many came up .that they might [*ritually*] *purify* (ἁγνίσωσιν) themselves"—but still, probably, with a notion of disparagement

THE NEW LAW OF PURIFICATION

be called the drama of the Washing of the Feet of the Disciples by Christ. Several details in it suggest that a contrast is intended between this new purification introduced at the Christian meal and the old one practised at the Jewish meal. The old one concerned the hands; this concerned the feet. The old one was before, this one was during, or after, the meal[1]. The old one was a self-purifying; the new one was altruistic, a purification of others[2]. Jesus, in this scene, girding Himself with a napkin, appears to be symbolically wiping off on Himself (as Origen says) the sins and infirmities of the disciples[3], and saying to us, in effect, that we are to do the same thing for one another. Such a work is not to be achieved except by those who can say with some truth (as Paul said) that they have "the mind of Christ[4]." But even for those who fail it is well to recognise the difficulty of the task, and to know that it is something very different from the mere attempt to save their own souls. In proportion as we have within us "the mind of Christ," "the good eye," "the fountain of life," we shall be enabled to "wash one another's feet" by kindness, and consideration, and forgiveness of wrong, even at the cost of some self-humiliation or sacrifice. Those who can do this will be purifying the souls of others as well as their own, and will be fulfilling the precept of Christ which He gave us through His Apostle,

---

(as Origen in his comment indicates) But no doctrine of Jesus on "purifying" is introduced till Jn xiii 10—11.

[1] Origen *ad loc* (Lomm ii 380) notes that the usual time for washing the feet was before the meal, but that Jesus deliberately "passed beyond that time (ὑπερβὰς δὲ τὸν καιρὸν ἐκεῖνον)"

[2] Jn xiii 12—14 "Know ye what I have done to you? Ye call me, Master, and Lord. ..If I then, the Lord and the Master, have washed your feet, ye also ought to *wash one another's feet*"

[3] See *Notes* **2964** quoting Origen (Lomm ii 401) τάχα δὲ ἵνα τὸν ἐν τοῖς ποσὶ τῶν μαθητῶν ῥύπον ἀναλάβῃ εἰς τὸ ἑαυτοῦ σῶμα διὰ τοῦ λεντίου ...αὐτὸς γὰρ (Is. liii 4 and Mt. viii 17) τὰς ἀσθενείας ἡμῶν φέρει.

[4] 1 Cor ii. 16.

THE NEW LAW OF PURIFICATION

"Bear ye one another's burdens and so fulfil the Law of Christ[1]."

---

[1] Gal vi 2 Self-purification, when mentioned by John, is expressed by ἁγνίζω. This word means ritual purification There is irony in the description of the Jews as coming to Jerusalem (xi 55) "to *purify* themselves" before "*the Passover of the Jews*" "The true self-purification (ἁγνισμός)," says Origen, "was not before the Passover, but *in the Passover*," that is, when Christ died as the Lamb of God There seems an allusion to this in 1 Jn iii. 1—3 "Behold what manner of love the Father hath bestowed on us... and everyone that hath this hope [set] on him *purifieth* (ἁγνίζει) *himself* even as *he* [i e Jesus Christ] is *pure* (ἁγνός)," that is to say, Christians are to purify themselves not by self-mortification for the mere purpose of saving their own souls, but by being conformed to the Passover in Christ, fulfilling the Pauline precept "present your bodies a living sacrifice, holy, acceptable to God" Before this "self-purification" can be achieved we must have received a "purification" But that is described by a different word, the Synoptic καθαρίζω (1 Jn i. 7—9) "If we walk in the light, as he [i e God] is in the light, we have fellowship one with another, and the blood of Jesus, his Son, *purifieth* (καθαρίζει) us from all sin . . If we confess our sins, he is faithful and righteous to forgive us our sins and *to purify* (καθαρίσῃ) us from all unrighteousness"

This is a case where John uses in his Epistle a word for which he has prepared the way in his Gospel, not by using the word, but by representing Jesus dramatically as setting before us the word's essential meaning

463 (Mark vii. 1—23)

CHAPTER XI

THE NEW LAW OF SACRIFICE
[Mark vii. 24—ix. 1*]

§ 1. *The Syrophoenician woman*[1]

AFTER the Pharisees had been alienated by His protest against their traditions of purification Jesus is said to have

---

* For comment on Mk viii 1—9, 14—21, see above, Chapter VIII; and for reference to particular passages see p 208, n 1, also Textual Index

[1] Mk vii 24—30 (R V)

(24) And from thence he arose, and went away into the borders of Tyre and Sidon (*some anc auth omit* and Sidon) And he entered into a house, and would have no man know it and he could not be hid.

(25) But straightway a woman, whose little daughter had an unclean spirit, having heard of him, came and fell down at his feet

(26) Now the woman was a Greek (*or*, Gentile), a Syrophoenician by race. And she besought him that he would cast forth the devil out of her daughter

(27) And he said unto her, Let the children first be filled for it is not meet to take the children's bread and cast it to the dogs

Mt. xv. 21—8 (R V)

(21) And Jesus went out thence, and withdrew into the parts of Tyre and Sidon

(22) And behold, a Canaanitish woman came out from those borders, and cried, saying, Have mercy on me, O Lord, thou son of David, my daughter is grievously vexed with a devil

(23) But he answered her not a word. And his disciples came and besought him, saying, Send her away, for she crieth after us

(24) But he answered and said, I was not sent but unto the lost sheep of the house of Israel

(25) But she came and worshipped him, saying, Lord, help me.

(26) And he answered and said, It is not meet to take the children's bread and cast it to the dogs

(27) But she said, Yea, Lord:

THE NEW LAW OF SACRIFICE

withdrawn "to the borders of Tyre [and Sidon]¹" The execution of John the Baptist can hardly have failed to play some part in causing this withdrawal, and in shaping the new utterances of Jesus to His disciples. But there is very little trace of such an effect in Mark's narrative On the surface, Mark seems to say (as we found Victor asserting above) that Jesus was never more sought after by the multitudes. Looking, however, below the surface, we find indications that the Gospel was not really succeeding. Jesus was making no way—at least on the lines on which He desired to appeal to His countrymen. When Mark, after describing a long round of journeying, brings us at last to Caesarea Philippi, we shall find that, according to the confession of Christ's own disciples, the multitudes did not recognise in Him anything really new. Even among admirers, He was "one of the prophets (*or*, of the old prophets)" or "Elijah." He was not recognised as the Christ, nor as being—in any unique and divine sense—what He called Himself, the Son of Man.

In this drama of rejection, the first scene is devoted to the healing of the daughter of the Syrophoenician woman. After

Mk vii. 24—30 (R V.) *contd.*	Mt. xv. 21—8 (R.V.) *contd.*
(28) But she answered and saith unto him, Yea, Lord even the dogs under the table eat of the children's crumbs	for even the dogs eat of the crumbs which fall from their masters' table
(29) And he said unto her, For this saying go thy way, the devil is gone out of thy daughter	(28) Then Jesus answered and said unto her, O woman, great is thy faith be it done unto thee even as thou wilt And her daughter was healed from that hour.
(30) And she went away unto her house, and found the child laid upon the bed, and the devil gone out.	

¹ Mk vii. 24. Elijah, when he had incurred the enmity of Ahab, retires first to Cherith, and then to (1 K xvii 9) "Zarephath which belongeth to Zidon" Jesus, after the execution of John the Baptist, might similarly retire from Galilee, as being under the jurisdiction of Herod Antipas According to Luke, the Pharisees themselves—perhaps for no kindly reasons—said to Jesus (Lk xiii. 31) "Herod would fain kill thee"

THE NEW LAW OF SACRIFICE

being virtually classed among the "dogs," that is to say, unclean animals not worthy to partake of the children's food, and after humbly accepting this bitter appellation, she receives as it were a tacit cancelling of this stigma from Jesus, "Go thy way, the devil is gone out of thy daughter." There are reasons for thinking that the disciples, not Jesus, classed this woman with the "dogs"; but in any case the narrative marks a preparation for the enlargement of the scope of the Gospel, since one of those that had been classed among the "dogs" was now admitted to the privileges of the "children" seated at the Father's table[1].

A comment preserved by Victor of Antioch says that Jesus "called the Jews 'children'...and that, until they had laid their hands on Him, He did not transfer [His] favour to those who are without—naming the Gentiles 'dogs,' *which [appellation] afterwards came round to Israel when* it [*i.e.* Israel] was also deprived of the divine food[2]." Such language would go far to encourage some Christians in addressing an Israelite as "dog of a Jew" It makes us realise the need of some antidote against misinterpretations of the dialogue under consideration. Some counter-doctrine of Jesus was desirable, shewing His kindness and consideration to such women as this Canaanite

Such an antidote—whether intended as one or not—is certainly to be found in the Johannine account of Christ's dialogue with the woman of Samaria who had had "five husbands" Assuredly it helps the readers of Mark's dialogue

---

[1] On the story of the Syrophoenician woman see *Son* **3353** (iv) *a* foll To the facts there collected add Exod vi. 15 "Shaul the son of *a Canaanitish woman*," LXX ὁ ἐκ τῆς Φοινίσσης (οἱ Γ'. Χαναναίας). This illustrates the difference between Mk vii 26 Συροφοινίκισσα (marg Σύρα Φοινίκισσα) and Mt. xv 22 Χαναναία The story is commented on, and allegorized at great length, by Origen; but he does not lessen the great difficulty of supposing that Jesus, even indirectly or tentatively, sanctioned the Jewish habit of calling certain Gentiles "dogs"

[2] Cramer, pp 337—8

THE NEW LAW OF SACRIFICE

to feel that Jesus could not have meant literally that which Mark records Him to have said[1].

§ 2 *The first "sighing" of Jesus, in Mark*[2]

After the dialogue with the Syrophoenician, Jesus comes through the north of Palestine to the neighbourhood of the sea of Galilee[3]. Here, according to Matthew, Jesus heals four

---

[1] The Diatessaron places the Johannine Dialogue (§ 21) after the Marcan Dialogue (§ 20), with nothing between them except Mk vii 31—7 (the healing of the "stammerer ($μογιλάλος$)"). Ephrem's comment, making no mention of the healing, passes from the Marcan to the Johannine Dialogue without anything intervening

[2] Mk vii 31—7 (R V)

Mt xv 29—31 (R V)

(31) And again he went out from the borders of Tyre, and came through Sidon unto the sea of Galilee, through the midst of the borders of Decapolis

(32) And they bring unto him one that was deaf, and had an impediment in his speech, and they beseech him to lay his hand upon him

(33) And he took him aside from the multitude privately, and put his fingers into his ears, and he spat, and touched his tongue,

(34) And looking up to heaven, he sighed, and saith unto him, Ephphatha, that is, Be opened

(35) And his ears were opened and the bond of his tongue was loosed, and he spake plain.

(36) And he charged them that they should tell no man but the more he charged them, so much the more a great deal they published it

(37) And they were beyond measure astonished, saying, He hath done all things well he maketh even the deaf to hear, and the dumb to speak.

(29) And Jesus departed thence, and came nigh unto the sea of Galilee, and he went up into the mountain, and sat there.

(30) And there came unto him great multitudes, having with them the lame, blind, dumb, maimed, and many others, and they cast them down at his feet, and he healed them

(31) Insomuch that the multitude wondered, when they saw the dumb speaking, the maimed whole, and the lame walking, and the blind seeing and they glorified the God of Israel.

[3] Mk vii 31 "From the borders of Tyre he came through Sidon to ($εἰς$) the sea of Galilee, through the midst of the borders of

THE NEW LAW OF SACRIFICE

classes of sufferers, "the lame, blind, dumb, maimed" (besides "many others") so that people see "the dumb speaking, the maimed whole, and the lame walking, and the blind seeing "

"Deafness" is not mentioned by Matthew. But the parallel Mark, which mentions only one sufferer, describes him as "deaf" and (literally) "stuttering[1]." Mark tells us at great length that Jesus, after resorting to means not elsewhere

---

Decapolis " See above, p 409 This route was very circuitous Prof Swete says (*ad loc*), "the long *détour* may have served the double purpose of defeating the immediate designs of His enemies"—to arrest Him in Galilee—"and providing for the Apostles the rest which He had desired to give them before (Latham, p 333) " But the variations in Mark's text, and Matthew's curt substitute for it (xv. 29 "came by the sea of Galilee.. ") shew that it was regarded as difficult at a very early date If Jesus at this time (comp. Mk vii 24) "did not wish to be known," it seems unlikely that He would pass "through Sidon," even with only a few disciples (but Prof Swete says "in so large and busy a place He may easily have escaped notice")

We have therefore to consider the possibility that Mark, though right in the main fact—namely, that Jesus did make a circuit so as to avoid Galilee—may be inexact in detail because he was influenced by O T narrative such as that quoted above by Origen (p 409, n 1) concerning "*the widow in Sarepta of Sidōnia* " In the same context, Origen quotes Lk iv 25—6 (Lomm v 211) "There were many widows in the people of Israel, but unto none of them was Elias sent, *save in Sarepta, to a widow woman (nisi in Sareptis ad mulierem viduam)* " Here Origen (or his translator) has omitted "*of Sidōnia*," and it is corrupted into "*of Sidon*" by some authorities (also *e* has *Sidonae*, L Σιδωνας) These two quotations deserve all the more attention because Sidon is not mentioned *by itself* in the whole of N T —apart from Acts xxvii 3 "we touched at Sidon "—anywhere except in two places (1) Mk vii 31, immediately after the story of the Canaanite woman, (2) Lk. iv 25—6 about the widow of Sarepta Elsewhere in the Gospels "Sidon" occurs only in the phrase "Tyre and Sidon." Mark's original may have referred to "Sidon" —or, more probably, to "Sidōnia"—because the early Evangelist regarded Jesus as following in the path of Elijah But it is not likely that Jesus as a fact ever "came through Sidon "

[1] Mk vii 32 "one that was deaf *and had an impediment in his speech* (καὶ μογιλάλον) "

468 (Mark vii 31—7)

THE NEW LAW OF SACRIFICE

mentioned by the Synoptists to heal this sufferer, looked up to heaven, and sighed, and said, in Aramaic, "Be opened " Then follows the "opening" ("his ears *were opened*") and the "loosing" ("the bond of his tongue *was loosed*"). After this minute description of the healing of a single sufferer, it is strangely spoken of (by the multitude) as a healing of more than one · "He hath done all things well, he maketh both (*or*, even) the deaf (pl) to hear and the speechless (pl) to speak[1] "

Of these two accounts Mark's is apparently the earlier and undoubtedly the more suggestive of poetic imagery Turning to LXX for illustrations of it, we find that his word for "stuttering" occurs nowhere except in Isaiah's description of the return of Israel from captivity: "Then the eyes of the blind shall be opened, and the ears of the deaf shall be unstopped; then shall the lame man leap as an hart, and the tongue of *the dumb* shall sing," where LXX has "[the] tongue of [*the*] stutterers shall be clear-of-speech[2]." The Hebrew "dumb," rendered here uniquely by LXX "*stutterer*," means etymologically "*bound*[3]" The

---

[1] Besides these divergences in the words of Mark and Matthew, there is also a divergence in their interpretations of the same word Matthew (W H txt) uses κωφός (*i e* deaf or dumb) to mean dumb ("see the *dumb* speaking"), (but W H marg (substituting "hearing" for "speaking") to mean *deaf*) Mark uses it to mean deaf ("the *deaf* to hear") As for "*dumb*," Mark represents it by two other words His first word is "*a stutterer*" ("they bring to him one that was deaf and *a stutterer*") His second word is "*speechless*" ("he maketh . *the speechless* to speak") See Mk ix 17 πνεῦμα ἄλαλον "a speechless spirit," *ib* 25 τὸ ἄλαλον καὶ κωφὸν πνεῦμα "speechless and deaf spirit," where the parall Mt xvii 15, 18 and Lk ix 39, 42 do not define the nature of the "spirit " Lk ix 39 κράζει perhaps seemed to Luke inconsistent with dumbness, but in Mk ix. 25—6 κράξας masc is applied to the πνεῦμα ἄλαλον.

[2] Is xxxv 5—6, LXX ὀφθαλμοὶ τυφλῶν...ὦτα κωφῶν ..χωλός, τρανὴ δὲ ἔσται γλῶσσα μογιλάλων, preceded by a mention of (*ib.* 3) "weak hands and.. feeble (*or*, tottering) knees " Τρανός, in LXX, occurs elsewhere only in Wisd vii. 22 πνεῦμα ..τρανόν, x 21 γλώσσας νηπίων ἔθηκε τρανάς.

[3] Gesen 47—8 The verb אלם "bind" = (Tromm.) ἄφωνος (1),

469 (Mark vii. 31—7)

THE NEW LAW OF SACRIFICE

adjective occurs for the first time where the Lord says to Moses "Who maketh [a man] *dumb*, or deaf...?" where LXX has "*badly-deaf* (meaning *dumb*) and deaf," but Aquila and the rest have "*stuttering*" (for "dumb")[1], while a scholiast has a word meaning "*maimed*" or "*lame*." This connection between "*dumb*" and "maimed" or "lame" may be illustrated by the context in Exodus where Moses says to the Lord "I am (lit) *heavy* of speech" but the Jerusalem Targums have "I am *lame* of speech," using a word that means in Hebrew "bound [with a girdle]" but in Aramaic "bound [as with a chain round one's feet]" and hence "lame[2]." Matthew, while omitting one of Isaiah's four classes, "the deaf," substitutes a word meaning "maimed," but primarily "bent," so that it may very well point back to the thought of a sufferer in some way "*bound*" by Satan[3].

If we ask why the LXX should have chosen that particular word ("stutterer") to express the Hebrew "dumb" in Isaiah, we may find some answer in the Targum, which uses a word that in Hebrew approximates to the English "curbed" or

---

κατανύσσω (1), συνέχω (1), δεσμεύω (1), forms of κωφόω (4), ἄλαλος γίνομαι (1). The adj אלם = ἄλαλος (1), δύσκωφος (1), ἐνεός i e dumb or silly (1), κωφός (1), μογιλάλος (1)

[1] Exod iv 11 δύσκωφον (אלם) καὶ κωφόν (חרש), Aq, Sym, Theod. μογιλάλον, Schol βωβόν, on which Field quotes Hesych Βωβός πηρός Βωβούς χωλούς Δύσκωφος (L S) might be used of one who, never having heard anything, has never been moved to speak

[2] Exod. iv 10 Jer I חגר, Jer II חגיר used elsewhere by Onk. to express פסח a "limper" Lev xxi 18, Deut xv 21 See Levy ii 14 *b* Comp 1 K xx 11 "him that *girdeth on* [*his armour*] (חגר)," LXX ὁ κυρτός "the *humpbacked*," apparently taking it as "bent forward," "bent down " Comp Lk xiii 11, 16 "bowed together (συνκύπτουσα)," and "Satan had bound," about the woman whom Jesus (*ib* 13) "made straight " Also comp *Acta Pil.* (B) vi 2 Κυλλὸς ἤμην...εὐθὺς ἠγέρθην with (A) Κυρτὸς ἤμην καὶ ὤρθωσέ με λόγῳ.

[3] Mt xv 30 κυλλούς, s. preceding note Justin Martyr (*Tryph* § 69), after quoting Is xxxv. 1—7, describes Jesus as healing τοὺς πηροὺς καὶ κωφοὺς [i e deaf, as shewn by his comment, τὸν δὲ καὶ ἀκούειν] καὶ χωλούς, but not (Mk) μογιλάλος, nor (Mt) κυλλοί.

THE NEW LAW OF SACRIFICE

"muzzled[1]" The Targumist takes it to mean that the children of Israel who have hitherto had their mouths muzzled in their captivity and desolation will now be able to praise God for His salvation[2] It does not therefore mean exactly "dumb," but rather implies that the mouth is gagged by a "bond," which is now removed. But this word in New Hebrew and Aramaic may also mean "lamed[3]." Thus we are brought round again from "stuttering," in Mark and LXX, through the Targumistic "muzzled" or "lamed," to something like Matthew's "lame," or "maimed," so as to recognise that "stuttering" and "lame" and "maimed" may be derived from one Semitic original

Hence we are led to the conclusion that both Mark and Matthew are probably based on Isaiah's description of the Return of the Redeemed Before the enumeration of the sufferings from which Israel is to be saved, Isaiah says "He [i e. the Lord] will come and save you[4]" Both Mark and Matthew regard Jesus as thus "coming" to "save" But while Matthew emphasizes the variety of the evils from which He saves, Mark emphasizes the radical evil implied by the "loosing" of a "bond" or "chain"—the binding by Satan when he takes men captive and binds them with the chain of their sins and infirmities Mark also mentions a command "Be thou opened" This suggests the thought of a prison-house, a place of imprisonment with hard labour, over which Satan is task-master[5].

---

[1] Ps xxxii 9 בלם, Gesen 117 *b*

[2] "*Laudabit* lingua eorum quae erat quasi muta (בלים)" Comp. Wisd x 21 γλώσσας νηπίων ἔθηκε τρανάς, and Ps viii 2 "out of the mouth of babes and sucklings hast thou established strength," quoted in Mt xxi 16 "out of the mouth of babes and sucklings thou hast perfected *praise*."

[3] In Aramaic and New Hebrew (Levy *Ch* 1. 99 and Levy 1 234) בלם means both "muzzled" and "lamed"

[4] Is xxxv 4

[5] Comp Acts x. 38, a Petrine utterance describing Jesus as "doing good and healing all that were *oppressed* (καταδυναστευομένους) (Mark vii. 31—7)

THE NEW LAW OF SACRIFICE

The thought of a prison leads us to think of the Psalmist's mention of "the sorrowful crying" or "groaning" of "prisoners" mentioned in the Psalms[1] and to ask whether there is any allusion to it in Mark, as if the Messiah were regarded as "sighing" in sympathy with them. If there is, it is probable that the allusion goes further back. For the Psalmist appears to be alluding to the "sighing" and "crying" and "groaning" of Israel in Egypt. "And the children of Israel sighed by reason of the bondage, and they cried, and their cry came up unto God...and God heard their groaning[2]." The word here rendered *"sighed"* occurs nowhere else in the historical books of Scripture. But it occurs in Ezekiel where the Lord says "All flesh shall know that I the Lord have drawn forth my sword out of its sheath....*Sigh*, therefore, thou son of man, with the breaking of thy loins and with bitterness *shalt thou sigh* before their eyes[3]."

These two passages present two aspects in which the Son of Man, or Messiah, might be regarded as "sighing." The first is that in which He might look up as an intercessor for Israel in bondage so that their cry may "come up unto God," and their bonds be loosed, and their prison-door thrown open. This appears to be represented by Mark here, where Jesus looks up to heaven, and sends up the cry for deliverance, *Ephphatha*,

---

by the devil," and note the first Biblical instance of καταδυναστεύω, Exod 1 13 "The Egyptians *made* the children of Israel *to serve* with rigour," κατεδυνάστευον βίᾳ. Egypt, or Sin, is regarded as an "ergastulum," a place of imprisonment with hard labour, and Pharaoh, or Satan, is regarded as the Master of it.

[1] Ps lxxix 11, cii 20, τὸν στεναγμὸν (אנקה, Gesen. "crying," "groaning") τῶν πεπεδημένων

[2] Exod ii 23—4 "sighed (אנח) κατεστέναξαν," "cried (זעק) ἀνεβόησαν," "cry (שועה) βοή," "groaning (נאקה) στεναγμόν" Gesen 58 b renders אנה "sigh, groan." Tromm gives אנה and אנחה as = forms of στένω, στενάζω etc (noun or verb) about twenty times.

[3] Ezek xxi 5—6

THE NEW LAW OF SACRIFICE

"be opened," and the cry is heard and the "bond" is "loosed," and the door is "opened¹."

The second aspect is that in which the Messiah must be regarded in the character of a judge, looking down on Israel with sadness because, having been rejected as an intercessor, He is compelled to send down judgment rather than to send up intercession That will come before us in the next section when we study a tradition peculiar to Mark, about a second sighing of Jesus in reply to the demand of the Jews for "a sign²" Meantime, before passing to that, we have to ask whether there are any traces of Johannine Intervention, as to this first kind of sighing³.

The Fourth Gospel nowhere intervenes by any repetition of this particular Marcan word But it does intervene, in word as well as thought, by using another Marcan word implying emotional rebuke with groaning⁴. This it applies to Jesus at the grave of Lazarus. There, as here in Mark, Jesus lifted up His eyes to heaven, there He also uttered something, perhaps unutterable in words, expressive of His sorrow and anger at the bondage of human nature to sin and death; there He also cried an *Ephphatha*, or summons to be "opened," in the words "Lazarus, come forth"; and then there followed also a literal

---

¹ Isaiah's description of the Healing of the Ransomed concludes with the words (xxxv 10) "And sorrow and sighing shall flee away " Is it fanciful to suppose that the originator of Mark's tradition inserted the "sighing" of Jesus, not only because it was a fact that Jesus *did* "sigh" over a particular act of healing, but also because there was a fitness in the fact? "The sighing of Israel," he might say, "cannot 'flee away' till it is driven out by the sighing of the Saviour In all their affliction He was afflicted (Is lxiii 9) "

² Mk viii 12, Mt xvi 4, Lk xi 29

³ The question is confined to the sighing We do not deal with Mk vii 33 which connects healing with spitting and which will be discussed in the comment on Mk viii 23 Mark and John (ix 6—7) are the only Evangelists who connect healing with "spitting "

⁴ See *Son* and *Joh Voc* Indices on ἐμβριμάομαι used in Jn xi 33, 38 R V. "groaned," marg "was moved with indignation."

THE NEW LAW OF SACRIFICE

as well as spiritual "loosing" when "he that was dead came forth *bound* hand and foot with bands of the grave," and Jesus said, "*Loose him*, and let him go[1]."

§ 3. *The second "sighing" of Jesus, in Mark*

After the acts of healing described in the last section Mark and Matthew place the Feeding of the Four Thousand, which has been discussed above[2], and then a request for a sign from heaven[3]. It is this that, according to Mark, draws a sigh a second time from Jesus, not mentioned by Matthew[4]. The request is made, in Mark, by the Pharisees, but in Matthew by the Pharisees and Sadducees. In John, a similar request is made for "a sign"—meaning "a sign from heaven"—after the Feeding of the Five Thousand, and apparently by some of the Five Thousand themselves. "What then doest thou *for a sign*,

---

[1] Jn xi 44.

[2] For comment on Mk viii 1—9 in Chapter VIII, see p 208, n 1, and Textual Index

[3] Mk viii 11 (R V)   Mt xvi 1 (R V)   Lk xi 16

Mk viii 11 (R V)	Mt xvi 1 (R V)	Lk xi 16
And the Pharisees came forth, and began to question with him, seeking of him a sign from heaven, tempting him	And the Pharisees and Sadducees came, and tempting him asked him to shew them a sign from heaven	And others, tempting [him], sought of him a sign from heaven.

This is preceded by —

Mk viii. 10 (R V)	Mt xv 39 (R V)
And straightway he entered into the boat with his disciples, and came into the parts of Dalmanutha	And he sent away the multitudes, and entered into the boat, and came into the borders of Magadan

The variations in the texts of these passages will be found discussed in detail in *Corrections* **498** *g—h* To the remarks there made should be added the hypothesis of an allusion in Dalmanutha (see above, pp 242—3) to the rare word rendered by R V "haven" in Ps cvii 30, and the suggestion that a "haven" may be implied in the tradition peculiar to Mark (vi 53) "they moored to the shore (προσωρμίσθησαν)" (see p 443)

[4] Mk viii 12 "And he sighed deeply in his spirit (ἀναστενάξας τῷ πνεύματι αὐτοῦ) and saith,...."

THE NEW LAW OF SACRIFICE

that we may see and believe thee?...Our fathers ate the manna ...as it is written, He gave them bread out of heaven to eat[1]"

Luke describes a request for a sign from heaven as proceeding from "others"—not very clearly defined—immediately after the "marvel" of "the multitudes" at the exorcism of "a dumb devil," and after the assertion of "*some of them*" that Jesus "casteth out devils in Beelzebub[2]." It will be seen below that

---

[1] Jn vi 30, 31. Jesus has previously said to them "Ye seek me, not because ye saw signs, but because ye ate of the loaves" By "ye saw signs" Jesus seems to refer to a previous mention of "beholding signs" in *ib* vi 2, "A great multitude followed him because *they beheld the signs that he did on them that were sick*" The context indicates that John now regards Jesus as saying to these seekers after a new sign "Ye are not like those who followed me because they beheld the signs performed in the healing of sufferers. Ye speak of the ancient 'bread *out of heaven*,' meaning that ye demand a sign of the same kind—*a sign from heaven*" So Westcott *ad loc* "They ask, as in the Synoptists, for 'a sign from heaven'"

[2] See *Proclam* pp 424 and 428. Luke is printed fully below in order to shew the difficulty of ascertaining the meaning of "*some of them*" and "*others*" Luke has said nothing about Scribes or Pharisees as being among the "multitudes" whom he has just mentioned

Mk iii. 20—23 *a* (R V)	Mt xii 22—5 (R V)	Lk xi 14—17 (R V)
(20) And he cometh into a house..	(22) Then . one possessed with a devil, blind and dumb . the dumb man spake and saw	(14) And he was casting out a devil [which was] dumb. And it came to pass, when the devil was gone out, the dumb man spake, and the multitudes marvelled
(21) And when his friends heard it. for they said, He is beside himself	(23) And all the multitudes were amazed Is this the Son of David?	
(22) And the scribes which came down from Jerusalem said, He hath Beelzebub..	(24) But when the Pharisees heard it, they said, This man .. by Beelzebub .	(15) But *some of them* said, By Beelzebub the prince of the devils casteth he out devils.
(23) And he called them unto him, and said unto them in parables ..	(25) And knowing their thoughts he said unto them ...	(16) *And others, tempting* [*him*], *sought of him a sign from heaven.*
		(17) But he, knowing their thoughts, said unto them ..

475 (Mark viii. 10—12)

THE NEW LAW OF SACRIFICE

the parallel Mark and Matthew mention no such demand. But it is not perhaps—as it appears at first sight to be—irrelevant It means that, although the multitudes marvelled, the upper classes refused to accept a "sign" of exorcism as proving anything The dumb devil might be driven out by an agent of the devil on earth What they wanted was "a sign from heaven," where the devil could work no sign This agrees with the above suggested explanation of the Johannine words "Ye seek me, not because ye saw *signs*," that is, "not because ye saw *the signs of healing performed on the sick*[1]."

It is implied by John that those who asked Jesus for "a sign from heaven" did not know what "heaven" meant. Defining it as a place, or perhaps as seven places ("seven heavens") of material glory, they did not recognise it as the region of the Supreme Love and Righteousness, the divine Father whose "signs" were to be seen issuing from every son of man, so far as that son of man identified himself with God in love and righteousness, as his Father in heaven This led them to accuse Jesus—who did identify Himself with the divine nature—of blaspheming God and of making Himself the agent of Satan in the act of curing the diseases of men Such a perversion of mind, such a determination to call good evil, could not but result in a distortion of the divine image and a substitution of Satan for God, and this it appears to have been that made Jesus, as Mark says, "sigh deeply in his spirit[2]."

---

[1] See p 475, n 1

[2] Comp *Mart Polyc* § 9 ὁ δὲ Πολύκαρπος ἐμβριθεῖ τῷ προσώπῳ εἰς πάντα τὸν ὄχλον τὸν ἐν τῷ σταδίῳ ἀνόμων ἐθνῶν ἐμβλέψας καὶ ἐπισείσας αὐτοῖς τὴν χεῖρα, στενάξας τε καὶ ἀναβλέψας εἰς τὸν οὐρανόν, εἶπεν, Αἶρε τοὺς ἀθέους

The Proconsul had said to Polycarp, "Say, *Away with* (lit *take away* (αἶρε)) *the atheists !*" The narrative, in a passage that suggests reminiscences of the two Marcan descriptions of Christ's "sighing," says that Polycarp "sighed" while he called on God to "take away" the *real* "*atheists*," that is, those who denied the true God by setting up false gods

476 (Mark viii 10—12)

THE NEW LAW OF SACRIFICE

A similar sense of sad and indignant condemnation is implied in the phrase "this generation," which appears, as part of Christ's answer to the demand for a sign, in all the Synoptists[1]. It has been shewn elsewhere that in the whole of O.T. "this generation" occurs but twice and means "this evil generation[2]." In the Gospels it means a transient and rebellious generation that is rejecting the will of Him who abides to all generations. It is a generation like the one that fed on the manna in the wilderness and yet provoked the Lord so that they were not allowed to enter the Promised Land. John never mentions the word "generation," but he implies it in the discourse of Jesus after the Feeding of the Five Thousand. The Jews ask Him for a sign, like the manna, from a local heaven, and say with complacency "Our fathers ate the manna in the wilderness." Jesus replies, in effect, "They did indeed. But your 'fathers' were not the true Israel. They were but a passing generation. They ate the manna, but what was the end? Not the Promised Land, but death. They ate—*and died*[3]."

Can we find anywhere in John a parallel to this second

---

[1] Mk viii 12—13 (R V)
(12) And he sighed deeply in his spirit, and saith, Why doth this generation seek a sign? Verily I say unto you, There shall no sign be given unto this generation
(13) And he left them, and again entering into [the boat] departed to the other side

Mt xvi 4 (comp xii 39) (R V)
(4) An evil and adulterous generation seeketh after a sign, and there shall no sign be given unto it, but the sign of Jonah. And he left them, and departed

Lk xi 29 (R V)
(29) And when the multitudes were gathering together unto him, he began to say, This generation is an evil generation it seeketh after a sign; and there shall no sign be given to it but the sign of Jonah

[2] See *Son* on "This Generation" 3362 v (b)—(f) "This generation," in O T, occurs only in Gen vii 1, Ps xii 7

[3] Jn vi 49 "Your fathers ate the manna in the wilderness—*and died*," *ib* 58 "not as the fathers ate—*and died*" That is to say, the bread from the local "heaven"—called by the Jews (*ib* 31) "bread out of heaven"—had no power to give heavenly life

THE NEW LAW OF SACRIFICE

"sighing" of Jesus recorded by Mark? If anywhere, it is perhaps in the passage describing how He was troubled in the spirit "When Jesus had thus said, *he was troubled in the spirit* and testified and said, Verily, verily, I say unto you, that one of you shall betray me"—where what "Jesus had thus said" was "I speak not of you all I know whom I have chosen, but—that the scripture may be fulfilled, He that eateth my bread lifted up his heel against me[1]." Jesus had previously taken upon Himself the responsibility ("Was it not I that chose?") for choosing the Twelve, of whom He said "one of you is a devil[2]," and now He is "troubled in the spirit" by the result This combines a sense of inevitable evil with a sense of responsibility for it, as in Genesis, "It repented the Lord that he had made man on the earth, and it grieved him at his heart[3]."

§ 4 *The disciples are said for the second time to have their "heart hardened," in Mark*[4]

On this "hardening of the heart" of the disciples Victor records the following comment. "At one and the same time

---

[1] Jn xiii 18—21 On ἀλλ' ἵνα, see *Joh. Gr* 2105—9

[2] Jn vi 70

[3] Gen vi 6. This, however, is not very much like the Marcan "sighing" over "this generation," which rather resembles the weeping of Jesus over Jerusalem (Lk xix 41—4)

Comp *Berach* 3 a, where a Jewish Rabbi amid the ruins of Jerusalem hears "a Voice cooing like a dove and saying 'Alas, that I have desolated my House, burned my Temple, and banished my children among the nations'"

[4]

Mk viii 17	Mt. xvi 8
And Jesus perceiving it, saith unto them, Why reason ye, because ye have no loaves? Do ye not yet perceive, neither understand? Have ye your heart hardened?	And Jesus perceiving it, said, O ye of little faith, why reason ye among yourselves, because ye have no loaves?

For the context, see above, pp. 210—11, where Mk viii 14—21, Mt xvi. 5—12 are printed in parallel columns; see also Textual Index.

the Lord reproaches their faithlessness and makes the meaning of what He had just said clear: 'Remembering the [miracles of feeding] already performed' (He says), 'ye ought neither to be troubled, on your part, about the absence of loaves, nor to suppose that I, for my part, am speaking to you about this. For it would not be hard for me to bring before you, now as formerly, the loaves that are not here, and to satisfy (*lit.* fulfil) your need. How then do ye not yet understand? But have ye your heart still hardened?' This He says while gradually leading the disciples forward to perception and faith[1]"

The defect in this explanation is that it fails to recognise the force of "hardened." It mentions at the beginning "faithlessness", but that is in Matthew, not in Mark. It implies, at the end, a want of "*perception*" as well as of faith; but "hardness" of heart is a much more grievous defect than a want of "perception." "Hardness" has been mentioned before by Mark in the word *pōrōsis*, or "callousness," as causing Jesus grief and indignation[2] There it denoted absorption in one's own interests and indifference to the suffering of others, uniting the Pharisees with the Herodians[3] in a jealous antagonism to Jesus the Healer, and in a determination to destroy Him And here again the Marcan context mentions "the leaven of the Pharisees and the leaven of Herod[4]," before warning the disciples against a callousness that made them fail to understand the moral implied by all Christ's acts, and by the words in which He inculcated the doctrine of the living

---

[1] Cramer on Mk viii 14—16 ending thus Ἀλλ' ἔτι τὴν καρδίαν ἔχετε πεπωρωμένην, Ταῦτα δέ φησι κατὰ βραχὺ προβιβάζων τοὺς μαθητὰς εἰς αἴσθησίν τε καὶ πίστιν.

[2] See *Proclamation* p 362 foll on "the hardening of their heart" in Mk iii 5.

[3] Mk iii. 6

[4] Mk viii 15 "See, beware of the leaven of the Pharisees and the leaven of Herod," Mt xvi 6 "the leaven of the Pharisees and Sadducees," Lk xii. 1 "the leaven (which is hypocrisy) of the Pharisees." On this, see *Proclamation* p 365 foll

THE NEW LAW OF SACRIFICE

Bread. For that doctrine was in fact a doctrine of self-sacrifice. And the opposite doctrine is that of self-worship—whether in those who profess religion or in those who profess irreligion

Matthew seems to have softened down the Marcan phrase ("the heart hardened") as being inapplicable to Christ's disciples And doubtless it is difficult But its very difficulty confirms its genuineness, and indicates that Jesus used some strong term of this kind to warn His disciples against a worship of this world, a worship of visible and material success, which, if they allowed it to enter into their hearts, would alienate them from Himself, just at the critical time when He was purposing to appeal to them to cast in their lot with Him in spite of apparent failure. Mark, in his own person, has already said about the disciples "they understood not concerning the loaves, but *their heart was hardened*[1]"; and now he represents Jesus Himself as, in effect, saying the same thing, "*Understand ye not concerning the loaves* even now? Is your heart still *hardened against the doctrine of the living Bread?*"

We might object that Mark, in relating the Feeding of the Five Thousand, has said nothing about the doctrine of the living Bread as being part, and an integral part, of Christ's acts and words on that occasion. But Mark might reply "It was not my business to record Christ's words I have left that to others. But I told my readers that Jesus, before feeding the multitudes, 'began to teach them many things.' And, in effect, what He did teach them was the New Law of the New Kingdom of God. The whole of the day was spent thus[2]." The reply would justify the Evangelist. And on examining the Synoptic

---

[1] Mk vi. 52

[2] Mk vi. 34 "And he began to teach them many things," Mt. xiv. 14 "...and healed their sick," Lk. ix 11 "and. he spake to them of the kingdom of God, and them that had need of healing he healed" (See above, Chapter viii § 15, and for a more literal rendering see p 184, n 4, comp *Proclam* p 208 foll) Matthew probably believed that the Sermon on the Mount (v 1—vii 29) contained the "many things" mentioned by Mark

THE NEW LAW OF SACRIFICE

parallels we shall find that Luke actually describes Jesus as speaking about the Kingdom of God Matthew does not. But that is explicable because Matthew believed that he had already given in detail the "many things" mentioned by Mark in the form of the Sermon on the Mount. That Sermon, or Teaching—Mark might say—contained the New Law, and the Eucharist that followed bestowed, in a rudimentary form, the power to perform the New Law

John, although he does not follow Mark verbally in applying to the disciples the same word ("harden") that has been applied to the Pharisees[1], nevertheless follows Mark to this extent, that he describes a critical occasion when even the Twelve, stumbling over Christ's doctrine of Bread, seemed in danger of abandoning Him First· "the Jews" contend, questioning the doctrine Then "many of his disciples"—after "murmuring," and after they had been asked by Jesus whether they were "made to stumble"—finally "went back and walked no more with him" Thus Jesus is led at last to make an appeal to the inmost circle of them· "Jesus said therefore unto the twelve, Can it be that ye, too, desire to go away[2]?" This is not exactly the same thing as Mark's "Have ye your heart hardened?" But in effect it resembles Mark. It means "Do ye too share in the hardness of heart and blindness of sight predicted by Isaiah and common to all Israel except the remnant[3]?" We may fairly say that John intervenes in favour of Mark to shew how Christ's doctrine of Bread was followed by a recalcitration of unbelief on the part of many of His disciples into which Mark has given us two faint glimpses, while Matthew and Luke have given us none at all

It must be admitted, however, that Luke had some justification in putting aside these expressions of Mark, about "the hardening of the heart," in the contexts in which he found

---

[1] Mk iii 5
[2] Jn vi 66—7
[3] See *Proclam* p 362 on Jn xii. 40 which paraphrases Is vi. 10.

them, and also in rejecting the tradition about "the one loaf," and indeed the whole of the Feeding of the Four Thousand with its mention of the *sphurides* as distinct from *cophinoi*[1]. Many others beside Victor of Antioch probably interpreted Mark's representation of Christ's argument as follows: "You are afraid because you have only one loaf But I fed five thousand men with five loaves and you took up twelve *large baskets* (*cophinoi*) of fragments; I afterwards fed fewer men, only four thousand, with more loaves, seven, and you took up only seven *small baskets* (*sphurides*) This should convince you that my power to give you bread does not depend on the number of your loaves, but simply on my will" If Luke put this aside either as being inappropriate to Christ's teaching, or as being based on misunderstanding, or for both these reasons, we ought to be very cautious in condemning him

Luke certainly knew that at a very early period the twelve *cophinoi* in the Feeding of the Five Thousand were regarded as symbols The *cophinos* was known everywhere as the "basket" of the Jews that tramped about the Roman Empire[2]. Luke also probably knew that there were traditions about other Eucharistic meals connected with the Lord Jesus before and after His resurrection, some of which were regarded as typical of the admission of the Gentiles to the feast of the Gospel For these, the *cophinos* would be inappropriate. A Gentile term such as the *sphuris* (corresponding to the Roman *sporta*, or "food-basket") would be more suitable. The same tendency of tradition that led Mark to insert the story about a Syrophoenician woman—called "*Hellenis*" or "*Greek*," as distinct from Jews—and to mention her prayer for the metaphorical "crumbs" from the table of the Jews, would lead Mark also to insert a mention of Gentile "baskets" or "*sphurides*" in an account of one of Christ's Eucharistic meals so as to balance the narrative about the Jewish *cophinoi*.

---

[1] Mk viii. 8, comp *ib* viii 20
[2] Juvenal iii 14, vi. 542
(Mark viii 17)

THE NEW LAW OF SACRIFICE

But although Luke may be right in rejecting a large part of the Marcan Gospel bearing on the miracles of feeding, he may have included in his rejection some things that it was desirable to retain. In developing the moral teaching deduced from these Eucharistic meals it was very natural that they should need to be distinguished In the earlier ones, the doctrine of taking up the cross, or denying oneself, would be latent, as it is in the Sermon on the Mount, in the later ones, it might become more prominent, and even so prominent as to overshadow the doctrine of the brotherhood of the children of God In all of them, however, there was a spiritual doctrine, which could not be rejected without bringing on those who rejected it the reproach of "hardening their heart" If Luke, in omitting Mark's duplicate of the Eucharistic meal, has also omitted a warning actually uttered against a spiritual danger, it would be ungrateful and presumptuous in us—having regard to the difficulty of eliciting the truth—to blame him for this omission, but we ought to be grateful to John for not only supplying what was omitted (the doctrine of sacrifice implied in the breaking of the bread) but also amplifying and emphasizing it in a positive as well as a negative aspect.

§ 5. *Jesus lays His hands twice on a blind man and heals him, in Mark*[1]

The only Johannine account of the healing of blindness resembles this narrative (which is peculiar to Mark) in two

---

[1]   Mk viii 22—6 (R V)

(22) And they come unto Bethsaida And they bring to him a blind man, and beseech him to touch him

(23) And he took hold of the blind man by the hand, and brought him out of the village, and when he had spit on (εἰς, *lit* into) his eyes, and laid his hands upon him, he asked him, Seest thou aught?

(24) And he looked up (ἀναβλέψας), and said, I see men, for I behold [them] as trees, walking

(25) Then again he laid his hands upon his eyes, and

respects. (1) The healing may be said, from one point of view, to be not accomplished at once but by stages (2) In the first of these stages there is "spitting" These two details point to Johannine Intervention. In other respects, however, John differs widely from Mark There is no ancient comment of much value on either narrative[1], but some verbal peculiarities in Mark demand attention

Our English Versions do not reveal the peculiarities of Mark's language. They say that the man when healed "saw *clearly*[2]." But the word rendered "*clearly*" means, etymologically, and frequently in Greek poetry, "far-beaming" like the sun or moon Hence it is naturally used of heavenly

---

Mk viii 22—6 (R V) *contd*
he looked stedfastly (διέβλεψεν), and was restored, and saw all things clearly (ἐνέβλεπεν τηλαυγῶς ἅπαντα)
(26) And he sent him away to his home, saying, Do not even enter into the village
Comp Jn ix 1—7 (R V). And as he passed by, he saw a man blind from his birth. (2) And his disciples asked him, saying, Rabbi, who did sin, this man, or his parents, that he should be born blind ? (3) Jesus answered, Neither did this man sin, nor his parents · but that the works of God should be made manifest in him. (4) We must work the works of him that sent me, while it is day the night cometh, when no man can work (5) When I am in the world, I am the light of the world. (6) When he had thus spoken, he spat on the ground, and made clay of the spittle, and anointed his eyes with the clay (*or*, and with the clay thereof anointed [his] eyes), (7) And said unto him, Go, wash in the pool of Siloam (which is by interpretation, Sent) He went away therefore, and washed, and came seeing

[1] Chrysostom's comment on Jn ix 5—7 "Go, wash," has the merit of calling attention to the faith of the blind man as superior to that of Naaman (2 K v 10 foll)

[2] Mk viii 25 ἐνέβλεπεν τηλαυγῶς Comp Philo 1 579 of Moses seeking to see God, ἐζήτει τὸν τριπόθητον καὶ μόνον τηλαυγῶς ἰδεῖν Commenting on God's command to Abraham (Gen xv 5) to look up to heaven and count the stars, Philo (1 95) thanks God for having implanted in the soul seeds "far-beaming" like the stars, σπέρματα ...τηλαυγῆ ὡς τοὺς ἀστέρας ἐν οὐρανῷ Philo ii 344 likens the sun, shewing its τηλαυγὲς φέγγος, after eclipse, to Truth, ἥξει πάλιν ἡ ἀλήθεια καὶ ἀναλάμψει φῶς ἀπαστράπτουσα τηλαυγέστατον

THE NEW LAW OF SACRIFICE

light, as in the only passage where the adjective occurs in the Psalms, "The commandment of the Lord is (Heb) *pure*, enlightening the eyes[1]"

Further, Mark uses here, in the phrase "having spit into (*not*, upon) his eyes," a word for "eye," *omma*, which he himself does not repeat when he describes Jesus as afterwards putting His hands on the man's "eyes" (where "eye" is *opthalmos*). *Omma* is used by Philo, Clement of Rome, and Justin Martyr (following Plato) to mean "the eye of the soul or mind[2]," but is practically unused in the Greek Testament, Old and New, except in Proverbs[3].

Lastly, as regards the gradual nature of the healing, Mark's words, if interpreted as usual in N.T., would imply four stages The man (1) "*recovered sight*[4] (R.V. *looked up*)," (2) "*saw*

---

[1] Ps xix 8 τηλαυγής In Job xxxvii 21 "bright (τηλαυγές)" is applied to "light" said to be (Heb) "in the skies" But in Lev xiii 2—24 it means "a bright spot" in the flesh

[2] See Clem Rom § 19 ἐμβλέψωμεν τοῖς ὄμμασιν τῆς ψυχῆς εἰς τὸ μακρόθυμον αὐτοῦ βούλημα Justin Mart *Tryph* § 4 quotes Plato on τὸ τοῦ νοῦ ὄμμα as given to us to behold things divine, after saying that τὸ θεῖον cannot be seen ὀφθαλμοῖς, ib § 123 speaks of the "opening of the *eyes* (ὄμματα) of proselytes" These are the only instances in Goodspeed Philo i 333 (rep ii 607) contrasts ὀφθαλμοί and ὄμματα in connection with τηλαυγῶς

[3] Ὄμμα, in canon. LXX, occurs only in Proverbs (four times representing the Heb "eye" and once in an interpolation) In N T it occurs only in Mk above, and in Mt xx 34 "he touched *their eyes* (ὀμμάτων)," where Matthew describes the healing of two blind men, but the parall Mk x 52, Lk xviii 42 mention only one

[4] Ἀναβλέπω in N T (Acts as well as Gospels), when used absolutely, (without εἰς τὸν οὐρανόν) mostly means "recover sight" Lk xix 5, xxi 1—of Jesus "looking up" to Zacchaeus in the tree, and to the almsgiving in the Temple—are exceptional Ἀνάβλεψις, unique in Lk iv 18 τυφλοῖς ἀνάβλεψιν, from Is lxi 1, means "recovery of sight" Hence, in answer to the question "Dost thou see aught?" we may naturally infer that Mk viii 24 καὶ ἀναβλέψας ἔλεγεν, Βλέπω... means "and having [immediately] recovered sight he said, I see .." On Mk xvi 4 ἀναβλέψασαι see *Corrections* 527 *a, l*

THE NEW LAW OF SACRIFICE

clearly[1] (R V *looked stedfastly*)"—which is emphasized by adding (3) "and he was restored," and (4) "*saw-with-insight in-bright-clearness* all things (R.V. *saw* all things *clearly*)." The Greek for "see-with-insight," in canonical LXX, is almost peculiar to Isaiah where it is used of "*seeing with insight* the works of the Lord*[2]*"; and the three Translators use it where Hezekiah says "I shall not see the Lord...I shall not *look-upon man*[3]."

This last passage suggests a partial explanation of the very difficult utterance of the blind man in the first stage of his recovery (about seeing men "as trees"). Hezekiah, when delivered from the impending darkness of death and restored to health, might have said "It has been given to me to see yet again the works of the Lord and to look upon man." Somewhat similarly, here, it is given to the blind man, first, to "see man," but only imperfectly, not clearly nor face to face, but faintly and dimly, shadowy moving objects "as it were trees," and then afterwards to see both man and all other things in the bright light of the perfect truth[4].

---

[1] Mk viii 25 διέβλεψεν Διαβλέπω occurs elsewhere in N T only in Mt vii 5, Lk vi 42 διαβλέψεις "thou shalt see clearly," i e with discrimination In Mk, R V has "looked stedfastly " But διαβλέπω has not quite the meaning of insight, or stedfastness, that is in ἐμβλέπω.

[2] "Saw with insight," ἐνέβλεπεν. Ἐμβλέπω occurs nine times in Isaiah, and only six or seven times in the rest of canon. LXX (with various readings)

[3] Ἐμβλέπω with εἰς or dative is freq , but rare with accus Comp. however Is v 12 τὰ δὲ ἔργα κυρίου οὐκ ἐμβλέπουσιν "see with insight," "see the meaning of," and Is xxxviii 11 (the complaint of Hezekiah) "I shall not see Jehovah...I shall not any longer *look-upon man* (Aq , Sym , Theod , οὐκ ἐμβλέψω ἄνθρωπον ἔτι).. "

[4] On Is xxxviii 11 Ibn Ezra says "The pleasure that man has in this world in understanding the works of the Almighty is first mentioned, and then, in the words, 'I shall behold man no more,' his pleasure in seeing his fellow men " The passage is differently explained by the Targum as though the first clause meant "I shall not appear before the Lord in His Temple "

THE NEW LAW OF SACRIFICE

These indications of a typical and allusive meaning in Mark's narrative are not inconsistent with its historical character, which is favoured by many of its details. For example, it takes place at Bethsaida. Now Bethsaida is denounced, in the Double Tradition of Matthew and Luke, for its rejection of the evidence of Christ's mighty works[1]. Accordingly Jesus first takes the man out of the town, as though out of an atmosphere of unbelief. Then He resorts to external processes such as those mentioned in the recent healing of "the stammerer." And in this miracle the cure is at first only partial. We may reasonably infer that the man's faith was weak and needed strengthening against Bethsaida influences. Finally comes the warning not to re-enter the place[2], "Do not so much as go into the village[3]." A similar suggestion of the infection of unbelief will be found later on, where the disciples absolutely fail to cast out a devil from a child, and Jesus Himself will not attempt it, as long as the father is in the atmosphere of "If thou canst[4]."

In passing out of an atmosphere of darkness and faithlessness into an atmosphere of light and faith, Abraham led the way. To Abraham Philo represents God as saying—with a play on

---

[1] Mt xi. 21, Lk x. 13   [2] Mk viii. 26

[3] Bethsaida was a city, not a village. And "village" is hardly explicable from the mere fact that (Schurer II. i. 160) the capitals of districts in Syria are described sometimes as πόλεις sometimes as κῶμαι. But possibly (Swete on Mk viii. 22—3) "Bethsaida Julias may have kept its old style in the popular speech, or one of the villages in its territory may be intended." The latter hypothesis might be illustrated by the reading of D, *a, b, i* in Mk viii. 27 "*Caesarea Philippi*," where Mark has "*the villages* (κώμας)" (and Mt xvi. 13 "*the parts* (μέρη)") of "Caesarea Philippi." Mark's original, "to a village of Bethsaida," may have been taken as "to a village [named] Bethsaida", and "village" may have been dropped there as superfluous, but retained in the following narrative. In LXX, κώμη represents seven different Hebrew words, see *Proclam* pp 240—1, on Mk i. 38 κωμοπόλεις, Lk iv. 43 πόλεσιν.

[4] Mk ix. 22 foll. This "if thou canst" is in Mark alone.

the Greek word meaning either "look-up" or "regain-sight"—
"*Look-up*, in order to convict the human herd that seems to see, but is blinded[1]" Philo also comments on the apparent superfluity of words in the statement that God "led him *out outside*" when He bade him "look up to heaven" This word "*outside*" (he says) means that "the mind that is really desirous of being 'led *out*' by God, so as to be in perfect freedom, must pass *outside all bodily things*, constraints, organs of perception, sophistic classifications, rhetorical tricks of persuasion—and *finally* [*outside*] *its own self*[2]" Here we have, in a Philonian form, Christ's doctrine of "*denying oneself*" Regarded in this light, the Marcan miracle about the blind man who is "*brought out outside*[3]" Bethsaida—for there is the same verbal superfluity here as in the passage commented on by Philo[4]—and who is then restored to sight but with the command not to return to the town, comes not inappropriately at this stage of the Gospel where Jesus is on the point of proclaiming the doctrine of "*denying oneself*[5]."

[1] Philo 1 483 Ἀνάβλεψον, εἰς ἔλεγχον τοῦ τυφλοῦ τῶν ἀγελαίων ἀνθρώπων γένους, ὃ, βλέπειν δοκοῦν, πεπήρωται.
[2] Philo 1 95 (on Gen xv 5) πάντων ὑπεκστῆναι σωματικῶν τὰ τελευταῖα καὶ ἑαυτοῦ
[3] Mk viii 23 ἐξήνεγκεν...ἔξω So the best MSS. It is not surprising that many MSS read ἐξήγαγεν, but comp Ezr viii 17 ἐξήνεγκα αὐτούς, parall to 1 Esdr viii 44 εἶπα αὐτοῖς ἐλθεῖν.
[4] Philo, on Gen xv 5 (1 95), notes, and corrects, one's first impression, namely, that it is "beside the mark" to add ἔξω to ἐξήγαγεν
[5] From the literal point of view no satisfactory explanation has ever been given (as far as I know) of Mk viii 24 "I see men (*or*, the men, *or* mankind) (τοὺς ἀνθρώπους), because I behold [people] as trees, walking (περιπατοῦντας)" But, if the story was applied mystically and typically as being an "opening of the eyes of man" for salvation, it would be natural to contrast it with the first "opening of the eyes of man," in Genesis, which followed close on his fall There, as here, a mention is made of "walking," the first Biblical instance of περιπατέω (Gen iii 8) But there it is God, not man, who "walks" And "the trees of the garden" are there mentioned merely as man's hiding-place Rashi testifies to the abundance of mystical interpretations

THE NEW LAW OF SACRIFICE

§ 6. *The Johannine healing of blindness*

In John's description of the healing of a blind man, "spitting" is mentioned as follows, "He spat on the ground and made clay from the spittle, and placed the clay thereof on the eyes[1]" Thus he avoids the Marcan expression, a somewhat repellent one, that Jesus spat, literally, "into the eyes of the blind man" The original phrase was also perhaps ambiguous, since "in (*or*, into) the eyes of" might be taken to mean "in the presence of," "face to face with," or "in front of[3]" It would therefore be possible, without much straining of the original tradition, to suppose that Jesus spat, not into the eyes of the blind man but straight forward on the ground. Then in describing the anointing with the spittle, it would

---

of this narrative, and Philo gives us a specimen of them There is no external evidence to shew that Mark's narrative, in its original form, contained allusions to Genesis, but internal evidence, and the omission of the narrative by Matthew and Luke, point to some early Marcan misunderstanding

[1] Jn ix 6 W H txt ἐπέθηκεν, marg ἐπέχρισεν The text varies greatly, SS has "formed clay from his spittle, and took [it] up [and] smeared [it] upon the eyes of that blind man " Nonnus says ἀνέρος ἔπλασεν ὄμμα τὸ μὴ φύσις εὗρεν ὀπάσσαι. ὀφθαλμοὺς τελέων νεοτευχέας, apparently meaning that the man, being born blind, had practically received from nature no eyes and that Jesus made eyes for him Chrysostom perhaps means something of the same kind when he says "the power that came forth from His mouth by itself both fashioned and opened (αὐτὴ καὶ διέπλασε καὶ ἀνέῳξε) the eyes "

[2] Deut xxv 9 "she shall spit *in his face*" is explained by Rashi as "*on the ground*," and by Breithaupt as "*before his face*, 1 e *on the ground*" Onk has באנפוהי, Walton "*in faciem ejus*," but Jer Targ. "she shall spit *before his face* (קדמוי) abundant spittle visible to the judges" Comp J *Jebam* xii g E, 13 *a* (Levy iv 436 *a*) where the judges say "The Jebama spat *before our faces* (קודמנא) spittle that was visible [to us] *on the ground*" *Hor Heb* on Jn ix 6 describes how R Meir, for a kind purpose, feigning an ailment in his eyes, said to a woman "Spit seven times *upon my eyes* " Levy iv 436*a* gives a version that has "speie *in mein Gesicht* (באנפי)", Levy i 113*a* says that באנפ with suffix means "*in the face of*" as in *Baba M* 86 *a* "he shut the door *in his face* "

489 (Mark viii 22—6)

THE NEW LAW OF SACRIFICE

naturally follow that the earth and the moisture were combined into what might be called "clay" No Jewish precedent appears to exist for anointing with such clay[1]; but having in view the fact that the Deuteronomic "spitting" which according to the Law was "spitting *in the face*," was interpreted by the Talmud as meaning "spitting *on the ground*," we may not unreasonably suppose that John was at all events right in substituting "the ground" for "the eyes"

When "the ground" had been thus substituted, other circumstances of the healing might naturally be modified so as to suit the change. Nonnus regards the manipulation of the clay as being of a creative nature, as if Jesus created new eyes for the blind man. But the meaning might be that Jesus closed up with clay even the sockets of the bodily eyes in order that the man might entirely give up the old before passing into the new[2].

It may be said that John, if he has Mark in view, finds no place for the partial and at first imperfect character of the Marcan act of healing. But that, though true, would not be an adequate statement of the fact from a Johannine point of view, which includes spiritual healing. Physically regarded, when the blind man, his eyes plastered up with clay, moves off to the waters of Siloam, he is just as he was before, only with his blindness proclaimed as it were on his face. There is no partial cure at any time Before he washes he is not

---

[1] None is alleged by *Hor Heb*, Wetstein, Schottgen, and Schlatter, on Jn ix 6

[2] *Introd* p 22 says "In the new-born proselyte, the old eye must be closed before the new one is opened, see Levy iv 154b quoting *Lev r.* (on Lev xii 2)." But Levy, interpreting "das Glied das im Mutterleibe geschlossen war" as "die Augen, Ohren u dgl.," goes rather beyond the text of *Lev r* which seems to refer to the mouth Philo i 92 dwells on the need of "concealing and destroying" the passions and says (*ib* 94) that the self-glorifying intellect must "die" if man is to escape the charge of "murder ($\phi\acute{o}\nu o s$)" The doctrine of "dying to oneself" in order to "live unto the Lord" is Pauline and based on Christ's own teaching

THE NEW LAW OF SACRIFICE

healed When he has washed he is healed and healed completely. The plastering cannot be confidently alleged to have produced any physical result It may have been a mere test of faith

Spiritually, however, there are two distinct stages. In the first, the man born blind is so far enlightened that he maintains, boldly and passionately, that his Healer is "a prophet" and "from God[1]." In the next stage, Jesus meets him after he has been cast out of the synagogue and asks him "Believest thou in the Son of man[2]?" The man does not know what this means, but is certain that he has but to know and he will believe· "Who is he, Lord, that I may believe on him?" When he knows, he at once believes and worships, and Jesus contrasts him with the Pharisees "For judgment came I into this world, that they that see not may see and that they that see may become blind[3]"

This accords with Christ's saying in Matthew and Luke about God's "hiding" truth from the wise and understanding while "revealing" it to babes[4], and with many passages in the Epistles to the same effect; and it is easy to understand that John would attach importance to a miracle of healing wrought on one born blind, who might seem to him a type of the Gentile world Still, it is startling to find this man described as "worshipping" Jesus—the only mention of actual "worship" in the Fourth Gospel, and the only Johannine instance of the word at all, apart from the worship of God repeatedly mentioned in the Dialogue with the Samaritan Woman and in the brief mention of "Greeks[5]"

---

[1] Jn ix 17, 33
[2] Jn ix 35 The reading "Son of Man" (not "Son of God") is confirmed by SS, see *Son* **3452**
[3] Jn ix 39
[4] Mt xi 25, Lk x 21
[5] Προσκυνέω, apart from Jn ix 28, occurs in iv 20—24 (nine times), and xii 20 "Greeks.. going up to *worship* at the feast."

THE NEW LAW OF SACRIFICE

Perhaps, among many traditions about the healing of blindness (beside the Marcan one under consideration) which John had in view in writing this story, there were some based on the prophecy of Isaiah concerning the twofold blindness of Israel —the blindness of the learned, to whom "the book" of revelation is "sealed," and that of the unlearned, who confess "I am not learned[1]" The context in Isaiah bears on our investigation. For these words of the prophet precede others quoted by Jesus about the "hypocrites" ("Well did Isaiah prophesy of you *hypocrites*[2]") Then follow, at a little interval, words predicting a better time, when "The deaf shall hear the words of the book, and the eyes of the blind shall *see out of obscurity and out of darkness*[3]" This last phrase was in early times variously interpreted as meaning either "see *darkness*," i e *see what was once dark now made light*, or "*see by passing out of darkness*[4]" Ibn Ezra, adopting the latter, says "Those blind men will not see *until they have already been in darkness*." Perhaps the Marcan story may be based on one that took the meaning to be "*see at first obscurely and then clearly*," and the Johannine on one that took the meaning to be "*see the light after passing through a phase of darkness made darker than before*"

These remarks do not concern themselves with the question whether, or how far, the Johannine narrative is unhistorical, or whether it is merely a version of the Marcan narrative. The object is to shew that there were probably many floating traditions about Christ's healing of blindness besides those mentioned in the Synoptic Gospels[5]. It is practically certain

---

[1] Is xxix 11—12
[2] Is xxix 13 quoted in Mk vii 6 foll , Mt xv 8 foll
[3] Is xxix 18
[4] See Jerome *ad loc* , who says that Aquila, Theodotion, and Symmachus translated it "*tenebras et caliginem* .*videbunt*, ut ostenderent gentium populo qui prius caecus erat, Christi Sacramenta pandenda ."
[5] The first mention of blindness in Mark is in viii 22 foll But

THE NEW LAW OF SACRIFICE

that the language of these stories would be affected in the earliest days of the Church by the language of the prophets, and especially Isaiah[1]. It is certain that Jesus had Isaiah in view when He attacked the blindness of the Pharisees, and probable that He had it in view when He healed blindness. These considerations, although they do not justify confident inferences about the precise results of Isaiah's influence in the Johannine narrative, confirm the conclusion that we have, in the healing of the man born blind, an instance of Johannine Intervention. John intervenes, in view of the Marcan miracle of healing blindness by spitting, to shew that the spitting was but a small detail in a similar miracle of a still more wonderful nature.

Inferring that the spitting was "on the ground" and that "clay" was thus compounded, John leads us to a further inference—natural for those who were familiar with the thought of God's creation of man out of the ground and with the language of Hebrew poets and prophets, "I also am formed out of the clay," "Thou art our father, we are the clay[2]." Christ's act is regarded, not as ameliorative, but as creative. The Psalmist said "Make anew in me a right spirit[3]." Jesus creates "a new eye"—for the man born blind, the representative of the Gentile world.

§ 7. "Prophet," "Son of Man," "Christ"

The parallel texts below shew that Matthew differs from Mark and Luke by representing Jesus as saying, not "I," but

---

Matthew mentions it as being healed at an earlier date, while John the Baptist was still in prison, Mt ix 27 foll., xi 5 (comp. Lk vii 21), and also xii 22 (τυφλὸν καὶ κωφόν), and xv 30—31. Then follows xx 30 δύο τυφλοί, parall. to Mk x 46 (Bartimaeus) (Lk xviii 35 τυφλός τις), and then xxi 14 ("blind and lame in the temple," pec. to Matthew).

[1] Strong's Concordance gives "blind" as occurring in Isaiah eleven times, as against four times in all the rest of the Prophets.

[2] Job xxxiii. 6, Is. lxiv 8 etc.

[3] Ps li 10, parall. to "*Create* in me a clean heart."

THE NEW LAW OF SACRIFICE

"the Son of Man," when He questions them about men's opinions concerning Himself[1]. Reasons have been given for

[1]

Mk viii 27—29 (R V)	Mt xvi 13—16 (R V)	Lk ix 18—20 (R V)
(27) And Jesus went forth, and his disciples, into the villages of Caesarea Philippi and in the way he asked his disciples, saying unto them, Who do men say that I am?	(13) Now when Jesus came into the parts of Caesarea Philippi, he asked his disciples, saying, Who do men say that the Son of man is? (*many anc auth* that I the Son of man am?)	(18) And it came to pass, as he was praying alone, the disciples were with him and he asked them, saying, Who do the multitudes say that I am?
(28) And they told him, saying, John the Baptist and others, Elijah, but others, One of the prophets	(14) And they said, Some [say] John the Baptist, some, Elijah and others, Jeremiah, or one of the prophets	(19) And they answering said, John the Baptist, but others [say] Elijah, and others, that one of the old prophets is risen again
(29) And he asked them, But who say ye that I am? Peter answereth and saith unto him, Thou art the Christ	(15) He saith unto them, But who say ye that I am? (16) And Simon Peter answered and said, Thou art the Christ, the Son of the living God	(20) And he said unto them, But who say ye that I am? And Peter answering said, The Christ of God.

Caesarea Philippi might be thought by readers of Mark to be called after the Philip (Herod Philip) previously mentioned in Mark (vi 17) But it was called after Philip the Tetrarch About a d 55 it was called Neronias (Madden p 116) and subsequently resumed its old name Paneas Luke (iii 1) mentions Philip the Tetrarch, but does not mention Herod Philip by name though referring to him in iii 19 "Herod the tetrarch, being reproved by him for Herodias his brother's [i e. Herod Philip's] wife " John abstains from these names—perhaps as being void of interest for his readers The only Philip that John mentions—eleven times as against once in each of the Synoptists—is the Apostle.

As regards Mk viii 27 "*in the way*," omitted by Matthew and Luke, we should note that it is used for "the way [of the Christians] " in Acts xix 23, "no small disturbance about *the Way*," xxiv 22 "having more exact knowledge about *the Way*," so that it might sometimes be used about Jesus leading His disciples on "*in the Way*," i e in the revelation of the Way of Life When Mark (alone) says that Bartimaeus (x 52) "followed Jesus *in the way*," it is very probable that there was a poetic play on the phrase "He was restored to sight and followed Jesus *in the Way [of Light]*" Mark also alone

THE NEW LAW OF SACRIFICE

believing that Matthew is right Jesus had deliberately called Himself "Son of Man" (or "Son of Adam," like Ezekiel) and wished to be known by that title, and not by that of "Prophet" But He used it, without defining it, always having in view the likeness suggested in Scripture between "the son of man" and God. We appear to have reached a turning point in Christ's use of the title, when, for the first time, after hearing the definitions of the multitudes, He asks the disciples to define it according to their own experience[1].

If this is so, it would seem that Jesus felt the multitudes to have done Him no honour, but on the contrary to have misunderstood Him, when they called Him the greatest of the Prophets, or the wonder-working Elijah It was not as a prophet nor as a wonder-worker that He desired to appeal to them It was as "the Man"—in Hebrew or Aramaic "the son of man," or perhaps "the son of Adam " The Man or the Son of Man was to be felt by them to be so divine as to be one with God, or with the Son of God Peter, in Mark, responds to the appeal by giving his Master a title distinguishing Him from all the prophets, "Thou art the Christ " This is amplified by Matthew as "the Christ, the Son of the living God," and by Luke as "the Christ of God "

Matthew and Luke seem to have deemed Mark to be abrupt and obscure And they seem right "The Christ," *i e.* "the Anointed," would mean little or nothing to most Gentiles unless one added something connecting the title with God This is not an instance where Luke omits anything that is in Mark Luke adds something. But as the addition is of the nature of an alteration we naturally ask what, if anything,

---

speaks of Bartimaeus as "*casting away* (ἀποβαλὼν)" *his cloak* Comp. Clem Rom § 35 "Let us *follow the Way of Truth having cast off* (ἀποῤῥίψαντες) from ourselves all unrighteousness ..." Hermas, who often uses Marcan expressions, speaks metaphorically of "coming to *the Way,*" and of "not abiding in *the Way,*" meaning "in the Christian Faith" (see *Vis* III 2 9 and III 7 1).

[1] See *Son* 3179—81.

THE NEW LAW OF SACRIFICE

John has to say, bearing on this addition (as also on Matthew's) when he represents Peter, or others, as making a confession similar to that in the Synoptists

What John says, in effect, is this: "To say, *Thou art the Christ* was, in itself, nothing All depended on the spirit in which the confession was made '*Christ*' is only a translation of the Aramaic '*Messiah*' About this matter, I have said something early in the Gospel, as soon as one of the disciples for the first time spoke concerning the Lord Jesus 'Andrew first findeth his own brother Simon and saith unto him, We have found the Messiah (which is, being interpreted, *Anointed*)[1].' Thus it has been seen that Andrew was the first disciple to call Jesus 'Messiah' and that Peter heard the title from his brother But Jesus pronounced no blessing on Andrew. Nor did He praise Nathanael, a little later, when Nathanael said, '*Thou art God's Son.*' On the contrary, the Lord implied that there was in store for Nathanael a higher revelation or vision not about the Son of God, but about the Son of Man, in which he would see *God's angels ascending and descending on the Son of man*[2]

"Wherein then consisted the special merit of Peter's Confession? In two respects First, in the things around Peter at the time The multitudes had failed to understand the sign given by the Lord Jesus to the Five Thousand They had called Him merely 'the prophet,' and they purposed to snatch Him away and 'make' Him 'king' His own disciples also had failed to understand His doctrine about the living Bread, and had mostly abandoned Him. Secondly, there was something special, or new, in Peter's own heart. Peter did

---

[1] Jn 1 41 "Anointed, $X\rho\iota\sigma\tau\acute{o}s$" John cannot interpret "anointed," because it is Greek already The Greek reader is supposed to know that *christos* means "anointed for a sacred or royal office" and not "anointed for secular purposes ($\dot{a}\lambda\eta\lambda\iota\mu\mu\acute{e}\nu os$)" See above, p 175, n 5, on the two kinds of anointing, and comp p 183

[2] Jn 1 51

not now think of Jesus as 'Messiah' in the same sense in which he accepted Him as 'Messiah' on the day when Andrew called Him by that title. Now he knew Jesus through experience, as his only hope in his search after truth ('Lord, to whom shall we go?') and as one from whose presence there breathed the very holiness of God Perhaps Peter actually said merely *Thou art the Messiah,* as Mark has handed down But in any case he meant more than the formal meaning of that title. He meant that Jesus was, to him, one who had the words of eternal life, not a saint, but the saint of saints, the Holy One of God In this form the confession will be such as may be understood by Greeks, and in this form it will be right for me to record it[1]."

Looked at in this way, Peter's confession is seen to be the result as it were of natural religion It is a kind of tribute to humanity and to its divine nature Christ came to be man, and to be loved as man, and by being loved thus, to attract His brethren, the sons of man, into the love of God the Father in heaven, in whose image man is made. This attraction may be illustrated by the progress or spiritual ascent of the man born blind The man's conviction about Jesus at first extends no further than this, "he is a prophet" Then he declares that Jesus must be "from God." Lastly, in answer to the appeal "Dost thou believe in the Son of man?" he replies "And who is he, Lord, that I may believe on him?" Then he "worships" Jesus[2].

---

[1] Jn vi 68—9 "Lord, to whom shall we go? Thou hast words of eternal life And we [firmly] believe and [assuredly] know that thou art the Holy One of God," on which see *Joh Gr* **2442—3**

[2] On Jn ix 35—6 and on the reading "Son of man" as preferable to "Son of God," see *Son* **3452—3**

THE NEW LAW OF SACRIFICE

§ 8 *"Get thee behind me, Satan," in Mark and Matthew*[1]

Although Mark does not say that Peter "worshipped" Jesus we perceive from the Three Gospels, in the light of the Fourth, that Peter had reached to a combination of love, trust, and awe, of such a nature as to constitute true worship Now therefore the time had come when Jesus deemed it right to set before Peter (and his companions) what Peter's confession meant. For it did not mean what Peter consciously thought it meant. He had said "Thou art the Messiah."

---

[1] Mk viii 30—33 (R V)

(30) And he charged them that they should tell no man of him

(31) And he began to teach them, that the Son of man must suffer many things, and be rejected by the elders, and the chief priests, and the scribes, and be killed, and after three days rise again

(32) And he spake the saying openly And Peter took him, and began to rebuke him.

(33) But he turning about, and seeing his disciples, rebuked Peter, and saith, Get thee behind me, Satan for thou mindest not the things of God, but the things of men

Mt xvi 20—23 (R V)

(20) Then charged he the disciples that they should tell no man that he was the Christ

(21) From that time began Jesus (*some anc auth* Jesus Christ) to shew unto his disciples, how that he must go unto Jerusalem, and suffer many things of the elders and chief priests and scribes, and be killed, and the third day be raised up

(22) And Peter took him, and began to rebuke him, saying, Be it far from thee (*or*, [God] have mercy on thee), Lord this shall never be unto thee

(23) But he turned, and said unto Peter, Get thee behind me, Satan thou art a stumbling-block unto me for thou mindest not the things of God, but the things of men

Lk ix 21—22 (R V)

(21) But he charged them, and commanded [them] to tell this to no man,

(22) Saying, The Son of man must suffer many things, and be rejected of the elders and chief priests and scribes, and be killed, and the third day be raised up.

THE NEW LAW OF SACRIFICE

But he had unconsciously meant "Thou art Thyself, whose saving helpfulness and sustenance to my soul I cannot express, but I try to express it by giving thee the name commonly bestowed on the Saviour of Israel"

But to Jesus the title implied, and had perhaps implied for some time, even before the execution of John the Baptist, a great deal more than this[1]. It implied suffering And Peter's Confession came to Him as a confirmation of a revelation from the Father that He, the Son, was to be the Sufferer: "Thou art the Suffering Servant of the Lord. Thou art the representative of the spiritual Israel, God's Firstborn, destined to be delivered up by the Father to humiliation and suffering for the sins of others, and not to rise out of them till an interval shall have elapsed according to the words of Hosea which speak of God as having 'smitten' Israel 'He *hath smitten* and he will bind us up After two days will he revive us, on the third day he will raise us up, and we shall live before him[2]'"

Here, the Hebrew for "smitten" is ambiguous[3] It is not surprising therefore if Mark, or Mark's original, in rendering

---

[1] The Epistle to the Hebrews appears to teach us that Jesus (Heb v 8) "learned," as time went on, things not revealed at first, namely, that He was to be "rejected" and "smitten." There is nothing to indicate that this anticipation of rejection was—and much to indicate that it was not—taught by Jesus, or definitely recognised by Jesus, at the beginning of His preaching

[2] Hos vi 1—2, "hath smitten," LXX πατάξει

[3] "Smite (πατάσσω)" is used by Jesus Himself (Mk xiv 27, Mt xxvi 31) (in quoting Zechariah (xiii 7)) "*I will smite* (Heb נכה 'smite,' LXX πατάξατε) the shepherd and the sheep shall be scattered" The Heb נכה (LXX diff) occurs also in Isaiah's prophecy about the Suffering Servant (liii 4) "Yet we esteemed him *smitten* by God" In both these passages it might naturally be interpreted as "smitten unto death," that is to say, "killed," and that is the rendering of the word nine times in LXX, and our Authorised Version renders it "*kill*" repeatedly where the Revised Version has "*smite*", but in some cases the latter, too, has "*kill*," as the sense often absolutely demands These facts are taken from *Son* **3198—9**, which see for detailed references

THE NEW LAW OF SACRIFICE

into Greek the prediction of Jesus based on Hosea and meaning "*shall be smitten,*" has paraphrased it as "*shall be killed*" Yet the context, "*he will bind us up,*" shews that the word did not in Hosea imply "killing"

The phrase in the three Synoptists, "suffer many things," appears to allude mainly to Isaiah's description of the Suffering Servant[1]. This is confirmed by the fact that Justin Martyr, in his Apology, after saying that Jesus "endured to *suffer,*" and appealing to his hearers to "hear the prophecies that relate to this," proceeds to quote nearly the whole of that description in Isaiah[2]

In this prediction of the Passion there is no deviation of Luke from Mark and therefore no call for Johannine Intervention[3]. But in what follows, Luke omits both the remonstrance made by Peter, and the rebuke addressed to Peter, "Get thee behind me, Satan." If John could not be proved to intervene here, the law of Johannine Intervention would conspicuously fail. Reasons can be given for believing that it does not fail Luke's omission, if his honesty, research, and accuracy are to be assumed, is to be explained on the supposition that the tradition about Peter and Satan is erroneous An error, very slight indeed, merely the disarrangement of one or two letters, appears to have resulted in substituting a rebuke for what was originally a warning, or an appeal. It was a moment when crowds of Christ's disciples were ceasing to follow Him, and " departing backward " to follow in the ways of the Ruler of this world If Jesus said to Peter, "Goest thou, too, behind [i e after] Satan?"—meaning "Art thou following (or,

---

[1] For the proof of this, see *Son* **3184—5**
[2] *Apol.* § 50, quoting Is liii 12, lii 13—15, liii. 1—8, comp. *Apol* § 51.
[3] John, of course, does in some sense intervene, but not as between Mark and Luke He intervenes to indicate that the Passion was a Glorification. Instead of "crucify" he says "lift up," and other expressions he alters in the same way See *Son*, Index "lift up"

500 (Mark viii 30—33)

THE NEW LAW OF SACRIFICE

Thou art following) Satan"?—this would be easily mistaken for "Go thou behind me, Satan."

In this misunderstood tradition, it would seem that John perceived "Satan" to mean "the ruler of this world," the spirit of worldliness, which, at a critical moment in Christ's career, was urging the multitudes—not without some support from Christ's own disciples, and especially Judas—to constrain Him to resort to arms in order to avenge the death of John the Baptist. In doing this, they were not "going after the Son of Man", they were "going after Satan." John suggests this in the context, though very indirectly. He represents Jesus as saying, in effect, to the Twelve, after Peter's loyal confession, "Ye are not all like Peter; he is following after me; but one of you, you the Twelve, you whom I myself have chosen—one of you is a servant of Satan[1]." It is highly probable that John is historically right in thus intervening, but it is more than probable that he does intervene.

§ 9. *Variations in the expression of the New Law*[2]

We have now reached the point where Jesus proclaims the

---

[1] Jn vi. 67, 71 *From Letter* **891** *b* and *Son* **3528** *b* give this explanation of Mk viii 33, Mt xvi 23. Also note that Mt. *ib* σκάνδαλον εἶ ἐμοῦ (Mk om) might contain some corruption of σκανδαλόω, a verb freq in Aquila The passive σκανδαλοῖ would mean "*thou art offended*"

[2]

Mk viii 34—ix 1 (R V)	Mt xvi 24—8 (R V)	Lk ix 23—7 (R V)
(34) And he called unto him the multitude with his disciples, and said unto them, If any man would come after me, let him deny himself, and take up his cross, and follow me	(24) Then said Jesus unto his disciples, If any man would come after me, let him deny himself, and take up his cross, and follow me	(23) And he said unto all, If any man would come after me, let him deny himself, and take up his cross daily, and follow me.
(35) For whosoever would save his life (*or*, soul) shall lose it, and whosoever shall lose his life (*or*, soul) for my sake	(25) For whosoever would save his life (*or*, soul) shall lose it and whosoever shall lose his life (*or*, soul) for my sake	(24) For whosoever would save his life (*or*, soul) shall lose it, but whosoever shall lose his life (*or*, soul) for my sake,

THE NEW LAW OF SACRIFICE

Law of the New Kingdom, the Law of the Gospel or Good Tidings of "great peace." The New Kingdom is the Kingdom in which there reigns, as king, not Satan the Adversary, but God the Father; and there obey, as subjects, not a horde of quarrelling competitors, but a family of concordant brothers; and the Law is not that of greedy or envious desire but that of brotherly love and zeal for the common welfare. That being

Mk viii 34—ix 1 (R V) *contd*	Mt. xvi 24—8 (R V) *contd*	Lk ix 23—7 (R.V) *contd*
and the gospel's shall save it	shall find it	the same shall save it
(36) For what doth it profit a man, to gain the whole world, and forfeit his life (*or*, soul)?	(26) For what shall a man be profited, if he shall gain the whole world, and forfeit his life (*or*, soul)? Or what shall a man give in exchange for his life (*or*, soul)?	(25) For what is a man profited, if he gain the whole world, and lose or forfeit his own self?
(37) For what should a man give in exchange for his life (*or*, soul)?		
(38) For whosoever shall be ashamed of me and of my words in this adulterous and sinful generation, the Son of man also shall be ashamed of him, when he cometh in the glory of his Father with (?) the holy angels*.	(27) For the Son of man shall come in the glory of his Father with his angels, and then shall he render unto every man according to his deeds (*lit* doing)	(26) For whosoever shall be ashamed of me and of my words, of him shall the Son of man be ashamed, when he cometh in his own glory, and [the glory] of the Father, and of the holy angels*
(ix 1) And he said unto them, Verily I say unto you, There be some here of them that stand [by], which shall in no wise taste of death, till they see the kingdom of God come with power	(28) Verily I say unto you, There be some of them that stand here, which shall in no wise taste of death, till they see the Son of man coming in his kingdom	(27) But I tell you of a truth, There be some of them that stand here, which shall in no wise taste of death, till they see the kingdom of God

In John, the doctrine about "losing" the soul by "loving" it, and "keeping" the soul by "hating" it, seems addressed to (xii 23) Andrew and Philip ("Jesus answereth them") but overheard by (*ib* 29) "the multitude." Comp Mk viii 34 "the multitude with his disciples," where Mt xvi 24 has "his disciples," and Lk. ix 23 "all"

---

* Mk τῶν ἀγγέλων τῶν ἁγίων, but Lk τῶν ἁγίων ἀγγέλων, see p 518

THE NEW LAW OF SACRIFICE

the case we might expect Jesus, when proclaiming this New Law, to announce it as one that brings peace under divine protection, according to the saying in Proverbs, "When a man's ways please the Lord he maketh even his enemies to be at peace with him[1]"

Epictetus represents his ideal philosopher as exclaiming—under the protection of a peace proclaimed, not by Caesar but by God—"Now no evil can befall me...all things are full of peace, full of untroubled calm In road or city, among crowds or neighbours or companions—nothing and no one can harm me[2]" And how, it might be asked, could a Christian fail to enjoy the same peace if he fulfilled the New Law, as set forth in the Sermon on the Mount? If a man "loves his enemies," how can he fail to be at "peace" with them, and much more with all the rest of the world?

Mark with peculiar frequency mentions that "gospel," or "good tidings," which Isaiah has taught us to connect with peace, yet in his own Gospel he hardly ever mentions the word "peace[3]" In Matthew, the opening of the Sermon on the Mount makes it clear to Christ's disciples that although they are to "love," they are to expect to be hated and persecuted; and Matthew places a benediction on *those persecuted in the past* before the benediction on those that are to be persecuted in the future[4]—as if to shew that such persecution is according

---

[1] Prov xvi 7 One of the many Jewish interpretations of this passage (see *Gen r* on Gen xxi 22, Wu p 257) declared that a man's "enemies" are in his own heart, his own evil tendencies Comp Origen on Ps cxix 157 "many are my persecutors," on which he quotes Mt v 10 "blessed are they that have been persecuted" and says "The [mention of] multitude hints at enemies visible and invisible . ."

[2] Epict iii 13 13

[3] Is lii 7 "good tidings. peace" Mark has εἰρήνη only in v 34 "go in *peace*" (but he has εἰρηνεύω in ix 50 "*be-at-peace* with one another")

[4] Mt v 10 "Blessed are those *that have been persecuted* because of righteousness, for theirs is the kingdom of heaven"—where

THE NEW LAW OF SACRIFICE

to precedent. "Princes," says the Psalmist, "have *persecuted* me without a cause...but thy law do I love...great *peace* have they that love thy law, and they have none occasion of stumbling[1]"

These words may explain the language of Jesus, proclaiming the New Law at a time when John the Baptist had recently been imprisoned and when the Pharisees, who had not raised a finger in the prophet's behalf, appeared to be preparing for Jesus a similar fate. Jesus was at "peace," and He desired all His disciples to be at "peace," and He sent to John a message of blessing for those who should find no occasion of stumbling[2] But it was "peace" internal and spiritual It rejected all servile bowing and bending to tyrannical kings and to tyrannical priests or scribes, even more absolutely and on higher grounds than did the "peace" of Epictetus; who was a friend to all, but a slave to none, and an inflexible foe to evil in every form. The peace promised in Proverbs was conditional.—"*When a man's ways please the Lord."* The same condition is recognised in Luke, "peace on earth among *men with whom* [God] *is well pleased*[3]." It was not possible that Jesus could patch up a "peace" with those Pharisees of His day with whom God was *not* "*well pleased*" They seemed to Him to be destroying the Temple of God, being the direct successors of those ancient prophets (spoken of by Ezekiel) who "daubed" the wall with untempered mortar "saying, 'Peace,' and there was no peace[4]."

Returning to Mark, and bearing in mind that he omits almost all the utterances in the Sermon on the Mount, we

---

A V "*they which are persecuted*" misses the meaning There is no parallel to this in Luke A partial parallelism is taken up in the next verse Mt v 11 "Blessed are ye when [men] shall revile you .," Lk vi 22 "Blessed are ye when men (οἱ ἄνθρωποι) shall hate you "

[1] Ps cxix 161—5
[2] Mt xi 6, Lk vii 23 ὃς ἂν (Lk ἐὰν) μὴ σκανδαλισθῇ ἐν ἐμοί
[3] Lk ii 14
[4] Ezek. xiii 10

THE NEW LAW OF SACRIFICE

ought to study with special care any Marcan sayings that appear to be equivalent to the blessing pronounced on the endurance of persecution—any that shew *how* a man is to fulfil the condition that his "ways" shall "please the Lord," so that, even in the face of "enemies," he may obtain the "peace" promised to those "with whom God is well pleased." Such a condition is expressed in Mark, first, negatively and obscurely ("let him deny himself"), then positively but, as we shall see, still very obscurely ("take up his cross"), then again positively ("follow me"). It is implied that those who thus "follow" Jesus must be ready to "lose" their life (*or*, soul) for His sake, but, while "losing" it in one form, they will "save" it in another form, wherein it is the most precious of all possessions.

Mark concludes with a prediction of Jesus about what the Son of Man, when He "comes" in glory, will do to those who have been "ashamed" of Him in this adulterous and sinful generation. He will be "ashamed" of them as they have been "ashamed" of Him. The meaning apparently is that He will say to those who have ignored or renounced or denied Him, that He also ignores or renounces or denies them. Such a "denial" is attributed to Jesus elsewhere by Matthew, and it is implied in the parallel Luke[1]. In the parallel to the present passage of Mark, Luke alone retains the statement that the Son of Man will "be ashamed," while Matthew—apparently softening down an expression that might repel some readers—paraphrases the words as meaning that those who sinned shall receive, by a *lex talionis*, a punishment proportioned to their offence[2]

---

[1] Mt x 33 ἀρνήσομαι, Lk xii 9 ἀπαρνηθήσεται. Comp Mt vii 23 "I never knew you," parall to Lk xiii 27 "I know not whence ye are."

[2] On Matthew's deviation, see *Son* 3211 foll where it is illustrated (3213) by the Targum which paraphrases Ps xviii 26 "*thou* [i e God] wilt *shew thyself froward* with the perverse" into "*thou didst cause the Egyptians who devised evil devices to be confounded in their own devices.*"

THE NEW LAW OF SACRIFICE

These variations of expression, which somewhat obscure the doctrine underlying them, must now be investigated, phrase by phrase. It will be found that under the phrases "denying oneself," "taking up the cross," "losing one's life," there is latent a doctrine inculcating the higher life, the life of the spirit as compared with that of the flesh, the life of Abraham the friend of God and man, as compared with that of Nimrod the rebel against God and hunter of the souls of men

§ 10 *"Denying oneself"*

The Greek Thesaurus gives several instances of "denying" in the sense of "declining"—or (perhaps better) "renouncing" —a practice or habit, and (in later Greek) a mother may be said to "deny," i e "renounce," a daughter, or a husband a wife[1]. But it gives no instance of "denying *oneself*." Hermas, who is a storehouse of Marcan phrases, contains abundant instances of Christians "denying the Lord," or "denying their own Law [i e the Law of the City of God in which they dwell]," or "denying their own Life [i.e. the Lord who is their life]"; but not (as far as I know) an instance of "denying oneself[2]"

Epictetus to a boastful sensualist, enslaved by his passions yet pretending to be a philosopher and free, addresses the

---

[1] Steph *Thes*, under ἀρνέομαι, quoting Nonnus *Dion* iv 36 Μῆτερ . τεὴν ἠρνήσαο κούρην, and other passages

[2] Harnack's Index gives none I have not tested all those in Goodspeed For "denying" Law or Life, see Hermas *Sim.* 1 5, viii 3 7, *Vis* ii 2 7 Denying, in the sense of ignoring or renouncing persons, is (in effect) imputed in the Song of Moses to Levi (Deut xxxiii 9) "Who said of his father and of his mother, 'I have not seen him', neither did he acknowledge his brethren, nor knew he his own children" Philo allegorizes this, so that Levi "kills," not his "brethren," but "the body that is 'brother' to the soul" (1 559) καὶ κτείνει ἕκαστος ἀδελφὸν.. ἀδελφὸν μὲν ψυχῆς τὸ σῶμα, i e. "mortifies" the body Comp *ib* 1 367 (also on Deut) "separated from the pleasures that are according to the 'brother' body (ἀπηλλαγμένος τῶν κατὰ τὸ ἀδελφὸν σῶμα ἡδονῶν)"

THE NEW LAW OF SACRIFICE

following rebuke "Speak the truth, slave, and do not play the runaway from your masters, and *deny* [*them*][1]" And Hermas says, "If the Gentiles punish their slaves when one *denies his master*, what (think you) will the Master do to you?[2]" Jesus assumes that man will serve one of two Masters, God and Mammon, and cannot serve both[3] In Scripture, God is the One Husband and Lord of Israel The forms of Mammon may be represented by the false gods sought after by Israel when the nation fell into that idolatry which their prophets regarded as adultery, but in fact they are forms of the lower Self rebelling against the higher Hence Philo says concerning Adam and Eve, when they ran away from God and hid themselves in the trees after the Serpent had misled them, "He that runs away from God flees into himself[4]" That is to say, he runs away from the freedom of serving the righteous Father of all, into the slavery of serving demons, his own unrighteous and selfish desires[5] Later on, Philo presents us a contrast in Abraham, whose mind is led out from slavery to freedom, making its way out, as the free mind must, from all the constraints and shackles of the fleshly nature, until finally it passes even "out of itself[6]"

§ 11 "*Taking up the cross*" *and* "*following*"

At this point we come to a Synoptic expression, avoided by John, which does not seem capable of being explained from Jewish thought and expression alone If we look beneath the Synoptic expression we may see the Jewish thought, but not otherwise An original Jewish tradition about "*taking up the*

---

[1] Epict iv 1 146 ἀπαρνοῦ
[2] Hermas *Sim* ix 28. 8
[3] Mt vi 24, Lk xvi 13
[4] Philo 1 93 ὁ γὰρ ἀποδιδράσκων θεὸν καταφεύγει εἰς ἑαυτόν.
[5] Comp Rom vi 16
[6] Philo 1 95 χρὴ γὰρ τὸν μέλλοντα νοῦν ἐξάγεσθαι . ὑπεκστῆναι... τὰ τελευταῖα καὶ ἑαυτοῦ

THE NEW LAW OF SACRIFICE

yoke" appears to have been transmuted into a Greek tradition about *"taking up the cross."* How this may have taken place has been explained in previous parts of *Diatessarica*[1].

Reasons have been there given for believing that the "cross" here mentioned was originally "the cross-piece of the yoke," and that it represented "the yoke of the Lord" as compared with "the yoke of this world," or of Mammon, or of the flesh. The Targum on Lamentations, "It is good for a man that he bear *the yoke* in his youth," explains the meaning to be *"the yoke of the precepts,"* and then adds as a paraphrase of the next verse, "He will sit alone and be silent and will bear the chastisements that befall him, *for the sake of the unity of the Name of God* ...[2]" As a fact, "chastisements" befell Christians in the same way *"for the sake of the Name"* of Christ the Crucified. *"The yoke of Christ"* was the symbol not only of allegiance to the Crucified, but also of a willingness to share in His sufferings, and even (if need arose, as in the case of Peter, who is related to have been crucified) in His Cross itself. It was therefore very natural that "the yoke" should be transmuted into "the cross."

Yet, owing to the transmutation, there arose a danger of missing one aspect of the meaning that comes out more clearly in the Jewish metaphorical contrast between the yoke of the ruler of this world and the yoke of the Kingdom of God. "If any one desires to come after me as my follower, let him *renounce the yoke of sin, the yoke of his own fleshly nature*, and let him take on himself the yoke that I bear, *the yoke of the New Law, the yoke of filial service to the Father in heaven* and of brotherly service to His children on earth."

In this sense, a Christian is called on to take up his cross

---

[1] See *From Letter* **928** (1)—(x) and *Notes* **2842**—9 for the reasons for the disuse of such traditions as Mt xi 29 "Take my yoke upon you," which represented Christ's fundamental doctrine

[2] Lam iii 27—8 It is added that the chastisements in this world are sent to spare the sufferer chastisements in the next world.

THE NEW LAW OF SACRIFICE

"*daily*," and Luke is justified in inserting the word. But, even with that insertion, there is some danger of misunderstanding "the cross" by separating it from the thought of service to men in the name of the Lord Jesus, and by taking it to mean mere suffering—"putting oneself in the way of persecution," or "imperilling one's life," or "subjecting oneself to hardship or discomfort." It is perhaps in allusion to Christian action (based on such a misunderstanding) that Epictetus warns his disciples to make up their minds which of two courses they will take, when standing before a judge's tribunal. If they decide to be silent, or to defy the judge, let them be prepared for the consequences "For if you have a mind to be crucified, only wait [silently for it] and the cross will come." If they decide to plead for their lives, let them do it in a manner consistent with a philosopher's self-respect[1].

John never mentions "yoke" and never speaks of "taking up the cross" as a duty imposed on Christ's followers. In the only passage where he mentions "cross" he uses it literally, though perhaps there is a symbolism in the first mention of it: "They therefore received Jesus [from Pilate], and he, *carrying the cross for himself*, went forth unto the place called The place of a skull[2]." Yet the *thoughts* of "cross" and "yoke" both find a place in his Gospel. The "cross" implies persecution and tribulation, and Jesus says "If they have persecuted me they will also persecute you," and "The hour cometh that every one that killeth you will think that he offereth service to God,"

---

[1] Epict. ii 2 20 This is the only mention of "cross" in Epictetus See Ign *Rom* § 4 for illustrations of the passion for martyrdom, "Let me be given to the wild beasts," "Entice the wild beasts that they may become my sepulchre"

[2] Jn xix 17 βαστάζων αὐτῷ τὸν σταυρὸν .. On this, see *Joh Voc.* 1792 *b* "Cross" is repeated, literally, in *ib* 19, 25, 31. Comp. Heb xiii 11—13 "without the camp Wherefore also Jesus.. suffered without the gate Let us therefore go forth unto him without the camp, *bearing his reproach*"

THE NEW LAW OF SACRIFICE

and, "In the world ye have tribulation, but be of good cheer, I have gained the victory over the world[1]"

Again the "yoke" implies service. And Christ's "yoke" implies willing service. It may be called that of a *doulos*, *i e* "bondservant" or "slave"—provided that the slave is willing. But it is more appropriately called that of a *diaconos*, *i e* "minister." Such a service, implying a sacrifice of one's own will or comfort to the welfare of others, is dramatized in the scene where Jesus washes the feet of the disciples. But the preparation for that scene comes a little earlier, just after Jesus has proclaimed "The hour is come that the Son of man should be glorified." How is He to be "glorified"? The answer is, "By losing His life in order to gain it," or, in the words of the Gospel, "Except a grain of wheat fall into the earth and die, it abideth by itself alone; but, if it die, it beareth much fruit. He that loveth his soul [*i e* life in the flesh] loseth it [*i e* life in the spirit], and he that hateth his soul in this world shall keep it unto life eternal. If any man [be minded to] be ministering unto me, let him follow me, and where I am, there shall also my minister be. If any man be ministering unto me, him will my Father honour[2]."

Here all the Synoptic thoughts are expressed in Johannine words as being fulfilments of the Law of life through death, the death of the lower principle preparing for the life of the higher. "Denying oneself" is expressed by "hating the soul in this world", "taking up the cross" (on the supposition that "cross" means "the yoke of service") is expressed by "ministering unto me." "Following" Jesus is partially defined—or at all events partially explained as being metaphorical not literal—by the context, which adds "where I am, there shall my minister be." But the Evangelist reserves a further doctrine about "following Jesus" for the conclusion of his Gospel. There we are shewn how the beloved disciple and Peter, each

---

[1] Jn xv. 20, xvi. 2, 33.   [2] Jn xii 23—6.

(Mark viii 34—ix 1)

THE NEW LAW OF SACRIFICE

in his appointed path, may "follow" Jesus Peter follows literally, on the path of the cross, the beloved disciple not literally, but spiritually—"following" and yet perhaps "tarrying" till the coming of the Lord[1]

§ 12 *"For my sake and the gospel's," in Mark*[2]

Matthew and Luke omit *"and the gospel's,"* and the omission gives force to the language if it is to be regarded as an expression of personal loyalty But it should be noted that in the later context, Mark has "Whosoever shall be ashamed of me *and of my words*" (not "of me" alone); and there, though Matthew deviates, Luke exactly follows Mark Also, in Mark here, several authorities have *"for the sake of the gospel,* or *my gospel"* (without *"for my sake"*)[3] Origen, too, has *"for the sake of the gospel"* (without *"for my sake"*) in a passage where he expressly quotes Mark by name at full length after quoting

---

[1] Jn xxi 19—23
[2] Mk viii 35 W H txt ἕνεκεν [ἐμοῦ καὶ] τοῦ εὐαγγελίου. Several authorities omit either ἐμοῦ καὶ or καὶ τοῦ εὐαγγελίου SS has "because of my gospel" In martyrological phrases variations might be expected to spring up in the days when martyrdom was common. For example, in a comment on Mt v 10 "Blessed are they that have been persecuted for the sake of righteousness, for theirs is the kingdom of heaven," Clem Alex 581—2 first (1) quotes rightly except that he substitutes "shall be called sons of God" for "theirs is the kingdom of heaven," μακάριοι οἱ δεδιωγμένοι ἕνεκεν τῆς δικαιοσύνης, ὅτι αὐτοὶ υἱοὶ θεοῦ κληθήσονται Then he adds (ἢ, ὥς τινες τῶν μετατιθέντων τὰ εὐαγγέλια) as variants, (2) δεδιωγμένοι ὑπὸ τῆς δικαιοσύνης, "persecuted [or (?) pursued, and taken] *by righteousness"* (comp Phil iii 12) *"for they shall be perfect,"* and (3) "persecuted *on account of me,* for they shall have a place where they shall not be persecuted" In Hermas, the endurance of persecution is freq. expressed by "suffer (πάσχω)" *"on account of* (εἵνεκα, διά, ὑπέρ)" *"the Name* (ὄνομα)"—used absolutely or with *"of the Lord,"* "of the Son of God" etc (See Resch *Paralleltexte* on Mt v 10) Perhaps there would be a tendency to drop the use of *"gospel"* in such phrases as these, where it has a quasi-personification, when the word came to be generally used to mean "a *written Gospel* "
[3] D and the best Latin MSS om. "me."

Matthew and Luke[1]. This, then, is a case that perhaps calls for Johannine Intervention. That is to say, we might expect to find somewhere in John a distinction drawn between Jesus Himself, and—not indeed "the gospel," a word that John never uses, but—the message of the Gospel, the essence and spirit of its vivifying and cleansing truth.

One aspect of such a distinction will be found immediately before the Washing of Feet, and a little after the exposition of the service of "ministering" as being the means of "keeping" the soul. It contains the last words of Christ's public doctrine "If any man hear *my sayings* and keep them not, I (*emph*.) judge him not...*the word* that I spake—*that will judge him in the last day*[2]." But a much more important aspect is that presented to us in the Johannine "Paraclete." This does indeed convict the world, but has for its main work the guidance and strengthening of the disciples, dwelling in their hearts as Christ's Other Self. John helps us to feel—though he does not expressly say—that as we can "grieve" this holy Spirit[3] and "rebel" against it, so also we can be, and should be, loyal to it and willing to "lose life" for its sake.

§ 13. *"For what could a man give in exchange for his soul?" in Mark and Matthew*[4]

The fact that Luke omits these words obliges us to ask whether there is any Johannine equivalent. But we have first to ask their precise meaning and Luke's (possible or probable) reasons for omitting them.

The Marcan word for "a thing given in exchange" is used by Euripides, "The crowd is an absurd *substitute* for the sterling friend," and Ben Sira (LXX), "There is no *substitute* for a

---

[1] Origen *Exhort. ad Mart.* § 12.
[2] Jn xii 47—8.
[3] Comp. Is lxiii 9—10 "In all their affliction he was afflicted... But they rebelled, and grieved his holy spirit."
[4] Mk viii 37, Mt xvi 26 ἀντάλλαγμα

THE NEW LAW OF SACRIFICE

disciplined soul[1]." It is the "equivalent," in money or kind, given in exchange for anything[2] "If a man has lost his soul, has he another soul to give to the captor as an equivalent so as to buy it back again?"—this question Chrysostom finds in Matthew and answers with a negative[3]. Origen puts the case rather differently: "But having once for all lost his own soul ...a man will not be able to give an *equivalent* for the soul that is perishing (*lit.* in the condition of being lost). For the [soul] fashioned according to the image of God is more precious than all things. There is only One who has been able to give an *equivalent* for our formerly *perishing* soul—He that bought us with His own precious blood[4]." This gives to Mark's word a meaning that approaches "ransom," and a form of the word is used in a parallel to "ransom" in the Epistle to Diognetus[5].

Thus interpreted, Mark's words contain a warning against the attractive yoke of Mammon, the ruler of this world—that selfish greediness which Paul calls idolatry[6]. If a man sells his soul to this Master, how will he buy it back again? What is the price, equivalent and effectual for such a purpose[7]?

---

[1] Eurip *Orest* 1156—7 ἀλόγιστον δέ τι Τὸ πλῆθος ἀντάλλαγμα γενναίου φίλου, where τι seems to apologize ("so to speak") for the strangeness of the epithet, which perhaps plays on two meanings, (1) "not worth reckoning," (2) "absurd" (but ? ὀλιγοστὸν or ὀλίγιστον), Sir xxvi 14 οὐκ ἔστιν ἀντάλλαγμα πεπαιδευμένης ψυχῆς.

[2] See *Oxf Conc* ἄλλαγμα and ἀντάλλαγμα, to which add that in Sir. xliv 17 ἀντάλλαγμα = תחליף

[3] Chrys on Mt xvi 26 *ed.* Field vol ii p 126

[4] Origen *Exhort ad Mart* § 12 ἅπαξ δὲ ἀπολέσας τις τὴν ἑαυτοῦ ψυχήν, ἢ ζημιωθεὶς αὐτήν, κἂν τὸν ὅλον κερδήσῃ κόσμον, οὐ δυνήσεται αὐτὸν δοῦναι ἀντάλλαγμα τῆς ἀπολλυμένης ψυχῆς 'Η γὰρ κατ' εἰκόνα θεοῦ δεδημιουργημένη, τιμιωτέρα ἐστὶ πάντων Εἷς μόνος δεδύνηται δοῦναι ἀντάλλαγμα τῆς ἀπολλυμένης πρότερον ψυχῆς ἡμῶν, ὁ ὠνησάμενος ἡμᾶς τῷ ἑαυτοῦ τιμίῳ αἵματι (1 Pet 1 19)

[5] *Epist. ad Diognet.* ix. 2—5 Αὐτὸς τὸν ἴδιον υἱὸν ἀπέδοτο λύτρον ὑπὲρ ἡμῶν...ὦ τῆς γλυκείας ἀνταλλαγῆς

[6] Coloss iii 5.

[7] Comp Rom vii 14—24 "But I am a creature of flesh (σάρκινος) sold under sin...who shall deliver me out of this body of death?"

THE NEW LAW OF SACRIFICE

If we ask why Luke omitted the words, a partial answer may be found in the obscurity of the context in Mark and Matthew, where they speak of "*being mulcted in his own soul*[1]." It may not have seemed clear to Luke that "*soul*" here meant "soul in the higher sense." Luke at all events substitutes "*himself*," meaning "*his true self*," and adds "having lost (*or*, destroyed)" to "being mulcted," in order to keep up the connection with what precedes ("*losing* the soul") and also to shew the active culpability of the "*loser* (or, *destroyer*)." Luke may also have had some other motive. For elsewhere, in a parallel to a Mark-and-Matthew tradition that Jesus "came to give his soul as a ransom for many[2]," Luke omits these words. Now we have seen above, from Origen, that the Marcan phrase "in exchange" naturally suggests thoughts about "ransom of the soul." Perhaps Luke may have argued that there was some inconsistency (at all events on the surface) in two traditions one of which said, in effect, that there was *no* ransom, and another, that there *was* a ransom. More probably Luke declined to record doctrine about so deep a subject in language so brief as to leave loop-holes for errors or perversions[3].

---

[1] Mk viii. 36 ζημιωθῆναι τὴν ψυχὴν αὐτοῦ, Mt. xvi 26 τὴν δὲ ψυχὴν αὐτοῦ ζημιωθῇ, Lk ix 25 ἑαυτὸν δὲ ἀπολέσας ἢ ζημιωθείς. Comp Philo ii 649 μεῖζον ἀνθρώπῳ κακὸν ἀφροσύνης οὐδέν ἐστι...τὸν νοῦν ζημιωθέντι.

[2] Mk x. 45, Mt xx. 28. Luke, in his introduction to this narrative, mentions vaguely (xxii 24) "a contention among them" where Mark and Matthew mention severally "indignation" concerning "James and John" or "the two brothers." Then he (*ib* 25—6) at first follows Mk-Mt. as to Christ's words But he breaks away (*ib* 27) at their conclusion. No doubt Luke followed, and did not invent, a different version of the narrative. But that need not have prevented him from inserting such an important saying as that about "ransom," in some other part of his Gospel—if he believed that it was uttered on some occasion, though not on the one described by Mark.

[3] Jerome, on Mt xvi. 26, says that the "equivalent (commutatio)" for Israel is (Is. xliii. 3) Egypt and Ethiopia, but, for man's soul, "Illa sola est *retributio* quam Psalmista canit 'Quid *retribuam*...? Calicem salutis accipiam (Ps. cxvi 12—13)...'" Jerome's comment

(Mark viii. 34—ix. 1)

THE NEW LAW OF SACRIFICE

John, although he nowhere mentions "ransom" or "equivalent," brings the thought before his readers in several ways First, he represents Jesus as Himself saying "Whence shall we *buy* bread that these may eat?"—mystically implying that Christ "*buys*" life for His disciples[1]. Secondly, in the Good Shepherd, he shews us Jesus "laying down life" for the sheep in conflict with the wolf—which implies ransom in a certain sense, and yet no compromise, but victory over the enemy[2]. Also, John repeatedly represents the disciples as being "in" the Son, so that they must share in His sufferings and in His glory. In his Gospel, Jesus does not indeed expressly say, with Pauline metaphor, "I am the body of which you are the limbs, so that I take your imperfect life into myself and give you my life in its place as the *equivalent*"; but He does express the Johannine aspect of this truth when He says "*I am the vine*, ye are the branches[3]."

§ 14. "*In this adulterous...generation,*" in Mark[4]

Luke omits these words, probably for the same reason for which he omits "adulterous" elsewhere[5], namely, that

---

on the Psalm says "*calicem* passionis martyrium esse," quoting "Pater, si possibile est, transeat iste *calix* a me"

As an instance of difficulties attending the use of "equivalent," see Sir xliv 17 "In a season of destruction he [i e. Noah] became the *equivalent*, or *successor* (תחליף) (ἀντάλλαγμα)"—i e he became the substitute, successor, representative, and remnant, of perished humanity—where Syr has (Walton) "mundi vicarius (חלפתא לעלמא)."

[1] Jn vi 5   See Chapter VIII § 18
[2] Jn x 15—18.   [3] Jn xv 5
[4] Mk viii. 38, om. in parall Lk ix. 26   The parall. Mt xvi. 27 paraphrases the whole sentence

[5] Mk viii 12	Mt. xvi 4 (rep xii 39)	Lk. xi. 29
Why doth this generation seek a sign? verily I say unto you, There shall no sign be given unto this generation.	An evil and adulterous generation seeketh after a sign; and there shall no sign be given unto it, but the sign of Jonah.	This generation is an evil generation it seeketh after a sign, and there shall no sign be given to it but the sign of Jonah

THE NEW LAW OF SACRIFICE

"adulterous" might be misunderstood by Greeks in such a context. "Adulterous," in the Prophets, meant that the generation was unfaithful to Jehovah and followed after false gods. Jesus declared that "this generation" had, as Jeremiah says, "broken the yoke" of the Lord, the yoke of freedom and wedlock[1]. They had gone back to the yoke of slavery to the flesh, the yoke of Egypt, concerning which the Lord had said to Israel "I am the Lord your God, who brought you forth out of the land of Egypt...and I have *broken the bars of your yoke* and made you go upright[2]."

John does not use the word "adulterous," but he takes pains to shew Greek readers the meaning of the term in a dialogue bearing on freedom. In reply to Christ's promise to make them "free" the Jews say "We be Abraham's seed and have never yet been in bondage to any man how sayest thou, ' Ye shall be made free'?" Hereon Jesus shews them that a man may be "the bondservant of sin" Afterwards He contrasts their conduct in seeking to kill Him with that of Abraham, as shewing that they are not truly Abraham's children or God's children. The Jews protest "We were not *born of fornication*; we have one Father, [even] God" Jesus replies, "If God were your Father, ye would love me," and finally says "Ye are of [your] father the devil[3]."

"Abraham" comes in again when Jesus says that the first of the Fathers of Israel exulted in the vision of His "day[4]." The "day"—as is shewn by the whole dialogue—means the triumph of humanity over inhumanity. That means a reign

---

[1] Jerem v 5 The context indicates spiritual as well as literal adultery

[2] Lev xxvi. 13 It might be objected that "going upright" is incompatible with the bearing of *any* "yoke," even that of the Lord But that is not the view taken by the Hebrew prophets of that service of the Lord which is perfect freedom In Jerem. v. 5, "broken the yoke" is paraphrased by the Targumist "revolted from the Law" Comp Jas 1 25 "the law of liberty."

[3] Jn viii. 32—44   [4] Jn viii. 56

THE NEW LAW OF SACRIFICE

of filial and brotherly love Such a triumph also implies the supersession of constrained obedience to Law by willing obedience to a Father's will. That is "freedom."

In *Johannine Grammar*[1] it was maintained that "man" is emphatic in the sentence "Ye seek to kill me, a *man*, [one] that told you the truth" The foregoing considerations rather favour that view They indicate that Jesus regarded Himself as "man," or "son of man," standing up for humanity against inhumanity or non-humanity, and they explain the importance Jesus attached to the personality of Abraham, as being the harbinger or promise of that Spirit of Humanity which He felt to be identified with Himself, and which was to result in the triumph of the Son of Man at the right hand of the Father[2].

The Law said "Honour thy father." Jesus, in the Fourth Gospel, calling Himself Son of Man, is regarded mystically as the Son of divine Humanity, the eternal, and only begotten Son of that God who has revealed Himself as Father to mankind, whom He created in His own image and destined to be conformed to His own likeness Believing that God Himself was, in the highest sense of the word, *humane*, and that humanity (rather than power or wisdom) was His most divine attribute, Jesus felt that in honouring human beings—provided that they were *humane*, even though very degraded specimens of humanity —He was honouring the Father. This the Pharisees could not understand because they did not understand man's divine nature. They attempted to exalt God ("give glory to God") by lowering His Son, "this man" ("we know that *this man* is a sinner[3]") —an attempt that Jesus had previously described in the words "I honour my Father and ye dishonour me[4]." It is not for nothing that Jesus, speaking of the evidence resulting from the combined action of the Father and the Son, illustrates it by saying "The testimony of *two human-beings* is true. I am he

---

[1] *Joh Gr* **2412** *a* [2] See *Son* **3216** *d—f*
[3] Jn ix 24 "this man (οὗτος ὁ ἄνθρωπος)," emphatic
[4] Jn viii. 49.

THE NEW LAW OF SACRIFICE

that beareth witness of myself, and the Father that sent me beareth witness of me[1]" The great fault of the Jewish "rulers" and scribes in Christ's time was that they were not humane, and their study of the Law merely hardened their inhumanity.

§ 15. *"With the angels that are holy," in Mark*[2]

This passage has been previously discussed, and the following conclusions have been reached[3]. Mark's original had *"with the holy ones"* or *"saints,"* that is, as the Epistle to the Hebrews says, "the spirits of righteous men made perfect[4]." This was taken by Mark to mean *"angels,"* and he conflated it in the phrase, *"the angels that are holy,"* meaning emphatically the angels that are of light, not of darkness[5]. Matthew expressed the same thing in the phrase "with *his* [i.e. *God's*] *angels.*" Luke adopted Mark's conflation, but with a slight alteration so as to take away the emphasis that suggested contrast. He has, not *"the angels that are holy,"* but simply *"the holy angels"* (a title of respect rather than of distinctive definition). The Revised Version (see p. 502) conceals this difference.

These conclusions were supported by collections of facts bearing on the Biblical use of the terms "holy [ones]" and

---

[1] Jn viii 17—18 See *Son* **3450** *a* on the emphasis created by inserting ἄνθρωποι, not meaning "men of special distinction (ἄνδρες)," but of "human beings" "Men" is not in the Hebrew or the Greek of the original (Deut xvii 6, comp Deut xix 15)

[2] Mk viii 38, comp Mt xvi 27 Lk ix 26 [3] *Son* **3220** foll

[4] See Heb xii 22—4, which mentions, in the following order, (1) "Mount Zion and the City of the living God, the heavenly Jerusalem," (2) "the full assembly of myriads of angels," (3) "the Church of the firstborn that are enrolled in the heavens," (4) "God the Judge of all," (5) *"the spirits of righteous* [*men*] *who have been perfected* (πνεύμασι δικαίων τετελειωμένων)," (6) "Jesus the mediator of a new covenant," (7) "the blood of sprinkling .. " It would seem that some of these categories might overlap one another

[5] On the rareness of the reduplicated article (τῶν ἀγγέλων τῶν ἁγίων) in the Synoptists, except in a few special phrases, see *Joh Gr.* **1983** In Barnabas, the only instance of "*angels*" pl is § 18 "*angels* of God...*angels* of Satan"

THE NEW LAW OF SACRIFICE

"angels" It was also pointed out that Paul regarded the "holy ones," or "saints," as destined to be assessors with Christ in the Last Judgment In that assessorship saints seem more appropriate than angels. Those who accept the Incarnation will recognise the reasonableness of the Christian belief that the Son assumed flesh in order that He might be subjected to the temptations of the flesh, and thus might be fitted to judge men as well as to help them. The same thing is true of saints. But it is not true of angels if they are regarded as beings that have never been tempted.

The Fourth Gospel, at all events, implies that judgment was committed to the Son of Man *because He was "the Son of Man,"* and therefore able to sympathize with, and make allowance for, men's infirmities[1]. Unless therefore Mark's original here mentioned "holy ones," there would seem to be an omission of something, if not essential, at all events contributive to the fairness and fulness of any judgment implied in the coming of the Son of Man But on the other hand if Mark's original spoke of the Son as coming "in glory" and "with holy ones," then we see how this prepares for the mention (in the next verse) of a foretaste of the "coming" for some "standing here," who "shall not taste death till they see the kingdom of God having come in power " This foretaste all the Synoptists appear to discern in the Transfiguration. And here Jesus appeared in glory with Moses and Elijah, who are called by Luke emphatically "two *men* (viri)"—as being the fit representatives of the preparatory testimony of Israel, testifying to the One God through the Law and the Prophets[2].

---

[1] Jn v 22—7
[2] Mk ix 4, Mt xvii 3 In Lk. ix 30 ἄνδρες δύο suggests the question whether we are to contrast it with the δύο ἄνθρωποι, above (pp 517–18) mentioned in Jn Is Luke, as well as John, thinking of the Law of Evidence in Deut xvii 6 (xix 15) "at the mouth of two witnesses"? If so, we must suppose that the two Evangelists regard the "witnesses" from different points of view Luke regards them as ἄνδρες, "men of repute, famous and credible", John regards

THE NEW LAW OF SACRIFICE

According to Matthew, Jesus spoke about "the angels of the little ones in heaven" as always beholding the face of the Father[1]. According to all the Synoptists, Jesus said that the righteous, in the Resurrection, are "*as angels in the heavens*," or are "*fellows-with-angels*," and "*sons of God*," being "*sons of the resurrection*[2]." Language like this points, not to such conceptions as Michael or Raphael, but to what we may call human angels, "the spirits of righteous men made perfect[3]." And these appear to be contemplated here in the Marcan tradition about the coming of the Son of Man[4]

What, if any, is the Johannine equivalent of an assessorship of "saints," taking part in the judgment pronounced by the Son of Man on the sinful world? It is difficult to answer without appearing to be fanciful—so completely does the Fourth Gospel depart from the popular conception of a judge sitting in judgment We cannot say that John departs from Mark, for Mark never mentions the word "judge"—nor "judgment" either, except as to the abundant "judgment," or "condemnation," which will be received by the Pharisees[5] But we can

---

them as "human beings," i e types or images of the divine Nature in the likeness of which God created man

[1] Mt xviii 10
[2] Mk xii 25, Mt xxii 30 ὡς ἄγγελοι, but Lk xx 36 ἰσάγγελοι... καὶ υἱοί εἰσιν θεοῦ, τῆς ἀναστάσεως υἱοὶ ὄντες.
[3] Heb xii 23
[4] To the facts collected in *Son* **3220** foll add that Clem Rom frequently mentions "angels" in the pl, but mostly in quotations from O T or from the Epistle to the Hebrews On one occasion (§ 39) he mentions "*holy angels*," quoting from LXX of Job v 1 "To which of the *holy ones* (or, *saints*) wilt thou turn?" but LXX εἴ τινα ἀγγέλων ἁγίων ὄψῃ (v r ἁγίων ἀγγέλων, and so Clem ἁγίων ἀγγέλων) Here we find, in fact, all that was put forward (in the above-mentioned four conjectures) about Mk viii. 38 1st, the original has "*holy ones*"; 2nd, this was taken to mean "*angels*", 3rd, it was conflated as "*holy angels*," a phrase occurring nowhere (*Son* **3219**) in O T, 4th, the MSS vary, as Mk and Lk. vary, in the order of "*holy*" and "*angels*"
[5] Mk xii 40

THE NEW LAW OF SACRIFICE

say that John departs from the tradition of Matthew and Luke that the Twelve shall "sit on thrones judging the Twelve Tribes of Israel[1]." Nowhere does the Fourth Gospel verbally favour such an exaltation of the Twelve, or of any human beings, into a position of judicial authority.

Yet, if we look beneath the words to the thoughts, we shall find that John does imply, or assume, in his conception of the judgment of the world, some co-operation of Christ's disciples with Christ Himself, such as might be represented in a picture by "assessors" For in the Fourth Gospel "judgment" means a *crisis*, or *division*, of the children of light from the children of darkness, a *crisis* caused by an effluence from the Light that attracts the former and repels the latter[2].

Through what channel, or by what instrumentality, is this effluence to go forth? Jesus says "I came not to judge the world...*the word that I spake shall judge*[3]" But is "the word" merely the doctrine uttered by Jesus and committed to writing by the Evangelists? Is it not also the expression of that doctrine in the words and deeds of all the faithful followers of Jesus, in all generations so far as they live as the children of light, and put to shame, and convict, the works of darkness? These therefore, the children of light, may be called—and indeed must be called—producers of the *crisis*, or division, or, in another metaphor, "assessors in judgment"

The same thing is implied in the Johannine doctrine of "conviction (*elenchos*)." It means the judgment pronounced on oneself by one's own conscience· "Every one that doeth evil hateth the light and cometh not to the light lest his deeds

---

[1] Mt xix 28, Lk xxii. 30

[2] Jn iii 16—21

[3] Jn xii 48 Comp viii 50 ἔστιν ὁ ζητῶν καὶ κρίνων, "There is he that seeketh and judgeth" Yet (v 22) "the Father judgeth no man" Who is it then that judges? It is the Word, or Spirit, of justice Though the Son did not "*come to judge*," He cannot help *judging*, any more than a lamp can avoid revealing that which, until the light came, lay hid in darkness

521 (Mark viii 34—ix. 1)

THE NEW LAW OF SACRIFICE

should be convicted," and "When he [*i e* the Spirit or Paraclete] is come, *he will convict* the world[1]." But through what channel was the Spirit to go forth to the world? It would seem to be those disciples to whom Jesus said "Receive ye the Holy Spirit. Whose soever sins ye forgive, they are forgiven unto them; whose soever [sins] ye retain, they are retained[2]." This was, in effect, an imparting of authority to "judge"; it constituted what might be represented in a picture as "assessorship"

§ 16. "*When he cometh in the glory of his Father*"

This is Mark's first mention of a future "coming" of the Son of Man. As it is mentioned also in the parallel Matthew and Luke, and as Luke closely agrees with Mark, there is no reason why John should intervene, so far as this verse is concerned. But in the following verse, where Mark and Matthew speak of bystanders who shall "see *the kingdom of God having come in power*," or "see the Son of man *coming in his kingdom*," Luke omits "*come*," thus: "till they see *the kingdom of God*[3]." The reason for the omission appears to be this Luke regards the words as an introduction to the Transfiguration, which immediately follows. But this, he seems to say, though it was a revelation, giving the disciples a glimpse of "the kingdom of God," was not a "*coming*" of the Lord: "The two things must be kept distinct. The time will arrive when men 'will see the Son of Man *coming* in a cloud.' Predictions of this I shall insert in the Gospel and in the Acts of the Apostles[4]. That will be the day of judgment. But that is far distant."

According to Origen, however, the "*coming*" here mentioned as being "in the glory of the Father" is rather of the nature of a revelation than of a local "*coming down*" from heaven to

---

[1] Jn iii 20, xvi. 8   [2] Jn xx 22—3
[3] Mk ix 1 τὴν βασιλείαν τοῦ θεοῦ ἐληλυθυῖαν ἐν δυνάμει, Mt xvi 28 τὸν υἱὸν τοῦ ἀνθρώπου ἐρχόμενον ἐν τῇ βασιλείᾳ αὐτοῦ, Lk ix 27 τὴν βασιλείαν τοῦ θεοῦ, all preceded by ἕως ἂν ἴδωσιν.
[4] Lk xxi 27, comp. Acts i. 11.

THE NEW LAW OF SACRIFICE

earth. This view accords with Jewish thought   In the Bible, when God says "*I will go down*"—as for example, to see the tower of Babel, or to see Israel in Egypt—the Targums render it by "*I will manifest myself*[1]"   So here, Origen says that the "*coming*" did not mean—or at all events did not mean merely—coming down from the clouds, or from one of the seven heavens, but coming into the heart   The vision, or feeling, of that "coming" must depend on the acceptance by the disciples of that spiritual preparation which has been offered to them by Jesus· "To the perfect He 'comes in the glory of His Father,' and they can say [with John the Evangelist] 'We beheld His glory, the glory as of the only begotten from the Father, full of grace and truth[2].'"

John suggests a "glory" of this kind in his account of a Voice from Heaven—the only one mentioned in the Fourth Gospel   In answer to Christ's prayer "Father, *glorify* thy name," the Voice replied, "I have both glorified it and will *glorify* it again[3]."   Jesus had previously said, "*The hour is come that the Son of man should be glorified*[4]"   The context speaks of judgment: "Now [*i.e.* in this moment] is there *a judgment of this world,* now [*i.e.* in this moment] shall the ruler of this world be cast out outside [*i.e* utterly], and I, if I be lifted up from the earth, will draw all [men] unto myself   But this he said, signifying by what kind of death he was destined to die[5]."   The context also speaks of "an *angel,*" but only perhaps in a kind of irony, along with "*thunder*"—as one of

---

[1] So Onkelos on Gen xi 5, 7, xviii 21, Exod iii 8 etc rendering ירד "go down," by hithp of גלה "reveal"   And so Jer Targ in Gen xviii 21, Exod iii 8 etc

[2] Origen, on Mt xvi 27 (Lomm iii 177—8), quoting Jn i 14. See *Son* **3234**

[3] Jn xii 27—8

[4] Jn xii 23

[5] Jn xii 31—3 ἐκβληθήσεται ἔξω   Without ἔξω, the verb might have suggested the "*casting out*" of an evil spirit, an action never mentioned by John.

523 (Mark viii 34—ix 1)

THE NEW LAW OF SACRIFICE

the *non-causes* which the materialistic multitude is always ready to substitute for a real and spiritual cause[1].

Taken as a whole, this Johannine narrative seems to convey—besides its direct dramatization of the revelation of the Law of Self-sacrifice—a lesson about the *"coming"* of Christ as revealed in the Synoptic account of the Transfiguration. John suggests to us that we need not find difficulty in the old tradition which said about the three "pillar apostles," Peter, James, and John, that they "should not taste death till they had seen the kingdom of God [having] come in power." For they did, in effect, "see" it when the Son revealed to them the Law of Self-sacrifice as the Law of that Kingdom, and Himself as being at once the Sacrifice and the King. The multitude did not hear the Voice, but the beloved disciple heard it and recorded it. When Jesus said, "The hour hath come that the Son of man should be glorified," it *had* "come." And He, too, "came," not from material clouds down to material earth, but from the bosom of God into the hearts of those who were ready to receive Him. That, or something like that, seems to be John's meaning.

If we turn to the final Johannine mention of the "coming" of the Lord, we shall find that its doctrine is of the same kind—at first sight, indefinite, thin, and unsatisfying, but ultimately helpful. It is preceded by teaching that seems intended to force us to delocalise our conceptions of "coming." Jesus has previously said, "Where I am, there shall also my minister be[2]," and "If a man love me...my Father will love him, and we will come unto him and make our abode with him[3]." That being the case, what need is there (we ask) of any future definite or local "coming" to the world at large? And yet such a coming is suggested toward the close of the Fourth Gospel in

---

[1] Jn xii 29 "The multitude therefore that stood by and heard it [with their outward ears] said that it had thundered, others said, An angel hath spoken unto him."

[2] Jn xii 26   [3] Jn xiv 23

524 (Mark viii 34—ix 1)

THE NEW LAW OF SACRIFICE

Christ's words to Peter about the beloved disciple· "If I desire him to remain [or, wait] *while I am coming*, what is that to thee? Follow thou me[1]."

If we are inclined to say "This is distracting," let us add "But perhaps it is purposely distracting." John does not set before us a picture—corresponding to that in the first chapter of the Acts—of the whole band of the disciples on the Mount of Olives, or of Peter as their representative, looking up from earth to heaven and "waiting" for the "coming" of the Lord from a visible cloud. He sets before us only two disciples— only two out of the little group of only seven. Both are described as "following" Jesus, or as bidden to "follow[2]." But concerning the one that follows, without being bidden to follow, Jesus says to the other, who follows because he is bidden to follow, "If I desire him to *remain* while I am coming, what is that to thee?"

In this sentence, it is little short of a disaster that our Revised Version renders "*while*" by "*till*[3]." The mistranslation prevents us from realising how the Evangelist knits together

---

[1] Jn xxi 22 On ἕως ἔρχομαι, "*while I am coming*" (not "till I come"), see *Joh Gr.* **2089.** Two of the best Latin MSS (*a* and *e*) have "*dum venio*"

[2] Jn xxi 19, 20 "*Follow* me...Peter seeth the disciple whom Jesus loved *following*"

[3] Jn xxi 22 ἕως ἔρχομαι, R V "till I come" There is no authority for such a rendering There is also much against it—including a passage in the Fourth Gospel itself where Jesus says (Jn ix 4), "We must work the works of him that sent me *while* it is day" R V., however, gives "till" without alternative, and supports it by marginal references, not one of which is to the point. Indeed they are all inconsistent with R.V, since they shew that N T. writers, when wishing to express "*until*" by ἕως, *do not use it with the indicative* Westcott, after quoting A V "tarry *till* I come," says "The exact force of the original is rather 'while I am coming' (ἕως ἔρχομαι) The 'coming' is not regarded as a definite point in future time, but rather as a fact which is in slow and continuous realisation " *The comment is excellent except for the insertion of "rather."* "*On the contrary*" would have been preferable

525 (Mark viii 34—ix. 1)

the beginning and the end of his Gospel in his use—a spiritual use—of this indefinite word "*coming*," which he contrasts with the definite "*came.*" Near the beginning of his Prologue, after speaking of the Life that was "the light of men," he says "There was a human being, sent from God, named John; he *came* to [be] a witness, that he might witness concerning the light.... He was not the light, but [*came*] that he might witness concerning the light. There was [from all eternity] the light that is the true light, which enlighteneth every human being [*by its continual*] *coming* into the world[1]." So now, at the end of the same Gospel, the incarnate Word, Life, Light, and Son, stands before us as if applying the title of the Coming One to Himself in order to still our impatient souls under the trial of waiting: "The beloved disciple 'followed,' and yet 'waited.' And how long the period of 'waiting' shall be is not revealed. Light, though it comes quickly and constantly, has never completed its coming It will not burn out like a torch. A torch gives its light and dies. The Light gives its light and does not die. It gains by giving itself to whatever receives it. The Life, the Light, and the Son, are to be thought of as continually giving and as continually coming."

---

[1] Jn i 6—9

INDICES

INDICES

		PAGE
I.	SCRIPTURAL PASSAGES	529
II.	ENGLISH	543
III.	GREEK	570

INDEX

I. SCRIPTURAL PASSAGES

GENESIS

		PAGE
	3	237
	7	76
	9	64
	11	306
	14	140
	22	319
2	4 foll	306
3	8	433, 488
	17–18	38
	18–19	305
	19	365
6	5	372
	6	478
	17–18	385
	18	388–9
7	1	477
9	3	306
10	20	87
	31	87
11	5	523
	7	523
	28	87
	31	87
12	1	110
	2	160, 319
13	16	351
14	20	164
15	1	387
	3–8	387
	5	484, 488
	7	87
	9–10	316
16	7	35, 461
	8	270
	10	351
	13	295, 461
	14	35, 295
17	2	386
	4	388
18	2	228, 285
	4	233
	6	31, 372
	7	288

GENESIS

		PAGE
18	8	332
	14	139
	21	523
	28	276
21	22	503
22	1	285
	3–5	265
	4	228, 265
	13	228
24	10	390
25	1	40
	11	164
26	12	39, 287
	12–13	38
	17	327
27	40	32
28	11	63–4
	12	16
	18	63–4
	20	257
29	4	270
	11	380
31	18	293
32	10	159
34	29	349
37	15	290
40	13	90
	19	90
	20	90
41	56–7	272
42	25	239
43	8	349
	25	223
	28–9	251
	30	251
45	21	239
46	21	97
48	15–16	258
	16	333
49	11	301, 395
	20	333
	27	332–3
50	10	101

EXODUS

		PAGE
1	6–7	20
	13	472
2	6	288–9
	10	433
	23	289
	23–4	472
3	1	259
	8	523
	18	225, 265
4	10	470
	11	470
	27	380
5	1	238
	3	265
6	15	466
7	16	238
8	20	238
	27	225, 265
	28	238
10	7	126
	9	246
	10	349
	11	245, 349
12	1	292
	10	340
	37	245–6, 349–50
	39	239
	46	322, 340
13	2	326
	18	312
14	29	304
15	22	265
16	4	203–5
	13	204
	14	204
	19	203
	27	336
19	7	332
	11	267
	15	267
	17	30
20	2	259
	8	394

A L.   529   34

INDEX

EXODUS

		PAGE
20	12	292
	17	131
21	1	332
	30	277
23	2	232
	25	319
	33	126
24	8	393
	9–11	357
	10	282
	11	358
25	31	36
	37	32
26	32	291
	32–7	354
	37	291
30	12	277
	12–13	278
33	1	12
	3	12
	5	100
	11	289, 291
38	26	350

LEVITICUS

2	13	221
4	3	178
5	7	99
7	12	319
10	8	357
	10	448
11	3	323
	37	45
12	2	490
13	2	53
	2–24	485
14	9	115
18	6	86
	12	86
	13	86
19	14	126
21	14–15	7
	18	470
25	5	38
	11	38
	49	336
26	8	293
	13	516
	26	159
27	8	99

NUMBERS

1	45–6	350
	47	90

NUMBERS

		PAGE
2	32	350
3	14	289
4	3	311
	7	323
	47	311
7	6	316
	48	233, 286
	66 foll.	292
9	12	322
11	4–6	347
	8	239
	13	270, 275
	21	245, 349–50
	21–2	275
	22	270–71, 334
14	30	347
16	26	17
	35	311
17	1 foll	350
18	19	221
21	17	233
	30	32
24	3	144
26	2	350
27	16 foll	255
	17	258
28	3	277
32	17	312

DEUTERONOMY

1	5	325
6	4	8
7	13	319
15	21	470
17	2–6	180
	6	518–19
19	15	156, 518–19
21	23	115
22	5	349
23	13	163
25	9	489
26	2–4	208, 342
	3	209, 342–3
	5–15	342
	10	342
28	5	342–3
	17	342–3
	60	312
	66	114
32	29	205
33	3	246
	9	506
34	5	382

JOSHUA

		PAGE
1	14	312
4	12	312
6	5	39
9	6–16	386
	11	218
13	6	333
23	13	126

JUDGES

2	3	126
7	11	312
8	27	126
14	12–19	4
15	19	100
16	26	287
19	7	262
	8	262
	9–11	262
	30	308

RUTH

1	14	380

1 SAMUEL

2	25	180
9	13	318, 324
10	1	380
16	14	76
17	40	160, 170
	43	161
	45	161
18	21	126
19	13	63
	14	238
21	3	293
	4	448
24	3	72
25	31	126
26	12	63
	18	271
	19	221
30	12	100

2 SAMUEL

6	19	330
12	13	179
15	16–18	245
17	23	387
22	17	433
24	19–20	244

SCRIPTURAL PASSAGES

1 KINGS

		PAGE
3	26	251
11	36	32
13	7	223
17	9	409, 465
	12	330
18	4	310
19	5	317
	6	317, 367
	11	54
20	11	470

2 KINGS

4	42	275, 286, 292
	43	287, 332, 338, 340
	44	332, 338, 340
5	10 foll	484
6	27	270
9	13	218
	16	99
19	29	39
20	1	387

1 CHRONICLES

7	29	443
8	35	87
	36	87
9	42	87
11	8	325
16	3	330
20	1	205
21	19–20	244

2 CHRONICLES

24	13	118
	21	118
25	12	117

EZRA

| 8 | 17 | 488 |
| 9 | 8 | 163 |

NEHEMIAH

1	3	87
5	14	159
7	40	87

ESTHER

		PAGE
2	1	76
	2	76
4	4	218
7	7	297

JOB

1	19	53
	20	218
5	1	520
	4	321
7	5	73
10	1	176
12	12	271
20	8	431
24	24	39
28	12–19	272
29	4	15
30	8	134
32	7	257
33	6	493
37	21	485
40	24	126

PSALMS

1	4	30
8	2	471
12	7	477
13	3	185
17	15	279
18	16	433
	26	505
19	1	140
	8	485
	12	180
23	1	258–9
	4–5	160
25	14	15
32	5	179
	9	471
35	2	162
	19	21
36	5–9	34
	9	35, 460–61
41	9	346
42	1	298
	7	422
45	7	175
49	4	4
	20	4
50	14	362
51	6–10	457
	10	493
	17	362

PSALMS

		PAGE
59	6	85
66	10	422
	12	422, 428
68	11	20
69	22	126
72	16	334
	17	333
73	10	294
76	3	162
77	2–10	176
78	1	7, 8
	2	4, 8, 46
	14–37	259
	15	238
	19	238
	20	347
	24	239
	25	239
	52	259
	70–72	7, 259
	72	256
79	11	472
80	1	258
	5	179
82	6	21
88	7	422
91	4	162
	12	133
102	20	472
104	8–9	64
	27	234, 237
105	16	159
	21	251
106	20	304
	36	126
107	2–5	264
	17–19	424
	20	20–21
	30	242–3, 443, 474
110	3–4	44
116	12–13	514
119	157	503
	161–5	504
	165	126, 130
126	5	39
128	1–2	38
140	7	381
141	4	221
145	15	237
	16	258

PROVERBS

| 1 | 14 | 449 |
| 3 | 11 | 176 |

531

34—2

INDEX

PROVERBS

		PAGE
3	28	205
	32	15
4	21	460
5	4	271
6	2	127
10	21	257
11	17	86
13	8	278
	14	460–61
14	6	271
	27	460–61
15	23	237
16	7	503
	15	358, 362
21	4	32
	9	449
25	24	449
27	1	204
	16	188
	25	304
31	20	326

ECCLESIASTES

4	9	157
	12	157
11	5–6	40

SONG OF SONGS

2	1–2	30
	16	259–60
5	12	339
	13	298
7	1	168
8	1	133

ISAIAH

1	22	173, 297
3	2–3	310
	3	311
	5	134, 136
	17	432
4	4	233
5	2	14
	4	14
	11	185
	12	486
	22	185
6	6	317, 368
	10	5, 438, 481
	10–11	8
11	1	355

ISAIAH

		PAGE
11	5	174
	12	264
12	1	320
14	19	73
15	6	304
18	2	74
22	23	163
24	9	185
25	3	320
26	17–19	44
	19	30
28	7	185, 431
	12	220
29	9–10	185
	11	492
	12	492
	13	492
	18	492
30	17	293
33	21	245
35	1–7	470
	3	469
	4	78, 471
	5–6	469
	6	264
	10	473
37	14	326
	30	39
38	1	387
	11	486
	19	320
40	1	78
	2	78
	6–8	303
	11	258, 263
41	27	78
42	6	389
43	3	514
45	15	5
49	1	30
	2	30
	3–4	5
	8	389
51	4	259
	12	78
	18	78
52	7	168, 503
	13–15	500
	14 foll	134
53	1–8	500
	2–3	136
	3	134–6, 426
	4	232, 462, 499
	10	426
	11	27, 232
	12	232, 500
54	1	409

ISAIAH

		PAGE
54	11	78
55	1	214, 272, 348
	9–11	17
	10	25
56	6	386
57	17	5
	19	265
58	7	323–4
	10	361, 376, 457
59	15–17	144
	16	144
	21	391
61	1	485
	11	45
63	5	144
	9	473
	9–10	512
	17	5
64	8	493
66	8	353

JEREMIAH

2	2	288
	13	460–61
3	4	29
4	3	32
5	1	243
	5	516
	13	20
6	4	262
	9	209
	16	220
12	5	245
13	18	64
16	7	323–4
24	6	460
31	31–3	391
46	16	110
50	44	87
51	39	185

LAMENTATIONS

1	1	87
	5	121
2	19	243
3	7	173
	27–8	508
	41	375
4	4	264, 323–4

EZEKIEL

3	20	131

SCRIPTURAL PASSAGES

EZEKIEL		
		PAGE
13	10	504
	18	64
	18–20	64
14	3	131
16	9	233
	10	168
	15	132
	26	132
17	7	299
	10	299
19	12	321
20	49	5, 198
21	5–6	472
22	18	173
	26	448
27	8	245
	26	245
34	2	273
	15	307
	16	307
	18	302
38	2	97
	3	98
39	1	98
42	20	448
44	23	448

DANIEL		
1	12	45
	16	45
4	19	244
	25–33	304
	27	200
5	25	324
	28	324
9	13	125
	25	125
11	14	125
	19	125
	33	125
	35	125, 127, 130
	41	125–6
12	2	72
	4	230–31, 424

HOSEA		
4	16	258
	18	297
6	1–2	499
	2	266, 326
	6	363
7	4	370
11	7	114

JOEL		
		PAGE
1	20	298

AMOS		
8	11–12	230
	12	230–31

JONAH		
1	4	53
	13	245

NAHUM		
3	7	270

ZECHARIAH		
2	4	289
9	7	75
	10	230
10	4	163
12	5	75
	6	75
13	7	252, 499

MATTHEW		
2	18	78
3	10	368
	11	167
4	5	56
	6	133
	8	56
	13	153
	23	152
	24	193
5	4	78
	6	307
	8	455
	10	503, 511
	11	504
	13	373
	14	32
	14–16	28 foll
	15	32
	16–17	32
	17	453
6	1	279
	11	203
	19–22	32
	20	171, 279

MATTHEW		
		PAGE
6	21	32
	22 foll	459
	22–3	33
	24	507
	30	303, 305
	33	29
7	2	28 foll
	5	486
	9–11	335
	11	27
	22	358
	23	505
	27	133
8	2	140
	6	422
	10	143
	11	230, 358
	16	261
	17	232, 462
	18	54 foll
	22	82
	23–7	54 foll
	27	430
	28	69–74
	28–34	66 foll
	31	79
	32	76
	33	81
	33–4	80
	34	71, 80
9	1	128, 241
	8	27
	13	363
	18	99
	18–26	94 foll
	20	98
	22	100
	24	101
	27	74
	27 foll	493
	35	148 foll, 152–3, 252
	36	154, 214,
	37	154, 252
	38	154
10	1	148 foll, 252
	2	142, 155
	5–6	151
	5–15	148 foll
	6	155
	9	170, 172
	9–10	158
	10	160
	19–20	166
	23	155
	26	28 foll
	27–8	382

INDEX

MATTHEW			MATTHEW			MATTHEW		
		PAGE			PAGE			PAGE
10	33	505	14	3–12	195 foll.	15	17	453
11	1	80, 221		9	201		18	448
	2–24	221		12	217, 218		19	459
	5	493		12–14	216 foll		20	448
	6	125, 504		13	218, 227,		21	408
	15	28 foll			237 foll, 241,		21–8	464 foll
	21	487			245 foll		22	409, 466
	25	320, 491		14	184, 227,		27	337
	25–7	221			247 foll, 256,		29	80, 409 468
	28	220			480		29–31	467 foll
	28–9	219, 223		14 foll	214		30	470
	28–30	221		15	215, 225,		30–31	493
	29	508			261 foll		31	264
12	4	293		15–16	269–74		32	220, 263 foll,
	7	363		16	273, 341, 355			267
	9	80		16–18	283 foll		32–4	283 foll
	22	493		17	290, 294 foll		33	225, 269 foll
	22–5	475		18	294 foll, 356		33–7	306
	39	477, 515		19	297, 302–3,		34	330
	48–50	380			315, 328 foll,		35	297, 302
13	1–23	1 foll			332, 340		36	315 329 foll
	3	8		20	306, 336, 339		37	336
	8	7, 18		21	246, 269, 309,		38	246, 314, 348
	10	10, 46			314, 344 foll,		39	242, 409, 443,
	11	14–15, 46			348			474
	12	29 foll		22	238, 240, 408,	16	1	474
	13	6			413		4	473, 477, 515
	15	438		22 foll	425		4–5	410
	18–19	19		22–33	403 foll		5	292
	21	124		23	238, 413		5–12	210 foll, 478
	22	127		23–4	422		6	371, 479
	23	7		24	244, 403, 418,		8	478
	23–4	31			421		9–10	208
	24	328		24–5	418		13	48, 408, 412,
	24–7	36 foll.		26	58, 429–30			487
	26	37		27	58		13–16	494 foll
	30	37		28	404		16	412
	31	328		29	404		20–23	498 foll
	31–2	41 foll		29–31	425		23	130, 501
	33	80–81, 370–72		30	53		24	204, 502
	34	20		31	421		24–8	501 foll
	34–5	45 foll		32	404		25	501
	35	4, 46		33	248, 429–30,		26	179, 512–14
	44	30			438, 440		27	515, 518, 523
	51	45		34	241, 244, 408,		28	522
	53–4	111			414	17	3	519
	53–8	107 foll.		34–6	442–4		12	135
	54	109–11, 119		35	243		15	469
	55	120, 128		36	79, 176		17	296
	55–7	112	15	1–20	445 foll		17–20	42
	56	111, 124		2	447–8		18	469
	57	109, 124,		7	452		20	80
		133–4		8 foll	492		24–7	280
	58	110, 137		10	452	18	6	53, 124
14	1	193, 201		11	412, 448, 450		8 foll	127
	1–2	190 foll		12	411, 413		10	255, 520
	2	191, 193		15	12		12	224, 254 foll

534

SCRIPTURAL PASSAGES

MATTHEW		MARK		MARK	
	PAGE		PAGE		PAGE
18 16	156	3 7–8	231	5 18	79
19–20	157	9	241	19	81, 85
19 19	279	13–14	142	21	241
25	114	14	217	21–43	94–106 *passim*
26	139	20–23	475		
28	358, 521	24	332	22	97
20 2–13	275	33–5	380	23	79, 99, 176
15	459	4 1–20	1–27 *passim*	25	98
28	231, 514	1–34	1–51 *passim*	26	99
30	493	2	11, 199	34	99, 169, 176, 503
34	485	2–3	8		
21 14	493	3	8 foll	41	98
15–16	114	8	7, 18	42	98–9
16	471	10	10–14, 48	43	98
42	191	11	5, 14 foll	6 1	109–11
22 18 foll	277	12	6	1 foll	122
30	520	13–14	19–21	1–6	107–47 *passim*
37	8	17	124, 129		
23 16	451	19	127, 131	2	111, 113, 119
25–6	455–8	20	7	3	1, 120–24, 128
26	361, 455	21	31–4	4	109–10, 133–6
24 11–12	166	21–5	28–36		
24	142	22	27 foll	4–5	175
38	345	25	27	5	112, 137 foll, 185
43	420	26–9	36–41		
26 26	316	27	36 foll	6	143, 152–3, 252
28	231, 385–6	28	36 foll, 267, 305		
29	394–5			6–13	148–89 *passim*
31	127, 129, 252, 499	29	39		
		30–32	41–4	7	155, 157
38	427	31	41–2	8	158–61, 170 foll, 206
41	127, 372	32	41–2		
53	77	33	20	9	167
56	146–7	33–4	45–51	10	193
60	74	34	45–6	12–13	186
27 27	56	35	241	13	175, 182, 184 foll, 193
51–3	73	35–41	52–65 *passim*		
52–3	70	36	55 foll, 60 foll	14	193, 200, 201
		38	62 foll.	14 foll	197 foll
		39	53	14–16	190–94
MARK		41	430	15	191
1 15	169	5 1	71–3	16	191, 200
22	113	1–20	66–93 *passim*	17	494
25	53	2	69, 81	17–29	195–202
32	261	3	69, 81, 83	20	192, 219, 348
38	153, 487	4	83–4	22	201
39	152–3	5	69, 73, 81–4	25	201
40	140	10	79, 83, 86–9, 199	26	201
41	247			27	201
45	199	10–23	78	29	218
2 1	128	12	79	29–34	216–63 *passim*
2	21	13	74, 76		
12	27	14	80–81, 429	29–44	203–402 *passim*
26	293	15	83	30	217–19
3 5	479, 481	16	81	30–35	233
6	479	17	71, 79–82	31	219 foll, 223,

INDEX

MARK		MARK		MARK	
	PAGE		PAGE		PAGE
6 31	225 foll, 233–7	7 1–23	445–63 *passim*	8 15	370, 479
31–4	226	2	448, 450	17	206, 478–83
32	219, 225, 237 foll, 241–2	3	448	19–20	208
		4	448	20	482
33	226, 228, 245–7	6	452	22	79
		6 foll	492	22 foll	487, 492
33–4	243	7	452	22–6	410, 412, 483–93
34	184, 199, 214, 227, 247 foll, 252–3, 256–7, 263, 327, 359, 480	14	452	23	473, 488
		15	412, 448	24	320, 485, 488
		17	12, 411–12	25	484–6
		19	453	26	487
		20	448	27	48, 408, 412, 487, 494
35	225, 261 foll	22	459		
35–7	269–82	23	448	27–9	494–7
36	215	24	408, 411, 465, 468	29	412
37	215, 274 foll., 355 foll			30–33	498–501
		24–30	464–6	33	130, 501
37–8	283–96	26	409, 466	34	204, 502
38	284, 294 foll	27	206	34–9 1	501–26
39	296 foll, 302 foll	28	337	34–8	501–26
		31	409, 467–8	35	511
39–40	297–314	31–7	467–74	36	514
40	296, 299, 309–14	32	79, 264, 468	37	512–17
		33	473	38	515–22
41	315 foll, 321 foll, 328–9, 332	33–6	411	9 1	502 foll, 522
		34	326	2	55
		37	114, 264	4	519
42	306	8 1 foll	343	12	135
42–3	336–43	1–3	263–8	17	469
43	336, 339	1–9	208, 474	19	296
44	246, 269, 275, 309, 344 foll, 348 foll	2	263 foll	22 foll	487
		2–5	283–96	23	138
		3	220, 263 foll	25	469
45	238, 240, 408, 413–17	4	225, 269, 271, 294–5	26	199, 469
				42	124
45–52	403–41 *passim*	4–8	306	43 foll	127
		5	283	49	221
46	413–17	6	297 329	49–50	373
47	238, 261, 418–19	6–7	315 foll, 322, 329	50	169, 503
48	227, 244, 418 foll, 421 foll, 424	7	318, 329–30	10 2	348
		8	336 foll, 339, 482	12	348
				21	279
49	58, 429–32	9	348 foll.	26	114
49–50	429	10	242, 409, 443, 474	27	139
50	58			32	55
51	438	10–11	411	42	432
52	206, 248, 438–41, 480	10–12	474–7	45	231–2, 377, 514
		11	474	46	405, 493
53	241, 243, 408, 414, 443, 474	12	473–4, 515	51	320
		12–13	477	52	485, 494
53–6	442–4	13–14	410	11 18	114
54	438, 480	14	292	12 4	135
54–5	243	14–21	208, 210 foll, 478	16 foll	277
56	79, 243, 443			18–27	188
7 1	218, 411	14–16	479	25	520

SCRIPTURAL PASSAGES

MARK		LUKE		LUKE	
	PAGE		PAGE		PAGE
12 29	8	4 25–6	409, 468	8 37	71, 80
33	363	25–30	108	39	81, 85
40	520	28	108	40	80
41	173	29	115 foll	40–56	94 foll
13 11	166	30	118	42	98–9
13	429	32	113	43	98–9
20	142	35	53	48	100, 176
22	142	40	261	50	176
35	420	43	487	53	100
14 5	280	44	152–3	55	98, 100
11	168	5 6	323	56	99
19	155	7	52	9 1–6	148 foll
24	231, 385	12	140	2	148
25	394	17	21	3	158, 171
27	127, 129, 252, 499	26	27	6	193, 218
		6 4	293	7	192–3, 200, 201
33	55	13	142		
34	427	17	231	7–9	190 foll
36	138	22	504	8	191
38	127, 372	38	28 foll	9	406
49	146–7	42	486	10	217–18, 237 foll, 411, 413
54	32	7 2 foll	422		
15 3	199	3	176	10–11	216 foll, 241
18	168	9	143	11	184, 227–8, 246–8, 256, 359, 414, 480
16 4	485	13	248		
12	432	19	202		
16	429	21	493	11 foll	214
17–18	185	23	125, 504	12	225, 239, 261 foll, 294–5
18	221	45	379		
		46	175	12–13	269 foll
		8 4–5	8	13	215, 294, 355, 357
LUKE		4–15	1 foll		
		8	7, 18	13–14	283 foll, 352
1 3	48	9	10, 14	14	269, 297, 309, 348
17	191	10	6, 14–15		
72–3	392	11	19	14–15	297 foll, 302
2 14	504	13	1, 124, 127, 129	15	309
23	326			16	315, 318, 321, 328, 332
34	368	14	127		
48	113, 117	15	7, 31	17	306, 336, 339
49	109	15–16	31	18	48, 238, 408, 412
3 1	494	16	28, 31–4		
9	368	16–17	28 foll	18–20	494 foll
18	71, 78	18	28 foll	20	412
18–20	195 foll, 201	21	380	21–2	498 foll
19	494	22	241	23	204, 502
4 5–6	87	22–5	54 foll.	23–7	501 foll
11	133	25	430	25	514
16	109	26	71	26	515, 518
16–17	107 foll.	26–39	66 foll	27	522
16–22	112	27	69, 83–4	30	519
18	485	29	84, 424	39	469
21–4	107 foll	31	86–91	41	296
22	112, 128	32	79	42	469
23	119, 136	33	76	43	113
23–30	112	34	80, 81	46	405
24	109, 133, 135	36	81, 176	49–50	405

INDEX

LUKE		LUKE		LUKE	
	PAGE		PAGE		PAGE
9 51–3	405	14 12	222	24 32	326
57	405	33	417	37	58, 431–2
60	82	34	373	37–8	58
61	417	35	28 foll	43	15
10 1	155	15 4	224, 254	45	326
1–2	154	4–6	261	48	156
4	148, 170–71	7	255		
7	80	20	248		
13	487	16 11	22	JOHN	
13 foll	221	13	507		
18	91	25	78	1 1	27
19	221	17 2	124	6–9	526
21	320, 491	27–8	345, 359	9	22
27	8	18 13	362	11	56
33	248	26	114	11–12	57
40	377	27	139	12	26, 42
11 3	203	35	493	14	27, 523
11–13	335	42	485	14–17	120, 318
13	27	19 5	485	14–18	34
14–17	475	41–4	478	17	26
16	474	47–8	114	18	27
29	473, 477, 515	20 11	135	21	194
32–4	82	24	277	23	49
33	34	36	520	32–4	157
34	459	21 1	173, 485	39	292
34–6	33	14–15	166	40	151
37	222	18	168	41	496
38	450	27	522	44	240
39–41	361, 455–8	28	168	46	281, 292
40–41	455	22 3	351	51	496
12 1	210 foll, 292, 479	15	394	2 5	377
		16	394	6	368, 460–61
3–4	382	17	316–17, 385	7	342
9	505	18	394	9	377
28	303	19	392	11	140
31	28 foll	20	231, 385, 392	13	212, 461
32	255	21	392	19–21	268
33	171, 279	24	514	25	144
38	420	25–6	514	3 3	256
41	420	27	231–2, 377, 514	3–8	9
13 1	406			5	256
11	470	29	393	6	40
13	470	29–30	358	8	40
15	373	30	521	10	10, 41
16	84, 470	31	127, 423, 425	12	146
18–19	41 foll	36	170	16	27, 342, 384
19	44	39 foll	252	16–21	521
20	371	47	228	19–20	131
21	30, 370–71	53	146–7	20	522
22	148, 152–3, 252	23 11	135	22	150, 193
		24 16	432	22 foll	150
26	358	18	15	24	202
27	505	27	15, 326	24–30	151
29	230, 358	29	261–2	25	460, 461
31	406, 465	30	322	26	191
32–3	266	30–35	322	30	150, 194, 202
33	406	31	326	31	194

SCRIPTURAL PASSAGES

JOHN		JOHN		JOHN	
	PAGE		PAGE		PAGE
3 31–6	202	6 5–7	269 foll	6 59	47, 260
35	384	5–9	283 foll	60	22, 128, 198
4 1	193	6	274, 285	61	128
1–2	150, 186	7	270, 274–82	63	401
3	406	9	275, 286–92	66	411
5	85	10	51, 297, 302,	66–7	129, 481
6	85		308 foll,	67	501
8	215, 274		348–51	67–70	236
11	85	11	315 foll, 328,	68	260
12	85		332, 356, 366	68–9	497
14	85	12	51, 337–8, 342	70	129, 141–2,
17–18	132	12–13	336 foll		478
19	461	13	332, 339–42	71	129, 501
20–24	491	14–15	236	7 1	406
23	28	15	129, 198, 224,	1–35	407
29	461		238, 253, 351,	3	80, 406
32	274		406	4–5	146
35	25, 51, 228	15–21	403 foll	5	124
36	189	16	241, 261	14	260
37	21–7	16–17	408	28	23, 260
38	40, 150	17	414	33	42
39	22	18	53	36	22
43–5	107	19	58, 227, 244,	37–8	461
44	109, 135		418, 433	43	113
45	109, 119, 135	20	58	8 12	35, 194
46–54	153	21	57, 425, 433,	16	23, 24
47	406		438, 443	17–18	156, 517–18
48	146	22	241	20	260
53	98	23	60	32–44	516
54	406	26	214, 236, 274,	37	338, 407, 444
5 2	240		307, 360, 444	39	43
13	182	26–65	440	44	132
18	253, 407	27	236, 308	49	135, 517
19	137, 140	30	475	50	521
22	521	31	203, 225, 239,	51	21
22–7	519		475, 477	52	21
24	80	31 foll	285	55	21
25	9	32	23, 214, 239,	56	229, 516
26	333		333	57	311
28–9	69	35	300, 333	59	118, 135
30	137, 140	37	140	9 1–7	484
32–6	85	39	342	4	525
35	191, 194	42	128	5–7	484
36	140	44	434	6	489–90
42	384	45	112	6–7	473
44	144	49	225, 477	11	320
6 1	241	51	300, 344	15	320
1–5	217, 228	51–9	249	16	113
2	246–7, 475	52	128, 347	17	491
2–3	224	52–3	300	18	320
3	228	52–8	347	24	517
3–5	228	54	346	28	491
4	212, 246, 263,	54–6	300	33	491
	287, 308	55	395	35	491
4–5	213	56	301, 346	35–6	497
5	214–15, 320,	57	346	39	6, 491
	515	58	346–7, 477	10 6	47, 281

INDEX

JOHN		JOHN		JOHN	
	PAGE		PAGE		PAGE
10 8	253	12 32	434	16 1	133
11 foll	261	32–3	19	1–2	129
12	252–3	35	42	2	510
15–18	515	38	22	8	522
16	256	39	144	11	89
19–21	113	39–40	6	17	13
28	253, 342	39–43	440	20	169
29	253	40	5, 8, 481	21	169
31	113, 118	47–8	512	21–2	43
35	21	48	521	22	169
39	118	49	396	24	169
41	194	50	396	25	13
11 3	104, 381	13 1	80	25 foll	47
5	104, 381	4 foll	232	29–32	14
7	406	5	155, 232	32	130, 158, 224
9	133	10	51	33	133, 169, 510
10	133	10–11	461–2	17 1	228, 321
11	101, 104, 189	12–14	462	3	23
14	100–106	16	150	11	140
23	189	17	396	12	145, 342
24	189	18	141–2, 145, 345–6	15	142
25	189			18	150
33	104, 473	18–21	478	26	395
33 foll	381	21	145	18 9	22, 342
34	292	27	361	20	47
35	104	29	274, 360, 376	28	213, 412
36	104	33	43	32	22
38	104, 473	34	51, 395	36	256
39	101	34–5	384	19 4	395
41	103, 228, 320–21	35	396	12	77, 383
		14 3	55–6	13	115–16
44	474	8	282	15	77
48	77	9	16	16–17	56
52	264	15	396	17	509
55	212–13, 461, 463	18	255, 398	19	509
		23	16, 158, 384, 396, 524	24	323
12 2	377			25	509
6	341	27	169, 398	29	369
7	51	30	89	31	509
10	105–6	15 1	23	35	23, 157
13	319	2	141, 460	36	322
20	491	3	461	20 7	64
20 foll	19	3–4	51	8–9	441
21	240, 282	4	301	12	63
21–2	158	5	395, 515	19	58
23	502, 523	7	396	21	150
23–6	510	9 foll	384	22	382
24	10, 18, 20, 267, 309	10	396	22–3	522
		11	169	29	437
24–5	27	12	396	21 4	427, 434
25–6	91, 377	13	395	9	211, 317, 365–6, 370
26	524	13–15	382		
27–8	523	14	383, 396	10	337
28–9	10	16–19	141–2	11	323
29	502, 524	20	21, 510	12	222–3, 435
31	89, 91	25	21	13	211, 316, 318, 322, 365–6
31–3	89, 523	27	157		

SCRIPTURAL PASSAGES

JOHN

		PAGE
21	15 foll	259
	15–17	256
	15–22	223, 383
	17	426
	19	525
	19–23	511
	20	525
	22	525
	25	49

ACTS

1	3	436
	4	221
	6–12	48
	8	156
	11	522
	15	14
	22	156
2	1 foll	343
	12	200
	32	156
	40	71, 82
	41	352
	46	234–5
	47	352
4	4	351–3
	9	176
	16	105
	29–30	21
5	24	200
6	7	19–20, 353
7	56	326
9	37–8	182
10	12	453
	14	450
	15	412
	17	200
	28	450
	34–8	21
	38	471
12	10	38
	24	19
14	9	176
15	5	41, 374
	8	41
16	14	326
17	3	326
	21	235
18	7	80
	7–17	363
	18	416
	21	416–17
19	23	494
20	35	25, 317
22	20	156

ACTS

		PAGE
24	22	494
	24–7	199
	25	235
26	2–27	198
	11	180
27	3	468

ROMANS

6	16	507
7	7	131
	14–24	513
9	4	391
	21	136
	27	351
10	15	168
11	7–25	441
	11	178
	15–32	338
	22	178
	25	6
	25–33	6
	27	391
12	8	72
	14	319
13	9	131
14	1	126
	4	178
	13	126
	14	437, 450
	15 foll	458
	20	126
	21	126
15	1	126
16	16	378–9

1 CORINTHIANS

1	13	328, 332
	17–22	119
2	1	17
	16	462
3	2	299
	6	299
	12	304
	15	179
4	7	317
	20	21
5	6 foll	371
	7	370
	8	213
7	31	90
8	1 foll	458
10	4	335
	12	178

1 CORINTHIANS

		PAGE
10	16–17	211
	17	363–4
11	20	237
	23	393
	25	392
	30	184
12	13	299
13	8	178
	12	5
15	12	189
16	20	378–9

2 CORINTHIANS

2	2	427
	13	416
3	6–14	391
	14–15	441
4	10	16
	14	176
5	20	396
7	10	427
13	1	156
	5	285
	12	378

GALATIANS

3	13	115
	15	386
	15 foll	390
	17–29	390
4	1	391
	3	387
	19	43
	24	391
5	6–9	374
	9	370, 372
6	2	463

EPHESIANS

2	12	391
	17	265
3	19	17
4	20–21	57
5	14	189
6	14	174

PHILIPPIANS

2	6	253
3	12	511
4	12	307

541

INDEX

COLOSSIANS		
		PAGE
2	2	17
	5	313
	6	57
	8	34
3	5	513

1 THESSALONIANS		
1	5	21
2	13	57
5	26	378–9

1 TIMOTHY		
1	19	425
4	1	127
6	9	52

2 TIMOTHY		
2	15	324
	18	189
3	2	280
4	14	121

TITUS		
1	15	455, 456

PHILEMON	
10	249
12	249

HEBREWS		
1	9	175
5	8	499

HEBREWS		
		PAGE
6	18	158
8	8–10	391
9	4	37
	16–17	390
	19–20	393
10	28–31	180
12	3	176
	5	176
	22–4	518
	23	520
13	11–13	509

JAMES		
1	10	303
	11	303
	25	516
2	15	205
3	4	424
5	10–11	175
	13	175
	13–15	175–6 fol
	14	175, 179, 193
	15	176 foll.
	18	37

1 PETER		
1	6–7	422
	19	513
	24	303
4	12	422
5	1	158
	14	878

2 PETER		
2	8	423
	10	185
	17	424

1 JOHN		
		PAGE
1	1–2	157
	7–9	463
2	1	43, 78
	7	395
	8	395
	9–10	130
	12 foll.	27
	17	90
	18–28	187
	20	187
	27	187
3	1–3	463
	2	57
	14	80
	16	249
	17	247, 249
4	1	285
5	6–7	157
	8	158
	14–16	188
	16	177–80

3 JOHN	
14	383

REVELATION		
1	4	267
	5	156
	13	174
2	2	285
	13	156
3	14	156
5	6	355
7	9	351
11	3	156
12	9	91
17	6	156
20	5–6	189

INDEX

II. ENGLISH

["*c w*" means "*confused, or confusable, with*", "*conn w*" means "*connected with*", "*interch w.*" means "*interchanged, or interchangeable, with*"]

Aaron, an apostle 288, the sons of 357
Able, "I am a [to]" =Heb and Gk "I find [how to]" 271, "not a," applied to Jesus 137–42, to Zeus 139
Aboth, i e *Sayings of the Jewish Fathers*, on —the teacher that hides his knowledge 29, "the banquet" 358, subduing one's nature 372, s also 305
About, before numbers of men 348–9, (Heb)like,(LXX)[amounting] to 349, in phrases of time 419
Above, "from a " 9, 12, 194
Abraham, the country of 87, the recompense of 228 foll, 286, 332, the feast of 230, the lad, or messenger, of 288, the covenant (LXX *diathēkē*) with 387 foll, the inheritance of 387–8, the mind of, passes out of itself 507, the vision of, of the triumph of humanity 516, lifting up his eyes 228, 265–7, 285, bidden to look up 484, looking up, or receiving insight 487–8, on the third day 265–7, tempted by God 285, taking [a heifer] for God 316, s also 229, 358, 382, 487–8, 517
Abyss, the, in Lk 86, 91
Acceptable, for "not without honour" 136
Acknowledge [God's greatness etc.], rendered in LXX bless 320
Acknowledgment, includes confession and thanksgiving 362
Acts of John, the, on —"one loaf" 318, 360, Christ's disciples as "dancing" 399
Acultha, in Mk (e) *Tabea acultha* 98

Adam, the curse on, changed 305, son of A 495
Admiration, marvelling, or wonder 143–5
Adulterous 516, how expressed by Jn 516, conn w generation, why om by Lk 515–16
Advocate, s Paraclete
Afar 265, s Far
After, s Behind, Following
Agapè, Gk, love, called *vox mere biblica* 384, in LXX almost confined to Cant 384, in Jn 384, s. Hermas, Wisdom of Solomon
Ain (or *En*), Heb, eye or fountain 35, 460, s *En*
Akiba, R 40, 447
Alectorophōniā, a new word in Gk 420, s Cockcrowing, *Gallicinium*
Aleiphein, Gk, anoint medically 175, anoint for wrestling, hence train 183
Alēthēs, Gk, "true," not to be confused with *alēthinos* "real-and-true" 22
Alēthinos, Gk, "real-and-true" 22
Alexander, a sensualist described by Lucian 381
Alexander the Coppersmith 121
Alexander the Great, posing a Gymnosophist 199
"All that the Father giveth" 140
Allegorizing 280, 506
Allusive narrative, may be historical 487
Almightiness and foreknowledge, the problem of 141
Almighty, not a correct rendering of *Shaddai* 139
Alms(giving), the ransom of man's soul 278; interch w. righteousness

543

INDEX

279, 456, in Lk, but not in parall. Mt 455

Alone 10 foll, 48, applied to Jesus in all the Gospels 238, 407, God is not a 34, he that is a is not necessarily deserted (Epict) 224

Alteration, in the risen Saviour, the 435, Chrysostom on 435–6

Altruism, in Jn 18

Altruistic purification 462

Amazement, c w hearing 99

Ambiguity, conn w —"they" 80, 218, 228, 337, "they that were in the boat" 429–30, "them" 415, aorist c w pluperf 182, affirmative c w interrogative 273, indicative c w imperative 187, "beseech" 79, raising up 176 foll, 186, arising and awaking 189, "it is [fit] for us" 273, said 291, here 295, superabound 337, broken pieces 338, wind c w spirit 424, men 430, inside c w the inside of 456, in his face c w before his face 489, smite c w kill 499, soul, in two senses 514, s also Metaphor

Ammonius, Origen resembles 341, on —"foods of luxury" 274, the Five Thousand 340–41, the basketful of Judas 341

Anachronisms, apparent 413

And, Heb, may mean "even" 160

Andrew, sayings of, Papias on 282, 289, comp 291, the first to call Jesus "Christ" 496, A and Philip, in Jn, addressed by Jesus 502

Angel (Heb) = some one (LXX) 317, A of Punishment, the, in Hermas 423

Angels, three, visit Abraham 286, c w holy ones or saints 518, the a that are holy (Mk) = the holy a (Lk) 518, human, diff from Michael and Raphael 520

Anoint, (1) medically or for training, Gk *aleiphein* 175, 183, a the sick 175 foll, among the Jews 180, metaph 183, the Logos anoints, i e trains, the wrestler Jacob 183

Anoint, (2) for consecration, Gk *chriein* 175, comp 187

Anointed, the, i e Christ, Messiah 495–6

Anointing, perhaps c w baptizing 186–7

Antedating 14, 46, 52–3, 186–7, 207, 222, s Post-resurrectional

Antichrists 187

Antipas, s. Herod

Aorist tense, the, c w pluperfect 182, 438, 440, combined with perfect 353

Apart from children, in Exod and Mt 348–9

Aphraates, on Christ thrown down and not hurt 117

Aploia, Gk, weather not fit for sailing 61

Apocalypse of Ezra, the, s Ezra

Apocrypha, Jewish 30

Apologists, Early, the, words rare or unused in 48, 52, 72, 168, 184, 287, 306, 307, 321, 333, 354, 371–2, 423, 431

Aporein, Gk, perplex or pose 199

Aposiopesis 146

Apostatize, parall to "be offended" 127

Apostle, or *Sheliach*, Moses a 233, 288, Aaron a 288

Apostles, the Sending of the 148 foll, in pairs 155, 158, "whom also he named a" 217–18

Apostolic Fathers, the, words rare or unused in 48, 52, 72, 136, 168, 183, 184, 287, 306, 307, 321, 333, 354, 371–2, 431

Apotassomai, Gk, "bid farewell to" 415 foll, renounce, hence renounce the old for the new 416, a and salute (Phrynichus) 417, contrasted w dismiss or let go (*apoluein*) 417

Apparition 430–4, R V, more correct than A V spirit 430, of Samuel to Saul, the 432, s *Phantasma*

Appear before the Lord, interch w see the Lord 486

Aquila (the translator of O T), Jerome on 298, uses *prasiai* and the verb derived from it 298, has *eucharistia* where LXX has praise 319, comp 362, substitutes *sunthēkē* for *diathēkē*, rarely using the latter 386, s also 221

Aramaic 85, 110, 126, 246–7, 324, 469–71, diff from Hebrew 470, Palestinian, has no word but *diathēkē* for "will and testament" 389–90

Archdemon, an 92

Arise, c w awake 189

Aristân, Gk, break one's fast, or breakfast (vb) 222, wrongly transl dine 222

Armed, c w in the fifth [day or generation] 312

ENGLISH

Arms (military), c w. peg, nail, or shovel **162-3**
Article, definite, inserted or omitted **238**, *e g* boat, the or a **241**, wilderness, the or a **238**
Article, reduplicated, rare in Synoptists **518**
Artos, Gk, loaf or bread, first mention of, in LXX **305**
Ascending **12, 496**
Ashamed, the Son of Man will be **505**
"Asking the parables" **10** foll
Asleep, applied to Christ **59**, to Lazarus **105, 189**, s Sleeping
Assembled with, or eating with **221**
Assessors, human, in divine judgment **519**, perhaps implied in Jn **521**
Astonished **113** foll
Atheism, imputed to Christians **398**
Atheists, "away with the a " **476**
Athenagoras, on —the kiss of love **379-80**, the charges brought against Christians **398**
Atīmos, Gk, R V "without honour" **133-7**, =outlawed etc **133-4**, how used by Justin Martyr **134**
Atonement, s Ransom
Attraction, spiritual **497**
Authority, s Control
Automatic, in Mk and Acts **38**, in LXX **38-9**
Avarice, s Covetousness
Awake, metaph **189**

Babe and child **288**
Babel, the king of **253**, the tower of **523**
Bacchus or Dionysus, the orgies of **399**
Backward, departing, misunderstood **129**, comp **500**
Banquet, of the saints, in *Aboth* **358**
Baptism, called the seal **267**, daily **446-7**
Baptist, John the, called "the lamp" **35**, "a voice" **49**, "Elijah" **194**, the death of **190** foll, **465**, Johannine non-intervention in matters concerning **219**
Baptize, v r sprinkle **448**, s. Immerse
Baptizing, by Christ's disciples **150**; omitted by Mk in the Precepts to the Twelve **186**, the b of 4000 in the Acts **352**
Barley, first Biblical mention of **287**, Heb, c w estimation **287**, a sign of rudimentariness **343**, b harvest, the **208**, b loaves, conn w Elisha **286-7, 338**
Barnabas (the writer), on a parable **12**, mentions angels (pl) only in one passage **518**, s also **78**
Bartimaeus **106, 493**
Basanizein, Gk, test by torture, lit and metaph **421**, in Plato, of testing the righteous **422**, in LXX, only once with Heb equiv **422-3**, rare in early writers except Hermas **423**, differently applied by Mk and Mt **421** foll
Baskets, in the Miracles of Feeding **208** foll, **336-44**, the carrying of, Ammonius and Origen on **341**, s *Cophinoi, Sphurides*
Baskets, the Feast of **208**, Philo on **208, 342**, Jewish traditions on **343**
Be, c w become **352**
Bear, s Carrying
Bear witness, s Witness
Beckon, s Signs, make
Become, c w be **352**
Begin, in Mk **155**
Behind, "Get thee b me, Satan," perhaps an erroneous tradition **498** foll, "go b," "go after," or "follow" **500-501**
Believe, "I know and b " (Ign) **436**, "believed," substituted for "knew" **436**
Beloved disciple, the, pp xii-xiii, **383, 435, 510-11**
Ben Sira, on —the teacher that hides knowledge **29**, prayer for the sick **181**, the physician as appointed by God **181**, discipline as bringing "rest" **219**, paying a vow **234**, righteousness (or, almsgiving) **279**, "watering a garden-bed" **298**, Wisdom as testing [by torment] **422-3**, "there is no substitute for a disciplined soul" **512-13**, s also **515**
Benediction before a meal, the **324**
Berîth, Heb, covenant, but not testament **386** foll, rendered by LXX *diathēkē* but by Aquila *sunthēkē* **386**
Beseech, exhort, or comfort, ambig. **78-9**
Beth, s House, Bethsaida
Bethel, Jacob at **257**
Bethesda, the healing at **138**
Bethsaida **237-40, 413, 487**, parall to Capernaum **408**, a city, not a village **487**, means House of Provision **238**, conn w *episitismos*,

INDEX

provision **239-40**, **242**, Lk omits what intervenes between two Marcan mentions of **410**, coming to, in Lk **411**, s also **488**
Bid farewell, in Mk **413**, and dismiss **415** foll
Bind, Heb, var renderings of in LXX **469-70**, bound, c w lame and lame-of-speech **470**
Blaspheme, Christ **180**
Bless, not in Jn except once, as passive participle **319**, distinguished by Philo from "blessed" (adj) **319**, "bless (food)," in Lk, parall to "bless" (absol) in Mk-Mt **315**, and to "give thanks (*eucharistein*)" in Jn **315**, comp **320**, blessing God, Origen on **319**, "bless [God]," conn w bread, confusable with "break [bread]," in Heb and Aram **324**, s also **318-28**
Blessing, God's, implies increasing **319**
Blind, in the prophets 15 times (11 of these in Isaiah) **493**, in SS, = (Mk) hardened **438**
Blindness, healing of, in Mk and Jn **483** foll, in Jn **489** foll, in Isaiah and the Gospels **492-3**, of Israel, the **440**, twofold **492**
Blood, water and **157**, of the grape, the **395**, of Christians, the, is seed **39**
Board, go on, in Mk **410**
Boat, the, in Mk **55** foll, **241-2**, Jesus received in the, in Mk-Mt, but not in Jn **425**, of temptations, the **425**, those in the, ambig **429**, Origen on **429**, Jerome on **430**, c w teaching **241**, "other boats," in Mk **60** foll
Bodiless demon, a, in Ignatius **58**, **431**
Body, the, the vessel of the soul **458**, brother to the soul **506**, the eye is the lamp of **32** foll, bodies, called tombs **73**
Body, Christ's, the temple of **268**
Bond-servant, s *Doulos*
Bonds, loosed **470-72**, s Bind
Books, Jn on the inadequacy of **49**, Papias on, as compared with "living voice" **49**, **282**
Bowels, implied, for Jews, son and love, for Greeks, resentment **249-50**, perhaps parall to Jn's "only begotten" **250**, of Joseph, the **251**, s Compassion
Brass, money **172**, meaning dross **173**

Bread, in the Precepts to the Apostles **159**, the staff of **159**, daily **203**, in the Lord's Prayer **203-205**, in Mk **206**, *lit* loaves **213**, a famine, not of **230**, c. w here **294**, c w for them **323**, first mention of, conn w. a curse **305**, Targum on **365**, a martyr's body like **369**, unleavened, the Feast of **210**, **212**, s *Epiousios*, Loaf
Break, Heb, *i e* cut off, gain by violence **325**
Break [bread], c w spread out [the hands in blessing] **319**, c w. bless [over bread] **324**
"Breaking of bread, in the" **325**
Break-in-pieces **321** foll, used by Mk and Lk (Five Thousand) but not by Jn **321-2**
Breakfast (vb), or break one's fast, diff from dine **222**, s *Aristân*
Breath, c w wind or spirit **9**, **40**
Brethren, Christ's **80**, **124**
Bring word, parall to declare **217**
Broken pieces, or crumbs **337**; Origen on **338**
Brother to the soul, the body is **506**; brothers, s Brethren
Bushel, under the **28**, **34**, **36**
But, Gk, c w other **60**
"But—in order that," in Jn **146**
Buy, in Synoptists, only in the Feeding of the Five Thousand **215**, **269**, in Jn **269**, **274**, **277**, **281**, parall to "find" **271**, b food **269-73**, "b and eat," in Isaiah **348**, s. also Ransom
Buy-corn, Heb *shâbar*, first instance of **272**

Caesar, Jn on **77**, Epictetus on the thunders of **77**, tribute to **277-8**, a friend of **383**
Caesarea Philippi **48**, **405**, **408**, **487**, **494**, not in Lk **412**, s Philippi
Cakes, in the days of the Messiah **334**, hidden in the embers, Clem. Alex on **372**
Calling, the men of the, diff from the elect **142**
Callous, hearts made **206**, s Hardening, *Pōroun*
Callousness, *pōrōsis* **441**, **479-80**, s. *Pōrōsis*
Cana, the miracle at **342**, **368**, servants [at table] at **377**
Canaanitish woman, the **409**, s. Syrophoenician

546

Capernaum, in Mk, parall to his own city in Mt **128**, in Jn, parall to Bethsaida in Mk **408**, s also **136, 414**

Captain over fifty **310–11**, the Messiah a **311**

Captivity, the Return from **469**

Carpenter, a complimentary term in Talmud **120** foll, Origen denies that Jesus was called a **121**, Justin Martyr on the works of a **122**

Carrying the basket, Judas, Ammonius on **341**, carrying the loaves and fishes, Origen on **356**

Carrying-about God (Epict) **16**

Cast down, or cast out **91**, cast down from a precipice, c w hang **115**

Casting out, the, of the ruler of this world **89**, of a spirit **523**

Celsus, on Christ's neglect of "just persons" **255**

Certain man (*vir*), a, interpr as Gabriel **290**, "a c [person]" (LXX)=angel (Heb) **317**

Chains, bound in **74, 84**, c w garments **83–4**

Chaldeans, Ur of the **87**

Charcoal fire, s Coal-fire

Charity, c w alms **279**

Chief, or head, Heb, c w thousand **74**, c w the name *Rôsh* **97**

Child or babe **288**

Children, said to include women **245–6, 350**, apart from, in Exod and Mt **348–50**, duty of, to parents **451**, in LXX freq rendered "baggage" **349**

Children of God, in Jn, =little ones in Synoptists **42, 44**

Choke, "the legions that c you" **76**

Choosing of the Apostles, including Judas, the **128–9, 141–2**

Chortāzein, Gk, fill [cattle] with grass, i e satisfy in Synoptists **306, 336**, depreciatively used in Jn **306–7**, and in literary Greek **304, 307**

Chortos, Gk, grass or hay, green, in Mk **302–9**, in literary Greek, depreciative **302–3**, metaph in Paul **303–4**, rare in early Christian writers **306**, in LXX =two Heb words **304**, used by Mk for blade of corn **305**, in LXX, first mention of, conn w. a curse **305**

Chrism, the **187–8**

Christ, s Jesus, the Coming of **522–6**, s Coming

"Christ, the," a title obscure to Gentiles **495**, first given to Jesus by Andrew **496**, "thou art the C," meaning of **496**, its meaning to Jesus **499**

Christians, in first century, charges against **398–9**

Chronological arrangement **65, 268**

Chrysippus **138**, on *phantasma* and "drawing" **431, 433**

Chrysostom, on —the lad with the barley loaves **286**, the Feeding of the Seven Disciples **435**, the post-resurrectional recognition of Jesus **435–6**, Peter's use of the word parable **454–6**, "Go, wash," and Naaman **484**, the healing of blindness **489**; s also **24, 60, 337, 422, 425–6, 513**

Chullin, Heb, common or unconsecrated food **448**, a Talmudic tract **448**

Church, the **25, 268**, of Jerusalem **105**, the growth of **351** foll, churches, the seven **375**

City, or province **87**, or village **238, 487**, or haven **443**

Clasma, Gk, broken-thing, i e the bread in the Eucharist **364**

Clay, anointing with, no precedent for **490**, in Jn, suggestive of creation by the Father **493**

Clean, and cleansing, Jn on **50–51**, the Logos described as, by Epictetus **50**, make clean **453**, s Purifying

Cleansing the vessel (Epict) **457–8**

Clearly, conn w "see," in Mk, lit "[with a] far-beaming [ray]" **484**

Clement of Alexandria, on —mustard-seed **42**, the Logos anointing the wrestler Jacob **183**, Alexander the Great posing a Gymnosophist **199**, three days **267**, baptism as the seal **267**, the five loaves, connected with the things of sense **291, 354**, the mystical seven **355**, *puros* as fire or wheat, and Christ's flesh as prepared by fire **369–70**, [cakes] hidden in the embers **372**, the abuse of the kiss of love **379**, "behold, I am my *diathēkē*" **388**, the Dionysiac *ōmophagiai* **399**, "being pursued (?) by righteousness" **511**, s also **31, 132, 136, 142, 255**

Clement of Rome, on —the Sower **17–18**, lifting up the weak **176, 186**, filling (*chortāzein*) the hungry **307**, the 600,000 in the

INDEX

wilderness 350, the eyes (*ommata*) of the soul 485, angels 520, s also 52, 78, 136, 495

Clementine Homilies, the 46, 199

Cloak, would not put on a 83

Clods, a congregation seen as, by George Fox 73

Coal, a live 368, coal(s), only twice in O T 317, conn w Elijah and Isaiah, prepared for prophetic work 317

Coal-fire, or fire-of-coals 366–8, symbolical 368, 428, Peter denied and confessed near a 368

Cockcrowing, in Mk, *alectorophōniā*, a new word 419 foll

Coin of fire, a 277

Coinage of David, the 172

Come, "c and see [a mystery]" 292

Comfort, exhort, or beseech, ambig 78

Comforter, the, a rendering of the Paraclete, *qu vid*

Coming, of Christ, Lk's view of, diff from Mk's 522, Jn's view of 524–6, Origen on, not local but spiritual 522, s also 366

Coming, of God, in Heb, =self-revealing, in Targum 523

Command, expr by Heb "say" 98

Commandment, a new 395, commandments, in Jn, not expressed imperatively 51, regarded as gifts 396

Common, in Heb (but not Gk) unconsecrated 448

Common hands, in Mk 448–50, s. also *Koinos*

Common, make 412, 448

Communion, in one loaf 365

Communions, or *Erubin* 363 foll

Companies, in Mk 296, s *Symposia*

Compassion, *lit* bowels, in I Jn 247, parall to child or son 249–50, s. Bowels

Compassion, have, *lit* "have-bowels," why not in Lk 247 foll, a new word in Mk 247

Concourse, the, of "many" 226

Confession of Peter, the, the merit of 496–7

Confession of sins, Origen on 179

Conflations 81, 99–100, 243–4, 518, the correct and the incorrect rendering in 299

Conscience 521

Consequently, implied in LXX by "hearing" 218

Consider, c w set yourselves on 308–9

Constrain, Jesus constraining the disciples 414, 417

Control, internal and external 92

Conviction, *elenchos*, the doctrine of, in Jn 521

Cophinoi, Gk, baskets, in the Miracle of the Five Thousand 208, 342–3, 375, 482, conn w Jews by Juvenal 344

Coppersmith, Alexander the 121

Corah, the censers of, Origen on 18

Corban 376, 451

Corn, from heaven, *i e* manna 239, 259, provisioning with, or *episitismos* 239, the grain of corn (or, wheat) 27, 30, 267, 309, 510, buy-corn, Heb *shâbar* 272

Cosmopolitan doctrine 374, yet homely 383

Cosmos, the, ambig 90

Country, of Abraham, the 87, Christ's own c 109–11, "outside the c," in Mk 86 foll

Covenant, of salt, a 221

Covenant, or testament, *diathēkē* 384–91, s *Berîth*, *Diathēkē*, *Sunthēkē*

Covetousness or greediness, called idolatry 513, s. also 132

Creation, spiritual 493, the second day of 76

Crisis, a division or judgment 521

Cronos, mysteries of 399

Cross, the, only in one passage of Jn 509, terminates the Law 453–4, in Epictetus 509, in *Evang Petr* 70, taking up the, p viii, 507 foll, conn w yoke 507 foll

Crucifixion, p xiii, 89 foll

Crucify, expr by "lift up" 90, 500

Crumbs, or broken pieces 337

Cup, the, at the Eucharist 394

Cure and heal 184, s Heal, Iatric, Therapeutic

Curse, the, pronounced on Adam 305, comp. 365

Cushion (rower's), in Mk 62 foll, mostly diff from pillow 63

D, codex D, or Bezae, readings of 10, 24, 58, 60, 63, 233, 238, 318, 419, 429, 432, 511

Daily, day by day, for the coming day 203, d baptism 446–7, ins by Lk. after "take up his cross" 509, s. *Epiousios*

Dalmanutha, unique mention of 243, parall to Magadan 242, 409, 443, 474

ENGLISH

Dancing, disciples, in *Acts of John* 399

Daniel, on stumbling 130, on running to and fro 230, conflations in 244

Dark sayings, p vii, 13, 47

David, the staff and scrip of 160 foll, the coinage of 160, 172, requests five loaves 293, divides food to Israel 329–30

David, the Son of 405

Day, a, c w to-day 204–5, the third 265–8, 499, far spent 261 foll, that he might see my 516, d by d, or for the coming d 203, s *Epiousios*

Days, four 101, three 70, 101, 265–8, two 102, after two 326, 499

Daybreak 427

Deacon, s *Diaconos*

Dead, metaph 82, c w sleeping 101 foll

Deaf or dumb 469

"Deal (Heb *pâras*) thy bread to the hungry," Talmud, Jerome, and Ibn Ezra on 323, s *Pâras, Pârash*

Death, life through 17, 377, of the grain of corn 27, 30, 267, 309, 510, spiritual 102, c w sleep 101 foll, the sin unto, Origen on 177–9, a decree of 180

Debt, owe as a, p ix foll

Deceived, Gk, c w loved 279

Declare, parall to bring word 217

Declining day, the 261

Decree, of death, spiritual 180

Defilement 412, 448, 452

Delphian oracle, the 33

Deluge, the 77

Demeter, Epictetus on 16

Demon (*daimonion*), or devil, bodiless (Ign) 58, 431, d, spirit, and *phantasma* 430 foll

Demons (*daimones*), an army of (Tatian) 431

Demoniac, the, and the swine 66 foll, apocryphal versions of 82 foll, demoniacs, two 70

Denarius, a labourer's daily wage 275, gold, a 276, of fire, a 277, of redemption, a 284, denarii, two hundred 274–82

Denars, an income of two hundred 274

Denial, Peter's 420–21, Levi's, of his brethren 506, a runaway slave's, of his master 506–7, in Hermas 127, 507

Denying oneself, Philonian aspect of 488, not in Gk literature 506

Depart backward 129, 500

Depart from, and bid farewell 415

Descensus ad Inferos, the 74, 84

Descent into Sheol, the 59

Desert (n), in Lk, parall to mountains in Mt 224, the or a 225, s *Midbar*

Desert place, a, ambig 223, parall to Bethsaida 237, s *Midbar*

Deserted, diff from alone 224

Desertedness or a desert, *erēmia*, Epictetus on 224

Desire (n), a neutral term 131–2, Origen on 132, only once in Jn, plur 132

Destroy, or lose 514

Detail, diffuse, in Mk 244, 445

Devil, in SS = Gk *phantasma* 430, one of you is a d 141, 414, s Demon, *Phantasma*

Diaconein, Gk, serve at table, in Jn 377

Diaconos, Gk, servant [at table], c. w deacon 377, in Mk and Jn, but not in Lk 377, diff from *doulos*, bondservant or slave 510

Diatessaron, the 55, 152–3, 329, 356, 435, 438, describes two visits to Nazareth 112 foll, on the Samaritan and the Syrophoenician woman 467

Diathēkē, lit Gk and Aram "[last will and] testament," but LXX covenant (Heb *berîth*) 384–91, R V (of Eucharist) covenant or testament 385, first mention of (LXX) conn w Noah, Heb *berîth*, R V covenant 385 and Aq and Sym *sunthēkē*, compact 386, Philo on, implies inheritance 387–8, d the only word in Palestin Aram to express will and testament 389, in the Epistles, implies a testator 390, Paul, in mentioning, hampered by LXX 391, the new 392

Didachē, the, i e *The Teaching of the Twelve Apostles*, on —the receiving of bread 159, 206, Eucharistic ritual 364–5, comp 395

Didrachm, i e half shekel 280

Die, *i e* spiritual death 102, Philo on 490

Dilemma, a 199

Diligently, or with the fist 448

Diminutive, Gk, the 43, 60, 330–31

Dine, a wrong rendering of *aristân*, breakfast (vb) 222, in Lk 222

Diogenes, condemns Plato for never grieving a disciple 429

549

INDEX

Dionysus, the orgies of, Clem Alex on **399**
Disciple, the beloved, s Beloved
Disciples, described as "house" **14**, c w the [men] in the boat **430**, **440**, the seven **317, 322, 365** foll
Discipline, in Ben Sira and in Wisdom of Solomon **219, 384**
Dismiss, and bid farewell **415**
Distressed, or tormented **421** foll, differently applied by Mk and Mt **421**, Origen on **424–5**, s *Basanizein*
Distributing, c w breaking **325**, s Divide
Distribution of bread to the Five Thousand, Jn differs from Synoptists as to **332, 356**.
Divide [food] **329–30**, Mk's word not used by Jn **332**, c w divide by dissension **332**
Division or schism, in Jn **113**
Dogs, Gentiles called by Jews **466**, "cast it to the d," perhaps wrongly assigned **466**, Victor on **466**, allegorized by Origen **466**
Double meaning of words, *e g* spirit **40**, lift up **90**, staff **160**, save **176**, raise up **176**, smite **499** etc
Double Tradition of Mt and Lk, the **125, 279, 335, 373**
Doulos, Gk, bondservant or slave, diff from *diaconos* servant [at table] or minister **510**
Dove, cooing like a, of a divine Voice **478**
Down, or out **91**
Dramatic expression, in Jn **10, 213, 248–9, 331, 377, 462–3, 510, 524**
Draught of fishes, a, in Lk **426**, in Jn **426**, comp. **116**
Drawing out the soul to the hungry **361, 376**
Drawing power, the, of the Logos (Epict) **433**, of Nature (Epict) **433**, of the Father and the Son (Jn) p xii, **434**
Drawn-and-dragged (Epict) **434**
Drink (n and vb), in Jn **300**
Driving, in Gk, may mean rowing **424**
Dumb, in Isaiah (Heb) =stammering (LXX) **264**, Ibn Ezra on **264**, or speechless **469**, or deaf **469**, c w maimed or lame **470**, s Stuttering
Duplication, emphatic **452**
Dust, the, the ground of **72**, heaped up d or mound, uniquely mentioned by Justin Martyr **72**

Duty, of children to parents, Talmud on **451**

East and West **230**
Eating, Gk verbs signifying **345**, not distinguished in R V **347**, s *Esthiein, Phagein, Trōgein*
Eating, in the presence of the Lord **357–60**, e (*or*, being assembled) with, applied to Jesus **221**
Eating, common, *i e* common to the Gentiles **449**, s *Koinophagiā*
Eating, swine's flesh **452**
Egypt, Israel in **264, 472**, Joseph in **251**, or Sin, a prison **472**, comp **76**
Elbow, up to the **448**, s Fist
Elders, the **175–82**
Elect, the **142**
Election, God's **141**, the problem of **142**
Elements, the **387**
Elenchos, Gk, conviction, the doctrine of, in Jn **521**
Eleusis, the mysteries of **16**
Eliezer Ben Hyrcanus **451**
Elijah, stood up as fire **191**, and the Baptist **191, 194**, and Jesus, the retirements of **465**, and Moses **519**, s also **317, 409**
Elisha, and barley loaves **275, 287, 338**, bidding farewell to his home **415**
Emmaus, the narrative of **325**, shews traces of LXX **262**
Emotion, imputed to Jesus **104**
Emphasis **339, 396, 518**, insertion for **9, 23, 296, 355** etc
En (or *Ain*), Heb, =eye or fountain **460**
Enemies, a man's, in his own heart **503**
Enlighten and baptize **186**
Ephphatha **472–3**, in Mk, illustr by "come forth" in Jn **473**
Ephrem, *i e* Ephraemus Syrus, on —"he knoweth not how" **37**, Christ's flying in the air **117**, s also **76, 467**
Epictetus, on —man as carrying about God **16**, Demeter and the mysteries of Eleusis **16**, hiding, conn w sowing **31**, the Gods and the Logos, as clean and cleansing **50**, *aploia* (only once mentioned) **61–2**, Caesar's thunder **77**, "things possible," not to be discussed **138**, [shoes] fastened (metaph) **167**, anointing (only once mentioned) **184**; deserted-

ness or *erēmiā* 224, kings as metaph shepherds 252, *chortos* and *chortázein*, used depreciatively 304, 307, Caesar's friends 383, *apotassomai* 415–16, man as "the logical creature" 433, the drawing power of the Logos 433, the example of Socrates 434, *phantasiā* 433–4, cleansing the vessel 457, peace 503, a slave denying his master 506–7, the cross (only once mentioned) 509

Epiousios, Gk, perhaps = daily, Origen on 204, various explanations of 204–5

Epiphanius 91, 177

Episitismos, Gk, provisioning, c w Heb *Saida* in Beth Saida 238–9, only once in N T 239–40

Eponymous, place-names called, by Origen 71

Erubin, or communions 363 foll

Essenes, the, Hippolytus, Josephus, and Philo on 161–4, were anointed for fellowship (Philo) 183, the salt at the meals of 221

Esthiein, Gk, eat, never used by Jn 344, altered by Jn in quotation 345, s *Trōgein*

Estimation, c w barley 287

Eucharist, the passionateness of the 375, eucharistic doctrine preceded the 375, accounts of the 392

Eucharistein, Gk, give thanks, used by Jn for bless 318

Eucharistiā, Gk, in Aquila (LXX praise, or sacrifice of praise) 319, comp 362

Eucharistic food, Jn's view of 322

Eusebius, on Polycarp's martyrdom 369

Evangelistic paraphrase of words of Jesus 359

Evangelium Petri 56, 70

Even or evening, called the first watch 420

Evenings, between the two 262

Exalt, might mean crucify 90

Exarchs, a name given by Macarius to two demoniacs in Mt 74

Exchange, a thing to be given in, or equivalent, for the soul, in Mk, meaning of 512–13, why om by Lk 514, how expr by Jn 515, Origen and Chrys on 513, there is no e for a disciplined soul (Ben Sira) 512–13

Excommunication, the Talmud on 180, inflicted by the Sanhedrin 447

Exhort, beseech, or comfort, ambig 78

Exodus, the departure of Israel from Egypt 264, 349

Exodus, the Book of, and Numbers 350

Exorcism, Jn's attitude to 67, 89–93

Expounding, private, in Mk 45 foll

Eye, the, metaph 33, a good or single 327, 459, the only Marcan instance of 459, Gk *omma* 485, in Heb, c w fountain 460

Ezekiel, a speaker of parables 5, 198, a son of man, bidden to sigh 472

Ezra, the Apocalypse of 20, on reclining on the hay 309

Face, spit before the, c w spit in the 489, s Spitting

Faith, a co-operation of, in healing 137

Fame, or report 193

Family, c w flesh 86

Family meal, Jewish, the father at a 375

Famine, not of bread, a 230

Far, come from 264, him that is far off 265

Far-beaming (R V clearly) 484–5

Farewell, bid 413 foll, c w dismiss 415 foll, s *Apotassomai*

Father of a family, a, at a Jewish meal 375

Father's house, my, ambig 109

Fear, not conn w the Resurrection by Jn 58

Feast, c w foot 246, of the Jews, the 212–13

Feed, Heb, c w know, or cause to know, *i e* teach 257

Feeding, miracles of 203–402 *passim*

Feeding of the Five Thousand, the, Jn differs from the Synoptists as to 356

Feeding of the Four Thousand, the, a personal note in 263

Feeding of the Seven Disciples, the 317, 365, and of Elijah 317–18

Feet, at his, c w on their f 245

Feet, the Washing of 462

Felix, and Paul 199, 235

Few, expr by five 291, 293

Field, parall to garden 44–5, fields, or farms 443, s Market-place

Fifth, day or generation, c w armed 312

Fifths, *i e* sections of the Law 311

Fifty, the symbol of repentance 303,

INDEX

310, the Messiah, a captain over 310-11, c w five or fifths 311, c w arrayed for battle 311
Fifties, and hundreds 309–14, Origen on 310, captains of 310, Jerome on 310–11, Talmud on 311
Fill [lit with grass or fodder], s *Chortázein*
Find, i e am able 271, be found, or be bought 271, Isaac sowed and found (not reaped) 38
Fire, a denarius of 277, of coals, a 367–8, 428, testing by f and water 422, 428
First, prefixed to Peter's name 155
First Biblical mention of —sowing 38, signs 140, buy-corn (*shâbar*) 272, ransoming the soul 277, tempting 285, (LXX, an error) barley 287, lad (Heb *naar*) 287–8, here, or hither 294, bread (or, loaf) along with grass 305, and with a curse 365, taking (ritual) 316, superabound 340, about (with numbers of men) 349, *geber* (pl) men of military age 349, numbering 351, LXX *diathēkē*, Heb *berîth*, Aq *sunthēkē* 385–6, inherit 387, *Ain* or *En* meaning fountain 461, (LXX) the oppressed 472, walking 488
Fish, Gk, *ichthus*, a Christian symbol 335, Jewish traditions about 335, and serpent 335
Fishes, two, or a few, perhaps symbolic 290, 318, from the Well that followed Israel 334, s *Jinnon*
Fist, with the, or diligently 448
Fit, "it is [fit] for us," ambig 273
Five, c w fifth, fifty, and arrayed for battle 311–12, might mean a few 291, 293, regarded mystically 351, 354, f senses, Philo on 132
Five loaves, perhaps symbolic 290, Clem Alex on 354, requested by David 293
Five thousand, in Gk, c w two hundred 276
Five Thousand, the Feeding of the 203–402 *passim*
Five Thousand in the Acts, Irenaeus and Origen on 352 foll
Flesh, his own, c w his family 86, of swine, the 452, f and blood 401, "who shall give us f to eat?" 347
Flock, in Lk and Jn 255
Flowers, trampling on (Jerome) 302, an error 303, 308–9

Following Jesus, ways of 510–11, f Satan 501, s Behind
Food, blessing God over 315 foll
Foods, all, purified by Jesus 453
Fool, Heb, c w rowing 424
Foot, c w feast 246, c w on account of 247, on foot, ambig 245–7, s also Feet
Footsoldiers, c w on my account 350
For (prepos), "for them," c w bread 273
Foreknowledge, and almightiness, the problem of 141, Christ's 103
Form, in another 432
Fountain, or well 35, 460, of life, the 35, me, the f 460, Heb, c w eye 460
Four, regarded mystically 354
Four Thousand, the Feeding of the, a more personal note in, than in the Feeding of the Five Thousand 263, conn w three days 263–7
Four Thousand, the baptizing of, in the Acts 352
Fourth Gospel, the, s John
Fourth watch of the night, the 418–21, 427
Friend, Caesar's, in Jn and Epict 383, friends, my, in Lk and Jn 382–3, the f, in 1 Jn 383
From, i e "some of" 336–7
Froward, "thou wilt shew thyself," addressed to God 505
Fulnesses of baskets, in Mk 336 foll
Fulvia, another Herodias (Jerome) 200
Funeral clothing 63

Gab, Heb, a ridge 115–16
Gab-batha 115
Gabriel, "a certain man" 290
Gadarenes 71 foll
Galilaeans 406
Galilee, perhaps an error for Judaea 152–3
Gallicinium, = *alectorophōniā* (Mk) 420
Garden, parall to earth and to field 44–5
Garden-beds 296, s *Prasiai*
Gargushta, Heb, i e clay or dirt 72–3
Garments, c w chains 83–4
Gate (SS), of a city called Bethsaida 238
Gather [themselves] together, in Mk 218
Geber, Heb, = man of military age 245, first pl instance of 349

ENGLISH

Generation, this, *i e* this evil g **477**, adulterous **515–18**
Gennesaret and Capernaum **414**
Gennesaret-traditions **65**
Gentile life, eating etc **449**, s *Koinophagiā, Koinos*
Gentiles, go not unto **151**
Gerasenes **71** foll
Gergesenes **71** foll, fellow-citizens of swine (Origen) **82**
Gird armour on, c w hump-backed **470**
Girdle, lit or metaph **170** foll, for money **172**, a golden **174**
Give, giving, etc, Jn's first mention of **26**, most freq in Jn **27**, given, applied by Jn to works **140**, and to commandments **396**, "all that the Father giveth me" **140**, "give ye them to eat," om by Jn **355**, "that he should give something to the poor" **360** foll
Giver, God regarded as the **140**
Give thanks **315, 319**, s *Eucharistein*, Thanks
Glorification, the Passion and the Crucifixion regarded as a **500, 510**, comp **90**
Glorifying, and glory, in Jn **523–4**
"Glory of his Father, the" **522–6**, Origen on **523**
Gnostic tradition **399–400**
"Go [and] see," in Mk **283, 289–93**
Go down, of God, Targ be manifested **523**
Go round, c w swine **85**
Go upright **516**
God, the secret of **15**, the foreknowledge of **141**, works by developing **373**, in the highest sense, humane **517**, the Giver, in Jn **140**, the most ancient of all fountains (Philo) **460**, the fountain of living waters (Jerem) **460**, smiting Israel **499**, "froward" **505**, "coming" or "going," in Heb, interpr as "being manifested" in Targ **523**
Gold, of the Temple, the **451**
Gold denarii **276**
Goliath and David **161**
Gospel, for the sake of the, in Mk **511**
Gospel of the Infancy, the Arabic **82**
Gospel of Peter, the, s *Evangelium Petri*
Gospels, the, s John, Luke, Mark, Matthew
Grace, in Lk and Jn **120**, and truth **26, 120, 318**

Grain of corn (or wheat), the death of the **27, 30, 267, 309, 510**
Grape, the blood of the, Origen on **395**
Grass, LXX *chortos*, Heb two words **304**, in Heb denotes transience but not degradation **304**, in Mk, called "green" **302–9**, in Mt, called by Jerome *arens foenum* **303**, winter the season of green g in Palestine **304–5**, of the field, conn w a curse **305**, diff from green [grass] (Philo) **306**, s *Chortos*
Grass, fill [cattle] with, feed full **306**, hence, depreciatively, cram **304**, s *Chortāzein*
Great, c w many **257**
Greediness, called by Paul idolatry **513**
"Greeks, certain" **18**
Green grass, in Mk **302–9**, green [grass] diff from grass (Philo) **306**
Grief, to cause, sometimes a teacher's duty **429**
Grieved, Peter was, by Jesus **426**
Groaning, Jesus described as **104, 473**
Ground, of the dust, the **72**

Hades and Satan **75**
Hagar **391**, and the woman of Samaria **35, 461**, by a fountain **461**, allusion to the story of **294–6**
Haggada, the **30**
Half-shekel or *didrachm*, the **280**
Hallowing, of the Sabbath, the **394**
Hands, the washing of **445** foll ; common h **448**, a phrase only in Mk **450**
Hang, lit and metaph **114**, *i e* crucify **115**, c w cast down from a precipice **115**
Haran **87**
Harbour, s Haven
Hardening, or blindness, of the heart in Mk, implied by Jn **438–40**, of the disciples **206, 478–81**, of Israel **441**, (SS) blind **438**, s *Pōrōsis*
Harvest, the heavenly **25**, in Mt, Lk, and Jn **154**
Hating one's life or soul **27, 91, 377, 502**
Haven (R V) the, of their desire **242**, Heb city, or market-place **243, 443**
Hay, in O T (A V) **304**, Jerome on **303**, reclining on the (*Ezr Apoc*) **309**, s *Chortos*

553

INDEX

Head, or chief, c w the name *Rôsh* 97
Headrest, or pillow, rarely means rower's cushion 63
Heal, c w save spiritually 176, 182, 185, by stages, in Mk and Jn 484–6, s Iatric, Therapeutic
Hear, passively or receptively 9, c w be amazed 99, "hear ye," in Mk 8, "hear, O Israel" 9, hearing, ins in LXX, implies "consequently" 218
Heart, hardness, blindness, or callousness of, s *Pōrōsis*
Heaven, meaning of, Jn on 475 foll
Heir, Abraham an 388
Hemerobaptists 447
Heracleon, on the heavenly harvest 25
Herbs, in O T and N T 44, greater than all the 41–2
Herd, the rational (Macarius) 92
Here (*or* hither), c w bread 294; first Biblical mention of 294–5, c w vision 295, ambig 295
Hermas, Mk illustrated from 12, 88, 127, 423, on —parables 12, the Lord of the Country 88, riches as leading to denial of the Lord 127, one understanding one love (*agapè*) 384, the Angel of Punishment 423, *basanizein* 423, never uses *diathēkē* 386, s also 48, 345, 416, 506–7, 511
Herod Antipas 465, and John the Baptist 190–202, 405
Herods, various, confused, s Philip
Herodias, not connected by Josephus with the Baptist's death 195–6, the daughter of 197, Fulvia another H 200
Hezekiah 486, in Talmud 89
Hidden, things 1, h in order to be manifested 27, comp 30, [cakes] h in the embers, Clem Alex on 372, was hidden, or hid himself 118, a God that hidest thyself 5, hiding knowledge, a teacher blamed for 29
Hillel 394, and Shammai 447
Hippolytus, on the Essenes 162
Hither, inserted for emphasis 296
Holy, the angels that are 518, the h angels 518, holy-ones, or saints, assessors in the Judgment 519, conflated as holy angels 520
Homeliness, of Christ's doctrines, the 373–4, comp 383
Honour, without, *i e* rejected 133 foll, s *Atīmos*

Horae Hebraicae, on —Gergesenes 72–3, the Legion 77, Gabbatha 116, "barley loaves" and "see" 292, common food 448, s also 89, 118, 172, 182, 447, 451, 489
Hosea, the third day in 266, quoted by Midrash on the third day in Genesis 266, on the smiting of Israel by God 499–500
Hosts, Lord of 139
Hours of the night, differently reckoned 419
House, disciples regarded as a 14, might be ambig 128, metaph. (Jerome) as Church 251
Householder, in Mt, parall to man in Mk 36–7
Human being, man meaning 517–18, comp 156–7
Humane, in the highest sense, God is 517
Humanity, the Son of Man the champion of 517
Hump-backed, c w he that girdeth on his armour 470
Hundred, the symbol of perfection (Jerome) 303, by hundreds 309
Husband 348
Hyperbole, not allowable in historians 331, h or metaphor? 416
Hypocrisy, tacitly condemned by Jn 131, 214
Hypocrites 452

Iatric and therapeutic healing, two Gk words 184–5, comp 480
Ibn Ezra, on —"a God that hidest thyself" 5, "dew of light" 44, "the dumb shall sing" 264; "deal (*i e* break) thy bread" 323, s also 144, 272, 348, 486, 492
Ichthus, Gk, fish, a Christian symbol 335, s Fish
Idolatry, covetousness, which is 513
Idols 83
Ignatius, on —the risen Saviour, not "a bodiless demon" 58, 431, new leaven 370, Peter and his friends 431, "be ye salted in Him" 373, "I know and believe" 436–7, "Let me be given to the wild beasts" 509, s also 183, 416
Immerse, and wash 448, 450
Impediment in speech 467 foll, s. Stuttering
Imperative, rare in Jn, p ix, c w. indicative 99, 187, pres imper, meaning of 203
In (*not* by) the Lord Jesus 437

ENGLISH

Incantations 187
Inclining, or declining, of the day 261 foll
Indefinite use of 3rd pers pl 80, 218, 228, 337
Indicative, c w imperative 99, 187
Infirm, not in Lk or early Christian writers 184, Origen on 184
Infirmity 176, the chain of in Mk, the variety of in Mt 471
Inheriting, Philo on 387–8, first mention of, conn w Abraham 387, s *Diathēkē*
Inside, or the inside of, ambig 456–7, c w in your power 457
Insight, see with 486
Intermediation of the Twelve, not in Jn 314–15, 332–3
Interrogative, ambig 273, 500–1 etc
Intervention, Johannine, s John
Irenaeus, on —rain and God's word 24–5, "living voice" 49, God's remembering the dead 72–3, heretical "redemption" of the dying 177, running-to-and-fro in Daniel 230, the 5000 in the Acts 352, s also 199, 354
Irony, Johannine 56, 254, 463, 523 etc
IS, WAS, and COMING, the 267
Isaac, the substitute for 228, Philo on the sacrifice of 265, sows and finds 38
Isaiah, on Israel ransomed and healed 264, 473, influence of, on Jesus 5–8, 500, (LXX) on Mark 264, 468–71, s also 492–3
Ishmael, regarded as the "lad" of Abraham 288
Israel (the nation), a lily among thorns 30, the return of, from captivity 264

Jabneh, the vineyard in 299
Jacob, the staff of 159, at Peniel 183, at Bethel 257
Jairus, or Ioarash 97, perhaps conn w *Rôsh*, head or ruler 97
James, the Epistle of, on anointing with oil 175 foll
Jerome, on —"sendeth his word" 21, faith as a grain of mustard-seed 42, Christ's country 110; "thy rod and thy staff" 160, Fulvia as "another Herodias" 200, "he made him [Joseph] lord of his house" 251, the wandering sheep 255, three days 267, the Johannine "lad" as Moses 290, the loaves and fishes 290, a garden-bed thirsting for rain 298, trampling on the flesh and its flowers 302, grass, in Mt, *arens foenum* 303, fifty, mystical significance of 310–11, Christ's sowing of food 340, he that cheweth my bread 346, the 5000 in the Acts 353, leaven (metaph) 372, Heb *berîth, foedus*, LXX *testamentum* 386, "those who were in the boat" and "the men" 429–30, Peter wrong in using the word parable 454, the ransom of Israel and of the soul 514–15, renders Gk "I know" by *vidi* 437, s also 9, 71–2, 157, 312, 323, 492
Jerome (i e Pseudo-Jerome on Mk), on —"he knoweth not how" 37, not dead but sleeping 101, the seven baskets etc 343, s also 39, 64, 175
Jesus, foreknowledge attributed to 103, emotion attributed to 104, the sense of responsibility in 478, attempts on the life of, in Jn 118 foll, homeliness of the doctrines of 373, revolutionary miracles of 383, temporary unpopularity of 405, 411, the doctrine of, on purifying 455 foll, 461, on the good eye 459, described as marvelling 143, tempting Philip 284, walking on the sea 403–41, journeying in North Palestine 407–12, 422, constraining the disciples 414, grieving Peter 426–9, purifying all foods 453, wiping off on Himself the sins of others (Origen) 232, 462, like Elijah, retiring to Sidon 465, sighing, on two occasions, in Mk 467, 474, looking up, in Lk 485, lifting up His eyes, in Jn 320
Jews, the, in Jn 213, 263, i e the rulers of the people 407, conn. w purification 461, s Passover
Jinnon, Heb, shall abound, (Schottg) shall be multiplied like fishes 333
Jochanan, R, called the Son of the Smith 121, on a threefold cord 157, on cakes in the days of the Messiah 334
Johannine Epistle, s John, the First Epistle of
Johannine irony, s Irony
John the Baptist, s Baptist
John, i e the (unknown) author of the Fourth Gospel, intervenes to explain or correct Mark, p vi and

INDEX

passim, regards all Christ's teaching as "proverbs," p vii, 13, avoids imperatives, p ix, 51, uses freq parentheses 62, varies metaphors 166, 281, does not invent 62, 289, prefers positives to negatives 214, avoids Synoptic names 124, 240, sometimes tacitly dissents where Lk agrees with Mk 322, expresses Synoptic thoughts in Johannine words 510, distinguishes passive from receptive hearing 9, deprecates the notion that Jesus taught in secret 47, calls miracles signs 140, emphasizes joy and peace 169 foll, tacitly contrasts "the Jews" with Christians 212, expresses truth dramatically 10, 213, 248–9, 331, 377, 462–3, 510, 524, ignores all distributors of bread except Jesus Himself 314–15, omits "Give ye them to eat" 355, omits all breaking of bread by Jesus 322, substitutes give thanks (*eucharistein*) for bless 318, alters *esthiein* to *trōgein* in quotation 345, meets the charge of *ōmophagiā* brought against Christians 400–1, supplies the doctrine of sacrifice implied in the breaking of bread 483, distinguishes "I" from "the word that I spake" 512, departs from the conventional conception of a judge 520, connects the end with the beginning of his Gospel 526, is perhaps influenced by Stoic doctrine on *phantasma* 434, s also Dramatic expression, Irony

John, on —"the word," as first mentioned by Jesus 21, "the word" as a whole 49–51, the Logos as cleansing 50–51, children of God 44, the Romans and Caesar 77, the ruler of this world 89, attempts on Christ's life 118, "offending" 128 foll, hypocrisy, not mentioned, but condemned, 131, 214, giving 26, 140, marvelling 143 foll, sending apostles 148, bearing witness 156, joy and peace 169 foll, John the Baptist 202, "the Jews," contrasted w Christians 212, snatching 253, the Passover of the Jews 212, 263, three days 268, metaphors of ransoming 281, Jesus, as tempting 284–5, *paidarion* 286–96, come and ye shall see 292, the Marcan *symposia* 300, "superabounding" 340, that nothing be lost 341, laid 368, *diaconos* and serving at table 377, the sisters of Lazarus 380, the drawing power of the Father and the Son 434, seeing 437, hardening 440–41, the doctrine of Jesus on purification 460–62, Jesus as groaning, equiv to (Mk) sighing 473, the raising of Lazarus, implying the Marcan *Ephphatha* 473, healing, conn w spitting 473, stumbling, perhaps parall to (Mk) callousness 481, the healing of blindness 489, "Thou art the Christ" 496, the Passion as a Glorification 500, the cross, mentioned only in one passage, perhaps symbolic 509, persecution 509, judgment 519–22, a crisis or division 521, the doctrine of conviction 521, glorifying and glory 523, Christ's coming, final mention of 524

John, words not mentioned in — parable 13, little-ones 42, 44, wisdom 119, hypocrisy and hypocrites 131, mighty-work (*lit* power) 139, witness (masc n) 156, infirm 187, bowels of compassion 248, bless (except as passive participle) 319, s also 155, 256, 460, 509

John, the First Epistle of, continuous with the Gospel 463, three stages of belief in 27, s also 57, 130, 247 etc

Jonah 61

Joseph, in Egypt 251, sold by Judah as Jesus by Judas (Tertull) 20, called (Philo) the bowels of Jacob 249, the bowels of, yearning for Benjamin 251

Josephus, on —the Essenes 161–2, Roman infantry 163–4, the Baptist's death 195–7, Elisha bidding farewell to his home 415–16, the common, *i e* Gentile life, manner of eating etc 449, uses *diathēkē* as meaning testament 386, avoids *diathēkē* as meaning covenant 386, s also 265, 297

Joshua 290, the son of Nun, a lad (Heb. *naar*) 291

Journeying of Jesus, the 407–12, 442

Joy and peace, more prominent in Jn than in Synoptists 168 foll

Judaea, ambig 111, Galilee perhaps an error for 152–3, Judaean land,

might be explained as not Samaria or not Gentiles **151**
Judas Iscariot **128–9, 141, 414**, the basketful of, Ammonius on **341**, s also **20**
Judge (vb and n) not in Mk **520**
Judgment, in Jn **519–22**, a crisis, or division **521**, of this world, a **523**, the saints as assessors in the day of **519**, mentioned by Mk only once, about Pharisees **520**
Jurisdiction, of Antipas **405**, of Pilate **406**
Justin Martyr, does not mention parable in his Apology **12–13**, charges Jews with corrupting Scripture **72**, adapts his vocabulary to Gentiles and Jews **386**, quotes Isaiah on the Suffering Servant **134, 500**, on —the Sower **6**, the works of a carpenter **122**, Christ's form as *atīmon* **134**, new leaven **371**, unleavened bread **372**, the water of life **373**, the assertion that Christians ate human flesh **399**, infirmities healed by Jesus **470**, the spiritual eye **485**, s also **136, 306, 416, 423, 457**
Juvenal, on the Jewish *cophinos* (basket) **344**

Kiddûsh, the, Sanctification of the Sabbath **207**
Kill, in A V and LXX, freq =smite in R V and Heb **499**
Kindred, or land of one's k , Gk *patris* **110**
King, Herod Antipas called a **197, 201**, and tetrarch **198**, of Babel, the **253**, the multitude purpose to make Jesus a **236**, kings, the wise are (Philo) **258**, regarded as shepherds **252**
Kingdom, freq in Mt **19**, rare in Jn **256**, the New **502**
Kiss, in Jewish tradition **379**, three kinds of **379–80**, in the Pauline Epistles **379**, salute with a (Lucian) **381**, c w arming **381**, Philo on **381**, of love, the **378–83**, Clem Alex on the abuse of **379**, of God, the, Moses died by **382**, s *Philēma*
Klasma, s *Clasma*
Know, cause to, *i e* teach, c w feed or shepherd (vb) **257**, c w. believe **436**, c w see **437**, "I k and believe" (Ign) **436**, "I k and am persuaded" **437**

Koinē dialectos, the common language of the empire **449**
Koinophagiā, Gk, common eating, s *Koinos*
Koinos, Gk, "common [to all, many, etc]," but not defiled **449**, thrice in canon LXX, "common purse" etc **449**, "common hands," unique in Mk **448–50**, the common life, *i e* to all Gentiles, hence (for Jews) unholy **449**, common eating, *i e*. unholy **449**

Lad, a, with barley loaves **286–96, 318**, Abraham's **288**, s *Paidarion*
Laid, in Jn **366–9**, perhaps appointed **368**
Lame of speech **470**
Lamp, Mk's single mention of **32**, John the Baptist a **35, 194**
Lampstand, the holy, Philo on **36**
Last Days, the Discourse on the **168–9**
Late **261**
Law (of Moses) the, sowing the (*Ezr Apoc*) **309**, and the Prophets **290**, the New **453**, of Purification **442** foll , and of Sacrifice **464** foll , variations in the expression of **501**, dramatized in Jn **524**
Lazarus, the Raising of **100** foll , **473–4**, the Synoptic silence about **105–6**
Learn, *i e* come to know, c w feed, shepherd (vb) **257**, Jesus described as learning **499**
Leave, take leave, inadequate for *apotassomai* **416**
Leaven, metaph in bad sense **209**, literal, not prohibited except at a stated season **210**, Christ's **370, 402**, conn by Tertull with the fire of hell **370**, in a good sense, not in Talmud **371**, a new (Ign and Justin M) **370–71**, Plutarch on **372**
Legion, the number in a **75**, why not mentioned by Mt **75**, transliterated into Heb **75**, ten legions (Caesar) **77**, "the legions that choke you" **76**
Leisure, have not, in Gk **235**, in Mk **233–7**
Levi, denying his brethren **506**
Levitical precepts, Origen on **454**
Lie [down] (vb) = to be laid, s Laid
Life, the fountain of **35**, Jesus restoring to **94** foll.

INDEX

Lift up, *i e* crucify 90
Lift up the eyes 228, first Abrahamic instance of 228, a precept of Jesus 228, in Jn 320, lift up the head, double meaning of 90, lift up the heart, how to 375-6
Light, heavenly, how denoted 484-5, no doctrine of, in Mk 32
Like, Heb, before numbers, *i e* about, = LXX [amounting] to 349
Literal, the, mixed with metaphorical, see Precepts to Apostles 158-89 *passim*, s also Metaphor
Little flock, in Lk 255
Little ones, not in Jn 42
Little sheep, in Jn 256
Living, a familiar epithet for water 300, a new epithet for bread 300
Living voice, the, Papias on 49
Loaf, or bread (Gk *artos*), first mention of, conn w a curse 305, conveyed to Jews suggestions of unity 365, one l, mentioned by Mk and Paul 211, contemplated by Jn 344, in *Acts of John* 360, we all partake of the 363, s Bread
Loaves, R V bread 213, comp 274, not in early Fathers etc 354, small, one for each guest 360, five 290, barley l and Elisha 287, s Five, and Miracles of Feeding, 203-402 *passim*
Logos, the, the cleansing nature of, in Epict and Jn 50-51, s. Word
Look up, or receive insight 488, in Synopt, c w recover sight 320, 485, to heaven 315 foll, 320, applied to Jesus in Lk 485
Loosing, in prophecy and Mk 469 foll, of Lazarus, the 474
Lose, Gk, double meaning of 514, l the soul, in Jn 502, lost, that nothing may be, in Jn 341
Love (n), Gk *agapê*, in Jn 384, a new kind of, in Jn 395-6, in Wisdom of Solomon 384, conn w understanding in Hermas 384, the kiss of 378-83, s Kiss
Loved, c w deceived 279
Lucian, on "salute with a kiss" 381
Luke, regards the Apostles as witnesses 156, shews traces of LXX 262
Luke, omits —many instances of *scandalizein* 127, (Mt) mountains (where Lk has desert) 224, traditions about a shepherd 252-6, *diaconos* 377, new wine, in the account of the Eucharist 394, journeyings of Christ 409-10, Caesarea 412, Marcan traditions on bread 481-2, other Marcan traditions 483, traditions about ransom 514
Luke, on —Christ's visits to Nazareth 112, Herodias 201, the risen Saviour, as eating 221, Bethsaida 237-40, *chortos* as grass, not hay 303, the number of the converted 351, a Petrine interrogation (not in Mk) 420, (Codex D) *phantasma* 432, (Ign) a bodiless demon 431, alms (not in parall Mt) 455, purifying (diff from parall Mt) 455 foll, the "daily" taking up of the cross 509, the coming of the Lord (diff from Mk) 522
Lyons, Elders of the Church of 399

Macarius, on mustard-seed 42, on two exarchs in Mt 74, views opposed by 86, 419, s also 91-3, 242, 419 foll
Machos, Heb city etc, R V. haven 243
Madmen, c w rowing 424, conn w *phantasma* 433 foll
Magadan and Dalmanutha 242, 409, 443
Maimed, lame, dumb, or bound 469-71
Maimonides, on *Erubin* or communions 363-4
Mammon 507, the yoke of 513
Man (*homo*), as champion of humanity 517, men, the, ambig 430
Man of military age (*vir*), Heb *geber* 245, a certain, *i e* Gabri-el 290, rendered ἀνήρ in Pentateuch only thrice 349, first Scriptural instance of pl *geber* 349, s Geber
Men, ἄνδρες, *i e* not women and children 350, two, in Lk, *i e* Moses and Elijah 519
Manna 203, 225, 239, 285
Many, freq in Mk 226, *i e* the majority 232, c w great 257; ransom for 231, m things, in Mk 199-200, suffer m things 500
Mark (s Chapter Headings in Contents), neglected by the ancients, p v, 439, typical and allusive meanings in 487, new words in 247, 420, signs of conflation in 243-4, 518, does not aim at variety 415, attitude of, toward Gentiles in traditions about bread 482, traces of Petrine tradition in 21, mentions lamp (metaph) but no

doctrine of light **32**, has man parall to Mt householder **36**, joy and peace latent in **168-9**, **503**, omits baptizing in the Precepts to the Twelve **186**, eye (sing) metaph in **459**, s Conflation

Mark, on —one loaf **211**, many **226**, ransom for many **231**, the boat **241-2**

Market-place, R V haven **243**, in fields (?) **443**

Martha, serving [at table] **377**, s *Diaconos*

Martus, Gk, a witness, or martyr, not in Jn **156**

Martyr, p xiii, **156**, martyrs, Jewish **452**

Martyrdom, Origen and Tertullian on the fruit of **39**, the passion for **509**

Martyrological phrases **511**

Marvelling, attributed to Jesus **143**, and to God **144**, deprecated by philosophers **143**, used in a bad sense by Jn **143**, explained as implying silence **144**

Materialistic, the multitude regarded as **524**

Matthew, mentions two demoniacs where Mk-Lk has one **70**, and two blind men where Mk-Lk has one **485**, has householder parall to Mk man **36**, omits legion **75**, has mountains parall to Lk desert **224**, mentions Peter, not in parall Mk **421**, differs from parall Lk as to purifying **455** foll, and as to metaphor **455-6**, on kingdom **19**, on retribution **505-6**

Meal, Jewish, the father of the family at a **375**

Meats, s Foods

Medinah, Heb, province or city **87-8**, **110**

Megalopolis, a **242**

Meir, R, attitude of, toward the Sabbath **181-2**, a kind action of **489**, on "a denarius of fire" **277**

Men, s Man

Mercury or Hermes, the sandals of **167**

Messenger, Moses a **288**, Abraham's **288**

Messiah, the, called the Nail **164**, a captain over fifty **311**, regarded as sighing **472-3**, cakes in the days of **334**, meaning of the title, to Jesus **499**

Metaphor, first-century misunderstandings of **398-9**, **401**; mystical, called tropology (Origen) **64**, obscure **33**, varied **166**, **281**, poetic **207**, military **313**, in the Precepts to the Twelve **148-87**, traces of, in the narratives about baskets **209** foll, of ransoming or buying **281**, of thirsty garden-beds **298**, of the vineyard in Jabneh, taken by some as literal **299**, of purification **460**, illustrating regeneration **373**, in Mt. but not in Lk **455-6**, mixed with non-metaphor **59**, **70**, **158** foll, **171-2**, **175** foll, **184-5**, **416**, **456-9**

Michael **520**

Midbar, Heb, (1) any open country, (2) the desert of Sinai **225**, c w. Aram take **238**

Military, age, man of **349**, m. metaphor **313**

Minister, s *Diaconos*, Servant

Miracles (*lit* powers), revolutionary **383**, in Synoptists, are signs in Jn **140**, of feeding **203-402** *passim*, s also Chapter Headings in Contents

Miriam, died by God's kiss **382**

Mishna, called the mysteries of God **17**, **20**, on —entering the Mount of the Temple **171**, washing before eating **448**, **450**, Corban **451**; common food **448**, s *Chullin*

Mission of the Twelve, the first **151**

Mixing, *i e* communion **363**

Modius, a Hebraized word **34**

Moment of time, c w plague **100**

Money, a girdle for **172**

Moored to the shore, in Mk **443**

Moses, God's *Sheliach* or apostle **233**, **288**, remonstrates with God ("Whence to me. ?") **270**, is shewn a denarius of fire **277**, is signified by the "lad" in Jn (Jerome) **290**, **318**, died by God's kiss **382**

Mount, of the Temple, the **171**

Mountain, conn w Jesus **407**; mountains in Mt, parall. to desert in Lk **224**

Mulcted, in one's soul or mind (Synopt and Philo) **514**

Multitude(s), the **415**, **524**

Mustard-seed, a grain of, faith as, how explained **42**

Muzzled or dumb, in Targum **470-71**, c w lamed **471**

Mystery, a Hebraized word **16**; in Gk and Heb **15**, of the seal, the **267**, the hardening of Israel a **6**, of the kingdom, the **15**, the m.

INDEX

that is the head of all things **48**, mysteries of Eleusis, the **16**, mysteries, some attacked by Philo but others praised **29**

Naar, Heb, lad **287**, might also imply service **291**, first Biblical instance of **287–8**, interpr in O T as Ishmael **288**, of Moses as "babe" **288**, s *Paidarion*
Nail, c w peg, shovel, arms **163** foll, *i e* the Messiah **163–4**, nails, the three, *i e* Abraham, Isaac, and Jacob **164**
Name, *i e* n of the Lord **188**, Heb, c w oil **188**, of God, the, unity of **508**
Names, Synoptic, avoided by Jn **124, 240**
Napkin, about Christ's head, the **64**
Nathanael **15**
Natural religion **497** foll
Nature, Philo on **39**, good or bad in man, Heb *yetzer* **372**, God in **373**, (Epict) drawing man **433**
Naught, set at, in Isaiah (Sym), Mk, and Lk **135**
Nazareth **109** foll, **153**
Nearing, they see Jesus n **433**
Negatives, as distinct from positives, avoided by Jn **214**
Nero **398**
New, in the accounts of the Eucharist **392–3**, om in Lk (shorter txt) **392–4**, n commandment, in Jn and I Jn **395**, n eye **493**, n kingdom **502**, the New Law **453**, of Purification **442** foll, of Sacrifice **464** foll, variously expressed **501**
New words in Mk **247, 420**, comp **125**
Nicodemus, the dialogue with **9–10, 40**
Night, fourth watch of the **418–22, 427**, hours of the, differently reckoned **419**
Nineveh **32**
Noah, the covenant with **385**, the equivalent, or successor, of perished humanity **515**
Non-causes **524**
Non-defilement, the doctrine of **412–13**
Non-intervention, Johannine, in matters affecting John the Baptist **219**, in Synoptic names **240**
Non-metaphor, c w metaphor **456**, s Metaphor
Nonnus, on —reclining on the hay

308, "not even Peter" ventured to say "who art thou?" **435**, Jesus making clay **490**, s also **60, 241, 337, 367, 369**
North and South **230**
North Palestine, Jesus in **407–13**
Not, Heb, c w to him **294**
Number, in Lk and Jn **351**, numbers, treated symbolically in Midrash **292**
Numbering, of Israel, ten occasions of **350**, perhaps differently regarded by Lk and Jn **351**, first instance of **351**, the seed of Abraham cannot be numbered **351**

Oath, of Herod Antipas, the **196–7**
Obscurity, a necessity in Christ's teaching, p viii, in an earlier writer, explained by a later **20**
Obvious interpretations, Origen's warning against **454**
Odes of Solomon, the **15, 114**
Oedipodean intercourse, imputed to Christians **398**
Offend, *i e* cause to stumble **125–6**, not in Gk literature **125**, not used actively in LXX **125**, in Synoptists **124–7**, in Jn **128–32**, in Mk, passive, parall to apostatize in Lk **127**, in Aram, has two Heb. meanings **126**, s *Scandalīzein*
Offspring of the vine, the **394**
Oil, anointing with **175** foll, curing with, Tertullian on **177**, in Heb, c w name **188**
Old, new and, in I Jn **395**
Old Testament, s First Biblical Mention
Omma, Gk, eye **485**, in LXX only in Prov **485**, in Gk literature means the eye of the soul **485**, in N T only conn w the healing of blindness **485**, *o* and *opthalmos* **485**
Ōmophagiai, Gk, eatings of raw flesh, Christians suspected of **399**, described by Plutarch and Clem Alex **399**
One loaf, in Mk and Paul **211**, contemplated by Jn **344**, in *Acts of John* **360**, we all partake of the **363** foll
Onkelos, on God's going down **523**
Only begotten son, implying uniquely beloved **250**, s Bowels
Opening, lit and metaph **326**, o the Scriptures **326**, be thou opened, implies a prison **471, 473**, s *Ephphatha*

ENGLISH

Oppressed (LXX), first mention of 472
Opthalmos and *omma*, Gk, eye 485
Order, chronological 65, 268
Origen, on —those who sow 7, the censers of Corah 18, "our Joseph" 20, "sendeth his word" 21, the harvest in heaven 25, the fruit from martyrs 39, faith as a grain of mustard-seed 42, Jesus, as appearing differently to the disciples and to the multitudes 46, the delivering up of Jesus 56, the sleeping of the Divine Word 59, Johannine "tropology" 64, eponymous place-names 71, bodies that are tombs 73, Gergesenes, fellow-citizens of swine 82, Abraham's country 87, the raising of Lazarus 103, Christ's country 110, Jesus, not called a carpenter 121, desire, a neutral term 132, *atīmos* 133, Christ's being "not able" 137, the *sumpraxis* or cooperation of faith 138, the claim of certain heretics to more than priestly power 177, sin unto death, and confession of sins 177–9, the infirm 184–5, the word *epiousios*, not in existence before the Lord's Prayer 204, the Jews, not knowing how to purify themselves 213, those who refresh themselves with the nourishment of Jesus 220, the Saviour, wiping off defilement 232, 462, the Four Thousand, and three days 267, the five loaves and the two fishes 290–91, lying down in (*sic*) the grass 303, ranks of the Five Thousand 310, blessing God 319, broken pieces of bread 338, he that cheweth my bread 346, the 5000 in the Acts 353–4, "give ye them to eat" 355–6, offspring of the vine, Christ's blood 394, the boat distressed 424–5, the boat of temptations 425, swimming through trials 425, the [men] in the boat 429, parables 454, "the obvious," contrasted with "the appointed scope" 454, Levitical precepts 454, true self-purification 463, invisible persecutors 503, "for the sake of the Gospel" 511, the equivalent, or exchange, for a man's soul 512–13, Christ's Coming 522–3, s also 10, 22–3, 31, 33, 43, 64, 70, 101, 155, 230, 274, 358, 409, 460, 466, 468

Originality of Christ's thought 374
Other, Gk, c w "but" 60
Ought, how expr in Heb 273
Outside, in Jn 89, 91, down substituted for 91, c w that which is o 456, o the country in Mk 86, o oneself (Philo) 488
Outstripping and running to and fro 231
Owe, p ix

Paidarion, Gk, freq = Heb *naar*, lad 287–8, in Jn "there is a l here" 286–96, unique in N T 287, interpr by Jerome as Moses 290, rare in early Christian writers 287, s *Naar*
Pairs, the Apostles said to be sent out in 158
Papias, on the living voice 49, on sayings of Andrew, Philip, and Thomas 282
Parable, the word, used in Justin Martyr's *Dialogue* but not in *Apology* 12–13, rare in early Fathers 12, in Hermas sometimes means paradox 12, Jn substitutes proverb for, p vii, 13, Peter blamed by Jerome and Chrys. for using 454
Parables, Christ's 1–8, of Sowing, the 1–59, "asking the p " 10 foll.
Paraclete, the, meaning of the term 78, 165, a personal testament 397
Pâras, Heb, break in half, R V. "*deal* thy bread" 323, v r. *pârash* separate, or spread out and explain 323–4
Pârash, Heb, spread out the hands in blessing, or separate Scripture into sections 324
Parentheses, freq in Jn 62
Parents, duty of children to 451
Paroimiā, Gk, i e proverb, Jn's substitute for parable 13, comp p vii
Partitive use of "from," i e some of 336–7
Parts, i e regions 242, c w villages 487
Paschal Lamb, first mention of the 340
Passion, of Jesus, the, a glorifying 500, 510
Passionateness, of the Eucharist, the 375, 378, 399
"Passover of the Jews, the," in Jn 212, 263, Origen on 213

INDEX

Patris, Gk, =Heb kindred, or land of one's kindred **109** foll
Paul, uses military metaphor **313**, on *diathēkē* **390–91**, s also **57, 441** etc
Peace, Epict on **503**, seldom in Mk **503**, of Jesus, the **504**, conditional **504**, the condition of, is self-sacrifice **505**, p and joy, more prominent in Jn than in the Synoptists **168–9**
Peniel, Jacob the wrestler at **183**
Penitence, s Repentance
Pennyworth, two hundred **274–82**
Pentecost, (Philo) conn w the square of seven **343**
Perfect tense, the, combined with aorist **353**
Perfection, a hundred the symbol of **303**
Perplexed, to be, prob. an error **192**, c w to pose **199**
Perplexity, of Herod Antipas, the **198**
Persecution, Jn on **509**
Persecutors, invisible, Origen on **503**
Peter, a martyr or witness, p xiii, the voice from heaven to (in Acts) **412**, the vision of "a sheet" to (in Acts) **452–3**, the denial of, reference to **420**, the merit of the confession of **496–7** foll , tested [and tormented] **425**, grieved by Jesus **426–7**, in Lk but not in Mk **420**, in Mt but not in Mk **421**, (?) called a stumbling-block in Mt. **130, 501**, said to have denied and confessed near a coal-fire **368**, blamed by Jerome and Chrys for using the word parable **454**, "not even Peter ventured to ask.." (Nonnus) **435**
Petrine reminiscences or speeches **21, 201, 420, 471**
Phagein, Gk, eat, interch by Jn with *trōgein* **347**
Phantasiā, Gk, in Epict **433–4**
Phantasma, Gk, various meanings or interpretations of **58, 430–34**, Chrysippus' definition of **431, 433**, Pliny on **431**
Pharaoh, the type of an oppressor **76**
Pharisees, definition of **448**, s also **451**
Philēma, Gk, kiss, and *philiā*, Gk, love, Philo on **381**
Philip the Apostle, the character of **273, 281–2**, sayings of, Papias on **282**
Philip (Herod) **494**

Philip the Tetrarch **405**, diff from Herod Philip **494**
Philippi, Caesarea, so called from Philip the Tetrarch **494**
Philo, attacks disreputable initiations and mysteries **29**, distinguishes shepherds from cattle-feeders **254–5**, blessed (particip) from blessed (adj) **319**, and *philēma*, kiss, from *philiā*, love **381**, rarely quotes prophecy **389**; on —the sun and the holy lampstand **36**, Isaac's finding (not reaping) **38–9**, things automatic and natural **39**, Abraham's country **87**, the seducer who acts through the five senses **132**, Jacob's staff **159**, the Essenes **161** foll , **183**, the nail or shovel **164**, the Feast of the Baskets **208, 342**, the salt at the meals of the Essenes **221**, "the Lord is my shepherd" **258**, the sacrifice of Isaac **265**, the third day **265–6**, the *symposia* of the Therapeutae **297–8, 313, 361**, grass and green [grass] **306**, "taking" for God **316**, the unity of the whole burnt offering **322–3**, the square of seven and the eve of Pentecost **343**, the four pillars and the five **354**, three measures of meal **372**, *diathēkai*, covenants or testaments **387–8**, God as a *diathēkē* **388**, God, the most ancient of all fountains **460**, *apotassomai* **415**, Abraham, bidden to look up **484, 488**, the eye (*omma*) of the soul **485**, bringing out outside **488**, Levi denying his brethren **506**, s also **31, 249–50, 253, 433, 488, 490, 507, 514**
Physical, the, c w the spiritual **182**, or moral **186**
Physicians, Ben Sira on **181**
Pilate, jurisdiction of **405–6**
Pillow **63–4**, s Cushion
Pistis Sophia, the **48**
Plague or stroke, c w moment **100**
Plato, blamed for never grieving a disciple **429**, followed by Philo and Justin Martyr **485**, on — *mȳthos* and *logos* **23**, the sun **36**; testing as if by torment **422**, s. also **11, 167, 458**
Pliny, acquits Christians that cursed Christ **180**, defines *phantasma* **431**
Pluperfect tense, c w aorist **182, 438, 440**, want of, in Heb **438**

Plural, c w singular 82, 469
Plutarch, quotes Chrysippus on *phantasma* and "drawing" 431, 433, quotes Diogenes to the effect that a teacher must "grieve" his pupils 429, on —the deprecation of marvelling by Pythagoras 143, brass rusted by lightning 173, grass, not dry but green 305, leaven 372, *ōmophagiai* 399, progressors as swimmers 425, s also 61, 307
Poetry, narratives of the nature of 59, traces of, in Mk's healing of the blind 484–6, comp 469
Polycarp, the martyrdom of 369
Poor, giving to the 360
Pŏrōsis, pŏroun, hardening, callousness, various kinds of 479–80, in Mk, Jn, and Paul 441
Positives, as distinct from negatives, Jn dwells on 214
Possible things, Epict declines to discuss 138, Jn's attitude towards 139
Post-resurrectional, acts and words of Christ 14, 374, possibly antedated 46, 52–3, 186–7, 207, 222, 432, 441, recognition of Jesus 435, Chrysostom and Nonnus on 435
Power, in one's p, c w inside 457
Powers, "these p work in him," in Mk-Mt 193–4, meaning "miracles," equiv to "signs" in Jn 140
Prasiā, Gk, *lit* greenery, and hence garden-bed 296, *prasiai*, in Mk 296–301, garden-beds thirsting for rain, Jerome on 298, equiv to, in Jn, if any 301
Prayer, in behalf of the sick 175 foll, for bread, the 203 foll, conn w Jesus 407
Preaching, to the spirits in prison 58, 70
Precepts, to the Twelve, the 148–87, literal or metaphorical 170 foll, regarded as gifts 396, the yoke of 508
Precipitation, the Rock of 117
Present imperative, implying continuous action 204
Priestly power, more than, Origen on 177
Priests 451
Prince, of this world, the 89, s Ruler
Prison, the spirits in 58, 70, Sin or Egypt a 472, sighing in the 472
Private expounding by Jesus 45, Jn's attitude towards 47

Profane or unholy (A V) = common (R V) 448, s Common
Pronoun, s They
Proofs, Thucydidean 436
Proper names, Synoptic, avoided by Jn 124, 240
Prophecy, influence of, s Hosea, Isaiah
Prophet, a term applied to Jesus 496
Prophets, the 290, 318
Proselyte, a, new-born 490
Prove, test, or try 285, by fire 422
Proverb, in Jn, = parable in the Synoptists, p vii, 13
Province or city 87, p and marketplace 443
Provisioning, Heb *saida*, Gk *episitismos* 237–40, s Bethsaida
Psalms, the 290, 318
Pseudo-Jerome, s Jerome
Punishment, the Angel of, in Hermas 423
Pure and impure, things 458
Purifier, the 460
Purifying, the New Law of 442 foll; Christ's doctrine on 455 foll, 461, the new and the old 462, two Gk verbs for 461–3, "p all foods" 453
Purse, lit or metaph 170 foll
Pursued (?) by righteousness (Clem. Alex) 511
Pythagoras, deprecates marvelling 143

Q, a name given to the Double Tradition of Matthew and Luke 125, 373
Quadratus 353
Quincunx 311, 314
Quotation, deviations in 6, 345, 499 etc

Rachel 380
Raising, ambig, morally or physically 176, 182
Ranks, of the Five Thousand, in Mk 296, Origen on 310, s *Prasiai*
Ransom 515, for the soul, the, revealed to Moses 277, 280, a denarius of fire 277, riches, or almsgiving 278, tradition about, om by Lk 514, for many, a 231, s Exchange
Ransomed, the, return of the 264
Raphael 520
Rashi, on —"with my staff" 159, Abraham's recompence 233, "this

INDEX

shalt thou give" 277, breaking [bread] 324, s also *passim*
Raw or living flesh, the Christians accused of eating 398 foll, s *Ōmophagiai*
Real-and-true, *alēthinos*, c w true, *alēthēs* 22, comp 50
Receiving Jesus 56
Recognition of Jesus, post-resurrectional 435
Recoil of disciples, in Mk but not in Mt -Lk 481, Jn intervenes as to 481
Recompensing, of Abraham, the 228 foll, 286
Recover sight, c w look up 320
Redeemed, the 264, comp 469, redeeming the dying, Irenaeus on 177, s Ransom
Reduplicated article, the, rare in Synoptists 518
Refresh oneself, with food, Origen on 220
Regeneration, in Jn 9–10, metaphors of 373, s also 42–4
Rejection, the drama of 465, anticipation of 499, s *Atīmos*
Religion, natural 497
Remnant or superabundance 338
Renounce, *apotassomai* 416
Repentance, fifty the symbol of (Jerome) 303, 310–11, applied to God 478
Report (n), or fame 193
Rest (n), under Christ's yoke 219
Rest (vb), in Gk, refresh [with food] 220, "come and r" might mean come and break your fast 219–23
Resurrection, for Israel (Hosea) 266, sons of the 520, Christ's, events placed before or after 46, s Post-resurrectional
Retribution, the Law of 76–7, in Mt 505
Return of the Captives, the, in Isaiah 264, Mk alludes to 468–71
Riches, the ransom of man's soul 278
Riddles 4–8
Righteousness, a name for almsgiving 279, c. w alms 456
Rise, s Arise
Rod, and staff, Jerome on 160, s Staff
Romans, the, Jn on 77
Rose, Israel compared to a 30
Rôsh, Heb, head or ruler 97, s Jairus
Round about, c w swine 88
Rowing, c w running to and fro 244–5, in Gk may mean driving

424, Heb *lit* "moving to and fro" may mean in Aram "mad" 424
Ruler of this world, the 89
Run away, Adam and Eve, from God (Philo) 507, running away from God is fleeing into oneself (Philo) 507
Runaway, a, denying his master (Epict) 507
Run to and fro, in Daniel and Mk 230, 244, c w row 244–5

Sabaoth, Lord of 139
Sabbath, the hallowing of the 207, 394, remember the, over the wine 394
Sacrifice (n), kindness and not 362–3, better than 363, the new law of 464 foll, s *Eucharistā* (Aquila)
Sacrifice (vb) 362
Said, or used to say, ambig 291
Saida, Heb., provision, in *Beth Saida*, House of Provisioning 238
Saints, s Holy
Sake, for the, of the Gospel, in Mk 511
Salt, at the meals of the Essenes 221, a covenant of 221
Salted, with fire 373, be ye s in Him (Ign) 373
Salute [for the last time] 416, s *Apotassomai*
Samaritans, "*not S*" 151
Samaritan woman, the, and the Syrophoenician 467, and Hagar 35, 460–61
Sandalon, a Hebraized word for sandal, with various meanings 168
Sandals, shod with 167 foll, of Mercury, the 167
Sanhedrin, the, on the washing of hands 447
Sarepta of Sidonia 409, comp 468
Satan, and Hades 75, regarded as binding 471, "Get thee behind me, S" 498, c w "Art thou going after S ?" 500–501
Save, c w heal 176
Say, *i e* command 98, used to say, c w said 291
Saying (n) interch w word 22
Scandalīzein, Gk, *i e* cause to stumble, not in Gk literature and only once in LXX 125, in Aram =two Heb words 126
Scandalon, Gk, stumbling-block, in LXX =two Heb nouns 126, there is no *s* in him 130

ENGLISH

Schism, in Jn 112
Scrip, conn w staff 161, or wallet 160, lit or metaph 170 foll
Scriptures, opening the 326
Sea, Jesus walking on the 403–41, by the 409, from s to s 230
Seal, the, of baptism, the mystery of 267
Season, *i e* leisure 235, have no good s 233–5
Secret, of God, the 15
See, the Lord, interch w appear before the Lord 486, saw, in Jerome, =Gk know 437
"See, come (*or*, go) and," conn w symbolism 289, 292 foll, w barley loaves 292
Seeing, metaph 33, in Jn 437, s the kingdom of God 524, s out of darkness, Ibn Ezra on 492, thou art a God of s 461
See-with-insight, Gk, construction with 486
Seed, the blood of Christians said to be 39, s Mustard-seed
Self, the lower, he that runs away from God flees into 507, the true 514
Self-purification 461–3, two Gk words for 461, 463
Self-sacrifice, the Law of 464–526, comp 27, 30, 267, 309, 510
Self-worship, implied in hardness of heart 480
Sending of Apostles, Jn on 148–51
"Separation," of Scripture into sections 324
Septuagint, the, amplifies for clearness 20, on *diathēkē*, covenant 385–91, paraphrases 469–70 etc
Servant, *i e* bondservant, s *Doulos*
Servant or young man (Heb *naar*) 288
Servant [at table] 377, s *Diaconos*
Service, filial, the yoke of 508
Set ye for yourselves (Heb)=set your hearts on (Targ) 308–9
Seven, mystically explained 355, seven baskets, loaves, churches 375, s *Sphurides*, seven disciples, the feeding of 222, 365, and that of Elijah 317
Seventy (*or*, seventy-two) missionaries, the 154, 221
Severus, the Emperor, "cured by oil" 177
Shâbar, Heb, buy [mostly corn] 272, first used of corn in Egypt 272
Shad, Heb, demon 432
Shaddai 139

Shadow, in Heb poetry 30
Shammai 160, and Hillel 394, 447
Shechinah, the, seen by Abraham and Isaac 266
Sheep, not having a shepherd 252–6, Jerome on the wandering 255, little, in Jn 256, three classes of 259
Shekel, or *stater* 280, half-shekel, the 280
Sheliach, Heb, *i e* one sent, or apostle, Moses a 233
Sheol, Descent into, the 59, s *Descensus*
Shepherd (n), the scrip of a 160 foll, metaph in Mk-Mt and Gk literature but not in Lk 252–6, a king as a 252, the compassionate 260, the Lord is my s, Jewish comments on 258–9, shepherds, diff from cattle-feeders (Philo) 254, Moses and David as 259
Shepherding, aspects of, in Lk and Jn 256, includes feeding, guiding, tending 256–7, is more than redeeming 258, c w knowing or teaching 257
Shod, with sandals 167 foll
Shoes, in the four Gospels 167
Sibylline Oracles, the, on *Ichthus* 335
Sick, anointing the 175 foll, praying over the 175 foll, s Heal
Sickness, physical and spiritual 182, comp 180
Sidon, c w Sidonia 468, perhaps derived from O T 468, through S, in Mk, om by Mt 409, 467–8
Sidonia, Sarepta of, the widow in 468, Origen on 409, comp. 468
Sighing, of Jesus, the first 467, the second 474, of prisoners 472, of Israel 289, 472, of Ezekiel, son of man 472, shall flee away 473
Sight, recover 485, c w look up 320, 485
Sign, from heaven, a, the demand for 474, the meaning of 475–6, signs, first Biblical mention of 140, in Jn, =miracles (*lit* powers) in Synoptists 140
Signs, "make s ," c w swim 52, 116, 426
Silence, and marvelling 144
Simon Magus, on mustard-seed 42
Simon Peter, s Peter
Sin, Egypt the prison of 472, against the light 373, unto death, Origen on 179, confession of, Origen on 179

565

INDEX

Sinai, the wilderness of **225**, the *diathēkē* of **391, 393**
Sinaitic Syrian Codex, the, readings of **115, 226, 435–6, 438** etc
Single, and singleness, of eye or heart **327**
Singular, c w plural **82, 218, 469**
Sister, my, in Mk, om by Lk **380**, Martha and her s, in Jn **381**
Sitting down, with Abraham and Isaac and Jacob **358**
Six hundred thousand, the, in Exodus and Numbers **349**, Jewish tradition about **349–50**
Slavery, to Mammon **507**
Sleeping, of the Divine Word, the (Origen) **59**, i e torpor **185**, i e death **101**
Smite, Heb, ambig **499**, =kill freq in LXX **499**, God described as smiting Israel **499**
Smith, the, or son of the, a name given to a Rabbi **121**
Snatching, Jn and Paul on **253**
Socrates **33, 167**, "Go and look at S" (Epict) **434**
Soldiers, Roman, Josephus on **163–4**
Some, in Lk, om in parall Mk-Mt **475**, some of, implied by "from" **336**, some one (LXX)=angel (Heb) **317**
Sometimes, insertion of, necessary **185**
Son of David **405**
Son of Man, why chosen as Christ's self-appellation **495**, the, regarded as sighing **472–3**
Son, the, speaks as a Testator **397**
Sons of the resurrection **520**
Soul, in two senses, ambig **514**
South, North and **230**
Sower, the **5** foll, **17**
Sowing, the parables of **1–51**, first Biblical mention of **38**, of the Law, the **309**
Speech, reported **99**
Speechless or dumb **469**, s Stuttering
Sphurides, Gk, the baskets in the Feeding of the Four Thousand **208, 342, 344, 482**, called the Seven Churches **343, 375**
Spirit, or wind, ambig **9, 424**, "his s returned," ambig **100**, i e apparition or phantasm **430–32**, s *Phantasma*, spirits in prison **58, 70**
Spiritual healing, c w physical **182**
Spitting, in his face, interpr as before his face **489**, and hence on the ground **489**, to heal blindness, in Mk and Jn **484** foll, in Mk in the face, but in Jn on the ground **489**, subordinated in Jn to "making clay" **493**
Spread out [the hands in blessing], Heb, c w break **323–4**
Sprinkle, v r baptize **448**
SS, s Sinaitic Syrian
Staff, a, in Mk **158** foll, in LXX, three Heb words **160**, conn w scrip **161**, Jacob's, allegorized by Philo **159**, in Heb and Aram **160**
Stages in healing **485**
Stammerer, the, in Isaiah (LXX) and Mk **264**
Stater or shekel **280**
Stephen, the Martyr, or *martus* **156**
Stoic doctrine, about "cleansing the vessel" **457**, about *phantasma* **434**, Jn perhaps influenced by **434**
Stoning in the Temple **118**
Strong drink **185**
Stumble, cause to (A V offend), s *Scandalizein*
Stumbling, at the Law of self-sacrifice **129**, different kinds of **130**, in Jn, perhaps parall to callousness in Mk **481** foll, s *Scandalizein, Scandalon*
Stumbling-block, s *Scandalon*
Stuttering (LXX), only in the Return of the Captives (Isaiah) **264, 469**, in N T only in Mk **264, 469**, in Aquila etc **470**, c w maimed or lame **470**
Subjunctive, deliberative **273**
Suetonius, on the Christians **398**
Suffer many things **500**
Suffering Servant, the **133–7, 500**
Suffice, in Jn, rare in LXX and Gospels **270**
Sumpraxis, Gk, co-operation, human, needed for Christ's healing (Origen) **137–8**
Sun, the, and the holy lampstand in Philo **36**
Sunthēkē, Gk, Aquila's rendering of *berîth*, covenant, LXX *diathēkē* **386**
Superabound, ambig **338–9**, they shall cause to s **338**, ye shall cause none of it to s **340**
Superabundance or remnant **338**, Jn's view of **340**, conn w first mention of the Paschal Lamb **340**
Sustaining Power, the **166**
Swim, **426–8**, c w make-signs **52, 116, 426**

ENGLISH

Swimmers, Plutarch on progressors as **425**
Swimming through trials, Origen on **425**
Swine, c w go round **85, 88**, the flesh of **452**, s Gergesenes
Symbolism, indicated by one loaf **211**, lift up the eyes **228**, "come (*or* go) [and] see" **292**, fire of coals **368**, s Metaphor, Seven
Symposia, Gk, lit drinking-parties, in Mk **296**, might imply thirst in Mk **297–8**, how expressed by Jn **300–301**, of the water-drinking Therapeutae, the **297**, contrasted by Philo with others **297–8**
Synoptists, the silence of about Lazarus **105**, the only mention of buying in **215**, the thoughts of, expressed in Johannine words **510**
Syrophoenician woman, the **464–6**, the story of, Jn perhaps influenced by **466**, and the Samaritan woman **466–7**

Tabea, s *Talitha*
Tabitha **182**
Table, serve at, in Jn **377**, s. *Diaconein*
Tacitus, on the Christians **398**
Take, i e receive a person **55**, to take (Aram) c w wilderness **238**, t ritually **315** foll, **367**, "t for me a heifer" **316**, explained by Philo **316**
Talitha, or *Tabea* **98**
Talmud, the, on —excommunication **180**, Rabbis and Roman Emperors **199**, captains of fifths, i e the five sections of the Law **311**, deal thy bread to the hungry **323–4**, the washing of hands **447**, Corban **451**, nowhere mentions leaven in good sense **371**
Targum **470–71**, amplifies for clearness **20**, alters "see the Lord" **486**, avoids anthropomorphism **523**
Teaching, c w boat **241**, might be expressed by shepherding **256–7**, in Heb , causing to know, c w shepherding **257**
Teaching of the Twelve Apostles, the **364**, s *Didachè*
Technical terms, avoided by Jn, p viii, **319**, conn w the washing of hands **447** foll
Temple, stoning in the **118**, the Mount of the **171**, the gold of the **451**
Temptations, the boat of (Origen) **425**
Tempting, first Biblical instance of **285**, for good **368**, Jesus uniquely described as **284–5**
Tertullian, compares Christ to Joseph **20**, connects leaven with the oven of hell **370, 372**, on — the blood of Christians as seed **39**, curing by oil **177**, *phantasma* **431**, charges against the Christians **400**, s also **46, 450**
Test, try, or prove **285**, test [as if by torment], applied to Peter **425**, to sailors or vessels **421, 425**, testing by fire and by water **422**
Testament, last will and, or covenant, Gk *diathēkē* **384–91**, in the Gospels **392–7**, a self-bequeathing **397**
Testator, the Son speaks as a **397**
Testify and testimony, s Witness
Tetrarch, and king **198**
Thanks, give, Gk *eucharistein* (Four Thousand and Jn) corresponds to bless (*eulogein*) (Five Thousand, Synopt) **315**, comp **319**, s *Eucharistein*
The, s Article
Therapeia, Gk, attendance, ambig **414**
Therapeutae, the, Philo on the *symposia* of **297, 313, 343, 361**, drink only running water **298**
Therapeutic and iatric healing **184–5**, comp **480**
They, ambig **429**, variously interpr by Mk and Mt **443**, them, ambig **415**, [they] ambig **80, 218, 228, 337**
Thing, Heb *dâbâr*, = also word **203**
Think, "they thought," conn w phantasm or spirit **432**
Third day and three days **225, 263, 265–8**, conn w perfection **266–7**, third watch, the **419**
Thirst, spiritual **300**
Thirsting like a garden-bed **298**
This generation, i e this evil g **477**, this world, a judgment of **523**
Thomas, the Apostle, sayings of, Papias on **282**
Thousand, Heb , c w chief **74**
Three, angelic visitors to Abraham **228, 286**, classes of sheep **259**, classes of fruit-bearers **27**, aspects of a shepherd **259**, measures of meal, Philo and Clem Alex on

567

INDEX

372, three days and third day 225, 263, 265-8
Threefold cord, a 157
Thucydidean proofs 436
Thunder, in Jn 10, 523-4
Thyestean banquets, imputed to Christians 398-9
Till (R V), an error for while, in N T not combined with an indicative 525
Timeless nature of the third day, the, Philo on 266
To and fro, running 230-31
To-day, Heb, c w a day 204-5
To him, Heb, c w not 294
Tombs, in the Gospels 69, bodies that are 73
Tormented, lit and metaph. 421-5, s *Basanizein*
Tradition, Papias on 49, 282
Trampling on the flowers 303
Transfiguration, the 519, 522
Transposition 98, 309
Trees, men as 488
Trial, the hour of 420
Trōgein, Gk, chew or eat, only once in Gk Bible exc Jn 345, Johannine use of 345-7
Tropology, Johannine, Origen on 64
True, c w real-and-true 22, comp 50, s *Alēthēs*, *Alēthinos*
Truth, grace and 26, 120, 318
Twelve, the, Precepts to 148-87, t baskets, the 336 foll, t years, variously applied 98, t hours in the day 133, s Apostles
Two, once in O T = "a few" 330-31, in Mt but not in Mk-Lk 70, 74, t demoniacs in Mt and t thousand swine in Mk 74, t fishes, the, Jerome and Origen on 290-91, t and t, applied to apostles, in Mk 155, t witnesses, s Twofold, t seasons (Philo) for the Feast of Baskets 342, t are better than one 157
Two hundred, pennyworth 274-82, denars, an income of 274-5, in Gk, c w five thousand 276
Twofold, witness 158, apostolic action 158
Typical narrative, may be historical 487
Tyre and Sidon 468, comp 408

Understanding, conn w love in Hermas 384
Unholy (A V), error for common (R V) 448

Unique words, in N T 5, 239, 274, 287, 460 etc, comp 37, 46, 62 foll, in the Gk Bible 243-4, 330, comp. 74, 117, 264
Unity, of the Eucharistic food, the, Johannine view of 322, of the Name of God 508
Unleavened 210, s Leaven
Unpopularity of Jesus, temporary 405, 411
Until, c w while 414
Uplift, s Lift
Upright, go 516
Ur of the Chaldeans 87

Verus, the persecution under 399
Vessel, cleanse the (Epict) 457, of the soul, the body 458, of thought, the soul 458, the only pure v is the Purifier 460
Viaticum, for the work of the Gospel 428
Vicarious, s Ransom
Victor of Antioch, on Mark, p v, 439, s also 158, 444, 453, 466, 478-9 etc
Village, c w city 238, 487, a v of, c w a v named 487, v in LXX =seven diff Heb words 487, villages, c w parts 487, cities sometimes called v 487
Village-cities 153
Vine, offspring of the, Christ's blood (Origen) 394
Vine-rows 296-301
Vineyard, in Jabneh, the 299
Vision, Heb, c w here 295, of a sheet, to Peter, the 452
Voice, the living, Papias on 49, divine, a, cooing like a dove 478
Vow, a, when to be relaxed 451

Waiting, after sowing 41, at table 377, s *Diaconos*
Walking, first instance of 488
Wallet or scrip 160
WAS, the 267
Wash, and immerse 448, washing of hands, the 445 foll, the undervaluing of, punished by excommunication 447
Washing of the Feet, the, in Jn 462
Watch of the night, the fourth 418-21, 427, the third, and cockcrowing 419
Water, and blood 157, and fire, as tests 422, 428

Way, the, of Christ, or of the Gospel **494-5**
Weakness, physical or moral **186**
Well, and fountain **460**, the w. that followed Israel **334**
West, the East and the **230**
Wheat, the law of the grain of **10, 18, 20, 267, 309**
"Whence [can]?," implying impossibility **269-74**, thrice in LXX, once in Pentateuch **270**
While, c w until **414**, till (R V.), an error for while **525**
Whole, make **176**, s Heal, Save
Widow of Sarepta, the **409, 468**
Wilderness, the, of Sinai **225**, the, and a **225**, s Desert place, *Midbar*
Wind, or spirit, ambig **424**, a great w, three instances of **53**
Wine, remember the Sabbath over the **394**, new w in Mk-Mt om. by Lk **394-5**
Wiping off sins, symbolical, Origen on **462**
Wisdom, not mentioned by Jn **119**
Wisdom of Solomon, the, on love, *agapè* **384**
Wise, the, are kings **258**
Withdrawal, of Jesus **237**
Within, s Inside
Without (adv), s Outside
Without (prep), without honour, or rejected, s *Atīmos*
Witness (n fem), i e testimony, twofold **158**
Witness (n masc), i e one testifying, not in Jn **156**, Lk's view of the Apostles as witnesses **156**, s. *Martus*
Witness (vb), i e. testify, in Jn **156-7**
Wonder, s Marvelling
Word, Heb. *dâbâr* =also "thing" **203**, in N.T. (A V and R V) interch w "saying" **22**; in Jn as a whole **49**, in Jn, how first mentioned by Jesus **21**; of God or of the Gospel **19**, sometimes ambig **21**, "the divine Word sleeps in the faithless" (Origen) **59**, "the w that I spake," in Jn, distinguished from "I" **512**, s. also *Logos*
Works, the, that the Father hath given me **140**
World, ambig **90**; a judgment of this w. **523**, s Ruler
Worship, true **498**, worshipping Jesus, in Jn **491**
Wounds, in Christ's hands, the **436**

"Ye" emph. **355**
Yetzer, Heb., i e nature, good or bad, in man **372**
Yoke, Christ's **219, 223**, y. and cross **507** foll, y of the precepts **508**; Heb break the y =Targ. revolt from the Law **516**
Young man (Heb *naar*) or servant **288**, "this y m" in Zechariah **289**, Joshua the son of Nun, a **291**

Zarephath **409**; s Sarepta

INDEX

III. GREEK

[This Index includes mainly such Greek words as cannot be expressed by one English word, e.g. χόρτος, "grass," "hay," "fodder," and not such ordinary words as βασιλεύς, "king," unless there is something noteworthy in their idiomatic use. "c.w." means "confused, or confusable, with."]

Ἄβυσσος 86
ἀγαπάω 104, c w. ἀπατάω 279
ἀγάπη 384, and φρόνησις 384, s *Agapè*
ἀγγεῖον 457-8
ἄγγελος 502, 518, 520, comp. 317
ἀγέλη 72, 92
ἅγιος 502, 518, 520
ἁγνίζω and καθαρίζω 463
ἁγνισμός 463
ἁγνός 463
ἀγοράζω 215, 272-4
ἀδυνατέω 139
ἀδύνατος 139
ἄθεος 476
αἴνιγμα 4-5
αἴρω, καθαίρω, and καθαιρέω 460
ἀκοή 193
ἀκούω imperat 8, with accus and with genit 9, ἀκούσας inserted 218
ἀκριβόω 379
ἄλαλος 469-70
ἄλειμμα 187
ἀλείπτης 183
ἀλείφω 175 foll , 183-4, ἀ- and χρίω 175, s *Aleiphein*
ἀλεκτοροφωνία 420
ἀληθής 23
ἀληθινός 21-6
ἁλίζω 221; ἁλίζομαι 373
αλλα ambig , "but" or "other" 60
ἄλλαγμα 513
ἅλς ἅλες 221

ἀναβιβάζω 56
ἀναβλέπω 328, 483, 485, 488
ἀνάγω 56
ἀνάπαυμα 220
ἀναπαύω 219 foll.
ἀναχωρέω and ὑποχωρέω 237
ἀνήρ 348,=Heb *geber* 349, ἄνδρες and ἄνθρωποι 518-19
ἀνθρακιά 366
ἄνθρωπος and ἀνήρ 518-19
ἀνίστημι ἀνάστα 189, ἀνέστη and ἠγέρθη 190-91
ἀνοίγω 4
ἀντάλλαγμα 512 foll
ἀξινάριον 162-4
ἀξινίδιον 162-4
ἀπαγγέλλω and διηγέομαι 81, 217
ἀπαρνέομαι and ἀρνέομαι 505
ἀπατάω ἠπάτησεν c w ἠγάπησεν 279
ἀπέρχομαι and πορεύομαι 269, 273
ἄπλοια 61-2
ἀπό, with θεραπεύω 99, ambig 336
ἀποθήκη 342
ἀπόλλυμι ἵναμὴἀπόληται 342
ἀπολύω and ἀποτάσσομαι 413-15
ἀπομαίνομαι 424, and διδάσκομαι 230
ἀποπνίγω 76

ἀπορέω 199, and διαπορέω 192, 200, ἀπορηθείς 199
ἀπόρημα 199
ἀποσκευή 349
ἀποστέλλω and πέμπω 150
ἀπόστολος 150
ἀποτάσσομαι and ἀπολύω 413-18, s *Apotassomai*
ἅπτω, parall to καίω and ἔρχομαι 32
ἀριθμός 351
ἀριστάω 222-3, ἀριστήσατε 222
ἀρκέω 270, 271
ἀρνέομαι 505-6
ἁρπαγμός 253
ἁρπάζω 252-3
ἀρρωστέω 184
ἀρρωστία 176, 184
ἄρρωστος 184
ἄρτος 206, for σῖτος 239; s. Bread, Loaves
ἄρχομαι 155
ἄρχων 89
ἀσθενέω 175-6, 186, ἀ- and προσκόπτω and σκάνδαλον 126
ἀσθενής 186
ἀσπάζομαι 416
ἀτιμάζω 134-5
ἄτιμος 133 foll.; s. *Atimos*
ἀτιμόω 134-5
αὔξω 18
αὔριον 204
αὐτάρκεια 132
αὐτεξούσιον, τό 92

570

GREEK

αὐτόματος 38-9
ἀφίστημι ἀφίστανται 127, 129
ἄφωνος 469

Βαλλάντιον 170
βαπτίζω v.r. for ῥαντίζω 448
βασανίζω 421-3, and δοκιμάζω 422, s. *Basanizein*
βάσκανος ὀφθαλμός 459
βαστάζω and φέρω 341
βλαστάνω 37
βυθίζω 52
βωβός 470

Γεμίζω 342
γένημα 394
γίγνομαι ἐγενήθη ambig 352
γινώσκω γνόντες 284

Δαιμόνιον ἀσώματον 58, 431, 437
δακρύω 104
δεῖ 273
δειπνέω 222
δεῖπνον 222
δεκτός 133, 135
δεσμεύω 470
δεῦτε 222
δέχομαι and λαμβάνω 3, 316-17
δή, s δηνάριον
δηνάριον δηναρίων c w. δὴ ἀνδρῶν 276
διά, ἕνεκεν, and ὑπέρ 511
διαβλέπω 484, 486
διαδίδωμι ambig. 333, "give in succession" 333, δ and δίδωμι and μερίζω 332
διαθήκη 385 foll, s. *Diathēkē*
διακονέω, -ος 232, 377, s *Diaconein, Diaconos*
διακρούομαι 416
διαμερίζω 318, 330
διανηχόομαι 425
διανοίγω, metaph. and lit 326
διανοέομαι and προσκόπτω 125
διαπεράω and διέρχομαι 241
διαπορέω and ἀπορέω 192, 200
διαρήσσω and σχίζω 323
διασώζω 176

διατάσσω 98
διαφθείρω 373
διδάσκω 260, διδάσκομαι and ἀπομαίνομαι 230
δίδραχμον 280
δίδωμι 203, pres. and aor imperat 203-4, δ and διαδίδωμι and μερίζω 332
διέρχομαι and διαπεράω 241
διηγέομαι and ἀπαγγέλλω 81, 217
δοκέω 432
δοκιμάζω and πειράζω 285, and βασανίζω 422
δοῦλος 510, s. *Doulos*
δύναμις 139
δυνατός 139
δύσκωφος 470
δωρεά 387

E, ι e ϵ, c w C 276
ἐγείρω ambig. 176, ἔ_γειρε 189, ἠγέρθη and ἀνέστη 190-91
ἐγκρυφίας 31, 372
εἰ μή and μή 159
εἰμί ἐστίν inserted for emphasis 23
εἰρηνεύω 503
εἰρήνη 503
εἰς, "[amounting] to" 349
ἐκβάλλω, with ἔξω 523
ἐκλέγομαι 142
ἐκλύομαι, absol. 176
ἐκπλήσσομαι 113-14, 117
ἐκτός 455
ἐκφέρω c w ἐξάγω 488
ἔκφυλος 417
ἐλαύνω ἐλαύνομαι ambig 424, and μαίνομαι 424
ἑλκύω and ἕλκω 434, and προσλαμβάνω 433
ἕλκω 433-4
ἐμβλέπω 484-6
ἐμβριμάομαι 104, 473
ἐμπλήθω 306
ἔνειμι 457, τὰ ἐνόντα 455, 457
ἕνεκεν and ὑπό 511, ἕ., διά, and ὑπέρ 511
ἐνεός 470
ἐγκρύπτω 31, 372
ἔνοπλος 161, ἔνοπλον c w ἐν ὅπλον 162
ἐντός 455

ἐνύπνιον and ἐνώπιον 295
ἐνώπιον and ἐνύπνιον 295
ἐνωτίζομαι 8
ἐξάγω c w. ἐκφέρω 488
ἐξέρχομαι ὁ ἐξελθών 177
ἐξετάζω 435
ἐξομολογέομαι 320
ἐξουδενόω 135
ἔξω, with ἐξάγω 488, with ἐκβάλλω 523, ἐκεῖνοι οἱ ἔ 14
ἔξωθεν 455
ἔπειμι 205, ἡ ἐπιοῦσα 204-5
ἐπερωτάω 12
ἐπί as prefix 205
ἐπιδημέω 353
ἐπιθυμέω 131
ἐπιθυμία 131-2
ἐπικείμενον 366
ἐπίλεκτος 358
ἐπιλύω 45-6
ἐπιοῦσα, ἡ 204
ἐπιούσιος 203 foll
ἐπισιτισμός 239
ἐπιστάτης 255
ἐπιστήμη 384
ἐπιτερπής 205
ἐπιτίθημι and ἐπιχρίω 489
ἐργάζομαι 308
ἐρέπτω 345
ἐρημία 225
ἔρημος 225, ἐν [τῇ] ἐρήμῳ 238
ἔρχομαι, parall. to καίω and ἅπτω 32
ἐρωτάω 11
ἐσθίειν 359, and φαγεῖν 345, and τρώγειν 345, s *Esthiein*
ἔσωθεν 455
εὐκαιρέω 233 foll
εὔκαιρον v r. εἰς καιρόν 234
εὐκαίρως 233-4
εὐλογεω 320, εὐλογημένος 319, ϵ and εὐχαριστέω 315, 318
εὐλογητός 319
εὔνοια 50
εὑρίσκω 271
εὐχαριστέω 315, 318, 319
εὐχαριστία 319, 323, 362
ἐφήμερος 205
ἕως with indicative 525

Ζημιόω τὸν νοῦν ζημιωθείς 514
ζώνη 163, 170

571

INDEX

Ἡμέρα, with κλίνει, κέκλικεν etc 261-2

Θαῦμα and φάσμα, v.r. for φάντασμα 431
θαυμάζω 143
θεραπεία ambig. 414
θεραπεύω and ἰάομαι 184, 256, θ. ἀπό 99, s. Therapeutic

Ἰάομαι and θεραπεύω 184, 256, s Iatric
ἵνα 79, ἵνα μή parall. to ὅτι οὐ 6
Ἰουδαία ambig. 111
ἰσχύω οὐκ ἰσχύει χείρ 99
ἰχθύδιον 330
ἰχθύς 328, 330, 335, and ὀψάριον 328, 330

καθαιρέω, καθαίρω, and αἴρω 460
καθαίρω 460, and αἴρω 460
καθαρίζω 460, and ἁγνίζω 463
καθαρισμός 460-61
καθαρός 455
καιρος 234-5, εἰς καιρόν, v r for εὔκαιρον 234, s. εὐκαιρέω
καίω, parall to ἅπτω and ἔρχομαι 32
κακοπαθέω 175
κάλαθος 343
κάμνω 176
κάρταλλος 208, 342
κατὰ πεντήκοντα 310
καταδυναστεύω 471-2
κατακλάω 321, 329
κατάκλισις 313
κατακρήμνημι 117
κατακρημνίζω 115, 117
καταλείπω and ἀφίημι 254
καταμόνας 48, 238
κατανεύω 52, comp. 116
κατανοέω 144
κατανύσσω 470
καταποντίζω 53
κατασιωπάω 199
κατορύσσω 31
κεῖμαι 366, 368-9, s. Laid
κλαίω 104
κλάσμα 337, 339, 364-5, s. Clasma
κλάω 322, 324, 329
κλίνει, with ἡμέρα 261-2
κλισία 297
κλυδωνίζω 423
κοιμάομαι 185

κοινός κοιναῖς χερσίν 448, κ βίος 449, κ. οἶκος 449, s. Koinos
κοινοφαγία 449
κοινόω, diff from μιαίνω 412, v r for κοινωνέω 449
κοινωνέω, v r. κοινόω 449
κοινωνία 364
κόφινος 211, 336, 482, s. Cophinos
κρεμάω 117
κρημνάω 117
κυλλός 470
κυρτός 470
κώμη 487, κῶμαι and πόλεις 487, and μέρη 487
κωμόπολις 153, 487
κωφός 469-70
κωφόω 470

Λαμβάνω and παραλαμβάνω 57, and δέχομαι 3, 316-17
λατρεία 358
λεγιών, s Legion
λιμήν, Hebraized 242
λόγος, s Logos, Word
λοιπός 131
λυπέω 427, 429
λυχνία 36
λύχνος 32

Μαίνομαι and ἐλαύνομαι 424
μαρτυρέω 156-7
μαρτυρία 156-7
μάρτυς 156-7
μεθύω, and πρασιά 298
μέλλω 274, 341
μένω μένετε ambig. 187
μερίζω 328, 332
μέρος μέρη 242, 487
μεταβαίνω 80
μή and εἰ μή 159
μιαίνω, diff from κοινόω 412
μιαροφαγέω, -ία 449
μικρόν (adv.) 42
μικρός 42, 255
μνήμη 69
μνημεῖον 69
μογιλάλος 264, 467-70
μόδιος, Hebraized 34
μόνος 238, κατὰ μόνας 48
μορφή and σχῆμα 432
μυστήριον 15

Ναυαγέω 425

νήπιος 349
νήχομαι 425

Ξυλάριον 331

Ο, dropped in MS 24
οἶδα 437
οἴησις 458
ὄμμα and ὀφθαλμός 485
ὀπίσω, s. Behind
ὅπλον 162, 165
ὀρφανία 255
ὄσπρια 45
ὅτι οὐ, parall to ἵνα μή 6
οὐσία, Hebraized 205
οὗτος resumptive 191
ὀφθαλμὸς βάσκανος 459, ὁ and ὄμμα 485
ὀφρύς 115
ὄχλος and πλῆθος 80
ὀψάριον 366, for ἰχθύς 328, 330
ὀψία 261

Παιδάριον 286 foll.; s. Paidarion
παιδεύω 341
παιδίον 288
παντοκράτωρ 139
παραβολή 4-5, 10-13
παρακαλέω 71, 78-9
παράκλησις 78
παράκλητος, s Paraclete
παρακολουθέω 16
παραλαμβάνω 55-6, and λαμβάνω 55, 57
παρατίθημι 328-9, 332
παρηγορέω 78
παροιμία 4, 13
πάσσαλος 163
πατάσσω 499
πατρίς 109-10
πειράζω and δοκιμάζω 285
πεζῇ v.r πεζοί 245
πεμπταῖζω 312
πέμπτος πέμπτη γενεά 312
πέμπω and ἀποστέλλω 150
περιάγω 152
περιούσιος 205
περιπατέω 488
περισσεία 338
περίσσευμα 337, 339
περισσεύω 337, 339
περιτρέχω 243
περιφέρω 16
πηγή 35, 461
πήρα 170
πηρός 470
πίπτω 178

572

GREEK

πλεονεξία 132
πληγή 100
πλῆθος and ὄχλος 80
πληθύνω 355
πλήρωμα 339, 342
πλοιάριον 60
πλοῖον 60
πνεῦμα 9, 58, 100, 424
πνίγω 76
ποιμαίνω 257-8
πόλις and κώμη 487
πολύς πολλά 226, with verbs of speech 199, ὥρα πολλή 261
πορεύομαι and ἀπέρχομαι 269, 273
ποτίζω 299
πραγματεία, Hebraized 122
πράσα, s. πρασιά
πρασιά 296-301, with μεθύω 298, with ποτίζω 299, πρασιαὶ πρασιαί 296 foll.
πρασιόομαι 298
πρόβλημα 4
προέρχομαι with accus 226, 228
προκόπτω 425
προσέχω 8
προσκεφάλαιον 62-3
πρόσκομμα 126
προσκόπτω 126, 133, π. and διανοέομαι 125, π and ἀσθενής and σκάνδαλον 126
προσκυνέω 491
προσκύνημα 379
προσλαμβάνω and ἑλκύω 433
προσνοέω 144
προσορμίζω 244, 443, 474
πυγμή 448
πωρόω 441
πώρωσις 206, 441, s. *Pōrōsis*

Ῥάβδος 160
ῥαντίζω and βαπτίζω 448

Σ, ι e C, c w. Ϛ 276
σάνδαλον 167-8
σίτα τρία 372
Σιδών 468
σῖτος c w ἄρτος 239
σκανδαλίζω 124 foll
σκάνδαλον 126, 130, 501
σκανδαλόω 501
σκεῦος 34
σπλαγχνίζομαι 247, 252

σπλάγχνον 249 foll, σπλάγχνα 247 foll
στατήρ 280
στεναγμός 472
στένω, στενάξω etc 472
στοιχεῖα 387
στοῖχος 310, κατὰ στοῖχον 313
συμπόσιον 296 foll, συμπόσια συμπόσια ibid
σύμπραξις 137
συνάγω συνάγομαι and ὑποστρέφω 218
συναλίζομαι 221
συνέχω 470
συνθήκη 386
συνίημι συνῆκαν rendered as pluperf 438
συντρίβω 322
σφραγίς 267
σφυρίς 211, 336, 482, s *Sphurides*
σχῆμα and μορφή 432
σχίζω and διαρήσσω 323
σχίσμα 113
σώζω 176
σῶμα 86

Τάγμα 310
τάλειθα 98
τάξις 313
τεκμήριον 436
τεκνίον 43
τέκνον 43
τέκτων 120 foll.
τελευτάω 177
τέλος 265
τηλαυγής 484-5
τηλαυγῶς 484
τίθημι θέσθε ὑμῖν 308-9
τις 317
τράγημα 346
τρανός 469
τράπεζα 347
τροφαί 274
τρώγω 345-7, s *Trōgein*

Ὕλη 50
ὑμεῖς, ὑμᾶς, emph. 9, 355
ὑπέρ, διά, and ἕνεκεν 511
ὑπηρέσιον 63
ὑπό and ἕνεκεν 511
ὑποδέω ὑποδεδεμένος 167
ὑποστρέφω and συνάγομαι 218
ὑποχωρέω and ἀναχωρέω 237

Φαγεῖν 345, 347, s. *Phagein*

φαίνω ἐφάνη 191
φάντασμα 58, 429, 431 foll., with v r φάσμα and θαῦμα 431; s. *Phantasma*
φάσμα, s. φάντασμα
φέρω and βαστάζω 341; ἐφέροντο (Orig) 356
φθορεύς 132
φίλαυτος 280
φιλέω 104 ἑαυτὸν φιλεῖν 280
φίλημα 379-82, diff. from φιλία 381, φ ἅγιον 378, φ ἀγάπης 378
φιλία 50, 381
φίλος 104, 382
Φοίνισσα v.r Χαναναία 466
φρέαρ 85
φρόνησις 384
φυλακή and ὥρα 419
φύραμα 320
φωνή ζῶσα 49
φῶς 32

Χαίρω 168
χαλεπός 74
χαλκεύς 121
χαλκοῦς 173
Χαναναία v.r.for Φοίνισσα 466
χείρ, s ἰσχύω
χλωρός 304-6, χ. χόρτος 302
χορτάζω 304-7, 360, comp 336, s *Chortāzein*
χόρτος 37, 302-6, χ. χλωρός 302, χ νόμενος 305, ὁ χ. τοῦ ἀγροῦ and ἐν ἀγρῷ ὁ χ 303, s. *Chortos*
χρίσμα 187
χριστός and ἀληλιμμένος 496
χρίω 175
χωλός 470
χῶμα γῆς 72
χώρα 86 foll.; s *Medinah*
χωρέω 444

Ψιχίον 337
ψυχή 514

Ὠμοφαγία 399
ὥρα and φυλακή 419, ὥ πολλή 261